Comprehension Instruction

Solving Problems in the Teaching of Literacy

Cathy Collins Block, *Series Editor*

Engaging Young Readers:
Promoting Achievement and Motivation
Edited by Linda Baker, Mariam Jean Dreher, and John T. Guthrie

Word Journeys:
Assessment-Guided Phonics, Spelling, and Vocabulary Instruction
Kathy Ganske

Learning to Read:
Lessons from Exemplary First-Grade Classrooms
Michael Pressley, Richard L. Allington, Ruth Wharton-McDonald,
Cathy Collins Block, and Lesley Mandel Morrow

Directing the Writing Workshop:
An Elementary Teacher's Handbook
Jean Wallace Gillet and Lynn Beverly

Comprehension Instruction:
Research-Based Best Practices
Edited by Cathy Collins Block and Michael Pressley

Comprehension Instruction

Research-Based Best Practices

Edited by

CATHY COLLINS BLOCK
MICHAEL PRESSLEY

THE GUILFORD PRESS
New York   London

KH

© 2002 The Guilford Press
A Division of Guilford Publications, Inc.
72 Spring Street, New York, NY 10012
www.guilford.com

Printed in the United States of America

This book is printed on acid-free paper.

Last digit is print number: 9   8   7   6   5   4   3   2

Library of Congress Cataloging-in-Publication Data

Comprehension instruction : research-based best practices / edited by Cathy
Collins Block, Michael Pressley.
      p. cm. — (Solving problems in the teaching of literacy)
   Includes bibliographical references and index.
   ISBN 1-57230-693-9—ISBN 1-57230-692-0 (pbk.)
   1. Reading Comprehension. 2. Cognitive learning. 3. Action research
in education.   I. Block, Cathy Collins. II. Pressley, Michael. III. Series.

LB1 050.45.C69 2001
428.4′3—dc21
                                                2001040933

11/22/04

About the Editors

Cathy Collins Block, PhD, has served on the graduate faculty of Texas Christian University since 1977. She has taught at Southern Illinois University–Carbondale, served as Research Assistant at the Wisconsin Research and Development Center for Cognitive Development, and taught kindergarten through high school in private and public schools. Dr. Block has directed and served as principal investigator of six nationally funded research projects and is presently serving on or has served on the board of directors for a number of organizations, including the National Center for Research and Training for Learning Disabilities and the National Reading Conference.

Michael Pressley, PhD, is the Notre Dame Chair in Catholic Education and Professor of Psychology at the University of Notre Dame. He is an expert in comprehension processing and in primary-level reading education, which is related to his career-long research on children's learning. He has published about 250 articles, chapters, and books. His most recent research involves exploration of how literacy can be motivated in classrooms.

Contributors

Peter Afflerbach, PhD, Department of Curriculum and Instruction, University of Maryland, College Park, Maryland

Richard C. Anderson, EdD, Center for the Study of Reading, University of Illinois at Urbana–Champaign, Champaign, Illinois

Linda Baker, PhD, Department of Psychology, University of Maryland, Baltimore County, Baltimore, Maryland

Pamela Beard El-Dinary, PhD, educational consultant, Clarksville, Maryland

Camille L. Z. Blachowicz, PhD, Department of Reading and Language, National-Louis University, Evanston, Illinois

Cathy Collins Block, PhD, Department of Education, Texas Christian University, Fort Worth, Texas

Edward Bouchard, MPH, Department of Psychology, The University of Chicago, Chicago, Illinois

Kathleen J. Brown, PhD, University of Utah Reading Center, University of Utah, Salt Lake City, Utah

Rachel Brown, PhD, Department of Reading and Language Arts, School of Education, Syracuse University, Syracuse, New York

Donald D. Deshler, PhD, Center for Research on Learning, University of Kansas, Lawrence, Kansas

Carol A. Donovan, PhD, College of Education, University of Alabama, Tuscaloosa, Alabama

Mariam Jean Dreher, PhD, College of Education, University of Maryland, College Park, Maryland

Gerald G. Duffy, EdD, Professor Emeritus, Department of Education, Michigan State University, East Lansing, Michigan

Nell K. Duke, EdD, College of Education, Michigan State University, East Lansing, Michigan

Thomas H. Estes, PhD, Curry School of Education, University of Virginia, Charlottesville, Virginia

Joseph B. Fisher, PhD, School of Education, Grand Valley State University, Allendale, Michigan

Paola Gaine, BA, graduate student, Masters of Education Program, University of Notre Dame, Notre Dame, Indiana

Linda B. Gambrell, PhD, School of Education, Clemson University, Clemson, South Carolina

John T. Guthrie, PhD, Department of Human Development, University of Maryland, College Park, Maryland

Gay Ivey, PhD, School of Education, James Madison University, Harrisonburg, Virginia

Joseph A. Joy, BA, graduate student, Masters of Education Program, University of Notre Dame, Notre Dame, Indiana

Patricia S. Koskinen, PhD, Department of Curriculum and Instruction, University of Maryland, College Park, Maryland

Lesley Mandel Morrow, PhD, Department of Learning and Teaching, Graduate School of Education, Rutgers University, New Brunswick, New Jersey

Darcia Narvaez, PhD, Department of Psychology, University of Notre Dame, Notre Dame, Indiana

Sherrie L. Nist, PhD, Division of Academic Assistance, University of Georgia, Athens, Georgia

Donna Ogle, EdD, Department of Reading and Language, National-Louis University, Evanston, Illinois

Sevgi Ozgungor, MA, Department of Human Development, University of Maryland, College Park, Maryland

P. David Pearson, PhD, College of Education, Michigan State University, East Lansing, Michigan

Michael Pressley, PhD, Masters of Education Program and Department of Psychology, University of Notre Dame, Notre Dame, Indiana

Ralph E. Reynolds, PhD, Department of Educational Psychology, University of Nevada, Las Vegas, Las Vegas, Nevada

Alina Reznitskaya, EdM, Center for the Study of Reading, University of Illinois at Urbana–Champaign, Champaign, Illinois

Joni L. Schaller, BA, Masters of Education Program, University of Notre Dame, Notre Dame, Indiana

Jean B. Schumaker, PhD, Center for Research on Learning, University of Kansas, Lawrence, Kansas

Michele L. Simpson, EdD, Division of Academic Assistance, University of Georgia, Athens, Georgia

Gale M. Sinatra, PhD, Department of Educational Psychology, University of Nevada Las Vegas, Las Vegas, Nevada

Laura B. Smolkin, EdD, Curry School of Education, University of Virginia, Charlottesville, Virginia

Hiller A. Spires, PhD, Department of Curriculum and Instruction, North Carolina State University, Raleigh, North Carolina

Diane H. Tracey, EdD, Communication Science and Educational Services Department, Kean University, Union, New Jersey

Tom Trabasso, PhD, Department of Psychology, The University of Chicago, Chicago, Illinois

Joanna P. Williams, PhD, Teachers College, Columbia University, New York, New York

Contents

III   COMPREHENSION INSTRUCTION
IN PRESCHOOL, PRIMARY, AND INTERMEDIATE GRADES

IV   INTENSIFICATION OF COMPREHENSION INSTRUCTION THROUGHOUT MIDDLE SCHOOL, HIGH SCHOOL, AND COLLEGE

IV   CONCLUSION

1

Introduction

CATHY COLLINS BLOCK
MICHAEL PRESSLEY

Between 1978 and 1981, three major publications thrust comprehension instruction to the forefront of educators' concerns. Teachers and researchers were riveted by Dolores Durkin's findings that our profession was allocating limited instructional time to improving students' reading comprehension (Durkin, 1978–1979). In the same year, Pearson and Johnson (1978) wrote *Teaching Comprehension* to address this need. In less than 250 pages, they reported as many research-based practices as were known at that time. Three years later, the International Reading Association published the first book dedicated solely to research about comprehension instruction: *Comprehension and Teaching: Research Reviews* (Guthrie, 1981). This volume contained 12 chapters, and was 292 pages long.

Twenty years have passed since that time, and many educators continued to work on improving students' understanding of what they read. The purpose of this volume is to bring together the latest works by many of the researchers in the reading-comprehension community to update the knowledge that now exists. The authors in this book describe studies that they have completed, as well as discuss how we can build on this base to provide the best possible comprehension instruction for all students.

We know that you can assume different points of view as you read this book. We recommend three overarching goals that can be achieved as you read *Comprehension Instruction: Research-Based Best Practices*. First, you could assume a historical perspective. You can mentally place the information you are about to read on a historical timeline, beginning in 1919 (Gray, 1919). It was at this point that research related to comprehension instruction was judged to have begun (Smith, 1978). In doing so, you might conclude, with us, that the amount of knowledge that we have obtained in 82 years is astounding, and yet simultaneously disheartening because so much still remains undiscovered. Second, you could assume an analytical perspective. You could note common themes between chapters. We were amazed at the similarities of thought among the 39 researchers in this book. When we read with a stance to discern these commonalities, we were equally enlightened by the different directions for future research that these leaders in the reading comprehension community recommended.

Third, you could assume a futuristic stance. When we did so, we noted more than 75 suggestions for future research and practice. Regardless of the stance that we took, however, we found that *Comprehension Instruction* led us to an expanded understanding of the present state and future potential for comprehension instruction.

READING WITH A HISTORICAL PERSPECTIVE

As we prepared to write this introduction, we reread the Durkin study, the Pearson and Johnson text, and the International Reading Association's edited volume on *Comprehension and Teaching: Research Reviews* (Guthrie, 1981). As these works described, at the turn of the 20th century, educators began to create new methods of teaching students how to comprehend. Pictures were placed in books, and controlled vocabulary was introduced. By 1946, Emmett Albert Betts's method, called the Directed Reading Activity (DRA), was used in more than 90% of the classrooms in North America (Smith, 1978; Stahl, 1999). This activity dominated instructional classroom reading periods and occurred more than once a week at every grade level, kindergarten through sixth grade. Although DRA did not teach comprehension, whenever teachers Directed students to Read silently as a classroom Activity (DRA) these directions were labeled as comprehension instruction in teachers' minds and lesson plan books. In DRA directions, teachers introduced new vocabulary terms, set the stage for reading, initiated external motivational techniques to build students' background and interest in a topic, supervised students' silent reading, and asked literal (as well as, more recently, interpretative and applied) questions about the information that students read. They did not actually teach how to comprehend, however.

As you will discover in reading this book, the question of "how to teach students to comprehend" is still being asked and with as much fervor today as it was in 1946. Our answers are becoming more specific, effective, and personalized, however. Current educators are employing multiple methods to deepen all people's (preschool to adult) pleasure and profit from reading. The scientific scope of our expertise has also expanded. For example, 12 researchers contributed to the International Reading Association's first book dedicated to comprehension instruction. In 20 years, the number of researchers examining comprehension processes and practices has greatly increased. More than 39 researchers were invited to participate in this book. Moreover, 9 of the 12 scientists represented in the 1981 book are still engaged in comprehension research today, and 4 have written chapters in this book. Their works provide us with their most recent analyses of the field.

Not only has our understanding of the influences on successful comprehension expanded, but additional issues have also emerged. Although today's scientists paint a more valid portrait of how we can increase comprehension abilities, we still do not know how to adddess specific developmental needs from preschool throughout the adult years. We have expanded our perceptions of comprehension. It now includes the intricate nature of networks of cognitive processes. We realize that understanding is based on ideas and relationships between people, texts, and technology that are, in turn, influenced by multiple temporal, personal, social, cultural, political, motivational, instructional, cognitive, and metacognitive factors. This definition has moved us beyond our infancy in positioning comprehension as merely a set of value-free rote skills that were taught by developing students' retrieval systems through repeated drill and practice with silent reading.

Today, we are also including formerly marginalized groups of students in our explorations for better methods of teaching comprehension. Presently, as we discovered in creating this book, what counts as comprehension of a text at a particular time and place depends on who has the power to define it and the characteristics of the person who is reading. Sadly, most classrooms are still not teaching comprehension processes as much as the researchers in this book recommend. All agree that more time and better instructional methods are necessary before we can empower all students to enjoy and profit from reading a wide variety of text and hypertext media.

ANALYZING COMMON THEMES BETWEEN CHAPTERS

One of the most interesting facets of editing this book was to discover how many commonalities existed among the work of present researchers. While you will undoubtedly note many that we did not, we were fascinated by the agreement among researchers about the following aspects of comprehension instruction.

- Comprehension programs must include ample reading, vocabulary and decoding development, and rich experiences with fiction, nonfiction, and technologically based texts.
- Comprehension involves more than 30 cognitive and metacognitive processes, including making connections to background knowledge, interpreting text structures, questioning, clarifying meaning, comparing, contrasting, summarizing, imaging, setting purposes, using fix-up strategies, monitoring, cognizing, interpreting authors' intentions, pausing to reflect, paraphrasing, analyzing, recognizing personal perspectives, identifying gists, changing hypotheses, adding hypotheses, searching for meaning, being alert to main ideas, creating themes, determining importance, drawing inferences, corroborating congenial and noncongenial data, contextualizing, engaging in retrospection, generating, using mnemonic devices, predicting, organizing, and reorganizing text.
- At least 14 programs for teaching comprehension are described in this book, including transactional strategies instruction; thinking-process development; reciprocal teaching; CORI; CSR; SAIL; QAR; K-W-L; explicit, elaborated instruction; informed strategies training; cognitive apprenticeships; imagery training; *Reason to Read* strategies; and WebQuests.
- Regardless of the program used to teach comprehension, instruction should include modeling, scaffolding, guided practice, and independent use of strategies so that students develop an internalized self-regulation of comprehension processes.
- Helping students become self-regulated comprehenders is hard work, and methods will likely take more than a year for most teachers to master.
- The quality of teacher–student interactions and collaborative talk, especially during scaffolded teacher assistance periods, can hasten students' development. Other aspects within the socially constructed nature of classroom discourse and climate must be attended to if all students are to reach their highest levels of comprehension abilities.

- In the past, educators were inclined to believe that if students knew some strategies or ways to approach text in general, they could transfer these skills to a variety of contexts and genres. We know now that such a lockstep heuristic leap is not possible.
- New labels for comprehension processes are being proposed. Several authors in this book suggest that the traditional categories of literal, interpretative, and applied comprehension are too restrictive. These researchers recommend that we explore a conceptualization of comprehension relative to the time of initiation and duration of mental energy that is expended throughout a reading to attain accurate and enriched understandings. Alternatively, we could group processes according to the goals that they are designed to achieve, such as whether or not they are to be used to repair a misunderstanding or to organize accurately interpreted information.

IDENTIFYING IMPLICATIONS
FOR FUTURE RESEARCH AND PRACTICES

When we view this book with a futuristic stance, the implications for research and practice are staggering. Already teachers are being asked to (1) take more time during the day to help students become enthralled with, and effectively read multiple topics; (2) tailor lessons so that all students overcome a multitude of decoding, memory, attentional, cognitive, and metacognitive challenges that present themselves in fictional, nonfictional, and technologically based texts; and (3) involve students more in their own making of meaning. As we increase our understanding about the complexity of the comprehension process itself, the number of such demands that are placed on teachers are likely to increase. Authors in this book suggest ways in which these expanded expectations can be addressed.

Every author·was asked to make recommendations for future research and practice, and we collapsed these projections into categories. Our intent was to provide an overview for future comprehension instruction before you read all authors' works. Recognizing their future goals in advance could enrich your understanding of their present thinking and provide connections between data that are presented in early and later, chapters. In this book, the recommendations fall into four categories of knowledge. Three of these were suggested by researchers in 1978 to 1981: (1) the nature of the comprehension processes, (2) student variables that influence comprehension, and (3) components that can be manipulated during comprehension instruction. The directions we are taking to answer questions related to these bodies of knowledge have altered dramatically. Furthermore, a new category of recommendations emerged in this book—to identify better methods of building teacher and parent expertise concerning comprehension instruction.

Looking at the first body of research, enormous differences have emerged as to how we describe the comprehension process itself. In 1981, comprehension was defined by fields such as visual perception, auditory processes, and visual–auditory integration at the word—as opposed to the phrase, paragraph, or story—level. At that time, scientists were only beginning to investigate the comprehension process as it related to "story structures, integration of sentences, drawing inferences, testing hypotheses, relating background knowledge to textual information, and reading to obtain information" (Guthrie, 1981, p. viii). Today researchers are asking questions such as:

- What methods will alert students to which strategies they need to comprehend and how can they initiate these processes at appropriate times in a text?
- How can we better teach metacognition?
- How does children's comprehension change based on the demands of specific books?
- How can we enable students to transfer comprehension processes to new contexts?
- Is there a preferred order for introducing strategies?
- How does the awareness of causal connections within a story strengthen comprehension?

Similarly, in the second body of knowledge, scientists have identified new student characteristics that influence comprehension. These characteristics are becoming increasingly important in the 21st century and were unknown as recently as 2 decades ago. Today's students must read instant, worldwide communications. They no longer have to wait for, or to be protected or limited by, the filters of having adults translate literature and media for them. As a result, they must have the comprehension competencies to interpret new knowledge simultaneously with the adults in their world. They also must learn how to analyze data critically, because credentialing, as a method of judging credibility, is becoming obsolete in Web-based reading. They need to learn how to comprehend stimulating visual input that makes non-lived-through experiences captivatingly real. They need to comprehend greater amounts of information exponentially faster and to assimilate infinitely greater bodies of information than did the authors in this book when we were children. By 2013, many educators predict that 100% of students will have access to the World Wide Web in unsupervised or non-instructionally guided situations (AT&T, 1998). Students must learn how to discern fact, opinion, and bias when reading alone. Students must become dissatisfied when they only create and comprehend mere sound bites as the soul and scope of knowledge.

In the early 1980s, researchers were beginning to examine student variables relative to reading comprehension through an anthropological lens. Qualitative researchers were documenting the interactions that occurred between large numbers of children, often grouped homogeneously for comprehension instruction. At that time, they were also examining different roles, expectations, activities, and social dimensions of students within such homogeneously grouped comprehension instructional settings. On the other hand, today's researchers are examining broader yet more specific questions, such as:

- How can we blend explicit, explanatory information smoothly and unobtrusively into an ongoing dialogue that continuously engages students with text content?
- How can we nudge students to synthesize knowledge from two sources as they form their own theories?
- With regard to sociocultural influences on comprehension, how can we honor students' cultural and linguistic differences and simultaneously accelerate their understanding of English?

- How can we build classroom comprehension programs that include a wide range of reading experiences for diverse students?
- How can we help children develop speed and accuracy in searching and using informational text?
- How can we develop comprehension skills for young learners in the information age?
- If middle school students demonstrate higher order comprehension when given appropriate and effective instruction, can younger children also do so?

Boundaries concerning the third body of knowledge, the instructional process, have also vastly expanded since 1980. Researchers within this volume spent less time making comparisons between methods and analyzing time-on-task variables than did scientists in the past. Today, researchers focus more attention on developing high quality teaching experiences for students from all lifestyles. Among the questions being posed are:

- How can we develop thought-filled, adaptive teaching episodes so that strategies can be described sensibly and meaningfully to students?
- What instructional supports can we create so students of all levels of ability comprehend deeply and broadly?
- How can we ensure that students are provided with texts that enable them to practice comprehension strategies that they have been taught?
- How can we teach and evaluate Web-based comprehension from a multidisciplinary stance?
- How can we include vocabulary in informational comprehension instruction, especially in light of the multicultural nature of the classroom populations and the explosion of technical vocabulary?

Finally, a new category of future research recommendations relates to teachers and parents. Researchers are seeking to identify better methods of building teacher and parent expertise concerning (1) comprehension, (2) students' development relative to comprehension processes, and (3) comprehension instruction. Questions that researchers are examining include:

- How can we teach teachers to explain well?
- How much support do teachers need to continue to teach comprehension effectively after their initial training has ended?
- How can we provide teachers with the variety of training needed to ensure that all students can read multimedia texts, hypertext, student-constructed texts, periodicals, nonfiction, and fiction?
- How can we teach educators to teach comprehension as an unfolding, ebb-and-flow process of interactive, strategic thinking, and not as a collection of strategies?
- How can we help teachers to identify the most effective blend of providing direct assistance and guiding students' discoveries of comprehension strategies?
- How can we help parents to improve their children's comprehension at home?

PREPARING TO READ THIS BOOK

We also wrote this introductory chapter with the intention of describing how this book is organized. We divided the book into four parts. Part I contains six chapters that explore new directions concerning the teaching of comprehension. Part II examines how research is expanding our understanding of comprehension in the four bodies of knowledge we described. Part III describes the current nature and potential for comprehension instruction in preschool, primary, and intermediate grades. Part IV describes how comprehension instruction can intensify at the middle school, high school, and college levels. Our concluding chapter summarizes novel and common themes, as well as provides a set of recommendations that collapses across the thinking presented in this book.

In this introductory chapter, we have attempted to "build background knowledge," "establish purposes for reading," "introduce new vocabulary," and "build motivation." Now, let's read the important information that flows throughout this book. After we have finished, our goal is to have learned how to introduce books better, and how to teach comprehension better to all students.

REFERENCES

AT&T. (1998, May). *Classrooms of the future*. Research conference report and videotaped demonstration, AT&T Communication Systems, Atlanta, GA.

Durkin, D. (1978–1979). What classroom observation reveals about reading comprehension instruction. *Reading Research Quarterly, 14*, 481–533.

Gray, W. S. (1919). Principles of method in teaching reading as derived from scientific investigation. *The Eighteenth Yearbook of the National Society for the Study of Education, Part II.* Bloomington, IL: Public School Publishing Company.

Guthrie, J. (Ed.). (1981). *Comprehension and teaching: Research reviews*. Newark, DE: International Reading Association.

Pearson, P. D., & Johnson, D. (1978). *Teaching comprehension*. New York: Harcourt Brace College Publishers.

Smith, N. (1978). *History of reading instruction*. New York: World Book.

Stahl, S. (1999). Why innovations come and go (and mostly go): The case of whole language. *Educational Research, 28*(8), 13–22.

I

Theoretical Foundations:
New Directions for the Future

2

Comprehension Strategies Instruction

A Turn-of-the-Century Status Report

MICHAEL PRESSLEY

I did my first research on comprehension strategies instruction in the school year 1974–1975 (Pressley, 1976), before many thought it was a good idea to teach comprehension strategies to children. During the quarter century since, a great deal of informative research has been done about comprehension and comprehension strategies instruction. Those of us producing this research should be justifiably proud of these accomplishments. Even so, for someone who had spent much of his career studying comprehension strategies instruction, 1998 was a very bad year—indeed, an absolutely depressing year. There were multiple indications in 1998 that educators were ignoring my work and the work of many of us who had focused on teaching comprehension skills to students.

First, one of the most painful articles I have ever written appeared in print. In the school year 1995–1996, Ruth Wharton-McDonald, Jennifer Mistretta-Hampston, Marissa Echevarria, and I spent a great deal of time observing the language arts instruction in 10 fourth- and fifth-grade classrooms in upstate New York (Pressley, Wharton-McDonald, Mistretta-Hampston, & Echevarria, 1998). The good news was that we observed lots of instructional practices that make very good sense based on research about effective literacy instruction. For example, we saw lots of literature-driven instruction, explicit teaching of vocabulary, one-to-one miniconferences between teachers and students, language arts–content integration, use of the plan–draft–revise model of writing, and cooperative learning. That said, we also saw very little comprehension instruction, very little of teaching students how to process text so that they might understand and remember it, although there was a great deal of testing of comprehension.

In the past, when I have related this finding to audiences, those with a historical understanding of reading instruction recall a study by Durkin (1978–1979). When Durkin observed upper elementary-grade classes more than 2 decades ago, she also encountered little teaching of comprehension, although there was much testing of comprehension. What is surprising about the more recent Pressley et al. (1998) observation, however, was that there has been a great deal of research in the past several decades on comprehension instruction. Indeed, the evidence is now overwhelming that upper-grade elementary students can be taught to use comprehension strategies, with substantial improvements in student understanding of text following such instruction (Pearson & Dole, 1987; Pearson & Fielding, 1991; Pressley, Johnson, Symons, McGoldrick, & Kurita, 1989). As one of the individuals who did quite a bit of research on comprehension strategies instruction for elementary students, I found it exceptionally disheartening to confront the reality that little to no comprehension instruction was being given in grades 4 and 5.

The second painful event of 1998 for researchers who had dedicated much of their careers to comprehension instruction came in the form of the National Research Council report *Preventing Reading Difficulties in Young Children* (Snow, Burns, & Griffin, 1998), which was released in the early spring of the year. On the positive side, the message was loud and clear in the volume that word-level processes were critical to comprehension and to making meaning from text, that comprehension depended on fluency in word recognition. Moreover, there was a good deal of acknowledgment that comprehension depends on vocabulary development and development of background knowledge. Unfortunately, much less was said about comprehension strategies. Yes, it was mentioned a few times that elementary students should be taught comprehension strategies, such as prediction, summarization, and monitoring of comprehension, but some well-validated strategies (e.g., construction of mental images) received no mention, and almost nothing was said about how comprehension strategies should be taught. In fact, the only comprehension strategies instruction given explicit endorsement was a very dated approach, reciprocal teaching (Palincsar & Brown, 1984). Although this approach is historically important (Pressley & McCormick, 1995) in that it was the first empirically validated approach to the teaching of a package of comprehension strategies (i.e., prediction, question generation, summarization, and seeking clarification), there has been a great deal of development of more flexible and longer term approaches to development of comprehension strategies in students. In general, I left my reading of the National Research Council volume feeling that comprehension strategies instruction had been very much ignored by the authors of a report who were charged to cover comprehensively the literature on prevention of reading difficulties in elementary students.

The third blow in 1998 came with the publication of my book *Reading Instruction That Works: The Case for Balanced Teaching* (Pressley, 1998). I tried to make the case in the book that effective elementary literacy instruction balances skills instruction, especially word-level skills and higher order competencies (i.e., composition and comprehension). Despite that intention, the reaction to my book centered entirely on its relevance to the debate over phonics versus whole language, with many comments (both pro and con) regarding my stances on beginning word-level instruction. There was hardly a mention in the reactions about comprehension, let alone instruction of comprehension strategies.

The fourth assault came near the end of 1998. On December 1, just as I arrived at the convention hotel for the National Reading Conference, I was confronted by P. David Pearson and Elfrieda Hiebert. They wanted to share with me an important finding from their first year of study at the recently funded Center for Improvement of Early Reading Achievement (CIERA). Researchers at the center had just spent a good deal of time observing grade 4 classrooms, generating quite a bit of data from sites across the nation.

What they had observed was what my colleagues and I had seen in upstate New York: very little comprehension strategies instruction. As Pearson put it, "It's as if that whole body of research on teaching of comprehension strategies did not exist; everything we did [referring to Pearson and Pressley] on comprehension instruction is being ignored!" Of course, Pearson was right. 1998 was a bad year for those of us who have worked hard to promote and improve comprehension strategies instruction in schools. Our work generally was being ignored by educators in 1998.

MOSAIC OF THOUGHT

With winter 1999 came some invitations to speak about reading instruction, mostly prompted by my book. It was heartening that there were a lot of questions about comprehension strategies from audiences at these talks. There was hope that someone remained interested in comprehension strategies instruction. Most intriguing, several members of one audience were emphatic that the summary of comprehension strategies instruction that I gave in my talk was identical to the perspective offered in a book by Ellin Oliver Keene and Susan Zimmermann (1997). Moreover, they described enthusiastically how the book was changing their teaching (and the teaching of others they knew). They claimed that in their classrooms, they now were teaching comprehension strategies.

I was intrigued enough by these assertions to buy and read a copy of Keene and Zimmermann's (1997) *Mosaic of Thought: Teaching Comprehension in a Reader's Workshop*. Some of the most important points in the book were the following:

- Reading is a very active process. Good readers question and challenge authors as they read. Sometimes the reader is confused by what is being read and makes efforts to resolve the confusions. The result of these efforts is a personal interpretation, which is affected by the reader's prior knowledge and experiences.
- Good readers use a relatively few thinking strategies consistently when they read (i.e., relating what is in text to their prior knowledge, figuring out the main ideas in text, questioning, constructing mental images of the meaning conveyed by text, making inferences beyond the information given in text, summarizing, seeking clarification when the meaning of text is confusing).
- Students' meaning making from text (i.e., understanding and memory) can be improved by teaching them to use the comprehension strategies used by good readers.
- The best way to teach comprehension strategies is to teach them one at a time, with a great deal of time devoted to each one. Teachers should model use of each strategy with a wide variety of texts. Students then should practice each strategy with a variety of texts, with the teacher encouraging student self-regulated use of the strategies by gradually releasing control of the strategies from the teacher to the student (Pearson & Gallagher, 1983).
- An important step in becoming a good teacher of comprehension strategies is to become a user of comprehension strategies. Thus teachers benefit from learning about comprehension strategies and attempting to use the strategies in their own reading. By learning to use and using the strategies, teachers become aware of the positive effects of using comprehension strategies.

- Comprehension strategies should be taught to students as they are immersed in the reading of excellent literature.
- Meaning of text can be socially constructed when readers of a text talk about it. Hence one mechanism for increasing active reading in children is to engage them in conversations about texts they are reading. Their interpretations of the particular texts read will be affected by such dialogue, and they will begin to learn how to engage texts actively themselves as they read them.

Keene and Zimmermann's (1997) book is mostly about the teaching of individual strategies, with whole chapters devoted to each of the comprehension strategies they believe are important (viz., relating to prior knowledge, identifying main ideas, questioning, mental imagery, making inferences, summarizing, and clarifying). There are many examples in the book of what happens when classroom teachers become comprehension strategies instructors.

In particular, there are many teacher–student and student–student dialogues included in the book. These dialogues illustrated instruction in using comprehension strategies, as well as the type of thinking that results when students do use strategies instruction. Comprehension strategies instruction as Keene and Zimmermann envision it is very active teaching, with teachers engaging students in using strategies to understand and interpret texts.

WHAT IS RIGHT WITH THE FRAMEWORK IN *MOSAIC OF THOUGHT*

There is much to admire in the Keene and Zimmermann text. In fact, most of their assumptions and their methods can be defended in light of substantial research on comprehension strategies.

Reading as an Active Process

Good readers are very active as they read, using a number of strategies as they proceed through text. The most revealing studies relative to this point used think-aloud methodology. Basically, readers were asked to verbalize their thought processes as they read. More than 40 such studies were included in a review of think-alouds during reading published by Pressley and Afflerbach (1995).

Before Reading

Before reading a text, the good reader has a goal (i.e., she or he knows what she or he wants to get out of the text). Often they overview a text before reading it, skimming to determine generally what is covered in the text. Based on such an overview, the good reader sometimes constructs a hypothesis about what the text says.

During Reading

Most good readers read text generally from front to back. They may skim some parts and concentrate intensely on others. Sometimes they repeat the reading of a section of text, perhaps making notes or pausing to reflect on parts of the text. Typically, they are especially alert to ideas that relate to their reading goal (i.e., information pertinent to what they want to find out). They check whether their tentative hypothesis about the meaning of text is borne out in the reading, typically changing hypotheses about the text meaning as new information is encountered and reflected on. The good reader is alert to the main ideas in a text, particularly main ideas that are relevant to the reader's goals or ones that are novel ideas. The good reader makes many inferences during reading, often conscious ones (e.g., inferring the meaning of a word encountered in the text based on context clues). These inferences often involve relating what is stated in text to the reader's prior knowledge. Sometimes the reader infers the author's intention (e.g., "The author wants me to think that . . ."). Part of this inference making is integrating ideas across different sections of text. The good reader's inferences often are interpretations of what is being read, paraphrases capturing the whole meaning of paragraphs or sections in a phrase or a sentence or two.

Throughout reading, the good reader is always monitoring, always aware of characteristics of the text (e.g., relevance to reading goal, whether reading is easy or difficult, whether the main ideas are being comprehended). The good reader monitors problems during reading, including loss of attention, words that are not known, or text that does not seem to make sense. Sometimes this awareness results in fix-up strategies being activated, such as rereading to seek clarification when text meaning is unclear.

Throughout reading, good readers also are evaluating the text. Thus, they are deciding whether they believe the information in the text or not. They decide whether they think the text is well written or poorly constructed. Good readers come to conclusions about whether the text is interesting enough to give to others. Such evaluations can be quite emotional, for example, as during a teary-eyed reading of a story about a heroic battle with a disease.

After Reading

On completion of a text, the good reader sometimes rereads selectively, sometimes consciously constructs a summary of what was in the text, and sometimes reflects on the text. Sometimes she or he thinks about how the information in the text might be used in the future.

Summary

Quite a bit goes on when good readers read. Does it make sense to conclude, as Keene and Zimmermann (1997) did, that skilled reading involves a relatively few strategic processes: relating to prior knowledge, identifying main ideas, questioning, mental imagery, making inferences, summarizing, and clarifying? In fact, all of the processes identified by Keene and Zimmermann (1997) were noted prominently in the Pressley and Afflerbach (1995) review of strategies reported by good readers as they read. Keene and Zimmermann's (1997) many admonitions that readers must learn to be aware when they read are consistent with the many reports of monitoring during reading by skilled readers. Moreover, the many evaluative interpretations of texts in the discussions reported by Keene and Zimmermann (1997) are very consistent with the portrait of skilled reading presented by Pressley and Afflerbach (1995). In particular, Keene and Zimmermann's emphasis on prior knowledge affecting understanding and interpretation of text also makes sense, with much of the monitoring, strategy use, and interpretation summarized in Pressley and Afflerbach (1995) clearly reflecting the extensive prior knowledge of very good readers.

In short, Keene and Zimmermann's (1997) conception of excellent reading is, in fact, consistent with the conception of skilled reading that emerges from studying the protocols of excellent reading analyzed by Pressley and Afflerbach (1995). Excellent reading does involve the strategies featured in Keane and Zimmermann's book, with lots and lots of monitoring of reading, and massive interpretation of what is read, with such interpretations often affected by the reader's prior knowledge.

Students Should Be Taught Strategies One at a Time

There is a great deal of evidence consistent with Keene and Zimmermann's (1997) assumption that students can be taught the strategies used by good readers and that when they are taught those strategies, their understanding and memory of texts read improves. Many experiments were conducted in the 1970s and 1980s of the following form: One group of students were taught to use some particular strategy while reading (e.g., imagery, summarization), with their reading compared with that of students who were not given such an instruction. In general, the students taught to use the comprehension strategy outperformed the students not given instruction; this result was obtained with a number of different strategies and with reading comprehension measured in a variety of ways.

Particularly relevant in this chapter directed at teaching in the upper elementary grades is that a number of individual strategies were validated as effective in improving comprehension in students in grades 4 through 8 (Pressley et al., 1989)—most prominently, the following:

- *Relating to prior knowledge.* Students were taught to compare their lives with situations in the text or to make predictions based on prior knowledge about what might happen in the text.
- *Mental imagery.* Students were taught to construct images in their heads consistent with the meanings conveyed in text.
- *Questioning.* Students were taught to develop questions pertaining to information represented in several different parts of the text. Students were also taught to evaluate their questions as to whether the questions covered important material and could be answered based on what was in the text.
- *Summarization.* Students are taught to find the big ideas in paragraphs and in longer passages by deleting trivial information. Sometimes students were taught to generate an outline of the passage.

That is, there is fairly definitive evidence that upper-grade elementary students can be taught to relate what they are reading to prior knowledge, to construct mental images of text content, to question themselves about ideas in text, and to summarize what has been read. I am less convinced, however, that we know how to teach upper elementary students to makes inferences when they are reading and to monitor their comprehension while they read.

With respect to making of inferences, there have been some successes in teaching children how to construct appropriate inferences when processing texts (Yuill & Oakhill,

1991). My reading of the literature, however, is that we are a long way from knowing how to teach children to make the many inferences they should make to get the most out of text. The challenge of teaching students to make inferences is obvious simply from considering the many types of inferences the good reader makes when processing text. Good readers infer all of the following (Pressley & Afflerbach, 1995): referents of pronouns; meanings of unknown vocabulary; subtle connotations in text; explanations for events described in text; examples of concepts explained in text; elaborations of ideas based on knowledge of the text or author or subject area; how ideas in a text relate to one's own opinions and theories; the author's purposes in writing the text; the author's assumptions about the world; the author's sources and strategies in writing the text; the text characters' intentions and characteristics; the nature of the world in which the written text takes place; and conclusions suggested by the text. There is high motivation to determine whether young readers can be taught to be highly inferential as they read, for skilled comprehension of text definitely depends on making inferences (Cain & Oakhill, 1998; Oakhill, Cain, & Yuill, 1998).

With respect to teaching children how to monitor their text comprehension, there also have been some limited successes (Elliott-Faust & Pressley, 1986; Ghatala, Levin, Pressley, & Goodwin, 1986; Lodico, Ghatala, Levin, Pressley, & Bell, 1983; Rao & Moely, 1989). However, even a very generous reading of the relevant studies does not permit the conclusion that we know how to teach children to do the many types of monitoring required during reading (Pressley & Afflerbach, 1995). Good readers can monitor all of the following: whether text is relevant to a current reading goal, the difficulty level of the text, the style of the text, the text's linguistic characteristics, the biases in a text, the relationship of parts of a text to larger themes in the text, the relationship of this text to other texts, when text is ambiguous, the relationship of the reader's background knowledge to the text, the tone of the text, and problems encountered in reading (e.g., loss of concentration, reading too quickly or too slowly, poorly written text, lack of background knowledge to understand text). Moreover, the skilled reader not only monitors but also shifts reading in reaction to what is monitored, and we are certainly a long way from knowing how best to teach readers to do such shifting. Shifting includes the following: attempting to figure out the meaning of a word detected as unknown; deciding whether to interpret text strictly or liberally; deciding whether to attend to or read carefully only certain parts of text that are most likely to be understood or most likely to be helpful; deciding to look up background material (e.g., a word in the dictionary) before continuing to read the text; attempting to pinpoint the parts of text that are confusing; and deciding to reread material that was not understood initially but that might be understood with more effort. There also are a few approaches to difficult text that good readers do not take, and monitoring plays an important role in stopping these behaviors from occurring; for example, as they read, good readers do not think about things other than the text, fall asleep, or simply give up on trying to understand the text. Unfortunately, however, we do not know how to teach weaker readers to monitor whether their attention is waning as they read.

In summary, Keene and Zimmermann's (1997) commitment to teach individual strategies one at a time can be defended by the many demonstrations of improved comprehension and memory for text when some individual strategic processes are taught. It remains unclear, however, whether it is possible to teach in the classroom all of the individual processes that Keene and Zimmermann favored in *Mosaic of*

Thought. Both inference making and monitoring are very complicated processes, with only limited understanding at this point of how to develop these competencies through instruction.

WHAT IS WRONG WITH THE FRAMEWORK IN *MOSAIC OF THOUGHT*

Even though some of Keene and Zimmermann's (1997) assumptions are well supported by research, I was sometimes frustrated by their book.

Little about the Teaching Model

There is not much of a model of teaching specified in *Mosaic*. The authors do make reference to Pearson and Gallagher's (1983) gradual release of control approach to instruction, beginning with teacher modeling and continuing with increasingly greater control of processing by students. Even so, it is very difficult from the descriptions of teaching to envision how modeling occurs in actual classrooms or the many ways in which teachers can support student efforts to use strategies.

A prominent claim in the book is that comprehension strategies should take place in the context of a "readers' workshop," although the specifics of that approach also are not provided. It is clear that such a workshop approach includes student reading of and interaction over literature, but that is about all I could conclude from Keene and Zimmermann's (1997) book.

Little about Student Outcomes

There also is little information about how students read differently as a function of the strategy instruction. That is, it is not at all clear whether students became autonomously strategic readers as a function of the comprehension strategies instruction they received. That seemed to be the goal, for near the end of the book, one of the authors describes her own reading in these terms:

> As I read, I consciously and subconsciously use the strategies we've discussed in this book. I synthesize. I question. I infer. I create vivid sensory images. I relate the piece to my own experience. I tease out what I think is most important. I draw conclusions about what I think the key points of the passage are. Sometimes I use the strategies purposefully, other times they surface randomly. They are tools I use, sometimes effortlessly, sometimes purposefully to construct meaning. They intertwine and merge and I switch quickly among them, frequently using them simultaneously. They are the instruments which, as I become more familiar with them, gave me the ability to read more quickly. They are a means to an end. For proficient readers, they are second nature. (Keene & Zimmermann, 1997, p. 216)

I wish Keene and Zimmermann had provided information about whether K–12 students were learning to read this way because of comprehension strategies instruction as they conceive of it and describe it in their book. There is a need for a lot of research on the Keene and Zimmermann (1997) approach and its effects on student reading.

Assumptions about Teachers' Reading

Despite the fact that Keene and Zimmermann (1997) insist that teachers using their approach learn to read differently than they did previously, I was frustrated during my reading of the text by the relative lack of attention by the authors to the changes in teachers' reading as a function of their becoming strategies instructors. An important research agenda should be to determine whether and how awareness of strategies increases as a function of learning to teach comprehension strategies to students and whether and how such increased awareness affects teaching *per se*.

The possibility that teachers can become strategic readers and aware of their own use of strategies is heartening. If that is so, then it should make it easier to sell teachers on the value of teaching comprehension strategies. This is critical, for if teachers do not buy into such comprehension strategies instructional models, it is unlikely that they will change their classroom teaching much in the direction of encouraging their students to use comprehension strategies. (This last assertion is discussed more fully later in this section.)

Teaching One Strategy at a Time

Keene and Zimmermann's (1997) focus on the teaching of individual strategies contrasts somewhat with other conceptions about how to teach comprehension strategies, including conceptions that define how comprehension strategies are taught when they are taught in American elementary schools. These conceptions begin with the recognition that multiple strategies are articulated by good readers as they read (e.g., Brown, Bransford, Ferrara, & Campione, 1983; Levin & Pressley, 1981), and hence it makes good sense to teach young readers to coordinate multiple strategies as they read.

For example, my colleagues and I studied classrooms that implemented comprehension strategies instruction (Brown & Coy-Ogan, 1993; El-Dinary, Pressley, & Schuder, 1992; Gaskins, Anderson, Pressley, Cunicelli, & Satlow, 1993; Pressley, El-Dinary, Gaskins, et al., 1992; Pressley, El-Dinary, Stein, Marks, & Brown, 1992; Pressley, Gaskins, Cunicelli, et al., 1991; Pressley, Gaskins, Wile, Cunicelli, & Sheridan, 1991; Pressley, Schuder, SAIL Faculty and Administration, Bergman, & El-Dinary, 1992). Consistently, we observed teaching of small repertoires of comprehension strategies, with students taught to articulate and coordinate strategies such as predicting from prior knowledge, relating to prior knowledge, generating images, seeking clarification, and summarizing. Although initially strategies were sometimes taught individually to acquaint students with a strategic process, typically such individual instruction yielded rather quickly to an emphasis on the repertoire of strategies and on learning to choose which strategy would be useful in a particular reading situation.

Consistent with the gradual release of responsibility approach favored by Keene and Zimmermann (1997), strategies typically were first modeled and explained, with student practice of the strategy (or repertoire) then following. Following the introduction of the strategies, students were coached as they attempted to use the strategies, particularly in the context of small group lessons. This was possible because students were encouraged during small group to model use of strategies for one another, thinking aloud as they read. Students did a lot of explaining to one another during these small group lessons, letting each other know how they were actively processing text. The students let one another know how useful the strategies were to them, reinforcing the teacher's instruction about how strategies improve understanding and memory of text. Although teacher modeling of strategies was reduced as students increased and improved their use of strategies, teachers continued to think aloud when they read to students, consistently modeling for them the flexible use of the repertoire of strategies being taught in the classroom.

Consistent as well with Keene and Zimmermann's (1997) emphasis on dialogue, the small group lessons my associates and I observed were filled with dialogue, and use of the strategies animated the discussions. That is, the discussions were filled with predictions about what might be in the stories, associations to the readings on the basis of prior knowledge, explanations of the images constructed during reading, commentaries about the parts of the text that were difficult to understand and alternative interpretations of such sections, and summaries of what readings were about. It was clear to us that strategies instruction is a powerful tool for stimulating rich conversations between students about the texts they are reading.

Eventually, my colleagues and I (Pressley, El-Dinary, Gaskins, et al., 1992) came to think of this type of instruction as transactional strategies instruction because the readers' transactions with text (i.e., interpretations) were so obvious as students applied strategies to text (Rosenblatt, 1978). We made the case that, as children practiced use of repertoires of comprehension strategies in small reading groups, they internalized the strategic processes, eventually using them on their own when reading.

There have been three published experimental evaluations of long-term transactional strategies instruction. Rachel Brown and I, in collaboration with Peggy Van Meter and Ted Schuder (Brown, Pressley, Van Meter, & Schuder, 1996), studied the effects of 1 year of transactional strategies instruction on weak grade 2 readers. Grade 2 readers who participated in classrooms that emphasized use of a small repertoire of comprehension strategies were compared with grade 2 readers in classrooms with conventional reading instruction. The particular strategies taught were predicting, questioning, seeking clarification, creating mental imagery, associating to ideas in text, and summarizing, with a strong emphasis on self-regulated use of these strategies. That is, it was emphasized that choosing an appropriate strategy was important and that different strategies apply in different situations. At the beginning of the year, the students in the two types of classrooms did not differ on standardized reading measures or on word attack measures. By the end of the year, striking differences on these measures favored the students in the transactional strategies instruction classrooms. Indeed, by the end of the year the students receiving transactional strategies instruction were more strategic as evidenced in their thinking aloud as they read and on measures of interpretive recall of text. The students who received a year of transactional strategies instruction were much better readers than control participants in the Brown et al. (1996) study.

Others besides my group, however, have also obtained positive results from long-term transactional instruction of repertoires of comprehension strategies. Cathy Collins Block (Collins, 1991) studied students in grades 5 and 6 as they received comprehension strategies instruction over a semester. The particular repertoire of strategies taught in her study included predicting, seeking clarification, looking for patterns and principles in ideas presented in text, analyzing decision making while reading, backward reasoning, mental imagery, summarizing, adapting and interpreting ideas in text, and negotiating interpretations of texts with others (i.e., discussing text with others, including how strategies are being applied in text). At the beginning of the study, the strategies-instructed students performed similarly to control participants on reading tasks, including standardized test measures. By the end of the 6 months of strategies instruction, the instructed students read much better than the control participants, including on standardized test measures.

Valerie Anderson (1992) provided 3 months of transactional strategies instruction to struggling readers in grades 6 through 11. Instruction was provided in small groups. The reading of students receiving strategies instruction was compared with the reading of other students who participated in small groups not receiving strategies instruction. By the end of the 3 months, strategies-instructed students were more willing to try challenging reading, more active while they read, and better able to interact with classmates to interpret texts read. After the instruction, the strategies-instructed students also outperformed control students on a standardized test of reading.

In summary, there is quite a bit of evidence that elementary, middle school, and secondary students benefit from instruction in the use of a small repertoire of reading comprehension strategies. In recent years especially, teaching of comprehension strategies has followed a common model, beginning with teacher modeling and explanation of strategies and continuing with student practice of strategies with the teacher then coaching students' use of strategies. Not only does such teaching work to increase reading comprehension but it does so by encouraging the kind of active reading done by proficient readers, as described earlier in this paper.

Teachers Are Motivated to Develop Strategic Readers and Be Comprehension Strategies Teachers

Keene and Zimmermann (1997) assume that most teachers will agree that students are too passive when they read. They also assume that teachers will agree that it is a good thing to stimulate use of strategies that encourage more active reading, strategies that encourage reading as good readers read. These assumptions may be too strong.

When my associates and I did our work on comprehension strategies instruction, we spent a great deal of time in classrooms of teachers who did it well. After all, we were interested in excellent comprehension strategies instruction. From time to time, however, we also observed teachers who were struggling with comprehension strategies instruction or were downright hostile toward it, for example, believing students were better off simply reading on their own. We also heard plenty of stories about teachers who tried comprehension strategies instruction and decided it was not for them or their students.

A particularly illuminating analysis was provided by Pamela Beard El-Dinary in her dissertation study (see Pressley & El-Dinary, 1997). She studied seven teachers as they attempted to become transactional strategies instruction teachers over the course of a school year. What became apparent early in the year was that learning to be a strategies instruction teacher was very challenging. For example, some of the teachers felt that transactional strategies instruction conflicted with their own beliefs about reading and teaching of reading. Some felt it conflicted with the whole-language methods they learned in their teacher education courses (i.e., strategies instruction seemed too teacher directed). Some teachers felt that comprehension strategies instruction and use of comprehension strategies during reading group took too much time, with the result that students were not reading nearly as many books and stories in reading groups. Also, there were teachers who had problems with the many interpretations emanating from reading group discussions that used the strategies: Some permitted any interpretation that emerged, regardless of whether it seemed consistent with the reading, and others seemed uncomfortable with anything except standard interpretations. By the end of the year of observations, only two of the seven teachers were committed comprehension strategies instruction teachers. El-Dinary's (1994) work made clear that comprehension strategies instruction, or at least the transactional strategies instructional approach, is not for every teacher.

Summary

In this section, I tried to place Keene and Zimmermann's (1997) book in the context of the larger comprehension strategies instructional literature. Compared with much of the work preceding it, *Mosaic of Thought* is relatively inattentive to details about how instruction should occur and how readers change as a function of the instruction they favor. More positively, I am certainly willing to accept as hypotheses that teaching individual strategies as Keene and Zimmermann (1997) conceived of it might improve teachers' comprehension processing and awareness of comprehension processes, might be a powerful approach to teaching of comprehension to elementary students, and might be an acceptable form of instruction for teachers. Indeed, I hope that all of these hypotheses will be supported as research on the model proceeds.

Even the most enthusiastic strategies instructionist, however, has to pause at the single-mindedness of Keene and Zimmermann (1997) with respect to comprehension: They advocate only for teaching of comprehension strategies. Thus, in the next section, I make the case that after a quarter of a century of research on comprehension strategies instruction, it is very clear that comprehension is not just about strategies and that instruction to improve comprehension should not be just about strategies.

WHAT SHOULD COMPREHENSION INSTRUCTION BE ABOUT?

There has been a great deal of work in recent decades establishing that comprehension depends very much on word-level skills and background knowledge, as well as on the processes stimulated by comprehension strategies instruction. Thus, as the century closes, it is well understood that if a child cannot decode a word, he or she will not comprehend the meaning intended by the word (Adams, 1990; Metsala & Ehri, 1998). Indeed, beyond accurate word recognition, if the child cannot decode words fluently, comprehension will be impaired (Breznitz, 1997a, 1997b; Gough & Tummer, 1986; LaBerge & Samuels, 1974; Tan & Nicholson, 1997). It is also well understood that comprehension depends on vocabulary, with good readers having more extensive vocabularies than weaker readers (e.g., Anderson & Freebody, 1981; Stanovich, 1986). When an elementary-level reader improves her or his vocabulary, reading comprehension improves (Beck, Perfetti, & McKeown, 1982; McKeown, Beck, Omanson, & Perfetti, 1983; McKeown, Beck, Omanson, & Pople, 1985).

Good readers also have extensive knowledge of the world that they relate to ideas in text in order to understand what they are reading (Anderson & Pearson, 1984). Making of inferences beyond the information given in text depends heavily on prior knowledge (Hayes-Roth & Thorndyke, 1979; Kintsch, 1988; van Dijk & Kintsch, 1983). Good readers use prior knowledge to make inferences required to understand a text (McKoon & Ratcliff, 1992), in contrast to weak readers who often make associations to prior knowledge that are only remotely related to ideas in the text (e.g., Williams, 1993).

There are a number of instructional recommendations (Pressley, 2000) that follow directly from the literature about word-level and prior knowledge contributions to comprehension:

- *Teach decoding skills.* Developing word recognition skills in the primary years pays off with comprehension gains in the upper elementary grades (e.g., Juel, 1988).
- *Encourage the development of sight words.* Sight words are recognized with less effort than words that must be decoded, freeing up cognitive capacity for comprehension (LaBerge & Samuels, 1974).
- *Teach vocabulary meanings.* Although more words are learned incidentally than through instruction (Sternberg, 1987), teaching of vocabulary often encountered in texts improves comprehension (Beck et al., 1982; McKeown et al., 1983; McKeown et al., 1985).
- *Encourage extensive reading.* Reading a great deal provides additional exposure to words, which affects fluency (LaBerge & Samuels, 1974). Reading increases young readers' vocabulary (e.g., Dickinson & Smith, 1994; Elley, 1989; Fleisher, Jenkins, & Pany, 1979; Pellegrini, Galda, Perlmutter, & Jones, 1994; Robbins & Ehri, 1994; Rosenhouse, Feitelson, Kita, & Goldstein, 1997; Valdez-Menchaca & Whitehurst, 1992; Whitehurst et al., 1988), as well as the knowledge of the world that mediates reading comprehension (Stanovich & Cunningham, 1993).
- *Encourage students to relate prior knowledge to text.* (Anderson & Pearson, 1984; Levin & Pressley, 1981).

In short, there are multiple ways to improve comprehension, with all of them potentially affected by instruction. Although a good case can be made for teaching comprehension strategies to elementary students, it is most defensible to do so in the context of a reading program that includes teaching to promote word recognition skills, vocabulary knowledge, and extensive reading of books filled with the world knowledge that young readers need to acquire.

In *Mosaic of Thought*, Keene and Zimmermann (1997) argue for a reader's workshop approach, which should go far in promoting a great deal of reading, which in turn should affect fluency, vocabulary development, and construction of background knowledge. Thus it is possible that their call for adding comprehension strategies instruction to reading of literature is an effective approach to development of comprehension abilities. For myself, I would like to see some formal comparisons of the "strategies instruction plus readers workshop" method recommended by Keene and Zimmermann (1997) with literature-based instruction filled with explicit teaching and encouragement of comprehension strategies, development of fluency, vocabulary learning, and coverage of critical world knowledge. That is, I do not think we have yet created and evaluated the best comprehension instruction possible based on what is known at the end of the 20th century about how to promote comprehension abilities. It seems to me that the time is ripe to do so.

REFERENCES

Adams, M. J. (1990). *Beginning to read.* Cambridge, MA: Harvard University Press.

Anderson, R. C., & Freebody, P. (1981). Vocabulary knowledge. In J. T. Guthrie (Ed.), *Comprehen-*

sion and teaching: Research reviews (pp. 77–117). Newark, DE: International Reading Association.

Anderson, R. C., & Pearson, P. D. (1984). A schema-theoretic view of basic processes in reading. In P. D. Pearson (Ed.), *Handbook of reading research* (pp. 255–291). New York: Longman.

Anderson, V. (1992). A teacher development project in transactional strategy instruction for teachers of severely reading-disabled adolescents. *Teaching and Teacher Education, 8,* 391–403.

Beck, I. L., Perfetti, C. A., & McKeown, M. G. (1982). Effects of long-term vocabulary instruction on lexical access and reading comprehension. *Journal of Educational Psychology, 74,* 506–521.

Breznitz, Z. (1997a). Effects of accelerated reading rate on memory for text among dyslexic readers. *Journal of Educational Psychology, 89,* 289–297.

Breznitz, Z. (1997b). Enhancing the reading of dyslexic children by reading acceleration and auditory masking. *Journal of Educational Psychology, 89,* 103–113.

Brown, A. L., Bransford, J. D., Ferrara, R. A., & Campione, J. C. (1983). Learning, remembering, and understanding. In J. H. Flavell & E. M. Markman (Eds.), *Handbook of child psychology: Vol. III. Cognitive development* (pp. 77–166). New York: Wiley.

Brown, R., & Coy-Ogan, L. (1993). The evolution of transactional strategies instruction in one teacher's classroom. *Elementary School Journal, 94,* 221–233.

Brown, R., Pressley, M., Van Meter, P., & Schuder, T. (1996). A quasi-experimental validation of transactional strategies instruction with low-achieving second grade readers. *Journal of Educational Psychology, 88,* 18–37.

Cain, K., & Oakhill, J. (1998). Comprehension skill and inference-making ability: Issues and causality. In C. Hulme & R. M. Joshi (Eds.), *Reading and spelling: Development and disorders* (pp. 329–342). London: Erlbaum.

Collins, C. (1991). Reading instruction that increases thinking abilities. *Journal of Reading, 34,* 510–516.

Dickinson, D. K., & Smith, M. W. (1994). Long-term effects of preschool teachers' book readings on low-income children's vocabulary and story comprehension. *Reading Research Quarterly, 29,* 104–122.

Durkin, D. (1978–1979). What classroom observation reveals about reading comprehension instruction. *Reading Research Quarterly, 14,* 481–533.

El-Dinary, P. B. (1994). *Teachers learning, adapting and implementing strategies-based instruction in reading.* Ann Arbor, MI: Dissertation Services (Order No. 9407625).

El-Dinary, P. B., Pressley, M., & Schuder, T. (1992). Teachers learning transactional strategies instruction. In C. K. Kinzer & D. J. Leu (Eds.), *Literacy research, theory, and practice: Views from many perspectives. 41st Yearbook of the National Reading Conference* (pp. 453–462). Chicago: National Reading Conference.

Elley, W. B. (1989). Vocabulary acquisition from listening to stories. *Reading Research Quarterly, 24,* 174–187.

Elliott-Faust, D. J., & Pressley, M. (1986). Self-controlled training of comparison strategies increase children's comprehension monitoring. *Journal of Educational Psychology, 78,* 27–32.

Fleisher, L., Jenkins, J., & Pany, D. (1979). Effects on poor readers' comprehension of training in rapid decoding. *Reading Research Quarterly, 15,* 30–48.

Gaskins, I. W., Anderson, R. C., Pressley, M., Cunicelli, E. A., & Satlow, E. (1993). Six teachers' dialogue during cognitive process instruction. *Elementary School Journal, 93,* 277–304.

Ghatala, E. S., Levin, J. R., Pressley, M., & Goodwin, D. (1986). A componential analysis of the effects of derived and supplied strategy-utility information on children's strategy selections. *Journal of Experimental Child Psychology, 22,* 199–216.

Gough, P. B., & Tunmer, W. E. (1986). Decoding, reading, and reading disability. *Remedial and Special Education, 7,* 6–10.

Hayes-Roth, B., & Thorndyke, P. W. (1979). Integration of knowledge from text. *Journal of Verbal Learning and Verbal Behavior, 18*, 91–108.

Juel, C. (1988). Learning to read and write: A longitudinal study of fifty-four children from first through fourth grade. *Journal of Educational Psychology, 80*, 437–447.

Keene, E. O., & Zimmermann, S. (1997). *Mosaic of thought: Teaching comprehension in a reader's workshop*. Portsmouth, NH: Heinemann.

Kintsch, W. (1988). The role of knowledge in discourse comprehension: A construction–integration model. *Psychological Review, 95*, 163–182.

LaBerge, D., & Samuels, S. J. (1974). Toward a theory of automatic information processing in reading. *Cognitive Psychology, 6*, 293–323.

Levin, J. R., & Pressley, M. (1981). Improving childrens' prose comprehension: Selected strategies that seem to succeed. In C. M. Santa & B. L. Hayes (Eds.), *Children's prose comprehension: Research and practice* (pp. 44–71). Newark DE: International Reading Association.

Lodico, M. G., Ghatala, E. S., Levin, J. R., Pressley, M., & Bell, J. A. (1983). Effects of meta-memory training on children's use of effective learning strategies. *Journal of Experimental Child Psychology, 35*, 263–277.

McKeown, M. G., Beck, I. L., Omanson, R. C., & Perfetti, C. A. (1983). The effects of long-term vocabulary instruction on reading comprehension: A replication. *Journal of Reading Behavior, 15*, 3–18.

McKeown, M. G., Beck, I. L., Omanson, R. C., & Pople, M. T. (1985). Some effects of the nature and frequency of vocabulary instruction on the knowledge and use of words. *Reading Research Quarterly, 20*, 522–535.

McKoon, G., & Ratcliff, R. (1992). Inference during reading. *Psychological Review, 99*, 440–466.

Metsala, J., & Ehri, L. (Eds.). (1998). *Word recognition in beginning reading*. Mahwah, NJ: Erlbaum.

Oakhill, J., Cain, K., & Yuill, N. (1998). Individual differences in children's comprehension skill: Toward an integrated model. In C. Hulme & R. M. Joshi (Eds.), *Reading and spelling development and disorders* (pp. 343–367). London: Erlbaum.

Palincsar, A. S., & Brown, A. L. (1984). Reciprocal teaching of comprehension-fostering and monitoring activities. *Cognition and Instruction, 1*, 117–175.

Pearson, P. D., & Dole, J. A. (1987). Explicit comprehension instruction: A review of research and a new conceptualization of instruction. *Elementary School Journal, 88*, 151–165.

Pearson, P. D., & Fielding, L. (1991). Comprehension instruction. In R. Barr, M. L. Kamil, P. B. Mosenthal, & P. D. Pearson (Eds.), *Handbook of reading research* (Vol. 2, pp. 815–860). New York: Longman.

Pearson, P. D., & Gallagher, M. (1983). The instruction of reading comprehension. *Contemporary Educational Psychology, 8*, 317–344.

Pellegrini, A. D., Galda, L., Perlmutter, J., & Jones, I. (1994). *Joint reading between mothers and their Head Start children: Vocabulary development in two text formats* (Reading Research Report No. 13). Athens, GA, and College Park, MD: National Reading Research Center.

Pressley, G. M. (1976). Mental imagery helps eight-year-olds remember what they read. *Journal of Educational Psychology, 68*, 355–359.

Pressley, M. (1998). *Reading instruction that works: The case for balanced teaching*. New York: Guilford Press.

Pressley, M. (2000). What should comprehension instruction be the instruction of? In M. L. Kamil, P. B. Mosenthal, P. D. Pearson, & R. Barr (Eds.), *Handbook of reading research* (Vol. III, pp. 546–561). Mahwah, NJ: Erlbaum.

Pressley, M., & Afflerbach, P. (1995). *Verbal protocols of reading: The nature of constructively responsive reading*. Hillsdale, NJ: Erlbaum.

Pressley, M., & El-Dinary, P. B. (1997). What we know about translating comprehension strategies instruction research into practice. *Journal of Learning Disabilities, 30*, 486–488.

Pressley, M., El-Dinary, P. B., Gaskins, I., Schuder, T., Bergman, J., Almasi, L., & Brown, R. (1992). Beyond direct explanation: Transactional instruction of reading comprehension strategies. *Elementary School Journal, 92*, 511–554.

Pressley, M., El-Dinary, P. B., Stein, S., Marks, M. B., & Brown, R. (1992). Good strategy instruction is motivating and interesting. In A. Renninger, S. Hidi, & A. Krapp (Eds.), *The role of interest in learning and development* (pp. 333–358). Hillsdale, NJ: Erlbaum.

Pressley, M., Gaskins, I. W., Cunicelli, E. A., Bardick, N. J., Schaub-Matt, M., Lee, D. S., & Powell, N. (1991). Strategy instruction at Benchmark School: A faculty interview study. *Learning Disability Quarterly, 14*, 19–48.

Pressley, M., Gaskins, I. W., Wile, D., Cunicelli, E. A., & Sheridan, J. (1991). Teaching literacy strategies across the curriculum: A case study at Benchmark School. In S. McCormick & J. Zutell (Eds.), *40th Yearbook of the National Reading Conference* (pp. 219–228). Chicago: National Reading Conference.

Pressley, M., Johnson, C. J., Symons, S., McGoldrick, J. A., & Kurita, J. A. (1989). Strategies that improve children's memory and comprehension of text. *Elementary School Journal, 90*, 3–32.

Pressley, M., & McCormick, C. B. (1995). *Advanced educational psychology for educators, researchers, and policymakers.* New York: HarperCollins.

Pressley, M., Schuder, T., SAIL Faculty and Administration, Bergman, J. L., & El-Dinary, P. B. (1992). A researcher–educator collaborative interview study of transactional comprehension strategies instruction. *Journal of Educational Psychology, 84*, 231–246.

Pressley, M., Wharton-McDonald, R., Mistretta-Hampston, J. M., & Echevarria, M. (1998). The nature of literacy instruction in ten grade 4/5 classrooms in upstate New York. *Scientific Studies of Reading, 2*, 159–194.

Rao, N., & Moely, B. E. (1989). Producing memory strategy maintenance and generalization by explicit or implicit training of memory knowledge. *Journal of Experimental Child Psychology, 48*, 335–352.

Robbins, C., & Ehri, L. C. (1994). Reading storybooks to kindergartners helps them learn new vocabulary words. *Journal of Educational Psychology, 86*, 54–64.

Rosenblatt, L. M. (1978). *The reader, the text, the poem: The transactional theory of the literary work.* Carbondale: Southern Illinois University Press.

Rosenhouse, J., Feitelson, D., Kita, B., & Goldstein, Z. (1997). Interactive reading aloud to Israeli first graders: Its contribution to literacy development. *Reading Research Quarterly, 32*, 168–183.

Snow, C. E., Burns, M. S., & Griffin, P. (1998). *Preventing reading difficulties in young children.* Washington, DC: National Academy Press.

Stanovich, K. (1986). Matthew effects in reading: Some consequences of individual differences in the acquisition of literacy. *Reading Research Quarterly, 21*, 360–407.

Stanovich, K. E., & Cunningham, A. E. (1993). Where does knowledge come from? Specific associations between print exposure and information acquisition. *Journal of Educational Psychology, 85*, 211–229.

Sternberg, R. J. (1987). Most vocabulary is learned from context. In M. G. McKeown & M. E. Curtis (Eds.), *The nature of vocabulary acquisition* (pp. 89–105). Hillsdale, NJ: Erlbaum.

Tan, A., & Nicholson, T. (1997). Flashcards revisited: Training poor readers to read words faster improves their comprehension of text. *Journal of Educational Psychology, 89*, 276–288.

Valdez-Menchaca, M. C., & Whitehurst, G. J. (1992). Accelerating language development through picture book reading: A systematic extension to Mexican day care. *Developmental Psychology, 28*, 1106–1114.

van Dijk, T. A., & Kintsch, W. (1983). *Strategies of discourse comprehension*. New York: Academic Press.

Whitehurst, G. J., Falco, F. L., Lonigan, C. J., Fischel, J. E., DeBaryshe, B. D., Valdez-Menchaca, M. C., & Caulfield, M. (1988). Accelerating language development through picture book reading. *Developmental Psychology, 24,* 552–559.

Williams, J. P. (1993). Comprehension of students with and without learning disabilities: Identification of narrative themes and idiosyncratic text representations. *Journal of Educational Psychology, 85,* 631–641.

Yuill, N., & Oakhill, J. (1991). *Children's problems in reading comprehension*. Cambridge, England: Cambridge University Press.

3

The Case for Direct Explanation of Strategies

GERALD G. DUFFY

It has been 14 years since we reported that direct teacher explanation of strategies results in significant achievement gains for struggling readers (Duffy et al., 1987). Given today's standard-based world, with its emphasis on raising low readers' achievement, one would expect this finding to be heavily emphasized. However, the reading literature tends to favor less explicit techniques for teaching comprehension and places relatively little emphasis on direct explanation of comprehension strategies. Consequently, this chapter: (1) reiterates the importance of direct explanation, particularly when teaching struggling readers; (2) describes what teachers do to make explanation effective; and (3) argues for developing teachers who use both explicit and less explicit techniques as the instructional situation demands.

BACKGROUND

In my work in classrooms, I often see teachers using instructional techniques such as Directed Reading Lessons, in which teachers introduce students to the selection, guide their reading of it, and discuss its contents with them. Historically, the Directed Reading Lesson has been the favored technique for teaching comprehension. However, Durkin (1978–1979) brought us all up short by finding that such instruction may be little more than "interrogation." Thus a sustained search began for ways to improve comprehension instruction. Four broad lines of research resulted: (1) research on the relationship between prior knowledge and comprehension; (2) research on metacognition; (3) research on classroom discourse; and (4) research on explicit teaching.

Instructional Strategies Capitalizing on Prior Knowledge Research

Richard Anderson, David Pearson and their colleagues at the Center for the Study of Reading at the University of Illinois pioneered this line of research. Basing their studies in a schema-theoretic orientation, they established a link between prior knowledge and readers' construction of meaning (Anderson & Pearson, 1984). A number of instructional techniques for guiding comprehension grew out of this research.

The one I see most often in classrooms is Donna Ogle's (1986) K-W-L technique. When using K-W-L, teachers guide students to think about what they already know about a topic (K), what they want to learn (W), and what they learned as a result of their reading (L). This technique results in improved comprehension of text content because readers make connections between their prior knowledge and what they are reading. Additionally, there is the expectation that if we practice K-W-L (and/or other guided reading techniques) with students enough, they will infer that they should use these techniques themselves.

Instructional Strategies Based in Understandings about Metacognition

A second line of research grew from studies of metacognition (Baker & Brown, 1984; Garner, 1988). Metacognition is "thinking about one's thinking," usually for the purpose of assuming metacognitive control of one's thinking, or what Clay (1991) calls "inner control."

Metacognition research spurred study of how to help readers become conscious of the strategic nature of comprehension. In the 1980s, two particularly important techniques were developed. The first was Taffy Raphael's Question-Answer-Relationship (Q-A-R) technique (Raphael & McKinney, 1983; Raphael & Wonnacott, 1985). This technique teaches students to be consciously aware of whether they are likely to find the answer to a comprehension question "right there" on the page, or between the lines, or beyond information provided in the text. By being aware of the requirements posed by a question, students are in a better position to seek answers to those questions.

The second was Annemarie Palincsar's reciprocal teaching (Palincsar & Brown, 1984). Students are taught to emulate a teacher's question asking, with an emphasis on self-questioning, summarizing, predicting, and clarifying. In posing such questions, teachers encourage students to think strategically.

As with K-W-L, both Q-A-R and reciprocal teaching operate on the assumption that after repeated experiences students will infer that they should employ these strategies themselves when reading independently.

The same is the case with Reading Recovery's version of guided reading, which also has a strong metacognitive flavor (Fountas & Pinnell, 1996). In this technique for teaching comprehension, the teacher typically introduces the text, works with individuals as they read the text, selects one or two teaching points to emphasize following reading, and asks children to extend their reading afterward (Fountas & Pinnell, 1996). Again, the purpose is to guide students' comprehension of text content in hopes that they will infer from these experiences how to use strategies when the teacher is not available to guide them. Fountas and Pinnell (1996) explicitly state that the purpose is *not* to teach strategies.

Research on Classroom Discourse

A third major line of research was spurred by discomfort with Durkin's (1978–1979) findings about "interrogation." Its focus was the quality of classroom discourse. Courtney Cazden (Cazden, 1986) led this effort, but others also made important contributions (see, for instance, Au & Mason, 1981; Heap, 1982; Heath, 1983; Gaskins, Anderson, Pressley, Cunicelli, & Satlow, 1993). This work helped us understand the socially constructed nature of learning and that oral language determines much of the classroom culture (Bloome & Green, 1984). It also revealed that classroom discourse is not easy to change (Alvermann, O'Brien, & Dillon, 1990). As Alvermann and Hayes (1989) explain:

> Convincing teachers to change their verbal interaction patterns for the purpose of effecting higher levels of response to text appears difficult to accomplish. . . . Teachers have their own experiences, beliefs, and intuitions that are translated into practical arguments and instructional goals to which they are firmly committed. (pp. 333)

Classroom discourse is complex and, as such, is not associated with particular instructional techniques. This line of research has, however, influenced instructional thinking regarding teacher–student interactions and is reflected in various discussions of scaffolded teacher assistance (Duffy & Roehler, 1987; Pressley et al., 1992; Taylor, Pearson, Clark, & Walpole, 1999).

Explicit Teaching

The previously mentioned three broad research areas all emphasize strategic behavior but avoid intentional and direct teaching of strategies and how they work. Instead of directly teaching strategies, they provide guidance in the expectation that repeated exposure will cause students to become strategic comprehenders.

Explicit teaching rose out of concern for struggling readers. Because struggling readers do not pick up on the relatively subtle cues and prompts provided by other activities, research was conducted on a number of instructional techniques designed to provide more explicit information about how reading works. One of these—direct explanation of strategies—is the focus of this chapter. Others include main idea techniques as studied by Jim Baumann (1984); metacognitive strategies as studied by Scott Paris and his colleagues (Paris, 1986; Paris, Cross, & Lipson, 1984); inference training as studied by Peter Dewitz and his colleagues (Dewitz, Carr, & Patberg, 1987); prereading strategies as studied by Jan Dole and her colleagues (Dole, Brown, & Trathen, 1996; Dole, Valencia, Greer, & Wardrop, 1991); explanatory feedback as studied by Phil Winne and his colleagues (Winne, Graham, & Prock, 1993); and transactional strategy instruction as studied by Michael Pressley and his colleagues (Brown, Pressley, Van Meter, & Schuder, 1996; Pressley et al., 1992).

Explicit teaching differs from other approaches to comprehension instruction in two important ways. First, explicit teaching uses "strategy" to mean a technique that *readers* learn to control as a means to better comprehend (see, for instance, the comprehension strategies described in Dole, Duffy, Roehler, & Pearson, 1991, and in Keene & Zimmermannn, 1997); other approaches, on the other hand, use "strategy" to mean a technique the *teacher* controls to guide student reading (such as the K-W-L). Second, explicit teaching is intentional and direct about teaching individual strategies on the assumption that clear and unambivalent information about how strategies work will put struggling readers in a better position to control their own comprehension; other approaches, on the other hand, emphasize quality interaction with text content but avoid explicit teacher talk designed to develop student metacognitive awareness of when and how to use a particular strategy.

To illustrate, note how teachers are usually told to use K-W-L (taken from (Cunningham & Allington, 1999, pp. 56–58):

- first, the teacher has students brainstorm what they know about the topic at hand and list those things on a chart under the heading "What we know";
- then the teacher has students think about what they would like to know and list that under the heading "What we want to find out";
- then students read the selection to see which of their questions were answered and to find other interesting information; and
- after checking to see which questions were answered, the teacher encourages kids to return to the text to clarify points.

The teacher, not the student; is in control of the strategy; the goal is student comprehension of the text, not student control of how a strategy works; and assessment focuses on whether students comprehend text content, not on whether they can control a strategy and use it independently when comprehending on their own.

When a teacher wants students to comprehend text content, less explicit techniques such as K-W-L and reciprocal teaching are unbeatable. However, when a teacher wants students to assume "inner control" (Clay, 1991) of a strategy so that they can use it independently of the teacher, these approaches often leave something to be desired. Many struggling readers cannot, by simply watching a teacher guide their reading, figure out what they are supposed to do on their own. Consequently, they remain mystified and do not achieve the desired "inner control."

This is not to imply that K-W-L, reciprocal teaching, and other similar techniques cannot be taught in ways that put struggling readers in control of the strategy the teacher is using. It means that, typically, these techniques are explained by reading educators and applied in classrooms in ways that emphasize understanding text content, not in ways that emphasize student control of the mental processes involved in using a particular strategy.

DIRECT EXPLANATION OF STRATEGIES

Direct explanation of strategies is the particular form of explicit teaching emphasized in this chapter. It is based on studies conducted by Laura Roehler and I and our colleagues at the Institute for Research on Teaching at Michigan State University (Duffy, Roehler, Meloth, Vavrus, Book, Putnam, & Wesselman, 1986; Duffy, Roehler, Sivan, et al., 1987).

Like other studies of explicit instruction, direct explanation provides struggling readers with explicit information. But our work was distinct in three ways. First, we focused on the mental processing (i.e., the reasoning) that is the guts of comprehension strategies, with the intent of making visible to readers what Clay (1991) calls "in the head" mental activity. Second, we combined explanation with application, so that strategic mental activity was immediately applied in the reading of text. Finally, because we believed struggling readers would be able to assume control of what had previously seemed like a magical act if they were metacognitive about the thinking one does when comprehending, we sought to make explicit for students the declarative, conditional, and procedural knowledge about the strategies being learned.

With those three ideas as the basis, we conducted two year-long experimental studies of classroom reading instruction (Duffy, Roehler, Meloth, Vavrus, Book, Putnam, & Wesselman, 1986; Duffy, Roehler, Sivan, et al., 1987). The hypothesis in both studies was that low-reading group students of teachers who provide explicit explanations about how to reason with strategies would be (1) more metacognitively aware of how to comprehend and would (2) demonstrate better reading achievement.

Studying Direct Explanation

Our intervention with experimental teachers emphasized six interrelated instructional actions (Duffy, Roehler, Meloth, & Vavrus, 1986):

- First, teachers introduced the selection to be read (almost always the text was from the basal textbook adopted by the district).
- Second, instead of immediately jumping into the reading of the selection, the teacher made an explicit statement about what strategy needed to be learned (declarative knowledge), when it would be used in the upcoming selection (conditional knowledge), and the critical attribute one must attend to in order to do the strategy successfully (procedural knowledge).
- Third, teachers provided students with a model of how to think when using the strategy, which we described as "mental modeling" (Duffy, Roehler, & Herrmann, 1988) because it involved "thinking out loud" about the mental processing one does when using strategies, thus providing students with a "window into the mind" of a successful strategy user.
- Fourth, scaffolded practice was provided in which students practiced using the strategy with gradually diminishing amounts of coaching assistance from the teacher. We called this phase "responsive elaboration" (Duffy & Roehler, 1987) because it required creative teacher responses to students' restructuring of their understandings about strategy use.
- Fifth, teachers had students read the selection for two purposes: for text content and for application of the newly learned strategy.
- Finally, lesson closure included explicit statements about the strategy, its use in understanding text in other settings, and how to implement it.

Control teachers, in contrast, relied on guided reading, usually the Directed Reading Lesson. Typically, they introduced a selection to be read (again, usually from the basal textbook required by the district), set purposes for the reading, reviewed vocabulary, directed students to read the selection, and led a discussion of the selection. Strategy (or skill) instruction was provided after reading the selection and was typically limited to basal textbook practice exercises.

In both studies, we observed experimental and control teachers as they taught their respective low reading groups across an entire academic year. Following each observed lesson, students from the low reading group were interviewed to assess their metacognitive awareness. Achievement was measured in the first study with a standardized test at the end of the school year; in the second study, achievement was measured throughout the school year, at the end of the year with a standardized test, and 6 months later with a state-mandated assessment test.

Results from Studies of Direct Explanation

In both studies, experimental group students were more aware of strategies and how to use them. Achievement was not significantly better for experimental students in the first study; but when more extensive instruction was provided for teachers in the second experiment, experimental group students not only outperformed control students on a standardized test but also did significantly better on achievement gains during the school year and on the state assessment test administered 6 months later.

In retrospect, three implications are particularly important.

Can Strategies Be Directly Taught?

First, the findings substantiated that strategies can be directly taught and that direct teaching of strategies benefits struggling readers.

Despite these results, however, leaders in the field of reading generally continue to resist the benefits of directly explaining strategies. For instance, almost a decade after we reported the effectiveness of direct explanation, Fountas and Pinnell (1996) continue to insist that strategies cannot be directly taught. This resistance is difficult to understand given (1) our empirical findings, (2) the absence of any contradictory data, and (3) the many related studies documenting that struggling readers benefit from explicit teaching (see, for instance, Baumann, 1984; Paris et al., 1984; Dewitz et al., 1987; Pressley et al., 1992; Winne et al., 1993; Dole et al., 1996).

What Teacher Actions Are Important?

A second implication regards the nature of explanation itself. Teacher actions that proved to be important were:

- establishing that the student needed to learn the strategy being taught;
- making an explicit tie between the strategy being taught and its application in a story, ensuring that the newly learned strategy was immediately applied in that day's reading selection;
- repeatedly stating and modeling the "secret" to doing it successfully so that students "saw" the mental workings involved;
- providing students with multiple opportunities to perform the strategy themselves, at first with coaching but gradually moving to independent use;
- basing assessment on both the students' use of the strategy and their comprehension of text content; and
- maintaining lesson alignment—that is, maintaining a consistent focus on the strategy to be learned throughout the reading of the text, a feature political campaigners call "message discipline."

What Does Direct Explanation Demand of the Teacher?

The most important implication of our findings is what it says about the crucial role of the teacher. Specifically, good explainers thoughtfully adapt their explanations to fit the instructional situation. Three examples are illustrative.

First, good explainers thoughtfully adapt their plans. For instance, we frequently observed teachers picking up on cues from students and changing plans "on the fly" during lessons. This led us to note that "teachers' lesson plans are temporary documents that must be modified as the dynamic and responsive instructional exchange unfolds" (Duffy & Roehler, 1989, p. 27) and that explanations "unfold in unpredictable ways depending on how students restructure what teachers say" (Duffy & Roehler, 1987, p. 519). In short, explaining comprehension strategies is not like lecturing or other rigid forms of explanation. To the contrary, "explanation involves subtleties not normally associated with traditional views of explanation where information is presented in a one-way, teacher-dominated lecture" (Duffy & Roehler, 1989, p. 31).

Second, good explainers thoughtfully adapt the modeling they provide. For instance, when we noted that some treatment students were more metacognitively aware than students in other treatment classes who supposedly received the same kind of explanations, we did a post hoc analysis of treatment teachers' lesson transcripts. We found that all the experimental teachers were explicit but that the modeling of the most effective experimental teachers was more substantive (Duffy, 1993a; Duffy, Roehler, & Rackliffe, 1986). In a typical main-idea lesson, for instance, less effective teachers just defined the main idea, pointed out some examples, and inserted prompts during guided reading; but the most effective teachers made thoughtful and substantive adjustments, based mainly on student cues, as they modeled how to link an author's ideas together.

Finally, good explainers thoughtfully adapt across lesson boundaries (Roehler, Duffy, & Warren, 1988). For instance, effective teachers would explain a strategy in one way on some days, and on another day the same teacher would explain the same strategy in a different way. Similarly, effective teachers linked a strategy taught on one day with a strategy taught on another day to build the understanding that strategy use is a coherent thinking process, not a matter of memorizing a long list of isolated strategies (Duffy, 1993b). Additionally, the most effective teachers situated instruction within larger, authentic projects or problems that often took weeks to complete (Duffy, 1997). For instance, a teacher might involve students in solving a schoolwide safety problem, assign various readings on that topic, and then use those readings as occasions for explaining needed comprehension strategies.

Summary

In addition to establishing that strategies can be directly explained and that doing so benefits struggling readers, our research also established that explanations cannot be scripted, proceduralized, or packaged. Instead, good explanations require thoughtfully adaptive teachers who "harness various ideas, select from a variety of principles and create different instructional combinations" (Duffy, 1992, p. 447).

Unfortunately, the thoughtful component of teacher explanation is often overlooked. Instead, teacher explanation is sometimes assumed to be a rigid, proceduralized technique in the tradition of scripted instruction such as DISTAR (Englemann & Bruner,

1974). Nothing could be further from the truth. Although direct explanation, like DISTAR, is direct, clear, and unambiguous, the similarity ends there. A teacher, not a program, decides what strategies to teach; a teacher, not the program, develops an explanation; a teacher responds to cues from students and does not compliantly follow a script; the instructional emphasis throughout is on development of high-level, not low-level, student responses; and a priority is placed on situating explanations in authentic learning occasions. These are not DISTAR-like characteristics.

It is true, of course, that thoughtless teachers who provide bad explanations can make students into passive recipients of information (see, most recently, the concern expressed by Fountas & Pinnell, 1996; earlier similar concerns were expressed by Pearson, 1984, and by Tierney & Cunningham, 1984). However, as we reported in our comparisons of less effective and more effective explainers (Duffy, 1993a; Duffy, Roehler, & Rackliffe, 1986; Roehler et al., 1988), thoughtful teachers do *not* do so. For instance, when I was demonstrating direct explanation of comprehension strategies recently with sixth graders in a local school, teacher-observers commented on how I blended explicit explanatory information about strategy use into an ongoing dialogue in which students were intensely engaged with text content.

That is what good explanation is. It blends explicit information giving and sensitive responsiveness to students in order to develop both conscious awareness of how a strategy works *and* richly textured understandings of text content (Duffy, 1997; Duffy, Roehler, Meloth, & Vavrus, 1986). Rather than rejecting explanation because some teachers explain poorly, it would seem that we would be better off teaching teachers to explain well.

WHAT RESEARCH REMAINS TO BE DONE?

No doubt we could profit from more research on the inner workings of direct explanation. For instance, we need more descriptive data about mental modeling and what ingredients make it work. Similarly, we need more substantive information on how to scaffold, such as the study recently reported by Rodgers (1999). Additionally, we need to learn more about how mental modeling interacts with coaching or scaffolding, about how to maintain lesson alignment, and about how teachers create cohesive networks of understanding across lessons.

However, I do not believe that direct explanation per se should be the focus of future research efforts. There are two reasons for this.

The first is that direct explanation is not a panacea—something that works all the time with all students. Such practices do not exist in the real world of classroom teaching. Rather, different practices are appropriate in different situations. K-W-L is the best technique to use in some situations, reciprocal teaching is the best choice in other situations, and direct explanation is best in still other situations. All are tools in the teacher's repertoire. The trick is to select the right tool for the right situation, not to rigidly insist on using only one kind of technique.

Second, direct explanation, like any instructional technique, is effective only to the extent that a teacher is analytical and adaptive in applying it. Comprehension is a multilayered conceptual endeavor, not a technical one. Instruction must be similarly multilayered and conceptual, not technical. Hence the technique itself is not as important as the teacher's ability to be thoughtful and sensitive in making adaptations that account for the multilayered and situational nature of comprehension instruction.

Hence the research focus must not be on the instructional technique; the research focus must be on thoughtfully adaptive teaching. Specifically, we need to abandon the search for "foolproof" instructional techniques and concentrate instead on research that helps us develop teachers who possess the psychological mindset to be adaptive. Six broad concerns need to be addressed in this regard.

1. *We must stop basing policy and teacher education on a "what works?" notion.* Such thinking is rooted in the flawed assumption that what makes comprehension instruction effective is a technique, a method, a program, or a procedure when, in reality, it is a teacher's *use* of these that makes the difference (Duffy, 1991). Favoring one method or approach and disparaging others disempowers teachers, creating in their minds the expectation that success lies outside themselves. The expectation we *should* be developing is that what makes the difference is teachers' professional decision making when using a method or technique, not the method or technique itself. Consequently, policy makers and researchers should stop looking for answers to put in teachers' heads ahead of time and focus instead on developing teachers who think for themselves.

2. *Teacher analysis is essential.* Four levels of analysis are needed. First, teachers must decide which students need explicit explanations and which will benefit from less explicit instruction. Second, if it is determined that a reader is struggling, teachers must determine specifically what strategy (or strategies) must be taught to put the student on the road to successful reading. Third, when conducting instruction, teachers must be able to analyze students' statements during instructional interactions, to make judgments about students' interpretations, and to decide how to intervene in ways that promote learning. Fourth, at a very high level of complexity, teachers must be able to analyze instructional situations across lessons and to determine how to establish conceptual congruity, alignment, and authenticity. Although informal, on-line data collection is important at all four levels, what teachers do with the data once they are collected is crucial. We need research that helps us learn how to develop teachers whose instructional actions are situationally appropriate because they are rooted in data-based analysis.

3. *We need to study teacher disposition as well as teacher knowledge.* Being analytical is not enough if one does not also have the will to follow up on what an analysis reveals. Having the will means having a certain spirit, a willingness to risk, and courage. As Cuban (1992) points out, teaching requires teachers to act; to act, teachers must choose. Choosing inevitably creates conflicts with values, beliefs, and preferences. In reading comprehension instruction, for instance, a teacher may have a strong preference for a particular form of guided reading; consequently, it may not be easy to switch to direct explanation for a particular struggling reader. Similarly, providing alternative instruction for a few struggling readers creates a classroom management and time resource problem involving difficult choices, to say nothing of teacher energy. Being able to persevere and make tough choices about such issues is as much a matter of the spirit as of the mind (Duffy, 1998). Improving comprehension instruction means helping teachers develop such spirit. The key to doing so lies with freeing them from the expectation that we (i.e., reading educators, program developers, etc.) have answers. Instead, we must develop in teachers the fundamental principle that good teaching is not so much a matter of following the advice of various "authorities" as it is a matter of inventing instructional re-

sponses to situational demands. Only by being put in charge can teachers develop the spirit and strength to make the kinds of choices Cuban (1992) describes.

4. *We need to abandon the concept of teacher "training."* As I have argued in the past (Duffy, 1994) and as Hoffman and Pearson (2000) have argued more recently, training works only when the task is done the same way repeatedly. The reality of comprehension instruction, however, is that it is never done in exactly the same way twice. Sometimes one technique or method is appropriate; sometimes other techniques or methods are appropriate. Sometimes a technique or method is used in one way; sometimes it is used in another way. Training, however, encourages adherence to rigid procedures, a characteristic that is incompatible with the realities of comprehension instruction.

5. *We need longitudinal study of teacher learning.* Becoming a thoughtfully adaptive teacher is a career-long endeavor. It can be initiated in preservice settings. But as studies of teacher change indicate (see, for instance, Duffy, 1993a), in-service teachers continue to learn the more subtle aspects of thoughtfully adaptive teaching long after completing preservice teacher education. The extent to which they engage in such adaptive thinking is often a function of school context. Teachers can be creative and thoughtfully adaptive to the extent that the school leadership promotes and supports it, to the extent that such thought is congruent with the school's traditional way of doing things, to the extent that required curriculum materials allow it, to the extent that assessment practices do not suppress it, and countless other contextual variables (Duffy, 1993b; Elmore, 1997). We need research, such as recent initiatives by Grossman, Valencia, and their colleagues (Grossman et al., 2000) and by Hoffman and Roller (1999), that examines teacher education from the preservice level into actual on-the-job teaching in schools having different culturally embedded ways of doing things.

6. *We need to learn how to integrate teachers' voices into the teacher-learning enterprise.* We want teachers who are thoughtfully adaptive professionals who control their own work and are analytical, creative, flexible problem solvers in their classrooms. Those characteristics cannot just be talked about in teacher education. Teachers must live those characteristics during teacher education if they are to be thoughtful later in their own classrooms. This means reading professors need to promote and authorize thoughtful professional decision making, even when student thinking diverges from a professor's favored ways of doing things. Similarly, in-service professional education must be rooted in the voices of teachers (see, for instance, Afflerbach, 2000). Learning how to do this well requires careful study.

In sum, because teacher judgment is a key to effective comprehension instruction, the dominant research question must be, How do we develop teachers who have both the ability and the will to make such judgments?

CONCLUSION

The world has changed since we reported our teacher explanation findings in 1987. In those days, it was commendable to teach struggling readers well; today, however, it is *mandatory* that we teach them well. Consequently, all teachers should be prepared to switch to tools such as direct teacher explanation when readers do not respond to less explicit forms of reading instruction.

Unfortunately, however, most reading methods texts deemphasize explicit, direct explanation. Although such texts often make vague reference to the need to be "explicit," direct explanation is seldom developed in detail. With the exception of Keene and Zimmermann's (1997) *Mosaic of Thought,* teachers are seldom taught how to provide mental modeling, how to scaffold students' understanding of mental processing, how to maintain lesson alignment, and other difficult instructional abilities associated with direct explanation. In today's world, we cannot afford such omissions.

Both teacher educators and policy makers have important roles to play in correcting this omission. Teacher educators must make clear that success does not lie in subscribing to their particular ideology or to their favored methods of instruction and cultivate instead thoughtfully adaptive teachers who use a broad range of comprehension techniques, regardless of what the teacher educator may personally prefer. Policy makers, for their part, must abandon the "quick fix" mentality in which restrictive instructional programs are mandated. This practice has two negative consequences. First, it tends to polarize the debate, with teacher educators defending the methods they favor and attacking the mandate, rather than aggressively encouraging teachers to use a variety of instructional techniques. Second, it conveys to teachers the erroneous message that teacher compliance to authority, rather than teacher responsiveness and judgment, is the key to effective instruction.

The bottom line is that there are many effective ways to teach comprehension. Success depends on thoughtfully selecting and then adapting techniques that fit the situation. Sometimes direct explanation is appropriate; sometimes something else is. Consequently, the question is not whether direct explanation is a "best practice." The question is whether we can stop investing ourselves in particular techniques, methods, or approaches as if they are universal panaceas and, instead, invest ourselves in authorizing teachers to make pedagogical choices based on what an instructional situation demands.

REFERENCES

Afflerbach, P. (2000). Our plans and our future. In J. Hoffman, J. Baumann, & P. Afflerbach (Eds.), *Balancing principles for teaching elementary reading* (pp. 75–102). Mahwah, NJ: Erlbaum.

Alvermann, D., O'Brien, D., & Dillon, D. (1990). What teachers do when they say they're having discussions of content reading assignments: A qualitative analysis. *Reading Research Quarterly, 25,* 296–322.

Alvermann, D., & Hayes, D. (1989). Classroom discussion of content area reading assignments: An intervention study. *Reading Research Quarterly, 24,* 305–335.

Anderson, R., & Pearson, P. D. (1984). A schema-theoretic view of basic processes in reading. In P. D. Pearson, R. Barr, M. Kamil, & P. Mosenthal (Eds.), *Handbook of reading research* (pp. 255–291). New York: Longman.

Au, K., & Mason, J. (1981). Social organizational factors in learning to read: The balance of rights hypothesis. *Reading Research Quarterly, 17,* 115–135.

Baker, L., & Brown, A. (1984). Cognitive skills and reading. In P. D. Pearson, R. Barr, M. Kamil, & P. Mosenthal (Eds.), *Handbook of reading research* (pp. 352–394). New York: Longman.

Baumann, J. (1984). Effectiveness of a direct instruction paradigm for teaching main idea comprehension. *Reading Research Quarterly, 20,* 93–108.

Bloome, D., & Green, J. (1984). Directions in the sociolinguistic study of reading. In P. D. Pearson,

R. Barr, M. Kamil, & P. Mosenthal (Eds.), *Handbook of reading research* (pp. 395–421). New York: Longman.

Brown, R., Pressley, M., Van Meter, P., & Schuder, T. (1996). A quasi-experimental validation of transactional strategies instruction with low-achieving second grade readers. *Journal of Educational Psychology, 88,* 18–37.

Cazden, C. (1986). Classroom discourse. In M. Wittrock (Ed.), *Handbook of research on teaching* (3rd ed., pp. 432–463). New York: Macmillan.

Clay, M. (1991). *Becoming literate: The construction of inner control.* Portsmouth, NH: Heinemann.

Cuban, L. (1992). Managing dilemmas while building professional communities. *Educational Researcher, 21*(1), 4–11.

Cunningham, P., & Allington, R. (1999). *Classrooms that work: They can all read and write.* (2nd ed.). New York: HarperCollins.

Dewitz, P., Carr, E., & Patberg, J. (1987). Effects of inference training on comprehension and comprehension monitoring. *Reading Research Quarterly, 22,* 99–121.

Dole, J., Brown, K., & Trathen, W. (1996). The effects of strategy instruction on the comprehension performance of at-risk students. *Reading Research Quarterly, 31,* 62–89.

Dole, J., Duffy, G., Roehler, L., & Pearson, P. D. (1991). Moving from the old to the new: Research on reading comprehension instruction. *Review of Educational Research, 61*(2), 239–264.

Dole, J., Valencia, S., Greer, E., & Wardrop, J. (1991). The effects of prereading instruction on the comprehension of narrative and expository text. *Reading Research Quarterly, 26,* 142–159.

Duffy, G. (1991). What counts in teacher education? Dilemmas in empowering teachers. In J. Zutell & C. McCormick (Eds.), *Learning factors/teacher factors: Literacy research and instruction 40th yearbook of the National Reading Conference* (pp. 1–18). Chicago: National Reading Conference.

Duffy, G. (1992). Let's free teachers to be inspired. *Phi Delta Kappan, 73,* 442–446.

Duffy, G. (1993a). Re-thinking strategy instruction: Teacher development and low achievers' understandings. *Elementary School Journal, 93*(3), 231–247.

Duffy, G. (1993b). Teachers' progress toward becoming expert strategy teachers. *Elementary School Journal, 94*(2), 109–120.

Duffy, G. (1994). How teachers think of themselves: A key to creating powerful thinkers. In J. Mangieri & C. Block (Eds.), *Creating powerful thinking in teachers and students* (pp. 3–26). Ft. Worth, TX: Harcourt Brace.

Duffy, G. (1997). Powerful models or powerful teachers? An argument for teacher-as-entrepreneur. In S. Stahl & D. Hayes (Eds.), *Instructional models in reading* (pp. 351–356). Mahwah, NJ: Erlbaum.

Duffy, G. (1998). Teaching and the balancing of round stones. *Phi Delta Kappan, 79,* 777–780.

Duffy, G., & Roehler, L. (1987). Improving classroom reading instruction through the use of responsive elaboration. *Reading Teacher, 40*(6), 514–521.

Duffy, G., & Roehler, L. (1989). The tension between information-giving and mediation: Perspectives on instructional explanation and teacher change. In J. Brophy (Ed.), *Advances in research on teaching* (Vol. 1, pp. 1–33). New York: JAI Press.

Duffy, G., Roehler, L., & Herrmann, B. (1988). Modeling mental processes helps poor readers become strategic readers. *Reading Teacher, 41*(8), 762–767.

Duffy, G., Roehler, L., Meloth, M., & Vavrus, L. (1986). Conceptualizing instructional explanation. *Teaching and Teacher Education, 2*(3), 197–214.

Duffy, G., Roehler, L., Meloth, M., Vavrus, L., Book, C., Putnam, J., & Wesselman, R. (1986). The relationship between explicit verbal explanation during reading skill instruction and student awareness and achievement: A study of reading teacher effects. *Reading Research Quarterly, 21,* 237–252.

Duffy, G., Roehler, L., & Rackliffe, G. (1986). How teachers' instructional talk influences students' understanding of lesson content. *Elementary School Journal, 87*(1), 3–16.

Duffy, G., Roehler, L., Sivan, E., Rackliffe, G., Book, C., Meloth, M., Vavrus, L., Wesselman, R., Putnam, J., & Bassiri, D. (1987). Effects of explaining the reasoning associated with using reading strategies. *Reading Research Quarterly, 22*(3), 347–368.

Durkin, D. (1978–1979). What classroom observation reveals about reading comprehension instruction. *Reading Research Quarterly, 14,* 481–533.

Elmore, R. (1997, August). *Investing in teacher learning: Staff development and instructional improvement in Community School District #2, New York City.* New York: National Commission on Teaching and America's Future.

Englemann, S., & Bruner, E. (1974). *DISTAR: Reading Level I.* Chicago: Science Research Associates.

Fountas, I., & Pinnell, G. (1996). *Guided reading: Good first teaching for all children.* Portsmouth, NH: Heinemann.

Garner, R. (1988). *Metacognition and reading comprehension.* Norwood, NJ: Ablex.

Gaskins, I., Anderson, R., Pressley, M., Cunicelli, E., & Satlow, E. (1993). Six teachers' dialogue during cognitive process instruction. *Elementary School Journal, 93,* 277–304.

Grossman, P., Valencia, S., Evans, K., Thompson, C., Martin, S., & Place, N. (2000). Transitions into teaching: Learning to teach writing in teacher education and beyond. *Journal of Literacy Research, 32*(4), 631–662.

Heap, J. (1982). Understanding classroom events: A critique of Durkin, with an alternative. *Journal of Reading Behavior, 14,* 391–411.

Heath, S. (1983). *Ways with words: Language, life and work in communities and classrooms.* Cambridge: Cambridge University Press.

Hoffman, J., & Pearson, P. D. (2000). Reading teacher education in the next millennium: What your grandmother's teacher didn't know that your granddaughter's teacher should. *Reading Research Quarterly, 35*(1), 28–45.

Hoffman, J., & Roller, C. (1999, December). *A longitudinal study of reading teacher education.* Paper presented at the annual conference of the National Reading Conference, Orlando, FL.

Keene, E. O., & Zimmermann, S. (1997). *Mosaic of thought: Teaching comprehension in a reader's workshop.* Portsmouth, NH: Heinemann.

Ogle, D. (1986). K-W-L: A teaching model that develops active reading of expository text. *Reading Teacher, 39,* 564–570.

Palincsar, A., & Brown, A. (1984). Reciprocal teaching of comprehension-fostering and monitoring activities. *Cognition and Instruction, 1,* 117–175.

Paris, S. (1986). Teaching children to guide their reading and learning. In T. Raphael (Ed.), *The context for school-based literacy* (pp. 115–130). New York: Random House.

Paris, S., Cross, D., & Lipson, M. (1984). Informed strategies for learning: A program to improve children's reading awareness and comprehension. *Journal of Educational Psychology, 76,* 1239–1252.

Pearson, P. D. (1984). Direct explicit teaching of reading comprehension. In G. Duffy, L. Roehler, & J. Mason (Eds.), *Comprehension instruction: Perspectives and suggestions* (pp. 222–233). New York: Longman.

Pressley, M., El-Dinary, P., Gaskins, I., Schuder, T., Bergman, J., Almasi, L., & Brown, R. (1992). Beyond direct explanation: Transactional instruction of reading comprehension strategies. *Elementary School Journal, 92,* 511–554.

Raphael, T., & McKinney, J. (1983). Examinations of fifth- and eighth-grade children's question-answering behavior: An instructional study in metacognition. *Journal of Reading Behavior, 15,* 67–86.

Raphael, T., & Wonnacott, C. (1985). Heightening fourth grade students' sensitivity to sources of information for answering comprehension questions. *Reading Research Quarterly, 20,* 282–296.

Rodgers, E. (1999, December). *Language matters: When is a scaffold really a scaffold?* Paper presented at the annual conference of the National Reading Conference, Orlando, FL.

Roehler, L., Duffy, G., & Warren, S. (1988). Adaptive explanatory actions associated with effective teaching of reading strategies. In J. Readance & S. Baldwin (Eds.), *Dialogs in literacy research 37th Yearbook of the National Reading Conference* (pp. 339–346). Chicago: National Reading Conference.

Taylor, B., Pearson, D., Clark, K., & Walpole, S. (1999, September 30). *Beating the odds in teaching all children to read* (Ciera Report no. 2-006). Ann Arbor: University of Michigan, Center for the Improvement of Early Reading Achievement.

Tierney, R., & Cunningham, J. (1984). Research on teaching reading comprehension. In P. D. Pearson, R. Barr, M. Kamil, & P. Mosenthal (Eds.), *Handbook of reading research* (pp. 609–656). New York: Longman.

Winne, P., Graham, L., & Prock, L. (1993). A model of poor readers' text-based inferencing: Effects of explanatory feedback. *Reading Research Quarterly, 28,* 52–69.

4

Process-Based Comprehension Instruction

Perspectives of Four Reading Educators

CATHY COLLINS BLOCK
JONI L. SCHALLER
JOSEPH A. JOY
PAOLA GAINE

Skilled readers process many thoughts as they read (e.g., Pressley & Afflerbach, 1995). They (1) make strategic decisions, (2) employ numerous strategies, and (3) adapt their thinking to an authors' intentions and to the constraints of a particular text, time, and reading objective. As described in previous chapters, and as many students are so painfully aware, such complex cognitive, metacognitive, attentional, and emotional processes are difficult to negotiate. Their mental states have also been influenced by the quality of their prior instruction, by their background knowledge, by their decoding abilities, and by the social, historical, and political context in which a reading experience occurs.

Unfortunately, many readers cannot engage such complex, interactive processes or locate comprehension clues. These limitations often fuel their already fragile self-images, which have been created by other challenges that less able readers face, such as (1) a limited knowledge of English, (2) living in poverty, (3) having few reading materials, and (4) interacting with adults who do not demonstrate literacy's personal and professional benefits. Their inadequate comprehension abilities engage a downward achievement that is not eradicated in schools. This is true because many less able readers spend most of their time with their teachers merely *listening* to comprehension instructions and questions or having stories read to them. For instance, in the first 4 years of school, a large majority spend 70% of their time performing non-reading-related tasks, such as cutting and pasting (Pressley, Allington, Wharton-McDonald, Block, & Morrow, 2001).

By third grade, most children who have not learned to wield comprehension processes enjoyably and profitably will have fallen so far below their peers that they will never regain their lost ground, even if they have decoding skills that are on grade level (Block, 2000; Hesselbrink, 1998; King, 1994). If we allow this cycle to continue, more students are likely to regularly disengage from comprehending. In so doing, they are likely to limit their worlds, their power in the Internet/information society, their vocabularies, and their intrinsic motivation to read (Block, 2000b). Before more students disengage, we must begin to teach comprehension in a new way, as an enjoyable, controllable process and not as the difficult mastery of separate, segmented strategies. We must also design more cognitively, socially, and pedagogically rich instructional lessons than ever before.

The long-term benefits of strategy-based comprehension instruction have been documented (e.g., Brown, Pressley, Van Meter, & Schuder, 1996, with grade 2 students; Collins, 1991; Block, 1993, with grades 5, 6, 7, and 8 students; Block, 1999, with grade 1 through grade 6 students; and Anderson, 1992, and Anderson & Roit, 1993, with middle and high school students). As we enter the 21st century, many educators want to teach comprehension as the seamless, complex interaction of thoughts that good readers use. This instruction must be neither too prescriptive nor too free-flowing. When instruction is too teacher dominated, students do not learn how to apply the skills without prompting (Block, 2000b; Taylor, Pearson, Clark, & Wolpole, 1999; Wood, Willoughby, McDermott, Motz, & Kaspar, 1999). Alternatively, when instruction is too sparse or unmonitored, pupils do not develop tools to think strategically as they read. Many struggle to attain a semblance of meaning, do not contemplate a detail's relevance, and make up vague meanings of unfamiliar words merely to "keep on" reading. As a result, comprehension becomes such a challenge that they avoid it.

Process-based comprehension instruction is designed to overcome these difficulties. It is defined as lessons that develop the ability to engage an effective set of thought processes at strategic points in a text so that the interaction releases a deep, fulfilling, and personally valuable understanding of print or technologically driven text. Process-based comprehension instruction moves beyond reminding students, before and while they read, to "think about a comprehension strategy that we just learned." It teaches students how to relate multiple strategies at specific points in a text when they are needed. The purpose of this chapter is to describe the research and practices that we have completed relative to teaching comprehension as a process. We describe three strands of process-based comprehension lessons that:

- Cast comprehension processes as large, multicomponent nets.
- Assist students to use comprehension processes automatically, habitually, and independently.
- Portray effective comprehension as resulting from a unique mixture of processes that students select to use.

Our data suggest that when comprehension is taught as a continuous thought process that ebbs and flows as new processes are interrelated at points of need, the making of meaning can become an enjoyable, lifelong process that comes more directly under students' control (Beck & Dole, 1994; Block, 2000a). Our hypotheses were based on two bodies of research. The first database suggested that we should differentiate the types of comprehension instruction that we provide students so that they develop different types of processing abilities. This rationale follows the success of offering different types of decoding lessons to students. These methods assist students to break the code of printed English. For instance, when we teach students how to decipher print, we provide many tools, through a wide variety of lessons (i.e., we teach phonics, English letter patterns, context clues, picture clues, structural analysis, content-specific sight words, basic sight words, word parts, etc.). Following this logic, it seems reasonable to assume that we should teach comprehension by differentiating the types of lessons and variety of tools that we provide.

A second body of research concerned expert readers' comprehension processes and self-teaching abilities (see Pressley & Afflerbach, 1995, and Block, 2001a, for reviews of this research). When we engage students in identifying, designing, and implementing instruction that builds the processes that they need to comprehend better, our lessons stand a greater chance of serving the multiple intellectual needs, varied personalities, and diverse literacy abilities of individuals who populate our classrooms in the 21st century. During the past year, we have examined and field tested numerous process-based comprehension lessons to encourage students to think strategically as they read. When students comprehended as a process and described parts of the process that they used, their comprehension abilities increased significantly (as measured by standardized and criterion-reference scores, Block, 2000a).

How can we teach process-based comprehension lessons? Such instruction is more than richly enhanced teacher-directed strategy lessons or highly elaborated think-alouds. It moves beyond telling students to read literally, inferentially, and appreciatively. It moves beyond setting purpose for students to demonstrating how *purposes can be set by students* as they read a text's setting, introduction, and initial events. It moves beyond telling students how to find the main ideas to showing how *main ideas find readers* (because main ideas are the anchoring thoughts that tie concepts together as they read). We must move beyond teaching how to draw conclusions to showing students *how conclusions are drawn* during the process of connecting possibilities to these anchoring thoughts.

We propose that today's reading programs should differentiate comprehension instruction into three strands. Each develops students' abilities to interrelate comprehension processes. Strand 1 lessons are intended to teach students how to use two comprehension processes simultaneously. Strand 2 lessons provide extended time for students to practice setting purposes for and to enjoy reading, and to make strategic decisions as they read. Strand 3 lessons enable students to demonstrate comprehension processes that they have discovered themselves and to tell teachers what they want to learn next. When these three strands were interspersed throughout each week, we found that pupils in grades 2–8 developed a breadth of thinking processes that enabled them to fully comprehend and appreciate narratives, poetry, and nonfictional texts (Block, 2001b, in press-a).

STRAND 1: CASTING COMPREHENSION
PROCESSES AS MULTICOMPONENT NETS

Strand 1 lessons teach how to use two comprehension processes together to eliminate a misunderstanding. They develop students' abilities to apply and coordinate at least two, and then many, comprehension processes sequentially before a specific comprehsnion need emerges. Three lessons in Strand 1 have been demonstrated to help students (1) set their own purpose; (2) sequence facts until main ideas mold them into a coherent body of knowledge; (3) relate main ideas vertically until themes and treatises emerge; (4) verify and make connections within and outside of a text during and after reading; and (5) apply data to their lives and mental data banks as they read. Examples of Strand 1 lessons that have been field tested and proven to reach these goals are (1) teaching how to interrelated comprehension strategies; (2) the TRIO teaching cycle; and (3) the power of three lessons.

Teaching How to Interrelate Comprehension Strategies

These lessons begin with teachers selecting two comprehension processes to instruct. This selection is based on the needs of their students and the particular set of processes that would be most valuable to comprehend a specific text that is to be read. Teachers can choose to teach:

1. How to add depth and breadth to one's knowledge through intertextuality, summarizing, inferring, imaging, interpreting author's intentions, reflecting, paraphrasing, identifying gist, organizing, predicting, and making connections between words, facts, and concepts and the historical and political context in which they are written and read.
2. How to comprehend literally, inferentially, and applicably simultaneously by setting efferent and aesthetic purposes for reading.
3. How to think metacognitively and to clarify by using fix-up strategies and continuous self-monitoring.
4. How to fill gaps in narrative and expository text by tilling a text continuously as one reads.

Most important, these lessons emphasize that two of these processes (at the initial sessions, and eventually all of these processes) are to occur interactively and synergistically, in relation to one another.

Once two of these processes have been selected, lessons can open with a think-aloud to demonstrate how students can employ these two processes together as they read. Students have the text before them either in a book; or on an overhead screen, blackboard, felt board, or computer screen. After the teacher demonstrates two processes in action to comprehend one paragraph, she can read a second with the students. The teacher can stop after the first sentence and ask students to describe how they are relating the two processes that she demonstrated in the prior paragraph. This discussion should continue for several minutes, using at least five subsequent paragraphs.

The next step is to ask students to volunteer to read a paragraph aloud to classmates and to pause when they can describe the processes that they are using to comprehend. When students are ready to be assessed in their abilities to relate processes, a teacher can listen to them individually as they read in a text and stop them periodically to describe their comprehension processes. One source of texts for these lessons appears in *Qualitative Reading Inventory—3* (Leslie & Caldwell, 2001). The passages in this work are marked at points at which fruitful think-alouds should occur if students are interrelating processes successfully.

The following example illustrates how these lessons can be introduced. Ms. Turner elected to teach her sixth graders (1) how to add depth and breadth to their knowledge by inferring how the characters felt, and making connections between the historical and political context in which the texts were written; and (2) how to comprehend literally, inferentially, and applicably by setting an efferent and aesthetic purpose for reading about a specific event in history. She selected a paragraph from the class history chapter that students were about to read. Before she displayed that paragraph on the overhead, she told the students that many processes would be working in their minds each time that they comprehend (Kintsch, 1988, describes each of these processes in more depth). She described the following processes and wrote the underlined words on the board. First, the mind decodes words and puts their meanings together into sentences to determine the *local meaning* of each sentence. Second, the mind uses relational processes to generate a gist, to organize local meanings to determine a *global meaning* when all paragraphs are put together. Third, the mind engages *linguistic parsers* to interpret words that have been eliminated in phrases; for example, in the paragraph that they were about to read, they would interpret the author's intention in saying "the old man and woman" to indicate both the man and the woman were old. Fourth, the mind uses *inference processes* to instill human emotions in events as they unfold.

Then the teacher drew double-headed arrows between each of these processes to demonstrate how they work together simultaneously to make meaning. Next, she wrote "Set a Purpose to Gain Information and Understand Characters' Emotional Responses" as a title above these phrases and arrows. She asked students to set two purposes each time they began to comprehend movies, television, computer screens, and books—one emotional and one intellectual. Then students posed two purposes they set in reading this history chapter that opened with two old people and occurred in 1929. These purposes were written around the title of the graphic that the teacher and students made previously. Then the teacher and students read the following paragraph and discussed how they felt and what they thought as each of the preceding processes, related together, generated their comprehension:

> Their stomachs churned with fear and emotions. The old man and woman clasped
> each other's hands and looked up and down the enormous gray bank. There was no
> way to enter. They were paralyzed by fear, and all their lives' dreams flashed before
> them in an instant.

Students discussed the processes that they used to (1) infer something about the bank that must have frightened the people, (2) extract the gist, and (3) integrate world experiences to reenact the scene. Then the teacher demonstrated how imagery could assist in comprehension. She asked students to describe their images. Then she asked them to notice how those images were altered when they interrelated the process of making connections between words, facts, and concepts and the historical and political context in which they were written. She described two historical contexts that existed in 1929 that would have affected the four sentences that they had just read: Most rivers swelled often and few bridges existed to cross them, and the U.S. economy fell to create the most disastrous depression that the country has ever experienced. Next, she asked the students to image the paragraph by relating it to the 1929 historical context in which it was written. They were to image the paragraph as if the following three sentences had appeared right before the paragraph that they had just read:

The old man and woman raised their heads and saw the bear at exactly the same instant. He was running toward their riverbank camp at top speed. Their stomachs churned with fear and emotions. The old man and woman clasped each other's hands and looked up and down the enormous gray bank. There was no way to enter. They were paralyzed by fear, and their all lives' dreams flashed before them in an instant.

Then she asked students to read, image, and relate the two comprehension processes of gaining information and understanding characters' emotional responses as if the second set of sentences had appeared immediately before the paragraph that they just read. She also asked them to pay attention to how the processes change in their interrelationship as they read the following historical context right before the paragraph:

It was October 29, 1929, Black Tuesday. As they heard about the stock market crash, the old man and woman drove all night from their New Hampshire farm to reach New York City's World Bank at dawn. Their stomachs churned with fear and emotions. The old man and woman clasped each other's hands and looked up and down the enormous gray bank. There was no way to enter. They were paralyzed by fear, and all their lives' dreams flashed before them in an instant.

Metacognitive processes (no. 3 on page 45) and tilling the text processes (no. 4 on page 45) can be taught in similar lessons. We can pause at difficult points in texts at which pupils could have problems and teach them how to relate two comprehension processes to overcome misunderstandings and dense concepts. To illustrate, we can say: "Here's a difficult point in this story, and one that will occur in other similar texts in the future. Whenever you come to this paragraph (and at others like it in the future), I suggest that you call upon several processes such as . . . and do something like this to craft the deepest, most fulfilling meaning." In a fourth-grade class, for example, Ms. Mackey taught students to till the text with the following demonstration before students read. She told them to use the sea of thoughts surrounding a story as a context clue. Then she demonstrated how to let individual words that an author selects suggest the horizons of possibilities: "The characters have strange names—Arsenic, Venom, and Hemlock. I know that a hemlock is a tree with a poisonous berry or leaf. Why would the author give characters names that mean poison? Is he trying to tell me something about the characters? Maybe I should pay attention to subtleties in this author's writing style. I think he is depending on me to infer a lot to gain a deeper, more global application to my life."

The TRIO Teaching Cycle

The TRIO cycles can be used in many classroom organizational plans, including guided reading groups, block grouping plans, and literature anthology schedules. TRIO lessons begin with Teaching a new concept to an entire class. During this initial introduction, teachers can give three distinct examples of the comprehension process in action using modeling, with a text to be read and expanded explanations through hands-on demonstrations. This T in the TRIO cycle occurs in a whole-group setting (1 teacher to 22 or more students). The second step is Reteaching in a small group in a different manner, using a different learning modality for those students who did not learn to process text in the manner instructed in the initial teaching session. This small-group Reteaching uses a new learning style and method to instruct the same comprehension strategies in a novel manner (in a 1-to-5 teacher–student ratio).

As one of us (JLS) explains: "If a group of students just had a hard time on comprehension processes that I taught in a Strand 1 lesson, I pull these pupils together the next day and work with them until they understand that concept. Students who learned the concept during the Strand 1 lesson choose to read books in pairs, silently write or go to centers while I Reteach those who need it." At the end of small group Reteaching episodes, teachers ask each student to use the comprehension processes independently as they read. Those who cannot are retaught in the third step in the teaching cycle.

The third step is Individualized instruction. It occurs in one-to-one sessions and contains personalized, individualized scaffolding (through a 1-to-1 teacher–student experience). Different books and examples are used individually as teacher and student read texts together. After this interaction, if a student does not use the comprehension processes independently, Others are asked to join the instructional team. Among those invited are peer teachers, parent volunteers, and specialized teachers. They might use specialized materials and teacher-made adaptations that are personalized to that student's interests, using that student's name and familiar words in the text. For example, one of us (CCB) created a personalized lesson for Tyler, who could not till the text or think metacognitively after having had instruction in the first three TRIO steps in the process. After step 4 (Others) using a teacher-made personalized teaching episode, Tyler did comprehend, and said:

> Ms. Block taught me how to put two thoughts together when I don't understand something. I do that now. When I read something I do not know, I think about the main idea of the paragraph. You know, like the other day I came to the word "Indians" and I did not know it. Just sounding it out did not fill my mind enough. So, I thought about what word the author would write for the main idea he was telling me. He was telling me about the first Thanksgiving and the people who were invited. Then the word just came to me. Because the word began with *I* and the people invited to the first Thanksgiving were Indians, I learned the word all by myself. I'll never forget it either!

TRIO lessons are learned more easily by some students because graphics are used to depict comprehension processes. These graphics illustrate *the direction their thoughts can take* to summarize, conclude, compare, and so forth, as they read. These graphic thinking guides (as shown in Figures 4.1, 4.2, and 4.3) become unique icons and models for processes-in-action. After the introduction and discussion of the process, students can read silently from the text, having two or more of these thinking guides before them on their desks. When silent application periods cease, teachers can ask: "How did these processes help while you read? How did they help you stay involved in the story? How did they help you overcome distractions in the room? How did you reference them to craft interactively, using all the processes that we have learned previously?"

Graphics that depict comprehension processes have been demonstrated to assist students to independently integrate thinking processes and to increase their strategic decisions during reading (Block & Mangieri, 1996; Schruder, 1987). Moreover, when such graphics are included in the comprehension program, we no longer have to hope that all students will reach a deep level of comprehension simply by "practicing or memorizing processes." These graphics are placed two at a time on students' desks as they read. Examples of process graphics appear in Figures 4.1, 4.2, and 4.3.

The Power of Three

The "power of three, third time's a charm" philosophy distinguishes these lessons. The power of three means that teachers consciously describe three highly distinct applications of the processes that they teach. These examples build a larger comprehension bridge by which students can cross difficult waters until they discover the value of using their own variations of the comprehension processes without prompting to do so. In these lessons,

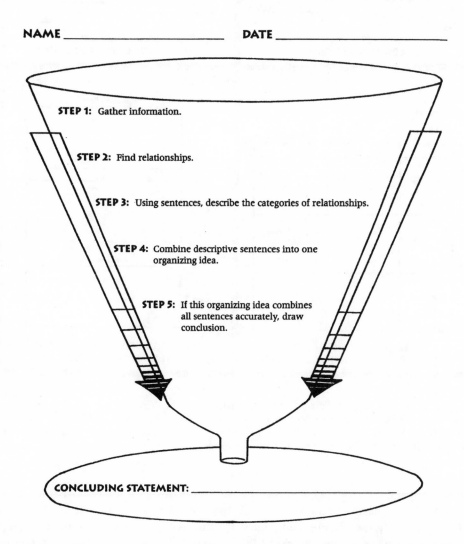

NAME _____   DATE _____

STEP 1: Gather information.

STEP 2: Find relationships.

STEP 3: Using sentences, describe the categories of relationships.

STEP 4: Combine descriptive sentences into one organizing idea.

STEP 5: If this organizing idea combines all sentences accurately, draw conclusion.

CONCLUDING STATEMENT: _____

FIGURE 4.1. Thinking Guide: Graphic that can be used to depict drawing conclusions, and that can be placed beside books (with a second thinking guide) that students read so two strategies can be referenced simultaneously. From Block and Mangieri (1996). Copyright 1996 by Pearson Learning. Reprinted by permission.

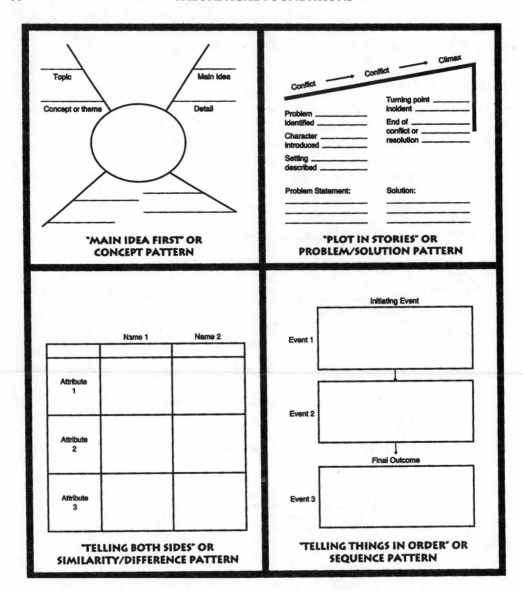

FIGURE 4.2. Recognizing the Pattern that the Author Used in Writing This Text: Graphic that illustrates how several comprehension processes can be depicted on the same page to remind students to use more than one thinking tool at a time as they read. From Block and Mangieri (1996). Copyright 1996 by Pearson Learning. Reprinted by permission.

processes are taught repeatedly, specifically, and consecutively to emphasize both the process and the outcome simultaneously. An example could be using three different pictures of the concept being taught, modeling one way of thinking through a comprehension process, then a second, and then a third "think aloud." For example, Figure 4.2 demonstrates four pictures of processing story grammar. When such examples are contained in comprehension instruction, students gain courage to speak up in class. At the beginning, you may find that some students will not become successful even after four examples are

1. **DELETE DUPLICATION.** ··

   ■ *Example:* There was a rabbit and in the beginning he was really splendid. He was fat and bunchy as a rabbit should be.

   ■ *Summary:* The splendid rabbit was fat and bunchy.

2. **COMBINE IDEAS WITH THE SAME SUBJECT.** ····················

   ■ *Example:* He has a brown coat with white spots. He had thread whiskers and his ears were lined with pink satin. His spots made him stand out among plain red stockings.

   ■ *Summary:* His brown coat, white spots, and pink-lined ears made him stand out among the plain red stockings.

3. **RESTATE IN FEWER WORDS.** ·····································

   ■ *Example:* There were other things in the stocking, nuts and oranges, and a toy engine, and chocolate almonds, a mouse and candy canes, but the rabbit was the best of all.

   The stocking was adorned with Christmas treats and decorations, but the rabbit was the best gift.

   ■ *Summary:* The stocking was filled with Christmas treats, but the rabbit was the best gift.

4. **USE SUMMARY WORDS.** ···

   ■ *Example:* Summary words include: *almost all, in conclusion, in brief, the main point, on the whole, ultimately, to sum up.*

5. **REMOVE DETAILS THAT ARE NOT** ·································
   ABOUT THE MAIN SUBJECT.

   ■ *Example:* On Christmas morning when he sat wedged in the top of the boy's stocking with a spring of holly between his paws, the Velveteen Rabbit looked charming.

   ■ *Summary:* The Velveteen Rabbit looked charming.

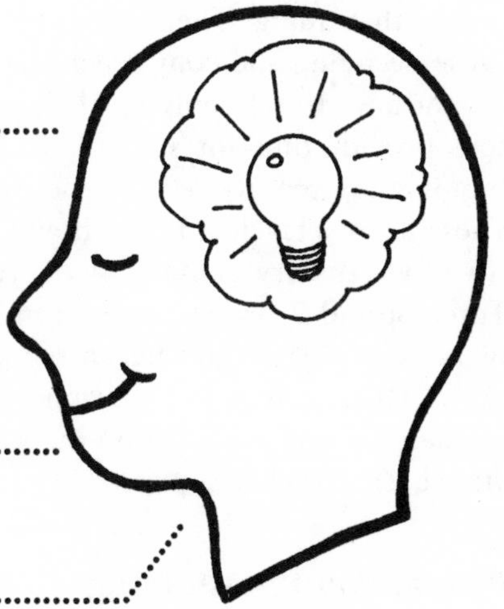

A GREAT SUMMARY SENTENCE COULD BE:

FIGURE 4.3. Summarization Thinking Guide: Graphic for students to refer to as they read, which reminds them to integrate strategies to connect and combine text within and between paragraphs. From Block and Mangieri (1996). Copyright 1996 by Pearson Learning. Reprinted by permission.

depicted. In time, however, after several power of three lessons, the effects of using contrastive examples begin to appear (Bransford & Vye, 2000). Students begin to choose the best of the three methods for them to use to comprehend.

In summary, in Strand 1 lessons teachers explain how to use the *teacher-within* (i.e., their own metacognition, prior experiences, and personal goals) and *teachers-without* (i.e., peers, teachers, textual clues, and other print, visual, or oral media as resources) when a lack of prior knowledge about the subject matter creates comprehension difficulties (Cain-Thoreson, Lippman & McClendon-Magnuson, 1997; Pressley & Afflerbach, 1995). Strand 1 lessons teach deeply through expanded explanations, monitored mentoring, and repeated guided-practice sessions. After repeated uses of these lessons, students can explain why they engaged a particular set of comprehension processes and the outcome of using them (Block, 2001b).

STRAND 2: ASSIST STUDENTS TO COMPREHEND PROCESSES AUTOMATICALLY, HABITUALLY, AND INDEPENDENTLY

The purpose of this strand of comprehension instruction is to assist students to fall in love with reading. Their minds can more completely enjoy the making of meaning because decoding and comprehension tools are handed to them at points of need. Students do not have to rely only on their unassisted making of meaning processes. Strand 2 lessons provide time for students to fall in love with reading because obstacles to understanding are removed at the specific points in a silent reading when students face them. These lessons teach students how to stop and think strategically in a text when the density of vocabulary, complexity of syntax, or idea density overwhelms their understanding. Three Strand 2 lessons have been demonstrated to increase students' abilities to intertwine several strategies into a self-guided crafting process: (1) Pivotal point scaffolding, (2) STAR lessons, and (3) diagnostic whisper reads (Block, in press-a). In these lessons, teachers do not teach before the whole class or small groups. Instruction is totally individualized. Teacher support is provided when students request it.

Pivotal Point Scaffolding

Pivotal point scaffolding is a process-based instructional lesson that occurs when students read silently. To begin, teachers allocate a developmentally appropriate number of minutes for SSR (sustained silent reading time). Students can transport themselves into texts during such extended reading and live within a book, so that the meaning-making process becomes their own. While students craft their personal purposes for a reading, experience their worth as valid comprehenders, respond to print in their unique manners, and care deeply about an author's message, teachers are available to assist them on a one-on-one basis when students need them. Teachers become master craftpersons, roaming the room as students raise their hands when texts become confusing. Without pivotal point scaffolding, teachers report that they feel as if they are "having to do all of their students' thinking for them and establishing all of their purposes for reading." By contract, these lessons stress that complete comprehension cannot occur if authors' messages are merely accepted without reflection. Teachers can be assured that they are leaving something for their students to be proud of concerning their own literacy. Students can be sure that they have the time and support to savor meaning in personally fulfilling contexts. Their teachers monitor comprehension with, and not for, them.

At these moments, teachers engage in pivotal point scaffolds in which their feedback statements are on *PAR* (*Praise–Ask–Raise*). Through pivotal point scaffolds, teachers Praise students for specific comprehension processes that they demonstrate. Then, they Ask individuals how they knew to use that comprehension process and what they need to continue their comprehension. Last, they Raise students' abilities by demonstrating the next higher type of support and process that the student requested. Teachers can also use PAR to address individual comprehension needs when single pupils encounter a confusion that halts their independent navigation of that particular text. When the specific question on a student's mind is answered (at the point in the text when needed), students can more rapidly interject new ideas into the text as well as the broader contexts of their lives (Block & Dellamura, 2000–2001). The last step is to record the difficulty that halted a student's making of meaning on a Pivotal Point Scaffolding Record Form that teachers carry with them. These forms can be used to group students into comprehension process-based groups for a Strand 1 lesson in an upcoming week.

STAR Lessons

STAR (Student-initiated Talk After Read-alouds) lessons are distinct from traditional shared reading experiences. In STAR lessons, teachers pause in a read-aloud only (1) *if students want to report how they are making meaning*; or (2) to *answer students' questions about how to make meaning at a specific point in a text*. In STAR lessons, teachers do not say the first words after a read-aloud. Students do. This is necessary because we have discovered that whoever manages and initiates the dialogue after a read-aloud controls the construction of meaning. In STAR lessons, students begin and sustain these conversations. They report how they integrated processes by naming them and describing how they enriched their comprehension. Such lessons are most powerful when books that are read contain: (1) a surprise that reversed the plot; (2) action-filled segments that required all four processes on page 119; (3) characters whom students could easily relate to and who repeatedly attempted to resolve problems and said or did insightful things; or (4) events that triggered a change in the usual order of events that traditionally occur in students' lives.

To illustrate, one of us (JAJ) began his second graders' STAR lesson when students selected *Do Tornadoes Really Twist? Questions and Answers about Tornadoes and Hurricanes* (Scholastic Reference Book Series, 2000) as the STAR book that he was to share in a read-aloud. Students decided whether they wanted him to stop the reading periodically for students to make comments, or if the reading was to be completed without anyone interjecting their ideas. Because they selected the latter for this particular STAR lesson, Mr. Joy asked Ms. Maria Martinez, his adult volunteer, to list students' names in the order that they raised their hands. Students raised their hands to discuss the results of comprehension processes that they were relating together in their minds. Ms. Martinez listed the page at which Mr. Joy was reading beside each student's name. Mr. Joy began reading. No one spoke. Several students raised their hands as book pages were turned. After the reading, Ms. Martinez asked Mr. Joy to turn to the page that was written beside the first child's name on her list. Mr. Joy asked that child to begin the conversation about processes used to comprehend *Do Tornadoes Really Twist?* As students talked, they pointed to sentences in the book or to two or more comprehension processes on the chart before them that they had learned in Strand 1 lessons and that they had used at that specific point in the text to make meaning. This and other STAR lessons end with students suggesting a process that they want to learn to deepen their construction of meaning. This suggestion becomes the basis for a Strand 3 lesson in the future, and teachers refer to this students' request to begin that Strand 3 lesson.

In summary, STAR lessons build more time for students to develop the habit of curling up with good books and permitting books to become mirrors in which they can discover how to use comprehension processes independently. In these lessons, students have teachers and peers as master comprehenders to serve as coaches at points of need.

Diagnostic Whisper Reads: What Students Are Processing Correctly during Silent Reading

This process-based lesson occurs in guided reading groups. When students begin their whisper reading, teachers do not stay seated. Instead, they take their record-keeping form and stand behind individuals as they read to make a note of comprehension growth. A teacher listens for points in a reading in which a student has successfully navigated a comprehension process to obtain meaning, stops that child's reading momentarily, and asks: (1) "What processes did you use?"; (2) "What were you thinking as you read that section?"; (3) "How did you comprehend that section successfully?"; (4) "What are you learning to do to comprehend better?"; and (5) "What is bothering you about your reading abilities?" If the child describes the meaning-making processes accurately, the teacher notes such on the record form and reinforces the exact growth that this child demonstrated. If the child does not describe the processes accurately, the teacher notes this on the form and performs an individually tailored pivotal point scaffold for that student at this point in the text. Teachers return in the next day's whisper-read text, in which the same processes would need to be engaged, and ask that child one or more of the three questions listed for a second time. These procedures are repeated as the next child whisper reads. On average, five students can receive a diagnostic whisper-read lesson in 15 minutes.

STRAND 3: COMPREHENSION PROCESSES THAT STUDENTS ELECT TO LEARN

Comprehension should be a self-initiated, deliberate, flexible, adaptable, and free-flowing process. Without effective instruction, poorer readers tend to dive into every text inflexibly, using the same approach to read all (Block, 2001a). After time, reading becomes boring because comprehension processes have not been adapted when confusions occur. Their ineffective processing dulls their abilities to discover and savor subtle meanings, which, in turn, limits their drive and desire to read.

Strand 3 lessons assist poorer readers to overcome these limitations. They create time for students to suggest what they want to learn to comprehend better. In Strand 3 lessons, teachers schedule time to listen to students' stories about their lives as readers, their reading abilities, and their literacy goals. Students can tell teachers what they depend on in order to read, as well as what they need to comprehend more completely. Strand 3 lessons have also been demonstrated to increase students' intrinsic motivation by making them aware of what they might do to improve their comprehension. Four types of Strand 3 lessons are: (1) discovery discussions; (2) correction journals; (3) teacher–readers; and, (4) entering into a text figuratively.

Discovery Discussions

Discovery discussions are a special type of one-to-one conference whereby students became aware of and expand their capabilities to comprehend. Such self-knowledge is essential, as students themselves are the people who are most aware of the level of effort (and are most sensitive to the level of drive) that they are willing to expend to become more powerful crafters (Caine & Caine, 1997). Discovery discussions increase the level of effort and drive that developing readers expend to become a better reader (Block, in press-b).

Teachers proactively prepare for each discovery discussion so that they can productively move a student to a higher level of processing text. A regular time is scheduled for discovery discussions, and both students and teachers can schedule one. During these lessons, teachers do not rush from one student to another. Teachers give individuals their undivided attention throughout, as the most important part of a discovery discussion often occurs at session's end. It is at these times that many students gain the confidence to risk asking an important question about their reading weaknesses.

Discovery discussions encourage students to talk about their reading abilities, their literacy goals, what they depend on to read well, and what they need to comprehend more completely. Much as when knowledge was fostered through fireside family conversations and time spent in by-the-bench mentoring, discovery discussions permit teachers and students to ask more questions of each other, such as "What do you think?" "What are you learning?" "What do you think I need to learn?" and "What is bothering you about your comprehension?" During these conversations, students tell very specific stories about their reading abilities. They also learn intensely in their zone of proximal development (Vygotsky, 1978). This theory emphasizes how tasks are learned more rapidly through collaborative interactions with more able mentors and how comprehension processes are co-constructed. Discovery discussions provide the time for students to communicate the exact action that they want to take to become better comprehenders. This ensures that students do not spend so much time in the "zone of the already known," which can occur in the classrooms that do not contain discovery discussions.

Discovery discussions also help to create a learning community in which inside jokes, shared personal insights, and laughter enable students and teachers to bond together as a group and with reading. Discovery discussions increase the number of questions that students ask about reading (Block, 2001b). This in turn expands students' comprehension, as students who pose questions score higher on standardized comprehension tests than do students who simply discuss the material that they read (Block, 1993; Graham & Block, 1994; King, 1994).

Correction Journals

These Strand 3 lessons enable students to keep journals in which they record what they learned to comprehend better. The first half of a *correction journal lesson* involves students in its design and asks students to examine their own comprehension processes to demonstrate how they learned and to gain insight into their hopes and desires concerning reading comprehension. For instance, consider Alex, a second grader, who was almost retained by his first-grade teacher because of his low comprehension. During the correction journal lesson, Alex expressed his desire to read, saying that reading was fun but difficult. He wanted to read *The 100th Day of School* by Angela Medearis because of the repetition throughout the book. He explained what he found to be a good reading process. As he read, Alex stopped to point out how he was personalizing the comprehension process and what he felt he needed to learn to better understand what he read: "*ai* equals *ay* as in rain. I didn't know that *ai* and *ay* make the same sound, did you? This is the same as *ou* and *ow*, in *flour* and *ourselves*, *ground*. I like to read books where it talks about similar words over and over again."

At this point, the second phase in the correction journal lesson begins. The teacher implemented a lesson using the decoding and repetition of ideas that Alex reported that he needed to comprehend. Because the choice of processes for instruction was Alex's, he felt ownership of the lesson, which in turn served as a new source of motivation. When the teacher explained the need to maintain an achievement press (i.e., sustaining a constant challenge during reading so comprehension power builds), Alex chose *The Little Red Hen*. It consisted of words of medium difficulty for Alex and had a substantial amount of repetition, as Alex requested. As Alex read the story, the teacher asked him to maintain a correction journal for some personal devices he was using to improve his comprehension process.

One example of the types of entries Alex made that day occurred when he discovered that every word that he stumbled to pronounce contained the "ou" pattern, as found in the word "ground." When Alex struggled with several such words, he paused and said that if he was ever going to free his mind to make meaning, he had to correct errors with these words. He recorded in his correction journal a method he was going to use to remember "ou" words. Alex wrote what he called an equation, that is, $ou = ow$. The teacher then wrote several other words with that same pattern below Alex's strategy (equation), and Alex read each perfectly. Once they finished reading *The Little Red Hen*, Alex asked to read *The 100th Day of School*. The teacher agreed to his request and asked him to point out all of the words containing the patterns that he struggled with that day. As Alex read the story, he pointed to and read nearly all of the words containing the patterns that he had struggled with earlier. Alex referred back to his correction journal several times as he read six pages, until he eventually no longer needed that correction journal entry as a reference. He was able to recognize the pattern successfully because of his own personally developed method of integrating decoding and comprehension processes.

The correction journal lessons that Joy and Alex performed together developed Alex's ability to comprehend. The interview provided additional insights for Joy about how Alex guided his comprehension processes. Alex took ownership of the comprehension process and the correction journal lessons provided a concrete support to do so. This was important to Alex's growth.

Teacher–Reader Lessons

Teacher–reader lessons begin when students tell their teachers what processes they want to learn. Then, students join a group in which that aspect of the comprehension process is taught. They bring one of their favorite books (or a book that they want to read) to the group meeting. During that meeting, the processes they want to learn are discussed in a more focused way than in Strands 1 and 2 lessons. Students talk about what they do to accomplish a particular aspect of comprehension and illustrate it by reading and doing think-alouds from their books. Students and teachers offer suggestions for overcoming specific reading problems. For example, one of the students in a teacher–reader group that one of us (CCB) conducted reported: "Yesterday, during our meaning-makers teacher–readers group, you asked me what I wished that I could do to comprehend better. For the first time I realized that I wanted to cling to meanings more. What everyone suggested worked! Today, I'm reading the words more rapidly and the thoughts more slowly. I don't read every word that the author says so slowly that I can't know each idea. Today, ideas just jump off the page. I must rush down the lines to capture them all as they leap into the pictures in my mind."

These meetings are normally held only once a week. Between meetings, students practice the suggestions they learned. In the next teacher–reader group, meeting peers confer about what they did to apply the processes that they previously discussed. At the third group meeting, students make icons or paraphrase the description of comprehension processes that they used. These graphic and word images became references similar to the icons on computer bars, reminding students of the comprehension tools that they can bring into play to become better comprehenders. Usually, no more than three teacher–reader groups meet each week. In this way, students have three choices of different comprehension processes that they want to apply. The groups created by fourth graders in a study by Block (1999) appear in Table 4.1.

Asking Students to Insert Themselves Figuratively into Text

One of us (JLS) has had success with emotionally laden sensory stimuli to engaging students to process text more completely. She believes that all children can identify with emotions and employ them to identify the tone of an author. She reasons that an author's emotional connection with his or her readers determines the tone, theme, and impact of any writing. When students can comprehend with their emotions and cognitive processes simultaneously, they can reinterpret both the content and the intent of a piece, making an immediate connection of textually based experiences to their own lives. Schaller helps them do this by asking students to rewrite a text in another medium, such as a pop culture communication form, a speech, song, screenplay, movie, television series, or piece of visual art. As she explains, when students create modality

TABLE 4.1. Student-Initiated Literacy Learning Groups

Meaning Makers	We want to learn how to understand better, make more in-depth responses to material read, and learn new strategies to craft understanding.
Transformer Titans	We want to learn how we can more rapidly apply what we read to our lives.
Breadth Builders	We want to find more genres that we want to read so we can enjoy more types of books.
Word Wanters	We want to learn more decoding strategies. We will bring a book we are reading to group meetings to model how we decoded a difficult word. We will ask classmates to find similar words using these methods in their books and try out their strategies in our books.
Speed Mongrels	We want to increase our speed of oral and silent reading.
Memory Menders	We want to find ways to retain more of what we read.
Critical Analyzers	We want to learn how better to connect what we read to other readings and aspects of the world. We also want to learn how to reflect more on what we read.
Author Askers	We want to confront the author with such questions as "What does he or she mean here? Does this make sense with what he or she told us before?" (Beck, McKeown, Hamilton, & Jucan, 1997, p. 332). We also want to learn how to consider the author's ideas and fallibility, grappling with his or her text to dig for deeper meanings; to write to authors about fictional writing decisions they have made; and to call on experts in fields related to our nonfictional quests.

Note. From Block (1999). Copyright 1999 by Guilford Press. Reprinted by permission.

shifts, "multiple intelligences ram right into, intensify, and enrich comprehension processes."

Another of us (PG) has developed lessons that accomplish this by asking students to "figuratively insert themselves into a text." She encourages students to be cheerleaders for an author. When students step inside the book and take the author's place, they identify more fully with the story because they root for the author to tell a successful story. They work their comprehension processes harder because they care about the author and want him or her to write the best possible book. As she stated, "When I was growing up, I never read for the sake of reading, because I always considered reading a chore. Even now, I sometimes struggle to understand the meaning and purpose of some of the literature that I read. If I had know when I was a child that reading could lead to a better understanding of oneself and others, then I would not have viewed reading as such a chore."

By asking students to insert themselves figuratively into the text (either as a cheerleader for the author or as a producer transforming the book into another art form), students begin to view comprehension as a living process. Students can also write biographies of the characters they encounter (i.e., text friends), including predictions about the characters' lives. Sometimes students rewrite the stories they read, changing endings to reflect what would be occurring if they were "in the story." Students can also bring illustrations to life in their own words as they write books from photos or wordless picture books. When teachers provide background lessons about authors, the authors in fact become human beings outside of their books. Students come to realize that when they write they are like adult authors, and reading becomes more interesting (Block, 2001a).

WHAT DO WE NEED TO DO IN THE FUTURE?

We, and other members of the Research-based Comprehension Consortium, are implementing Strand 1, 2, and 3 lessons over a 2-year period. This study involves students in grades 2–8. During this research, students' comprehension, affective responses to reading, fluency, vocabulary, and reading power will be further analyzed. As we do this, we will be exploring the following needs for future research and improvements in present practices of teaching comprehension.

1. *How can we teach comprehension in ways that are more like the process that expert readers experience, and not as a collection of separate, segmented strategies to be memorized?* Using differentiated purposes for our instruction and three strands of lessons can be a first step in reaching this goal. Ten lessons in this chapter have demonstrated to build grade 2–8 students' independence in comprehension. Students as young as 8 years can describe the processes that they employ to comprehend and experience the ebb and flow of increased processing when difficult concepts are read (Block, 1999, 2001b, in press).

2. *How can we decide when to provide explicit instruction for learners? How can we find an effective blend between giving assistance and guiding learners to discover their own comprehension processes* (e.g., Zecker, Pappas, & Cohen, 1998)? The evidence presented in this chapter suggests that much more time must be spent with teachers instructing differentiated strands of lessons and asking students what they are thinking while they are reading before this answer can be attained.

3. *How can we provide more opportunities (during the school day) for students to*

tell us which comprehension processes they need and want to learn? We need to provide more opportunities during the weekly literacy class schedule for students to tell us what they need. Data in this chapter suggest that time for asking students what they need and teaching it to them must be allocated weekly before some students (ages 8–14) reach their full potential as lifelong lovers of literacy. Discovery discussions, correction journals, teacher–reader lessons, and asking students to insert themselves figuratively into the text have demonstrated to be four methods that we can employ to do so.

SUMMARY

It is an exciting time to be a teacher and researcher in the field of reading comprehension. We are discovering how to teach comprehension more effectively than at any other time in history. In this chapter, we proposed that comprehension instruction should become more differentiated and taught more as it occurs in the minds of expert readers (process-based instruction). We recommended that we can begin to so by teaching three strands of lessons. (1) Strand 1 teaches how to use two processes together to eliminate misunderstandings by teaching how to interrelate comprehension processes, (2) utilizing *the TRIO teaching cycle*, and (3) conducting *the power of three lessons*. Strand 2, assisting students to use comprehension processes automatically, habitually, and independently, can be implemented through *pivotal point scaffolding, STAR lessons,* and *diagnostic whisper reads*. Strand 3 portrays effective comprehension as resultant from a unique mixture of processes that students select to use. They can begin through *discovery discussions, correction journals, teacher–reader lessons,* and *asking students to insert themselves figuratively into text.* We are expanding the time we spend answering students' questions at the exact point in a text at which confusions arise. We have learned how to model, give examples, provide think-alouds, and monitor guided practice sessions so that students can intertwine the three strands of comprehension processes.

To enhance our success, future instruction should (1) assist students to overcome comprehension challenges as they present themselves; (2) include more opportunities for students to become enthralled with reading and exploring topics of importance, with the individualized support of their teachers; and (3) involve students in making decisions about what reading difficulties they want to overcome. This three-strand approach is demonstrating effectiveness in improving the comprehension abilities in children aged 7–14 (e.g., Block, 1994, 1999, 2000a, in press-a, in press-b).

REFERENCES

Anderson, V. (1992). A teacher development project in transactional strategy instruction for teachers of severely reading-disabled adolescents. *Teaching and Teacher Education, 8,* 391–403.

Anderson, V., & Roit, M. (1993). Planning and implementing collaborative strategy instruction for delayed readers in grades 6–10. *Elementary School Journal, 94,* 121–137.

Beck, I., & Dole, J. (1994). Engaging readers in nonfictional text. In C. Collins & J. Mangieri (Eds.), *Teaching thinking: An agenda for the twenty-first century* (pp. 233–254). Mahwah, NJ: Erlbaum.

Beck, I., McKeown, M., Hamilton, R., & Jucan, L. (1997). *Questioning the author: An approach for enhancing student engagement with text.* Newark, DE: International Reading Association.

Block, C. (1993). Strategy instruction in a literature-based program. *Elementary School Journal*, *94*, 103–120.

Block, C. (1994). Developing problem-solving abilities. In J. N. Mangiei & C. C. Block (Eds.), *Creating powerful thinking in teachers and students: Diverse perspectives* (pp. 141–161). Fort Worth, TX: Harcourt Brace.

Block, C. (1999). Comprehension: Crafting understanding. In L. Gambrell, L. Morrow, S. Neuman, & M. Pressley (Eds.), *Best practices in literacy instruction* (pp. 98–118). New York: Guilford Press.

Block, C. (2000a). The case for exemplary instruction especially for students who come to school without the precursors for literacy success. *National Reading Conference Yearbook*, *49*, 155–67.

Block, C. (2000b). Reading instruction in the new millennium. In A. Costa (Ed.), *Developing minds* (3rd ed., pp. 472–490). Alexandria, VA: Association for Supervision and Curriculum Development.

Block, C. (2001a). *Teaching the language arts* (3rd ed.). Boston, MA: Allyn & Bacon.

Block, C. (2001b, May). *Comprehending non-fiction: Reading to learn*. Paper presented at the Annual Meeting of the International Reading Association, New Orleans, LA.

Block, C. (in press-a). *Teaching reading comprehension*. Boston, MA: Allyn & Bacon.

Block, C. (in press-b). *Literacy difficulties: Diagnosis and instruction*. Boston, MA: Allyn & Bacon.

Block, C., & Mangieri, J. (1996). *Reason to read: Thinking strategies for life through literature* (Vols. 1–3). Menlo Park, CA: Addison.

Block, C. C., & Dellamura, R. Y. (2000–2001). Better book buddies. *The Reading Teacher*, *54*(4), 364–370.

Bransford, J., & Vye, J. (2000, April). *The case for comparison cases*. Paper presented at the annual meeting of the American Educational Research Association, San Francisco, CA.

Brown, R., Pressley, M., Van Meter, P., & Schuder, T. (1996). A quasi-experimental validation of transactional strategies instruction with low-achieving second grade readers. *Journal of Educational Psychology*, *88*, 18–37.

Caine, R. N., & Caine, G. (1997). *Education on the edge of possibility*. Alexandria, VA: Association of Society of Curriculum and Development.

Cain-Thoreson, C., Lippman, M. Z., & McClendon-Magnuson, D. (1997). Windows on comprehension: Reading comprehension processes as revealed by two think-aloud procedures. *Journal of Educational Psychology*, *89*(4), 579–592.

Collins, C. (1991). Reading instruction that increases thinking abilities. *Journal of Reading*, *34*, 510–516.

Graham, M., & Block, C. (1994). Elementary students as co-teachers and co-researchers. *Greater Washington Journal of Literacy*, *12*, 334–348.

Hesselbrink, T. (1998, May). *Overcoming the cycle of reading failure*. Paper presented at the annual meeting of the International Reading Association, Orlando, CA.

Kintsch, W. (1988). The role of knowledge in discourse comprehension: A construction–integration model. *Psychological Review*, *95*(2), 163–182.

King, A. (1994). Guiding knowledge construction in the classroom: Effects of teaching children how to question and how to explain. *American Educational Research Journal*, *31*(2), 338–368.

Leslie, L., & Caldwell, J. (2001). *Qualitative Reading Inventory—3*. Boston, MA: Allyn & Bacon/ Longman.

Pressley, M., Allington, R. L., Wharton-McDonald, R., Block, C. C., & Morrow, L. M. (2001). *Learning to read: Lessons from exemplary first-grade classrooms*. New York: Guilford Press.

Pressley, M. (1999). Self-regulated comprehension processing. In L. Gambrell, L. Morrow, L., S. Neuman, & M. Pressley (Eds.), *Best practices in literacy instruction* (pp. 90–97). New York: Guilford Press.

Pressley, M., & Afflerbach, P. (1995). *Verbal protocols of reading: The nature of constructively responsive reading.* Hillsdale, NJ: Erlbaum.

Schruder, T. (1987). The SAIL Program: Effects on students' reading achievement. *Educational Leadership, 44*(6), 345–349.

Taylor, B., Graves, M., & van den Broek, P. (2000). *Reading for meaning: Fostering comprehension in the middle grades.* New York: Columbia University, Teachers College.

Taylor, B., Pearson, P. D., Clark, K. F., & Wolpole, S. (1999). Effective schools/accomplished teachers. *The Reading Teacher, 53*(2), 156–159.

Vygotsky, L. (1978). *Mind and society.* Cambridge, MA: Harvard University Press.

Wood, E., Willoughby, T., McDermott, C., Motz, M., & Kaspaar, V. (1999). Developmental differences in study behavior. *Journal of Educational Psychology, 91*(3), 527–536.

Zecker, L., Pappas, C., & Cohen, S. (1998). Finding the "right measure" of explanation for young Latina/o writers. *Language Arts, 76*(1), 49–56.

5

Implications of Cognitive Resource Allocation for Comprehension Strategies Instruction

GALE M. SINATRA
KATHLEEN J. BROWN
RALPH E. REYNOLDS

During the 1980s and early 1990s, comprehension strategies instruction received considerable research attention. Initially, researchers investigated how readers of varied abilities used comprehension strategies and whether lower achieving readers could be taught to use the strategies that successful readers employed (see Alexander & Judy, 1988; and Duell, 1986, for reviews). Gradually, as findings from controlled short-term studies converged to indicate that strategies training was effective (see Garner, 1987, for a review), researchers moved to apply strategies instruction in classroom settings (see, for example, Duffy et al.,1987; Gaskins, Anderson, Pressley, Cunicelli, & Satlow, 1993; Block & Mangieri, 1996).

Overall, empirical evidence on the effectiveness of comprehension strategies instruction has been favorable (Pressley et al., 1990; Swanson, Hoskyn, & Lee, 1999). However, the evidence also indicated that such effects were hard won in that they required a great deal of time and effort from teachers (Pressley, Goodchild, Fleet, Zajchowski, & Evans, 1989; see also El-Dinary, Chapter 13, this volume). Also, even when sufficient time and effort was invested, not all students seemed to benefit from strategies instruction (see Dole, Brown, & Trathen, 1996), nor were effects demonstrated on all comprehension measures (see Duffy et al., 1987). In addition, some researchers questioned whether strategies instruction was the most effective way to help students improve their comprehension (Beck, McKeown, Sandora, Kucan, & Worthy, 1996). These researchers suggested that students' comprehension might be better served by developing a general disposition toward an "active search for meaning" (Beck et al., 1996, p. 386). With these issues in mind, we agree with Alexander, Graham, and Harris (1998) that, "despite the past decades of programmatic investigations, there are still many unanswered questions and unresolved issues about strategies that are worthy of attention" (p. 129). One of the questions that we believe deserves increased attention is: Why is it so difficult to achieve results from comprehension strategies instruction?

In addition to the well-documented challenges that teachers face in learning how to execute this approach effectively, we suggest that part of the answer may lie in a feature of the learner's cognitive processing system—specifically, the *limitations* of that system. When students attempt to learn from text, that is, when they identify words, use basic comprehension techniques, or use comprehension strategies, they expend cognitive resources, reducing availability for other purposes. Put another way, comprehension strategies are among the many cognitive processes competing for limited resources during the reading process. This constraint leads us to consider a number of related issues: To what extent can readers maintain conscious, effortful strategy use? While thus engaged, what other kinds of processing are hampered? Do all readers—especially lower achievers—have the cognitive resources necessary to use comprehension strategies? Although issues of resource limitations related to lower-level reading processes such as word identification have been the subject of considerable research (for example, see Stanovich, 1986), they have not been explored thoroughly by researchers examining higher level processes such as comprehension strategy use. Accordingly, this chapter (1) provides a brief overview of comprehension strategies instruction and its documented empirical effectiveness, (2) explores the likely relation between conscious, strategic processing and automatic processing during reading, (3) describes how strategies instruction might be modified to address the issue of cognitive resource limitations, and (4) outlines a direction for future research.

COMPREHENSION STRATEGIES INSTRUCTION: AN OVERVIEW

Strategies typically are defined as goal-directed cognitive operations over and above the processes that are a natural consequence of carrying out a task (Pressley, Forrest-Pressley, Elliot-Faust, & Miller, 1985). With regard to reading comprehension, strategies may include determining importance, drawing inferences, generating questions about text, summarizing, or monitoring comprehension (for a review, see Dole, Duffy, Roehler, & Pearson, 1991). Strategic readers typically are characterized as "self-regulated" (Paris, Wasik, & Turner, 1991). They are motivated and persistent, controlling and monitoring strategy use and background knowledge as they read (Pintrich & De Groot, 1990; Schunk, 1990; Zimmermann, 1989). Using the "strategic reader" as their model, researchers have designed instructional interventions to help lower achieving students develop the cognitive, metacognitive, and motivational abilities to become self-regulated. Researchers have hypothesized that if teachers can help lower achieving students learn how and when to use reading strategies and to attribute subsequent reading success to strategy use, then students are more likely to use strategies successfully when they read on their own. This hypothesis informs most versions of comprehension strategies instruction—including explicit comprehension instruction (Pearson & Dole, 1987), transactional strategies instruction (Pressley et al., 1992), informed strategies training (Paris, Cross, & Lipson, 1984), cognitive apprenticeship (Collins, Brown, & Newman, 1989), reciprocal teaching (Palincsar & Brown, 1984), and self-instructional training (Miller & Brewster, 1992).

Comprehension strategies instruction typically includes two components: direct explanation and scaffolding (Harris & Pressley, 1991). To provide direct explanation of reading strategies, Winograd and Hare (1988) suggest that teachers employ the following instructional actions. First, they must describe strategies sensibly and meaningfully to students. Second, teachers need to motivate students to learn by informing them how strategies are useful and what performance benefits accrue from strategy use. Third, teachers must explain how to use strategies step by step. This can be accomplished through modeling (Collins et al., 1989), talk-alouds (Hansen & Pearson, 1983), and think-alouds (Roehler & Duffy, 1991). Fourth, teachers should help students understand the conditions under which certain strategies are appropriate by providing diverse contexts for strategy use. Finally, teachers need to show students how to monitor, evaluate, and improve their own strategy use.

The second component of a strategies instructional model—scaffolding—includes instructional actions designed to shift responsibility for strategy use from teachers to students (Paris et al., 1991; Roehler & Duffy, 1991). Sometimes known as "fading" or the "gradual release of responsibility" (Pearson & Gallagher, 1983), scaffolding requires teachers to operate in students' zone of proximal development (Vygotsky, 1978). This means that teachers help students use strategies to succeed when they could not succeed alone. Then, with time, practice, feedback, and coaching, students gain the knowledge and motivation to use independently what they have learned. In short, the goal is for students to become self-regulated in their strategy use.

COMPREHENSION STRATEGIES INSTRUCTION EFFECTIVENESS: FAVORABLE, BUT DIFFICULT TO ACHIEVE

Researchers have conducted a large number of studies evaluating the effectiveness of the comprehension strategies instruction model. Viewed collectively, those studies seem to indicate that comprehension strategies instruction does help students improve their comprehension performance—especially among students with learning disabilities (see Swanson et al., 1999).

For example, data from classroom-based studies have indicated that lower achieving students who received comprehension strategies instruction improved their performance on researcher-constructed measures of comprehension (Dewitz, Carr, & Patberg, 1987; Dole et al., 1996; Gaskins et al., 1994). Students in the strategies groups typically received explicit instruction in one or more comprehension strategies for several weeks, after which they outperformed other instructional treatment and control groups when asked to complete short-answer questions about texts they read independently. Moreover, students from the strategies group continued to use the strategies they learned and maintained their comprehension edge for weeks even after instruction had ceased.

Evidence of effects on standardized measures is somewhat more mixed. Large-scale long-term interventions conducted by Duffy, Paris, and their respective colleagues (Duffy et al., 1987; Paris et al., 1984) demonstrated that, in comparison with control group peers, students who received comprehension strategies instruction improved metacognitively. That is, strategy group students showed greater awareness of the reading process and steps they could take to read successfully. However, these students did not transfer those gains to standardized measures of reading comprehension. In contrast, the original empirical work on reciprocal teaching (Palincsar & Brown, 1984) did show such transfer—even on standardized tests of content area knowledge.

It must also be noted that even in studies in which strategies instruction produced an overall statistical advantage, not all students improved their comprehension performance. Why do some students appear to benefit from strategies instruction whereas others do not? As noted, the challenge of teaching strategies effectively has been well documented (El-Dinary & Schuder, 1993; Pressley et al., 1992; Roehler, 1992). Duffy (1993) reported that it took years for teachers to acquire expertise in strategies instruction. And, even with time, some teachers do not. Teaching strategies well requires a deep understanding of the cognitive processes involved in comprehension and an ability to scaffold students through an apprenticeship in executing those processes successfully. Thus, if some teachers become adept at strategies teaching and others do not, the lack of consistency may affect students' performance, leading some students to improve their comprehension abilities, others to maintain their current abilities, and still others to perform less well.

In addition to teacher variables, students themselves—through their mediation of instruction—may influence the effectiveness of instruction (Winne & Marx, 1982). Dole et al. (1996) taught lower achieving students in fifth and sixth grades a story-mapping strategy. They then examined how two individual students (both lower achieving, but one more able than the other) responded to the instruction. They found that the less able reader made clear gains in strategy use and comprehension. Interview data suggested that this student found the instruction helpful and worthwhile. In contrast, the more able reader appeared to learn how to use the story-mapping strategy, but her comprehension declined over the course of the intervention. Interview data suggested that she found the instruction unnecessary and irritating. Dole et al. (1996) concluded, "it could be that the strategy instruction . . . forced her into making an easy task difficult and cumbersome" (1996, p. 81).

These findings were replicated on a larger scale in Brown's (2000) investigation of a classroom's mediation of one strategy lesson. The instruction focused on using a story map to find the main idea in expository text. Evidence confirmed that the 24 students in the classroom did not respond to the lesson uniformly. Rather, they engaged in a variety of cognitive and motivational thought processes. For example, students who reported being attentive and engaged and who had high self-efficacy regarding their abilities to meet their teacher's instructional expectations did improve on postlesson measures. In contrast, some students reported being attentive and engaged during the lesson but also reported experiencing confusion and feelings of low self-efficacy. These students failed to improve, as did those who reported uninterest in the lesson because they "already knew how to find the main idea"—despite the fact that they had room for improvement, as indicated on baseline measures. These data seem to suggest that the ways students think and feel about strategies instruction may influence what and how much they learn.

Also, the effectiveness of strategy instruction may rest—to some extent—on the type of strategies taught. Gallini, Spires, Terry, and Gleaton (1993) investigated the effect of teaching macroprocessing or microprocessing strategies on struggling adolescent readers' comprehension. Strategies instruction in the macroprocessing group focused on the relation among concepts and ideas at a text level. Students were taught to develop concept maps to depict the relations among ideas they read in text. Strategies instruction for the microprocessing group focused on links within and between sentences, such as linking an anaphor ("it") with its referent ("the horse"). The macroprocessing strategies were more effective. Gallini et al. (1993) explained the poor performance of the microprocessing group as follows: "it is possible that the students directed their attention toward . . . learning the strategy . . . at the neglect of also utilizing the detailed cues to promote comprehension" (1993, p. 175). Also, it might be the case that students were processing anaphoric references with few resources prior to instruction and that the instruction brought this previously automatic process back into their conscious awareness.

The concern that strategies instruction itself may draw too much of students' attention away from comprehension has been expressed by other researchers (Pearson & Fielding, 1991; Beck et al., 1996). Beck et al. (1996) noted that "a potential drawback of strategy-based instruction . . . is that attention may become focused on the surface features of the strategies themselves rather than on reading for meaning" (p. 386). In fact, Beck and her colleagues recommend an instructional alternative: Questioning the Author (Beck et al., 1996). Rather than teaching a specific set of strategies, teachers who use Questioning the Author ask questions that encourage students to "grapple with and reflect on what an author is trying to say in order to build a representation [of the text]" (Beck et al., 1996, p. 387). This may reduce demands on cognitive resources because it promotes a general disposition toward text comprehension as a problem-solving process rather than executing strategies performed *in addition to* comprehension itself.

COGNITION AND RESOURCE ALLOCATION: THE ROLE OF AUTOMATICITY

Learning and using comprehension strategies affects students' management of cognitive resources as they read. This is important because cognitive resources are limited (Kahneman, 1973). Limitations have been described as *storage capacity limits* (such as Miller's famous estimate of 7 plus or minus 2 items for short-term memory capacity; Miller, 1956), *allocation of limited attentional resources* (Reynolds, 2000), or *working memory limits* on how much information can be held in active awareness at one time (Kintsch, 1998). Despite differences in characterization, researchers agree that the management of finite resources is a critical issue for successful cognitive processing (see Perfetti, 1988; Reynolds, 2000; Stanovich, 1980). The limitations of the system impose tradeoffs. When students devote resources to one cognitive process, fewer resources are available for others. Thus how students "spend" their resources could have weighty implications for successful reading and learning.

Some types of cognitive processing drain more resources than others. For example, cognitive activities that require conscious attention and effort demand more from the system than activities that can proceed almost automatically. However, individuals can become more cognitively efficient over time. Functions that were originally conscious and effortful can become virtually automatic and below the level of awareness with practice (e.g., proficient drivers shifting their cars into second gear). This frees up resources for more effortful (less practiced) activities such as talking on your cell phone while negotiating traffic.

What it means to become automatic at cognitive task performance is a subject of some debate (see Speelman & Maybery, 1998, for a review of differing theories of automaticity). However, automatic processes typically are characterized as those that are executed quickly, accurately, and almost effortlessly. This characterization is in marked contrast to controlled, strategic processes that require the "willful allocation of attention" (Speeling & Maybery, 1998, p. 80). Such processes are executed slowly, flexibly, and with a considerable drain on cognitive resources.

It has been suggested that automaticity develops as the learner's declarative knowledge (factual knowledge) becomes bundled into proceduralized knowledge ("how to" knowledge) that can be applied with ease (Anderson 1983, 1990). Applied to strategies, this would suggest that strategies move from conscious and effortful to automatic and almost effortless as strategy users move from relying on knowledge *about* the strategy to relying on automatically activated knowledge about strategy *use*. Reynolds, Trathen, Sawyer, and Shepard (1994) refined this notion by suggesting that proceduralized knowledge about strategy use develops through three stages. Readers first acquire knowledge about (1) how to use the strategy in context, (2) when to use the strategy, and finally (3) how to use the strategy with increasing effectiveness and sophistication.

If we apply these notions to comprehension strategies instruction, it suggests that the initial phase of learning involves learning the strategy—which may include a number of sequential steps—and how to use the strategy in relation to text. This first stage of strategy learning necessitates that students engage self-regulated cognitive processes that are slow, rule based, and very demanding of attentional resources. With practice and experience, students begin to strengthen the effective features of the strategy and weaken less effective ones by utilizing feedback. During this second stage of strategy learning, using the strategy requires both controlled and automatic processing. Finally, as knowledge about the strategy compiles into a procedure strengthened by repeated use, the components of the strategy begin to operate more automatically. At this point, the strategy is less subject to cognitive control, demands fewer resources, and is executed when the situation (or text) demands it.

Thus automatic processes develop through repeated use in which a particular set of circumstances invokes the same response. For example, when skilled readers allocate attention to what they consider important information in the text, they may do so without deliberate awareness (Reynolds, 1992). They do not consciously tell themselves, "Pay attention to the important text segments." In fact, they may not be aware that they are selectively attending to different elements of the text at all. Contrast this automatic use of a comprehension strategy with the initial attempts of younger, more inexperienced readers. What changed? With practice and experience, the strategic allocation of resources to important text elements became proceduralized and no longer required conscious effort. For these students, the strategy simply occurs in response to the appropriate situation (i.e., motivation to learn text information). It has been argued that many, if not most, of the cognitive processes we use every day are executed like a skilled readers' use of selective attention—without conscious attention and effort (Bargh & Chartrand, 1999).

COGNITIVE RESOURCE ALLOCATION, AUTOMATICITY, AND COMPREHENSION: IMPLICATIONS FOR STRATEGIES INSTRUCTION

When reading educators discuss reading skills that have become automatic, they generally are referring to lower level processes such as word identification. However, when they discuss comprehension, they use terms such as "conscious," "deliberate," and "strategic." Indeed, the instructional literature emphasizes this view of comprehension (Keene & Zimmermann, 1997).

In contrast, the research literature on comprehension has demonstrated convincingly that important aspects of the comprehension process are automatic—particularly for skilled readers (O'Brien, 1995; Reynolds, 2000; Speelman, 1998). For example, readers can activate relevant background knowledge quickly and need few resources to do so (Magliano, Trabasso, & Graesser, 1999). Some inferences, such as those required to maintain coherence, "are quickly and routinely made during reading" (Graesser & Bertus, 1998, p. 263). The activation of anaphoric references (the noun to which a pronoun refers) often occurs automatically (O'Brien, 1995). And readers even infer fictional characters' emotional states at little cognitive cost (Gernsbacher, Hallada, & Robertson, 1998). So many aspects of comprehension are automatic that O'Brien argues that, when explaining research findings, "an appeal to conscious comprehension processes should only be made when processes assumed to be automatic cannot account for particular results" (1995, p. 174).

Strategies instruction researchers have acknowledged that over time and through practice strategies may become automatic (Alexander et al., 1998; Paris et al., 1991). van den Broek and Kremer (2000) have explained that comprehension strategies instruction is conducted with the "hope that the practiced skills will become internalized and automatic, so that they can be applied spontaneously and effortlessly in future reading situations" (p. 22).

Despite the research evidence suggesting that automatic comprehension processes play a critical role in reading success and the acknowledgment that strategies must become efficient, little attention has been devoted to developing instructional methods that might foster automaticity of comprehension strategies. This lack of attention to automaticity issues in comprehension instruction may explain some of the challenge posed by the teaching of strategies. When teachers instruct students to use a comprehension strategy and students comply, they expend resources. Students employing a new, difficult, or cumbersome strategy may shift the bulk of their thinking to strategy use and have insufficient attentional resources left for simply making sense of the text.

Even if students prove able to apply the strategy and to make sense of text simultaneously, resource issues may still come into play. Specifically, if there is continued instructional emphasis on the reflective, deliberate use of strategies, the desired transition to automatic processing may be undermined. For example, students often are asked to produce concrete evidence (e.g., a story map) that they performed a strategy (e.g., finding the main idea). This serves two purposes: It provides students with guided practice in strategy use and it provides the teacher with a means of assessment. However, once students show prowess at strategy use, if they continue to execute the strategy in a very deliberate, concrete way (e.g., making a story map), they may be drawing valuable resources away from constructing meaning.

Finally, the number of strategies teachers ask students to learn may present a challenge for cognitive resource allocation. Magliano et al. (1999) explained that instructional programs that "emphasize the concurrent use of multiple strategies" may be problematic because some strategies "conflict with one another" (p. 625). They noted that "it is difficult to both explain and predict concurrently" (p. 625). Thus asking students to retell important text events while at the same time predicting future events may be asking too much—particularly if those processes are still unfamiliar. Moreover, if students are taught to apply a large number of strategies during the reading process, they also may develop the perception that all texts require ongoing, deliberate processing. As they attempt to do what they have been instructed, they may be overwhelmed by the sheer number of tasks they must perform, and comprehension may suffer.

COGNITIVE RESOURCE ALLOCATION, AUTOMATICITY, AND WORD IDENTIFICATION: IMPLICATIONS FOR STRATEGIES INSTRUCTION

One important factor in successful cognitive resource management and comprehension is the extent to which a reader has sufficient word processing ability to meet the demands of a given text. This issue has been thoroughly explored in the word recognition and reading disability literatures but has had less impact on comprehension research. Automaticity in word recognition is a necessary but not sufficient condition for successful comprehension (for a review, see Adams, 1990). Automaticity at the word level implies extremely fast, accurate, and nearly effortless identification of printed words with simultaneous activation of word meanings from memory. Such fast and efficient processing of print has an important effect. It allows good readers to spend their resources where they should be spent: on those aspects of comprehension that still require resources, such as newly acquired comprehension strategies. Thus good readers are not "strategic" about word identification because they do not need to be. They only become strategic when unfamiliar and difficult words necessitate conscious and deliberate processing.

In contrast, a signature characteristic of young or poor readers is lack of word recognition automaticity and an overreliance on context for identifying unfamiliar words (Perfetti, 1985; Stanovich, 1980). The consequences are obvious from a resource allocation point of view: When readers lack automaticity at the word level, they are forced to expend their resources on letter-by-letter decoding and/or contextual guessing—both inefficient and unreliable processes. In addition, these readers have insufficient resources left for making meaning from the print they do manage to process. In short, being "strategic" about word identification on a regular basis is a source of reading problems, not reading success.

What impact might word identification automaticity—or lack thereof—have on the effectiveness of comprehension strategies instruction? Primarily, it raises questions about appropriate texts for use in comprehension strategies instruction. Are lower achieving students—the traditional target population for strategies instruction—reading text that they can decode with a high degree of accuracy and at a reasonable rate of speed? If not, some students' failure to benefit from strategies instruction could be explained by frustration-level text that exceeds their word recognition abilities. Labored decoding drains resources, and even basic comprehension can be impaired. Thus, even if readers have clear knowledge about when, where, and how to employ a particular comprehension strategy, they may not do so if word identification requires too many cognitive resources. Thus it would not be surprising for readers who have difficulty with basic word identification skill to show lack of improvement or even to fare poorly on measures of comprehension performance following comprehension strategy instruction.

In conclusion, based on the resource allocation research reviewed, the description of skilled readers as "strategic readers" that has been traditionally used in the comprehension instruction literature may be somewhat misleading. It is likely more accurate to describe skilled readers as those who have automated as many decoding and comprehension processes as possible, thus allowing them to conserve adequate cognitive resources to behave in a strategic manner when necessary (Reynolds, 2000).

COPING WITH LIMITED RESOURCES:
SUGGESTIONS FOR COMPREHENSION INSTRUCTION

What are the implications of cognitive resource limitations for general classroom comprehension instruction? Regardless of the approach teachers take, we recommend that students learn and practice what they have learned in *instructional level text* that does not exceed their word identification abilities. Frustration-level texts direct students' attention to the word level. As a result, students are likely to have insufficient resources available to devote to basic comprehension—let alone to learning something new. Most classrooms are populated by students who manifest a wide range of reading abilities; thus "one-size-fits-all" text is not the most effective vehicle for comprehension instruction of any sort. Rather, teachers and students need access to a wide variety of leveled texts that meet students' word identification abilities and are appropriate for comprehension instruction (Brown, 1999/2000).

There are also implications of cognitive resources for comprehension strategies instruction in particular. Consideration of resource limitations raises the question of whether teachers should explicitly teach comprehension strategies or teach students to look at reading as problem solving. Adopting a problem-solving approach to text comprehension, as advocated by Beck, McKeown, and their colleagues, may be one way to circumvent the cognitive resource issues we have identified. Rather than teaching a set of strategies, the teacher asks certain types of questions that lead students to dig deeply into the text (see Beck, McKeown, Hamilton, & Kucan, 1997). For example, as the teacher guides students through a social studies chapter, she may ask, "What is the author telling us here?" or "Why do you think the author is telling us this piece of information now?" or "Does this make sense with what the author told us before?" (Beck et al., 1997, p. 45). This stance positions authors as real, fallible people who have a written message they want readers to understand—rather than as abstract, infallible authorities. The questions also are designed to encourage discussion about the text among students and to reduce the traditional format of teacher questions followed by monosyllabic student answers. With regard to cognitive resource issues, the advantage here is that teachers are not asking students to do something in addition to making sense of the text. Yet, by steadily asking certain types of questions, they help students adopt an active, strategic stance toward text.

At the same time, some students—especially lower achievers—do seem to benefit from explicit strategies instruction. If teachers wish to incorporate strategies into their comprehension curriculum, they need to take on cognitive resource issues directly. That is, instruction should be designed to move strategy use from deliberate to automatic. Toward this end, we make the following suggestions:

1. *Pare down the number of strategies and prioritize them.* Strategies instruction is challenging and time-consuming. Moreover, students can juggle only a limited number of

processes during reading. For these reasons, we suggest that the list of strategies worth teaching is a short one. In selecting which strategies to teach, we suggest teachers choose those that have demonstrated effectiveness at improving comprehension performance. A review conducted by Lysynchuk, Pressley, d'Ailly, Smith, and Cake (1989) found that few comprehension strategies studies met their criteria for methodological rigor—a finding that suggests caution in making those selections. Since publication of that review, Oakhill and her colleagues have shown that, once word identification has been ruled out as a source of comprehension difficulties, skilled and less skilled comprehenders differ in inferencing ability, use of text structure, and comprehension monitoring (Cain & Oakhill, 1999; Oakhill & Yuill, 1996). In particular, the ability to make causal inferences seems important for building a coherent understanding of text (Graesser & Bertus, 1998; van den Broek & Kremer, 2000). Students who have difficulty drawing important connections that are not explicitly stated may fail to infer, for example, that all members of the House of Slytherin hate Harry Potter because of their allegiance to Voldemort (Rowling, 1997, 1999a, 1999b). In failing to make this connection, they will have missed an important piece of the novel's plot and built an inadequate understanding. In such cases, instruction designed to help students learn to make these connections seems to have merit. However, despite these promising leads, it remains for researchers to establish exactly which strategies provide the most "cognitive bang for the buck." In the meantime, we suggest that only those strategies demonstrated to be effective are worthy of instructional time and effort.

2. *Make sure students are provided with texts that call for the strategy being taught.* For a strategy to become automatic, the text eventually must trigger that comprehension process. With this in mind, it makes sense for students to practice the strategy with texts that "call up that program." For example, if a teacher is introducing a strategy for making inferences, he or she should choose texts that clearly require the reader to make several inferences. At the same time, the texts cannot be contrived, because they must resemble texts that students will encounter in everyday situations. Selection of instructional texts is an important part of curriculum planning; teachers may wish to collaborate in finding, determining levels, and categorizing appropriate texts. Finding real texts that call for particular strategies is possible *if the set of instructed strategies is limited to those that apply to many texts.* For example, students can practice making causal inferences in any number of texts: by following the conflict between Harry Potter and his various adversaries (Rowling, 1997, 1999a, 1999b), by reading Winnie Foster's tombstone inscription along with the Tucks (Babbitt, 1975), or by listening to Tim, Sam, and their parents give divergent viewpoints about the American colonies' insurrection against the British (Collier & Collier, 1974).

3. *Make sure students know that strategies are a means to an end, not an end in themselves.* Comprehension strategies are no more than tools that readers employ in the service of constructing meaning from text. However, learning to use strategies can be such a challenging and time-intensive endeavor that students may place an undue emphasis on learning the strategy itself. In such cases, the text and comprehension end up taking a back seat. Teachers can help students put strategy use in its proper place by minimizing its "trappings" (e.g., numerous and/or intricate steps, written products) and by focusing on how the strategy aids comprehension. It also may help to remind students that the goal is to make sense of what they read and that the strategy is just a tool they can use to make that happen.

4. *As students become proficient at strategy use, fade out requirements.* Initially, asking students to produce concrete evidence of strategy use may help students learn and remember to use the strategy. For example, students who have been unsuccessful at determining the main idea of expository text likely will benefit from having their teacher model construction of a story map and then constructing their own as they read. Such tasks also provide important assessment information for teachers. However, ongoing requirements for students to demonstrate their use of the strategy overtly may keep them focused on its deliberate use. This may actually interfere with the development of automatic comprehension processes. After all, expert readers do not produce concrete evidence of strategy use every time they encounter a text; in fact, they may do so only under duress. With this in mind, once students develop satisfactory prowess at the tasks that demonstrate strategy use, teachers should fade out task requirements. From then on, assessment should center on students' comprehension of texts that lend themselves to the use of a particular strategy.

FUTURE DIRECTIONS FOR EMPIRICAL RESEARCH

Clearly, researchers need to further investigate how resource issues may affect the comprehension process—and by extension, comprehension instruction. For example, much work needs to be done to determine which type of comprehension instruction is effective for which students under what circumstances. In addition, strategies researchers must follow the lead of Oakhill and her colleagues and clearly rule out word identification resource demands as a factor affecting strategy use. In the past, it has been difficult to determine whether students in strategy studies were asked to read texts that were too difficult, because researchers usually did not provide information related to students' word identification abilities. Typically, student participants in strategies studies are chosen through a combination of teacher judgment and scores on standardized tests. We suggest that students be assessed on measures of word recognition accuracy *and* speed because, although some students may be highly accurate at identifying words, they also may be extremely slow at doing so. In such cases, the drain on resources from word identification demands could negatively influence their capacity to use strategies efficiently.

As noted, considerable research suggests that successful comprehenders perform basic aspects of the comprehension process very efficiently (O'Brien, 1985; Reynolds, 2000). However, because precise empirical work often necessitates the use of experimenter-designed texts, more work is needed examining how resource issues play out in texts students encounter in their instructional and everyday experience. In addition, more work must be directed at beginning readers and how they become automatic at certain comprehension processes over the course of reading development.

This raises another important question. Does the development of automaticity of basic comprehension processes emancipate cognitive resources for use with higher level comprehension processes? Reynolds (2000) has suggested this, but more empirical work is needed to investigate this intriguing possibility.

Finally, the traditional methods of investigating the effectiveness of strategy instruction are not necessarily adequate for identifying automaticity of comprehension processes. Resource issues can not be explored with outcome measures alone. We suggest that strategies researchers use multiple lines of evidence when investigating resource issues and strategy instruction. Specifically, strategies researchers must consider the use of on-line measures—along with interviews and other post-hoc measures—to fully explore resource issues in strategies instruction.

REFERENCES

Adams, M. J. (1990). *Beginning to read: Thinking and learning about print.* Cambridge, MA: MIT Press.

Alexander, P. A., Graham, S., & Harris, K. R. (1998). A perspective on strategy research: Progress and prospects. *Educational Psychology Review, 10*(2), 129–154.

Alexander, P. A., & Judy, J. E. (1988). The interaction of domain-specific and strategic knowledge in academic performance. *Review of Educational Research, 58,* 375–404.

Anderson, J. R. (1983). *The architecture of cognition.* Cambridge, MA: Harvard University Press.

Anderson, J. R. (1990). *The adaptive character of thought.* Hillsdale, NJ: Erlbaum.

Babbitt, N. (1975). *Tuck everlasting.* New York: HarperCollins.

Bargh, J. A., & Chartrand, T. L. (1999). The unbearable automaticity of being. *American Psychologist, 54*(7), 462–479.

Beck, I. L., McKeown, M. G., Hamilton, R., & Kucan, L. (1997). *Questioning the author: An approach for enhancing student engagement with text.* Newark, DE: International Reading Association.

Beck, I. L., McKeown, M. G., Sandora, C., Kucan, L., & Worthy, J. (1996). Questioning the author: A yearlong classroom implementation to engage students with text. *The Elementary School Journal, 96*(4), 385–414.

Block, C. C., & Mangieri, J. (1996). *Reason to read: Thinking strategies for life through literature* (Vols. 1–3). Palo Alto, CA: Addison-Wesley.

Brown, K. J. (1999–2000). What kind of text for whom, and when? Textual scaffolding for beginning readers. *The Reading Teacher, 53,* 292–307.

Brown, K. J. (2000). *Student mediation of a comprehension strategy lesson: An exploration of cognition, motivation, and performance.* Manuscript in preparation.

Cain, K., & Oakhill, J. V. (1999). Inference making ability and its relation to comprehension failure in young children. *Reading and Writing, 11*(5–6), 489–503.

Collier, J., & Collier, C. (1974). *My brother Sam is dead.* New York: Scholastic.

Collins, A., Brown, J. S., & Newman, S. E. (1989). Cognitive apprenticeship: Teaching the craft of reading, writing, and mathematics. In L. B. Resnick (Ed.), *Knowing, learning, and instruction: Essays in honor of Robert Glaser* (pp. 453–494). Hillsdale, NJ: Erlbaum.

Dewitz, P., Carr, E. M., & Patberg, J. P. (1987). Effects of inference training on comprehension and comprehension maintaining. *Reading Research Quarterly, 40,* 514–521.

Dole, J. A., Brown, K. J., & Trathen, W. (1996). The effects of strategy instruction on the comprehension performance of at-risk students. *Reading Research Quarterly, 31*(1), 62–88.

Dole, J. A., Duffy, G. G., Roehler, L. R., & Pearson, P. D. (1991). Moving from the old to the new: Research on reading comprehension instruction. *Review of Educational Research, 61,* 239–264.

Duell, O. K. (1986). Metacognitive skills. In G. D. Phye & T. Andre (Eds.), *Cognitive classroom learning: Understanding, thinking, and problem solving* (pp. 205–242). New York: Academic Press.

Duffy, G. G. (1993). Rethinking strategy instruction: Four teachers' development and their low achievers' understandings. *Elementary School Journal, 93,* 231–247.

Duffy, G., Roehler, L., Sivan, E., Rackliffe, G., Book, C., Meloth, M., Vavrus, L., Wesselman, R., Putnam, J., & Bassiri, D. (1987). Effects of explaining the reasoning associated with using strategies. *Reading Research Quarterly, 22,* 347–368.

El-Dinary, P. B., & Schuder, T. (1993). Seven teachers' acceptance of transactional strategies instruction during their first year using it. *Elementary School Journal, 94,* 207–219.

Gallini, J. K., Spires, H. A., Terry, S., & Gleaton, J. (1993). The influence of macro- and micro-level cognitive strategies training on text learning. *Journal of Research and Development in Education, 26,* 163–178.

Garner, R. (1987). *Metacognition and reading comprehension.* Norwood, NJ: Ablex.

Gaskins, I. W., Anderson, R. C., Pressley, M., Cunnicelli, E. A., & Satlow, E. (1993). Six teachers' dialogue during cognitive process instruction. *The Elementary School Journal, 93,* 277–304.

Gernsbacher, M. A., Hallada, B. M., & Robertson, R. R. W. (1998). How automatically do readers infer fictional characters' emotional states? *Scientific Studies of Reading, 2*(3), 271–300.

Graesser, A. C., & Bertus, E. L. (1998). The construction of causal inferences while reading expository texts on science and technology. *Scientific Studies of Reading, 2*(3), 247–269.

Hansen, J., & Pearson, P. D. (1983). An instructional study: Improving the inferential comprehension of good and poor fourth-grade readers. *Journal of Educational Psychology, 75,* 821–829.

Harris, K. R., & Pressley, M. (1991). The nature of cognitive strategy instruction: Interactive strategy construction. *Exceptional Children, 57,* 392–404.

Kahneman, D. (1973). *Attention and effort.* Englewood Cliffs, NJ: Prentice-Hall.

Keene, E. O., & Zimmermann, S. (1997). *Mosaic of thought: Teaching comprehension in a reader's workshop.* Portsmouth, NH: Heinemann.

Kintsch, W. (1998). *Comprehension: A paradigm for cognition.* Cambridge, England: Cambridge University Press.

Lysynchuk, L. M., Pressley, M., d'Ailly, H., Smith, M., & Cake, H. (1989). A methodological analysis of experimental studies of comprehension strategy instruction. *Reading Research Quarterly, 24,* 458–470.

Magliano, J. P., Trabasso, T., & Graesser, A. C. (1999). Strategic processing during comprehension. *Journal of Educational Psychology, 91*(4), 615–629.

Miller, G. A. (1956). The magical number seven, plus or minus two: Some limits of our capacity for processing information. *Psychological Review, 63,* 81–97.

Miller, G. E., & Brewster, M. E. (1992). Developing self-sufficient learners in reading and mathematics through self-instructional training. In M. Pressley, K. R. Harris, & J. T. Guthrie (Eds.), *Promoting academic competence and literacy in school* (pp. 169–221). San Diego, CA: Academic Press.

Oakhill, J., & Yuill, N. (1996). Higher order factors in comprehension disability: Processes and remediation. In C. Cornoldi & J. Oakhill (Eds.), *Reading comprehension difficulties: Processes and intervention* (pp. 69–92). Mahwah, NJ: Erlbaum.

O'Brien, E. J. (1995). Automatic components of discourse comprehension. In R. F. Lorch & E. J. O'Brian (Eds.), *Sources of coherence in reading* (pp. 159–176). Hillsdale, NJ: Erlbaum.

Palincsar, A. S., & Brown, A. L. (1984). Reciprocal teaching of comprehension-fostering and comprehension-monitoring strategies. *Cognition and Instruction, 1*(2), 117–175.

Paris, S. G., Cross, D. R., & Lipson, M. Y. (1984). Informed strategies for learning: A program to improve children's awareness and comprehension. *Journal of Educational Psychology, 76,* 1239–1252.

Paris, S. G., Wasik, B. A., & Turner, J. C. (1991). The development of strategic readers. In R. Barr, M. L. Kamil, P. Mosenthal, & P. D. Pearson (Eds.), *Handbook of reading research* (Vol. 2, pp. 609–640). New York: Longman.

Pearson, P. D., & Dole, J. A. (1987). Explicit comprehension instruction: A review of research and a new conceptualization of instruction. *Elementary School Journal, 88*(2), 151–165.

Pearson, P. D., & Fielding, L. (1991). Comprehension instruction. In R. Barr, M. L. Kamil, P. Mosenthal, & P. D. Pearson (Eds.), *Handbook of reading research* (Vol. 2, pp. 815–860). New York: Longman.

Pearson, P. D., & Gallagher, M. (1983). The instruction of reading comprehension. *Contemporary Educational Psychology, 8,* 317–344.

Perfetti, C. A. (1985). *Reading ability.* New York: Oxford University Press.

Perfetti, C. A. (1988). Verbal efficiency in reading ability. In M. Daneman & G. E. McKinnon (Eds.), *Reading research: Advances in theory and practice* (Vol. 6, pp. 109–143). San Diego, CA: Academic Press.

Pintrich, P. R., & De Groot, E. V. (1990, April). *Quantitative and qualitative perspectives on student motivational beliefs.* Paper presented at the annual meeting of the American Educational Research Association, Boston.

Pressley, M., El-Dinary, P. B., Gaskins, I., Schuder, T., Bergman, J. L., Almasi, J., & Brown, R. (1992). Beyond direct explanation: Transactional instruction of reading comprehension strategies. *Elementary School Journal, 92,* 513–556.

Pressley, M., Forrest-Pressley, D. L., Elliot-Faust, D., & Miller, G. (1985). Children's use of cognitive strategies, how to teach strategies, and what to do if they can't be taught. In M. Pressley & C. J. Brainerd (Eds.), *Cognitive learning and memory in children: Progress in cognitive development research* (pp. 1–37). New York: Springer-Verlag.

Pressley, M., Goodchild, F., Fleet, J., Zajchowski, R., & Evans, E. D. (1989). The challenges of classroom strategy instruction. *Elementary School Journal, 89,* 301–342.

Pressley, M., Woloshyn,V., Lysynchuk, L. M., Martin,V., Wood, E., & Willoughby, T. (1990). A primer of research on cognitive strategy instruction: The important issues and how to address them. *Educational Psychology Review, 2(1),* 1–58.

Reynolds, R. E. (1992). Selective attention and prose learning: Theoretical and empirical research. *Educational Psychology Review, 4(4),* 345–391.

Reynolds, R. E. (2000). Attentional resource emancipation: Towards understanding the interaction of word identification and comprehension processes in reading. *Scientific Studies of Reading, 4(3),* 169–195.

Reynolds, R. E., Trathen, W., Sawyer, M., & Shepard, C. R. (1994). Causal and epiphenomenal use of the selective attention strategy in prose comprehension. *Contemporary Educational Psychology, 18,* 258–278.

Roehler, L. R. (1992). Embracing the instructional complexities of reading instruction. In M. Pressley, K. R. Harris, & J. T. Guthrie (Eds.), *Promoting academic competence and literacy in school* (pp. 91–127). San Diego, CA: Academic Press.

Roehler, L. R., & Duffy, G. G. (1991). Teachers' instructional actions. In R. Barr, M. L. Kamil, P. Mosenthal, & P. D. Pearson (Eds.), *Handbook of reading research* (Vol. 2, pp. 861–883). New York: Longman.

Rowling, J. K. (1997). *Harry Potter and the sorcerer's stone.* New York: Scholastic.

Rowling, J. K. (1999a). *Harry Potter and the chamber of secrets.* New York: Scholastic.

Rowling, J. K. (1999b). *Harry Potter and the prisoner of Azkaban.* New York: Scholastic.

Schunk, D. H. (1990). Goal setting and self-efficacy during self-regulated learning. *Educational Psychologist, 25,* 71–86.

Speelman, C. (1998). The automaticity of discourse comprehension. In K. Kirsner, C. Speelman, M. Maybery, A. O'Brien-Malone, M. Anderson, & C. Macleod (Eds.), *Implicit and explicit mental processes* (pp. 187–200). Mahwah, NJ: Erlbaum.

Speelman, C., & Maybery, M. (1998). Automaticity and skill acquisition. In K. Kirsner, C. Speelman, M. Maybery, A. O'Brien-Malone, M. Anderson, & C. Macleod (Eds.), *Implicit and explicit mental processes* (pp. 79–98). Mahwah, NJ: Erlbaum.

Stanovich, K. E. (1980). Towards an interactive compensatory model of individual differences in the development of reading fluency. *Reading Research Quarterly, 16,* 32–71.

Stanovich, K. E. (1986). Matthew effect in reading: Some consequences of individual differences in the acquisition of literacy. *Reading Research Quarterly, 21,* 360–407.

Swanson, H. L., Hoskyn, M., & Lee, C. (1999). *Interventions for students with learning disabilites: A meta-analysis of treatment outcomes.* New York: Guilford Press.

van den Broek, P., & Kremer, K. K. (2000). The mind in action: What it means to comprehend during reading. In B. M. Tayor, M. F. Graves, & P. van den Broek (Eds.), *Reading for meaning: Fostering comprehension in the middle grades* (pp. 1–31). New York: Teachers College Press.

Vygotsky, L. S. (1978). *Mind in society: The development of higher psychological processes.* Cambridge, MA: Harvard University Press.

Winne, P. H., & Marx, R. W. (1982). Students' and teachers' views of thinking processes for classroom learning. *Elementary School Journal, 82*(5), 493–518.

Winograd, P., & Hare, V. C. (1988). Direct instruction of reading comprehension strategies: The nature of teacher explanation. In C. E. Weinstein, E. T. Goetz, & P. A. Alexander (Eds.), *Learning and study strategies: Issues in assessment, instruction, and evaluation* (pp. 121–139). Berkeley, CA: Academic Press.

Zimmermann, B. J. (1989). Models of self-regulatory learning and academic achievement. In B. J. Zimmermann & D. H. Schunk (Eds.), *Self-regulated learning and academic achievement: Theory, research, and practice* (pp. 1–25). New York: Springer-Verlag.

6

Metacognition in Comprehension Instruction

LINDA BAKER

Metacognition is a term that is now widely used to refer to the knowledge and control we have of our own cognitive processes. The knowledge component of metacognition is concerned with the ability to reflect on our own cognitive processes, and it includes knowledge about ourselves as learners, about aspects of the task, and about strategy use. The control component is concerned with self-regulation of our own cognitive efforts, and it includes planning our actions, checking the outcomes of our efforts, evaluating our progress, remediating difficulties that arise, and testing and revising our strategies for learning (Baker & Brown, 1984). In the domain of reading, comprehension monitoring is the control component of primary importance. It involves deciding whether or not we understand (evaluation) and taking appropriate steps to correct whatever comprehension problems we detect (regulation). This chapter examines theory, research, and practice on the place of metacognition in comprehension instruction.

CRITICAL RESEARCH ON METACOGNITION IN COMPREHENSION INSTRUCTION

Establishing Consensus That Metacognition Is Important to Reading

Research on metacognition had its origins 25 years ago in the work of developmental psychologists John Flavell (1976) and Ann Brown (1978), whose initial concerns focused on how and when children develop knowledge and control of their cognitive processes. Almost immediately, educational researchers turned to metacognition as an explanation for why some students were more successful in reading than others. Instructional interventions to promote metacognition soon followed, along with recommendations to practitioners.

Metacognition is now firmly established in theories of reading and learning. For example, the engagement perspective that guided the National Reading Research Center includes a role for metacognition (Alvermann & Guthrie, 1993; Baker, Afflerbach, & Reinking, 1996; Baker, Dreher, & Guthrie, 2000). Engaged reading involves the interplay of motivation, knowledge, strategies, and social interaction. "Developing engaged readers involves helping students to become both strategic and aware of the strategies they use to read" (McCarthey, Hoffman, & Galda, 1999).

The American Psychological Association has also acknowledged the importance of metacognition in its Learner-Centered Principles for education (Lambert & McCombs, 1998). In documenting the research base for the principles that involve strategic processing and executive control, Alexander and Murphy (1998) noted, "The ability to reflect on and regulate one's thoughts and behaviors is essential to learning and development" (p. 31). Other principles address knowledge, motivation, and social interaction, providing broader support for the critical elements identified in the engagement perspective.

Just as the engagement perspective and the learner-centered principles have made it clear that we need to go beyond cognitive factors to understand reading comprehension and learning, so too do we need to recognize that motivation and social interaction also influence metacognition. Indeed, metacognitive theorists were aware some time ago of the need to examine motivational and affective, as well as metacognitive, factors (Hacker, 1998; Paris & Winograd, 1990; Borkowski, Carr, Rellinger, & Pressley, 1990). Strategy use is effortful, and readers will not learn or use strategies effectively unless they are motivated to do so (Alexander & Murphy, 1998; Guthrie et al., 2000; Pressley et al., 1994).

Social interaction is also an important mediator of metacognitive development (Baker, 1996). Many theorists believe that the origins of metacognitive skills lie in adult–child or expert–novice interactions (Rogoff, 1990; Wertsch, 1978), whereas others emphasize the important role of peer interactions (Almasi, 1996). The first view comes from Soviet psychologist Lev Vygotsky (1978), who proposed that children first learn how to engage in cognitive tasks through social interaction with more knowledgeable others, usually parents or teachers. The expert initially takes the responsibility of regulating the novice's activity by setting goals, planning, evaluating, and focusing attention on what is relevant. Gradually the expert gives over more and more responsibility to the novice as the novice becomes capable of assuming it, until finally the novice internalizes the regulatory mechanisms and can perform without expert assistance. In other words, there is a sequence of development from other-regulation to self-regulation. This notion provides the framework for virtually all instructional programs in which the goal is to enable students to take responsibility for their own learning (Pressley, 2000; Rosenshine & Meister, 1997).

The second view on social interaction comes from Swiss psychologist Jean Piaget, who emphasized the important roles that peers play in challenging one another's thoughts and thus advancing cognitive development. Discussion and collaboration help students to monitor their own understanding and build new strategic capabilities (Almasi, 1996; Hacker, 1998; McCarthey et al., 1999). Many instructional programs now supplement an emphasis on individual cognition with an emphasis on social support for monitoring, reflection, and revision (Brown & Campione, 1998; Vye, Schwartz, Bransford, Barron, & Zech, 1998).

Consensus among scholars is high that metacognition plays an important role in reading comprehension (e.g., Baker & Brown, 1984; Garner, 1987; Gourgey, 1998; Hacker, 1998; Mastropieri & Scruggs, 1997; Mayer, 1998; Paris, Wasik, & Turner, 1991;

Schraw, 1998). Two highly visible national committees recently concluded, on the basis of the available empirical research, that metacognition and comprehension monitoring should be fostered in comprehension instruction (National Reading Panel, 2000; Snow, Burns, & Griffin, 1998). Writing for the National Research Council and Snow, Burns, and Griffin (1998) concluded that children must have "opportunities to develop and enhance language and metacognitive skills to meet the demands of understanding printed texts" (p. 278) and that "adequate progress in learning to read English beyond the initial level depends on [among other things] control over procedures for monitoring comprehension and repairing comprehension" (p. 223).

Comprehension monitoring is often considered to be a comprehension strategy in itself. Comments about its importance and recommendations for its instruction are often found within broader discussions of comprehension strategy instruction. For example, the National Reading Panel (2000) identified comprehension monitoring as a strategy shown through reliable and replicable research to affect comprehension. Similarly, in a comprehensive research synthesis, Braunger and Lewis (1997) included self-monitoring as one of five strategies critical to reading.

Documenting Children's Metacognitive Knowledge and Comprehension Monitoring

Beginning with the seminal studies of Scott Paris (Myers & Paris, 1978) and Ellen Markman (1977), research has been consistent in showing that younger children and poorer readers have less knowledge and control of their comprehension processes than older children and better readers. (For reviews, see Baker, 1985; Baker & Brown, 1984; Garner, 1987; Hacker, 1998; Paris, Wasik, & Turner, 1991.) Information about knowledge and control is often gained by asking students directly what they know or what they do. Students may be asked to think aloud about what they were doing and thinking as they read a text (Bereiter & Bird, 1985; Pressley & Afflerbach, 1995). Or they may be asked to complete interviews or questionnaires regarding strategies they use (Myers & Paris, 1978; Paris, Cross, & Lipson, 1984; Hall, Bowman, & Myers, 1999; Pereira-Laird & Deane, 1997).

Information about comprehension monitoring is often gained through the "error detection paradigm" (Baker, 1979; Garner, 1987; Otero, 1998; Kinnunen & Vauras, 1995; Winograd & Johnston, 1982; Zabrucky & Ratner, 1992). The reader is presented with texts that contain embedded problems or errors and is asked to identify them. The assumption is that these problems disrupt comprehension, so the reader who is checking his or her ongoing comprehension should notice them. Various measures have been used to determine if readers detect the errors: performance measures, such as underlining errors when they are encountered; verbal reports collected during or after reading; and on-line measures, such as patterns of eye movements, reading times, and look-backs.

Research shows that neither children nor adults are very successful at identifying embedded problems in text (see Baker, 1989b; Baker & Brown, 1984, for reviews). However, many failures to report problems are not due to failures to evaluate comprehension but rather to the use of fix-up strategies for resolving comprehension difficulties. That is, readers attempt to evaluate *and* regulate their comprehension, using strategies such as rereading and looking ahead for clarification. Skilled readers go to great lengths to make sense of text, especially if they have no reason to suspect that the texts were altered to be difficult to understand. We also now know that readers use a variety of different criteria or standards for evaluating their understanding (Baker, 1985). Failure to notice a particular type of problem in a text does not necessarily imply poor comprehension monitoring. For example, the reader who fails to notice a contradiction within a passage presumably was not evaluating his or her understanding with respect to a standard of internal consistency; however, he or she may have been using alternative criteria for evaluating comprehension, such as consistency with prior knowledge.

Increasing Metacognition through Instructional Interventions

Fostering Metacognitive Awareness and Comprehension Monitoring

The evidence of developmental and ability-related differences in metacognition cited in the previous section led researchers to attempt to "train" metacognitive skills. Simple interventions were conducted in laboratories by the researchers themselves, often within a single session. More complex interventions were carried out in classrooms over extended periods of time, often with teachers providing the instruction. Both sorts of studies have provided solid evidence that the comprehension monitoring skills of good and poor readers alike can be enhanced through direct instruction (e.g., Baker & Zimlin, 1989; Baumann, Seifert-Kessell, & Jones, 1992; Bereiter & Bird, 1985; Bossert & Schwantes, 1995–1996; Miller, 1985, 1987; Paris et al., 1984; Payne & Manning, 1992).

One line of research is aimed at increasing children's knowledge and use of appropriate standards for evaluating their comprehension. For example, Baker and Zimlin (1989) found that providing fourth-grade children with instruction in the use of three particular standards for evaluating their comprehension generalized to their use of three other standards and that both groups of students who received instruction identified more embedded problems in text than the no-treatment control group. Instruction in evaluation criteria is also useful in helping children revise their own writing (Beal, 1996).

Another line of research draws on Vygotsky's (1978) premise of a transition from other-regulation to self-regulation. Children were taught via adult modeling and guided practice to use self-instruction (Miller, 1985, 1987) or think-alouds (Baumann et al., 1992) to monitor their own comprehension during reading. Think-aloud instruction improved children's comprehension, as well as comprehension monitoring in a classroom study (Payne & Manning, 1992).

Children have also been taught to regulate their comprehension once an obstacle arises. For example, Bereiter and Bird (1985) first identified strategies that expert readers use when they encounter comprehension difficulties. Then they taught students to use a set of fix-up strategies, including rereading and reading ahead in search of clarification. Not only did students show increased use of the strategies, but they also showed improved comprehension.

Perhaps the most comprehensive instructional intervention designed to promote metacognitive skills was Paris et al.'s (1984) Informed Strategies for Learning (ISL). Children were given lessons in the classroom over a period of months on the use of various strategies for improving comprehension and comprehension monitoring. The program was effective in promoting metacognitive knowledge about reading and comprehension monitoring, although it did not boost standardized reading test scores.

The National Reading Panel (2000) identified 20 instructional studies of comprehension monitoring that met scientifically rigorous criteria for inclusion in their analysis of what works in reading instruction. The panel concluded that comprehension monitoring can be taught and that it can have an impact on student comprehension. The National Research Council (Snow et al., 1998) also concluded that training in metacognitive skills is effective for improving comprehension and that comprehension monitoring skills can improve with training. Similar conclusions were reached in an earlier research synthesis by Haller, Child, and Walberg (1988).

Fostering Comprehension through Metacognitively Oriented Strategies Instruction

Countless studies have demonstrated the efficacy of instruction in single strategies (National Reading Panel, 2000), but the focus here is on interventions that involve multiple strategies, including comprehension monitoring. Students are explicitly taught when, where, and why to use the strategies, promoting metacognitive awareness for flexible use under appropriate circumstances. Teacher modeling, discussion, and guided practice are prominent in these studies, with gradual transfer of responsibility for regulating performance from the adult to the child (Blair-Larsen & Vallance, 1999; Dole, 2000; Pressley, 1998; Rosenshine & Meister, 1997). Peer collaboration and cooperative learning are also common features of the instructional approach.

The first multiple strategies intervention, and the one that remains best known, is reciprocal teaching, developed by Palincsar and Brown (1984). The strategies taught were predicting, clarifying, summarizing, and questioning. These particular strategies were those that had the potential to promote comprehension, as well as to provide information about how well comprehension was proceeding. Clarifying is essentially comprehension monitoring; children are taught to ask themselves whether everything makes sense. The intervention was successful in promoting strategy use and comprehension. Two other well-known and well-regarded approaches are transactional strategies instruction (TSI; Pressley et al., 1994) and Peer-Assisted Learning strategies (PALS; Fuchs, Fuchs, Mathes, & Simmons, 1997).

A recent intervention that combines comprehension strategy instruction with cooperative learning is Collaborative Strategic Reading (CSR; Klingner & Vaughn, 1999). CSR teaches four strategies: preview (activate knowledge and predict what the passage will be about); click and clunk (monitor comprehension during reading by identifying difficult words and concepts and using fix-up strategies when the text does not make sense); get the gist (restate the most important ideas in sections or paragraphs during reading); and wrap-up (summarize after reading what has been learned and generate questions that a teacher might ask). The teacher uses direct explanation and modeling with the full class, and students then break into small groups in which each student has a defined role. Results revealed greater improvement on a standardized reading comprehension test relative to peers who did not use CSR. The approach was implemented successfully in culturally and linguistically diverse classrooms that included struggling readers, English-language learners, and average and high achieving students.

The National Reading Panel's (2000) analysis of 38 multiple strategies studies led them to conclude that "the evidence supports the use of combinations of reading strategies in natural learning situations" (p. 4-83). This conclusion is consistent with that of an earlier analysis of 10 reciprocal teaching studies (Rosenshine & Meister, 1994).

Researchers have also begun to examine multiple strategies instruction in the context of content learning. The National Reading Panel (2000) referred to such studies as "curriculum plus strategies" and concluded that the research evidence attests to their promise. One example of such a program is Concept-Oriented Reading Instruction (CORI; Guthrie et al., 1996; Guthrie et al., 1998), which integrates science instruction with reading and writing. Strategy instruction is situated in an intrinsically interesting and conceptually compelling context. Direct explanation, teacher modeling, and peer interaction are incorporated here as well. Students in CORI classrooms made significant gains over comparison classrooms in strategy use, comprehension, and motivation.

Strategies instruction research today looks considerably more sophisticated than in years past. Dowhower (1999) aptly summarized the trends:

1. Students' use of comprehension strategies is situated within a broader context of what a competent reader does, consistent with the engagement perspective.
2. Strategy development is seen in a more constructivist and collaborative light; strategies are used to construct meaning in interaction with others.
3. As opposed to strict teacher control, strategy learning is more cognitively situated in student needs and demands of the reading task; strategies are taught in context.
4. Because of this cognitively situated viewpoint, strategy development and use is best supported "in flight."
5. Isolated strategy teaching is being replaced by an emphasis on learning a repertoire of strategies, as well as the coordination and flexible orchestration of those strategies.
6. There is a greater emphasis on self-assessment of multiple comprehension strategies, increasing students' awareness of the strategies and their positive effects.

This new look is well exemplified in the "communities of learners" (COL) research of Brown and Campione (1998). Reading comprehension instruction is fully integrated with science, combining coherent content and complex strategies. Students collaborate with one another in research and knowledge sharing. The promise of this approach comes from data showing that students in the COL classrooms made even greater improvement in reading comprehension than those in classrooms in which traditional reciprocal teaching was used.

APPLYING WHAT IS KNOWN

Most comprehension instruction techniques recommended for use in schools today are characterized as metacognitive (Snow et al., 1998), and the scientific evidence is compelling that this is the way to go. The techniques incorporate the principles of instruction documented as effective in the multiple strategies research and described elsewhere in this volume. Increasing students' knowledge about how, when, and why to regulate their own comprehension is an important component of comprehension instruction. However, metacognition should not be promoted as a goal in itself, taught in isolation, but rather as a means to an end, integrated with comprehension instruction (Baker, 1994; Paris & Winograd, 1990). Moreover, instructional contexts should be intrinsically motivating, for as Guthrie et al. (2000) commented, "Teachers rarely hear students say, 'I really want to learn how to monitor my comprehension'" (p. 212).

Very early on in the history of metacognitive research, recommendations began to appear in the literature for teachers, summarizing the research findings, emphasizing their educational significance, and suggesting ways for teachers to promote metacognition in the classroom and to assess it informally in their students. Unfortunately, sometimes these recommendations have been put forward without solid research evidence behind them (Baker & Cerro, 2000; Paris, Wasik, & Van der Westhuizen, 1988), or they reflect misapplications of research to practice.

Consider the case of strategy instruction. Reciprocal teaching (Palincsar & Brown, 1984) has been widely picked up by teachers and textbook publishers in such a way as to cause Brown and Campione (1998) concern: "The surface rituals of questioning, summarizing, and so forth are engaged in, divorced from the goal of reading for understanding that they were designed to serve. These strategies are sometimes practiced out of the context of reading authentic texts" (p. 177). And as Beck, McKeown, Hamilton, and Kucan (1997) noted, a "potential drawback of strategy-based instruction is that the attention of teachers and students may be drawn too easily to the features of the strategies themselves rather than to the meaning of what is being read" (p. 16). These concerns get to the very heart of the definition of a strategy: "To assume that one can simply have students memorize and routinely execute a set of strategies is to misconceive the nature of strategic processing or executive control. Such rote applications of these procedures represents, in essence, a true oxymoron—nonstrategic strategic processing" (Alexander & Murphy, 1998, p. 33).

Are Teachers Today Providing Metacognitively Oriented Comprehension Instruction?

Researchers continue to express concern that, despite a quarter century of research on comprehension, teachers still lack understanding of the process. And despite the major advances in our knowledge of how to teach comprehension effectively, classroom observations indicate that research still has not had much impact on classroom practice (Dole, 2000; Pressley, 2000). Schmitt and Baumann (1990) observed teachers during classroom basal reader instruction and concluded that teachers tended to do little spontaneously to promote children's metacognitive awareness and ability. Observations conducted by Pressley, Wharton-McDonald, Mistretta-Hampston, and Echevarria (1998) in 10 grade 4 and 5 classrooms revealed that most teachers were weak in facilitating students' self-regulation.

Self-report data provide a somewhat more encouraging picture than do the observations of the current status of metacognitively oriented instruction. In a comprehensive survey of elementary reading instruction practices, Baumann, Hoffman, Duffy-Hester, and Ro (2000) found that 88% of 1,207 pre-K to grade 5 teachers indicated that one of their goals for reading instruction was to produce readers who were skillful and strategic. Intermediate teachers (grades 3–5) were also asked whether they regularly (three or more times per week) provided instruction in comprehension strategies and in comprehension monitoring. Examples of comprehension strategy instruction were making inferences and drawing conclusions; examples of comprehension monitoring instruction were self-questioning and applying fix-up strategies such as rereading. Eighty-nine percent of the teachers responded affirmatively to the strategies question, whereas 71% responded affirmatively to the monitoring question (J. Baumann, personal communication, August 9, 2000). Of course, teachers may well endorse practices they know to be valuable because of a social desirability bias. Nevertheless, these survey results at least indicate that most teachers are aware of the value of such practices, an important first step toward adopting them.

Helping Teachers Promote Metacognitive Knowledge and Control

Information for teachers on how they might promote metacognitive knowledge and control is readily available, but the information is often very general and sketchy. For example, although basal reading series give considerable attention to lessons and activities that would foster strategic reading (Schmitt & Hopkins, 1993), they tend not to give information dealing with where and when to apply the particular strategies that are taught (Pressley et al., 1994).

Teachers are routinely encouraged to model how to monitor comprehension and use comprehension strategies, but many teachers find that modeling thinking processes is difficult (Dowhower, 1999; Jongsma, 2000). Increasing teachers' own metacognitive awareness of their reading processes is an important first step in preparing them to increase students' awareness (Edwards, 1999). Teacher education programs are a good place to begin, as shown in a recent study by Thomas and Barksdale-Ladd (2000).

These researchers had been addressing metacognition in their reading methods courses for many years but noticed that their students rarely used this knowledge in practice. They therefore redesigned their courses with a much more explicit focus on metacognition and executive control. Students were required to think aloud about assigned readings and to discuss their reading processes with classmates. Students were asked to keep a journal of the metacognitive strategies they used when reading self-selected materials. They were also encouraged to use the strategies talked about in class in their tutoring of a young reader and to keep a record of what they did. The think-aloud protocols and journals showed that these preservice teachers used many cognitive and metacognitive strategies characteristic of effective readers and that these strategies increased over the course of the semester as they became more aware of their own comprehension processes. However, the increased metacognitive awareness had little impact on their interactions with their tutees; the most common instructional activity was to ask students to read aloud. The students seemed to think that metacognition was irrelevant for young readers who were still mastering the mechanics of reading.

Many of the researchers who have developed effective ways to promote metacognitive awareness and comprehension monitoring have taken their results directly to teachers, often by publishing in practitioner journals such as *The Reading Teacher*. For example, Baumann, Jones, and Seifert-Kessell (1993) described to teachers how to enhance students' comprehension monitoring ability through think-alouds, based on their empirical research (Baumann et al., 1992). Similarly, Klingner and Vaughan (1999) described for teachers how they could implement their Collaborative Strategic Reading program (Klingner, Vaughn, & Schumm, 1998) in the classroom. Other researchers who have translated their findings into practice for teachers are Palincsar (Palincsar & Ransom, 1988), Garner (1992), Paris (1991a, 1991b), and Guthrie (Guthrie & Cox, 1998). Teachers who do not wish to use an instructional "package" may find Dowhower's (1999) comprehension strategies framework useful. Drawing on a large body of empirical research, Dowhower identified strategies students could be taught to use before, during, and after reading, including monitoring and learning to repair faulty comprehension.

The common element in all of the approaches for teaching students to monitor their comprehension is that teachers need to make explicit their own comprehension and comprehension monitoring processes. The approach I have used is to focus on the variety of ways that text can be difficult to understand. Students can be taught through teacher think-alouds to ask themselves questions such as the following: Are there any words I don't understand? Is there any information that doesn't agree with what I already know? Are there any ideas that don't fit together (because of contradictions, ambiguous referents, misleading topic shifts)? Is there any information missing or not clearly explained? Teachers can use authentic texts to illustrate the process, or they may choose to modify simple texts to contain inconsistencies, difficult words, conflicts with prior knowledge, ambiguous referents, and so on. Teachers then model how they would go about resolving the comprehension difficulties, using fix-up strategies such as rereading, looking ahead in the text for clarification, or consulting an outside source. Transferring responsibility for thinking aloud to the students themselves helps them take ownership of the monitoring process.

Some might be concerned that embedding errors in texts creates a task that is too contrived. But in fact texts are often "inconsiderate," lacking sufficient background information and explicit connections among ideas. Teaching students about different standards for evaluating comprehension through an error detection approach can help make them aware that texts are fallible. They become more willing to acknowledge comprehension difficulties and are less apt to blame themselves, as many poorer readers do (Baker, 1989a; Hacker, 1998). In their "Questioning the Author" approach, Beck, McKeown, Worthy, Sandora, and Kucan (1996) give students a subtle change in goal from trying to understand to making text understandable, thereby "deposing" the authority of the text. Seeking help in the face of comprehension difficulty is a valid comprehension monitoring strategy and figures prominently in reciprocal teaching. Help seeking illustrates an important interconnection of motivation and metacognition: Students need to have sufficient confidence in themselves as readers to ask questions and request clarifications.

Assessing Metacognitive Knowledge and Comprehension Monitoring in the Classroom

In an effective reading program, comprehension instruction and comprehension assessment are seamlessly integrated (Afflerbach, 1996; Paris, 1991b). Many approaches are available for teachers to track the development of metacognitive strategies in their students, including interviews, questionnaires, think-alouds, error detection procedures, anecdotal records and observation, and student self-assessment. (See Baker & Cerro, 2000, for an extended discussion of metacognitive assessment.)

Interviews and Questionnaires

Almost every article written for teachers about metacognition includes recommendations to interview students about their metacognitive knowledge and strategy use. Verbal reports have their imitations, but they can be valid and reliable sources of information (Pressley & Afflerbach, 1995). It is important, however, that teachers keep in mind that children may not be able or willing to express their thoughts and experiences, that the questions may not be understood, and that children may respond based on how they think they should respond (social desirability). And, from a practical perspective, open-ended interview responses are often difficult and time-consuming to score.

Garner (1992) suggested that teachers can interview readers to get a sense of their views of the reading process and their knowledge of reading and study strategies using questions originally designed for research purposes. Several authors have recommended using interview questions like those originally used by Paris and his colleagues (e.g., Yochum & Miller, 1990; Zabrucky & Ratner, 1990), such as, "What do you do if you come to a word and you don't know what it means? When you come across a part of the text that is confusing, what do you do?"

A number of multiple-choice questionnaires have been recommended for classroom use. Best known is the Index of Reading Awareness (IRA), developed originally as a research tool (Paris et al., 1984) and subsequently recommended for use to classroom teachers as an informal assessment instrument (Jacobs & Paris, 1987; Paris, 1991a; Zabrucky & Ratner, 1990). The IRA assesses "children's knowledge about reading and their abilities to evaluate tasks, goals, and personal skills; to plan ahead for specific purposes, to monitor progress while reading, and to recruit fix-up strategies as needed" (Jacobs & Paris, 1987, p. 268). In a rare independent validation of a metacognitive questionnaire, McLain, Gridley, and McIntosh (1991) concluded that the IRA was suitable for use a measure of the reading process but should not stand alone. Other multiple choice instruments are Schmitt's (1990) Metacognitive Strategy Index, Miholic's (1994) Metacognitive Reading Awareness Inventory, Pereira-Laird and Deane's (1997) Reading Strategy Use scale, and Yore, Craig, and Maguire's (1998) Index of Science Reading Awareness.

Multiple-choice instruments have their own associated limitations. For one, the multiple-choice format suggests there is a single right way to think about using a particular strategy (Duffy et al., 1987; Rhodes & Shanklin, 1993). Another limitation is that children might simply learn to mimic stock answers to the questions without real understanding (Paris, 1991a). Teachers and students should not put undue emphasis on scores; rather, the questionnaires are best used as opportunities to help increase students' awareness of strategies.

Think-Aloud Assessments

The growing popularity of think-aloud procedures in research on cognitive processing and metacognition has led, not surprisingly, to recommendations for its use as a diagnostic tool (see Kucan & Beck, 1997). Factors that teachers need to keep in mind are the following: (1) think-aloud procedures may disrupt the reading process itself; (2) cognitive processes may not be accessible to consciousness for report; (3) personal characteristics such as age, motivation, anxiety, verbal ability, and willingness to reveal oneself may influence responding; (4) the instructions, types of questions, and probes that are used can cue children to give particular kinds of responses; (5) children may not reveal the use of monitoring strategies unless the materials are sufficiently difficult, and (6) think-aloud protocols are often difficult and time-consuming to score.

Clay (1998), among others, has expressed concern about the recommended practice of asking even young children to talk about what they are doing while reading: "Adults are so expert at reading that what they do is little guide to what young readers need to learn in order to become experts. At this beginning stage, teachers have to work with children's vague awareness and try to work out what cognitive confusions impede their progress" (p. 68). This issue is addressed more fully in the final section of the chapter.

Error Detection

Several investigators who have conducted research using the error-detection paradigm have gone on to write articles for teachers recommending its use in assessment (e.g., Garner, 1992; Paris, 1991a; Zabrucky & Ratner, 1990). Garner (1992) suggested that teachers could assess children's use of different standards of evaluation by embedding errors of different types in short expository passages, asking children to underline anything troublesome, and having them explain the nature of the problem. Teachers she has worked with reportedly found this procedure useful in revealing whether children overrelied on particular standards.

Paris (1991a) also recommended adapting the error detection approach for diagnostic and remedial purposes. He identified the following advantages of the approach: It can be used with regular curriculum materials and may be particularly useful in content area reading; it can be used with individuals, small groups, or large classes; and it can be either used as a paper-and-pencil silent reading task or given orally. "Besides the flexibility, quick administration, adaptability to the reading level of each student, and the savings in time and money with a locally designed task, error detection tasks promote a thoughtful, inquisitive interaction while reading, so that the goals of instruction and assessment are congruent" (p. 39).

Although I have used error detection in my own research (Baker, 1979, 1984a, 1984b). I recommend caution in using the approach to assess children's ability to monitor their comprehension. It is a useful instructional tool for helping readers to see the variety of ways in which comprehension can fail and the variety of things that can make text difficult to understand, as discussed earlier. But given the difficulties researchers have had in disentangling explanations for poor detection performance, it should not be used for formal assessment purposes. Whether or not a problem will be reported depends on several factors, including the students' goals for reading, the criteria they adopt for evaluating their understanding, their knowledge about the topic, and their confidence in themselves as readers.

Observation and Analysis of Oral Reading

Observations have an advantage over verbal reports in that they can provide teachers with evidence of what children do instead of what they say they do. Observational checklists are available in many books for teachers, including Rhodes (1993) and Rhodes and Shanklin (1993). Running records are useful for evaluating children's oral reading strategies and comprehension monitoring (Paris, 1991a; Rhodes & Shanklin, 1993). As the child reads aloud, the teacher records oral reading miscues, including self-corrections. Self-corrections reveal metacognitive awareness that a word does not make sense in the context of the larger passage.

Paris (1991a, 1991b) recommended that teachers use a "think-along" approach in which the student reads aloud and the teacher asks interspersed questions. The questions assess not only understanding but also how students know that they know the answers, or, if they do not know, how they can find out. The teacher probes students' thinking with questions about their strategies and also observes spontaneous strategy use. For example, the teacher might question the child about an unfamiliar word: "What do you think 'trat' means in the sentence you just read? How could you tell? If you don't know, how could you find out?" Commercial materials for think-alongs are available, including the *Heath Reading Strategies Assessment* (1991), recommended by Paris, and *Think-Alongs: Comprehending as You Read,* recommended by Jongsma (2000).

Metacognitive knowledge can also be revealed as teachers observe peer tutoring, with the tutor the focus of particular interest. Listening to how the tutor describes strategies to a child who is not using them spontaneously provides insight into the tutor's own metacognitive knowledge (Garner, 1992). Does the tutor show awareness, for example, of how to use rereading to locate information in a text that the tutee could not remember?

Student Self-Assessment

An excellent way to integrate comprehension instruction and assessment, while at the same time fostering metacognitive awareness and control, is to help students develop the ability to assess and evaluate their own progress in reading (Afflerbach, 1996). Students can be taught to use portfolios to set goals, check their progress, and monitor their understanding (Paris, 1991b; Valencia, 1998). Enabling self-assessment is important, "especially if the goal for instruction is to develop strategic readers who monitor their own performance" (Leipzig & Afflerbach, 2000, p. 163).

Thinking aloud provides another means of self-assessment for students, helping them gain an awareness of whether or not comprehension is occurring (Baumann et al., 1993). Similarly, dialogue and discussion are valuable ways for readers to test their understanding of text, as they see that their peers have other perspectives on the meaning of the material (Hacker, 1998; Walker, 1996).

WHAT STILL NEEDS TO BE KNOWN ABOUT METACOGNITION IN COMPREHENSION INSTRUCTION?

Considerable progress has been made over the past 25 years, but important questions remain to be answered, four of which are raised in this section.

1. *When should children be taught to monitor their comprehension?* Opinions are diverse with respect to this question. Braunger and Lewis (1997) argued that children learning to read need access to their own reading processes, but Clay (1998) suggested such an emphasis would only confuse them. Graham and Harris (2000) advocated for explicit instruction in comprehension strategies for young readers with teacher modeling, whereas Chall and Squire (1991) suggested that direct instruction in metacognitive skills related to literacy may be inappropriate during the early years of schooling. The National Research Council (Snow et al., 1998) recommended explicit instruction in monitoring for understanding throughout the early grades, beginning in grade 1. However, the Baumann et al. (2000) survey of teachers' instructional practices did not even inquire about comprehension monitoring instruction in grades pre-K to 2, implying either that it is not or should not be taught.

Clay (1998) pointed out that strategic reading, including comprehension monitoring, is seen by many educators as something that older readers learn, a view held by the preservice teachers studied by Thomas and Barksdale-Ladd (2000). However, evidence that earlier forms of comprehension strategies occur in the young reader if instruction allows for it "is inconsistent with the advocacy of decoding first and comprehension later" (Clay, 1998, p. 253). For example, Baker (1984a) found that young children could monitor their listening comprehension effectively in an error-detection paradigm if specifically told that problems would be present. The processes of monitoring for comprehension are similar in listening and reading situations, and certainly children could be sensitized to the need to check their understanding through such everyday classroom activities as teacher read-alouds. Others have also demonstrated early acquisition of metacognitive strategies (Glaubman, Glaubman, & Ofir, 1997; Juliebo, Malicky, & Norman, 1998). Further research is needed to document the truth of the assertion that "an effective reader is an effective reader irrespective of age, and the ability to monitor comprehension is a hallmark of all successful readers" (Thomas & Barksdale-Ladd, 2000, p. 79).

2. *At what level are children most likely to benefit from metacognitively-oriented strategies instruction?* Several syntheses of the research literature raise questions as to the efficacy of metacognitively oriented strategies instruction with young students. Rosenshine and Meister's (1994) meta-analysis revealed that multiple strategies instruction (reciprocal teaching) is most effective for older students, with consistently significant effects only for grades 7 and 8. Similarly, Haller et al. (1988) concluded that the positive effects of teaching metacognition on reading comprehension do not appear until grade 7. Chall (Chall, Jacobs, & Baldwin, 1990) interpreted these results as support for her stage model of reading, which holds that higher level comprehension processes begin to appear when children are reading at grade levels 7 and 8.

Clay (1998) expressed concern that the popular instructional technique of gradual transfer of responsibility through verbal guidance is not appropriate for the teacher working with beginning readers who are aware of very little. "It is not enough to have children adopt our verbal statements about what they are doing. We want them to think about their thinking and not merely parrot teacher talk" (p. 68). Nevertheless, approaches such as transactional strategies instruction (Pressley et al., 1994) have proven effective even with second graders at risk for reading difficulties. The National Reading Panel (2000) calls for more research on this issue.

3. *Is comprehension monitoring necessarily a conscious process?* For those who consider comprehension monitoring to be a strategy, the answer to this question must be "yes," because there is a general consensus that strategies are deliberately deployed (Alexander & Murphy, 1998). But perhaps it is not really appropriate to classify comprehension monitoring along with question generating, summarizing, and predicting. Consider Clay's (1998) assertion, "We need to have children successfully monitoring and controlling their literacy acts, but with minimal conscious attention" (p. 68). A model proposed by Butterfield, Hacker, and Albertson (1996) allows for monitoring to take place at two different levels: "Readers can decide consciously which standards to use when monitoring comprehension, or . . . they may decide implicitly and automatically" (p. 277). When the decision is made at a conscious level, it competes for valuable working memory resources that are involved in comprehension per se. Less competent readers will have little capacity available for comprehension monitoring, as shown by Kinnunen, Vauras, and

Niemi (1998); first graders who were struggling with decoding were less likely to detect inconsistencies in the texts they were reading than their more advanced classmates.

4. *Does frequent independent reading promote metacognitive awareness and control?* Research indicates that children who read frequently tend to be better readers, but a link between reading frequency and metacognition has not been empirically established. Nor do we know whether independent reading, regardless of its frequency, is sufficient for metacognitive development. Pressley (1998) noted with concern the current practice in many intermediate classrooms to provide extensive opportunities for independent reading but little teaching of comprehension strategies. Research clearly shows that children who receive strategies instruction are more strategic in their reading and that those who are explicitly taught to monitor their comprehension do so more effectively than those who are not. But it is also well established that good readers are more metacognitively sophisticated than poor readers. Is this because good readers engage in more independent reading and develop these skills on their own? Perhaps the majority of children first need explicit strategies instruction in order to benefit metacognitively from independent reading. The possibility that independent reading is necessary but not sufficient is consistent with a conclusion reached by Byrnes (2000): Teachers will not enhance student achievement simply by allocating more time to silent reading; rather, they need to provide instructional scaffolds.

REFERENCES

Afflerbach, P. (1996). Engaged assessment of engaged reading. In L. Baker, P. Afflerbach, & D. Reinking (Eds.), *Developing engaged readers in school and home communities* (pp. 191–214). Hillsdale, NJ: Erlbaum.

Alexander, P. A., & Murphy, P. K. (1998). The research base for APA's Learner-Centered Psychological Principles. In N. M. Lambert & B. L. McCombs (Eds.), *How students learn: Reforming schools through learner-centered education* (pp. 25–60). Washington, DC: American Psychological Association.

Almasi, J. F. (1996). A new view of discussion. In L. B. Gambrell & J. F. Almasi (Eds.), *Lively discussions! Fostering engaged reading* (pp. 2–24). Newark, DE: International Reading Association.

Alvermann, D. E., & Guthrie, J. T. (1993). The National Reading Research Center. In A. P. Sweet & J. I. Anderson (Eds.), *Reading research into the year 2000* (pp. 129–150). Hillsdale, NJ: Erlbaum.

Baker, L. (1979). Comprehension monitoring: Identifying and coping with text confusions. *Journal of Reading Behavior, 11,* 365–374.

Baker, L. (1984a). Children's effective use of multiple standards for evaluating their comprehension. *Journal of Educational Psychology, 76,* 588–597.

Baker, L. (1984b). Spontaneous versus instructed use of multiple standards for evaluating comprehension: Effects of age, reading proficiency and type of standard. *Journal of Experimental Child Psychology, 38,* 289–311.

Baker, L. (1985). How do we know when we don't understand? Standards for evaluating text comprehension. In D. L. Forrest-Pressley, G. E. MacKinnon, & T. G. Waller (Eds.), *Metacognition, cognition, and human performance* (pp. 155–206). New York: Academic Press.

Baker, L. (1989a). Developmental change in readers' responses to unknown words. *Journal of Reading Behavior, 21,* 241–260.

Baker, L. (1989b). Metacognition, comprehension monitoring, and the adult reader. *Educational Psychology Review, 1,* 3–38.

Baker, L. (1994). Fostering metacognitive development. In H. Reese (Ed.), *Advances in child development and behavior* (Vol. 25, pp. 201–239). San Diego, CA: Academic Press.

Baker, L. (1996). Social influences on metacognitive development in reading. In C. Cornoldi & J. Oakhill (Eds.), *Reading comprehension difficulties: Processes and interventions* (pp. 331–351). Hillsdale, NJ: Erlbaum.

Baker, L., Afflerbach, P., & Reinking, D. (1996). Developing engaged readers in school and home communities: An overview. In L. Baker, P. Afflerbach, & D. Reinking (Eds.), *Developing engaged readers in school and home communities* (pp. xiii–xviii). Mahwah, NJ: Erlbaum.

Baker, L., & Brown, A. L. (1984). Metacognitive skills and reading. In P. D. Pearson, M. Kamil, R. Barr, & P. Mosenthal (Eds.), *Handbook of research in reading* (pp. 353–395). New York: Longman.

Baker, L., & Cerro, L. (2000). Assessing metacognition in children and adults. In G. Schraw & J. C. Impara (Eds.), *Issues in the measurement of metacognition* (pp. 99–145). Lincoln, NE: Buros Institute of Mental Measurements, University of Nebraska Press.

Baker, L., Dreher, M. J., & Guthrie, J. T. (2000). Why teachers should promote reading engagement. In L. Baker, M. J. Dreher, & J. T. Guthrie (Eds.), *Engaging young readers: Promoting achievement and motivation* (pp. 1–16). New York: Guilford Press.

Baker, L., & Zimlin, L. (1989). Instructional effects on children's use of two levels of standards for evaluating their comprehension. *Journal of Educational Psychology, 81,* 340–346.

Baumann, J. F., Hoffman, J. V., Duffy-Hester, A. M., & Ro, J. M. (2000). The First R yesterday and today: U.S. elementary reading instruction practices reported by teachers and administrators. *Reading Research Quarterly, 35,* 338–377.

Baumann, J. F., Jones, L. A., & Seifert-Kessell, N. (1993). Using think alouds to enhance children's comprehension monitoring abilities. *Reading Teacher, 47,* 184–193.

Baumann, J. F., Seifert-Kessell, N., & Jones, L. A. (1992). Effect of think-aloud instruction on elementary students' comprehension monitoring ability. *Journal of Reading Behavior, 24,* 143–172.

Beal, C. R. (1996). The role of comprehension monitoring in children's revision. *Educational Psychology Review, 8,* 219–238.

Beck, I. L., McKeown, M. G., Hamilton, R. L., & Kucan, L. (1997). *Questioning the author: An approach for enhancing student engagement with text.* Newark, DE: International Reading Association.

Beck, I. L., McKeown, M. G., Worthy, J., Sandora, C. A., & Kucan, L. (1996). Questioning the author: A year-long implementation to engage students with text. *Elementary School Journal, 94,* 358–414.

Bereiter, C., & Bird, M. (1985). Use of thinking aloud in identification and teaching of reading comprehension strategies. *Cognition and Instruction, 2,* 131–156.

Blair-Larsen, S. M., & Vallance, K. M. (1999). Comprehension instruction in a balanced reading classroom. In S. M. Blair-Larsen & K. A. Williams (Eds.), *The balanced reading program: Helping all students achieve success* (pp. 37–52). Newark, DE: International Reading Association.

Borkowski, J. G., Carr, M., Rellinger, E., & Pressley, M. (1990). Self-regulated cognition: Interdependence of metacognition, attributions, and self-esteem. In B. F. Jones & L. Idol (Eds.), *Dimensions of thinking and cognitive instruction* (pp. 53–92). Hillsdale, NJ: Erlbaum.

Bossert, T. S., & Schwantes, F. M. (1995–1996). Children's comprehension monitoring: Training children to use rereading to aid comprehension. *Reading Research and Instruction, 35,* 109–121.

Braunger, J., & Lewis, J. P. (1997). *Building a knowledge base in reading.* Newark, DE: International Reading Association.

Brown, A. L. (1978). Knowing when, where, and how to remember: A problem of metacognition. In R. Glaser (Ed.), *Advances in instructional psychology* (Vol. 1 , pp. 77–165). Hillsdale, NJ: Erlbaum.

Brown, A. L., & Campione, J. C. (1998). Designing a community of young learners: Theoretical and practical lessons. In N. M. Lambert & B. L. McCombs (Eds.), *How students learn: Reforming schools through learner-centered education* (pp. 153–186). Washington, DC: American Psychological Association.

Butterfield, E. C., Hacker, D. J., & Albertson, L. R. (1996). Environmental, cognitive, and metacognitive influences on text revision: Assessing the evidence. *Educational Psychology Review, 8,* 239–297.

Byrnes, J. P. (2000). Using instructional time effectively. In L. Baker, M. J. Dreher, & J. T. Guthrie (Eds.), *Engaging young readers: Promoting achievement and motivation* (pp. 188–208). New York: Guilford Press.

Chall, J. S., Jacobs, V. A., & Baldwin, L. E. (1990). *The reading crisis: Why poor childrn fall behind.* Cambridge, MA: Harvard University Press.

Chall, J. S., & Squires, J. R. (1991). The publishing industry and textbooks. In R. Barr, M. L. Kamil, P. Mosenthal, & P. D. Pearson (Eds.), *Handbook of reading research* (Vol. 2, pp. 120–146). White Plains, NY: Longman.

Clay, M. M. (1998). *By different paths to common outcomes.* York, ME: Stenhouse.

Dole, J. A. (2000). Explicit and implicit instruction in comprehension. In B. M. Taylor, M. F. Graves, & P. van den Broek (Eds.), *Reading for meaning: Fostering comprehension in the middle grades* (pp. 52–69). New York: Teachers College Press.

Dowhower, S. L. (1999). Supporting a strategic stance in the classroom: A comprehension framework for helping teachers help students to be strategic. *Reading Teacher, 52,* 672–688.

Duffy, G. G., Roehler, L. R., Meloth, M. S., Polin, R., Rackliffe, G., Tracy, A., & Vavrus, L. (1987). Developing and evaluating measures associated with strategic reading. *Journal of Reading Behavior, 19,* 223–246.

Edwards, M. (1999). The aim is metacognition: For teachers as well as students. In J. Hancock (Ed.), *The explicit teaching of reading* (pp. 80–96). Newark, DE: International Reading Association.

Flavell, J. H. (1976). Metacognitive aspects of problem solving. In L. B. Resnick (Ed.), *The nature of intelligence* (pp. 231–235). Hillsdale, NJ: Erlbaum.

Fuchs, D., Fuchs, L. S., Mathes, P., & Simmons, D. (1997). Peer-assisted learning strategies: Making classrooms more responsive to student diversity. *American Educational Research Journal, 34,* 174–206.

Garner, R. (1987). *Metacognition and reading comprehension.* Norwood, NJ: Ablex.

Garner, R. (1992). Metacognition and self-monitoring strategies. In S. J. Samuels & A. E. Farstrup (Eds.), *What research has to say about reading instruction* (pp. 236–252). Newark, DE: International Reading Association.

Glaubman, R., Glaubman, H., & Ofir, L. (1997). Effects of self-directed learning, story comprehension, and self-questioning in kindergarten. *Journal of Educational Research, 90,* 361–374.

Gourgey, A. F. (1998). Metacognition in basic skills instruction. *Instructional Science, 26,* 81–96.

Graham, S., & Harris, K. R. (2000). Helping children who experience reading difficulties: Prevention and intervention. In L. Baker, M. J. Dreher, & J. T. Guthrie (Eds.), *Engaging young readers: Promoting achievement and motivation* (pp. 43–67). New York: Guilford Press.

Guthrie, J. T., & Cox, K. E. (1998). Portrait of an engaging classroom: Principles of Concept-Oriented Reading Instruction for diverse students. In K. Harris (Ed.), *Teaching every child every day: Learning in diverse schools and classrooms* (pp. 70–130). Cambridge, MA: Brookline.

Guthrie, J. T., Cox, K. E., Knowles, K. T., Buehl, M., Mazzoni, S. A., & Fasulo, L. (2000). Building toward coherent instruction. In L. Baker, M. J. Dreher, & J. T. Guthrie (Eds.), *Engaging young readers: Promoting achievement and motivation* (pp. 209–236). New York: Guilford Press.

Guthrie, J. T., Van Meter, P., Hancock, G. R., Alao, S., Anderson, E., & McCann, A. D. (1998). Does concept-oriented reading instruction increase strategy use and conceptual learning from text? *Journal of Educational Psychology, 90*, 261–278.

Guthrie, J. T., Van Meter, P., McCann, A. D., Wigfield, A., Bennett, L., Poundstone, C. C., Rice, M. E., Faibisch, F. M., Hunt, B., & Mitchell, A. M. (1996). Growth of literacy engagement: Changes in motivations and strategies during Concept-Oriented Reading Instruction. *Reading Research Quarterly, 31*, 306–332.

Hacker, D. J. (1998). Self-regulated comprehension during normal reading. In D. J. Hacker, J. Dunlosky, & A. C. Graesser (Eds.), *Metacognition in educational theory and practice* (pp. 165–191). Mahwah, NJ: Erlbaum.

Hall, K., Bowman, H., & Myers, J. (1999). Metacognition and reading awareness among samples of nine-year-olds in two cities. *Educational Research, 41*, 99–107.

Haller, E. P., Child, D. A., & Walberg, H. J. (1988). Can comprehension be taught? A quantitative synthesis of "metacognitive" studies. *Educational Researcher, 17*(9), 5–8.

Heath Reading Strategies Assessment. (1991). Lexington, MA: Heath.

Jacobs, S. E., & Paris, S. G. (1987). Children's metacognition about reading: Issues in definition, measurement, and instruction. *Educational Psychologist, 22*, 255–278.

Jongsma, K. (2000). Instructional materials: Vocabulary and comprehension strategy development. *Reading Teacher, 53*, 310–311.

Juliebo, M., Malicky, G. V., & Norman, C. (1998). Metacognition of young readers in an early intervention programme. *Journal of Research in Reading, 21*, 24–35.

Kinnunen, R., & Vauras, M. (1995). Comprehension monitoring and the level of comprehension in high-and low-achieving primary school children's reading. *Learning and Instruction, 5*, 143–165.

Kinnunen, R., Vauras, M., & Niemi, P. (1998). Comprehension monitoring in beginning readers. *Scientific Studies of Reading, 2*, 353–375.

Klingner, J. K., & Vaughn, S. (1999). Promoting reading comprehension, content learning, and English acquisition through collaborative strategic reading (CSR). *Reading Teacher, 52*, 738–747.

Klingner, J. K., Vaughn, S., & Schumm, J. S. (1998). Collaborative strategic reading during social studies in heterogeneous fourth-grade classrooms. *Elementary School Journal, 99*, 3–21.

Kucan, L., & Beck, I. (1997). Thinking aloud and reading comprehension research: Inquiry, instruction, and social interaction. *Review of Educational Research, 67*, 271–299.

Lambert, N. M., & McCombs, B. L. (1998). Introduction: Learner-centered schools and classrooms as a direction for school reform. In N. M. Lambert & B. L. McCombs (Eds.), *How students learn: Reforming schools through learner-centered education* (pp. 1–22). Washington, DC: American Psychological Association.

Leipzig, D. H., & Afflerbach, P. (2000). Determining the suitability of assessments: Using the CURRV framework. In L. Baker, M. J. Dreher, & J. T. Guthrie (Eds.), *Engaging young readers: Promoting achievement and motivation* (pp. 159–187). New York: Guilford Press.

Markman, E. M. (1977). Realizing that you don't understand: A preliminary investigation. *Child Development, 46*, 986–992.

Mastropieri, M. A., & Scruggs, T. E. (1997). Best practices in promoting reading comprehension in students with learning disabilities: 1976 to 1996. *Remedial and Special Education, 18*, 197–213.

Mayer, R. E. (1998). Cognitive, metacognitive, and motivational aspects of problem solving. *Instructional Science, 26*, 49–63.

McCarthey, S. J., Hoffman, J. V., & Galda, L. (1999). Readers in elementary classrooms: Learning goals and instructional principles that can inform practice. In J. T. Guthrie & D. E. Alvermann (Eds.), *Engaged reading: Processes, practices, and policy implications* (pp. 46–80). New York: Teachers College.

McLain, K. V. M., Gridley, B. E., & McIntosh, D. (1991). Value of a scale used to measure metacognitive reading awareness. *Journal of Educational Research*, 85, 81–87.

Miholic, V. (1994). An inventory to pique students' metacognitive awareness. *Journal of Reading*, 38, 84–86.

Miller, G. E. (1985). The effects of general and specific self-instruction training on children's comprehension monitoring performance during reading. *Reading Research Quarterly*, 20, 616–628.

Miller, G. E. (1987). The influence of self-instruction on the comprehension monitoring performance of average and above average readers. *Journal of Reading Behavior*, 19, 303–317.

Myers, M., & Paris, S. G. (1978). Children's metacognitive knowledge about reading. *Journal of Educational Psychology*, 70, 680–690.

National Reading Panel (2000). *Teaching children to read: An evidence-based assessment of the scientific research literature on reading and its implications for reading instruction.* Bethesda, MD: National Institute of Child Health and Human Development.

Otero, J. (1998). Influence of knowledge activation and context on comprehension monitoring of science texts. In D. J. Hacker, J. Dunlosky, & A. C. Graesser (Eds.), *Metacognition in educational theory and practice* (pp. 145–164). Mahwah, NJ: Erlbaum.

Palincsar, A. S., & Brown, A. L. (1984). Reciprocal teaching of comprehension-fostering and comprehension-monitoring activities. *Cognition and Instruction*, 1, 117–175.

Palincsar, A. S., & Ransom, K. (1988). From the mystery spot to the thoughtful spot: The instruction of metacognitive strategies. *Reading Teacher*, 41, 784–789.

Paris, S. G. (1991a). Assessment and remediation of metacognitive aspects of children's reading comprehension. *Topics in Language Disorders*, 12, 32–50.

Paris, S. G. (1991b). Portfolio assessment for young readers. *Reading Teacher*, 44, 680–682.

Paris, S. G., Cross, D. R., & Lipson, M. Y. (1984). Informed strategies for learning: A program to improve children's reading awareness and comprehension. *Journal of Educational Psychology*, 76, 1239–1252.

Paris, S. G., Wasik, B. A., & Turner, J. C. (1991). The development of strategic readers. In R. Barr, M. Kamil, P. Mosenthal, & P. D. Pearson (Eds.), *Handbook of reading research* (Vol. 2, pp. 609–640). White Plains, NY: Longman.

Paris, S. G., Wasik, B. A., & Van der Westhuizen, G. (1988). Meta-metacognition: A review of research on metacognition and reading. In J. E. Readence, B. S. Baldwin, J. P. Konopak, & P. R. O'Keefe (Eds.), *Dialogues in literacy research: 37th yearbook of the National Reading Conference* (pp. 143–166). Chicago, IL: National Reading Conference.

Paris, S. G., & Winograd, P. (1990). How metacognition can promote academic learning and instruction. In B. F. Jones & L. Idol (Eds.), *Dimensions of thinking and cognitive instruction* (pp. 15–51). Hillsdale, NJ: Erlbaum.

Payne, B. D., & Manning, B. H. (1992). Basal reader instruction: Effects of comprehension monitoring training on reading comprehension, strategy use and attitude. *Reading Research and Instruction*, 32, 29–38.

Pereira-Laird, J. A., & Deane, F. P. (1997). Development and validation of a self-report measure of reading strategy use. *Reading Psychology*, 18, 185–235.

Pressley, M. (1998). Comprehension strategies instruction. In J. Osborne & F. Lehr (Eds.), *Literacy for all: Issues in teaching and learning* (pp. 113–133). New York: Guilford Press.

Pressley, M. (2000). Comprehension instruction in elementary school: A quarter century of research progress. In B. M. Taylor, M. F. Graves, & P. van den Broek (Eds.), *Reading for meaning: Fostering comprehension in the middle grades* (pp. 32–51). New York: Teachers College Press.

Pressley, M., & Afflerbach, P. (1995). *Verbal protocols of reading: The nature of constructively responsive reading.* Hillsdale, NJ: Erlbaum.

Pressley, M., Almasi, J., Schuder, T., Bergman, J., Hite, S., El-Dinary, P. B., & Brown, R. (1994).

Transactional instruction of comprehension strategies: The Montgomery County, Maryland, SAIL program. *Reading and Writing Quarterly: Overcoming learning difficulties, 10,* 5–19.

Pressley, M., Wharton-McDonald, R., Mistretta-Hampston, J., & Echevarria, M. (1998). Literacy instruction in 10 fourth- and fifth-grade classrooms in upstate New York. *Scientific Studies of Reading, 2,* 159–194.

Rhodes, L. K. (Ed.). (1993). *Literacy assessment: A handbook of instruments.* Portsmouth, NH: Heinemann.

Rhodes, L. K., & Shanklin, N. L. (1993). *Windows into literacy: Assessing learners K–8.* Portsmouth, NH: Heinemann.

Rogoff, B. (1990). *Apprenticeship in thinking.* New York: Oxford University Press.

Rosenshine, B., & Meister, C. (1994). Reciprocal teaching: A review of the research. *Review of Educational Research, 64,* 479–530.

Rosenshine, B., & Meister, C. (1997). Cognitive strategy instruction in reading. In S. A. Stahl & D. A. Hayes (Eds.), *Instructional models in reading* (pp. 85–108). Mahwah, NJ: Erlbaum.

Schmitt, M. C. (1990). A questionnaire to measure children's awareness of strategic reading processes. *Reading Teacher, 43,* 454–461.

Schmitt, M. C., & Baumann, J. F. (1990). Metacomprehension during basal reading instruction: Do teachers promote it? *Reading Research and Instruction, 29*(3), 1–13.

Schmitt, M. C., & Hopkins, C. J. (1993). Metacognitive theory applied: Strategic reading instruction in the current generation of basal readers. *Reading Research and Instruction, 32,* 13–24.

Schraw, G. (1998). Promoting general metacognitive awareness. *Instructional Science, 26,* 113–125.

Snow, C. E., Burns, M. S., & Griffin, P. (Eds.). (1998). *Preventing reading difficulties in young children.* Washington, DC: National Academy Press.

Thomas, K. F., & Barksdale-Ladd, M. A. (2000). Metacognitive processes: Teaching strategies in literacy education courses. *Reading Psychology, 21,* 67–84.

Valencia, S. W. (1998). *Literacy portfolios in action.* Fort Worth, TX: Harcourt Brace.

Vye, N. J., Schwartz, D. L., Bransford, J. D., Barron, B. J., & Zech, L. (1998). SMART environments that support monitoring, reflection, and revision. In D. J. Hacker, J. Dunlosky, & A. C. Graesser (Eds.), *Metacognition in educational theory and practice* (pp. 305–346). Mahwah, NJ: Erlbaum.

Vygotsky, L. S. (1978). *Mind in society.* Cambridge, MA: MIT Press.

Walker, B. J. (1996). Discussions that focus on strategies and self-assessment. In L. B. Gambrell & J. F. Almasi (Eds.), *Lively discussions! Fostering engaged reading* (pp. 286–296). Newark, DE: International Reading Association.

Wertsch, J. V. (1978). Adult–child interaction and the roots of metacognition. *Quarterly Newsletter of the Institute for Comparative Human Development, 2,* 15–18.

Winograd, P., & Johnston, P. (1982). Comprehension monitoring and the error detection paradigm. *Journal of Reading Behavior, 14,* 51–76.

Yochum, N., & Miller, S. D. (1990). Classroom reading assessment: Using students' perceptions. *Reading Psychology: An International Quarterly, 11,* 159–165.

Yore, L. D., Craig, M. T., & Maguire, T. O. (1998). Index of Science Reading Awareness: An interactive–constructive model, test verification, and Grades 4–8 results. *Journal of Research in Science Teaching, 35,* 27–51.

Zabrucky, K., & Ratner, H. H. (1990). Children's comprehension monitoring: Implications of research findings for the classroom. *Reading Improvement, 27,* 46–54.

Zabrucky, K., & Ratner, H. H. (1992). Effects of passage type on comprehension monitoring and recall in good and poor readers. *Journal of Reading Behavior, 24,* 373–391.

7

Teaching Reading
Self-Assessment Strategies

PETER AFFLERBACH

In this chapter I examine the teaching of reading assessment as a means for helping students achieve independence in reading. I provide an overview of research related to metacognition, self-evaluation, and teaching reading strategies that supports the notion that children can and must learn to assess their own reading. Next, I focus on common classroom reading assessments to describe how they can provide the opportunity to teach children about reading assessment. I finish the chapter by charting a theoretical and practical course that should lead to effective teaching and learning of reading assessment strategies and students' independent use of them.

Across classrooms, school districts, and states, the teaching and learning of reading is perceived as a means to help students achieve success (National Council of Teachers of English/International Reading Association [NCTE/IRA], 1996). The ability to read contributes to students' personal, intellectual, and social development, in school and out of school (Snow, Burns, & Griffin, 1998). Success in reading helps students become informed citizens and contributing members of society (Donahue, Voelkl, Campbell, & Mazzeo, 1999). Such success is currently framed in terms of the decoding, vocabulary, and comprehension strategies and knowledge that are taught in classrooms. Reading self-assessment is often absent from this list, yet it is this assessment that allows students to be truly independent readers.

Support for the importance of teaching reading assessment can be found in the reading and learning standards that proliferate throughout districts and states. When we help a student develop phonemic awareness, learn sound–symbol correspondences, and decode words, our ultimate goal is that children will use these critical skills on their own. When we teach comprehension strategies so that students make appropriate inferences or summarize a paragraph, our intention is that students soon will be able to use these strategies themselves. And when we ask student readers to critically evaluate the content of text and use what they have learned from a text in complex performances, we expect that this will be done independently and successfully. Every reading standard that demands students' independence implies students' ability to assess their own reading effectively. Yet there may be little or no overt emphasis on reading assessment strategies in published standards, mandated curricula, or classroom practice. These strategies are as critical to reading development as decoding and comprehension strategies, and there is a precarious disconnect in reading instruction that does not include the teaching of reading self-assessment strategies.

The ability to self-assess is central to success in reading (Clay, 1993; Goodman & Goodman, 1977), yet it eludes many student readers. To realize the promise of reading, children must be able to select, comprehend, and use a variety of texts. They must be able to read increasingly complex texts on their own, concurrently building sophisticated reading strategies and independence. Fostering independence in reading should be an instructional priority, and teaching reading assessment is central to helping students develop this independence. Teaching reading assessment must accompany the teaching and learning of other important reading skills and strategies. Fortunately, there is voluminous research that describes the details of self-assessment strategies and that anticipates the need to teach them.

WHAT WE KNOW ABOUT ACCOMPLISHED READERS' SELF-ASSESSMENT EXPERTISE: MONITORING AND EVALUATION STRATEGIES

Talented readers assess their own reading processes and products. These evaluative and regulative strategies contribute to better reading (Baker & Brown, 1991; Hacker, 1998; Paris, Wasik, & Turner, 1991; Pressley & Afflerbach, 1995). Comprehension monitoring research builds on foundational work by Markman (1977) and Flavell (1978) that describes the importance and development of metacognitive ability and self-evaluation. Metacognition is the ability to understand one's understanding and to manage the meaning construction process. Metacognition and comprehension monitoring are demonstrated by a young reader who realizes that a word has been misread and self-corrects the word. For example, a third grader reads "Allie rode off into the sunset on the house," for "Allie rode off into the sunset on the horse." Asking the question, "Does that make sense?" the reader uses semantic cues to determine that "No, the sentence really doesn't make much sense." The third grader regulates the reading act by rereading and paying particular attention to the letters that make up the troublesome word. The student determines that the word "horse" has been misread as "house," self-corrects this, and continues to construct meaning from the text. A more experienced reader monitors comprehension of a paragraph within a text on space travel and exploration. Based on knowledge of text structure, as well as knowledge gathered through museum visits, previous study of solar systems, and familiarity with *Star Wars*, a reader anticipates that the paragraph is of some importance (it concludes a section within the chapter). The reader constructs meaning while checking text information in light of what is already known about the heavens. For both of these readers, metacognition involves the continuous self-assessment of critical components of reading (Garner, 1987).

Accomplished readers evaluate their progress toward a goal at both micro- and macrolevels. Pressley and Afflerbach (1995) provided a comprehensive catalog of the comprehension monitoring used by accomplished readers. Their review of think-aloud protocol data indicated that accomplished readers evaluate and regulate the meaning construction process comprehensively. The processes of evaluation and regulation consistently inform one another when reading is working. Expert readers are aware of problems that arise while processing text to construct meaning, including blockages of this process at and beyond the word and phrase level (Olshavsky, 1976–1977). All accomplished readers regularly regulate their reading. They vary the rate of reading, proceeding quickly when the text is well understood and when feedback from their evaluation tells them that meaning construction is proceeding smoothly. In contrast, regulation may result in rereading sections of text and in slower rates of reading when text is more challenging. Here, evaluative strategies inform the reader that "slow and sure" is a good approach. For example, a reader may determine that the just-read paragraph is not easily integrated with previously read paragraphs. This evaluation leads to a regulatory decision to reread with the goal of better synthesis of information across paragraphs (Baker & Brown, 1991). Accomplished readers check to see that words, clauses, and sentences are understood. They also check to see that their comprehension is adequate for meeting a goal, be it memorization of text for a test, understanding and using the scientific process as described in a content area text, or sharing the latest *Harry Potter* in the schoolyard. Readers' evaluation that a text is too difficult suggests that regulation may take the form of stopping reading and finding out more about the content of a text through more comprehensible means.

In addition to assessing their progress at the reading task at hand, talented readers may evaluate the content and structure of a text for accuracy and coherence, the style of the text, the legitimacy of claims made by an author, and an author's purpose. These assessment abilities help place students in a position to critically evaluate their knowledge and progress in relation to the text. Independent and successful reading involves being alert enough to notice difficulties when reading and using sophisticated repertoires of strategies to identify and fix problems while reading (Johnston & Afflerbach, 1985). Accomplished readers set goals for their reading and gauge progress toward these goals while reading (Baker & Brown, 1991). For example, readers can monitor text characteristics so that they may determine if the text content is relevant to their reading goal. While they monitor strategy use, talented readers also assess their prior knowledge related to text content and text structure (Bazerman, 1985). A reader's assessment and determination that she has extensive prior knowledge of the text topic can drastically change the reading process, just as a determination that there is little or no applicable prior knowledge may (Hacker, 1998). For example, a reader with the goal of understanding a complex chapter on the causes of the American Revolution may evaluate his own prior knowledge and determine that there is not enough of it to strive toward the goal of sophisticated understanding of the text. This evaluation results in the regulation move to find a more suitable book with which the reader may construct a more rudimentary understanding of causes. On the other hand, a reader with broad and deep content knowledge related to ecosystems may decide that there is little new in a text and forgo reading it. Or the reader will use her prior knowledge to help shift into a critical reading mode, in which examination of the veracity and accuracy of text are a primary goal (VanSledright & Afflerbach, 2000).

Evaluative and regulative strategies are the benchmarks of talented readers' self-assessment. Accomplished readers are flexible in their routines of metacognition and comprehension monitoring, as demanded by the particular act of reading. The ability to self-assess is multifaceted, and good readers apply their self-assessment strategies on demand. Given that accomplished readers regularly assess their knowledge, their strategies, and their progress toward goals, we need to specify the means for helping less able readers develop self-assessment mind-sets and strategies. There is considerable research evidence that good readers self-assess and that developing readers need to learn to do so. Reading standards that invoke independence as the worthy goal of learning to read add to the already compelling argument for the centrality of self-assessment to student success, in spite of the fact that they do not always provide the details of how to teach reading assessment.

A SHIFT IN PERSPECTIVE ON READING ASSESSMENT

Using assessment to foster students' reading independence requires that we adopt a particular perspective on reading assessment in the classroom. We must use assessment to help teach children how to assess, in addition to the more prevalent use of assessment to describe and measure student reading growth and achievement. The use of assessment to foster student independence in reading requires that we conceptualize reading assessment, in part, as a set of opportunities to model and teach. We must look for contexts in which we can help students become familiar with the culture of reading assessment and encourage them to develop self-assessment strategies. In fact, we must become metacognitive about our reading instruction and assessment programs to determine the best opportunities for teaching reading assessment. This involves making inventory of existing assessments to determine where and when teaching reading assessment is feasible. It requires that we introduce students to reading assessment materials and procedures and help them become familiar with assessment routines. Too many students have reading assessment done to them, or for them. Only reading assessment that is done with students and eventually by students can foster true independence and success in reading.

Successful reading self-assessment revolves around the teaching and learning of specific strategies. There is compelling evidence of the effectiveness of teaching reading strategies. These strategies may include prediction and summarization (Palincsar & Brown, 1984), asking questions of the text and author (Beck, McKeown, Hamilton, & Kucan, 1997), and negotiating the meaning of text (Pressley et al., 1992). Just as learning and using comprehension strategies has a positive effect on students' reading performance, I believe that learning and using related self-assessment strategies is mandatory for student success in reading. Palincsar and Brown's reciprocal teaching program, in which middle school special education students learned clarification, summarization, and question-asking strategies, demonstrates this. Reciprocal teaching also taught students to monitor their reading. The success demonstrated by this program suggests that a comprehensive approach to teaching strategies renders reading self-assessment an attainable goal.

Dedicating classroom time to teach reading assessment is often a challenge (Afflerbach, 1997). Reading assessment must serve many different audiences and purposes, and statewide assessments, district assessments, and daily assessment routines all compete for valuable class time. Rarely are these assessment agendas well integrated. High-stakes assessments are often accompanied by implicit and explicit requirements, including an emphasis on helping students prepare to take assessments. There may be much time dedicated to teaching to the test but little time given to teaching reading assessment. If the teaching of reading assessment strategies is not already practiced, mandated high-stakes assessments may make it even more difficult to initiate. Many high-stakes assessments are not particularly useful to classroom teachers. However, a more important point for this chapter is that such tests reflect the practice of *doing* reading assessment rather than *teaching* reading assessment. We must help students become familiar with how reading assessment works so that they can eventually assess and evaluate their own learning. Without this experience, all the good teaching that is done related to decoding, fluency, comprehension, critical reading strategies, and the appreciation of reading may have a less positive immediate and lifelong impact.

FACTORS THAT CONTRIBUTE TO SUCCESSFUL TEACHING OF READING ASSESSMENT

Given the importance of self-assessment in reading, we need to develop the expertise to teach reading assessment effectively. The nature of expertise is well documented (Chi, Glaser, & Farr, 1988; Ericsson & Smith, 1991). Experts have broad and deep knowledge that is declarative, procedural, and conditional (Alexander, 1997). For the teaching of reading assessment, this includes the ability to identify the reading assessment strategies, routines, and materials that are helpful to students moving toward independence in reading. It also requires the ability to identify the contexts and situations in which reading assessment can be taught and learned. We must become experts in what we know and do related to reading assessment (Afflerbach & Johnston, 1993). Experts' knowledge development is the result of frequent opportunities to work with particular materials and procedures, repeated exposures to salient features to be learned, and encouragement and meaningful outcomes as a result of the time and effort invested in such work. For example, the success of early reading intervention programs often revolves around teacher expertise in conducting, interpreting, and using reading assessment to inform daily instruction (Clay, 1993). Teachers who reliably use running records and performance assessment scoring rubrics are assessment experts (Johnston, 1997). To the degree that teachers are good assessors, they may be effective teachers of reading assessment.

Teachers' assessment expertise includes broad and deep knowledge of a range of reading assessment materials and procedures. To teach reading assessment, knowledge of the nature and suitability of formative and summative assessment, process and product assessment, and individual and group assessment is necessary. Detailed knowledge of the varied audiences and purposes of assessment is necessary. Expertise in reading assessment also implies understanding of the validity, reliability, and consequences of the mandated and chosen materials and procedures that make up a school's reading assessment regimen (Liepzig & Afflerbach, 2000). To help students develop self-assessment ability and confidence, teachers must be expert at both the practice of reading assessment and the teaching of reading assessment (Afflerbach, 1997).

Comprehension strategy instruction research (e.g., Palincsar & Brown, 1984) demonstrates that students become strategic when instruction is geared to their developmental needs. Just as we model and explain reading comprehension strategies, we should model and explain reading assessment strategies to help students move toward independence in reading. Strategy instruction should be geared to students' current levels of assessment knowledge and ability, and it should anticipate their next levels of competence (Vygotsky, 1978). For example, an important cluster of reading assessment strategies helps readers apprehend a reading difficulty, identify the difficulty, apply fix-it strategies, check on the success of the fix-it strategies, and press on with the larger reading task. Over time, the external model of evaluating and assessing one's own reading that is provided by the teacher can become internalized by students. Students may develop the ability to use the self-assessment strategies independently. This approach demands that we consider teachable moments in terms of the reading assessment strategies that we use and how we may model, explain, and teach these strategies.

Teachers must also become expert at identifying students' needs in relation to their developing ability to self-assess. This may be best accomplished through the careful examination of students' reading processes and products. Through observation of student reading, the nature of development of students' self-assessment abilities can be better examined and understood. We can observe students to determine if they are mindful and reflective while reading and if they demonstrate an ability to identify problems during reading, to focus on them, and to fix them. We can observe if students read and attend to the text at hand while keeping track of the purpose for reading and if their performances and responses reflect the mindfulness and attention to detail that are necessary for successful reading. We may conclude that their reading self-assessment strategies are effective. In contrast, if our observations describe students who do not realize when the reading process has gone astray, who do not know how to correct an apparent difficulty, or who are not monitoring reading in relation to the goal for reading, this indicates the need for instruction that leads to able self-assessment. Teachers may regularly identify and work within these students' zones of proximal development, providing scaffolding in the form of models and explanations to help students build independence as self-assessors. Specifically, reading assessment strategy instruction should include detailed models of the strategies to be learned, explanations of the importance of the strategies and how to use them, and demonstrations of the strategies themselves as they are used in reading (Kucan & Beck, 1997).

The development of the ability to teach reading assessment and an increased understanding of what individual students need must be complemented by the teacher's ability to identify the classroom contexts in which we may most effectively teach reading assessment. That is, the teacher must anticipate those reading assessment situations in which clear focus, detailed modeling, and precise explanation may take place. An example is using performance assessment rubrics. Such rubrics may inform students about what a good performance is, providing a context in which to teach students to begin to judge their own work against a detailed and consistent rubric. The determination of appropriate contexts for using and teaching reading assessment strategies is especially crucial given the amount of time that we may be required to devote to high stakes assessments, including helping students to prepare for the test and administer the tests. A good starting point is to conduct an inventory of reading assessment that is practiced in the school and classroom and to use the inventory to help determine the opportunities for teaching reading assessment. For example, if there is a reading comprehension checklist used throughout the middle school grades, the commonality of the checklist and its contents suggests that it could be a major focus of teaching reading assessment. Students may eventually internalize the consistent model and instructional focus related to checklists. If there is a schoolwide (or countywide) initiative to develop performance assessments, then the use

of performance assessment rubrics to help teach assessment is a suitable goal. A result of
the inventory process can be the rank ordering of the frequency of types of assessments
and the appropriateness of the assessments, in relation to the teaching of reading assessment and students' development as independent readers.

USING SPECIFIC READING ASSESSMENT MATERIALS AND PROCEDURES TO TEACH READING ASSESSMENT

In this section we consider reading assessment materials and procedures that lend themselves to the teaching of reading assessment. These include teacher questioning and feedback, checklists, portfolios, and performance assessments. Evaluative materials and procedures, used in a classroom context that encourages student mindfulness and reflection,
may provide opportunities to teach reading assessment. We must help students internalize
what are at first external models of how to do assessment. Helping our students learn
reading assessment strategies to improve their ability to read independently is the goal.

Teacher Questioning and Oral Feedback to Students

Classroom talk is a first promising context for the explicit teaching of assessment strategies, including asking questions of one self while reading challenging text. For example,
when students are reading aloud, the teacher may ask questions at the end of a clause,
sentence, or paragraph. Asking "Does that make sense?" and "How do I know?" helps
focus students' attention on the meaning-making goal of reading. The questions call students' attention to the current portion of text read and remind them that they need to be
mindful and to check on their comprehension. Good question asking also provides a
model of the type of questions to ask and when to ask them. These questions may be
strikingly simple and direct from the perspective of the accomplished independent reader.
Yet, for readers who are beginning to evaluate their own reading, the questions represent
a foundation on which future independent reading is based. Teachers can build on these
foundations to introduce student readers to more complex self-assessment routines and
actions based on asking questions. For example, if the question, "Does that make sense?"
can be answered with an unequivocal "No," then the self-assessment serves as a call to
action that is followed by application of fix-it strategies. If there is a difficulty, attention is
given to that critical aspect of the meaning-making process. Students can reread if the
word seems out of place. This inward-looking stance represents a watershed event in students' development as self-assessing readers and mindful students in general. For more
accomplished readers, a suitable question might be, "Does the author's account of the
Mayaguez incident square with what you already know about it?"

Discourse research demonstrates that the I-R-E (Initiate–Respond–Evaluate) pattern
is a prevalent form of classroom talk (Cazden, 1986). Within this discourse pattern, the
teacher *Initiates* talk with a question, a student *Responds* to the question, and the teacher
then *Evaluates* the student's response. At its core, the IRE pattern can be evaluative: The
teacher evaluates the student's response. A challenge for teachers is to identify the good
assessment that can happen within an IRE pattern and to call students' attention to it.
For example, there is the opportunity for teachers to "talk around" the IRE. Thinking
out loud about why they are asking a particular question and how they are understand-

ing and evaluating the students response to the question helps teachers model the assessment behind the discourse. Consider a 5th-grade middle school classroom and the following interaction:

TEACHER: I am interested in how well each of you understood this section of the chapter. Remember, we will be writing about this chapter later today, so we need to check on our understanding of what we're reading. So I want to ask you about the main idea of the paragraph. What is the main idea? [Initiate]

STUDENT: It's about weights and levers . . . and gravity. [Response]

TEACHER: That's a good beginning, because you've identified important information in the text. [Evaluate] I am thinking about your answer in relation to our upcoming writing task.

In this classroom discourse excerpt, the teacher has taken the familiar IRE pattern and thought around it to inform students about self-assessment and to uncover details of how the student reading and response are evaluated. The teacher's thinking aloud may be done according to particular criteria, including a student's response in relation to the reading goal, the student's attention to the task at hand, and the student's progress. A key is to focus on the assessment process and the evaluative intent that are embedded in the IRE interaction. The feedback we give students should provide guidance on how they may improve their reading while illuminating the assessment process (Black & William, 1998).

Teacher thinking out loud during classroom discussion provides students with examples of how assessment happens. This uncovering of assessment makes the process more familiar to students and presents a model that students may eventually internalize. The seeds of successful student self-assessment are often planted by teachers' thoughtful questions and comments that help students focus their attention on details of critical importance. I note that effective classroom learning environments include a variety of classroom talk, including peer-led discussions and discussions that are not always initiated by the teacher. There are legitimate criticisms of IRE patterns when they restrict discourse and thought (Cazden, 1986; Mehan, 1979). However, should a teacher determine that IRE patterns are useful in the classroom, they may serve triple duty in modeling for children how to ask questions related to their reading, how to go about answering the question, and how to assess the ongoing question-asking and question-answering processes.

Checklists and Observation Forms

Checklists and observation forms provide students with concrete examples of what to focus on when conducting self-assessment and how to do so in a sequential and logical manner. Teachers may use checklists to monitor and describe students' decoding ability, sound–symbol correspondence knowledge, comprehension strategies, fluency, and motivation to read. Good teaching revolves around informed instructional decision making, and good teaching employs written and mental checklists that help us take note of a broad range of student reading behavior to fuel the decision-making process (Harp, 1996; Hill, Ruptic, & Norwick, 1998). Teachers' able use of checklists is normally formed over time in relation to particular teaching, curriculum, and student characteristics. These checklists may be written or mental, teacher made or commercially produced. In a manner similar to rubrics in performance assessment, checklists help map the problem terrain that students must cross to achieve in reading.

Critical to teaching reading assessment is having checklists and observation forms that are palpable—clearly understood by students and capable of giving guidance to developing student readers. How might students use checklists? Students may benefit from learning the contents of an observational checklist used by their teacher, be it a series of prompts to use comprehension strategies, to check on near term progress, or to align the reading performance at hand with a long-term goal. We may use a checklist to determine that students are reflecting while reading to see if they understand each paragraph that they read and if they regularly remind themselves of the purpose for reading a particular text and if they progress toward reading goals. A sample checklist that gives attention to these critical points in assessing one's own reading is provided in Figure 7.1.

A teacher's mental checklist can be revealed to students through teacher talk about reading assessment events. Teachers render private or public evaluations of students' reading, including decoding, comprehension, fluency, and self-correction behaviors. Much in the manner of reading assessment within the IRE discourse pattern, teacher explanations of reading checklist criteria and processes help students to better know assessment. Using such a checklist in a consistent manner offers students an opportunity to begin to internalize a focused and logical means for judging their own performance and progress in reading. Our work should center on helping students to practice with an explicit and helpful checklist so that it becomes a consistent and self-prompted part of their reading routine. We may think of checklists as a type of rubric, geared toward the self-assessment processes of reading. For example, a teacher can share aspects of a reading strategy checklist that helps students reflect on and evaluate their work. "When I complete each paragraph, I stop and check if I am understanding all that I have read so far, and I focus on why I am reading. I remind myself that I am reading because I need to find examples of the evidence that the author provides to support her argument. So I am checking this paragraph to see if it contains evidence, and to make sure that I can remember the evidence that the author does provide." Publicly displayed checklists will remind students to use them and how to use them, as will classroom discussions that are centered on the uses of checklists.

Let's begin with your goal for reading today. What is your goal?

As you finish each paragraph of the chapter, review the checklist to determine if you have been assessing your own reading.

_____ I remember why I am reading and I keep this goal in mind.
_____ I regularly assess my reading in relation to this goal.
_____ I ask the questions, "Does that make sense?" and "How do I know?"
_____ If I find a problem or difficulty, I remember the "If, then . . ." strategies we learned.
_____ I ask the question, "Am I understanding the text well enough to meet my goal?"

Remember that you can ask for help, but try to do so only after you've gone through each item on this checklist.

FIGURE 7.1. A reading checklist.

Performance Assessments

Performance assessments hold great promise for helping us teach self-assessment (Marzano, Pickering, & McTighe, 1993). Performance assessments offer a potential advantage over traditional multiple-choice tests because of their focus on processes and complex performances and products. So, too, performance assessment can introduce students to new levels of reading assessment complexity and sophistication. Students must undertake and succeed at increasingly complex reading and reading-related tasks throughout their school careers. The task of assessing this growth also builds in complexity. Performance assessments offer teachers and students the opportunity to further advance their reading assessment abilities as required by more demanding teaching and learning. For example, developing readers may be familiar with the task of answering "who," "what," "where," and "when" questions related to a story. The skillful use of self-assessment strategies helps readers determine if they understand the story so that they can answer such questions successfully. These readers will eventually encounter more complex texts and tasks. In turn, readers will be required to use increasingly sophisticated performances, including summarizing across texts, comparing texts, using information from texts to conduct inquiry, and critically evaluating the texts they read. Learning self-assessment for such complex operations is clearly needed, and performance assessments are a rich context in which to practice and learn such assessment.

Although performance assessments may offer a valid match of assessment with real life performance, they are a compelling challenge: Increased complexity and sophistication of reading performance must be paralleled by the development of complex and sophisticated assessment. A key aspect of evaluating student work within such performance assessments is the use of rubrics. Performance assessment rubrics provide detailed information, in the form of samples of performances, examples of scoring points in relation to gradations of performance, and models of what students must do to get particular grades or scores. Rubrics can communicate to students both the nature of the performance and the means to assessing that performance. Many of us have internalized evaluation routines into more or less well-defined rubrics for areas in which we have some correspondingly defined standards. These may pertain to washing a car, cooking, or throwing a Frisbee. Rubrics can provide a model and explanation to students on what must be done to earn a particular grade for a performance. In this sense, rubrics serve as a guide or map for student process and product. Rubrics may be internalized over time so that students approach complex tasks knowing what is needed, what is acceptable, and what attention to evaluation will get them. This is important when students are asked to perform complex and lengthy tasks and to monitor their attainment, processes, and learning at specified points in time or at a task. Models are available when teachers use the public display of rubrics to teach and guide student self-assessment. Finding a place on the classroom wall for a public display of reading rubrics and regularly referring to the rubric in classroom discussions will provide students with a consistent model of how assessment works and how their work will be evaluated.

Consider the rubric outline in Figure 7.2, which allows for both student and teacher ratings of the different aspects of the student's reading performance. The categories, "Using prereading strategies" and "Demonstrating an understanding of text," contain four and three aspects, respectively, that make up good performance and that the student

Directions to students: Please rate your ongoing performance in relation to the following criteria.

My teacher's rating	Using prereading strategies	My rating
1 2 3 4 5	Preview and skim text	1 2 3 4 5
1 2 3 4 5	Anticipate and predict meaning	1 2 3 4 5
1 2 3 4 5	Determine difficulty of vocabulary	1 2 3 4 5
1 2 3 4 5	Identify helpful resources	1 2 3 4 5
My teacher's rating	Demonstrating understanding of text	My rating
1 2 3 4 5	Answers to questions at end of chapter	1 2 3 4 5
1 2 3 4 5	Creating questions for the author	1 2 3 4 5
1 2 3 4 5	Using what is learned from text in a complex performance	1 2 3 4 5

FIGURE 7.2. A reading performance assessment rubric.

would need to monitor. Comparison of the student and teacher ratings provides ideal discussion points at which scoring and assessment details can be clarified and better understood. For example, the student can recount for the teacher how and how well she conducted the determination of difficulty of vocabulary. Discussion about this and other points of the rubric are purposely focused on what students must do to do well in their reading and what they must undertake to self-assess their reading. This is an example of the talk that can surround reading assessment and the learning of reading assessment.

Detailed and step-by-step rubrics provide information that helps readers focus on different critical features of their reading performance. Well-constructed scoring rubrics are a guide for students to do good work. Such rubrics help students understand intermediate goals to which they can scaffold their own work and progress, as part of a self-evaluative routine. Samples of student work discussed in relation to a scoring rubric may help students internalize a schema for increasingly complex self-assessment routines. As teachers, we need to provide feedback to students that is well aligned with scoring rubrics, to provide students with a consistent message and means for better understanding how they might assess themselves using rubrics.

Portfolios

The portfolio is ideally suited to helping students develop self-assessment. In fact, the portfolio can serve as a meeting point for diverse reading assessment materials and processes, including checklists and performance assessments. Reading portfolios have a multiplicity of possible uses (Tierney, Carter, & Desai, 1991): They may serve as both repository for reading assessment materials and procedures and a context in which to practice assessment processes. It is important to dedicate a portion of the portfolio to student reflection and the development of reading assessment routines. Portfolios provide students with an ideal context in which to become familiar with and practice self-assessment. The portfolio helps students learn to accurately assess their progress toward long-term goals, such as the development of a report that is based on the reading of several chapters and books. Students may concurrently compare drafts of their writing with the goal they have set for good performance at a project, using checklists and rubrics stored in the portfolio. It is critical to provide guidance on how different sections in the portfolio might serve assessment and evaluation purposes. This means creating structured routines in which both literacy growth and self-assessment prowess develop hand in hand.

In addition to helping students work on their self-assessment strategies, portfolio use can prove motivating, as it demonstrates to students both their progress at the reading task and their metacognitive control of the act of reading. For example, a portion of the portfolio with three distinct sections can be used to help a student independently self-assess and determine what vocabulary words are "known," what words are "being learned," and what words are "unfamiliar." This dedicated area can help young readers develop sight word vocabulary or help older readers learn new and more complex meanings for familiar words. As a result, the student increases and refines word knowledge and the means to assess this learning. A routine of self-assessment is learned. For a more accomplished student reader, motivation may follow (and accompany) a reader's iterations of the dramatic presentation that is being written, revised, and kept in a portfolio section. Repeated work with such materials can help students develop confidence in assessing their own knowledge and the processes with which they learn. Fostering student use of portfolios in this manner requires that teachers regularly model and explain the different ways in which portfolios facilitate self-assessment. Further, the portfolio can help students become and remain motivated to do the often arduous work of learning to accurately assess their reading. Portfolios provide a context in which students can understand the initiative and ability that are necessary for assessing their own works. They also provide a means for students to reflect on the quality and scope of their work in relation to reading goals.

Paper-and-Pencil Tests

Because paper-and-pencil tests demand often-scarce class time and because they may wield undue influence on curriculum (Frederiksen, 1984), we may be reluctant to devote time to teaching reading assessment in relation to such tests. However, paper-and-pencil tests offer an opportunity for useful student discussion about the different purposes for assessment. To the extent that paper-and-pencil tests sample the important outcomes of reading instruction, they may represent the opportunity to help students better understand how they will be assessed, how the reading assessment maps onto the act of reading, and the consequences of assessment. To the extent to which paper-and-pencil tests represent the valued outcomes of a reading program, working with test items to describe the outcomes may help students better understand how and why tests are used and the means by which their reading is evaluated. The more clear the relationship between the daily teaching and learning routine of the classroom and the test, the more beneficial a test may be to helping teach students about assessment and having them understand how assessment and learning are related.

Conclusions

The effectiveness of reading programs must ultimately be judged by students' ability to read independently. That many students do not progress beyond basic reading ability (Donahue et al., 1999) may be related to the fact that preparing students to do their own effective assessment is not a universal instructional priority. Without self-assessment abilities, student readers cannot be strategic in their monitoring nor in their attempts to meet reading challenges. Such students will be needy when held to standards of independence. Reading programs are often evaluated in relation to students' decoding, vocabulary, and comprehension skills and strategies. These programs are also judged on the diversity of types of texts to which they expose students. To this worthy list of criteria we must add the critical element of development in self-assessment to reading program evaluation.

The ability to self-assess is critical for each student's progress toward independent reading. Student independence is a highly valued outcome of reading instruction that is supported by voluminous reading research. It is also alluded to in the many district, state, and national documents related to reading standards. However, the ability to evaluate and assess one's own reading is not often easily learned. What is at first external must be gradually internalized by developing readers. Teaching reading assessment to foster students' reading independence must receive appropriate attention in the reading classroom. We need to consider the ways and means of helping students develop the ability to self-assess. The findings of comprehension strategy research suggest that rich models and explanations of good assessment practice by the teacher can contribute to the gradual learning and assumption of reading assessment responsibilities by students. The diverse array of reading assessment materials and procedures that may be used in teaching reading assessment includes teacher questions and feedback to students, portfolios, performance assessments, and teacher checklists. Existing reading assessment materials and procedures may provide useful contexts for modeling, explaining, and demonstrating the detail of good assessment practice. We need to help students develop independence by teaching explicitly the means for students to monitor and assess themselves as readers and learners.

A THEORETICAL AND PRACTICAL COURSE FOR TEACHING READING ASSESSMENT

I hope that this chapter has hinted at the considerable work that must be done to fully realize the value of developing readers' self-assessment strategies. The importance of teaching reading self-assessment strategies requires that future work, both practical and theoretical, be focused in several areas. Practical points of importance include the following:

- Reading program development must include a clear focus on students' reading assessment ability. Reading instruction materials and processes must be conceptualized with attention to assessment as a critical component of learning to read. Efforts to help students develop decoding and comprehension strategies and to develop increased fluency and vocabulary must be complemented with self-assessment strategies that help students read independently and successfully.
- Conducting an inventory of the reading assessments that are used in classrooms and schools will help determine where to make initial attempts to teach reading self-assessment strategies within an existing assessment program. Identifying an assessment that can do double or triple duty is important. For example, running records may provide the teacher with detailed and useful information about a student's reading, convince parents that the teacher knows their child well, and present an opportunity to teach the reading self-assessment strategy of self-correction. An inventory of existing assessments might lead to the determination that there are few that provide rich opportunity for teaching assessment.

• Teachers must become assessment experts to identify teachable moments. Expert teaching of self-assessment strategies also demands that teachers know the details of the reading assessment materials and procedures they use. This knowledge is invaluable as teachers attempt to scaffold, model, and explain reading assessment strategies for developing readers.

• Organizing assessment across the different content areas may contribute to students' learning to monitor all aspects of schoolwork, from reading literature to conducting a science investigation. For example, the use of a consistent form of reading checklist in social studies, science, math, and reading can help students more quickly internalize an increasingly automatic routine for checking on their reading. Similarly, a rubric form that is used across content areas provides the repeated opportunity for students to learn the details and nuances that distinguishes a "2" level performance from a "4" level performance. Such coordination will provide students with repeated messages of the importance of developing the ability to self-assess and with numerous models of how to do so. A reflective and evaluative stance that is developed through students' learning reading assessment may be fruitful across school content areas and their related reading and learning tasks.

• Successful classroom and school efforts to bring teaching of self-assessment strategies into the spotlight and programs that identify a priori the importance of learning to be one's own best assessor of reading should be documented. Sharing a blueprint of what works for a classroom or school may be a valuable resource to other teachers and administrators interested on placing more attention on teaching self-assessment strategies.

Theoretical issues of importance include:

• Investigations that describe in detail the concurrent development of reading self-assessment ability and reading strategies in general. We know that both contribute to reading achievement. Details of how decoding, vocabulary, comprehension, and fluency grow in relation to the development of reading self-assessment strategies will help optimize instruction that intentionally links the two. In addition, such knowledge will contribute to increasingly refined models of reading development.

• Examinations of the relationship between an increased emphasis on teaching reading self-assessment strategies and developing readers' epistemologies and their strategy use. That is, with increased self-assessment may come a better sense of how texts are written, how believable the content of text is, and how talented authors are (Afflerbach & VanSledright, 2001). When self-assessment is going well, readers better understand themselves in relation to the texts they read. A result of concerted efforts to teach assessment may be increased critical reading ability and students' increased sense of agency in acts of reading.

REFERENCES

Afflerbach, P. (1997). Reading assessment and learning to read. In J. Osborn & F. Lehr (Eds.), *Literacy for all: Issues in teaching and learning* (pp. 239–263). New York: Guilford Press.

Afflerbach, P., & Johnston, P. (1993). Writing language arts report cards: Eleven teachers' conflicts of knowing and communicating. *Elementary School Journal, 94*, 73–86.

Afflerbach, P., & VanSledright, B. (2001). Hath? Doth? What! The challenges middle school students face when reading innovative history text. *Journal of Adolescent and Adult Literacy, 44,* 696–707.

Alexander, P. (1997). Mapping the multidimensional nature of domain learning: The interplay of cognitive, motivational, and strategic forces. In M. Maehr & P. Pintrich (Eds.), *Advances in motivation and achievement* (Vol. 10, pp. 213–250). Greenwich, CT: JAI Press.

Baker, L., & Brown, A. (1991). Metacognitive skills in reading. In R. Barr, M. Kamil, P. Mosenthal, P. Pearson (Eds.), *Handbook of reading research* (2nd ed., pp. 353–394). New York: Longman.

Bazerman, C. (1985). Physicists reading physics: Schema-laden purposes and purpose-laden schema. *Written Communication, 2,* 3–24.

Beck, I., McKeown, M., Hamilton, R., & Kucan, L. (1997). *Questioning the author: An approach for enhancing student engagement with text.* Newark, DE: International Reading Association.

Black, P., & William, D. (1998). Inside the black box. *Phi Delta Kappan, 80,* 139–148.

Cazden, C. (1986). Classroom discourse. In M. Wittrock (Ed.), *Handbook of research on teaching* (3rd ed., pp. 432–462). New York: Macmillan.

Chi, M., Glaser, R., & Farr, M. (1988). *The nature of expertise.* Hillsdale, NJ: Erlbaum.

Clay, M. (1993). *Reading recovery: A guidebook for teachers in training.* Portsmouth, NH: Heinemann.

Donahue, P., Voelkl, K., Campbell, J., & Mazzeo, J. (1999). *NAEP 1998 reading report card for the nation.* Washington, DC: United States Department of Education.

Ericsson, K., & Smith, J. (1991). *Toward a general theory of expertise: Prospects and limits.* Cambridge, England: Cambridge University Press.

Flavell, J. (1978). Metacognitive aspects of problem solving. In L. Resnick (Ed.), *The nature of intelligence* (pp. 231–255). Hillsdale, NJ: Erlbaum.

Frederiksen, N. (1984). The real test bias: Influences of testing on teaching and learning. *American Psychologist, 39,* 193–202.

Garner, R. (1987). *Metacognition and reading comprehension.* Norwood, NJ: Ablex.

Goodman, K., & Goodman, Y. (1977). Learning about psycholinguistic processes by analyzing oral reading. *Harvard Educational Review, 47,* 317–333.

Hacker, D. (1998). Self-regulated comprehension during normal reading. In D. Hacker, J. Dunlosky, & A. Graesser (Eds.), *Metacognition in educational theory and practice* (pp. 165–191). Mahwah, NJ: Erlbaum.

Harp, B. (1996). *The handbook of literacy assessment and evaluation.* Norwood, MA: Christopher Gordon.

Hill, B., Ruptic, C., & Norwick, L. (1998). *Classroom based assessment.* Norwood, MA: Christopher Gordon.

Johnston, P. (1997). *Knowing literacy: Constructive literacy assessment.* York, ME: Stenhouse.

Johnston, P., & Afflerbach, P. (1985). The process of constructing main ideas from text. *Cognition and Instruction, 2*(3–4), 207–232.

Kucan, L., & Beck, I. (1997). Thinking aloud and reading comprehension research: Inquiry, instruction, and social interaction. *Review of Educational Research, 67,* 271–299.

Liepzig, D., & Afflerbach, P. (2000). Determining the suitability of assessments: Using the CURRV framework. In L. Baker, M. J. Dreher, & J. M. Guthrie (Eds.), *Engaging young readers: Promoting achievement and motivation* (pp. 159–187). New York: Guilford Press.

Markman, E. (1977). Realizing that you don't understand: A preliminary investigation. *Child Development, 50,* 643–655.

Marzano, R., Pickering, D., & McTighe, J. (1993). *Assessing student outcomes: Performance assessment using the dimensions of the learning model.* Alexandria, VA: Association for Supervision and Curriculum Development.

Mehan, H. (1979). *Learning lessons: Social organization in the classroom*. Cambridge, MA: Harvard University Press.

National Council of Teachers of English/International Reading Association. (1996). *Standards for the English language arts*. Urbana, IL: National Council of Teachers of English.

Olshavsky, J. (1976–1977). Reading as problem solving: An investigation of strategies. *Reading Research Quarterly, 12,* 654–674.

Palincsar, A., & Brown, A. (1984). Reciprocal teaching of comprehension-fostering and monitoring activities. *Cognition and Instruction, 1,* 117–175.

Paris, S., Wasik, B., & Turner, J. (1991). The development of strategic readers. In R. Barr, M. Kamil, P. Mosenthal, & P. Pearson (Eds.), *Handbook of reading research* (Vol. 2, pp. 609–640). Hillsdale, NJ: Erlbaum.

Pressley, M., & Afflerbach, P. (1995). *Verbal reports of reading: The nature of constructively responsive reading*. Hillsdale, NJ: Erlbaum.

Pressley, M., El-Dinary, P., Gaskins, I., Schuder, T., Bergman, J., Almasi, J., & Brown, R. (1992). Beyond direct explanation: Transactional instruction of reading comprehension strategies. *Elementary School Journal, 92,* 511–554.

Snow, C., Burns, M., & Griffin, P. (Eds.). (1998). *Preventing reading difficulties in young children*. Washington, DC: National Academy Press.

Tierney, R., Carter, M., & Desai, L. (1991). *Portfolio assessment in the reading–writing classroom*. Norwood, MA: Christopher Gordon.

VanSledright, B., & Afflerbach, P. (2000). Reconstructing Andrew Jackson: Prospective elementary teachers' readings of revisionist history texts. *Theory and Research in Social Education, 28,* 411–444.

Vygotsky, L. (1978). *Mind in society: The development of higher psychological processes*. Cambridge, MA: Harvard University Press.

II

Branching Out and Expanding Our Horizons in the 21st Century

8

Reading in Web-Based Learning Environments

HILLER A. SPIRES
THOMAS H. ESTES

As teaching and learning increasingly take place within Web-based environments, literacy theorists, researchers, and practitioners are defining the nature of reading that occurs in the context of hypertext technology. We are only beginning to acquire insights into the potentials of emerging technologies that are saturating our society at an accelerated rate. Likewise, we are just beginning to create viable technological environments for literacy instruction. With its increasing capacity for access to an ever-growing body of information employing hypertext, hypermedia, and multimedia, the World Wide Web (WWW) affords exciting opportunities, as well as looming challenges, for literacy educators.

What exactly is the nature of *reading* within Web-based environments? How is reading traditional print different from reading hypertext? How can we design instruction that facilitates the developmental nature of the reading process within these new environments? What research should be conducted that will contribute to theoretical and practical constructs that will enable us to reasonably and effectively incorporate these technologies into teaching? In order to answer these questions, we examined existing research and theory to discern key characteristics involved in processing hypertext. Although research in specific Web-based instructional environments is in its infant stages, early research on hypertext provides an appropriate lens through which to begin viewing and interpreting the potential of Web-based instruction and ultimately helping to inform reading instructional practices.

WHAT IS HYPERTEXT?

Ted Nelson coined the term "hypertext" in the 1960s, referring primarily to text that was accessible in a nonsequential, user-directed format (Boyle, 1997). Long before Nelson offered the definition and in the years since, hypertext has been studied in a variety of do-mains, including education, computer science, psychology, linguistics, and graphic design. In 1945, Bush created the initial idea of user-assigned pathways among information with his *memex*. While nonlinear database text systems were implemented in the 1960s, it wasn't until the late 1980s and early 1990s that a relatively small number of stand-alone hypertexts were generated, including original works of fiction. One such work was Joyce's (1987) *Afternoon*, which used hypertext technology to create a very different experience for the reader, including shifting points of view within the narrative.

Currently, the most popular example of hypertext is the WWW, which incorporates a wide range of textual genres and subject domains and represents a radical departure from how we have historically obtained information. Using a variety of Web-search programs, an interested reader can locate articles and information on practically any topic. Magazines, newspapers, and reference sources of every description are available with a click or a keystroke. It is noteworthy that the *Encyclopedia Britannica* recently announced that it will no longer market its venerable hardbound collection to homes. Instead, this encyclopedia is now available free of charge on the Web or for a modest price on CD. Most of *Britannica*'s electronic articles contain embedded hyperlinks to topically related Web sites. Other encyclopedias, such as *World Book* and *Encarta*, offer similar hypertext features, as do a number of well-known dictionaries, including the complete *Oxford English Dictionary* (available on CD or on-line for a subscription fee). In the very near future, readers will commonly "buy" books by downloading electronic versions from the Web and paying a fee to the author or publisher. Recently, a short novel by mystery writer Stephen King was offered in e-book form for download to portable reading devices. The offer generated more than 400,000 orders in the first 24 hours of availability. Because the hypertext environment is so rapidly replacing traditional print offerings in a wide variety of genres, readers are challenged to accommodate the textual changes, both cognitively and aesthetically, that hypertext environments present to comprehension.

Hypertext challenges many long-standing assumptions and perspectives that have evolved from theory and research with print-based reading. Key differences between hypertext and traditional print relate to textual boundaries, mobility, and navigation. On the computer monitor, the reader sees less text at any given juncture and cannot easily transport text from one physical location to another but is allowed to choose from multiple paths through a body of text. Rather than reading from top to bottom across a page and front to back from page to page, readers navigate unique paths that they forge through a network of text nodes. Christina Haas (1996) refers to the challenge of "getting a sense of the text" on screen that the reader of traditional print texts does not face.

Another essential difference between text and hypertext, and one that is frequently cited by theorists, is that of linearity. Hypertext challenges the presumption of linearity—the need for a well-defined textual beginning and end. Rather than accepting the linear–nonlinear dichotomy, however, Bolter (1998) refers to the fluidity of hypertext. Typically, one thinks of standard text as being read in a linear fashion and hypertext in a nonlinear fashion. Bolter (1998) argues that hypertext is not nonlinear but rather multilinear. Traditional print is designed to be read in one direction, in one order, and in one predetermined pattern that may cause confusion when read in an order other than that offered by the author. Hypertext, by contrast, is designed to allow the reader to forge cross-connections among subtopics, to make directional choices.

One of the intriguing aspects of hypertext is that it provides a literal and physical dimensionality for "constructing" text that previous textual forms have not afforded. Readers traditionally relied on the author to select topics, to determine logical progression of ideas, and to signal essential relationships among the topics through the use of discourse conventions such as transitional words and phrases, subheadings, and paragraphs. In many ways hypertext provides the embodiment of the poststructural concept of a reader constructing a text or collaborating with the text to make meaning. Purves (1998) referred to this phenomenon as the difference between internal and external construction. Within a hypertext environment, the reader is literally constructing a text by the choices he or she makes and thus weakening the authority of the author and the dominance of the text. The result is a more egalitarian relationship between reader and writer (Bolter, 1991; Landow, 1992). Purves (1998) noted that in hypertext the reader can manipulate the text (e.g., record, delete, supplement, and ignore parts of the text) as he or she deems appropriate, thus providing a whole new sense of agency to the reader. With this invitation for readers to take a more involved role in the reading process, van Oostendorp and de Mul (1996) claim that students need more cognitive energy to "make meaning" as they actively determine optimal routes through information networks and constuct information frameworks based on the idiosyncratic nature of the paths they forged.

As we think historically about the theoretical definition and progression of comprehension processes, from behavioral to cognitive to social constructivist, it appears that Web-based reading may lead us to the threshold of a new theoretical domain, what may be called *Web transactions*. We use this term to imply a juxtaposition of Louise Rosenblatt's (1978) well-established notion of reader–text transaction to the salient features of Web-based reading, which are not physically and literally possible within traditional print environments. With the many freedoms, choices, and possibilities that the Web presents, challenges and potential negative consequences for learning also emerge.

It is possible that the freedom of choice and interest that drives the reading process in hypertext can become diverted by potential cognitive overload—hypertext may tend to amplify trivia and highlight seductive details that lead directly to recall of inappropriate knowledge (Harp & Mayer, 1998; Garner & Brown, 1992; Birkerts, 1995). Meyer and Rose (1998) offer this summary of the problem:

> As early as 1913, Dewey cautioned teachers against "fictitious inducements to attention." Studies have supported his warning, demonstrating the ineffectiveness of inserting intriguing detail in expository writing in an effort to attract students' attention and keep them engaged in the text. This "seductive detail" (as interesting but unimportant information added to text is called) does attract students' attention, but has no positive effect on reading comprehension because it is irrelevant to the subject itself. In some cases, it distracts from important information and actually diminishes student recall. (1998, p. 4)

An instructional assumption that is regularly made by educators is that the hypertext nature of the WWW and the freedom of choice that it affords will facilitate students' understanding and use of large amounts of textual information. In some studies of hypertext, however, readers actually found hypertext more difficult to read than linear text (see Gordon, Gustavel, Moore, & Hankey, 1988; Rouet, Levonen, Dillon, & Spiro, 1996). Related to this issue, Shapiro (1998) found that her hierarchical system of information did not present a reader advantage over a linearly ordered one with respect to knowledge retention or quality of written essays. Shapiro concluded that in order to make hypertext advantageous as a learning tool, supportive links must be included to prompt readers to think explicitly about the information relationships they are encountering. A second assumption often made by educators is that students can critically evaluate their Web-based resources, a task that has been historically relegated to editors of traditional print publishing companies. Because the flexibility inherent in Web-based learning may allow too much freedom for some students to handle, teachers must determine how much freedom is appropriate and simultaneously teach students strategies for handling their new freedom. Fortunately, a number of recently designed on-line tools and activities address the potential problem of unlimited freedom. One particularly promising organizational tool is the WebQuest (Dodge, 1995). This Web-based set of instructional activities can provide instructional scaffolding as teachers and students take advantage of the Web's informational resources in a directed, focused way.

WEBQUESTS: SCAFFOLDED INSTRUCTION FOR READING ON THE WORLD WIDE WEB

WebQuests are inquiry-oriented units of study that propose an open-ended problem for students to solve with the resources put at their disposal in the hypertext environment. These instructional modules incorporate information available on the Web with a variety of other resources. Though a WebQuest is presented as a Web page, much of what a student learns in the Quest is learned by textbook reading, supplemental reading, and study in other sources, as well as independent activities related to the topic of the unit. These might include interviewing and reporting, observation and note taking, survey research, and many other "real-life" experiences that students write about. A thorough description of WebQuests can be found at http://www.edweb.sdsu.edu/courses/edtec596/about_webquests.html. Examples of WebQuests done by students at the University of Virginia can be found at http://www.curry.edschool.virginia.edu/go/edis771/classwebquests.html. An index of WebQuests by students and teachers at a variety of schools and universities can be seen at http://www.edweb.sdsu.edu/webquest/webquest_collections.htm

WebQuests provide instructional scaffolding for the teacher and the learner, as they navigate Web resources. In this context, reading is no longer done for its own sake or merely to "know" what the textbook says in order to pass a test. The Quest has a purpose, a problem that reading can help to solve, and this puts reading and study in an entirely new light. Because the Quest directs readers to text of varying levels of difficulty on the same topic, all students have a chance to participate, to contribute to the project, and to learn. A WebQuest serves several useful functions: It is an organizing tool; it leverages the best features of the Web, namely the ability to make choices about types of information and the flexibility to access that information immediately; and it allows the reader to be involved in a construction of meaning.

The home page of a WebQuest on ancient China, created by a high school social studies teacher, Griffin Fernandez of Charlottesville High School, illustrates the general organizational structure of most WebQuests. This WebQuest was adapted from a lesson created by David Goldfarb, a ninth-grade world history teacher at Chantilly High School in Virginia. (These teachers never met face to face but were able to collaborate on the construction of a unit of study they were both interested in teaching.) This WebQuest exposes students to three of the most important philosophies that emerged from the "Era of a Hundred Schools" in China. Through role plays, students are exposed to the basic ideas underlying Confucianism, Taoism, and Legalism and are asked to consider the benefits and problems of governments based on these belief systems. In addition to providing an explanation of the task and the process that will engage the students, Fernandez articulated a clear evaluation rubric so students will understand his expectations for the assignment. The screen shots in Figure 8.1 give a flavor of the work Fernandez's students will do as they engage in the WebQuests.

WebQuests are undergirded by key instructional principles that (1) allow teachers and students to set a purposeful context for reading in which everyone can participate; (2) give readers access to information on a topic at several levels of readability/difficulty; (3) provide multimedia (e.g., audio, video) dimensions to enhance the learning/reading process; (4) create opportunities for students to participate in social construction of meaning and consensus building; (5) create opportunities for students to synthesize ideas across multiple source documents; and (6) provide scaffolding for cognitive processing of text.

The scaffolding instructional process occurs on two levels. First, students' cognitive processing of text is supported by small-group collaborations in which key textual ideas are socially constructed and agreed on by class members. Likewise, solutions to problem-solving activities that are based on essential text ideas are reached through negotiation and consensus building. Teachers and students create a shared intellectual and social space within the hypertextual zone of proximal development (ZPD). Reading practitioners and researchers alike have long relied on Vygotsky's ZPD to help explain the learner's acquisition of higher mental processes. Vygotsky (1978) defines this zone as "the distance between the actual development level as determined by independent problem-solving and the level of potential development as determined through problem-solving under adult guidance or in collaboration with more capable peers" (1978, p. 86). Stu-

TABLE 8.1. Cognitive Skills That May Be Included in WebQuests

Comparing	Identifying and articulating similarities and differences between things
Classifying	Grouping things into definable categories on the basis of their attributes
Inducing	Inferring unknown generalizations or principles from observations or analysis
Deducing	Inferring unstated consequences and conditions from given principles and generalizations
Analyzing errors	Identifying and articulating errors in one's own or other's thinking
Constructing support	Constructing a system of support or proof for an assertion
Abstraction	Identifying and articulating the underlying theme or general pattern of information
Analyzing perspectives	Identifying and articulating personal perspectives about issues

Note. From Marzano (1992, as cited in Dodge, 1995).

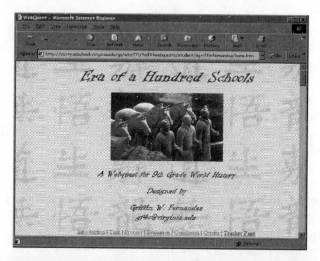

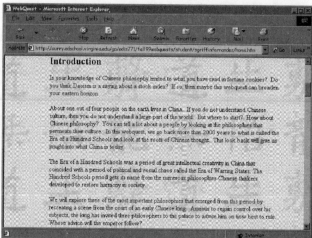

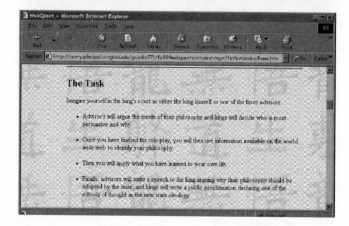

FIGURE 8.1. Sample Ninth-Grade World History WebQuest. For full viewing of this site, go to *http://www.curry/edschool.virginia.edu/go/edis771/fall99webquests/student/sgriffinferandez/home.htm.* Screen shots reprinted by permission of Microsoft Corporation.

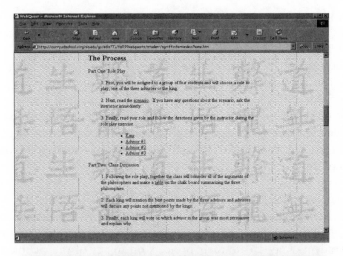

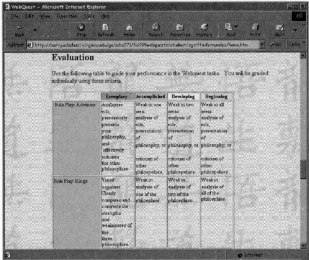

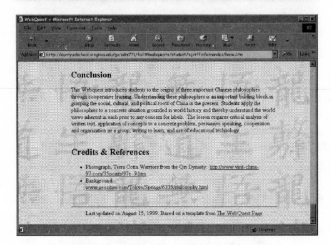

FIGURE 8.1. (*continued*)

dents may be involved in a range of higher order mental processes depending on how the Quest is designed. Table 8.1 depicts a possible range of cognitive processing activities that may be included.

Second, because key Web sources are predetermined by the teacher, the complexity of text-driven ideas from multiple Web sources may be controlled. The scaffolding process unfolds as the teacher thoughtfully guides students' reading and learning by designing increasingly difficult and more complex WebQuests. The ultimate goal is for students to internalize the cognitive processing skills necessary to complete a WebQuest by developing their own mental map of the process. Eventually, the scaffolded instructional process progresses to the point at which students create their own WebQuests on topics pertinent to their interests.

Teachers who are interested in developing WebQuests but who do not possess Web-development skills may visit the Filamentality site at http://www.filamentality.com/wired/fil/. This site provides complete directions, as well as a template, for creating WebQuests. Teachers and students may create their projects on topics of their choice employing the user-friendly template, as well as house their work free of charge for up to 6 months. We have used this site in the content-area reading courses that we teach at our respective universities in order to provide a relatively painless point of entry to Web-based instruction for both preservice and in-service teachers. In many ways, WebQuests may provide structure for bringing time-honored reading approaches such as the directed reading thinking activity (Stauffer, 1969), reciprocal teaching (Palincsar & Brown, 1984; Rosenshine & Meister, 1994), and literature study circles (Samway & Whang, 1996; Noe & Johnson, 1999) into the information technology age. Given the complex nature of reading in hypertextual, Web-based environments, WebQuests have the potential to help teachers and students use Web resources in a focused, directed way for reading and learning.

DIRECTIONS FOR FUTURE RESEARCH

Whether or not we believe that the Internet, and specifically the WWW, is the most revolutionary invention since the printing press, it is a medium with definite consequences for education. The WWW has captured the public imagination, and in that regard it is powerful and influential. As a result, several essential issues for educational researchers must be addressed.

1. *We believe that the evaluation of Web-based teaching and learning must be approached from a multidisciplinary stance.* Internet research reflects methodological paradigms from such disciplines as education, psychology, sociology, literacy criticism, anthropology, and communication, using both qualitative and quantitative approaches. Because no single discipline has cornered the market on Web-based research, borrowing from different areas based on the nature of the research can be beneficial for everyone.

2. *We believe that it is important to develop and continue parallel lines of research—the benefits of information technologies on learning and how best to support teachers in this endeavor.* One line of research will mutually and naturally inform the other. Leu and Kinzer (2000) argue that efficacy research on the use of information technologies often is less important than simple observation about the changing nature of literacy. Leu (2000) argues that research might be better spent in exploring issues of how to

support teachers' efforts to unlock the potentials of new technologies and not in demonstrating the learning gains from technologies we already know will be important to our children's success with life opportunities.

3. *We agree with Kamil and Lane (1998) that what is missing from the literature is systematic analysis of the relationship between reading hypertext and reading conventional text.* In the same way that researchers investigated the comprehension processes and comprehension instruction with traditional print in past decades (see Lysynchuk, Pressley, d'Ailly, Smith, & Cake, 1989; Pearson & Fielding, 1991; Pressley, 2000), we need to investigate comprehension processes on the WWW. For example, based on decades of research, we have extensive information on the roles of prior knowledge, metacognition, and rhetorical structures and how each construct affects comprehension with print. Within a Web-based reading environment, however, will these constructs serve similar functions, or will they evolve and change in ways not yet considered? And if these established theories do hold up, are they robust enough to paint a complete picture of Web-based comprehension? Or will we need new theories that will complement existing theories?

One potential avenue for answering these and related research questions is through the employment of verbal reports and protocol analysis. Although not without their methodological challenges (see Afflerbach, 2000), verbal reports and protocol analysis have been used constructively in the areas of literary response (Beach & Hynds, 1991), cognition and instruction (Pressley & Afflerbach, 1995), and computer interface design. It seems reasonable that this approach can be used to help uncover potential cognitive processes inherent in Web-based reading environments that have not yet been articulated. These findings may contribute to scaffolded reading instructional strategies that will support teachers and students as they negotiate the challenges of reading on the Web.

4. *We agree that future research does not need to focus on whether hypertext is more useful than traditional text. Rather, research should focus first on rich theoretical descriptions of comprehension processes during Web-based reading and learning and second on how to provide scaffolded instruction for students to read effectively on the Web in ways that facilitate established learning outcomes.* A possible venue for beginning this research agenda is through comprehensive and detailed study of Web-based instructional tools such as WebQuests. By incorporating both qualitative and quantitative methodologies and by casting a wide research net across a variety of disciplines, we will optimize our potential for forging research pathways that will boldly and wisely lead educators into the information technology era.

REFERENCES

Afflerbach, P. (2000). Verbal reports and protocol analysis. In M. Kamil, P. Mosenthal, P. D. Pearson, & R. Barr (Eds.), *Handbook of reading research* (Vol. 3, pp.163–179). Mahwah, NJ: Erlbaum.

Beach, R., & Hynds, S. (1991). Research on response to literature. In R. Barr, M. L. Kamil, P. B. Mosenthal, & P. D. Pearson (Eds.), *Handbook of reading research* (Vol. 2, pp. 453–489). New York: Longman.

Birkerts, S. (1995). *The Gutenberg elegies.* New York: Ballentine Books.

Bolter, J. (1991). *Writing space: The computer, hypertext, and the history of writing.* Hillsdale, NJ: Erlbaum.

Bolter, J. D. (1998). Hypertext and the question of visual literacy. In D. Reinking, M. McKenna, L. Labbo, & R. Kieffer (Eds.), *Handbook of literacy and technology: Transformations in a post-typographic world* (pp. 3–13). Mahwah, NJ: Erlbaum.

Boyle, T. (1997). *Design for multimedia learning.* London, England: Prentice Hall.

Bush, V. (1986). As we may think. In Lambert & S. Ropiequte (Eds.), *CD-ROM: The new papyrus.* Redmond, WA: Miscrosoft Press. [Reprinted from *The Atlantic Monthly* (1945, July). 101–108]

Dodge, B. (1995). *Some thoughts about WebQuests.* Retrieved 1/15/99 from the World Wide Web: http://www.edweb.sdsu.edu/courses/edtec596/about_webquests.html.

Garner, R., & Brown, R. (1992). Seductive details and learning from text. In A. K. Renninger, S. Hidi, & A. Krapp (Eds.), *The role of interest in learning and development* (pp. 239–254). Hillsdale, NJ: Erlbaum.

Gordon, S., Gustavel, J., Moore, J., & Hankey, J. (1988). The effects of hypertext on reader knowledge representation. In *Proceedings of the 32nd Annual Meeting of the Human Factors Society, 32,* 296–300. Santa Monica, CA: The Human Factros Society.

Haas, C. (1996). *Writing technology: Studies in the materiality of literacy.* Mahwah, NJ: Erlbaum.

Harp, S. F., & Mayer, R. E. (1998). How seductive details do their damage: A theory of cognitive interest in science learning. *Journal of Educational Psychology, 90*(3), 414–434.

Joyce, M. (1987). *Afternoon* [Computer program]. Cambridge, MA: Eastgate Press.

Kamil, M., & Lane, D. (1998). Researching the relationship between technology and literacy: An agenda for the 21st century. In D. R. Reinking, L. D. Labbo, M. McKenna, & R. Kieffer (Eds.), *Literacy for the 21st century: Technological transformations in a post-typographic world* (pp. 323–342). Mahwah, NJ: Erlbaum.

Landow, G. P. (1992). *Hypertext: The convergence of contemporary critical theory and technology.* Baltimore: Johns Hopkins University Press.

Leu, D. J. (2000). Literacy and technology: Deictic consequences for literacy education in an information age. In M. Kamil, P. Mosenthal, P. D. Pearson, & R. Barr (Eds.), *Handbook of reading research* (Vol. 3, pp. 743–788). Mahwah, NJ: Erlbaum.

Leu, D. J., & Kinzer, C. (2000). The convergence of literacy instruction with networked technologies for information and communication. *Reading Research Quarterly, 35,* 108–127.

Lysynchuk, L. M., Pressley, M., d'Ailly, H., Smith, M., & Cake, H. (1989). A methodological analysis of experimental studies of comprehension strategy instruction. *Reading Research Quarterly, 24,* 458–470.

Marzano, R. J. (1992). *A different kind of classroom: Teaching with dimensions of learning.* Alexandria, VA: Association for Supervision and Curriculum Development.

Meyer, A., & Rose, D. H. (1998). *Learning to read in a computer age.* Peabody, MA: Center for Applied Special Technology. Retrieved 1/15/2000 from the World Wide Web: http://cast.org/LearningToRead.

Noe, K., & Johnson, N. (1999). *Getting started with literature circles.* Norwood, MA: Christopher Gordon.

Palincsar, A., & Brown, A. (1984). Reciprocal teaching of comprehension-fostering and monitoring activities. *Cognition and Instruction, 1,* 117–175.

Pearson, P. D., & Fielding, L. (1991). Comprehension instruction. In R. Barr, M. L. Kamil, P. B. Mosenthal, & P. D. Pearson (Eds.), *Handbook of reading research* (Vol. 2, pp. 815–860). New York: Longman.

Pressley, M. (2000). What should comprehension instruction be the instruction of? In M. Kamil, P. Mosenthal, P. D. Pearson, & R. Barr (Eds.), *Handbook of reading research* (Vol. 3, pp. 545–561). Mahwah, NJ: Erlbaum.

Pressley, M., & Afflerbach, P. (1995). *Verbal protocols of reading: The nature of constructively responsive reading.* Hillsdale, NJ: Erlbaum.

Purves, A. (1998). Flies in the web of hypertext. In D. R. Reinking, L. D. Labbo, M. McKenna, &

R. Kieffer (Eds.), *Literacy for the 21st century: Technological transformations in a post-typographic world* (pp. 235–251). Mahwah, NJ: Erlbaum.

Rosenblatt, L. (1978). *The reader, the text, the poem.* Carbondale, IL: Southern Illinois University Press.

Rosenshine, B., & Meister, C. (1994). Reciprocal teaching: A review of nineteen experimental studies. *Review of Educational Research, 64,* 479–530.

Rouet, J., Levonen, J., Dillon, A., & Spiro, R. (Eds.). (1996). *Hypertext and cognition.* Mahwah, NJ: Erlbaum.

Samway, K., & Whang, G. (1996). *Literature study circles in a multicultural classroom.* York, ME: Stenway.

Shapiro, A. (1998). Promoting active learning: The role of system structure in learning from hypertext. *Human–Computer Interaction, 13*(1), 1–36.

Stauffer, R. G. (1969). *Directing reading maturity as a cognitive process.* New York: Harper & Row.

van Oostendorp, H., & de Mul, S. (Eds.). (1996). *Cognitive aspects of electronic text processing.* Norwood, NJ: Ablex.

Vygotsky, L. S. (1978). *Mind and society.* Cambridge, MA: Harvard University Press.

9

Using the Theme Scheme to Improve Story Comprehension

JOANNA P. WILLIAMS

Stories have been used through the ages not only to entertain but also to teach. From the epics of Homer to the anecdotes that mothers tell their children, narratives depict situations that reflect human complexities and conflicts. Information is presented in the form of concrete examples, which illustrate how the knowledge that is imparted is related to real-life situations.

The power of narratives to foster socialization and educational goals is reflected in the fact that fables and folk tales are universally featured in moral education (Tappan & Brown, 1989; Vitz, 1990). Discussions of case histories and problem instances are central to most clinical and educational programs in interpersonal problem solving (Shure & Spivack, 1978; Williams & Ellsworth, 1990). There is a program in child psychotherapy that is built around the exchange of stories by child and therapist (Gardner, 1987), and in bibliotherapy, stories are the primary vehicles for introducing and exploring problematic issues. School curricula also use a substantial amount of narrative in content area instruction, (e.g., biographies of notable figures in social studies classes).

Narrative is relatively easy to comprehend, partly because stories typically deal with familiar characters and situations. The structure of the text can also promote comprehension. Through exposure to countless stories during their early years—from being read to, as well as from movies, TV, even gossip—children develop a grasp of narrative structure. This structure provides an organizing framework that helps focus attention on the important information in the story (Hansen, 1978; Weaver & Dickinson, 1982; Williams, 1998). In other words, knowledge of text structure helps students discover what is likely to be most relevant for understanding the story.

Even preschool children are sensitive to story structure. In a classic study, Mandler and Johnson (1977) showed that when a story is presented in scrambled form so that the components of the underlying story grammar do not appear in their typical order, preschool children remember less of it. Thus, by the time they start school, children have developed at least a rudimentary grasp of narrative structure. The early ability to use this knowledge to aid comprehension continues to improve with age. Older children are better than younger ones at identifying important story information, such as characters and goals, as well as such subtle story events as the feelings of the characters (Beach & Wendler, 1987; van den Broek, 1997).

However, students with learning disabilities develop this knowledge of narrative text structure slowly. Compared with their normally achieving peers, they are poorer at such tasks as picking out important story information (van den Broek, 1997) and making inferences (Cain, 1996, Oakhill, 1984). Although there are few relevant studies that address higher order processing, there is evidence that students with learning disabilities are less able to identify the theme of a story (Williams, 1993).

The purpose of this chapter is to describe an instructional program that teaches children how to identify story themes and to present empirical evidence of the effectiveness of the program. First, I provide some background information about previous efforts at theme instruction, and at the end of the chapter I discuss implications for research and practice.

INTERVENTIONS GUIDED BY NARRATIVE TEST STRUCTURE

Many interventions addressing the comprehension of narrative text have been devoted to building a knowledge of text structure and then teaching students how to use it to analyze the stories they read. These interventions typically involve teaching the students to identify the principal components of a story and then to use this knowledge as an organizational guide when reading. That is, students learn to look for the main character, the central action, and the outcome as they read. Evidence from studies involving students with learning disabilities (as well as with nondisabled students) provide persuasive evidence that such instruction focused on text structure is effective.

Carnine and Kinder (1985), for example, taught elementary students with learning disabilities to generate four generic story grammar questions: "Who is the story about?" "What are they trying to do?" "What happens when they try to do it?" and "What happens at the end?" The use of this strategy, along with the incorporation of general principles of direct instruction (e.g., explicitness, repetition, and feedback; Brophy & Good, 1986; Gersten & Carnine, 1986), led to substantial improvement in performance on short-answer comprehension questions and on free-recall measures.

Idol and Croll (1987) worked with five elementary students with mild learning handicaps and poor reading comprehension. The instruction involved a story map instead of a series of questions. The components of the story map included setting (characters, time, and place), problem, goal, action, and outcome. Four of the five students gained from this training. They answered more comprehension questions, provided better story retellings, and scored higher on standardized reading tests. All four students also maintained their higher performance level when they were no longer directed to use the story-mapping strategy. In addition, three of the four evidenced some generalization to classroom reading materials.

In a related study, Idol (1987) used a similar mapping strategy to teach groups of children with varied abilities at the third- and fourth-grade levels. The instruction followed a typical teacher-model, teacher-assist, and independent-practice paradigm. A high performance level was achieved, was maintained when students were no longer required to use the strategy, and generalized to measures of listening comprehension, criterion-referenced tests, and spontaneous story writing.

THEME

The studies described here focused entirely on plot level. But the meaning of a story is not limited to its plot; many stories, including those that are traditionally told to young children, embody another level of meaning that goes beyond the specific plot. Full comprehension implies an understanding of this level, too; that is, of the general theme that the story exemplifies. Children gradually learn to comprehend this level of a story. Like other types of comprehension, it presents a challenge to some children, who require help in achieving success.

Lehr (1988) defined theme as a concept, such as friendship or courage. According to Lukens (1988), a theme is "the idea that holds the story together, such as a comment about either society, human nature, or the human condition" (p. 101). Our definition encompasses both of these notions: We define theme as a commentary attached to a core concept (Williams, Brown, Silverstein, & deCani, 1994). In the classic fable about the tortoise and the hare, for example, the theme is not "the tortoise did not stop; he kept moving slowly toward the finish line, and he won the race": This statement is at the plot level. Nor is the theme simply "perseverance": That is the core concept. The theme is based on the lesson that the tortoise learns (as does the hare): "You can succeed if you keep trying and don't give up." Readers can learn the lesson, too: "We should keep trying."

How does one identify the theme? Dorfman and Brewer (1994) investigated children's comprehension of one specific type of story, the fable, in which the theme is the didactic lesson embodied in the text. Dorfman and Brewer proposed that in order to identify the theme of a fable, one must attend to two of the basic plot components: the central event and the outcome. Given the event, one evaluates the outcome in terms of one's moral understanding; this evaluation is essentially a moral judgment. The combination of the plot components and the evaluation results in the theme. For example, if the event is an evil action such as stealing and the outcome is negative for the thief, the story communicates a lesson/theme such as "One should not steal." According to Dorfman and Brewer (1994), people make these judgments in terms of the "just-world" hypothesis, that is, the idea that the world is or should be just (Lerner, 1980).

Our definition of theme follows and expands on Dorfman and Brewer (1994). A theme expresses a relationship among story components in a form that is abstracted from the specific story context, and it comments on that relationship in some way. The commentary can take the form of a lesson (with a value judgment), as in a fable, or it can consist simply of an observation, with no value judgment attached ("Some people steal," or "When he is hungry, a man may do bad things"). This commentary operates at the concept level, not the plot level; that is, the lesson or the observation is generalized beyond the specifics of the particular story plot.

Although theme is an important concept, it has not been the focus of much research, and there have been less than a handful of instructional studies on theme. Gurney, Gersten, Dimino, and Carnine (1990) examined the effectiveness of a story grammar (text structure) instructional approach to teaching comprehension of literature to high school students with learning disabilities. Seven low-performing students whose reading skills ranged from fourth- to eleventh-grade levels were given either story grammar instruction or traditional basal literature instruction for a period of 9 weeks. In the story grammar instruction, *theme* was identified as a component, in addition to the story components typically taught to elementary students. In the other, traditional instruction treatment, typical procedures outlined in the teachers' guides for basal readers were followed. These included the teaching of related vocabulary, discussion of background information, and oral reading of (the same) stories, answering comprehension questions orally on story details, inferences, and literary techniques, and completing worksheets.

The story grammar instruction proved to be the more effective technique for teaching students to comprehend important elements in short stories, and the students who received this type of instruction gained in confidence. Interestingly, however, it did not improve students' ability to answer the basal literature questions that typically are found in high school literature anthologies. According to the authors, such questions generally focus on minor, literal details and do not represent the desired outcome of high school literature instruction.

Gurney et al. (1990) further reported that theme was the most difficult story component to teach. Even with extensive teacher modeling and direct explanation, they were not successful in improving students' ability to identify story themes. Nor was the same research team successful in another, similar study (Dimino, Gersten, Carnine, & Blake, 1990). In fact, theme is usually considered difficult to teach even to nondisabled students (Singer & Donlan, 1982).

A PROGRAM TO TEACH THEME IDENTIFICATION

Could we build on the few existing studies and develop instruction that would help children for whom reading and comprehension present a challenge? We began our work by considering current reading comprehension instruction. Most of today's instruction is constructivist; it views each reader as bringing a unique knowledge base to the reading of a text and ending up with a unique interpretation of the text. The instruction that follows from this type of approach is typically organized around discussion, in which students contribute their individual interpretations so that all can expand and refine their own meaning construction (Allington, Guice, Michelson, Baker, & Li, 1996). Teachers serve as facilitators who contribute their own interpretations without imposing them on the group. This constructivist paradigm has been found to be successful for many students (Allington et al., 1996).

However, this is relatively unstructured instruction. In addition, it presumes that all students have stable knowledge bases and interpretations to begin with, so that the class discussions can effectively modify and refine the interpretations and understanding of individual students. We decided that this constructivist approach would not fully meet the needs of students with learning disabilities, who have been shown to respond well to structured, direct instruction (Simmons, Fuchs, Fuchs, Mathes, & Hodge, 1995). Thus we designed our theme identification program to incorporate constructivist goals of comprehension instruction with an instructional approach that is effective for students with learning disabilities and for others at risk. That is, our program emphasizes the holistic and constructive nature of the comprehension process and the importance of integrating text meaning with concepts and experiences that are personally meaningful, but it also acknowledges the demonstrated value of structured, direct instruction for poor readers.

The purpose of our instructional program is to help students learn about the concept of theme, identify theme in stories, and apply themes to real life. The instruction follows the paradigm of teacher explanation and modeling, guided practice, and independent practice. It focuses on teaching plot-level components via organizing (schema) questions, as previous studies have done. Then it teaches theme identification via additional questions. A final set of questions helps students generalize the theme to relevant life situations. We call our set of questions the "Theme Scheme." We use simple stories with single, clear, and accessible themes. Some of the theme concepts that we have used include perseverance, cooperation, greed, and honesty. All of our themes are of the evaluative commentary type and are expressed in a simple, common format: "We should cooperate," "We should not be greedy."

The original version of the program consisted of a series of twelve 40-minute sessions, each organized around a single story and comprising five parts, as outlined in the following subsections. The 12 stories were taken from four basal reader series. In most cases, the stories had originally appeared in trade books. Five of the stories exemplified a single theme, "We should persevere." Each of the other 7 stories exemplified a different theme concept, such as cooperation, responsibility, and respect for others, all expressed in the theme format ("We should . . ."), described previously.

Prereading Discussion about Lesson Purpose and Story Topic

In the first part of each lesson, "theme" is defined as a lesson that you can learn from a story, the value of understanding themes is discussed, and background for the specific story for that lesson is introduced, including its relevance to personal experiences. This instruction is heavily scaffolded, with teachers initially modeling each step and students gradually taking on more responsibility. In the first three lessons, teachers define theme and lead the discussion on the importance of theme and the story topic, making associations between the story and personal experiences. Starting in Lesson 4, the students offer definitions of theme and lead the discussions themselves. As is the case throughout the lessons, only a general outline is given to the teachers, who use their own expertise in developing discussions and guiding the instruction.

Reading the Story

Next, the teacher reads the story aloud while students follow along with their texts (so that decoding difficulties do not interfere with comprehension). At various points during the reading, the teacher interposes questions. These questions are designed to encourage students to process the text actively (to make associations between their own knowledge and the text information and to clarify the text information). The teacher asks the students to make predictions about what would happen next in the story and to explain major story events. Student responses are discussed, and students are encouraged to ask their own questions.

After reading the story, the class discusses the main points and reads a summary highlighting the main events and outcome. This is done because students with learning disabilities are particularly likely to have trouble identifying the important story components (Wong, 1984) and their story comprehension is often idiosyncratic (Williams, 1993).

Discussion of Important Story Information Using Organizing (Schema) Questions

Teacher and students discuss five questions designed to help organize the important story components and derive the thematic material. Over the course of the lesson series, the teacher provides opportunities to practice these questions so that students can recall them on their own.

The first three organizing questions focus on the important story components from which a theme concept will be derived: main character, central event, and outcome. The questions are:

- Who is the main character?
- What did he or she do?
- What happened?

These questions direct students to focus on the important information and enable them to extract and organize important story components independently. Again, instruction is scaffolded.

The final two organizing questions are designed to encourage the students to make the judgments that, when combined with the theme concept, lead to theme identification. These questions are:

- Was this good or bad?
- Why was this good or bad?

Although teachers model their responses to the first four questions for four lessons, the final question—why was this good or bad—requires teacher modeling through Lesson 7. Also through Lesson 7, teachers model the way in which the answers to the five questions lead to a theme, and they state the theme. After Lesson 7, responsibility for identifying and stating the theme is gradually transferred to the students. Teachers provide feedback to help the students in this process.

Identification of the Theme in Standard Format

Students next learn to state the theme in a standard format, defined as a "should" statement. Teachers model two generic statement frames:

- (Main character) should have (should not have) _____.
- We should (should not) _____.

The first frame puts the theme into the *should* format. The second frame applies the theme to situations and people in general rather than just to those in the story. Students practice stating the theme in this format.

Application of Theme to Real-Life Experiences

The last two questions help extend the theme to specific and often personal real-life scenarios:

- To whom would this theme apply?
- When would it apply? (In what situation?)

In this step, too, instruction proceeds by means of scaffolding. For each story, more explicit forms of the questions are also included in the lesson, elaborating on "who" and "in what situation," to be used as prompts when necessary.

EVALUATION OF THE PROGRAM

First Evaluation

Our first evaluation involved fifth- and sixth-grade students in eight New York City classrooms that included both normally achieving students (n = 38) and those with disabilities that were mild enough to permit mainstreaming (n = 31). The mean age of the students was 11.2 years. Half the students were White, one third were Hispanic, and the rest were African American or Asian. This evaluation allowed us to assess the effectiveness of the theme identification program initially with children who were making satisfactory progress. Our assumption was that any difficulties that we found would not be attributable to the children's learning problems but rather would lie in the program. In this study, students were taught by their own teachers in classrooms that had been randomly assigned either to receive the instructional program or to serve in a control condition receiving no special instruction.

This initial study provided positive evidence for the effectiveness of our instructional program (Williams et al., 1994). Specifically, the students in the theme identification classrooms understood the concepts of theme and the concept of perseverance better, both of which represented content that they had been explicitly taught. They also did better on application of the perseverance theme (i.e., generating a story with that theme), which also had been explicitly taught. And they were better at identifying the theme of a previously unheard perseverance story, which can be considered a near-transfer task (Brown & Palincsar, 1989). Finally, they were better at identifying the theme of a novel story whose theme had not appeared at all during the instruction, a task we considered to qualify as far transfer. Both the students with mild disabilities and the nondisabled students performed at similar levels.

Encouraged by these results but recognizing the preliminary nature of the findings (they were based on a no-treatment control), we turned to the evaluation of our comprehension instruction for students with more severe learning disabilities (Williams et al., 1994). It was for those students, who do not respond well to normal classroom instruction, that our program was really designed.

Second Evaluation

Here we compared the performance of students who were given our theme identification program with students who were given more traditional instruction. Ninety-three students from 12 seventh- and eighth-grade special education classrooms in a small city near New York were the participants. There were approximately equal numbers of Hispanics, African Americans, and Whites. The mean age was 14.2 years. All students received all their instruction in their own classrooms; they were not mainstreamed. All had been certified by the school as having learning disabilities, although many of them had IQ scores below 85, the usual minimum for a learning disabilities classification.

We did not impose any further criteria on this school-identified group because we feel that instructional studies are most useful if conducted in ecologically valid settings; that is, in actual classroom situations as they exist in schools. Well-structured instruction should be effective with all students who are functioning at a low level, regardless of how they have been classified. This point of view is reflected in many schools' current grouping policies, written in terms of level of functioning and not of classification status (New York City Board of Education, 1991).

The students in the theme identification classrooms performed significantly better than the students in the traditional instruction classrooms. First, they understood the concept of theme and the concept of perseverance better, and they were also better at identifying the theme of a previously unheard perseverance story. Thus the theme identification program aided students in their comprehension and promoted near transfer. But they were not superior at applying the perseverance theme. And when we asked the students to identify the theme of a previously unheard story that had a novel theme, one that was not represented at all during the instruction, the two instructional treatments did not differ. Thus these students with severe learning disabilities, unlike the students in the first study, did not demonstrate any transfer to stories with novel themes.

However, it should be pointed out that, although it might seem that we achieved only a modest degree of generalization, the results actually demonstrated a level of transfer that represents substantial achievement for students with severe learning disabilities (Pressley & McCormick, 1995). Overall, the students with learning disabilities were able to respond positively to an integrated approach to comprehension when it was well structured.

Third Evaluation

We decided to work further on our program, because it appeared as if it could be modified so that it would lead to even greater transfer. To accomplish this, we made one major change in the program (Wilder & Williams, 2001). In its original version, almost half of the instruction focused on a single theme, and the rest included one instance each of several other themes. Recommendations concerning training-for-transfer propose that the transfer be built into the original instruction by using multiple instances in a variety of contexts (Pressley et al., 1990). Following these recommendations, we included three themes in the instruction, each one exemplified in four stories. These themes were "We should not prejudge," "We should be ourselves," and "We should keep trying." We presented these themes in a sequence that made it impossible to predict what the theme of the next story would be.

We also made some other changes in the program. We added three questions to the Theme Scheme (making it a 12–step program). We added one question at the plot level ("What was his or her problem"), and two redundant, reinforcing questions ("The theme of this story is . . . " and "In what situation will . . . [not] help?"). We also included additional activities that we thought would engage the students, such as drawing, role playing, and song writing.

This evaluation involved 10 classrooms for students with learning disabilities in three junior high schools in New York City, which were randomly assigned to either the theme identification program (n = 47 students) or the story comprehension program (more traditional instruction emphasizing vocabulary acquisition and plot-level comprehension; n = 44 students). The mean age of the students was 14.0 years. The enrollment across the three schools was almost all Hispanic (54%) and African American (43%). About 80% of the students in each school received state aid in the form of free or reduced-rate lunches.

Our efforts proved successful. In this study, the students in the theme identification classes were significantly better than the others, not only on the posttest measures (on which there had been differences in the previous study) but also on application of the instructed themes and on identification of the theme of a new story whose theme had not been part of the instruction ("We should be honest"). Students with serious learning disabilities did demonstrate far transfer. We believe that it was the combination of the sequencing of the lessons as recommended in the literature on transfer and the explicit and highly structured instruction, including the Theme Scheme, that were the effective elements of our instruction.

SUGGESTED INSTRUCTIONAL PRACTICES

Our comments here are phrased in relation to the specific goal of teaching students to identify story themes, but all of our suggestions are generalizable; that is, they also make sense in other instructional contexts. First, the teachers who have taught the theme identification program in the context of our several studies have ranged from those with many years of experience to others who were quite new at teaching. They have been quite varied in their delivery of the lessons. A variety of teaching styles can be effective, and teachers should be encouraged to keep to their own styles as they teach the program. From our observations, we have identified several general features that seem to be genuinely characteristic of successful teachers. Successful teachers probe for answers, and they keep probing (gently), giving students plenty of time to formulate their ideas in response. They often ask children to restate something that they, or other class members, have said, which promotes fluency. They often give reminders of earlier lessons (stories and themes), which helps integrate the elements of the program. Finally, they are willing to share their own experiences, which provides interest and perhaps even bonding.

The students in our evaluation studies learned what we taught them and also showed that they could generalize from what they were taught. This leads us to advise educators not to put off comprehension instruction, even of higher order concepts, until children can decode and can read with fluency. Some students take a long time to develop these basic skills. To focus all of their instruction on these skills during this period means that these children are losing valuable opportunities to work on higher order comprehension skills.

One way to start comprehension instruction early is to bypass reading altogether and work on an oral level. Because these children usually have adequate listening skills, stories can be read to them, and discussion can be the mode of instruction. Our first evaluation studies really dealt with listening comprehension. In our most recent study, with at-risk second- and third-graders, we continue to emphasize listening comprehension, but we also have included simple reading and writing tasks. We ask the children to read, on their own, short stories of only five or six sentences and to identify and discuss their themes. We also have the children write their own short stories, which they then read to the class. In this way the program allows students to develop their comprehension ability without being overburdened by requirements for written language skill that they do not yet possess. At the same time, they are bringing the rudimentary written language skills that they do have to bear on issues of higher order comprehension, thus promoting comprehension across spoken and written language.

Following are a few additional points that are worth keeping in mind. It is important to choose stories with one clear and simple theme to start with. In our studies we always had proficient readers (graduate students) identify the themes of the stories that we used, and we also had good readers of approximately the same age as our target population do the same thing, to make sure that the stories we selected were in fact clear and the themes accessible. It is better to save the more complicated stories for later on, when the students have definitely mastered the concept of theme and are able to identify the themes of simple stories. In the Dimino et al. (1990) and the Gurney et al. (1990) studies cited previously, the authors followed sound principles for devising instruction for students with learning disabilities, but their stories were complex, and their results were disappointing. Don't make the mistake of confounding complexity with interest and simplicity with dullness, because then you may well choose stories that are not interpretable by the students and therefore serve no pedagogical function.

It is also important to be sure that the steps in the Theme Scheme are thoroughly mastered. The steps should not be seen as merely a rote task, because they are what provide the framework for comprehension. When internalized, the Theme Scheme provides a structure that is useful for understanding most stories. Because we provide basic outlines of the instruction but tell teachers to use their own best teaching techniques, we have seen interesting variations in delivering the Theme Scheme instruction. For example, teachers sometimes have one student ask all of the Theme Scheme questions and choose from those students whose hands are raised the one to answer each question. There are many ways of handling this aspect of the instruction so that it incorporates drill in an appealing way. Proficiency with the Theme Scheme will guide the students to focus on the information they need in order to identify the story theme.

The discussion should be kept centered on the topic—the plot components and how to get from those to the theme. Some students, especially but not solely those with learning disabilities and others at risk, are easily distracted by the associations they make to the story information and to the comments of the other students (Williams, 1993). One of the most important things teachers must do is to monitor how well the discussion is staying on track. In addition, good teachers use every opportunity to pick up on students' offerings in discussion; that is, they take what a child offers as an example and elaborate on it. Focusing on what students are interested in will ensure their interest and make for a livelier and more meaningful discussion.

It is helpful to offer students the option of talking about others instead of themselves. In discussions about real-life experiences, sometimes students are shy about talking about themselves. At other times, by discouraging them from talking about themselves, the teacher can help them protect their families' and their own privacy. Also, teachers should not leave themselves vulnerable. Alice Wilder's dissertation study (Wilder & Williams, 2001) contained a story in which the main character was apprehensive about being placed in a class with a mean and grouchy teacher and was much relieved when he found out that his teacher was good-natured and fair (theme: "We should not prejudge"). In one discussion the teacher innocently asked what the students thought about her, which provoked giggles and comments about how old and wrinkled and unattractive she was.

One last point: It is important not to focus too much on the "meta" in instruction. A potential danger that accompanies some of today's metacognitive strategy instruction is that it can lead students to be so conscious of their own mental processes that those, and not the information in the story, become the object of their attention. The main focus of the instruction should be on the story, not on the student's thinking processes. Use of the Theme Scheme will help here. If the Theme Scheme is well learned, a student will not have to allocate a great deal of attention to it when a new story is encountered. In this way the focus will remain on the story, as it should.

IMPLICATIONS FOR FUTURE RESEARCH AND PRACTICE

Extension to a Younger Population

If middle school students are able to demonstrate higher order comprehension when given appropriate and effective instruction, can younger children also do so? It is well accepted that comprehension instruction should begin in the very early grades, though educators have only recently started to concentrate on this aspect of primary grade reading instruction (Brown, Pressley, Van Meter, & Schuder, 1996). As part of our work in the Center on Accelerating School Learning, we have just completed a study of second- and third-grade children at risk for school failure, similar in many details to our third evaluation study. Preliminary results are promising.

Selection of Stories

Might other media be used effectively? We were surprised to find out how difficult it was to find suitable stories for our program, stories that met the criteria that we determined would make them effective. Perhaps there are short films that could be included, along with conventional text stories. Visual presentation has an enormous impact on children. However, we would have to be careful. If our ultimate goal is reading comprehension, we do not want to overemphasize nontext presentation. That would reduce the amount of textual language the children hear, and familiarity with the linguistic features of written language fosters the acquisition of reading comprehension. Could we determine a good balance between media presentations that enhance comprehension and text presentations that specifically enhance reading comprehension? This is an important question that reaches beyond the scope of our program.

Nonresponders

Will all children achieve success with the program? The Theme identification program is appropriate for both whole-class and small-group instruction. The recent movement toward mainstreaming students with mild disabilities means that more such students will be receiving their instruction in large, heterogeneous classes. Educators recognize the challenge involved in designing instruction that will be equally effective for all members of these inclusion classes. Probably no instructional program, no matter how well designed, will result in every child succeeding. It would be valuable to examine the outcomes of a program that teaches higher order skills, as this one does, to determine how to identify nonresponders and to make adaptations of the program that will be more conducive to success on the part of these children.

SUMMARY

Our evaluation studies have clearly indicated that our theme identification program is effective with respect to achievement. We have demonstrated that children with learning disabilities, even severe disabilities, can acquire higher order comprehension skills. Specifically, our program is successful in helping students attain one important aspect of higher order comprehension, understanding story themes. Students also can generalize what they learn to other stories and to real-life experience.

We have had a positive and enthusiastic response from both teachers and students. Informal feedback from students indicated that they enjoyed the program. Teachers' responses on evaluation questionnaires indicated that they deemed the program educationally beneficial and enjoyable. The characteristics of the program that the teachers liked were its explicitness, repetition, and organization.

In conclusion, with appropriate materials and methods, low-functioning students can achieve competence in higher order comprehension. It is encouraging to see that these students respond well when an integrated approach to comprehension is used and to realize that there is no need to limit instruction for these students to low-level tasks.

REFERENCES

Allington, R., Guice, S., Michelson, N., Baker, K., & Li, S. (1996). Literature-based curricula in high poverty schools. In M. F. Graves, P. van den Broek, & B. M. Taylor (Eds.), *The first R: Every child's right to read* (pp. 73–96). New York: Teachers College Press.

Beach, R., & Wendler, L. (1987). Developmental differences in response to a story. *Research in the Teaching of English, 21,* 286–297.

Brophy, J., & Good, T. L. (1986). Teacher behavior and student achievement. In M. Wittrock (Ed.), *The third handbook of research on teaching* (pp. 328–375). New York: McMillan.

Brown, A. L., & Palincsar, A. M. (1989). Guided, cooperative learning and individual knowledge acquisition. In L. B. Resnick (Ed.), *Knowing and learning: Essays in honor of Robert Glaser* (pp. 395–451). Hillsdale, NJ: Erlbaum.

Brown, R., Pressley, M., Van Meter, P., & Schuder, T. (1996). A quasi-experimental validation of transactional strategies instruction with low-achieving second grade readers. *Journal of Educational Psychology, 88,* 18–37.

Cain, K. (1996). Story knowledge and comprehension skill. In C. Cornoldi & J. Oakhill (Eds.), *Reading comprehension difficulties: Processes and interventions* (pp. 167–192). Hillsdale, NJ: Erlbaum.

Carnine, D., & Kinder, B. D. (1985). Teaching low performing students to apply generative and scheme strategies to narrative and expository material. *Remedial and Special Education, 6,* 20–30.

Dimino, J., Gersten, R., Carnine, D., & Blake, G. (1990). Story grammar: An approach for promoting at-risk secondary students' comprehension of literature. *Elementary School Journal, 91*, 19–32.

Dorfman, M. H., & Brewer, W. F. (1994). Understanding the points of fables: A developmental study. *Discourse Processes, 17*, 105–129.

Gardner, R. A. (1987). *Therapeutic communication with children: The mutual storytelling technique.* Northvale, NJ: Aronson.

Gersten, R., & Carnine, D. (1986). Direct instruction in reading comprehension. *Educational Leadership, 43*, 70–78.

Gurney, D., Gersten, R., Dimino, J., & Carnine, D. (1990). Story grammar: Effective literature instruction for high school students with learning disabilities. *Journal of Learning Disabilities, 23*, 335–348.

Hansen, C. L. (1978). Story retelling used with average and learning disabled readers as a measure of reading comprehension. *Learning Disability Quarterly, 1*, 62–69.

Idol, L. (1987). Group story mapping: A comprehension strategy for both skilled and unskilled readers. *Journal of Learning Disabilities, 20*, 196–205.

Idol, L., & Croll, V. (1987). Story mapping training as a means of improving reading comprehension. *Learning Disability Quarterly, 10*, 214–230.

Lehr, S. (1988). The child's developing sense of theme as a response to literature. *Reading Research Quarterly, 23*, 337–357.

Lerner, M. J. (1980). *The belief in a just world.* New York: Plenum.

Lukens, R. (1988). *A critical handbook of children's literature.* Glenview, IL: Scott, Foresman.

Mandler, J. M., & Johnson, N. J. (1977). Remembrance of things parsed: Story structure and recall. *Cognitive Psychology, 9*, 111–151.

New York City Board of Education. (1991). *Educational services for students with handicapping conditions.* New York: Fernandez.

Oakhill, J. V. (1984). Inferential and memory skills in children's comprehension of stories. *British Journal of Educational Psychology, 54*, 31–39.

Pressley, M., & McCormick, C. (1995). *Advanced educational psychology.* New York: Harcourt Brace.

Pressley, M., Woloshyn, V., Lysynchuk, L. M., Martin, V., Wood, E., & Willoughby, T. (1990). A primer of research on cognitive strategy instruction: The important issues and how to address them. *Educational Psychology Review, 2*, 1–33.

Shure, M. B., & Spivack, H. (1978). *Problem solving techniques in childrearing.* San Francisco: Jossey-Bass.

Simmons, D. C., Fuchs, L. S., Fuchs, D., Mathes, P. G., & Hodge, J. P. (1995). Effects of explicit teaching and peer tutoring on the reading achievement of learning-disabled and low-performing students in regular classrooms. *Elementary School Journal, 95*, 387–408.

Singer, H., & Donlan, D. (1982). Active comprehension: Problem-solving schema with question generation for comprehension of complex short stories. *Reading Research Quarterly, 17*, 166–186.

Tappan, M. B., & Brown, L. M. (1989). Stories told and lessons learned: Toward a narrative approach to moral development and moral education. *Harvard Educational Review, 59*, 182–205.

van den Broek, P. (1997). Discovering the cement of the universe: The development of event comprehension from childhood to adulthood. In P. W. van den Broek, P. J. Bauer, & T. Bourg (Eds.), *Developmental spans in event comprehension and representation* (pp. 321–342). Hillsdale, NJ: Erlbaum.

Vitz, P. C. (1990). The use of stories in moral development: New psychological reasons for an old education method. *American Psychologist, 45*, 709–720.

Weaver, P. A., & Dickinson, D. K. (1982). Scratching below the surface structure: Exploring the usefulness of story grammar. *Discourse Processes, 5*, 225–243.

Wilder, A. A., & Williams, J. P. (2001). Students with severe learning disabilities can learn higher-order comprehension skills. *Journal of Educational Psychology, 93*, 268–278.

Williams, J. P. (1993). Comprehension of students with and without learning disabilities: Identification of narrative themes and idiosyncratic text representations. *Journal of Educational Psychology, 85*, 631–641.

Williams, J. P. (1998). Improving the comprehension of disabled readers. *Annals of Dyslexia, 48*, 213–238.

Williams, J. P., Brown, L. G., Silverstein, A. K., & deCani, J. S. (1994). An instructional program for adolescents with learning disabilities in the comprehension of narrative themes. *Learning Disability Quarterly, 17*, 205–221.

Williams, J. P., & Ellsworth, N. J. (1990). Teaching learning disabled adolescents to think critically using a problem-solving schema. *Exceptionality, 1*, 135–146.

Wong, B. Y. L. (1984). Metacognition and learning disabilities. In T. Waller, D. Forrest, & E. MacKinnon (Eds.), *Metacognition, cognition, and human performance* (pp. 137–180). New York: Academic Press.

10

"Oh Excellent, Excellent Question!"

Developmental Differences
and Comprehension Acquisition

LAURA B. SMOLKIN
CAROL A. DONOVAN

There is much we have learned from past research on comprehension instruction. From summaries provided by Pressley and his colleagues (Pressley, Johnson, Symons, McGoldrick, & Kurita, 1989) and Pearson and his colleagues (e.g., Dole, Duffy, Roehler, & Pearson, 1991; Pearson & Fielding, 1991; Pearson, Roehler, Dole, & Duffy, 1992), we know there are eight important cognitive acts that teachers should encourage their students to perform. These are activating their prior knowledge, monitoring comprehension (and employing "fix-up" strategies such as rereading when reading goes awry), generating questions, answering them, drawing inferences between and among pieces of text, creating mental imagery, bringing knowledge of text structure to bear, and, both during and after reading, creating summaries of what they have read. We have come, too, to understand the crucial role of teacher modeling in children's comprehension development (e.g., Beck, McKeown, Hamilton, & Kucan, 1997; Duffy, Roehler, & Herrmann, 1988; Pressley & Harris, 1990; Pearson, 1996). However, despite all we have learned, there are important points raised in prior research that we seem to have forgotten. For us, a critical need in this time when phonemes rule is to remind ourselves that comprehension is developmental in nature and to address the question of what type of comprehension-related work should be done at what grade levels.

So that we can move forward to frame and ultimately answer this question, we first look backward, attending to the findings and comments of researchers writing in the 1970s and 1980s (and some in the 1990s) as they discussed developmental aspects of comprehension, cognition, and language learning. We then shift our discussion to application of this knowledge and a particular context we have studied, the interactive information book read-aloud, that supports what we have come to call comprehension acquisition. Finally, we consider what remains to be learned about children's developing abilities to comprehend various types of texts.

RESEARCH ON THE DEVELOPMENTAL NATURE OF COMPREHENSION, COGNITION, AND LANGUAGE LEARNING

In the following sections, we consider the major research we believe forms the foundation for thinking about the development of abilities to comprehend written text, research that seems to us to have been forgotten, put aside in our current intensive interest in phonological awareness. We start with a look at the developmental nature of comprehension. Next, we look at issues of cognitive and language development that affect comprehension acquisition. We then consider implications of this research for comprehension instruction.

The Developmental Nature of Comprehension

When research on reading comprehension strategy instruction began, those working in cognition had already established that children's comprehension was developmental in nature (e.g., Flavell, Speer, Green, & August, 1981; Markman, 1977, 1979). Paris, in a series of articles written with various colleagues (Cross & Paris, 1988; Paris, Cross, & Lipson, 1984; Paris, Lipson, & Wixson, 1983; Paris & Jacobs, 1984), addressed this developmental aspect of reading comprehension as he researched informed strategies for learning (ISL). Paris argued (e.g., Paris & Jacobs, 1984) that metacognitive and reasoning abilities continue developing throughout the elementary grades. Although Paris and Jacob's third graders and fifth graders both improved in their comprehension abilities as a result of direct instruction in comprehension strategies, fifth graders "exhibited greater reading awareness and comprehension than 8–year-olds" (p. 2091). Based on his various findings, Paris and colleagues specifically addressed the need to consider appropriate ages for reading comprehension instruction (e.g., Paris, Saarnio, & Cross, 1986). They suggested that a certain threshold of decoding (and memory) would need to be exceeded before strategies such as skimming, rereading, using context, planning, paraphrasing, and summarizing could "play [a significant role] in children's reading comprehension" (Paris et al., 1986, p. 121). This threshold would likely be passed when children's reading had become fluent enough for comprehension to occur (LaBerge & Samuels, 1974).

Young Children Operate in Cognitively Different Ways from Older Children

Paris and colleagues' attention to memory reflected the discoveries of their contemporary developmental psychologists. In 1983, Brown, Bransford, Ferrara, and Campione's work indicated that young children's use of strategies, a planning effort requiring memory, could be enhanced through instruction; however, they noted, these gains were seldom sustained beyond the training sessions. This same point had been and would be repeatedly made by many working in the field of cognitive development. As early as 1965, Sheldon White had described the "five-to-seven shift" in children's cognition, a time when children moved from unidimensional thinking to the multidimensional thinking that comprehension strategy application would require. The classic balance-scale experiment (Siegler, 1976) is useful in distinguishing unidimensional and multidimensional thinking. This experiment has two variables—amount of weight on either side of a fulcrum and the distance of that weight from the fulcrum—that determine whether the scale will balance. Younger children tend to rely on one dimension—weight alone—in making their predictions of whether the scale would balance; by age 9, children comfortably consider two dimensions, weight and distance, in predicting the outcome of the task. Although in 1996 Siegler would acknowledge the many studies that did and did not indicate that young children could reason multidimensionally, he still felt it necessary to comment: "[D]emonstrating that 5–year-olds *can* reason multidimensionally does not explain why they fail to do so in many situations in which older children and adults do" (p. 77). A more appropriate "explanation for 5–year-olds' frequent unidimensional reasoning," suggested Siegler, "is that they encode situations more narrowly than do older children" (p. 80). White (1996), too, came to see the shift in cognition in relation to contexts: "What happens to children between 5 and 7 is not the acquisition of an absolute ability to reason; it is an ability to reason with others . . . to learn how to act in . . . [various] behavior settings" (pp. 27–28).

Contemplating Routes to Knowledge

Second-language researcher and theorist Stephen Krashen (1976, 1981) proposed his monitor theory of language acquisition and learning. Krashen suggested that there exist two separate knowledge systems underlying language performance. The first he termed "acquisition"; this he saw as operating in a largely subconscious fashion. The second, which he deemed less important in ultimately mastering a language, was the "learned" system, created during periods of formal instruction. To clarify his distinction, it may help to look at examples of 4-year-old girls of two different cultures learning dances. Young Pueblo girls can be seen dancing in the harvest dance either by the sides of their mothers or in the group of children who dance at the rear of the larger group's circle. They have received no explicit training in preparing to participate; they simply accompany parents to practice events, watching and sometimes imitating, acquiring the steps of the dance. Young Anglo girls can be seen carefully counting beats and steps as they dance sugarplum fairies in ballet recitals. They receive explicit training for these events, attending hours of after-school classes in which teachers focus on pointed toes, proper positioning of bodies, and careful attention to the point in the music at which particular actions will be performed. In Krashen's presentation, the Pueblo girls are acquiring the steps of the harvest dance, whereas the Anglo girls are learning the steps of the sugarplum-fairy dance.

As recast by Gee (1990), acquisition could be seen as resulting from exposures to models and through practice in social groups, accomplished without formal instruction. By contrast, learning occurred through conscious effort, a gaining of knowledge through a teacher, in which a task had been analyzed into useful parts. In contrast to Krashen, Gee recognized that these two processes were often mixed and that the balance would be different at different developmental stages.

These contrasting cognitive operations bear a remarkable resemblance to the "low roads" and "high roads" to transfer described by Salomon and Perkins (1989). Low roads to transfer, which would result in "the acquisition of habitual behavior patterns" and "cognitive strategies and styles" (p. 122), involved socialization and depended on "practice that occurr[ed] in a variety of somewhat related and expanding contexts" (p. 120). High roads to transfer depended on "the mindful abstracting of knowledge from a context" (p. 115). The key here was the notion of a decontextualizing of cognitive elements, resulting in abstractions that sometimes took the forms of rules or principles, something seen in virtually every form of strategy instruction.

Cazden (1992) discussed the socialization of attention in learning to read and chose to recast Krashen's terminology, borrowing her terms from Donaldson (1978), as "revealing" and "telling." Revealing, she suggested, might be particularly useful for young children, in that "told" information seemed often to be "indigestible for later use" and that abstractions often oversimplified a complex reality. However, for older children, telling was particularly useful in discussing previous actions or approaches, allowing a more critical look (more "mindful" would be Salomon and Perkins' term) at the phenomenon being advocated.

Revisiting Paris's Decoding Emphasis Suggestion

Given that young children have trouble thinking multidimensionally, given that they do not easily retain strategies, and given the preponderance of evidence that phonemic awareness has been shown to be critical to young children's reading success (see Snow, Burns, & Griffin, 1998), it would seem sensible to follow Paris and colleagues' (1986) suggestion to focus young children's attention on the associative learning tasks of attaching phonemes to letters and names to symbols. However, we now have some evidence that early reading instruction that stresses decoding but that fails to attend in some substantive fashion to children's concurrent growth in the comprehension of a range of texts may unintentionally put children in peril. In their 1996 chapter, Morrison, Griffith, and Frazier, examining the issue of transfer of literacy skills, suggested that instruction in decoding does not "naturally produce spin-off benefits in vocabulary skills and general knowledge" (p. 179). In their preliminary investigation of the effects of schooling, they examined two groups of students, distinguished from each other by school entry cutoff dates that placed 10 of their participants in kindergarten and the other 10 in first grade. Their results indicated that the "young" first-grade group made far more substantive progress in phonemic awareness than the "old" kindergarten group. In vocabulary, general knowledge, and narrative skills, both groups made significant gains from fall to spring testing; however, the two groups' gains were found to be equal. The researchers explained, "no evidence was revealed that unique experiences in schooling improved growth" (p. 179) in the three areas. These results call into question the assumption that primary grade instruction that focuses on decoding will necessarily lead to success in comprehension, which is so heavily dependent on all three of these areas of knowledge.

Looking for Guidance on Comprehension Building for Our Youngest Scholars

We take the various scholarly findings and suggestions we have reviewed to indicate that there is likely a developmentally "better" time to begin actual comprehension strategy instruction, telling, or learning, perhaps during children's second-grade year as children's ability to reason multidimensionally grows closer to adult forms. This leaves us with the important question of what types of comprehension activities will supply primary grade students with the "vocabulary skills and general knowledge," critical components in background knowledge, to which Morrison, Griffith, and Frazier (1996) alluded.

The answer, we believe, lies in the thoughtful creation of the social contexts and situations that shape children's cognition, a point stressed by author after author in the preceding review. From our review, we have come to see two elements as critical in the comprehension building period that we are calling "comprehension acquisition" (see Smolkin & Donovan, 2000, in press). For the first, we look to White (1996), who stressed that during the five-to-seven shift, children are *learning to reason with others*. For the second, we find it helpful to consider Salomon and Perkins's (1989) emphasis on practice. They stressed that social practice of the desired behavior (in our case, comprehension of texts) must occur in a *variety of contexts*, as it is the contrast in contexts that yields "more transfer by exercising a wider variety of related complexes" (p. 120) of procedures.

If we want children to reason their ways through texts during a time when they cannot yet read, then the social context for comprehension acquisition must be a read-aloud of text. We now have now many years of research documenting the benefits of reading aloud to children. From Cohen's (1968) study to Wells's (1986) longitudinal study, research has almost universally supported the idea that reading aloud to children leads to improved reading comprehension (but see Meyer, Stahl, Wardrop, & Linn, 1994, for a cautionary note on the amount of read-aloud time). If children are to learn to reason with others and later to reason for themselves, then these read-alouds must entail child-involved analytical interactions in discussions of the text being read (Dickinson & Smith, 1994). If the social practice must occur in contrasting contexts, then there must be a variety of texts that are read.

COMPREHENSION ACQUISITION: APPLYING WHAT WE KNOW

In the sections that follow, we further elucidate and demonstrate the key principles and acts involved in the settings we see as most supporting comprehension acquisition, so that teachers might put them into practice. To this end, we draw on examples from our own work (Smolkin & Donovan, 1993, 2000, in press), gathered when one of us (Donovan) was a first-grade teacher, first at a low to middle socioeconomic status (SES) elementary school and then at a middle to upper SES school, to show how comprehension can be supported and revealed for children as their first-grade teacher extends their reasoning efforts. First, we look at the role of the teacher and the nature of the discussions that support children's reasoning. Next we consider the variations in texts that should lead to greater transfer of comprehension ability. Then we supply examples of interactive information book read-alouds, showing how the cognitive acts identified through comprehension instruction research are put into play.

The Adult in the Reasoning Building Context: Interaction and the Read-Aloud

Since Cazden's (1965) dissertation, we have understood that, in terms of verbal interactions, different adult responses to children's verbal contributions produce different language outcomes. In that research on African American preschoolers, Cazden found that meaning-oriented adult extensions of children's meaning-making offerings yielded greater gains on six measures of syntactic development, including a sentence-imitation test and mean length of utterance, than did adult responses, termed expansions, that supplied Standard English syntactic forms. By 1983, Cazden had further considered adult "input," noting three types that occurred as parents communicated with young children in contexts that would ultimately allow the child to complete the same task (Cazden, 1983). Scaffolds, borrowed from Wood, Bruner, and colleagues (Wood, Bruner, & Ross, 1976; Wood, Wood, & Middleton, 1978), enabled children to complete tasks beyond their present capabilities. Models demonstrated a mature behavior deemed important in our larger society. Direct instruction occurred when an adult not only modeled but then also directed "the child to *say* or *tell* or *ask*" (1983, p. 14). Drawing on Cazden, we see that interactive read-alouds (see Oyler, 1996) in which children's initiations, efforts at meaning, are *extended* and key points of comprehension *revealed* by their teachers provide the rich cases from which younger learners can reason with others in particular behavior settings.

Considering the Interactive Read-Aloud

Presently, several researchers use the term "interactive" to describe read-aloud practices. Unlike Barrentine (1996), who used the term to describe a situation in which teachers carefully examined texts to determine at what point to insert their well-placed questions, we use the term as did Oyler (1996), to indicate a genuine sharing of authority. In this situation, which we distinguish from other types of read-aloud interactions in the next section, teachers can "gain insight into the connections students are making between the text" (Oyler, 1996, p. 150) and their lives, schemas, and other texts, building on those connections to extend and shape children's reasoning. Like Oyler, we are not describing a situation in which teachers abandon their authority but a situation in which the adult can reveal the way texts and information work at the very moment children are attempting to reason their way through these points.

What Happens during an Interactive Read-Aloud?

Consider this interchange between Donovan and her students. The underlining indicates text, in this instance, Tomie dePaola's *The Popcorn Book* (1978). This dual-purpose (see Donovan & Smolkin, in press-a, in press-b; Smolkin, Donovan, & Lomax, 2001) book consists of two texts. The first, a simple story displayed through cartoonlike characters with speech balloons, is about two brothers who have decided to make popcorn. The second is informational; one of the boys wonders why their mother keeps popcorn in the refrigerator, and he reads aloud to his brother from a hefty, encyclopedic tome to find his answer. Underlining indicates the actual text of the book.

TEACHER: In 1612, French explorers saw some Iroquois people popping corn in clay pots. They would fill the pots with hot sand, throw in some popcorn and stir it with a stick. When the corn popped, it came to the top of the sand and made it easy to get.

CHILD: Look at the bowl!

TEACHER: (*providing an oral commentary on the "story"*): Okay, now it's hot enough [for the brothers] to add a few kernels.

CHILD: What's a kernel?

CHILD: Like what you pop.

TEACHER: It's a seed.

ANNIE: What if you, like, would you think [of] a popcorn seed? Like a popcorn seed. Could you grow popcorn?

TEACHER: Oh, excellent, excellent question. Let's read and we'll see if this [book] answers that question, and if not, we'll talk about it at the end.

Note that the teacher provides her students a context that supports and extends their reasoning efforts. Within this context, in which meaning is being co-constructed, Annie (a pseudonym) feels free to pose her question—if you plant a popcorn seed, will popcorn grow? In response, the teacher compliments Annie's question (one of the eight cognitive acts we earlier noted), then directly instructs children in a method for answering questions ("let's read . . ."). Her interactive style in no way diminishes her right to supply correct information ("It's a seed"), nor to reveal how good comprehenders approach a text. This sharing, this co-construction indicates to children that they need to be actively processing text and pictures as books are read aloud.

This interactive style contrasts sharply with "interactive" examples supplied by Barrentine (1996, p. 40).

TEACHER: Can you think of a way that Little Sal and Little Bear are alike? Bart?

BART: They're both little.

TEACHER: They're both little. Yes, they are. Matt, what do you think?

MATT: They're both brown.

TEACHER: Okay. Um, somebody in the back. Ben. Do you want to look at the picture, Ben? Here's Little Sal, and here's Little Bear.

BEN: They're both girls.

TEACHER: Okay. Maybe so.

We see clearly that Barrentine's teacher is working toward enabling her students to compare and contrast the two stories simultaneously developing in Robert McCloskey's *Blueberries for Sal*, a major component of the humor of this text. However, their interchange is clearly marked with the standard I-R-E (teacher initiation, student response, teacher evaluation) instructional pattern so common in schools (see Cazden, 1988). In part, this may be due to the fact that the text is a story, a genre that we have found, as we discuss later, less supportive of comprehension-related acts than are information book read-alouds. Still, an approach such as Barrentine's, in our opinion, provides considerably less opportunity for a teacher to seize, extend, and support a child-posed reasoning effort than does Donovan's read-aloud.

Working toward Interactive Read-Alouds

A co-constructive, interactive style is not something that comes naturally to all of us. Anne Barry, a Chicago teacher who worked with both Christine Pappas and her student

Cynthia Oyler (Oyler, 1996; Oyler & Barry, 1996; Pappas & Barry, 1997), acknowledged that for her the move to an interactive style entailed hard work (Pappas & Barry, 1997). However, making this effort was worthwhile, for Barry then was better able to support, extend, and scaffold her students' verbal points as they reasoned their ways through various types of texts. And this process, she believed, ultimately allowed her to know both her students and their cognition better.

Variations in Texts: What We Think Teachers Should Know

Recently, Duke (1999, 2000) established the minimal presence of information books in first-grade classrooms. Having no reason to assume that the situation is different in preschool and kindergarten classrooms, we believe this absence of information books to be an extremely important problem. First, as the literature on transfer suggests, varied types of practice are critical for children's transfer of particular types of reasoning. Duke's (1999) study and Kamberelis's (1999) work clearly establish the dominance of story texts in young children's school lives. This early story dominance appears to have long-term results. It has, for example, been established that even good third-grade readers recall more information from, generate more connectors, and maintain the original ordering better in readings of narrative texts than they do in their readings of expository text (e.g., Bridge & Tierney, 1981). Certainly, this is not a surprising finding if we remind ourselves of the conditions for low-road transfers.

Storybook and Information Book Read-Alouds Are Different

For some time, we have been thinking our way through the differing natures of story and information book read-alouds. Strongly influenced by Pappas (1991), we decided to conduct a study in which one of us (Donovan) read aloud to her first-grade students. The books, quality trade literature named in Children's Choices in *The Reading Teacher*, included six information books and six storybooks. We decided to focus our attention on the discussion that occurred during the read-aloud itself and accordingly recorded from the time the actual reading began until the book was finished. Because Donovan transferred from a lower-middle-class school to a middle-upper-class school at the end of the year, we decided to replicate the study. Transcribing the tapes, we analyzed both teacher and student contributions through the reader response categories of Martinez, Roser, Hoffman, and Battle (1992).

In our first coding pass (Smolkin & Donovan, 1993), we placed children's responses into 17 different categories that ranged from children's *bids for turns* ("Mrs. Donovan!") to *literary associations* ("It could be like *Look, Look, Look*") to *predictions* ("They're gonna make a mess in there") to *wondering outside the text* ("Did God put the color on those eggs or how did it get there?") to *literary evaluations* ("This is getting weird"). In our next analysis (Smolkin & Donovan, 2000) we combined the categories titled *interpreting, telling, personal associations,* and *literary associations* into an overarching category that we called *comprehension.* (Since that publication, we have reexamined our thinking and our computations; the correct figures are as reported here.) As we noted in that Center for the Improvement of Early Reading Achievement report, there were considerable differences in these particular comprehension-related moves made by Donovan's students during information book read-alouds as contrasted with story read-alouds. At the lower-middle-class school, the students produced 256 comprehension-coded moves when listening to information books (83% of their total) as contrasted with their 52 moves in this category when they were listening to the six storybooks (17% of their total). The percentages in the transcripts from the upper-middle-class school looked quite similar—253 comprehension moves during the information book read-alouds (87% of the total), contrasted with 38 moves during the read-aloud of fiction (13% of the total).

In our most recent analyses (Smolkin & Donovan, in press), we have extended our comprehension category to include the additional subcategories of *elaborations* ("Look at that little baby. He's screaming"), *predictions* (demonstrated previously), and *wondering* (demonstrated previously). With all categories included, at the lower-middle-class school, Donovan's students produced 395 comprehension-coded moves while listening to information books (70% of their total) as contrasted with their 170 moves in this enlarged category while they were listening to the six storybooks (30% of the total). These percentages in the transcripts from the upper-middle-class school show a similar orientation—421 comprehension moves during the information book read-alouds (78% of their total) contrasted with 118 moves during the read-aloud of fiction (22% of their total).

Regarding teacher discourse categories, we have combined our earlier categories (Martinez et al., 1992) of *informing* ("You can plant it as long as you haven't cooked it"), *summarization* ("They were just eating plants"), *fostering predictions* ("The best thing about popcorn is . . ."), and *thinking about text* ("I think the book's going to tell us"). In our most recent analyses, Donovan produced 226 comprehension-related moves in the information book read-alouds with her lower-middle-class students as contrasted with 60 such moves during read-alouds of storybooks (79% vs. 21%). With her upper-middle class students, she produced 254 meaning-oriented moves during the information read-alouds as contrasted with only 34 such moves during the storybook read-alouds (88% vs. 12%).

Our findings are by no means unique. Mason, Peterman, Powell and Kerr (1989), Kerr and Mason (1994), and Oyler (1996), to name a few, have all observed that genre influences the types of discourse produced by participants in read-alouds.

Comprehension Activity Called for in Story and Information Book Read-Alouds Differs

It is our contention that these different types of texts call for different types (and amounts) of comprehension activity, whether they are read aloud or read silently. Consider the types of comprehension occurring in this excerpt from Donovan's read-aloud of Joanna Cole's folktale *It's Too Noisy*.

TEACHER: The wiseman closed his eyes. He thought and thought. "Here is what to do," he said. "Bring your rooster and your chickens into the house." "That is a funny thing to do," thought the farmer. But he did what the wiseman told him. He got his rooster and his chickens. He put them in the house.

C: The wiseman wants him to make it more noisy!

TEACHER: Will that make it better for the farmer?

C: (*many, in unison*): NO!

C: It's gonna get real noisy.

Stories contain much with which children are already familiar—people, their actions, and outcomes. Their structures are almost always similar; someone's problem is established and various episodes occur as the individual works to solve the problem (e.g., Hasan, 1984; Stein & Glenn, 1979). This is clearly not the case with informational or expository text. These texts not only come in a variety of structures (e.g., Donovan & Smolkin, in press-a, in press-b; Meyer, 1975; Taylor & Taylor, 1983) but they also contain numerous new concepts (and their attendant vocabulary). Moreover, their linguistic features vary considerably, stressing nominalization (e.g., Martin, 1993; Unsworth, 1999), a transformation of form virtually confined to written texts. For us, it is no stretch at all to accept the hypothesis suggested by Chall, Jacobs, and Baldwin (1990) that a contributing factor to the fourth-grade slump might be children's lack of familiarity with expository text.

We do not wish our message to be mistaken. We are not saying that teachers should not read stories aloud; far from that. Even our own prior research (Yaden, Smolkin, & Conlon, 1989) has clearly shown the benefits of reading stories aloud. We do, however, stress the importance for teachers of gaining greater familiarity with the varied types of informational texts, a task with which we hope our explorations may provide some assistance. Our analyses (Donovan & Smolkin, in press-a) have revealed, for instance, three separate subgenera of information books—narrative, nonnarrative, and dual-purpose texts. We also ask that teachers accept that, although it may at first be "hard to read aloud without a story line" (Chittenden, 1991, p. 13), their young students will gain much from learning to reason in these important contextual variations.

COMPREHENSION ACTIVITY DURING INFORMATION BOOK READ-ALOUDS

In the sections that follow, we present examples of Donovan's modeling, scaffolding, and explicitly instructing children as they worked interactively to co-construct the meanings of expository text. First, we consider some links that texts require. Second, we present a consideration of the role of text structure in comprehension. Finally, we focus on a type of explicit instruction that resulted from a comprehension failure.

Linking Pieces of Text Together

The examples in this section are taken from two texts that we classify as *narrative informational* texts. All three examples indicate the ways links are formed, from the level of a word and its meaning in a sentence to the creation of causal inferences.

Linking a Word to Contexts

As we indicated earlier, information books exist to acquaint children with new concepts in which vocabulary figures importantly. In our first example, the teacher (Donovan) reads from Gibbons' (1988) *Sunken Treasure*. This book, by noted information book writer Gail Gibbons, makes great use of the narrative, time-dependent structures (*now*, *next*, and *then*) that children have learned from story exposures. The teacher pauses to make sure the children comprehend the meaning of a particular word in the text.

TEACHER: <u>Now the treasure can be brought to the surface. Salvage boats are moved in. Divers descend and crewmembers lower baskets over the side to them.</u> What does descend mean? We learned this word when we talked about hot air balloons. Pete?

PETE: It's like . . .

CHILD: Lifting it up . . .

CHILD: Lifting it up . . .

TEACHER: Say what you were going to say, Pete.

PETE: It goes down.

TEACHER: Excellent. Down. That's right. And, you can tell that by the meaning of the sentence: <u>Divers descend and crewmembers lower baskets over the side to them.</u> So, they're going down.

In this example, the teacher clearly has moved into the role of authority on text as she demonstrates and discusses a number of important comprehension strategies. Concerned that the children will not understand the word *descend*, she first leads the children through a consideration of their prior knowledge, their previous experiences with this word. She also explicitly tells her students that they can double-check that information by examining it in the context of the sentence in which the word appeared, demonstrating Gee's (1990) point that acquisition and instruction are often mixed.

   Linking Pieces of Text Information to Consider Cause. In the following example from *Sunken Treasure*, Donovan works to scaffold the children's construction of an inference in a section of text that does not make a causal connection explicit.

TEACHER: All right, it hit the reef. Why did it hit the reef? Because it got. . . . (*No response from children*). What did it [the book] say? It said there was . . .

CHILD: A storm.

TEACHER: Storm, right.

CHILD: They couldn't see.

TEACHER: Right, it did [say that]. Because they couldn't see, and if they were out

CHILD: Were the people surprised?

CHILD: The storm blew it into the rocks.

TEACHER: Exactly.

Using scaffolding, the teacher guides the children backward in the text to the pieces of text information critical in understanding the cause of the shipwreck. The ascertaining of cause (Trabasso, 1994; Trabasso & Magliano, 1996) is critical in narratives, whether they constitute stories studied by Trabasso and Magliano or the recountings of factual events in narrative informational texts.

Our two examples thus far featured teacher-initiated comprehension activities. The information book read-alouds were genuinely interactive, allowing children to put forth their concerns. In the next example, a student initiates the comprehension effort, after carefully studying the picture in another narrative information book, Cole and Wexler's (1976) *A Chick Hatches*.

CHILD: That yellow stuff wasn't there. [Why did it disappear?]

TEACHER: Well, it might have dried up, or it might be a little bigger. Let's keep reading and see. <u>Inside the membrane, the fetus looks more and more like a chick. Notice how much of the yolk has been used up. Every day now until hatching some of the yolk will be drawn into the chick's body.</u>

CHILD: Why?

CHILD: Why? Does he eat the egg?

CHILD: Oh, gross.

TEACHER: Well, remember, remember the blood vessels are in the yolk and they get the food from the yolk, so yeah, it uses it up. He doesn't eat it with his mouth, but he eats it through his blood vessels.

CHILD: (*whispering*) Wow.

Between them, the teacher and the children put a number of cognitive acts and strategies into play. Like a good adult comprehender, the child poses a problem (an implied question). The teacher responds with two possible answers, then suggests that they try reading further to find their answer, a strategy we noted earlier in the example from *The Popcorn Book* (de Paola, 1978).

Further supporting the children's comprehension, the teacher models the formation of inferences, linking the current information on the yolk absorption to previously presented information on the location and function of the blood vessels. To accomplish this end, she directly indicates that the metacognitive act of remembering might be instantiated to locate an important piece of text information.

Attending to Text Structure

As comprehension research has shown repeatedly, awareness of text structure aids readers' comprehension. In the excerpt that follows, the teacher pauses to discuss the way de Paola's *The Popcorn Book* is structured.

TEACHER: <u>And 100–year-old popcorn kernels were found in Peru that could still be popped.</u> Now. This guy is doing different . . . [It's] kind of like two stories [are] going on. What is this part giving us?

CHILDREN: (*together*) Information.

TEACHER: It is. And what is this doing?

CHILD: It's telling you.

TEACHER: It's giving us, right, the steps of how to make the popcorn.

CHILD: And he has a big ole speech bubble.

TEACHER: Yes, because he's reading about this, remember? And so, his speech bubble is him reading from this book about this (*pointing to pictures of native peoples*).

By interrupting to comment on the way this book "works," the teacher models attention to text structure and then scaffolds her children in noting that a text's structure may be critical in understanding its presentation of ideas. In this particular *dual purpose informational* text, all information regarding the history of popcorn appears in the speech bubbles, whereas the narrative describes the steps the two brothers engage in as they prepare popcorn.

Modeling Fix-Up Strategies When Comprehension Failure Occurs

Monitoring comprehension, as we noted at the beginning of the chapter, is an important comprehension strategy. In the following example, Donovan reads from *Tree Trunk Traffic* (Lavies, 1989), a book that we classify as a *nonnarrative informational* text. Reading amidst the many comments her students are offering, the teacher suddenly pauses and begins again.

TEACHER: Insects live on the tree, too. This big cicada just crawled out of its brown, shell-like skin. For several years. . . . (*Teacher pauses. The next word in the text is "it."*) Let's start back here. Insects live on the tree, too. This big cicada just crawled out of its brown, shell-like skin.

CHILD: (*interrupting*): We already read this.

TEACHER: I know, but see, sometimes if you stop, it helps [to reread the previous sentences]. It didn't make sense just reading [further in the text].

This particular example seems very important for us. Opportunities to hear an adult speak of a comprehension failure are quite few. This particular opportunity arises because the teacher's genuinely interactive style allows her children to comment freely. Like many children, the child wants the reading of the text simply to move forward and complains when it doesn't. The teacher doesn't talk about the source of her comprehension difficulty, the distance between a noun ("skin") and its pronoun ("it"), but she does inform her students that when we have to stop during reading, it truly is helpful for comprehension to reread the previously read section.

WHAT REMAINS TO BE LEARNED ABOUT COMPREHENSION BUILDING IN THE EARLIEST GRADES

Our notion of comprehension acquisition contains within it many questions for future research. In this section, we pose six questions that we feel merit further attention to enhance our understanding of supporting young children's comprehension.

1. *What are the distinctions in the comprehension of stories and informational texts?* The first point we make is that our view of the distinctions between story and informa-

tion book read-alouds needs additional validation. Although we carefully studied both other researchers' reports and our own data, we believe that studies involving larger numbers of teachers are needed to support what we have found. We wish, ultimately, to substantiate our assertion that information book read-alouds contribute in some substantively different way from storybook read-alouds to children's long-term comprehension abilities.

2. *How do the subgenera of informational texts impact comprehension strategies used?* Within those studies, we would also like to address the types of comprehension fostered by the different subgenera of informational texts to which we have referred in this chapter. We are quite interested in teacher read-alouds of dual-purpose texts such as de Paola's (1978) *The Popcorn Book* and Joanna Cole and Bruce Degen's various "Magic School Bus" books. We have observed that read-alouds of nonnarrative informational texts such as Lavies's (1989) *Tree Trunk Traffic* produce many questions to which the authors have supplied no answer. This inevitably leads teachers and children to a consideration of where to read or look next to find the answer to those questions, emphasizing the important strategies of both asking and answering questions during reading. And, as we noted previously, narrative informational texts seem to produce many efforts toward establishing causal links. We believe that knowing what types of books support particular comprehension processes will facilitate both comprehension acquisition and comprehension instruction.

3. *What are the cognitive demands of different comprehension strategies?* We are also keenly interested in considering which of the eight identified cognitive acts place lesser and greater demands on younger readers in terms of cognitive abilities. Knowing this would be very important in designing developmental comprehension curricula to follow and support the period of comprehension acquisition.

4. *What support would teachers need to move toward interactive read alouds?* We need to know what types of teacher support are needed to move toward interactive read-alouds that highlight comprehension. Since the early 1990s (e.g., El-Dinary, Pressley, & Schuder, 1992; Rich & Pressley, 1990), we have known that teachers resist using instructional approaches that strike them as either too disembedded or too complex. We also understand, as was established earlier in this chapter, that not all teachers feel comfortable reading interactively with their students. Clearly, research that seeks to determine appropriate contexts for comprehension acquisition must attend carefully to teacher needs.

5. *What are the benefits of interactive information book read-alouds over time?* In that informational texts are deliberately instructive in concepts and vocabulary, we are interested in the long-term benefits of information book read-alouds. What impact will a greater early acquaintance with these texts offer in terms of children's vocabulary and concept knowledge? What impact might this have in terms of text structure knowledge or ease of comprehending lexico-grammatical structures particular to expository text?

6. *What are the long-term effects of establishing a comprehension acquisition approach?* Ultimately, this is the most important question to be addressed. Research to answer this question and the others posed here will require longitudinal studies. These studies will need to contrast children's reading comprehension progress over the course of their elementary years, comparing groups for whom a comprehension acquisition period was addressed with those whose school literacy diets have consisted virtually exclusively of decoding emphases in their primary grade instruction.

CONCLUSION

In this chapter, we have argued for increasing our research attention to young children's development of text comprehension. We suggest strongly that cognitive development occurring between the ages of 5 to 7 needs to be considered as part of this equation. To us, this seems particularly important in determining the types of situations that will ultimately lead children to transfer, through low roads and revealed information, the comprehension activities demonstrated by adult models to their own future text encounters. We have supplied a possible model for "comprehension acquisition instruction"—the interactive information book read-aloud—but stress that this model needs future research validation. We argue for attention to the situations and texts that will ultimately enable upper-grade elementary students to remark to themselves as they read, "Oh, excellent, excellent question! I wonder if it's answered in here?"

REFERENCES

Barrentine, S. J. (1996). Engaging with reading through interactive read-alouds. *Reading Teacher*, 50, 36–43.

Beck, I. L., McKeown, M. G., Hamilton, R. L., & Kucan, L. (1997). *Questioning the author: An approach for enhancing student engagement with text*. Newark, DE: International Reading Association.

Bridge, C. A., & Tierney, R. J. (1981). The inferential operations of children across text with narrative and expository tendencies. *Journal of Reading Behavior*, 13, 201–214.

Brown, A. L., Bransford, J. D., Ferrara, R. A., & Campione, J. C. (1983). Learning, remembering and understanding. In J. H. Flavell & E. M. Markman (Eds.), *Cognitive development* (4th ed., pp. 77–166). New York: Wiley.

Cazden, C. B. (1965). *Environmental assistance to the child's acquisition of grammar*. Unpublished doctoral dissertation, Harvard University, Cambridge, MA.

Cazden, C. B. (1983). Adult assistance to language development: Scaffolds, models, and direct instruction. In R. P. Parker & F. A. Davis (Eds.), *Developing literacy: Young children's use of language* (pp. 3–18). Newark, DE: International Reading Association.

Cazden, C. B. (1988). *Classroom discourse: The language of teaching and learning*. Portsmouth, NH: Heinemann.

Cazden, C. B. (1992). Revealing and telling: The socialisation of attention in learning to read. *Educational Psychology*, 12, 305–313.

Chall, J. S., Jacobs, V. A., & Baldwin, L. E. (1990). *The reading crisis: Why poor children fall behind*. Cambridge, MA: Harvard University Press.

Chittenden, E. (1991). The role of science books in primary classrooms. In W. Saul & S. A. Jagusch (Eds.), *Vital connections: Children, science, and books: Papers from a symposium sponsored by the Children's Literature Center* (pp. 127–141). Washington, DC: Library of Congress.

Cohen, D. (1968). The effect of literature on vocabulary and reading achievement. *Elementary English*, 45, 209–213, 217.

Cole, J. (1989). *It's too noisy*. New York: Crowell.

Cole, J., & Wexler, J. (1976). *A chick hatches*. New York: William Morrow.

Cross, D. R, & Paris, S. G. (1988). Developmental and instructional analyses of children's metacognition and reading comprehension. *Journal of Educational Psychology*, 80(2), 131–142.

de Paola, T. (1978). *The popcorn book*. New York: Holiday House.

Dickinson, D. K., & Smith, M. W. (1994). Long-term effects of preschool teachers' book readings on low-income children's vocabulary and story comprehension. *Reading Research Quarterly*, 29, 104–122.

Dole, J. A., Duffy, G. G., Roehler, L. R., & Pearson, P. D. (1991). Moving from the old to the new: Research on reading comprehension instruction. *Review of Educational Research*, 61, 239–264.

Donaldson, M. C. (1978). *Children's minds*. New York: Norton.

Donovan, C. A., & Smolkin, L. B. (in press-a). Considering genre, content, and other features important in the selection of trade books for science. *Reading Teacher*.

Donovan, C. A., & Smolkin, L. B. (in press-b). Genre and other factors influencing teachers' book selections for science instruction. *Reading Research Quarterly*.

Duffy, G. G., Roehler, L. R., & Herrmann, B. A. (1988). Modeling mental processes helps poor readers become strategic readers. *Reading Teacher*, 41, 762–767.

Duke, N. K. (1999). *The scarcity of informational texts in first grade* (CIERA Report #1-007). Ann Arbor: CIERA/University of Michigan.

Duke, N. K. (2000). 3.6 minutes per day: The scarcity of informational texts in first grade. *Reading Research Quarterly*, 35, 202–224.

El-Dinary, P. B., Pressley, M., & Schuder, T. (1992). Teachers learning transactional strategies instruction. In C. K. Kinzer & D. J. Leu (Eds.*)*, *Literacy research, theory, and practice: Views from many perspectives. 41st yearbook of the National Reading Conference* (pp. 453–462). Chicago, IL: National Reading Conference.

Flavell, J. H., Speer, J. R., Green, F. L., & August, D. L. (1981). The development of comprehension monitoring and knowledge about communication. *Monographs of the Society for Research in Child Development*, 46(5)[192], 1–65.

Gee, J. P. (1990). *Social linguistics and literacies: Ideology in discourses*. New York: Falmer.

Gibbons, G. (1988). *Sunken treasure*. New York: Harper Trophy.

Halliday, M. A. K. *An introduction to functional grammar* (2nd ed.). London: Arnold.

Hasan, R. (1984). The nursery tale as a genre. *Nottingham Linguistic Circular*, 13, 71–102.

Kamberelis, G. (1999). Genre development and learning: Children writing stories, science reports, and poems. *Research in the Teaching of English*, 33, 403–460.

Kerr, B. M., & Mason, J. M. (1994). Awakening literacy through interactive story reading. In F. Lehr & J. Osborn (Eds.), *Reading, language, and literacy: Instruction for the twenty-first century* (pp. 133–148). Hillsdale, NJ: Erlbaum.

Krashen, S. (1976). Formal and informal linguistic environments in language acquisition and language learning. *TESOL Quarterly*, 10, 157–168.

Krashen, S. (1981). *Second language acquisition and second language learning*. Oxford, England: Pergamon Press.

LaBerge, D., & Samuels, S. J. (1974). Toward a theory of automatic information processing in reading. *Cognitive Psychology*, 6, 293–323.

Lavies, B. (1989). *Tree trunk traffic*. New York: Dutton.

Markman, E. M. (1977). Realizing that you don't understand: A preliminary investigation. *Child Development*, 48, 986–992.

Markman, E. M. (1979). Realizing that you don't understand: Elementary school children's awareness of inconsistencies. *Child Development*, 50, 643–655.

Martin, J. R. (1993). Life as a noun: Arresting the universe in science and humanities. In M. A. K. Halliday & J. R. Martin (Eds.), *Writing science: Literacy and discursive power* (pp. 166–202). London: Falmer.

Martinez, M., Roser, N. L., Hoffman, J. V., & Battle, J. (1992). Fostering better book discussions through response logs and a response framework; A case description. In C. K. Kinzer & D. J. Leu (Eds.), *Literacy research, theory, and practice: Views from many perspectives. 41st yearbook of the National Reading Conference* (pp. 303–311). Chicago: National Reading Conference.

Mason, J. M., Peterman, C. L., Powell, B. M., & Kerr, B. M. (1989). Reading and writing attempts by kindergartners after book reading by teachers. In J. M. Mason (Ed.), *Reading and writing connections* (pp. 105–120). Boston: Allyn & Bacon.

Meyer, B. J. (1975). Identification of the structure of prose and its implications for the study of reading and memory. *Journal of Reading Behavior, 7*(1), 7–47.

Meyer, L. A., Stahl, S. A., Wardrop, J. L., & Linn, R. L (1994). Effects of reading storybooks aloud to children. *Journal of Educational Research, 88*(2), 69–85.

Morrison, F. J., Griffith, E. M., & Frazier, J. A. (1996). Schooling and the 5 to 7 shift: A natural experiment. In A. J. Sameroff & M. Haith (Eds.), *The five- to seven-year shift: The age of reason and responsibility* (pp. 161–186). Chicago: University of Chicago Press.

Oyler, C. (1996). Sharing authority: Student initiations during teacher-led read-alouds of information books. *Teaching and Teacher Education, 12,* 149–160.

Oyler, C., & Barry, A. (1996). Intertextual connections in read-alouds of information books. *Language Arts, 73,* 324–329.

Pappas, C. C. (1991). Is narrative "primary"? Some insights from kindergartners' pretend readings of stories and information books. *Journal of Reading Behavior, 25,* 97–129.

Pappas, C. C., & Barry, A. (1997). Scaffolding urban students' initiations: Transactions in reading information books in the read-aloud curriculum. In N. J. Karolides (Ed.), *Reader response in elementary classrooms: Quest and discovery* (pp. 215–236). Mahwah, NJ: Erlbaum.

Paris, S. G., Cross, D. R., & Lipson, M. Y. (1984). Informed strategies for learning: A program to improve children's reading awareness and comprehension. *Journal of Educational Psychology, 76,* 1239–1252.

Paris, S. G., & Jacobs, S. E. (1984). The benefits of informed instruction for children's reading awareness and comprehension skills. *Child Development, 55,* 2083–2093.

Paris, S. G., Lipson, M. Y., & Wixson, K. K. (1983). Becoming a strategic reader. *Contemporary Educational Psychology, 8,* 293–316.

Paris, S. G., Saarnio, D. A., & Cross, D. R. (1986). A metacognitive curriculum to promote children's reading and learning. *Australian Journal of Psychology, 38*(2), 107–123.

Pearson, P. D. (1996). Reclaiming the center. In M. F. Graves, P. van den Broek, & B. M. Taylor (Eds.), *The first R: Every child's right to read* (pp. 259–274). New York: Teachers College Press.

Pearson, P. D., & Fielding, L. (1991). Comprehension instruction. In R. Barr, M. L. Kamil, P. Mosenthal, & P. D. Pearson (Eds.), *Handbook of reading research* (Vol. 2, pp. 815–860). New York: Longman.

Pearson, P. D., Roehler, L. R., Dole, J. A., & Duffy, G. G. (1992). Developing expertise in reading comprehension. In S. J. Samuels & A. E. Farstrup (Eds.), *What research has to say about reading instruction* (pp. 145–199). Newark, DE: International Reading Association.

Pressley, M., & Harris, K. R. (1990). What we really know about strategy instruction. *Educational Leadership, 48,* 31–34.

Pressley, M., Johnson, C. J., Symons, S., McGoldrick, J. A., & Kurita, J.A. (1989). Strategies that improve children's memory and comprehension of text. *Elementary School Journal, 90,* 3–32.

Rich, S., & Pressley, M. (1990). Teacher acceptance of reading comprehension strategy instruction. *Elementary School Journal, 91,* 43–64.

Salomon, G., & Perkins, D. N. (1989). Rocky roads to transfer: Rethinking mechanisms of a neglected phenomenon. *Educational Psychologist, 24*(2), 113–142.

Siegler, R. S. (1976). Three aspects of cognitive development. *Cognitive Psychology, 8,* 481–520.

Siegler, R. S. (1996). Unidimensional thinking, multidimensional thinking, and characteristic tendencies of thought. In A. J. Sameroff & M. Haith (Eds.), *The five- to seven-year shift: The age of reason and responsibility* (pp. 63–84). Chicago: University of Chicago Press.

Smolkin, L. B., & Donovan, C. (1993, December). *Responses of first graders to information and picture storybooks within a classroom context*. Paper presented at the annual meeting of the National Reading Conference, Charleston, SC.

Smolkin, L. B., & Donovan, C. A. (2000). *The contexts of comprehension: Information book read alouds and comprehension acquisition* (CIERA Report #2-009). Ann Arbor: CIERA/University of Michigan.

Smolkin, L. B., & Donovan, C. A. (in press). The contexts of comprehension: The information book read aloud, comprehension acquisition, and comprehension instruction in a first grade classroom. *Elementary School Journal.*

Smolkin, L. B., Donovan, C. A., & Lomax, R. G. (2001). Is narrative primary? Well, it depends. In T. Shanahan & F. Rodriguez-Brown (Eds.), *National Reading Conference Yearbook, 49,* 511–520.

Snow, C. E., Burns, M. S., & Griffin, P. (Eds.). (1998). *Preventing reading difficulties in young children: Report of the Committee on the Prevention of Reading Difficulties in Young Children.* Washington, DC: National Academy Press.

Stein, N. L., & Glenn, C. G. (1979). An analysis of story comprehension in elementary school children. In R. O. Freedle (Ed.), *Advances in discourse processes, Vol. 2: New directions in discourse processing* (pp. 53–120). Norwood, NJ: Ablex.

Taylor, I., & Taylor, M. M. (1983). *The psychology of reading.* New York : Academic Press.

Trabasso, T. (1994). The power of narrative. In F. Lehr & J. Osborn (Eds.), *Reading, language, and literacy: Instruction for the twenty-first century* (pp. 187–200). Hillsdale, NJ: Erlbaum.

Trabasso, T., & Magliano, J. P. (1996). How do children understand what they read and what can we do to help them? In F. Graves, P. van den Broek, & B. M. Taylor (Eds.), *The first R: Every child's right to read* (pp. 160–188). New York: Teachers College Press.

Unsworth, L. (1999). Developing critical understanding of the specialised language of school science and history texts: A functional grammatical perspective. *Journal of Adolescent and Adult Literacy, 42*(7), 508–521.

Wells, G. (1986). *The meaning makers: Children learning language and using language to learn.* Portsmouth, NH: Heinemann.

White, S. H. (1965). Evidence for a hierarchical arrangement of learning processes. *Advances in Child Behavior and Development, 2,* 187–220.

White, S. H. (1996). The child's entry into the age of reason. In A. J. Sameroff & M. Haith (Eds.), *The five- to seven-year shift: The age of reason and responsibility* (pp. 18–30). Chicago: University of Chicago Press.

Wood, D., Bruner, J., & Ross, G. (1976). The role of tutoring in problem solving. *Journal of Child Psychology and Psychiatry, 17,* 89–100.

Wood, D., Wood, H., & Middleton, D. (1978). An experimental evaluation of four face-to-face teaching strategies. *International Journal of Behavioural Development, 1,* 131–147.

Yaden, D. B., Jr., Smolkin, L. B., & Conlon, A. (1989). Preschoolers' questions about pictures, print conventions, and story text during reading aloud at home. *Reading Research Quarterly, 24,* 188–214.

11

Individual Differences That Influence Reading Comprehension

Darcia Narvaez

Theories about reading have moved away from viewing the reader as a passive recipient of textual input, as a *tabula rasa* on which the author sketches his or her message. Under this view, reading comprehension is easily explained by the success of the textual input entering and staying intact within the mind of the reader. Adopting this view, some character educators can assert that reading moral stories to children will build moral literacy and moral character due to the nature of the stories themselves. That is, as long as the children "hear" the stories, they will absorb the story messages. This is the view promulgated by former secretary of education William Bennett in his wildly popular book, *The Book of Virtues*. Bennett (1993) contends that hearing moral stories will develop moral literacy, which then leads to moral character. There is no evidence for his claims. William Kilpatrick (1993) agrees with Bennett, saying that "good books do their own work in their own way" and "it is not necessary or wise for adults to explain the 'moral' in each story" (p. 268). In fact, recent research has disconfirmed a "passive reader" theory and the claims made by Bennett, Kilpatrick, and others. These findings are reviewed in this chapter.

We find that readers are active comprehenders. They use their knowledge and strategies to construct meaning from a text (Pressley & Afflerbach, 1995). The reading process resembles more closely the interaction of a breeze on a landscape. The breeze has an influence on the features, moving dirt and debris about and shaping erosion, but only so far as the structures of the landscape allow. Constructivist reading theory takes into account the nature of the reader (the landscape) in response to the textual input.

Constructivist reading research tells us that at least five things about the reader matter in reading comprehension: reader skills, reader knowledge, reader cognitive development, reader culture, and reader purpose. Leaving the discussion of general reading comprehension skills to others, this chapter address the influence of (1) reader expertise in the knowledge domain of the text, (2) the sociomoral cognitive development of the reader,

(3) the degree to which the cultural assumptions of the text match those of the reader, and (4) the reader's purpose for reading (e.g., for fun or to study). All four factors concern elements that the reader brings to the reading situation and that affect the reader's processing of the text.

READER KNOWLEDGE

Individuals who read or view the same text often end up with different mental models or understandings of the text. For example, a 16–year-old gunslinger named "Doug," who had performed nine drive-by shootings over the previous year in his hometown of Omaha, Nebraska, considered the films *South Central* and *Boyz 'n the Hood* to be affirmations of his aspirations and lifestyle (Hull, 1993). In contrast, most viewers of either one of these films created a mental model with an explicit moral lesson about which behaviors and life choices *to avoid*. What are the factors that lead to these radically different comprehensions of the same text?

Traditionally, reading researchers have studied the causes of individual differences in the comprehension of texts along two lines, reader skill and reader knowledge. Reader skill concerns basic reading and language abilities, including essential decoding skills such as word recognition, vocabulary, and memory, as well as higher level skills such as reading strategies and forming inferences. Readers with more of these skills are better at comprehending texts (e.g., Cunningham, Stanovich, & Wilson, 1990; Palmer, MacLeod, Hunt, & Davidson, 1985). "Doug"'s misunderstanding of an antigang movie may have been influenced by poorly developed text comprehension skills. But there are other sources for reader misunderstanding.

A second type of individual difference that researchers study is differences in the specific knowledge brought by the reader to the text. Constructivist theory generally assumes that an individual processes or interprets experience based on previous experience or knowledge. Cognitive schema theory (CST) suggests that when an individual is presented with information, a schema or knowledge structure is activated to interpret the information. Derry (1996) suggests that there are three types of schemas or knowledge structures that can be activated in an individual: memory objects (specific small units of related characteristics), cognitive fields (an activated set of memory objects), and mental models (an overall meaning structure of a particular situation or experience). Such mental activations occur during reading. If the reader lacks the knowledge (and therefore the activations) requisite for interpreting the information in the text, the reader will misunderstand or misinterpret the text.

In general, as a reader reads and remembers text, he or she attempts to create a coherent mental representation by integrating text information and by elaborating on the text with prior knowledge about the world (van den Broek, 1994). Prior knowledge often comes in the form of general knowledge structures. General knowledge structures, such as specific scripts (e.g., Brown, Smiley, Day, Townsend, & Lawton, 1977; Schank & Abelson, 1977) and schemas (e.g., Anderson & Pearson, 1984; Bartlett, 1932; Bobrow & Norman, 1975; Rumelhart, 1980; Rumelhart & Ortony, 1977), have been shown to affect how readers comprehend a particular text. For example, due to extensive familiarity with grocery stores, a reader likely has a general knowledge "script" (or cognitive field) of the type and order of events that occur in grocery stores (a grocery store script) that affects the reader's recall of a text about a grocery store visit. When a reader familiar with grocery stores reads a text such as the following, a grocery store script may be activated: "Carol had a long list of food to get, so she went to the store. After she got inside, it took over an hour before she was finished." The reader might add details (memory objects that were activated in the cognitive field) at recall that were not in the text, such as: "Carol parked the car in the parking lot. She entered the store and took a grocery cart, which she pushed through the store collecting her food. After everything on her list was placed in her cart, she went to the checkout line, and so on." Such additions suggest the existence of a grocery store script that influenced recall. Such scripts, schemas, or knowledge structures provide a means by which to understand the text.

A single word or event in the text may evoke a whole knowledge structure (such as a restaurant script or beach schema). Not only does the schema or knowledge structure help with current understanding, but related memory objects are also activated (i.e., a cognitive field). Later events in the text are interpreted according to the activated cognitive field. For example, "After she got inside, it took over an hour before she was finished" is an ambiguous sentence that is interpreted according to the grocery store schema activated by the previous sentence: "Carol had a long list of food to get, so she went to the store." Schemas provide a top-down tool for interpreting events in texts.

Sophistication in domain-specific schemas (more and better organized knowledge) often distinguishes experts from novices in that experts have more tools for interpreting the text. Domain knowledge generally refers to a specific, "studied" domain (Alexander, 1992) for which expertise may take an estimated 10,000 hours of study (Simon & Chase, 1973). Differences between experts and novices have been examined in many domains, for example, chess (Chiesi, Spilich, & Voss, 1979), dinosaurs (Chi & Koeske, 1983), baseball (Spilich, Vesonder, Chiesi, & Voss, 1979), and medical diagnosis (Johnson, Hassebrock, Duran, & Moller, 1982; Rikers, Boshuizen & Schmidt, 1997). Although it is still unclear what kind of knowledge and skill advantages the expert has, some have suggested that experts are distinguished by such things as (1) the ability to perceive larger, more complex, meaningful patterns in given information (Chase & Simon, 1973; Chi, Glaser, & Farr, 1988); (2) having better schema selection, as well as schema availability (Spiro, 1980); (3) the ability to immediately transfer information to or activate a larger long-term memory network (Charness, 1976; Ericsson & Kintsch, 1995; Frey & Adesman, 1976); (4) the ability to derive a set of retrieval cues that facilitate the recall of meaningful information later (Chase & Ericsson, 1981); and (5) the ability to efficiently suppress inappropriate associations (Gernsbacher & Faust, 1991). Many of these suggested mechanisms operate when experts read domain-relevant texts.

When researchers have looked at domain expertise in the context of reading, several findings have emerged. For example, greater comprehension of a text is related to (1) reader familiarity with the text topic (e.g., Chiesi et al., 1979; Fincher-Kiefer, Post, Greene, & Voss, 1988; Spilich et al., 1979; see also reviews by Alexander, 1992; Roller, 1990); (2) congruity between reader background and specific text content (e.g., Ohlhausen & Roller, 1988); and (3) a greater amount of knowledge considered analogous to subject matter knowledge (Alexander, Pate, & Kulikowich, 1989; Hayes & Tierney, 1982; Kulikowich & Alexander, 1990; Walker, 1987). Differences in comprehension between domain experts and nonexperts when reading domain-relevant text may reflect differences in schema activation that affect the ability to make inferences and to construct relevant schematic and conceptual models of text events.

When readers read, they apply prior knowledge in order to build a coherent mental model (overall meaning structure) of the text (McNamara, Miller, & Bransford, 1991; van Dijk & Kintsch, 1983). Texts are cognitively modeled or represented in several ways. In a vein similar to cognitive schema theory, van Dijk and Kintsch (1983) proposed three types of mental representations built in the process of reading: the surface structure (which words are presented in which order), the propositional text base (which propositions are presented in which organization), and the situation or mental model (what the text is depicting). Whereas the propositional text base is based primarily on the text itself, the *mental model* of a text tends to be knowledge dependent (e.g., van Dijk & Kintsch, 1983). Moravcsik and Kintsch (1993) found that high-knowledge readers achieved a deeper level of understanding, enabling them to construct an appropriate situation or mental model that allowed them to elaborate texts correctly. Low domain knowledge prevented readers from forming an adequate mental model, which led to erroneous elaborations and inferences during recall. When texts are inconsistent with the reader's activated knowledge structures and mental model, readers understand poorly (Bransford & Johnson, 1972), recall wrongly (Steffensen, Joag-Dev, & Anderson, 1979), and even distort memory to fit with their schematic structures (Bartlett, 1932; Narvaez, 1998; Reynolds, Taylor, Steffensen, Shirey, & Anderson, 1982). Inadequate schema activation or inappropriate mental modeling may explain "Doug"'s response to the antigang films. Inadequate schema activation is characteristic of differences in moral text comprehension.

THE SOCIOMORAL COGNITIVE DEVELOPMENT OF THE READER

Generally, research in sociomoral development has focused on moral judgment (i.e., reasoning used to advocate a certain action choice in a moral dilemma). In this tradition, researchers recognize that people conceptualize moral problems differently, based on developmental age and education (e.g., Kohlberg, 1984; Rest, 1986). As individuals develop in moral judgment, transformations occur in how they construe their obligations to others. These transformations can be viewed as changing moral schemas (memory objects and cognitive fields) about how it is possible to organize cooperation (Rest, Narvaez, Bebeau, & Thoma, 1999). As moral judgment matures, an individual's concerns expand, and he or she is able to consider the welfare of more and more "others" when conceptualizing ideal forms of cooperation (e.g., at the lowest schema, one is primarily concerned for self, whereas in the most developed type of schema, one includes concern for strangers). Perhaps "Doug"'s misunderstanding of the antigang message was influenced by developmentally limited moral judgment schemas.

The effect of moral judgment development on reading has been examined in several studies. Narvaez (1998) studied the effects of moral judgment development on the recall of narratives. Real-life, complex narratives were used with embedded moral reasoning at different stages of moral judgment. Moral arguments were presented in a stream of contextual detail. As in real life, the narratives intertwined events with people's rationalizations and interpretations of those events. Participants were asked not only to recall what actions generally occurred in the narrative but also what the protagonist was thinking about in the narrative. As in real life, the participant had to think over a decision situation while trying to sort out the reasoning and reconstruct what happened.

After reading the narratives, middle school and college students were asked to recall the narratives. Differences in recall corresponded to differences in moral judgment development as measured by the Defining Issues Test (DIT). Persons with higher scores in moral judgment on the DIT not only better recalled the texts and the high-stage moral arguments within them, but they also distorted their recall differently. Although all readers tended to distort the text in their recall, high-stage moral reasoners were significantly more likely to add new *high-stage* reasons to their recall of the narratives in comparison to lower stage reasoners. Explained by cognitive schema theory, those with higher levels of moral judgment had a larger and better organized set of memory objects activated (i.e., a different type of cognitive field) of both higher and lower moral judgment schemas, whereas those with lower levels of moral judgments had a more limited set of activations. Thus it was found that distortions were common, yet the type of distortion varied according to cognitive developmental structures.

In order to examine whether or not there is an expertise aspect to moral judgment development, Narvaez (2001) examined moral text comprehension between more expert and less expert groups in moral judgment. Three tasks were used: recall of moral narratives as in Narvaez (1998), giving advice after listening to a personal moral dilemma on tape, and thinking aloud while reading a narrative. Think-aloud protocols, in which a continuous record of thoughts is produced while reading aloud, have been used to study individual differences among readers (e.g., Whitney, Ritchie, & Clark, 1991), including both domain novices and experts (e.g., Lundeberg, 1987; Wineberg, 1991). In some studies, more skilled comprehenders generated more explanatory inferences while thinking aloud during reading (e.g., Chi, de Leeuw, Chiu, & LaVancher, 1994; Graesser, Singer, & Trabasso, 1994; Trabasso & Magliano, 1996; van den Broek & Lorch, 1993; Zwaan & Brown, 1996). Similarly, readers with expert background knowledge do more explaining (e.g., Chiesi et al., 1979), analysis of the text (e.g., Lundeborg, 1987; Wineberg, 1991), and evaluation (Wyatt et al., 1993).

Those with more moral judgment expertise exhibited superior performance: They were better at recalling higher stage moral arguments from narratives; they were more active in reading aloud domain-relevant texts, especially in terms of predictions, explanations, evaluations, text-based coherence breaks and responses to higher stage items; and they exhibited a more complex mental model after listening to a moral dilemma situation, recalling and advocating more high-stage reasons in their advice giving. Those with less expertise, on the other hand, did not recall as much from the moral texts, especially the high-stage reasoning; they were less active in reading aloud, reacted less to high-stage items, and exhibited less complex representations during advice giving, providing fewer high-stage reasons.

In another set of studies (Narvaez, Bentley, Gleason, & Samuels, 1998; Narvaez, Gleason, Mitchell, & Bentley, 1999), we examined developmental differences in the comprehension of themes in moral stories. We created well-constructed (i.e., with a beginning, middle, and end), nonreligious, literary, moral stories. A "moral story" has a theme about a specific aspect of getting along with others, such as being honest with strangers. The stories reflected the complex notion of moral behavior as theorized by Rest's four component model (Rest, 1983). In it, moral action requires moral sensitivity (e.g., awareness of cause–consequence chains of actions and reactions), moral judgment (e.g., selecting the most moral action), moral motivation (applying one's values and prioritizing a moral action), and moral action (implementing and following through on the moral choice). All four components were included in each story.

We examined whether children understood the themes of moral stories as intended. We selected themes that were understandable to younger children (e.g., persevere for the good of others, be honest with strangers, do not lie for friends, be responsible and trustworthy by completing your duties to others) rather than more adult themes, such as principles for sustaining constitutional democracies. We focused on correct versus incorrect choice of the moral theme from among distractors. Participants from third and fifth grades and from a university were tested on whether or not they understood the author-based lessons (i.e., the moral themes) from several moral stories. They were asked to identify the theme from a list of message choices and to identify which of four alternative vignettes had the same theme. Participants also rated the set of message and vignette choices for closeness of match to the original story. Reading comprehension was used as a covariate. Developmental differences in moral theme understanding were significant, even after accounting for reading comprehension differences. Younger participants were more attracted to lower moral judgment stage distortions of themes, suggesting that moral judgment development is a factor in moral theme comprehension. The reader seems to impose a level of cognitive moral sophistication (a set of moral schemas or cognitive field) on the initial interpretation of the moral story.

Imposing his moral schemas on the story, "Doug" may have been attracted to a more simplistic understanding of the theme. He may have ignored or missed the contradictory elements in the story because of a very personal, tacitly held understanding of causal and necessary events in the social world. Culture operates in a similar manner. As readers read or view a text, they seem to impose a culturally based cognitive field on the text as well.

THE DEGREE TO WHICH THE CULTURAL ASSUMPTIONS OF THE TEXT MATCH THOSE OF THE READER

What knowledge do people from different cultures draw on when they read culture-specific texts? Cultural knowledge seems to affect comprehension much like background knowledge. Similarly, when texts are inconsistent with the expectations or high-level knowledge structures of the reader, the reader will understand poorly (Bransford & Johnson, 1972), recall wrongly (Steffensen et al., 1979) and even distort memory to fit with the reader's mental schemas (Reynolds et al., 1982). A classic example is Bartlett's (1932) seminal work with the "War of the Ghosts'" folktale, in which participants showed an increasingly distorted recall over time of this Native American story, making it conform to familiar story schemas. Bartlett was the first in this century to provide evidence for the influence of cultural expectations on narrative recall. In subsequent research, Harris, Lee, Hensley, and Schoen (1988) found that routines from another culture were increasingly recalled erroneously over time by those from a different culture, indicating a conceptual influence during memory retrieval. Readers apply culture-based schemas to the way they mentally represent the text (e.g., Reynolds et al., 1982). For example, when Harris et al. (1988) asked participants to recall texts about events in a different culture, they found distorted recall, as in the following story. The text said:

"Ted was eager to go downtown to do some shopping for Carnival. He needed to buy some gifts for his parents and some new costumes for himself and his friends. . . . He got on the bus at the rear door and found a seat in the back. After getting settled, he pulled out his wallet. . . . He then carried a stack of fifties up to the cashier in the center of the bus. . . . Ted passed through the turnstile and found a seat just behind the driver. . . . When he arrived, he scrambled out the front door of the bus."

Participants from the United States tended to recall incorrectly that Ted got on the front of the bus, paid, and sat down in the back. Participants from Brazil did not make these errors because the particular bus experience was a familiar schema.

One large-group difference that has been studied in cross-cultural research is orientation to relationships in terms of individualism or collectivism (Triandis, 1995). As for religious and political differences, difference in orientation to human society and relationships can be a source of value conflicts. In an individualistic orientation, everyone is expected to look after self and immediate family, whereas with an orientation to collectivism, persons receive protection from a cohesive in-group in exchange for loyalty (definitions are from Hofstede, 1991). Triandis and his colleagues (e.g., Kim, Triandis, Kagitcibasi, Choi, & Yoon, 1994) have studied the individualism–collectivism construct and postulate that it reflects cultural syndromes for which evidence at the individual level is accumulating. So, for example, Triandis (1995) suggests that in a restaurant setting, waiters in places with different cultural orientations on individualism–collectivism will behave differently. A waiter in Brazil (collectivist) takes the order from the senior member of a group because he assumes that the group will build bonds by sharing the same food. In contrast, most waiters in Western (individualist) countries will assume that each person will order according to individual preference.

We designed a study to examine the influence of individualism–collectivism orientation on the on-line processing of moral texts. In Narvaez, Mitchell, and Linzie (1998), we tested two groups: Asians/Asian Americans and non-Asians, expecting that the Asian group would more reliably provide us with collectivists than other groups. Participants had native skills in English and read several stories on a computer about individuals who were asked for help by a relative (aunt, uncle, cousin). In half of these stories, the protagonist sacrificed his or her own goals in order to help ("help" stories); in the other half he or she did not help ("no-help" stories).

While they were reading, the participants were interrupted with a lexical decision task. Some of the letter strings were not (English) words, some were words irrelevant to what they were reading, and some of the words represented inferences assumed to take place by the reader at that point in the story. Two kinds of inferences were tested in the moral stories: reinstatements of information from earlier in the text necessary to understand a current sentence and moral inferences—elaborations on current text action based on cultural assumptions (cognitive field). The moral inferences occurred after the protagonist decided to help or not help in the story. In the "help" stories, the moral inferences were represented by words like "dutiful" or "loyal." For the "no-help" stories, the moral inferences were represented by words like "self-centered" or "shameful." Using the nonrelevant English words as a baseline, each participant served as his or her own control. We expected there to be a significant response-time difference for both kinds of moral stories between individualists and collectivists. We also expected that the collectivists would react more quickly especially to the moral probes in the "no-help" stories. Participants took an inventory of their orientation to individualism or collectivism. Reading skill differences were controlled by individually standardizing each reader's responses.

As expected, there were no significant differences in reaction time for reinstatement (nonmoral) probe words based on collectivism score. But we did find significant differences in reaction time to moral probe words based on collectivism scores. Further, significant differences in reaction time to moral probe words remained after holding cultural background constant. That is, collectivism scores, regardless of cultural–ethnic background, were significantly related to reaction time for moral inferences but not for nonmoral inferences. We concluded that cultural–ideological background can influence moral inferences while reading. The process of reading about helping or not helping relatives activated a cognitive field concerning relating to others and affected the mental model of the text.

Cultural influences on reading often transpire without awareness. Reading is also influenced by the reading context and the reader's conscious goals. Another factor in determining intraindividual variation in the pattern of inferential activity during reading is the purpose the reader has for reading (e.g., Walker & Meyer, 1980).

THE READER'S PURPOSE FOR READING

A critical role for reading purpose in the comprehension process is implied by findings that orientation to (or goal while reading) the text during reading influences recall (e.g., Pichert & Anderson, 1977; Anderson & Pichert, 1978). Readers claim to modify their reading strategies according to reading goal. For example, Lorch, Lorch, and Klusewitz (1993) asked readers what kinds of different reading tasks they experienced and how they perceived the processing demands for the different types of reading tasks. The participants broadly distinguished two categories of reading tasks, reading for school (study) purposes and reading for stimulation or entertainment.

School reading was perceived as less interesting, slower, involving less anticipation of future text events, more attempts at integration, and more rereading, and also as more taxing of understanding and memory. In contrast, reading for entertainment was perceived to involve an increased effort to find relations among ideas and events in the text, more anticipation of forthcoming text events, more interest, and more analysis of writing style. Lorch et al. (1993) provide a rich description of text types and reader perception of their demands.

Narvaez, van den Broek, and Ruiz (1999) reported that reading purpose influenced the pattern of inferences that readers generated as they read. Readers with a study goal were more likely to engage in rereading and evaluating the text and to indicate knowledge-based coherence breaks than were readers who were reading for entertainment. This pattern of findings corroborates readers' assessments of their own reading processes, in particular their perception that school/study reading involves more rereading and attempts at integration (Lorch et al., 1993). The findings also suggest that the "search-after-meaning" principle (Graesser et al., 1994; van den Broek, 1990)—according to which the reader attempts to explain each element in the text before continuing to the next element—applies particularly to readers who are reading to study rather than to readers who simply read for entertainment.

Narvaez, van den Broek and Ruiz (1999) also examined the interaction between reading purpose and the reading of two types of text, narrative and expository texts. The expository text evoked more study-type behaviors, specifically the generation of repetitions, evaluations, and the identification of knowledge-based coherence breaks. Processing of the narrative appeared to be much less affected by reading goal. Regardless of reading goal, readers gave more explanations and predictions when reading the narrative text than when reading the expository text. Conversely, the expository text evoked more associations, repetitions, evaluations, and indications of knowledge-based coherence breaks. The research literature provides various reasons for why one might expect different comprehension processes for narrative and expository text:

1. Narratives may elicit more interest, promoting more explanations and predictions than expository texts (e.g., Olson, Mack, & Duffy, 1981; Perrig & Kintsch, 1985; Schmalhofer & Glavanov, 1986; Trabasso & Magliano, 1996; van Dijk & Kintsch, 1983).
2. Narratives may promote increased inferencing, resulting, for example, in readers making nine times as many inferences during stories as during expository texts (Graesser, 1981).
3. Readers have early and extensive practice making inferences while reading stories because stories are used when learning to read and because everyday life is constructed much like a story (Britton, van Dusen, Glynn, & Hemphill, 1990).
4. The structure of expository texts is more variable than that of narratives (Bock & Brewer, 1985).
5. Narratives activate schema and script structures that support inference generation (Britton et al., 1990).
6. Narratives may rely more on familiar forms of causality than do expository texts, thus prompting more explanations and predictive inferences.

In summary, instructors need to be aware of the extent of individual differences among comprehenders. In general, readers vary in cognitive structures or schemas according to their experience and the interaction of experience with maturation. Reader schemas help determine what the reader extracts from a text. Schemas known to affect reading comprehension include world knowledge, developmentally based conceptual fields, and culturally based causal fields. Reading failure may occur due to lack of text-relevant schemas to make the requisite inferences and to activate related memory objects or ideas that the author assumes in the reader. Failure to comprehend the intended messages in a text can also occur during moral discourse comprehension. For example, young children may interpret a story about being responsible to others as a story about avoiding deleterious effects to the self. Specific implications for practice follow. These suggestions are grouped in terms of moral discourse comprehension, moral theme comprehension, cultural differences, and reading strategies.

Comprehension of Moral Discourse

Persuasive discourse that incorporates moral argumentation pervades our lives: news shows, talk shows, documentaries, political speeches, policy discussions, lawyers' arguments in jury trials. Often containing implicit moral reasoning, persuasive discourse of any kind may be understood distinctively by different comprehenders in correspondence to their levels of moral judgment development. As has been found in schema research (e.g., Bransford & Johnson, 1972; Dooling & Lachman, 1971), discourse that presents implicit or fragmented moral reasoning may activate moral schemas more strongly (as a means to fill in coherence breaks). When the textual information conflicts with reader knowledge, the reader's preexisting knowledge is likely to prevail unless the reader is dissatisfied with the level of explanation his or her knowledge provides (Anderson, 1983). This "dissatisfaction" with moral reasoning schemas can be generated through class discussion with peers (see Power, Higgins, & Kohlberg, 1989).

Explicit educational curricula and instruction concerning moral topics such as social behavior change (e.g., drug use prevention or abuse recovery) may not be properly understood if the moral judgment capacities of the audience are not accommodated. Instructors should be aware that students may be understanding texts in ways different from the author's intention or the perspective of the instructor. Just as teachers attempt to match the reading level of a text with the student's level of reading skill, moral and social education programs should attempt to match the moral reasoning level of a text with the level of the student's moral reasoning capacities. Of course, in order to create the context for cognitive growth, texts should be selected that contain familiar and slightly more advanced moral reasoning (to promote "dissatisfaction" with existing schemas). Curricula advocating behavior change, such as character education curricula, should be thoroughly piloted in order to gauge what is understood by the target audience. A curriculum that works with one age group may not work with another.

Comprehension of Moral Themes

In order to promote the development of general theme comprehension, the instructor should facilitate student practice of gist recall and generalizing from texts (see Williams, Brown, Silverstein, & deCani, 1994 for a direct teaching approach). For *moral* theme comprehension, instructors also can focus on specific moral aspects of texts. A list of actions that teachers can take based on the process model of moral behavior (Narvaez, Mitchell, Endicott, & Bock, 1999) follows.

1. Assist students to become aware that some demands in a story are in conflict with others (e.g., personal/inner, outer/social). This may be studied by discussing: What was the problem? What was the worst thing the character faced? Were there differences in what people wanted? What were the differences?

2. Increase students' moral sensitivity to the configuration of the situation. This may be accomplished by asking these questions: What was going on? Who was thinking about what was going on? Who could be affected? Who was affected?

3. Help students reason about possible actions (moral sensitivity and reasoning) by posing questions such as: What could be done? What would happen if____? What outcomes might occur? How might people react?

4. Focus students' attention on their own, as well as characters', personal identities and moral motivation, with questions like: What did the character think about when deciding/doing the deed? What kinds of ideals were driving the character in the story?

5. Increase students' awareness of sacrifice or sublimation of personal gratification for a greater good (moral motivation). Ask: How did the action affect each char-

acter in the story? How did the action affect the community (e.g., classroom, neighborhood)?

6. Help students notice follow through: How did the character carry out the action? When there were obstacles, what did the character do?

7. Develop students' skills in interpreting the social outcome and implicit or explicit positive judgment of action taken: How did the story end—good or bad? Why? For whom was it a good ending? For whom was it a bad ending?

8. Develop students' skills in reflecting on alternative endings: How could the outcome have turned out better for everyone?

To explore characteristics of moral themes and texts themselves, we (Narvaez, Bock, Endicott, Mitchell, & Bacigalupa, 2001) are developing methods to measure the moral content in stories. This will allow the study of particular content effects on particular comprehenders.

Culture and Reading Comprehension

Schema effects are strongest with ambiguous material in which referential specificity is low (what the sentence or phrase refers to is not clear), local coherence is weak (the phrases and sentences are not closely related), and the message is unclear or nonsensical until a theme or title is provided (Bransford & Johnson, 1972; Dooling & Lachman, 1971). To a non-native speaker of English, this is the way an average text may appear to a reader. Those whose first language is not English or who have immigrated to the United States. may find most school texts ambiguous. Students from diverse backgrounds are often novices in text-relevant knowledge and in knowledge of text structures. Their cognitive fields may be quite different in terms of understanding world events, and they may need assistance in learning the memory objects relevant to school learning. Instructors need to help all students build the cultural cognitive fields necessary for a particular text. Further, instructors should discuss readings during or soon after reading. The longer the interval before recall, the more inaccuracies, and the more likely memory reconstruction is affected by the individual's own perspectives (e.g., schemas) in terms of theme sharpening (embellishment, emphasis, rationalization) and theme leveling (discarding, condensation) of seemingly irrelevant material (Bartlett, 1932; Brown et al., 1977; Dooling & Christiaansen, 1977; Dooling & Lachman, 1971; Sulin & Dooling, 1974).

For students with a different language or cultural background: (1) different conceptual frameworks may become activated that misguide them in reading; (2) expectations of what is normal may differ and cause breakdowns in coherence; (3) cause–consequence chains can differ and/or may be more emotional, evoking strong reactions in the reader (e.g., showing disrespect to an elder by talking back); (4) symbols may differ and cause a breakdown in coherence (e.g., a black cat is related to bad luck in some European cultures; the color white is related to death in some Asian cultures); and (5) there may be differences in what to attend to, what to ignore, or what is superfluous (e.g., what a woman wears on the street is generally ignored by Western societies but highly important in Muslim countries). Instructors should make explicit the world knowledge a text requires for understanding, identifying cultural differences in terms of contextual features, actions, and interpretation of outcomes. Explicit discussion of text events and necessary inferences can help in fostering dialogue not only about the texts themselves but about differences in cultural and moral practice. In addition, using a variety of cultural texts may not only bring some relief to diverse students but also encourage the "mainstream" students to widen their views of the world.

Regardless of what the instructor does, the students may not understand what is intended due to developmental, cultural, and expertise differences. The instructor needs to continue to counter the related misconceptions by helping students hone study strategies that focus on comprehension and that develop thinking, knowledge, and multicultural reading skills.

Reading Purpose and Strategies for Comprehension

Strategies readers use are not always appropriate for comprehension. Readers tend to generate associative inferences with study texts. Instructors and students need to realize that associative elaborations alone are not enough for learning (see Trabasso & Magliano, 1996). Explanatory inferences are also vital (e.g., van den Broek & Kremer, 1999). Yet readers with a study purpose do not automatically use strategies that are related to increased understanding (Chi et al., 1994). Students need assistance in learning helpful reading strategies when reading expository texts. Reading strategies focused on comprehension—in which causal relations are central—are related to better reading comprehension (see also van den Broek & Kremer, 1999) than study strategies such as questioning or outlining. A focus on comprehending a text is more likely to "transform" knowledge into the type of mental representation that promotes long-term learning (Scardamalia & Bereiter, 1984).

Instructors (and texts) need to ask the questions that will lead the reader to make inferences that are related to increased retention, such as causal relations between elements of the text, predictions, and explanations. Students naturally perform these behaviors with narrative texts and need to activate such strategies when studying. Readers need instruction on how to transfer the strategies that they know and apply automatically when reading narrative texts to their reading of expository texts. Instructor coaching can assist readers to monitor their comprehension strategies and activate comprehension-enhancing techniques. Conscious strategic reading will help with comprehension and memory.

Most important, instructors should remember how complex is the interaction between reader and text. Based on the memory objects and cognitive fields built from experience, every reader will have a different mental model of a text. Only those with more expertise, development, and/or similarity in world knowledge to the author will have a mental model of the text that resembles that of the author.

OUR FUTURE RESEARCH AGENDA

Moral text comprehension research is in its early stages; hence there is much work to be done. Although we have studied moral theme comprehension, moral narrative recall, and on-line moral inferencing, it is still unclear what the key features of moral discourse comprehension are. How common is it? How is it used? For example, how does moral theme comprehension relate to persuasive discourse generally? What factors other than moral reasoning and background knowledge influence the interpretation of persuasive discourse? When persuasive discourse is used for prevention of risky behaviors, how do moral themes affect the power and influence of the discourse? For instance, Narvaez, Gardner, and Mitchell (2001) examine both the comprehension of and the effects of using antidrug use messages that depend on moral reasoning and/or evoke moral identity in their interpretation.

Relating moral theme comprehension research to general text comprehension, these questions might be explored:

1. What are the elements of moral theme comprehension? What is the difference between moral and nonmoral theme comprehension? Researchers find that extracting embedded information from a narrative is difficult and relies on factors such as the concerns of the reader at the time and the reader's perspective on the topic (Britton, 1984; Rosenblatt, 1991). General theme extraction is especially difficult for children, becoming better established by fifth grade (Goldman, Reyes, & Varnhagen, 1984). We know that story grammar categories such as initiating events, actions, goals, and outcomes are differentially recalled by children in contrast to adults (e.g., Collins; 1983; van den Broek, Lorch, & Thurlow, 1997). Does moral theme comprehension require something over and above these simpler elements, such as more sophisticated social knowledge?

2. What kinds of story structure and affective focus (Brewer & Lichtenstein, 1982) facilitate moral theme comprehension? How does causal connection strength (Trabasso & van den Broek, 1985) of a moral theme relate to its comprehension (i.e., is a theme with more causal connections to events in the story better comprehended)?

3. What determines whether a reader conjures a moral or a nonmoral theme for a story? For example, *The Little Engine That Could* (Piper, 1930) has both a nonmoral theme (keep trying and you will be successful) and a moral theme (persevere to help others). Does the generation of a moral theme (instead of a nonmoral theme) become a more automatic rather than a consciously controlled process with age?

Classroom research into the teaching of moral theme comprehension should address questions such as:

1. Where are the children failing in theme comprehension? In "picking up" the message through the integration of intention-action-outcome chains of events? In remembering the message? In putting it into words? In making a generalization and applying it? When are differences occurring—at encoding or at retrieval?

2. What skills can be developed for moral theme comprehension? Are the skills the same as for general theme comprehension? How should moral theme instruction be different? What works in teaching moral themes? Williams et al. (1994) have demonstrated that middle-level students can understand the theme of a narrative, but only with deliberate, structured guidance.

3. Are there developmental limitations to moral theme comprehension skills? Does a reader have to have a particular set of moral schemas in order to extract a theme based on such schemas? Are some moral themes understood sooner developmentally than other moral themes, or are some themes just easier to comprehend than others?

Research into the influence of culture on reading should include the study of such questions as: (1) What specific aspects of culture affect reading? (2) Is the cognitive field predictably different for bicultural readers? (3) How multicultural can someone become in terms of reading comprehension? How easy is it to change a reader's cultural cognitive field? (4) What are the specific, identifiable ways that cultural background influences reading comprehension?

There is abundant work to be tackled in the study of individual differences and text comprehension. The mapping of the variety of differences alone will take many years of study. Identifying the instructional strategies that increase reader abilities in each area will require ingenious and persevering research programs.

REFERENCES

Alexander, P. A. (1992). Domain knowledge: Evolving themes and emerging concerns. *Educational Psychologist, 27*, 33–51.

Alexander, P. A., Pate, P. E., & Kulikowich, J. M. (1989). Domain-specific and strategic knowledge: Effects of training on students of differing ages or competence levels. *Learning and Individual Differences, 1*, 283–325.

Anderson, R. C. (1983). *The architecture of cognition.* Cambridge, MA: Harvard University Press.

Anderson, R. C., & Pearson, P. D. (1984). A schema–theoretic view of basic processes in reading comprehension. In P. D. Pearson (Ed.), *Handbook of reading research* (pp. 225–291). New York: Longman.

Anderson, R. C., & Pichert, J. W. (1978). Recall of previously unrecallable information following shift in perspective. *Journal of Verbal Learning and Verbal Behavior, 17*, 1–12.

Bartlett, F. C. (1932). *Remembering.* Cambridge, England: Cambridge University Press.

Bennett, W. (1993). *The book of virtues.* New York: Simon & Schuster.

Bobrow, D., & Norman, D. (1975). Some principles of memory schemata. In D. Bobrow & A. Collins (Eds.), *Representation and understanding: Studies in cognitive science* (pp. 131–149). New York: Academic Press.

Bock, J. K., & Brewer, W. (1985). Discourse structure and mental models. In D. Carr (Ed.), *Development of reading skills* (pp. 55–75). San Francisco: Jossey-Bass.

Bransford, J. D., & Johnson, M. K. (1972). Contextual prerequisites for understanding: Some investigations of comprehension and recall. *Journal of Verbal Learning and Verbal Behavior, 11*, 717–726.

Brewer, W. F., & Lichtenstein, E. H. (1982). Stories are to entertain: A structural–affect theory of stories. *Journal of Pragmatics, 6*, 473–486.

Britton, B. K., Van Dusen, L., Glynn, S. M., & Hemphill, D. (1990). The impact of inferences on instructional text. *Psychology of Learning and Motivation, 25*, 53–70.

Britton, J. N. (1984). Viewpoints: The distinction between participant and spectator role in language research and practice. *Research in the Teaching of English, 18*, 320–331.

Brown, A. L., Smiley, S. S., Day, J. D., Townsend, M. A. R., & Lawton, S. C. (1977). Intrusion of a thematic idea in children's comprehension and retention of stories. *Child Development, 48*, 1454–1466.

Charness, N. (1976). Components of skill in bridge. *Canadian Journal of Psychology, 33*, 1–16.

Chase, W., & Simon, H. (1973). Perception in chess. *Cognitive Psychology, 4*, 55–81.

Chase, W. G., & Ericsson, K. A. (1981). Skilled memory. In J. R. Anderson (Ed.), *Cognitive skills and their acquisition* (pp. 141–189). Hillsdale, NJ: Erlbaum.

Chi, M. T. H., de Leeuw, N., Chiu, M., & LaVancher, C. (1994). Eliciting self-explanations improves understanding. *Cognitive Science, 18*, 439–477.

Chi, M. T. H., Glaser, R., & Farr, M. J. (1988). *The nature of expertise.* Hillsdale, NJ: Erlbaum.

Chi, M. T. H., & Koeske, R. (1983). Network representation of a child's dinosaur knowledge. *Developmental Psychology, 19*, 29–39.

Chiesi, H. L., Spilich, G. J., & Voss, J. F. (1979). Acquisition of domain-related information in relations to high and low domain knowledge. *Journal of Verbal Learning and Verbal Behavior, 18,* 257–274.

Collins, W. A. (1983). Interpretation and inference in children's television viewing. In I. Bryant & D. R. Anderson (Eds.), *Children's understanding of television.* New York: Academic Press.

Cunningham, A. E., Stanovich, K. E., & Wilson, M. R. (1990). Cognitive variation in adult college students differing in reading ability. In T. H. Carr & B. A. Levy (Eds.), *Reading and its development: Component skill approaches* (pp. 129–159). New York: Academic Press.

Derry, S. J. (1996). Cognitive schema theory in the constructivist debate. *Educational Psychologist, 31*(3/4), 163–174.

Dooling, J. D., & Christiaansen, R. E. (1977). Episodic and semantic aspects of memory for prose. *Journal of Experimental Psychology: Human Learning and Memory, 3,* 428–436.

Dooling, J. D., & Lachman, R. (1971). Effects of comprehension on retention of prose. *Journal of Experimental Psychology, 88,* 216–222.

Ericsson, K. A., & Kintsch, W. (1995). Long-term working memory. *Psychological Review, 12,* 211–245.

Fincher-Kiefer, R., Post, T. A., Greene, T. R., & Voss, J. V. (1988). On the role of prior knowledge and task demands in the processing of text. *Journal of Memory and Language, 27,* 416–428.

Frey, P. W., & Adesman, P. (1976). Recall memory for visually presented chess positions. *Memory and Cognition, 4,* 541–547.

Gernsbacher, M. A., & Faust, M. (1991). The mechanism of suppression: A component of general comprehension skill. *Journal of Experimental Psychology: Learning, Memory, and Cognition, 17,* 245–262.

Goldman, S. R., Reyes, M., & Varnhagen, D. (1984). Understanding fables in first and second languages. *NABE Journal, 8*(2), 35–66.

Graesser, A. C. (1981). *Prose comprehension beyond the word.* New York: Springer-Verlag.

Graesser, A. C., Singer, M., & Trabasso, T. (1994). Constructing inferences during narrative text comprehension. *Psychological Review, 101,* 371–395.

Harris, R. J., Lee, D. J., Hensley, D. L., & Schoen, L. M. (1988). The effect of cultural script knowledge on memory for stories over time. *Discourse Processes, 11,* 413–431.

Hayes, D. A., & Tierney, R. J. (1982). Developing readers' knowledge through analogy. *Reading Research Quarterly, 17,* 256–280.

Hofstede, G. (1991). *Cultures and organizations: Software of the mind.* London: McGraw-Hill.

Hull, J. (1993, May). A boy and his gun. *Time, 142*(5), 20–27.

Johnson, P. E., Hassebrock, F., Duran, A. S., & Moller, J. H. (1982). Multimethod study of clinical judgment. *Organizational Behavior and Human Performance, 30,* 201–230.

Kilpatrick, W. (1993). *Why Jonny can't tell right from wrong.* New York: Simon and Schuster.

Kim, U., Triandis, H. C., Kagitcibasi, C., Choi, S., & Yoon, G. (1994). *Individualism and collectivism: Theory, method, and applications.* Thousand Oaks, CA: Sage.

Kohlberg, L. (1984). *Essays on moral development: Vol. 2. The psychology of moral judgment.* San Francisco: Harper & Row.

Kulikowich, J. M., & Alexander, P. A. (1990). The effects of gender, ability, and grade on analogy performance. *Contemporary Educational Psychology, 15,* 364–377.

Lorch, R. F., Lorch, E. P., & Klusewitz, M. A. (1993). College students' conditional knowledge about reading. *Journal of Educational Psychology, 85,* 239–252.

Lundeberg, M. A. (1987). Metacognitive aspects of reading comprehension: Studying understanding in legal case analysis. *Reading Research Quarterly, 22,* 407–432.

McNamara, T. P., Miller, D. L., & Bransford, J. D. (1991). Mental models and reading comprehension. In R. Barr, M. L. Kamil, P. B. Mosenthal, & P. D. Pearson (Eds.), *Handbook of reading research* (Vol. 2, pp. 490–511). New York: Longman.

Moravcsik, J. E., & Kintsch, W. (1993). Writing quality, reading skills, and domain knowledge as factors in text comprehension. *Canadian Journal of Experimental Psychology, 47,* 360–374.

Narvaez, D. (1998). The effects of moral schemas on the reconstruction of moral narratives in 8th grade and college students. *Journal of Educational Psychology, 90*(1), 13–24.

Narvaez, D., & Gleason, T. (2001). *Expertise differences in comprehending moral texts.*

Narvaez, D., Bentley, J., Gleason, T., & Samuels, J. (1998). Moral theme comprehension in third grade, fifth grade and college students. *Reading Psychology, 19*(2), 217–241.

Narvaez, D., Bock, T., Endicott, L., Mitchell, C., & Bacigalupa, C. (2001). *Rating Content in Moral Stories Scale.*

Narvaez, D., Gardner, J., & Mitchell, C. (2001). *Comprehension of anti-drug use messages, ethical identity, moral judgment, and drug use.* Manuscript in preparation.

Narvaez, D., Gleason, T., Mitchell, C., & Bentley, J. (1999). Moral theme comprehension in children. *Journal of Educational Psychology, 91*(3), 477–487.

Narvaez, D., Mitchell, C., Bock, T., & Endicott, L. (1999). *Nurturing character in the middle school classroom: Teacher guidebook.* St. Paul, MN: Department of Children, Families, and Learning.

Narvaez, D., Mitchell, C., & Linzie, B. (1998, November). *Comprehending moral stories and the influence of individualism/collectivism.* Paper presented at the annual meeting of the Association for Moral Education, Hanover, NH.

Narvaez, D., van den Broek, P., & Ruiz, A. B. (1999). Reading purpose, type of text and their influence on think-alouds and comprehension measures. *Journal of Educational Psychology, 91*(3), 488–496.

Ohlhausen, M. M., & Roller, C. M. (1988). The operation of text structure and content schemata in isolation and interaction. *Reading Research Quarterly, 23,* 70–85.

Olson, G. M., Mack, R. L., & Duffy, S. A. (1981). Cognitive aspects of genre. *Poetics, 10,* 283–315.

Palmer, J., MacLeod, C. M., Hunt, E., & Davidson, J. E. (1985). Information processing correlates of reading. *Journal of Memory and Language, 24,* 59–88.

Perrig, W., & Kintsch, W. (19850. Propositional and situational representations of text. *Journal of Memory and Language, 24*(5), 503–518.

Pichert, J. W., & Anderson, R. C. (1977). Taking different perspectives on a story. *Journal of Educational Psychology, 69*(4), 309–315.

Piper, W. (1930). *The little engine that could.* New York: Platt & Munk.

Power, C., Higgins, A., & Kohlberg, L. (1989). *Lawrence Kohlber's approach to moral education.* New York: Columbia University Press.

Pressley, M., & Afflerbach, P. (1995). *Verbal protocols of reading: The nature of constructively responsive reading.* Hillsdale, NJ: Erlbaum.

Rest, J. (1983). Morality. In J. Flavell & E. Markham (Eds.), *Cognitive development.* In P. Mussen (Ed.), *Manual of child psychology* (Vol. 3, pp. 556–629). New York: Wiley.

Rest, J. (1986). *Moral development: Advances in research and theory.* New York: Prager.

Rest, J. R., Narvaez, D., Bebeau, M., & Thoma, S. (1999). *Postconventional moral thinking: A neo-Kohlbergian approach.* Mahwah, NJ: Erlbaum.

Reynolds, R., Taylor, M., Steffensen, M., Shirey, L., & Anderson, R. (1982). Cultural schemata and reading comprehension. *Reading Research Quarterly, 17,* 353–366.

Rikers, R. M. J. P., Boshuizen, H. P. A., & Schmidt, H. G. (1997). *Nonroutine problem solving by medical experts.* Paper presented at the annual meeting of the American Educational Research Association, Atlanta.

Roller, C. M. (1990). The interaction between knowledge and structure variables in the processing of expository prose. *Reading Research Quarterly, 25,* 79–87.

Rosenblatt, L. M. (1991). The reading transaction: What for? In B. M. Power & R. Hubbard (Eds.), *Literacy in process* (pp. 114–127). Portsmouth, NH: Heinemann.

Rumelhart, D. E. (1980). Schemata: The building blocks of cognition. In R. J. Spiro, B. C. Bruce, & W. F. Brewer (Eds.), *Theoretical issues in reading comprehension* (pp. 33–58). Hillsdale, NJ: Erlbaum.

Rumelhart, D. E., & Ortony, A. (1977). The representation of knowledge in memory. In R. C. Anderson, R. J. Spiro, & W. E. Matague (Eds.), *Schooling and the acquisition of knowledge* (pp. 99–135). Hillsdale, NJ: Erlbaum.

Scardamalia, M., & Bereiter, C. (1984). Development of strategies in text processing. In H. Mandl, N. L. Stein, & T. Trabasso (Eds.), *Learning and comprehension of text* (pp. 379–406). Hillsdale, NJ: Erlbaum.

Schank, R. C., & Abelson, R. (1977). *Scripts, plans, and goals.* Hillsdale, NJ: Erlbaum.

Schmalhofer, F., & Glavanov, D. (1986). Three components of understanding a programmer's manual: Verbatim, propositional, and situational representations. *Journal of Memory and Language, 25,* 279–294.

Simon, H., & Chase, W. G. (1973). Skill in chess. *American Scientist, 61,* 394–403.

Spilich, G. J., Vesonder, G. T., Chiesi, H. L., & Voss, J. F. (1979). Text processing of domain-related information for individuals with high and low domain knowledge. *Journal of Verbal Learning and Verbal Behavior, 18,* 275–290.

Spiro, R. J. (1980). Accommodative reconstruction in prose recall. *Journal of Verbal Language and Verbal Behavior, 19*(1), 84–95.

Steffensen, M., Joag-Dev, C., & Anderson, R. (1979). A cross-cultural perspective on reading comprehension. *Reading Research Quarterly, 15,* 10–29.

Sulin, R. A., & Dooling, D. J. (1974). Intrusion of a thematic idea in retention of prose. *Journal of Experimental Psychology, 103,* 255–262.

Trabasso, T., & Magliano, J. P. (1996). Conscious understanding during comprehension. *Discourse Processes, 21,* 255–288.

Trabasso, T., & van den Broek, P. (1985). Causal thinking and the representation of causal relations in stories. *Discourse Processes, 12,* 1–12.

Triandis, H. C. (1995). *Individualism and collectivism.* Boulder, CO: Westview Press.

van den Broek, P. (1990). The causal inference maker: Towards a process model of inference generation in text comprehension. In D. A. Balota, G. B. Flores d'Arcais, & K. Rayner (Eds.), *Comprehension processes in reading* (pp. 423–445). Hillsdale, NJ: Erlbaum.

van den Broek, P. (1994). Comprehension and memory of narrative texts: Inferences and coherence. In M. A. Gernsbacher (Ed.), *Handbook of psycholinguistics* (pp. 539–588). New York: Academic Press.

van den Broek, P., & Kremer, K. (1999). The mind in action: What it means to comprehend. In B. Taylor, P. van den Broek, & M. Graves (Eds.), *Reading for meaning* (pp. 1–31). New York: Teacher's College Press.

van den Broek, P., & Lorch, R. F., Jr. (1993). Network representations of causal relations in memory for narrative texts: Evidence from primed recognition. *Discourse Processes, 16,* 75–98.

van den Broek, P., Lorch, E., & Thurlow, R. (1997). Children and adults' memory for television stories: The role of causal factors, story-grammar categories and hierarchical level. *Child Development, 67*(6), 3010–3028.

van Dijk, T. A., & Kintsch, W. (1983). *Strategies of discourse comprehension.* New York: Academic Press.

Walker, C. H. (1987). Relative importance of domain knowledge and overall aptitude on acquisition of domain-related information. *Cognition and Instruction, 4,* 25–42.

Walker, C. H., & Meyer, B. J. F. (1980). Integrating different types of information in text. *Journal of Verbal Learning and Verbal Behavior, 19,* 263–275.

Whitney, P., Ritchie, G. G., & Clark, M. B. (1991). Working-memory capacity and the use of elaborative inferences in text comprehension. *Discourse Processes, 14*(2), 133–146.

Williams, J. P., Brown, L. G., Silverstein, A. K., & deCani, J. (1994). An instructional program in comprehension of narrative themes for adolescents with learning disabilities. *Learning Disability Quarterly*, *17*, 205–221.

Wineberg, S. S. (1991). On the reading of historical texts: Notes on the breach between school and academy. *American Educational Research Journal*, *28*, 495–520.

Wyatt, D., Pressley, M., El-Dinary, P. B., Stein, S., Evans, P., & Brown, R. (1993). Comprehension strategies, worth and credibility monitoring, and evaluations: Cold and hot cognition when experts read professional articles that are important to them. *Learning and Individual Differences*, *5*(1), 49–72.

Zwaan, R. A., & Brown, C. M. (1996). The influence of language proficiency and comprehension skill on situation-model construction. *Discourse Processes*, *21*, 289–328.

12

Teaching Readers How
to Comprehend Text Strategically

TOM TRABASSO
EDWARD BOUCHARD

CRITICAL RESEARCH ON READING COMPREHENSION

As a formal study, reading comprehension has received widespread scientific attention only during past 25 years. Among the first to focus on comprehension, Markman (1977, 1981) studied the reader's awareness of comprehension processes during reading itself. Did the readers know that they did not understand what they were reading? What they did do when they recognized that they had an understanding failure? An initial, surprising finding was that young and mature readers alike failed to detect logical and semantic text inconsistencies. Her discovery of comprehension failure was instrumental in the identification and teaching of cognitive strategies for readers that were aimed at enhancing their comprehension.

As a result of cognitive theories, the reader is now seen as an active participant who constructs meaning through intentional, problem-solving processes. Further, reading is viewed as an interaction between the text and the reader. During this interaction, thinking is jointly influenced by the text and the reader's prior knowledge (Anderson & Pearson, 1984; Durkin, 1993). Readers construct "mental representations" of what they read. These representations are stored in memory and contain the semantic interpretations that were made by the reader during reading (Kintsch & van Dijk, 1978). The memory representations enable subsequent use of what had been read and understood (Pressley & Afflerbach, 1995).

COGNITIVE STRATEGIES
FOR IMPROVING READING COMPREHENSION

The interest in comprehension strategies is not new. Highly skilled readers have known about and learned to use effective reading techniques before they were referred to as "strategies." For example, the autobiographies of Benjamin Franklin (1706–1790) and Frederick Douglass (1817–1895) reveal that they intuitively employed metacognitive strategies to improve their reading comprehension. From age 10, Franklin was largely a self-taught reader (he had a tutor for a year). To improve his reading comprehension, he copied passages, made short summaries, rewrote passages, turned essays into rhyming verse and other games, and avidly discussed what he read with peers. Douglass was also briefly tutored but then forbidden to read. Forced to learn on his own, he too invented reading and writing exercises, summarized passages, played word games, and practiced giving speeches and responding to issues in debate.

Before the 1970s, the explicit teaching of reading comprehension was not done through formal reading instruction. It was done mainly by learning skills acquired in content areas. Durkin (1979) observed reading instruction in grade 4 and found that teachers spent little time on comprehension instruction. Only 20 minutes of comprehension instruction was observed in 4,469 minutes of reading instruction. A study by Duffy, Lanier, and Roehler (1980) confirmed this omission of explicit comprehension instruction during the teaching of reading in classrooms.

Comprehension strategies are specific, learned procedures that foster active, competent, self-regulated, and intentional reading. Classroom teachers implement comprehension strategy instruction by demonstrating, modeling, or guiding their use during the reading of a text. When readers practice and acquire the procedures, they can interact effectively with a text without assistance. Most readers who are not explicitly taught cognitive procedures are unlikely to learn, develop, or use them spontaneously. Practice in their use with teacher assistance leads to their gradual internalization and independent mastery (Palincsar & Brown, 1984; Paris, Saario, & Cross, 1986; Pressley, Almasi, Schuder, Bergman, & Kurita, 1994).

In this chapter, we present a summary of text comprehension strategy instruction. The bottom line is that readers who are given cognitive strategy instruction make significant gains on comprehension compared with students who are trained with conventional instruction procedures (see Pressley, Johnson, Symons, McGoldrick, & Kurita, 1989; Rosenshine & Meister, 1994; Rosenshine, Meister, & Chapman, 1996).

Our summary reveals distinct trends over the past 25 years. Initial investigations of comprehension strategies focused on the training of an individual strategy and whether readers could use it. Then the focus shifted to whether combinations of strategies could facilitate text comprehension. The success of teaching multiple strategies then led to investigations of preparing teachers to teach comprehension strategies in natural, classroom contexts (Block & Mangieri, 1995, 1996a, 1996b).

Our literature review covers this history and is based on Trabasso and Bouchard (2000), a scientific review of teaching comprehension to readers mainly in grades 2 through 8 and from 1980 to the present. We carried out the review for the National Reading Panel, and our technical report was the basis for Chapter 4, Part 2, in the final National Reading Panel report (National Institute of Child Health and Human Development, 2000).

Our review began with our reading other important reviews of the comprehension strategy instruction literature, including those of Duffy and Roehler (1989); Lysynchuk, Pressley, d'Ailly, Smith, and Cake (1989); Pressley et al. (1989); Pressley (1998); Rosenshine and Meister (1994); and Rosenshine, Meister, and Chapman (1996). Using these reviews and our own electronic searches, we located 481 studies on the teaching of comprehension published since 1980. We focused on those studies that were relevant to instruction of reading comprehension. We excluded studies on comprehension instruction in reasoning and mathematics problem solving. We focused on experimental investigations published in scientific journals that involved at least one treatment and one control group—and in which participants were either randomly assigned to the treatment and control groups or matched on initial reading comprehension measures. Of the 481 studies examined, 205 met these criteria.

FINDING OUT AND EVALUATING WHAT IS KNOWN ABOUT INSTRUCTION OF COMPREHENSION

We coded the 205 studies for the rationale, instructional procedures, experimental treatments and controls, grade and reading level of readers, assessments, and findings of effectiveness. We identified 12 categories of instruction that contained a reasonable number of studies found to be effective in teaching comprehension strategies and improved comprehension. We also identified two categories on instruction of strategies, one aimed at preparing teachers to teach readers and the other aimed at peers teaching peers during reading. In these instructional studies, the ability of either the teachers or peers to learn and teach strategies in classroom contexts is studied. In addition, improvement in comprehension by readers as a result of learning the strategies from prepared teachers or peers was assessed.

In this chapter, we discuss each of the 12 kinds of strategy instruction in turn, providing a definition for each kind of instruction, describing the procedures, and indicating its effectiveness for particular grade levels. We then examine the teacher preparation and peer instructional (cooperative learning) studies in a similar manner.

We summarize across many studies for each kind of instruction. The many studies that were reviewed are not cited in the text. Rather, we list these studies under each form of instruction in an appendix. The references are given for each of the kinds of strategy instruction, in the order in which they are presented below.

COMPREHENSION INSTRUCTION: TYPES OF STRATEGIES

Comprehension Monitoring

Comprehension monitoring involves a process of readers self-listening (monitoring) or listening to others reading aloud (Elliott-Faust & Pressley, 1986). Readers learn this process to become aware of their own understanding during reading (Taylor & Frye, 1992). The teacher first models his or her own awareness of difficulties in understanding words, phrases, clauses, or sentences by "thinking aloud" during reading aloud. Readers then carry out the same procedures—identifying what is causing difficulty in understanding; using think-aloud procedures that show the reader and the teacher where and when understanding difficulties occur; looking back in text to try to solve a problem; restating a text in terms more familiar to them; and reading forward in a text to solve a problem.

We evaluated 20 studies on comprehension monitoring in which readers in grades 2 through 6 were taught to monitor their comprehension, to become aware when they have difficulty, and to overcome problems by use of strategies of guessing and looking back or reading forward in the text. Readers who were trained in comprehension monitoring improved on the detection of text inconsistencies, on memory for text, and on standardized reading comprehension tests.

Training in comprehension monitoring can be used successfully in grade levels 2 through 6. It can be taught through teacher modeling and practice by children during reading. Teachers can be trained in how to think aloud and to communicate their own understanding of monitoring processes to students. Training in comprehension monitoring can be part of a larger program of reading strategies and used in content area instruction.

Graphic Organizers

Teachers who use graphic organizers show readers how to display relationships of ideas with diagrams, pictorial devices, or story maps. These techniques are often used to instruct readers to organize their ideas with graphic representations of what they read, hence the term "graphic organizer" (Harris & Hodges, 1995, p. 101). Such teaching helps readers learn text structures, focus on concepts and relations between concepts, construct tools to represent text relationships visually, and assist in writing well-organized summaries. Graphic organizers are appropriate for expository texts in content areas such as science or social studies.

We reviewed 11 studies that used graphic organizers with readers in grades 4 through 8. Teaching readers to use systematic, visual graphs in order to organize ideas benefited readers in remembering what they read and improved reading comprehension and achievement in social studies and science. Teachers can be trained to teach students in grades 4 to 8 how to use graphic organizers (Block, 1991, 1993).

Listening Actively

Listening to another person read and following what is being read teaches students how to listen actively while reading (see Dickson, 1981). The teacher guides the students to listen while others read. The teacher poses questions for the students to answer while they listen to the teacher, who reads a text. Active listening training is aimed at improving critical listening, reading, and reading comprehension. It is also aimed at increasing the student's participation in discussions, engendering more thoughtful responses to questions, increasing memory for the text, and focusing interest on material.

We examined four studies on listening instruction for grades 1–6. Instruction in learning to listen to teachers or peers reading benefited the readers' comprehension as assessed by question answering or by standardized tests.

Mental Imagery

When the reader can construct an image of what is read, the constructed image serves as a memory representation of the reader's interpretation of the text. This should improve retention of information read.

We examined seven studies on mental imagery instruction. The main effects were to increase memory for the text that was imaged and to improve the reader's detection of text inconsistencies (Borduin, Borduin, & Manley, 1994; Levin & Divine-Hawkins, 1974).

Mnemonic Instruction

Mnemonic instruction uses an external memory aid—for example, a picture or concept—as a proxy for a person, concept, sentence, or passage in order to generate an internal association of the word or a picture with the information in the text (Peters & Levin, 1986). Suppose, for example, that the readers read passages about famous people. For Taylor, they might use a similar name that is familiar to them. For example, "tailor" might be the similar word, and the teacher might show a picture of a tailor making a suit. Another example is from Levin, Shriberg, and Berry (1983) in which attributes of fictitious towns were taught and the key word was the town name. The children were then shown an interactive picture that contained the key word and the town's attributes. When provided with the town name later, the children could recall more town attributes than those who were not provided with the pictures. Key word methods provide prompts that improve recall for complex passages about people, events, or places. Mnemonic instruction is appropriate for teaching unfamiliar concepts with different levels of readers in grades 2 through 8.

Prior Knowledge

Knowing a lot about Russian history helps one to understand historical texts about Russia. Teachers activate this knowledge prior to reading. The activation directs the readers' attention to relevant parts of a text. It encourages readers to infer and elaborate what they are reading. This enables them to fill in missing or incomplete information. It also enables them to construct memory representations that facilitate recall of what was read and understood (Anderson & Pearson, 1984).

We examined 14 studies in which readers were encouraged to activate prior knowledge. Prior knowledge activation has been studied for students in grades 1–9. In these studies, prior knowledge was activated by asking students to think about topics relevant to the passage, by teaching relevant knowledge, by using prereading activity, by having the readers predict what will happen based on personal experience, by making associations during reading, and by having the teacher preview the story or text. Recall and question answering, achievement in content areas, and standardized reading comprehension tests have been used as assessments. Activation of prior knowledge improved comprehension in all studies except one. The one failure was on grade 4 readers and used previewing the text as a form of prior activation (Spires, Gallini, & Riggsbee, 1992).

Question Answering

Question answering instruction (i.e., teach students how to find answers available in the text) focuses the reader on particular content. Question answering can facilitate reasoning through the use of "why" or "how" questions. Question answering can also increase memory for what was read. Readers can learn to discriminate questions that can be answered based on the text versus those that require the generation of inferences or conclusions. Questions after the reading of a passage can lead to reprocessing of relevant text.

We examined 17 studies on question answering instruction. Instruction of question answering leads to an improvement in memory for what was read, in answering questions after reading passages, and in strategies for finding answers. This improvement occurred over grades 3 through 8.

Question Generation

Question generation instruction teaches readers to self-question while reading a text. Teachers demonstrate through thinking aloud how to generate questions during the reading of a passage. Readers then practice generating answers as they read the text. The questions should integrate information in the text. Teachers provide feedback on the quality of the questions asked or assist the student in answering the question generated. Teachers teach the students to evaluate whether their questions covered important information, whether the questions were integrative, and whether they themselves could answer the questions.

There is strong evidence that question generation instruction during reading benefits reading comprehension in terms of improved memory, accuracy in answering questions, and better integration and identification of main ideas (Rosenshine et al., 1996). There is mixed evidence that standardized comprehension test performance is improved (Rosenshine et al., 1996).

Story Structure

Story content is systematically organized into episodes, and the story plot unfolds over a set of episodes. Suppose a child reads or hears the Little Red Riding Hood story. There is an episode in which Little Red Riding Hood meets a woodsman and then meets the disguised wolf in the woods. In another episode, the grandmother is deceived and eaten by the wolf. Another episode features the question exchanges between Little Red Riding Hood and the wolf. In the final episode, the real woodsman kills the wolf.

Knowledge of episodic content helps a reader to understand the *who, what, where, when*, and *why* of stories, *what* happened, and *what* was done and to infer causal relationships between events. For example, the reader could answer questions on the motivation of Little Red Riding Hood to go to her grandmother's house, on why the wolf disguised himself, and on why Little Red Riding Hood's questions forced the wolf to reveal itself. The reader could learn to answer questions about where the different scenes occur, when Little Red Riding Hood reached the grandmother's house, and where the wolf and the grandmother were at this time. This learning gives the reader knowledge and procedures for deeper understanding. It allows the reader to construct more coherent memory representations of what occurred in the story. Readers learn to identify the main characters of the story, where and when the story took place, what the main characters did, how the story ended, and how the main characters felt. Readers learn to construct a story map recording the setting, problem, goal, action, and outcome of the story as they unfold over time.

Teachers can be prepared to teach story structure through the use of questions and graphic organizers (sometimes called "story maps"). They teach readers to focus on the characters, the settings, what happened, how characters felt, what they thought, what they wanted to do, what they did, and how things turned out. When the reading material is narrative, question answering and generation strategies can be used by teachers to draw out the content and organization of stories crucial to the student building a representation of the episodic structure and causal relationships. The use of questions to learn story structure can be a part of a program of instruction of comprehension strategies in natural reading or content areas in which narratives occur, such as in social studies.

We analyzed 17 studies on story structure instruction that showed improvement. The story structure instruction improved comprehension of stories as measured by the ability of the reader to answer questions and recall what was read. There were also successes on standard comprehension test performance. The improvement is more marked for less able readers in grades 3 through 6. Story structure instruction benefited recall, question answering, and identifying elements of story structure. All studies on poor readers report successful improvement; the failures reported, while infrequent, were with normal readers.

Summarization

Summarization instruction can make readers more aware of how a text is structured and how ideas are related. To create a text summary, a reader must discern and stress central and important ideas, generalize, and minimize less relevant details. Through example and feedback, a reader can be taught to apply any various summarization rules, such as the identification of topic sentences, deletion of redundancy, deletion of trivia, recognition of superordination, and invention of a topic sentence. Readers can gain experience by summarizing single or multiple-paragraph passages (Brown & Day, 1983). They first summarize individual paragraphs and then they learn to construct a summary of summaries or to create a spatial organization of paragraph summaries. For example, the readers of or listeners to the "Little Red Riding Hood" story might first describe and summarize the episodes of the story. Then they might summarize each of their summaries of each episode. For example: Little Red Riding Hood leaves for Grandmother's house. She meets a woodsman in the forest. Disguised wolf meets Little Red Riding Hood in woods. Wolf goes to grandmother's house. Wolf eats grandmother. Wolf dons grandmother's clothes. Little Red Riding Hood arrives at grandmother's house with the wolf in her bed. Little Red Riding Hood asks the wolf questions. Wolf leaps at Little Red Riding Hood with intention of eating her, too. Woodsman rescues Little Red Riding Hood (and, in some versions, her grandmother) by killing the wolf (and cutting it open).

We found 18 studies on summarization instruction for grades 3–8. Readers improved the quality of their summaries of text not only by identifying the main ideas but also by leaving out detail, including ideas related to the main idea, by generalizing, and by removing redundancy. Further, the instruction of summarization improves memory for what is read, both in terms of free recall and answering questions.

Vocabulary Instruction and Reading Comprehension

Vocabulary instruction promotes word knowledge that enhances text comprehension. It is a part of normal content area learning. Having a strong vocabulary leads to better reading and listening comprehension and to improvement in course achievement.

In some forms of vocabulary instruction, the teacher models being a "word detective." The teacher looks for contextual clues to find a word's meaning. The teacher analyzes words and word parts and looks at the surrounding text for clues to a word's meaning. The teacher elaborates on a word's meaning and uses the word in different meaning contexts. The teacher adds activities to extend the use of learned words beyond the classroom, such as having the students find three uses of a word in a newspaper. The learning tasks provide definitions, knowledge, fluency, access of word meaning, context interpretation, and story comprehension. Students encounter words multiple times, highlight and use vocabulary terms to generate inferences, complete sentence stems, generate situations appropriate to target words, and fill in missing words in blanks in the text (the "Cloze" procedure, Adams, 1990).

There are many studies on the teaching of vocabulary but few studies on the relationship between teaching vocabulary and comprehension. The three studies on instruction of vocabulary and its effect on comprehension that we reviewed each involved grade 4 readers. Two studies reported success in learning of the words, use of word meanings, and in increased story comprehension (McKeown, Beck, Omanson, & Perfetti, 1983; McKeown, Beck, Omanson, & Pople, 1985). One study applied reciprocal teaching methods to teach vocabulary. Readers learned to derive word meanings but attained no standardized comprehension test improvement when instructed by this method (Tomeson & Aarnouste, 1998).

Multiple-Strategy Instruction

Skilled reading involves the coordinated use of several cognitive strategies. Readers can learn and flexibly coordinate these to construct meaning from texts.

Two classes of multiple strategy instruction have been studied: reciprocal teaching and a class of various multiple strategy packages that do not use the reciprocal teaching methods. Reciprocal teaching presumes basic decoding skill. Here, four main strategies are taught frequently: generation of questions, summarization, seeking clarification when confused, and prediction of what might occur later in the text (Palincsar & Brown, 1984; Lysynchuk, Pressley, & Vye, 1990). Optional additions include question answering, making inferences or drawing conclusions, listening, monitoring, thinking aloud, and elaborating. As a part of reciprocal teaching, the teacher models the strategies and explains as she models them. The teacher then turns use of the strategies over to a group of readers, one of whom is the leader for the group. The leader guides the group in applying the strategies in the presence of the expert teacher. By participating in a number of lessons with the role of leader rotated among group members, the use of the strategies is practiced and eventually internalized by group members.

Multiple strategy programs that do not use reciprocal teaching mainly have the student practice strategies with feedback from the teacher. The teacher may initially model the strategy. In explicit transactional approaches that use multiple strategies, the teacher explains a strategy before she models it during reading (Pressley, Johnson et al., 1989; Pressley, El-Dinary, et al., 1992).

Packages of strategies vary in the number of strategies taught from two to five: self-study of the passage, oral reading, rereading, retelling, review, summarization, question generation, testing hypotheses, deriving word meaning, training word recognition, vocabulary instruction, drawing conclusions, filling in blanks, monitoring comprehension, story structure, collaborative learning with partner including listening to partner reading, debating or arguing with the author of the text or with the teacher or partner, and classification of words, phrases, and sentences.

Multiple strategy instruction usually occurs in a dialogue between the teacher and the reader. Several strategies may be taught in conjunction with one another over the course of reading a passage. Readers are taught when and where individual strategies are appropriate. The teaching is usually done through modeling and explanation by the teacher. Readers learn to adapt the strategies and use them according to the reading situation by practicing them in teacher-led reading groups (Pressley, Gaskins, et al., 1991).

There is very strong empirical, scientific evidence that the instruction of more than one strategy in a natural context leads to the acquisition and use of reading comprehension strategies and transfer to standardized comprehension tests. Multiple strategy instruction facilitates comprehension as evidenced by performance on tasks that involve memory, summarizing, and identification of main ideas.

Rosenshine and Meister (1994) conducted a meta-analysis of 16 reciprocal training studies on grades 1–8, with most of the readers falling above grade level 3. The effect sizes were large (averaging about .80) for assessments other than standardized tests (which averaged .30). The effect sizes were large for good readers but were actually larger for poor readers. Effectiveness increased from none in grade 3 to mixed in grades 4–6 to high effectiveness in grades 7–8. These data indicate that multiple strategy instruction is more suited for grades 4 and above. Weaker and older readers benefit the most from reciprocal teaching. We located and examined 11 studies of reciprocal teaching in grades 1 through 6 that were not covered by Rosenshine and Meister (1994). There were also clear positive effects produced by reciprocal teaching in these investigations.

We found 17 multiple-strategy instruction studies that used an approach other than reciprocal teaching. These multiple strategy studies showed that this procedure is very powerful in teaching comprehension skills. It also improved general reading comprehension. Multiple strategy instruction does not seem to require reciprocal teaching to be effective.

STUDIES ON TEACHING TEACHERS OR PEERS TO TEACH STRATEGIES

Teacher Preparation for Text Comprehension Instruction

To teach comprehension strategies, teachers have to learn how to interact with students at the right time and right place during the reading of a text. This requires that teachers know and understand the cognitive processes that occur in reading, how comprehension strategies can be utilized by a reader, and how to teach these strategies through explanation, demonstration, modeling, and interactive techniques. Teachers need to know how to allow readers to learn and use individual strategies in the context of reading a text and in conjunction with several other reading comprehension strategies.

We found four studies on preparing teachers to teach text comprehension strategies. There was clear evidence in these studies that teachers can learn to implement multiple comprehension strategy instruction in the classroom under natural teaching circumstances from grades 2 through 11. All the studies were carried out on "poor readers," "disabled students," or "low achievers." With respect to the teachers' learning and being faithful to the treatment, all studies claimed success. Students benefit from the teachers who were prepared to teach multiple reading strategies. Successful improvement occurred on learning the subject matter of the instruction and on standardized reading comprehension test performance.

There is a need for more information on how teachers can be effectively prepared to teach comprehension strategies. The idea of teacher as a modeler and coach of thinking strategies is new to reading instruction. Few teachers have received practical preparation in cognitive strategy instruction (Anderson & Roit, 1993; Duffy, 1993). There is a need to carry out further teacher preparation studies on a wider range of readers in natural reading and content area instruction. The relation of successful learning and teaching by teachers and of successful learning and use of strategies by students in content area achievement needs to be assessed using a variety of methods rather than by measuring benefits only through general reading comprehension tests. One study that did this is reported by Brown, Pressley, Van Meter, and Schuder (1996). They showed that teaching teachers to use transactional strategies instruction for developing word attack skills in language arts led to student gains in learning content over the course of the school year.

Cooperative Learning by Peers

Readers may learn best when they are in social situations in which they are actively engaged with other learners who are near their same level of understanding (Vygotsky, 1978). Cooperative learning can be used to teach readers to read together with a partner or in small groups (Harris & Hodges, 1995). Readers read aloud and listen to others, are taught strategies for effective reading comprehension, and are encouraged to tutor each other on these strategies (Klingner, Vaughn, & Schumm, 1998).

The teacher models reading through her demonstrated use of the strategies during reading. Readers learn to carry out the demonstrated activities in partner or small reading groups. Readers take turns in activities including word recognition, asking and answering questions, summarizing, predicting, and clarifying. The emphasis is on oral reading and listening by the reader and peers.

In all 10 studies we reviewed on cooperative learning of comprehension strategies, reading strategies were successfully learned by students in grade levels 3 through 6. Training was assessed by analyses of peer talk during cooperative learning, by asking readers to summarize what they read, by having them generate and answer questions, and by their predictions of upcoming ideas in the text. Cooperative learning promoted intellectual discussion. It increased students' control over their learning, promoted social interaction with peers, and saved teacher time. For example, in two studies, the talk of the children showed an increased focus on reading content. In three studies, cooperative learning produced significant improvement in performance on standardized reading comprehension tests.

Cooperative learning can be effective for integrating academically and physically handicapped students into regular classrooms (Klingner et al., 1998). It also increases motivation toward learning and time spent by the learners on tasks (Bramlett, 1994).

IMPLICATIONS FOR FUTURE RESEARCH AND PRACTICE

Instruction of comprehension strategies has been successful for readers in grades 3 through 8. There are a number of unanswered questions, however:

1. *Which strategies?* Our review shows that strategy instruction, alone or in combination, is effective in improving reading comprehension. Are certain strategies more appropriate than others for readers of certain ages or abilities? Which reader characteristics are most likely to benefit from successful instruction of reading comprehension?

2. *Reader ability.* Which specific strategies and in which combinations are best for readers of different abilities? More positively, a strong case can be made that teaching comprehension strategies improves the reading of weaker readers.

3. *Content area instruction.* Instruction in comprehension in social studies, reviewed previously, showed that readers' achievement improved in this content area. Would instruction of comprehension strategies as a learning skill in content areas improve performance and achievement in other content areas, such as science or language arts?

4. *Texts.* Does successful instruction generalize across different text genres (e.g., narrative and expository) and texts from different subject content areas? In the research reviewed, we found little reporting on the kinds or difficulty levels of texts that were used. More attention needs to be paid to the texts that readers are asked to read, both in terms of difficulty and type of text.

5. *Teacher preparation.* What are the important teacher characteristics that influence successful instruction of reading comprehension? What are the most effective ways to train teachers to teach comprehension strategies? The art of instruction involves a series of "wh–" questions: knowing *when* to apply *what* strategy with *which* particular student(s). How do we develop teachers as masters of this art?

6. *Approaches to comprehension instruction.* Does the ability to develop independent, integrated strategic reading abilities require subtle instructional distinctions that go well beyond techniques of demonstration, direct explanation, or reciprocal teaching?

On the last issue, Duffy (1993) posited that teaching students to acquire and use strategies requires a fundamental "change in how teacher educators and staff developers work with teachers and what they count as important about learning to be a teacher." In this line of thinking, being strategic is not a skill that can be taught by drill; it is a method of approach to reading and reading instruction. Much more than knowing a strategy, being strategic calls for coordinating individual strategies, altering, adjusting, modifying, testing, and shifting tactics as is fitting until a reading comprehension problem is solved.

In the two decades since Durkin's 1979 study there has been a great deal of research on how to promote reading comprehension but not much on how well this knowledge has filtered into the classroom. Teachers seem not to teach comprehension instruction strategies without having themselves been prepared to teach them (Anderson, 1992; Bramlett, 1994; Brown et al., 1996; Duffy, 1993; Durkin, 1979; Pressley et al., 1989; Reutzel & Cooter, 1988). During intensive observation of 10 grade 4 and 5 classes in upstate New York in the 1995–1996 school year, researchers "observed explicit comprehension instruction only rarely" (Pressley, 1998, p. 198). Ironically, Pressley notes further that there has been a great deal of testing but little teaching of reading comprehension.

Perhaps, as Duffy (1993) argues, developing metacognitive readers requires meta-cognitive teachers, as well as school support for strategy learning.

When teachers applied strategy instruction in the classroom, even when they omitted crucial aspects of a strategy, their students improved their reading comprehension (Bramlett, 1994; Duffy, 1993; Pressley et al., 1989). Although it may not be easy for teachers or readers to develop strategic practice, the research suggests that helping teachers become good strategy teachers (making the creative adaptations involved in teaching students to be strategic) will help their students better confront the complexities of learning and living. To implement strategy instruction in the classroom will likely require more than providing prescriptions (including effective modeling and reciprocal teaching), more than providing students with opportunities to practice the comprehension strategies, and more than knowing how to use a strategy and sensing the value of applying it.

ACKNOWLEDGMENTS

The research review was supported by a research grant from the National Institute of Child Health and Human Development. Tom Trabasso carried out the review as part of his responsibilities as a member of the National Reading Panel. We benefited from the suggestions of Joanna Williams and Michael Kamil throughout the conduct of the review. Mike Kamil conducted the initial electronic searches that served as the database for the review.

REFERENCES

Adams, M. J. (1990). *Beginning to read: Thinking and learing about print*. Cambridge, MA: MIT Press.

Anderson, R. C., & Pearson, P. D. (1984). A schema-theoretic view of basic processes in reading. In P. D. Pearson (Ed.), *Handbook of reading research* (pp. 255–291). New York: Longman.

Anderson, V. (1992). A teacher development project in transactional strategy instruction for teachers of severely reading-disabled adolescents. *Teaching and Teacher Education, 8*(4), 391–403.

Anderson, V., & Roit, M. (1993). Planning and implementing collaborative strategy instruction for delayed readers in grades 6–10. *Elementary School Journal, 94*, 121–137.

Block, C. (1991). Reading instruction that increases thinking. *Journal of Reading, 35*, 136–142.

Block, C. (1993). Strategy instruction in a student-centered classroom. *The Elementary School Journal, 94*(2), 137–153.

Block, C. C., & Mangieri, J. (1995). *Creating a culturally enriched classroom*. Boston, MA: Allyn & Bacon.

Block, C. C., & Mangieri, J. (1996a). *Power thinking for success*. Cambridge, MA: Brookline Press.

Block, C. C., & Mangieri, J. (1996b). *Reason to read: Thinking strategies for life through literature* (Vol. 1). Reading, MA: Addison-Wesley.

Borduin, B. J., Borduin, C. M., & Manley, C. M. (1994). The use of imagery training to improve reading comprehension of second graders. *Journal of Genetic Psychology, 155*(1), 115–118.

Bramlett, R. K. (1994). Implementing cooperative learning: A field study evaluating issues for school-based consultants. *Journal of School Psychology, 32*(1), 67–84.

Brown, A. L., & Day, J. D. (1983). Macro rules for summarizing texts: The development of expertise. *Journal of Verbal Learning and Verbal Behavior, 22*, 1–14.

Brown, R., Pressley, M., Van Meter, P., & Schuder, T. (1996). A quasi-experimental validation of transactional strategies instruction with low-achieving second grade readers. *Journal of Educational Psychology, 88,* 18–37.

Dickson, W. P. (Ed.). (1981). *Children's oral communication skills.* New York: Academic Press.

Duffy, G. G. (1993). Rethinking strategy instruction: Four teachers' development and their low achievers' understandings. *Elementary School Journal, 93*(3), 231–247.

Duffy, G. G., & Roehler, L. R. (1989). Why strategy instruction is so difficult and what we need to do about it. In C. B. McCormick, G. Miller, & M. Pressley (Eds.), *Cognitive strategy research: From basic research to educational applications* (pp. 133–154). New York: Springer-Verlag.

Durkin, D. (1979). What classroom observations reveal about reading comprehension. *Reading Research Quarterly, 15,* 481–533.

Durkin, D. (1993). *Teaching them to read* (6th ed.). Boston, MA: Allyn & Bacon.

Elliot-Faust, D. J., & Pressley, M. (1986). How to each comparison processing to increase children's short- and long-term listening comprehension monitoring. *Journal of Educational Psychology, 78,* 27–33.

Franklin, M. R. (1993). Overcoming the reading comprehension barriers of expository texts. *Educational Research Quarterly, 16*(1), 5–14.

Harris, T. L., & Hodges, R. E. (Eds.). (1995). *The literacy dictionary: The vocabulary of reading and writing.* Newark, DE: International Reading Association.

Kintsch, W., & van Dijk, T. A. (1978). Toward a model of discourse comprehension and production. *Psychological Review, 83,* 363–394.

Klingner, J. K., Vaughn, S., & Schumm, J. S. (1998). Collaborative strategic reading during social studies in heterogeneous fourth-grade classrooms. *Elementary School Journal, 99*(1), 3–22.

Levin, J. R., & Divine-Hawkins, P. (1974). Visual imagery as a prose-learning process. *Journal of Reading Behavior, 6,* 23–30.

Levin, J. R., Shriberg, L. D., & Berry, J. K. (1983). A concrete strategy for remembering abstract prose. *American Educational Research Journal, 20,* 277–290.

Lysynchuk, L. M., Pressley, M., d'Ailly, H., Smith, M., & Cake, H. (1989, Fall). A methodological analysis of experimental studies of comprehension strategy instruction. *Reading Research Quarterly, 24,* 458–470.

Lysynchuk, L. M., Pressley, M., & Vye, N. J. (1990). Reciprocal teaching improves standardized reading-comprehension performance in poor comprehenders. *Elementary School Journal, 90*(5), 469–484.

Markman, E. M. (1977). Realizing that you don't understand: A preliminary investigation. *Child Development, 46,* 986–992.

Markman, E. M. (1981). Comprehension monitoring. In W. P. Dickson (Ed.), *Children's oral communication skills* (pp. 61–84). New York: Academic Press.

McKeown, M. G., Beck, I. L., Omanson, R. C., & Perfetti, C. A. (1983). The effects of long-term vocabulary instruction on reading comprehension: A replication. *Journal of Reading Behavior, 15*(1), 3–18.

McKeown, M. G., Beck, I. L., Omanson, R. C., & Pople, M. T. (1985). Some effects of the nature and frequency of vocabulary instruction on the knowledge and use of words. *Reading Research Quarterly, 20*(5), 522–535.

National Institute of Child Health and Human Development. (2000). *Teaching children to read: An evidence-based assessment of the scientific research literature on reading and its implications for reading instruction* [Report of the National Reading Panel]. (NIH Publication No. 00-4769). Washington, DC: U.S. Government Printing Office.

Palincsar, A. S., & Brown, A. L. (1984). Reciprocal teaching of comprehension-fostering and comprehension-monitoring activities. *Cognition and Instruction, 2,* 117–175.

Peters, E. E., & Levin, J. R. (1986). Effects of a mnemonic imagery strategy on good and poor readers' prose recall. *Reading Research Quarterly, 21,* 179–192.

Pressley, M. (1998). *Reading instruction that works: The case for balanced teaching.* New York: Guilford Press.

Pressley, M., & Afflerbach, P. (1995). *Verbal protocols of reading: The nature of constructively responsive reading.* Mahwah, NJ: Erlbaum.

Pressley, M., El-Dinary, P. B., Gaskins, I., Schuder, T., Bergman, J. L., Almasi, J., & Brown, R. (1992). Beyond direct explanation: Transactional instruction of reading comprehension strategies. *Elementary School Journal, 92,* 511–554.

Pressley, M., Gaskins, I. W., Wile, D., Cunicelli, E. A., & Sheridan, J. (1991). Teaching literacy strategies across the curriculum: A case study at Benchmark School. *National Reading Conference Yearbook, 40,* 219–228.

Pressley, M., Johnson, C. J., Symons, S., McGoldrick, J. A., & Kurita, J. A. (1989). Strategies that improve children's memory and comprehension of text. *Elementary School Journal, 90*(1), 3–32.

Reutzel, D. R., & Cooter, R. B., Jr. (1988). Research implications for improving basal skill instruction. *Reading Horizons, 28*(3), 208–215.

Rinehart, S. D., Stahl, S. A., & Erickson, L. G. (1986). Some effects of summarization training on reading and studying. *Reading Research Quarterly, 21*(4), 422–438.

Rosenshine, B., & Meister, C. (1994). Reciprocal teaching: A review of the research. *Review of Educational Research, 64*(4), 479–530.

Rosenshine, B., Meister, C., & Chapman, S. (1996). Teaching students to generate questions: A review of the intervention studies. *Review of Educational Research, 66*(2), 181–221.

Spires, H. A., Gallini, J., & Riggsbee, J. (1992). Effects of schema-based and text structure-based cues on expository prose comprehension in fourth graders. *Journal of Experimental Education, 60*(4), 307–320.

Taylor, B. M., & Frye, B. J. (1992). Comprehension strategy instruction in the intermediate grades. *Reading Research and Instruction, 32,* 39–48.

Tomesen, M., & Aarnoutse, C. (1998). Effects of an instructional programme for deriving word meanings. *Educational Studies, 24*(1), 107–128.

Trabasso, T., & Bouchard, E. (2000). *Text comprehension instruction. Report of the National Reading Panel: Report of the Subgroups* (Chap. 4, Pt. 2, pp. 39–69). NICHD Clearinghouse.

Vygotsky, L. S. (1978). *Mind in society: The development of higher psychological processes* (M. Cole, V. John-Steiner, S. Scriber, E. Souberman, Eds. & Trans.). Cambridge, MA: Harvard University Press.

APPENDIX: COMPREHENSION INSTRUCTION
CATEGORY REFERENCES

Comprehension Monitoring

Babbs, P. J. (1984). Monitoring cards help improve comprehension. *Reading Teacher, 38*(2), 200–204.

Baker, L., & Zimlin, L. (1989). Instructional effects on children's use of two levels of standards for evaluating their comprehension. *Journal of Educational Psychology, 81*(3), 340–346.

Baumann, J. F., Seifert-Kessell, N., & Jones, L. A. (1992). Effect of think-aloud instruction on elementary students' comprehension monitoring abilities. *Journal of Reading Behavior, 24*(2), 143–172.

Block, C. C. (1993). Strategy instruction in a literature-based reading program. *Elementary School Journal, 94*(2), 139–151.

Carr, E. M., Dewitz, P., & Patberg, J. P. (1983). The effect of inference training on children's comprehension of expository text. *Journal of Reading Behavior, 15*(3), 1–18.

Cross, D. R., & Paris, S. G. (1988). Developmental and instructional analyses of children's metacognition and reading comprehension. *Journal of Educational Psychology, 80*(2), 131–142.

Elliot-Faust, D. J., & Pressley, M. (1986). How to teach comparison processing to increase children's short- and long-term listening comprehension monitoring. *Journal of Educational Psychology, 78*, 27–33.

Hasselhorn, M., & Koerkel, J. (1986). Metacognitive versus traditional reading instructions: The mediating role of domain-specific knowledge on children's text processing. *Human Learning: Journal of Practical Research and Applications, 5*(2), 75–90.

Markman, E. M. (1977). Realizing that you don't understand: A preliminary investigation. *Child Development, 46*, 986–992.

Miller, G. E. (1985). The effects of general and specific self-instruction training on children's comprehension monitoring performances during reading. *Reading Research Quarterly, 20*(5), 616–628.

Miller, G. E. (1987). The influence of self-instruction on the comprehension monitoring performance of average and above average readers. *Journal of Reading Behavior, 19*(3), 303–317.

Miller, G. E., Giovenco, A., & Rentiers, K. A. (1987). Fostering comprehension monitoring in below average readers through self-instruction training. *Journal of Reading Behavior, 19*(4), 379–394.

Paris, S. G., Cross, D. R., & Lipson, M. Y. (1984). Informed strategies for learning: A program to improve children's reading awareness and comprehension. *Journal of Educational Psychology, 76*(6), 1239–1252.

Paris, S. G., & Jacobs, J. E. (1984). The benefits of informed instruction for children's reading awareness and comprehension skills. *Child Development, 55*(6), 2083–2093.

Paris, S. G., Saarnio, D. A., & Cross, D. R. (1986). A metacognitive curriculum to promote children's reading and learning. *Australian Journal of Psychology, 38*(2), 107–123.

Payne, B. D., & Manning, B. H. (1992). Basal reader instruction: Effects of comprehension monitoring training on reading comprehension, strategy use and attitude. *Reading Research and Instruction, 32*(1), 29–38.

Schmitt, M. C. (1988). The effects of an elaborated directed reading activity on the metacomprehension skills of third graders. *National Reading Conference Yearbook, 37*, 167–181.

Schunk, D. H., & Rice, J. M. (1984). Strategy self-verbalization during remedial listening comprehension instruction. *Journal of Experimental Education, 53*(1), 49–54.

Schunk, D. H., & Rice, J. M. (1985). Verbalization of comprehension strategies: Effects on children's achievement outcomes. *Human Learning: Journal of Practical Research and Applications, 4*(1), 1–10.

Silven, M. (1992). The role of metacognition in reading instruction. *Scandinavian Journal of Educational Research, 36*(3), 211–221.

Tregaskes, M. R., & Daines, D. (1989). Effects of metacognitive strategies on reading comprehension. *Reading Research and Instruction, 29*(1), 52–60.

Graphic Organizers

Alvermann, D. E., & Boothby, P. R. (1983). A preliminary investigation of the differences in children's retention of "inconsiderate" text. *Reading Psychology, 4*(3–4), 237–246.

Alvermann, D. E., & Boothby, P. R. (1986). Children's transfer of graphic organizer instruction. *Reading Psychology, 7*(2), 87–100.

Armbruster, B. B., Anderson, T. H., & Meyer, J. L. (1991). Improving content-area reading using instructional graphics. *Reading Research Quarterly, 26*(4), 393–416.

Armbruster, B. B., Anderson, T. H., & Meyer, J. L. (1992). "Improving content-area reading using instructional graphics": Erratum. *Reading Research Quarterly, 27*(3), 282.

Baumann, J. F. (1984). The effectiveness of an instruction paradigm for teaching main idea comprehension. *Reading Research Quarterly, 20*(1), 93–115.

Berkowitz, S. J. (1986). Effects of instruction in text organization on sixth-grade students' memory
for expository reading. *Reading Research Quarterly, 21*(2), 161–178.

Darch, C. B., Carnine, D. W., & Kameenui, E. J. (1986). The role of graphic organizers and social
structure in content area instruction. *Journal of Reading Behavior, 18*(4), 275–295.

Gordon, C. J., & Rennie, B. J. (1987). Restructuring content schemata: An intervention study.
Reading Research and Instruction, 26(3), 162–188.

Sinatra, R. C., Stahl-Gemake, J., & Berg, D. N. (1984). Improving reading comprehension of disabled readers through semantic mapping. *Reading Teacher, 38*(1), 22–29.

Vidal-Abarca, E., & Gilabert, R. (1995). Teaching strategies to create visual representations of key
ideas in content area text materials: A long-term intervention inserted in school curriculum.
European Journal of Psychology of Education, 10(4), 433–447.

Listening Actively

Boodt, G. M. (1984). Critical listeners become critical readers in remedial reading class. *Reading
Teacher, 37*(4), 390–394.

Shany, M. T., & Biemiller, A. (1995). Assisted reading practice: Effects on performance for poor
readers in grades 3 and 4. *Reading Research Quarterly, 30*(3), 382–395.

Shepherd, T. R., & Svasti, S. (1987). Improved sixth grade social studies test scores via instruction
in listening. *Journal of Social Studies Research, 11*(2), 20–23.

Sippola, A. E. (1988). The effects of three reading instruction techniques on the comprehension and
word recognition of first graders grouped by ability. *Reading Psychology, 9*(1), 17–32.

Mental Imagery

Borduin, B. J., Borduin, C. M., & Manley, C. M. (1994). The use of imagery training to improve reading comprehension of second graders. *Journal of Genetic Psychology, 155*(1),
115–118.

Gambrell, L. B., & Bales, R. J. (1986). Mental imagery and the comprehension-monitoring performance of fourth and fifth-grade poor readers. *Reading Research Quarterly, 21*, 454–464.

Peters, E. E., & Levin, J. R. (1986). Effects of a mnemonic imagery strategy on good and poor readers' prose recall. *Reading Research Quarterly, 21*, 179–192.

Pressley, G. M. (1976). Mental imagery helps eight-year-olds remember what they read. *Journal of
Educational Psychology, 68*, 355–359.

Shriberg, L. K., Levin, J. R., McCormick, C. B., & Pressley, M. (1982). Learning about "famous"
people via the keyword method. *Journal of Educational Psychology, 74*, 238–247.

Mnemonic Instruction

Levin, J. R., Shriberg, L. D., & Berry, J. K. (1983). A concrete strategy for remembering abstract
prose. *American Educational Research Journal, 20*, 277–290.

Levin, J. R., Levin, M. E., Glasman, L. D., & Nordwall, M. B. (1992). Mnemonic vocabulary instruction: Additional effectiveness evidence. *Contemporary Educational Psychology, 17*(2),
156–174.

McCormick, C. B., & Levin, J. R. (1984). A comparison of different prose-learning variations of
the mnemonic keyword method. *American Educational Research Journal, 21*, 379–398.

McCormick, C. B., Levin, J. R., Cykowski, F., & Danilovics, P. (1984). Mnemonic-strategy reduc-
tion of prose-learning interference. *Educational Communication and Technology Journal, 32*,
145–152.

Multiple Strategies

Reciprocal Teaching (Reviewed by Rosenshine & Meister, 1994)

Brady, P. I. (1990). *Improving the reading comprehension of middle school students through reciprocal teaching and semantic mapping strategies.* Unpublished doctoral dissertation, University of Oregon—Eugene.

Dermody, M. (1988, February). *Metacognitive strategies for development of reading comprehension for younger children.* Paper presented at the American Association of Colleges for Teacher Education, New Orleans, LA.

Fischer Galbert, J. L. (1989). *An experimental study of reciprocal teaching of expository test with third, fourth, and fifth grade students enrolled in chapter 1 reading.* Unpublished doctoral dissertation, Ball State University, Muncie, IN.

Jones, M. P. (1987). *Effects of reciprocal teaching method on third graders' decoding and comprehension abilities.* Unpublished doctoral dissertation, Texas A&M University, College Station.

Labercane, G., & Battle, J. (1987). Cognitive processing strategies, self-esteem, and reading comprehension of learning disabled students. *Journal of Special Education, 11,* 167–185.

Lysynchuk, L. M., Pressley, M., & Vye, N. J. (1990). Reciprocal teaching improves standardized reading-comprehension performance in poor comprehenders. *Elementary School Journal, 90*(5), 469–484.

Padron, Y. N. (1985). *Utilizing cognitive reading strategies to improve English reading comprehension of Spanish-speaking bilingual students.* Unpublished doctoral dissertation, University of Houston.

Palincsar, A. S. (1987, April). *Collaborating for collaborative learning of text comprehension.* Paper presented at the Annual Meeting of the American Educational Research Association, Washington, DC.

Palincsar, A. S., & Brown, A. L. (1984). Reciprocal teaching of comprehension-fostering and comprehension-monitoring activities. *Cognition and Instruction, 2,* 117–175.

Rich, R. Z. (1989). *The effects of training adult poor readers to use text comprehension strategies.* Unpublished doctoral dissertation, Columbia University.

Rush, R. T., & Milburn, J. L. (1988, November). *The effects of reciprocal teaching on self-regulation of reading comprehension in a post secondary technical school program.* Paper presented at the National Reading Conference, Tucson, AZ.

Shortland-Jones, B. (1986). *The development and testing of an instructional strategy for improving reading comprehension based on schema and metacognitive theories.* Unpublished doctoral dissertation, University of Oregon, Eugene.

Taylor, B. M., & Frye, B. J. (1992). Comprehension strategy instruction in the intermediate grades. *Reading Research and Instruction, 32*(1), 39–48.

Williamson, R. A. (1989). *The effect of reciprocal teaching on student performance gains in third grade basal reading instruction.* Unpublished Doctoral dissertation, Texas A&M University, College Station.

Other Reciprocal Teaching Studies (not reviewed by Rosenshine & Meister, 1994)

Carnine, D., & Kinder, D. (1985). Teaching low-performing students to apply generative and schema strategies to narrative and expository material. *Remedial and Special Education, 6,* 20–30.

Chan, L. D. S., & Cole, P. G. (1986). Effects of inference training on children's comprehension of expository text. *Remedial and Special Education, 7,* 33–40.

Gilroy, A., & Moore, D. W. (1988). Reciprocal teaching of comprehension-fostering and comprehension-monitoring activities with ten primary school girls. *Educational Psychology, 8*(1–2), 41–49.

Grant, J., Elias, G., & Broerse, J. (1989). An application of Palincsar and Brown's comprehension instruction paradigm to listening. *Contemporary Educational Psychology, 14*(2), 164–172.

Jacobs, J. E., & Paris, S. G. (1987). Children's metacognition about reading: issues in definition, measurement, and instruction. *Educational Psychologist, 22*, 255–278.

Klingner, J. K., Vaughn, S., & Schumm, J. S. (1998). Collaborative strategic reading during social studies in heterogeneous fourth-grade classrooms. *Elementary School Journal, 99*(1), 3–22.

Loranger, A. L. (1997). Comprehension strategies instruction: Does it make a difference? *Reading Psychology, 18*(1), 31–68.

Lysynchuk, L. M., Pressley, M., & Vye, N. J. (1990). Reciprocal teaching improves standardized reading-comprehension performance in poor comprehenders. *Elementary School Journal, 90*(5), 469–484.

Palincsar, A. S., David, Y. M., Winn, J. A., & Stevens, D. D. (1991). Examining the context of strategy instruction. *RASE: Remedial and Special Education, 12*(3), 43–53.

Pressley, M., El-Dinary, P. B., Gaskins, I., Schuder, T., Bergman, J. L., Almasi, J., & Brown, R. (1992). Beyond direct explanation: Transactional instruction of reading comprehension strategies. *Elementary School Journal, 92*, 511–554.

Soriano, M., Vidal-Abarca, E., & Miranda, A. (1996). Comparacion de dos procedimientos de instruccion en comprension y aprendizaje de textos: Instruccion directa y ensenanza reciproca. [Comparison of two procedures for instruction in comprehension and text learning: Direct instruction and reciprocal teaching]. *Infancia y Aprendizaje, 74*, 57–65.

Taylor, B. M., & Frye, B. J. (1992). Comprehension strategy instruction in the intermediate grades. *Reading Research and Instruction, 32*(1), 39–48.

Multiple Strategy Treatments Other Than Reciprocal Teaching

Adams, A., Carnine, D., & Gersten, R. (1982). Instructional strategies for studying content area texts in the intermediate grades. *Reading Research Quarterly, 18*(1), 27–55.

Anderson, V., & Roit, M. (1993). Planning and implementing collaborative strategy instruction for delayed readers in grades 6–20. *Elementary School Journal, 94*(2), 121–137.

Blanchard, J. S. (1980). Preliminary investigation of transfer between single-word decoding ability and contextual reading comprehension by poor readers in grade six. *Perceptual and Motor Skills, 51*(3), 1271–1281.

Brown, R., Pressley, M., Van Meter, P., & Schuder, T. (1996). A quasi-experimental validation of transactional strategies instruction with low-achieving second-grade readers. *Journal of Educational Psychology, 88*(1), 18–37.

Carr, E., Bigler, M., & Morningstar, C. (1991). The effects of the CVS strategy on children's learning. *National Reading Conference Yearbook, 40*, 193–200.

Pelow, R. A., & Colvin, H. M. (1983, Spring). PQ4R as it affects comprehension of social studies reading material. *Social Studies Journal, 12*, 14–22.

Reutzel, D. R., & Hollingsworth, P. M. (1991). Reading comprehension skills: Testing the distinctiveness hypothesis. *Reading Research and Instruction, 30*(2), 32–46.

Reutzel, D. R., & Hollingsworth, P. M. (1991). Reading time in school: Effect on fourth graders' performance on a criterion-referenced comprehension test. *Journal of Educational Research, 84*(3), 170–176.

Ritchie, P. (1985). Graduate research: Reviews and commentary: The effects of instruction in main idea and question generation. *Reading-Canada-Lecture, 3*(2), 139–146.

Smith, K., Johnson, D. W., & Johnson, R. T. (1981). Can conflict be constructive? Controversy versus concurrence seeking in learning groups. *Journal of Educational Psychology, 73*(5), 651–663.

Stevens, R. J. (1988). Effects of strategy training on the identification of the main idea of expository passages. *Journal of Educational Psychology, 80*(1), 21–26.

Stevens, R. J., Madden, N. A., Slavin, R. E., & Farnish, A. M. (1987). Cooperative integrated reading and composition: Two field experiments. *Reading Research Quarterly, 22*(4), 433–454.

Stevens, R. J., Slavin, R. E., & Farnish, A. M. (1991). The effects of cooperative learning and instruction in reading comprehension strategies on main idea identification. *Journal of Educational Psychology, 83*(1), 8–16.

Prior Knowledge

Au, K. (1980). Participation structures in a reading lesson with Hawaiian children. *Anthropology and Education Quarterly, 11,* 91–115.

Brown, A. L., Smiley, S. S., Day, J. D., Townsend, M. A. R., & Lawton, S. C. (1977). Intrusion of a thematic idea in children's comprehension and retention of stories. *Child Development, 48,* 1454–1466.

Dewitz, P., Carr, E. M., & Patberg, J. P. (1986). Effects of inference training on comprehension and comprehension monitoring. *Reading Research Quarterly, 22,* 109–119.

Dole, J. A., Valencia, S. W., Greer, E. A., & Wardrop, J. L. (1991). Effects of two types of prereading instruction on the comprehension of narrative and expository text. *Reading Research Quarterly, 26*(2), 142–159.

Hansen, J., & Pearson, P. D. (1983). An instructional study: Improving the inferential comprehension of good and poor fourth-grade readers. *Journal of Educational Psychology, 75*(6), 821–829.

Linden, M., & Wittrock, M. C. (1981). The teaching of reading comprehension according to the model of generative learning. *Reading Research Quarterly, 17*(1), 44–57.

Manzo, A. V. (1979). The ReQuest procedure. *Journal of Reading, 2,* 123–126.

Neuman, S. B. (1988). Enhancing children's comprehension through previewing. *National Reading Conference Yearbook, 37,* 219–224.

Palincsar, A. S., & Brown, A. L. (1984). Reciprocal teaching of comprehension-fostering and comprehension-monitoring activities. *Cognition and Instruction, 2,* 117–175.

Prince, A. T., & Mancus, D. S. (1987). Enriching comprehension: A scheme altered basal reading lesson. *Reading Research and Instruction, 27*(1), 45–54.

Roberts, T. A. (1988). Development of pre-instruction versus previous experience: Effects on factual and inferential comprehension. *Reading Psychology, 9*(2), 141–157.

Spires, H. A., Gallini, J., & Riggsbee, J. (1992). Effects of schema-based and text structure-based cues on expository prose comprehension in fourth graders. *Journal of Experimental Education, 60*(4), 307–320.

Tharp, R. G. (1982). The effective instruction of comprehension: Results and description of the Kamehameha Early Education Program. *Reading Research Quarterly, 17*(4), 503–527.

Wood, E. G., Winne, P., & Pressley, M. (1988, April). *Elaborative interrogation, imagery, and provided precise elaborations as facilitators of children's learning of arbitrary prose.* Paper presented at the American Educational Research Association, New Orleans.

Question Generation

Signal Word Prompts

Brady, P. I. (1990). *Improving the reading comprehension of middle school students through reciprocal teaching and semantic mapping strategies.* Unpublished doctoral dissertation, University of Alaska, Anchorage.

Cohen, R. (1983). Students generate questions as an aid to reading comprehension. *Reading Teacher, 36,* 770–775.

Davey, B., & McBride, M. (1986). Effects of question-generation on reading comprehension. *Journal of Educational Psychology, 22,* 2–7.

Lysynchuk, L. M., Pressley, M., & Vye, N. J. (1990). Reciprocal teaching improves standardized reading-comprehension performance in poor comprehenders. *Elementary School Journal, 90(5),* 469–484.

MacGregor, S. K. (1988). Use of self-questioning with a computer-mediated text system and measures of reading performance. *Journal of Reading Behavior, 20(2),* 131–148.

Palincsar, A. S. (1987, April). *Collaborating for collaborative learning of text comprehension.* Paper presented at the Annual Meeting of the American Educational Research Association, Washington, DC.

Palincsar, A. S., & Brown, A. L. (1984). Reciprocal teaching of comprehension-fostering and comprehension-monitoring activities. *Cognition and Instruction, 2,* 117–175.

Taylor, B. M., & Frye, B. J. (1992). Comprehension strategy instruction in the intermediate grades. *Reading Research and Instruction, 32(1),* 39–48.

Williamson, R. A. (1989). *The effect of reciprocal teaching on student performance gains in third grade basal reading instruction.* Unpublished Doctoral dissertation, Texas A&M University, College Station.

Self-Questioning

King, A. (1989). Effects of self-questioning training on college students' comprehension of lectures. *Contemporary Educational Psychology, 14,* 366–381.

King, A. (1990). Improving lecture comprehension: Effects of a metacognitive strategy. *Applied Educational Psychology, 29,* 331–346.

King, A. (1992). Comparison of self questioning, summarizing, and note taking-review as strategies for learning from lectures. *American Educational Research Journal, 29,* 303–325.

Main Idea Prompts

Blaha, B. A. (1979). *The effects of answering self-generated questions on reading.* Unpublished doctoral dissertation, Boston University.

Dreher, M. J., & Gambrell, L. B. (1985). Teaching children to use a self-questioning strategy for studying expository text. *Reading Improvement, 22,* 2–7.

Lonberger, R. (1988). *The effects of training in a self-generated learning strategy on the prose processing abilities of fourth and sixth graders.* Unpublished doctoral dissertation, State University of New York, Buffalo.

Ritchie, P. (1985). Graduate research: Reviews and commentary: The effects of instruction in main idea and question generation. *Reading-Canada-Lecture, 3(2),* 139–146.

Wong, Y. L., & Jones, W. (1982). Increasing metacomprehension in learning disabled and normally achieving students through self-questioning training. *Learning Disability Quarterly, 5,* 228–239.

Question-Type Prompts

Dermody, M. (1988, April). *Metacognitive strategies for development of reading comprehension for younger children.* Paper presented at the American Association of Colleges for Teacher Education, New Orleans, LA.

Labercane, G., & Battle, J. (1987). Cognitive processing strategies, self-esteem, and reading comprehension of learning disabled students. *Journal of Special Education, 11,* 167–185.

Smith, N. J. (1977). *The effects of training teachers to teach students at different reading ability lev-*

els to formulate three types of questions on reading comprehension and question generation ability. Unpublished doctoral dissertation, University of Georgia, Athens.

Story Grammar Prompts

Nolte, R. Y., & Singer, H. (1985). Active comprehension: Teaching a process of reading comprehension and its effects on reading achievement. *Reading Teacher, 39*(1), 24–31.

Short, E. J., & Ryan, E. B. (1984). Metacognitive differences between skilled and less skilled readers: Remediating Deficits through story grammar and attribution training. *Journal of Educational Psychology, 76*(2), 225–235.

No Prompts

Helfeldt, J. P., & Lalik, R. (1976). Reciprocal student-teacher questioning. *Reading Teacher, 33*, 283–287.

Manzo, A. V. (1969). *Improving reading comprehension through reciprocal teaching.* Unpublished doctoral dissertation, Syracuse University, Syracuse, NY.

Simpson, P. S. (1989). *The effects of direct training in active comprehension on reading achievement, self-concepts, and reading attitudes of at-risk sixth grade students.* Unpublished doctoral dissertation, Texas Tech University, Lubbock.

Other Question Generation Studies (not reviewed by Rosenshine, Meisler, & Chapman, 1996)

Hansen, J., & Pearson, P. D. (1983). An instructional study: Improving the inferential comprehension of good and poor fourth-grade readers. *Journal of Educational Psychology, 75*(6), 821–829.

Singer, H., & Donlan, D. (1982). Active comprehension: Problem-solving schema with question generation for comprehension of complex short stories. *Reading Research Quarterly, 17*(2), 166–186.

Question Answering

Anderson, R., & Biddle, W. (1975). On asking people questions about what they are reading. In G. H. Bower (Ed.), *The psychology of learning and motivation* (Vol. 9, pp. 90–132). New York: Academic Press.

Ezell, H. K., Hunsicker, S. A., Quinque, M. M., & Randolph, E. (1992). Use of peer-assisted procedures to teach QAR reading comprehension strategies to third-grade children. *Education and Treatment of Children, 15*(3), 205–227.

Fischer, J. A. (1973). Effects of cue synthesis procedure and post questions on the retention of prose material. *Dissertation Abstracts International, 34*, 615.

Garner, R., Hare, V. C., Alexander, P. A., Haynes, J., & Winograd, P. (1984). Inducing use of a text lookback strategy among unsuccessful readers. *American Educational Research Journal, 21*, 789–798.

Garner, R., Macready, G. B., & Wagoner, S. (1984). Readers' acquisition of the components of the text-lookback strategy. *Journal of Educational Psychology, 76*, 300–309.

Griffey, Q. L., Jr., Zigmond, N., & Leinhardt, T. (1988). The effects of self-questioning and story structure training on the reading comprehension of poor readers. *Learning Disabilities Research, 4*(1), 45–51.

Levin, J. R., & Pressley, M. (1981). Improving children's prose comprehension: Selected strategies that seem to succeed. In C. M. Santa & B. L. Hayes (Eds.), *Children's prose comprehension: Research and practice* (pp. 44–71). Newark, DE: International Reading Association.

Pressley, M., & Forrest-Pressley, D. (1985). Questions and children's cognitive processing. In A. C. G. B. Black (Ed.), *The psychology of questions* (pp. 277–296). Hillsdale, NJ: Erlbaum.

Raphael, T. E., & McKinney, J. (1983). An examination of fifth- and eighth-grade children's question-answering behavior: An instructional study in metacognition. *Journal of Reading Behavior, 15*(3), 67–86.

Raphael, T. E., & Pearson, P. D. (1985). Increasing students' awareness of sources of information for answering questions. *American Educational Research Journal, 22,* 217–235.

Raphael, T. E., & Wonnacott, C. A. (1985). Heightening fourth-grade students' sensitivity to sources of information for answering comprehension questions. *Reading Research Quarterly, 20*(3), 282–296.

Richmond, M. G. (Ed.). (1976). The relationship of the uniqueness of prose passages to the effect of question placement and question relevance on the acquisition and retention of information. In W. D. Miller & G. H. McNinch (Eds.), *Reflections and investigations on reading* (Vol. 25). Clemson, SC: National Reading Conference.

Rowls, M. D. (1976). The facilitative and interactive effects of adjunct questions on retention of eight graders across three prose passages: Dissertation in prose learning. *Journal of Educational Psychology, 68,* 205–209.

Serenty, M. L., & Dean, R. S. (1986). Interspersed post passage questions and reading comprehension achievement. *Journal of Educational Psychology, 78*(3), 228–229.

Sheldon, S. A. (1984). Comparison of two teaching methods for reading comprehension. *Journal of Research in Reading, 7*(1), 41–52.

Watts, G. H. (1973). The "arousal" effect of adjunct questions on recall from prose materials. *Australian Journal of Psychology, 25,* 81–87.

Wixson, K. K. (1983). Questions about a text: What you ask about is what children learn. *Reading Teacher, 37*(3), 287–293.

Story Structure

Baumann, J. F., & Bergeron, B. S. (1993). Story map instruction using children's literature: Effects on first graders' comprehension of central narrative elements. *Journal of Reading Behavior, 25*(4), 407–437.

Buss, R. R., Ratliff, J. L., & Irion, J. C. (1985). Effects of instruction on the use of story structure in comprehension of narrative discourse. In J. A. Niles & R. B. Lalik (Eds.), *Issues in literacy: A research perspective* (Vol. 34, pp. 55–58). Rochester, NY: National Reading Conference.

Fitzgerald, J., & Spiegel, D. L. (1983). Enhancing children's reading comprehension through instruction in narrative structure. *Journal of Reading Behavior, 15*(2), 1–17.

Gordon, C. J., & Rennie, B. J. (1987). Restructuring content schemata: An intervention study. *Reading Research and Instruction, 26*(3), 162–188.

Greenewald, M. J., & Rossing, R. L. (1986). Short-term and long-term effects of story grammar and self-monitoring training on children's story comprehension. In J. A. Niles & R. V. Lalik (Eds.), *Solving problems in literacy: Learners, teachers, and researchers* (pp. 210–218). Rochester, NY: National Reading Conference.

Griffey, Q. L., Jr., & et al. (1988). The effects of self-questioning and story structure training on the reading comprehension of poor readers. *Learning Disabilities Research, 4*(1), 45–51.

Idol, L. (1987). Group story mapping: A comprehension strategy for both skilled and unskilled readers. *Journal of Learning Disabilities, 20,* 196–205.

Idol, L., & Croll, V. J. (1987). Story-mapping training as a means of improving reading comprehension. *Learning Disability Quarterly, 10,* 214–229.

Nolte, R. Y., & Singer, H. (1985). Active comprehension: Teaching a process of reading comprehension and its effects on reading achievement. *Reading Teacher, 39*(1), 24–31.

Omanson, R. C., Beck, I. L., Voss, J. F., & McKeown, M. G. (1984). The effects of reading lessons on comprehension: A processing description. *Cognition and Instruction, 1*(1), 45–67.

Reutzel, D. R. (1984). Story mapping: An alternative approach to communication. *Reading World, 24*(2), 16–25.

Reutzel, D. R. (1985). Story maps improve comprehension. *Reading Teacher, 38*(4), 400–404.

Reutzel, D. R. (1986). Clozing in on comprehension: The Cloze Story Map. *Reading Teacher, 39*(6), 524–528.

Short, E. J., & Ryan, E. B. (1984). Metacognitive differences between skilled and less skilled readers: Remediating deficits through story grammar and attribution training. *Journal of Educational Psychology, 76*(2), 225–235.

Singer, H., & Donlan, D. (1982). Active comprehension: Problem-solving schema with question generation for comprehension of complex short stories. *Reading Research Quarterly, 17*(2), 166–186.

Spiegel, D. L., & Fitzgerald, J. (1986). Improving reading comprehension through instruction about story parts. *Reading Teacher, 39*(7), 676–682.

Varnhagen, C. K., & Goldman, S. R. (1986). Improving comprehension: Causal relations instruction for learning-handicapped learners. *Reading Teacher, 39*(9), 896–904.

Summarization

Afflerbach, P., & Walker, B. (1992). Main idea instruction: An analysis of three basal reader series. *Reading Research and Instruction, 32*(1), 11–28.

Armbruster, B. B., Anderson, T. H., & Ostertag, J. (1987). Does text structure/summarization instruction facilitate learning from expository text? *Reading Research Quarterly, 22*, 331–346.

Baumann, J. F. (1983). Children's ability to comprehend main ideas in content textbooks. *Reading World, 22*(4), 322–331.

Baumann, J. F. (1984). The effectiveness of an instruction paradigm for teaching main idea comprehension. *Reading Research Quarterly, 20*(1), 93–115.

Bean, T. W., & Steenwyk, F. L. (1984). The effect of three forms of summarization instruction on sixth graders' summary writing and comprehension. *Journal of Reading Behavior, 16*(4), 297–306.

Berkowitz, S. J. (1986). Effects of instruction in text organization on sixth-grade students' memory for expository reading. *Reading Research Quarterly, 21*(2), 161–178.

Brown, A. L., & Day, J. D. (1983). Macro rules for summarizing texts: The development of expertise. *Journal of Verbal Learning and Verbal Behavior, 22*, 1–14.

Brown, A. L., Day, J. D., & Jones, R. S. (1983). The development of plans for summarizing texts. *Child Development, 48*, 968–979.

Carnine, D. W., Kameenui, E. J., & Woolfson, N. (1982). Training of textual dimensions related to text-based inferences. *Journal of Reading Behavior, 14*(3), 335–340.

Doctorow, M., Wittrock, M. C., & Marcks, C. (1978). Generative processes in reading comprehension. *Journal of Educational Psychology, 70*, 109–118.

Jenkins, J. R., Heliotis, J., Stein, M. L., & Haynes, M. (1987). Improving reading comprehension by using paragraph restatements. *Exceptional Children, 54*, 54–59.

Reutzel, D. R., & Cooter, R. B., Jr. (1988). Research implications for improving basal skill instruction. *Reading Horizons, 28*(3), 208–215.

Reutzel, D. R., & Hollingsworth, P. M. (1988). Highlighting key vocabulary: A generative-reciprocal procedure for teaching selected inference types. *Reading Research Quarterly, 23*(3), 358–378.

Rinehart, S. D., Stahl, S. A., & Erickson, L. G. (1986). Some effects of summarization training on reading and studying. *Reading Research Quarterly, 21*(4), 422–438.

Sjostrom, C. L., & Hare, V. C. (1984). Teaching high school students to identify main ideas in expository text. *Journal of Educational Research, 78*(2), 114–118.

Taylor, B. M. (1982). Text structure and children's comprehension and memory for expository material. *Journal of Educational Psychology, 74*(3), 323–340.

Taylor, B. M. (1986). Teaching middle-grade students to read for main ideas. In J. A. Niles & R. V. Lalik (Eds.), *Solving problems in literacy: Learners, teachers, and researchers* (pp. 99–108). Rochester, NY: National Reading Conference.

Taylor, B. M., & Beach, R. W. (1984). The effects of text structure instruction on middle-grade students' comprehension and production of expository prose. *Reading Research Quarterly, 19,* 134–136.

Teacher Preparation

Anderson, V. (1992). A teacher development project in transactional strategy instruction for teachers of severely reading-disabled adolescents. *Teaching and Teacher Education, 8*(4), 391–403.

Brown, R., Pressley, M., Van Meter, P., & Schuder, T. (1996). A quasi-experimental validation of transactional strategies instruction with low-achieving second grade readers. *Journal of Educational Psychology, 88,* 18–37.

Duffy, G. G. (1993). Rethinking strategy instruction: Four teachers' development and their low achievers' understandings. *Elementary School Journal, 93*(3), 231–247.

Duffy, G. G., Roehler, L. R., Sivan, E., Rackliff, G., Book, C., Meloth, M., Vavrus, L., Wesselman, R., Rutnma, J., & Bassiri, D. (1987). Effects of explaining the reasoning associated with using reading strategies. *Reading Research Quarterly, 22*(3), 347–368.

Vocabulary and Comprehension

Beck, I. L., Perfetti, C. A., & McKeown, M. G. (1982). Effects of long term vocabulary instruction on lexical access and reading comprehension. *Journal of Educational Psychology, 74,* 506–521.

McKeown, M. G., Beck, I. L., Omanson, R. C., & Perfetti, C. A. (1983). The effects of long-term vocabulary instruction on reading comprehension: A replication. *Journal of Reading Behavior, 15*(1), 3–18.

McKeown, M. G., Beck, I. L., Omanson, R. C., & Pople, M. T. (1985). Some effects of the nature and frequency of vocabulary instruction on the knowledge and use of words. *Reading Research Quarterly, 20*(5), 522–535.

Tomesen, M., & Aarnoutse, C. (1998). Effects of an instructional programme for deriving word meanings. *Educational Studies, 24*(1), 107–128.

Cooperative Learning

Bramlett, R. K. (1994). Implementing cooperative learning: A field study evaluating issues for school-based consultants. *Journal of School Psychology, 32*(1), 67–84.

Guthrie, J. T., Van Meter, P., Hancock, G. R., Solomon, A., Anderson, E., & McCann, A. (1996). Growth of literacy engagement: Changes in motivations and strategies during concept-oriented reading instruction. *Reading Research Quarterly, 31*(3), 306–332.

Judy, J. E., Alexander, P. A., Kulikowich, J. M., & Wilson, V. L. (1988). Effects of two instructional approaches and peer tutoring on gifted and nongifted sixth-grade students' analogy performance. *Reading Research Quarterly, 23*(2), 236–256.

Klingner, J. K., Vaughn, S., & Schumm, J. S. (1998). Collaborative strategic reading during social studies in heterogeneous fourth-grade classrooms. *Elementary School Journal, 99*(1), 3–22.

Mathes, P. G., Fuchs, D., Fuchs, L. S., & Henley, A. M. (1994). Increasing Strategic Reading Practice with Peabody Classwide Peer Tutoring. *Learning Disabilities Research and Practice, 9*(1), 44–48.

Pickens, J., & McNaughton, S. (1988). Peer tutoring of comprehension strategies. *Educational Psychology: An International Journal of Experimental Educational Psychology, 8*(1–2), 67–80.

Soriano, M., Vidal-Abarca, E., & Miranda, A. (1996). Comparacion de dos procedimientos de instruccion en comprension y aprendizaje de textos: Instruccion directa y ensenanza reciproca. [Comparison of two procedures for instruction in comprehension and text learning: Direct instruction and reciprocal teaching.] *Infancia y Aprendizaje, 74,* 57–65.

Stevens, R. J., Madden, N. A., Slavin, R. E., & Farnish, A. M. (1987). Cooperative integrated reading and composition: Two field experiments. *Reading Research Quarterly, 22*(4), 433–454.

Stevens, R. J., Slavin, R. E., & Farnish, A. M. (1991). The effects of cooperative learning and instruction in reading comprehension strategies on main idea identification. *Journal of Educational Psychology, 83*(1), 8–16.

Uttero, D. A. (1988). Activating comprehension through cooperative learning. *Reading Teacher, 41*(4), 390–395.

13

Challenges of Implementing Transactional Strategies Instruction for Reading Comprehension

Pamela Beard El-Dinary

CRITICAL RESEARCH ON COMPREHENSION INSTRUCTION

Since the realization in the late 1970s that reading comprehension instruction was meager in elementary classrooms (e.g., Durkin, 1979), our understanding of ways to improve comprehension has come a long way. By the middle 1980s, it was evident that elementary students could profit from researcher-developed instruction in reading strategies, such as self-questioning, summarizing, rereading, visualizing, and analyzing story-grammar elements (e.g., Bereiter & Bird, 1985; Collins, 1991; Duffy et al., 1987; Palincsar & Brown, 1984). Educators began designing and implementing reading strategies instruction, and by the late 1980s several promising school-based programs were in place (see Gaskins & Elliot, 1991; Schuder, 1993; Pressley, Goodchild, Fleet, Zajchowski, & Evans, 1989).

School-based strategies programs were founded on the view that skilled reading develops through long-term teaching of coordinated use of comprehension strategies. This instruction was clearly more complex than interventions that had been evaluated by university researchers (Pressley et al., 1989). Yet there were no formal analyses documenting how school-based programs worked. Thus a research group then at the University of Maryland began a collaboration with curriculum developers who had designed strategies instruction and with teachers who were implementing it.

Transactional Strategies Instruction

Part of this research effort aimed to describe teaching practices that make up the school-based programs using ethnographies, case studies, and collaborative interviews (Bergman

& Schuder, 1992; El-Dinary, Pressley, Coy-Ogan, Schuder, & Strategies Instruction Teachers, 1994; Marks et al., 1993; Pressley, El-Dinary, et al., 1992; Pressley, Gaskins, Cunicelli, et al., 1991; Pressley, Gaskins, Wile, Cunicelli, & Sheridan, 1991; Pressley, Schuder, SAIL Faculty and Administration, Bergman, & El-Dinary, 1992; Schuder, 1993). These analyses revealed that the instruction involved a variety of transactions among teachers, students, and texts. The approach therefore came to be called transactional strategies instruction (TSI; see Pressley, El-Dinary, et al., 1992).

The instruction is transactional in at least three senses:

1. *Transactions among group members.* Instructional activities are determined by students and teacher together as they work with a text, based on students' immediate needs (Bell, 1968; Bjorklund, 1989; Sameroff, 1975). The teacher uses "teachable moments" to discuss, model, or coach a particularly appropriate strategy.
2. *Transactions between reader and text.* Interpretations develop as students learn how to apply their knowledge of the world when constructing meaning from text (e.g., Rosenblatt, 1978).
3. *Transactions of socially constructed meaning.* The interpretation created when a group of students and a teacher work together differs from the meaning any of the individuals would have created alone (e.g., Hutchins, 1991; Wegner, 1987). Students also are expected to learn about reading processes through the modeled thought processes of other group members (e.g., Day, Cordon, & Kerwin, 1989; Vygotsky, 1978).

The term "transactional" also emphasizes what effective strategies instruction is *not*: It is not instruction of isolated skills, a method that induces student passivity, one-way communication from teacher to students, or transmission of facts (cf. Poplin, 1988). Rather, TSI teachers and students act as a literary community, using strategies to construct and evaluate interpretations of text. The long-term goal of the instruction is that students will internalize strategic processes that are practiced in the group (Bergman & Schuder, 1992; Pressley, El-Dinary, et al., 1992).

Positive Impacts of TSI

Teachers and curriculum developers implementing transactional strategies instruction were confident that it was effective. Teachers cited a positive impact on students' comprehension and interpretation of text, general metacognitive and thinking skills, motivation, and content-area skills, such as awareness of story structure. Schools also had documented increases in standardized reading test scores after implementing strategies instruction (Gaskins & Elliot, 1991; Schuder, 1993).

A quasi-experiment comparing TSI classrooms to those with traditional reading instruction (Brown, Pressley, Van Meter, & Schuder, 1996; Brown & Pressley, 1994) verified a wide range of positive impacts: TSI students learned more from daily readings, developed richer, more personalized interpretations, and performed better on standardized reading measures. These striking improvements further supported the importance of understanding TSI.

Teaching Practices in TSI

A key research goal was to describe the strategies-teaching practices in sufficient detail that they could be implemented elsewhere. We learned that school-based transactional strategies instruction involves a rich repertoire of teaching practices (El-Dinary, 1993; El-Dinary et al., 1994), many of which support a direct-explanation model of instruction (Roehler & Duffy, 1984). That is, the instruction includes extensive modeling, explaining, and scaffolded coaching, with students taking increasing responsibility for independent strategies use over time.

Consistent with the direct-explanation model, the TSI teacher bears most of the responsibility for instruction at the beginning, defining and explaining strategies and modeling how to use them (Bereiter & Bird, 1985; Duffy, Roehler, & Herrmann, 1988). The teacher then *scaffolds* instruction, gradually giving responsibility to the students by coaching students as they practice using strategies and by elaborating on students' thought processes. (See Duffy et al., 1987; Pearson, 1985; Wood, Bruner, & Ross, 1976.) Eventually, the teacher fades out cues, encouraging students to choose appropriate strategies for themselves. As students practice using strategies, the teacher continues monitoring student progress and reexplaining strategies as necessary until students work well independently. In the school-based programs we have encountered, this instruction occurs over years of schooling.

Figure 13.1 summarizes 44 practices identified in El-Dinary et al. (1994), illustrating the variety of ways in which TSI teachers carried out the direct-explanation model of strategies instruction. That is, teachers had many ways of explaining and modeling strategies use. They extensively coached students to use strategies and reflect on strategic processing. They also had several ways of scaffolding instruction as they responded to students' attempts to use strategies. (See also El-Dinary, 1993, for in-depth descriptions of these teaching practices, including excerpts from classroom observations.)

Teacher explanations and modeling introduce strategies to students. From that start, a student's first attempts often fall short of the teacher's conception of successful application. So the teacher prompts strategies use and responds with feedback about how to use the new procedures. As students work at applying the strategies to a task at hand, their understanding of them increases (Pressley, Harris, & Marks, 1992). Yet teachers noted that, although their students often used strategies in the absence of cuing, independent use was not as extensive as it could be. Because teachers knew that strategies maintenance and generalization do not come easily (see also Pressley, Gaskins, Cunicelli, et al., 1991), coaching practices of prompting and responding were among the most frequent.

TSI did not always supersede teachers' existing instruction. Rather, it was interwoven with many elements of traditional teaching. Some of these elements, such as use of "wait time" (Anderson & Pearson, 1984; Tobin, 1987), appeared to support TSI and principles of direct explanation. In contrast, other elements of traditional teaching, such as factual question asking and answering (I-R-E cycles; Mehan, 1979) and steering interpretations, were inconsistent with the principles of TSI as presented by the program developers in this setting (Bergman & Schuder, 1992; Schuder, 1993). Thus, although TSI often replaces elements of traditional teaching, it does not do so completely—sometimes it is consistent with TSI but other times it is inconsistent with it.

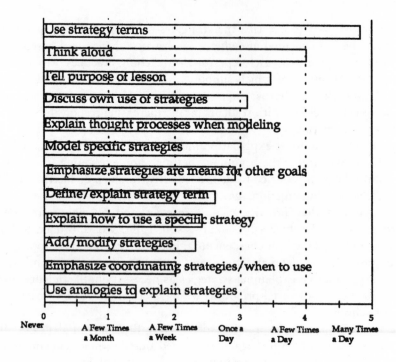

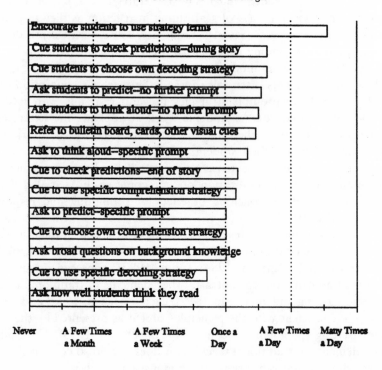

FIGURE 13.1. Teachers' ratings of the frequency of their instructional practices (means).

Respond to Student Strategy Attempts

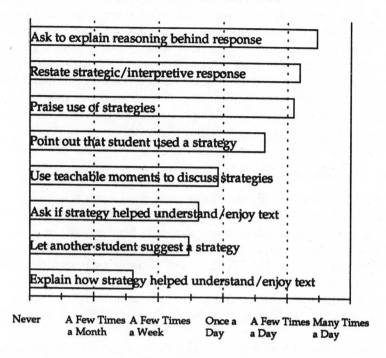

Conventional Teaching Behaviors

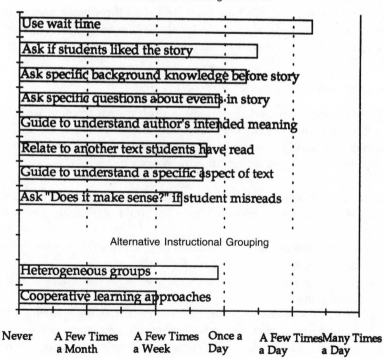

FIGURE 13.1. (*continued*)

On the other hand, we were particularly intrigued with what teachers did *not* do. Most critically, there was little use of some instructional procedures that enjoy solid support in the instructional literature: cooperative learning structures (see Slavin, 1985a, b), analogies to explain strategic procedures (e.g., Mayer, 1985), explicit discussion of the intercoordination of strategies (e.g., Meichenbaum, 1977), and explicit commentary about why and when particular strategies are useful (Pressley, Borkowski, & O'Sullivan, 1984, 1985). The instruction we studied, as good as it was, was still not all it could be. Future professional development should emphasize (and model and coach) how other effective instructional approaches can be integrated with TSI.

Challenges of Implementing TSI

Because of the complexity of TSI, one of our greatest concerns was how to enable other educators to implement what had been successful in the programs we observed. In addition to studying *what* skilled transactional strategies teachers did, we also studied *how* they learned to do it. Moreover, a critical facet of our work was identifying the challenges involved in learning to teach TSI. We spent considerable time with teachers, attending their professional development workshops, observing the formative stages of their transactional strategies instruction, and talking about how implementation was going (El-Dinary et al., 1994; El-Dinary, Pressley, & Schuder, 1992; El-Dinary & Schuder, 1993).

The findings reported here are based directly on a culminating questionnaire/interview used in El-Dinary et al. (1994). These findings are substantiated by observations, conversations, and focus groups in that study and the others listed previously. Teachers raised a variety of issues, including professional support requirements, implementation challenges, and confidence in their own implementation.

Professional Development Activities Supporting TSI

Recognizing TSI's complexity and the intensive professional training we had observed, we were interested in what activities teachers considered most critical in their development as strategies teachers. A variety of supports were provided, and the teachers rated them all as helpful. In order of importance, teachers valued:

- Expert models: instructional modeling through videos and live modeling in teachers' own classrooms demonstrating how TSI could work with their particular students.
- Coaching in the classroom: opportunities to practice strategies lessons while a curriculum developer observed and gave feedback.
- Conferring with peers: opportunities to discuss with colleagues how strategies instruction was going.
- Scripted practice lessons: opportunities to try TSI initially through scripted lessons, a useful form of scaffolding for beginning strategies teachers.
- Research reports: summaries of research that supports strategies instruction.
- Prepackaged materials: strategies-oriented bulletin board displays and other classroom materials.

Implementation Challenges of TSI

A number of concerns about implementing TSI were raised in focus groups and conversations. However, only three challenges were endorsed by the majority of teachers:

- Transactional strategies instruction takes a great deal of classroom time.
- TSI requires giving up some teacher control, which was considered difficult by many teachers.
- It can be difficult to locate texts appropriate for TSI: Many texts are not rich enough in meaning to warrant use of strategies. Some texts are too easy, others too difficult. For some stories, students have too little background knowledge, others are too familiar.

Other challenges were raised by a few teachers but were *not* endorsed by the majority. A few teachers experienced:

- Difficulty beginning strategies instruction
- Disruption to the flow of reading with strategies discussions
- Classroom management difficulties during strategies instruction (However, most teachers thought classroom management was better with TSI)
- Difficulty with reading assessment (Further clarification suggested that assigning objective reading grades was more challenging, even though teachers know more about students' progress through strategies discussions. Some teachers used traditional assessments for grading.)

Teacher Confidence with TSI

Lack of confidence in their strategies teaching was a prominent theme in teacher discussions. It turned out that teachers lacked confidence in specific aspects of instruction, with high variability across teachers. However, overall, teachers were uneasy with the following competencies:

- Knowing how to carry out strategies instruction across the curriculum
- Knowing whether there is a logical or preferred order for introducing strategies, including whether strategies should be introduced in clusters or individually
- Creating materials to support strategies instruction
- Teaching coordinated use of strategies

Summary of Challenges

Strategies instruction is challenging for teachers. Teachers reported needing all of the extensive professional support available. They were concerned with the amount of classroom time being devoted to strategies, the difficulty of identifying and developing appropriate texts and materials, and the challenges in grading strategic reading. They found it difficult to give up teacher control as they enabled students to become more independent. And they lacked confidence as they strived to coordinate use of strategies across the curriculum.

APPLYING WHAT IS KNOWN

Why Bother If TSI Is So Hard?

The teachers we worked with were definitely aware of the demands of transactional strategies instruction on them and on classroom life (see also Pressley, Gaskins, Cunicelli, et al., 1991). Despite the difficulties, however, the teachers enthusiastically accepted strategies instruction (see also Rich & Pressley, 1990). Why did these teachers "buy into" TSI? They recognized that it changed their students' reading for the better. Teachers cited improvements in comprehension and interpretation, critical thinking, awareness of reading processes, self-confidence, enjoyment in reading, use of background knowledge, and student interactions during reading. Moreover, teachers enjoyed teaching reading more when they used strategies instruction. In short, teachers perceived that reading instruction was a better experience for both them and their students because of TSI. The teachers perceived TSI to be demanding, but they were committed to it because they believed it worked.

Professional Development Support Is the Key

Testimonials from other teachers and evidence from research may help build enthusiasm for strategies instruction. Ultimately, however, interested educators and their school districts will have to follow the lead of successful TSI programs and invest time and money into the professional development required to build competent, confident, committed transactional strategies teachers. Teachers experienced in TSI said they needed the many professional supports available to them—modeling, coaching, peer discussion, scripted lessons, research summaries, and classroom materials (El-Dinary et al., 1994). In contrast, teachers who experienced less intensive professional development were far less likely to take ownership for TSI (El-Dinary & Schuder, 1993).

Through research reports, teachers can build motivation as they learn the power of strategies. Through live and videotaped modeling, teachers can learn about the large repertoire of teaching practices that make up TSI. Through scripted lessons teachers can "try on" the teaching for themselves. Through coaching and peer discussion teachers can build confidence as they refine their own strategies instruction.

It is no accident that this professional development approach follows the same direct-explanation model as TSI itself. Just as teachers treasure their classroom time and worry about spending intensive time on strategies, administrators and policy makers may be concerned about the cost of intensive professional development. But as with TSI, the professional development is scaffolded so that once teachers "have it," they can "take it and run with it." Many TSI teachers we worked with eventually served as peer trainers themselves. Moreover, teachers found that the impact of TSI went beyond reading, improving their instruction across the curriculum.

In addition to professional development support, teachers must have the support of their principals and other administrators to experiment with TSI. Teachers must be respected as professionals, honoring their rights to choose and to adapt innovations such as TSI to fit their own styles. This approach cannot be "mandated" to teachers. To be effective, it must become their own (see El-Dinary & Schuder, 1993).

Implications of Teachers' Specific Challenges

Teachers' challenges with TSI suggest potential focus areas for teachers, curriculum developers, professional developers, and policy makers. In this section, I address some of the implications of each issue teachers raised.

Taking Up Classroom Time

Transactional strategies instruction does indeed require more class time than traditional approaches, such as round-robin reading followed by factual question-and-answer sessions. As students engage in interpreting a story and applying strategies, it takes longer to finish a story. However, teachers should consider the rich quality of this instructional time versus other forms of instruction. Time spent in a TSI lesson is more than time spent reading an individual story. It is time spent learning ways of processing information and solving problems, strategies that students can carry with them not only to their independent reading but also to learning in other parts of the curriculum. Moreover, although strategy explanations and modeling are intensive at the beginning of instruction, students soon begin using strategies themselves. Eventually, students will internalize the strategies so that they can do much better in their independent work. Teachers experienced with TSI realize this payoff of time spent working on strategies (see El-Dinary et al., 1994).

Giving Up Control

Some teachers were uncomfortable giving up control over the direction of the lesson to allow students to apply strategies and interpret the text for themselves. In other studies we found that teachers who had comfortably relied on more traditional methods and a "knowledge transmission" model of instruction had difficulty implementing TSI (El-Dinary & Schuder, 1993). On the other hand, teachers philosophically predisposed to the role of facilitator were eager to use it. Thus, no matter how powerful this approach may be, it cannot be effective unless teachers truly "buy into" it for themselves.

Teachers should be reassured that their initial discomfort will be rewarded, as releasing teacher control can allow students to become more independent learners, capable of achieving much more. On the other hand, teachers should be reassured that they are not giving up total control of instruction, just taking a different role. As students become independent in using strategies, the teacher's role is to monitor and respond to ensure that students are applying appropriate strategies that fit the task and problem at hand. Experienced TSI teacher testimonials and student responses in videotaped lessons can illustrate the benefits, as well as model what the teacher's role looks like.

Identifying/Developing Appropriate Instructional Materials

In choosing texts, it is important to identify authentic literature in students' "zone of proximal development" (Vygotsky, 1978). That is, it has to be challenging enough that students actually need strategies to help them read it, yet not so difficult that students can't manage it even when they rely on appropriate strategies. If it is too easy or too difficult, students will not see the benefit of strategies and will not be motivated to internalize them.

TSI teachers who participated in El-Dinary et al. (1994) had difficulty finding readings rich enough to support strategies discussion. However, I believe the quality of available instructional materials is improving. The whole-language movement has led to the use of more authentic literary materials in classrooms, and these texts are also appropriate for integrating strategies instruction. Moreover, textbook developers have worked to ensure not only that readings are rich enough to promote strategies use but also that strategies instruction is integrated into their basal series.

Teachers also can work with media specialists and/or reading specialists to identify trade books appropriate for students' level and for introducing specific strategies such as visualizing or predicting. Teachers and their curriculum guides across grade levels should coordinate so that texts used for strategies discussions are not repeated across grades. That is not to say that students should not reread good books; teacher read-alouds and independent reading time are great opportunities to experience good literature again. However, TSI teachers have found that well-known books do not lend themselves as well to group discussions in which the focus is on strategies.

One way curriculum developers responded to teachers' concerns about appropriate TSI materials was to include a "make-and-take" segment in workshops, in which teachers brainstormed and created bulletin board displays and other instructional materials. Curriculum developers were available to offer suggestions and provide feedback. Such materials development is a critical component to TSI development, based on the needs of teachers in our studies. Simply providing time for teachers to discuss the materials they have developed on their own could also help teachers expand their own ideas.

Assessment

Teachers faced the challenge of how to assign objective grades when daily instruction includes more subjective, although telling, assessments of student progress. Teachers who did not have a problem assigning grades frequently relied on traditional assessments for grading. So the primary challenge is developing formal, practical assessment that is compatible with the goals of transactional strategies instruction, tapping thinking processes rather than just factual products of comprehension. Schools we worked with acknowledged this issue and had been developing formal system-wide assessment that focused on strategies use and thinking skills (Montgomery County Public Schools, 1998). Moreover, at the statewide level, the Maryland State Performance Assessment Program, or MSPAP (see Guthrie, Schafer, Afflerbach, & Almasi, 1994), has also emphasized higher order thinking skills, problem solving, and meaning construction.

Thus the focus of formal standardized assessment has been shifting away from recall of facts and use of strict formulas toward the application of thinking skills to real-life problems. I believe that this is a critical step in promoting strategies instruction in classrooms. Through national standards and the response of state and local testing programs, policy makers are showing that indeed this is the kind of deep learning that is valued and expected. I hope that as more examples of performance-based and criterion-referenced assessment become available, these can serve as models for teachers struggling with appropriate ways to assign grades to TSI students. Curriculum developers and teachers should work together to adapt such forms of assessment to the ongoing demands of the classroom.

Coordinating Strategies across the Curriculum

Some strategies lend themselves readily to use across the curriculum. For example, prediction works well for reading, mathematics, science, and social studies. Yet teachers often lacked confidence in their ability to coordinate use of strategies across the curriculum. Not surprisingly, much more strategies instruction occurred during reading than in other portions of the school day. This outcome is consistent with our observations in other settings in which TSI occurs (Marks et al., 1993; Pressley, Gaskins, Cunicelli, et al., 1991).

However, we have also witnessed individual classrooms in which strategies taught during reading are integrated across the curriculum (see Pressley, Gaskins, Wile, et al., 1991). Moreover, curriculum developers in the school system studied here had created lessons for a successful summer program in which a set of strategies was taught for both reading and math (see El-Dinary, 1993, Study 1; Schuder, Wenig, York, & Rowan, 1989).

Nonetheless, professional development for teachers we worked with tended to focus on extensive support for teaching strategies for reading, with the suggestion that teachers go ahead and carry out these strategies in other content areas. It is not enough, then, to simply suggest that teachers apply strategies to other content areas. Rather, professional development must include modeling of how to teach for transfer of strategies to other content areas. Likewise, teachers need coaching in transactional strategies instruction not only during reading but also in other content areas.

This suggestion is consistent with research on strategies transfer for students, which shows that transfer is not automatic but must be supported by instruction (Derry, 1990; Wong, 1994). Students often need explicit guidance in how to adapt strategies for other areas, including modeling and practice in the new area. Just as students need guidance in strategies transfer, so teachers need guidance in instructional transfer.

WHAT STILL NEEDS TO BE KNOWN
ABOUT COMPREHENSION INSTRUCTION

Challenges faced by TSI teachers illuminate areas ripe for further research and development. Just as teachers benefited from seeing research on strategies instruction, so future research can guide teachers in areas in which they lacked confidence.

Whether There Is a Preferred Order for Introducing Strategies

Teachers wondered whether to introduce strategies one at a time or in clusters and in what order. These questions are particularly important considering the goal of developing a coordinated repertoire of strategies. Introducing a cluster of strategies at the outset may emphasize flexible coordination. On the other hand, students may need to master one strategy before learning another. Also, some strategies may be more natural for students to use and thus a good introduction before taking on more complex strategies. Laboratory research settings could be useful in determining which strategies are learned most easily, which combinations are effective when taught together, and whether any one strategy impedes or fosters learning of any other strategy. Classroom research could also tap teachers' experiences, looking at instructional successes and failures in these areas.

How to Expand Strategies Instruction across Content Areas

A collective goal for the teachers in this school was to expand strategies instruction beyond reading and, in particular, to encourage use of the reading strategies across the school day. They found it difficult to do so, however. Thus, an important research and development direction for the future is to determine how teachers can encourage use of reading strategies during mathematics, science, and social studies. Several research questions could guide strategies instruction across the curriculum: (1) How appropriate are each of the reading strategies for transfer to the other content areas? (2) What adaptations are required to make each strategy appropriate to other tasks? How well do students adapt the TSI strategies to fit other content areas? (3) What instruction is most effective and efficient in promoting strategies transfer across content areas? For example, is modeling in the new area required, or is coaching of students' strategies attempts sufficient? (4) What instructional adaptations are required for smooth integration with other content areas? Finally, (5) What professional development support is required to help teachers transfer TSI from one content area to another?

How to Integrate Strategies Instruction with Other Powerful Teaching Practices

Although teachers integrated TSI into their existing instruction, we were struck by the infrequent use of other powerful practices like cooperative learning, analogies, strategies coordination, and explaining why and when particular strategies are useful. Thus it is important to look at how teachers successfully integrate multiple instructional innovations. Innovations never cease, yet when a new approach comes along, teachers may believe it is intended to replace everything else (El-Dinary & Schuder, 1993). This can lead to frustration, as teachers feel pulled in many directions. A critical goal of teacher education is for teachers to learn to smoothly coordinate instructional innovations into an approach that works for their own classrooms. Professional developers introducing an instructional innovation should focus on how it can be coordinated with other current approaches. Moreover, a goal of teacher educators should be to help teachers to be lifelong learners rather than just imparting the latest instructional fads.

CONCLUSION

So much has been learned in the past two decades about how to improve students' reading. Yet much of what is known has not made its way into mainstream practices in American classrooms. Perhaps what we know has been pushed to the wayside simply because the price seems too high. TSI is challenging to learn, requires high energy and commitment from teachers, and requires ongoing support from administrators and school districts. Yet some teachers, administrators, and curriculum developers have paid the price to implement transactional strategies instruction. These educators firmly believe that TSI's benefits—helping students become independent learners—justify its costs.

ACKNOWLEDGMENTS

I acknowledge the invaluable contributions of my collaborators in this research effort, including Michael Pressley, Lynne Coy-Ogan, Ted Schuder, and the transactional strategies instruction teachers. This research was funded in part by a grant from the U.S. Department of Education (Office of Educational Research and Improvement) to the National Reading Research Center headquartered at the Universities of Maryland and Georgia. No endorsement by the U.S. Department of Education or the NRRC should be inferred, however.

REFERENCES

Anderson, R. C., & Pearson, P. D. (1984). A schema-theoretic view of basic processes in reading. In P. D. Pearson (Ed.), *Handbook of reading research* (pp. 255–291). New York: Longman.

Bell, R. Q. (1968). A reinterpretation of the direction of effects in studies of socialization. *Psychological Review, 75,* 81–95.

Bereiter, C., & Bird, M. (1985). Use of thinking aloud in identification and teaching of reading comprehension strategies. *Cognition and Instruction, 2,* 91–130.

Bergman, J., & Schuder, R. T. (1992). Teaching at-risk elementary school students to read strategically. *Educational Leadership, 50,* 19–23.

Bjorklund, D. F. (1989). *Children's thinking: Developmental function and individual differences.* Monterey, CA: Brooks/Cole.

Brown, R., & Pressley, M. (1994). Self-regulated reading and getting meaning from text: The transactional strategies instruction model and its ongoing evaluation. In D. Schunk & B. Zimmerman (Eds.), *Self-regulation of learning and performance: Issues and educational applications* (pp. 155–179). Hillsdale, NJ: Erlbaum.

Brown, R., Pressley, M., Van Meter, P., & Schuder, T. (1996). A quasi-experimental validation of transactional strategies instruction with low-achieving second grade readers. *Journal of Educational Psychology, 88,* 18–37.

Collins, C. (1991). Reading instruction that increases thinking abilities. *Journal of Reading, 34,* 510–516.

Day, J. D., Cordon, L. A., & Kerwin, M. L. (1989). Informal instruction and development of cognitive skills: A review and critique of research. In C. B. McCormick, G. E. Miller, & M. Pressley (Eds.), *Cognitive strategy research: From basic research to educational applications* (pp. 83–103). New York: Springer-Verlag.

Derry, S. J. (1990). Learning strategies for acquiring useful knowledge. In B. F. Jones & L. Idol (Eds.), *Dimensions of thinking and cognitive instruction* (pp. 347–379). Hillsdale, NJ: Erlbaum.

Duffy, G. G., Roehler, L. R., & Herrmann, B. A. (1988). Modeling mental processes helps poor readers become strategic readers. *Reading Teacher, 41,* 762–767.

Duffy, G. G., Roehler, L. R., Sivan, E., Rackliffe, G., Book, C., Meloth, M., Vavrus, L. G., Wesselman, R., Putnam, J., & Bassiri, D. (1987). Effects of explaining the reasoning associated with using reading strategies. *Reading Research Quarterly, 22,* 347–368.

Durkin, D. (1979). What classroom observations reveal about reading comprehension instruction. *Reading Research Quarterly, 14,* 481–538.

El-Dinary, P. B. (1993). Teachers learning, adapting and implementing strategies-based instruction in reading (Doctoral dissertation, University of Maryland, 1993). *Dissertation Abstracts International, 54,* 5410A. (University Microfilms No. 9407625).

El-Dinary, P. B., Pressley, M., Coy-Ogan, L., Schuder, T., & Strategies Instruction Teachers. (1994). *The teaching practices of transactional strategies instruction teachers as revealed through collaborative interviewing* (Technical Report No. 23). Athens, GA: National Reading Research Center.

El-Dinary, P. B., Pressley, M., & Schuder, T. (1992). Teachers learning transactional strategies instruction. In C. K. Kinzer & D. J. Leu (Eds.), *Literacy research, theory, and practice: Views from many perspectives* (41st yearbook of the National Reading Conference, pp. 453–462). Chicago, IL: National Reading Conference.

El-Dinary, P. B., & Schuder, T. (1993). Seven teachers' acceptance of transactional strategies instruction during their first year using it. *Elementary School Journal, 94,* 207–219.

Gaskins, I. W., & Elliot, T. T. (1991). *The Benchmark model for teaching thinking strategies: A manual for teachers.* Cambridge, MA: Brookline Books.

Guthrie, J. T., Schafer, W. D., Afflerbach, P., & Almasi, J. (1994). *Systemic reform of literacy education: State and district-level policy changes in Maryland.* (Technical Report No. 27). College Park, MD: National Reading Research Center.

Hutchins, E. (1991). The social organization of distributed cognition. In L. Resnick, J. M. Levine, & S. D. Teasley (Eds.), *Perspectives on socially shared cognition* (pp. 283–307). Washington, DC: American Psychological Association.

Marks, M., Pressley, M., Coley, J. D., Craig, S., Gardner, R., Rose, W., & DePinto, T. (1993). Teachers' adaptations of reciprocal teaching: Progress toward a classroom-compatible version of reciprocal teaching. *Elementary School Journal, 94,* 267–283.

Mayer, R. E. (1985). Learning in complex domains: A cognitive analysis of computer programming. *Psychology of Learning and Motivation, 19,* 89–130.

Mehan, H. (1979). *Social organization in the classroom.* Cambridge, MA: Harvard University Press.

Meichenbaum, D. M. (1977). *Cognitive behavior modification.* New York: Plenum.

Montgomery County Public Schools. (1998). *Annual report on the systemwide outcome measures: Success for Every Student plan.* Rockville, MD: Author. (ERIC Document Reproduction Service No. ED 428 108)

Palincsar, A. S., & Brown, A. L. (1984). Reciprocal teaching of comprehension-fostering and comprehension-monitoring activities. *Cognition and Instruction, 1,* 117–175.

Pearson, P. D. (1985). Changing the face of reading comprehension instruction. *Reading Teacher, 38,* 724–738.

Poplin, M. S. (1988). The reductionist fallacy in learning disabilities: Replicating the past by reducing the present. *Journal of Learning Disabilities, 21,* 389–400.

Pressley, M., Borkowski, J. G., & O'Sullivan, J. T. (1984). Memory strategy instruction is made of this: Metamemory and durable strategy use. *Educational Psychologist, 19,* 84–107.

Pressley, M., Borkowski, J. G., & O'Sullivan, J. T. (1985). Children's metamemory and the teaching of strategies. In D. L. Forrest-Pressley, G. E. MacKinnon, & T. G. Waller (Eds.), *Metacognition, cognition, and human performance* (pp. 111–153). New York: Academic Press.

Pressley, M., El-Dinary, P. B., Gaskins, I., Schuder, T., Bergman, J. L., Almasi, J., & Brown, R. (1992). Beyond direct explanation: Transactional instruction of reading comprehension strategies. *Elementary School Journal, 92,* 511–554.

Pressley, M., Gaskins, I. W., Cunicelli, E. A., Burdick, N. J., Schaub-Matt, M., Lee, D. S., & Powell, N. (1991). Strategy instruction at Benchmark School: A faculty interview study. *Learning Disability Quarterly, 14,* 19–48.

Pressley, M., Gaskins, I. W., Wile, D., Cunicelli, E. A., & Sheridan, J. (1991). Teaching literacy strategies across the curriculum: A case study at Benchmark School. In S. McCormick & J. Zutell (Eds.), *Learner factors–teacher factors: Issues in literacy research and instruction* (40th yearbook of the National Reading Conference, pp. 219–228). Chicago: National Reading Conference.

Pressley, M., Goodchild, F., Fleet, J., Zajchowski, R., & Evans, E. D. (1989). The challenges of classroom strategy instruction. *Elementary School Journal, 89,* 301–342.

Pressley, M., Harris, K. R., & Marks, M. B. (1992). But good strategy instructors are constructivists!! *Educational Psychology Review, 4,* 1–32.

Pressley, M., Schuder, T., SAIL Faculty and Administration, Bergman, J. L., & El-Dinary, P. B. (1992). A researcher–educator collaborative interview study of transactional comprehension strategies instruction. *Journal of Educational Psychology, 84,* 231–246.

Rich, S. R., & Pressley, M. (1990). Teacher acceptance of reading comprehension strategy instruction. *Elementary School Journal, 91,* 43–64.

Roehler, L. R., & Duffy, G. G. (1984). Direct explanation of comprehension processes. In G. G. Duffy, L. R. Roehler, & J. Mason (Eds.), *Comprehension instruction: Perspectives and suggestions* (pp. 265–280). New York: Longman.

Rosenblatt, L. M. (1978). *The reader, the text, the poem: The transactional theory of the literary work.* Carbondale IL: Southern Illinois University Press.

Sameroff, A. J. (1975). Early influences on development: Fact or fancy? *Merrill–Palmer Quarterly, 21,* 267–294.

Schuder, T. (1993). The genesis of transactional strategies instruction in a reading program for at-risk students. *Elementary School Journal, 94,* 183–200.

Schuder, T., Wenig, J. J., York, M., & Rowan, T. E. (1989). *Report on the implementation of the Summer Institute of Achievement* (Research Report, November 6). Rockville, MD: Montgomery County Public Schools, Office of Instruction and Program Development.

Slavin, R. (1985a). An introduction to cooperative learning research. In R. Slavin, S. Sharan, S. Kagan, R. H. Lazarowitz, C. Webb, & R. Schmuck (Eds.), *Learning to cooperate, cooperating to learn* (pp. 5–15). New York: Plenum.

Slavin, R. (1985b). Team-assisted individualization: Combining cooperative learning and individualized instruction in mathematics. In R. Slavin, S. Sharan, S. Kagan, R. H. Lazarowitz, C. Webb, & R. Schmuck (Eds.), *Learning to cooperate, cooperating to learn* (pp. 177–209). New York: Plenum.

Tobin, K. (1987). The role of wait time in higher cognitive level learning. *Review of Educational Research, 57,* 69–95.

Vygotsky, L. S. (1978). *Mind in society: The development of higher psychological processes.* (M. Cole, V. John-Steiner, S. Scribner, & E. Souberman, Eds. and Trans.). Cambridge, MA: Harvard University Press.

Wegner, D. M. (1987). Transactive memory: A contemporary analysis of the group mind. In B. Mullen & G. Goethals (Eds.), *Theories of group behavior* (pp. 185–208). New York: Springer-Verlag.

Wong, B. Y. L. (1994). Instructional parameters promoting transfer of learned strategies in students with learning disabilities. *Learning Disability Quarterly, 17*(2), 110–120.

Wood, P., Bruner, J., & Ross, G. (1976). The role of tutoring in problem solving. *Journal of Child Psychology and Psychiatry, 17,* 89–100.

I I I

Comprehension Instruction in Preschool, Primary, and Intermediate Grades

14

Preparing Young Learners for Successful Reading Comprehension

Laying the Foundation

DIANE H. TRACEY
LESLEY MANDEL MORROW

Reading comprehension is an enormously complex task. Relatedly, the job of preparing young learners to be successful at reading comprehension is equally multifaceted. In this paper we examine the issue of reading comprehension from the perspective of the early-childhood literacy learner. The primary questions we seek to answer are the following:

1. What is the relationship between children's emergent literacy backgrounds and their reading comprehension abilities?
2. What are the factors that influence young children's reading comprehension capabilities?
3. How can educators facilitate the development of reading comprehension in their young students?
4. What conclusions can be drawn from our current knowledge bases regarding reading comprehension and the instruction of emerging literacy learners?

THE EMERGENT LITERACY FOUNDATION
AND READING COMPREHENSION

Although descriptions of the reading comprehension process and their implications for instruction vary and are complex enough to fill a volume such as this, it is widely accepted that the roots of the process lie in a child's emergent literacy phase of development (Morrow, 2000). It is impossible, however, to identify a single root that leads to successful reading comprehension. Successful reading comprehension occurs when a multitude of knowledge sources and processes are present and available to a child and when the child is able to effectively activate and integrate the use of that information (Adams, 1996; Pressley, 2000). These knowledge sources and processes include background life experiences, knowledge of oral language, book and print concepts, and attitudes toward literacy and learning, among others. Thus it is not an isolated skill developed in early childhood that leads to later successful reading comprehension but rather a strong, broad, multifaceted early literacy foundation that is built and eventually used by the reader for the purpose of constructing comprehension of a text. We think of the metaphor of laying a foundation for a house as illustrative of laying an early literacy foundation. Our premise is that children who are ultimately most likely to be successful comprehenders of reading are those who acquire the strongest literacy foundations during the early childhood years. In what follows we articulate those factors that influence the quality of the foundation from which the ability to engage in effective and efficient comprehension evolves.

Factors Influencing Young Children's Foundations for Successful Reading Comprehension

Applying an adaptation of Bronfenbrenner's (1979) ecological model of human development, children's reading comprehension ability can be viewed as influenced by multiple and concentric layers of contexts and constructs. Figure 14.1 illustrates one conceptualization of the concentric spheres of influence that affect children's reading comprehension

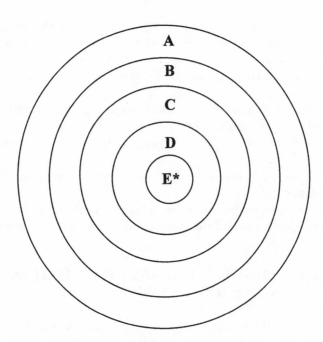

FIGURE 14.1. Spheres of influence on young children's comprehension development. A, sociocultural influences; B, school, classroom, and teacher influences; C, home and family influences; D, "Whole-Child" influences; E, the emergent literacy foundation; *, comprehension development.

ability. Below we highlight some of the most important findings regarding each area of influence and its effects on young children's literacy development.

Multicultural and Sociocultural Influences

In a current review chapter regarding the influence of multicultural factors on literacy achievement, children's literacy abilities were reported as significantly affected by the cultural variables of ethnicity, social class, and primary language (Au, 2000):

> In the United States, the students least well served by schools often are African American, Asian American, Latina/o, and Native American in ethnicity; come from poor and working-class families; and speak home languages other than standard American English. . . . Many of these children grow up in poverty. For example, in 1992, 44% of African American preschoolers lived in households with incomes under $10,000, a figure $5,000 below the poverty line for a family of four. At the same time, 2.3 million students in the United States spoke a first language other than standard American English and were considered to have "limited English proficiency" (U.S. Department of Education, 1992). . . . A gap between the literacy achievement of students of diverse background and students of mainstream backgrounds has long been recognized. (p. 835)

Despite the impact of these sociocultural factors, some writers question the value of such research, suggesting that focusing on broad, sociocultural constructs "minimizes the full range of factors that contribute to literacy learning," thus concealing critical differences between learners, learning tasks, and learning situations that may hold implications for instruction and student achievement (Gadsden, 2000). Thus, although sociocultural variables exert a significant influence on young children's literacy development and therefore their preparedness for the job of reading comprehension, their effects may be mitigated by other influences.

Teachers, Classrooms, Instructional Practices, and Text Materials

Within the socioeconomic sphere is the concentric sphere of a child's school life. Here we see evidence that a teacher's personality, classroom environment, instructional practices, and choice of text materials all influence young children's literacy foundations. Teachers who are most positively influential have the personality characteristics of warmth, high energy, sensitivity, and flexibility (Ruddell, 1997). Highly effective literacy teachers also have more extensive teaching experience and a deeper knowledge base and are more reflective and conscious of the decisions they make than are less effective literacy educators (Pressley, Allington, Wharton-McDonald, Block, & Morrow, 2001).

Highly effective literacy educators also create rich literacy environments in their classrooms. These classrooms are filled with print and an extensive and diversified collection of high-quality reading materials and contain literacy centers with varied opportunities for interacting with texts (Morrow & Gambrell, 2000; Pressley et al., 2001). Classrooms of highly effective literacy educators are additionally marked by unusually positive affective climates (Morrow, Tracey, Woo, & Pressley, 1999; Pressley et al., 2001).

A multitude of instructional practices have been linked to positive growth in young children's literacy development. Highly effective literacy educators have exceptionally strong classroom management skills (Morrow et al., 1999; Pressley et al., 2001). An important distinction, however, is that these management skills are designed to help young children become independent, self-regulated learners rather than traditional, teacher reliant, "obedient" students (Pressley et al., 2001). Highly effective early-literacy educators focus on teaching for meaning (Knapp, 1995) and make learning personally relevant for individual students (Ruddell, 1997). These teachers tend to be very child centered, rather than curriculum or test focused, and, accordingly, frequently individualize instruction (Pressley et al., 2001).

Another domain of effects stems from highly effective early-literacy educators' abilities to provide many and varied opportunities for reading in the classroom. These teachers frequently use cross-content thematic instruction and link reading with high-quality writing instruction (Morrow et al., 1999; Pressley et al., 2001). For instance, the use of extensive and explicit letter and sound-level instruction has been linked to children's early-literacy growth (Adams, 1996), as has the focus on higher order literacy competencies (Pressley et al., 2001). Other instructional practices that have been identified through a meta-analysis specifically to improve comprehension include comprehension monitoring, cooperative learning, using of graphic and semantic organizers, question answering, question generating, story structuring, and summarizing (Langenberg et al., 2000). (It is important to note, however, that these practices were identified as a result of a meta-analysis that included only experimental research and that, furthermore, was not specific to young learners.)

The quality and type of text materials used in the classroom are additional factors that influence students' literacy learning (Alexander & Jetton, 2000), with Alexander and Jetton concluding that "Quality depends on how effectively a text communicates its purpose or aim" (p. 289). Furthermore, they stated, "One consistent finding of the research of Garner and Alexander (1991) and Goldman and Varma (1995) is that the quality of text becomes differentially important depending on the readers' stage of academic development. Competent and proficient learners are better equipped to deal with vagueness, incoherence or other inconsiderate characteristics of domain-related texts than are acclimated (beginning) learners" (Alexander & Jetton, p. 302). The use of high quality children's literature has also been linked to early-literacy growth (Morrow & Gambrell, 2000; Pressley et al., 2001). The addition of literature to a basal reading program is associated with greater literacy gains than a basal-only approach (Morrow, 1992). Similarly, a science-text-and-literature approach produces greater literacy gains than a science-text-only-approach (Morrow, Pressley, Smith, & Smith, 1997).

In short, the effects of factors related to teachers, classrooms, instructional practices, and texts on children's early literacy foundations have been extensively documented. Each child's early literacy foundation is affected by his or her experiences with these factors. In turn, every child is differentially prepared for reading comprehension as a result.

The Home Environment

Yet another sphere of influence on a young child's literacy foundations is his or her home environment. The quality of a child's home environment exerts an extremely powerful effect on his or her literacy development (Purcell-Gates, 2000). The importance of the home environment was first captured by Durkin (1966) in her seminal work investigating young children who came to school already reading. In this groundbreaking research, Durkin determined that factors within the home, specifically the amount of books and writing materials available to the child, the frequency with which parents engaged in and discussed reading themselves, and the frequency with which parents took children to the library and bookstores, were all stronger correlates of children's early reading achievement than were the traditional factors of socioeconomic status and IQ. Subsequently, the finding that the quality of the home environment is more predictive of children's literacy achievement than traditional sociocultural factors has been repeatedly reported in the literature (Au, 2000) and has facilitated an abundance of research aimed specifically at further investigating this phenomenon.

Studies aimed at more carefully examining the home environment have most often focused on parent–child shared book reading. These projects show that both the frequency of shared reading and the quality of the reading episodes are related to children's literacy achievement (Yaden, Rowe, & MacGillivray, 2000). Predictably, more frequent shared reading episodes are related to greater early-literacy growth. In terms of quality, the elements of parent–child shared reading that have traditionally been linked to improved student performance include: (1) the total number of words spoken by children, (2) the number of preparatory questions asked by parents, (3) the number of poststory evaluative questions asked by parents, (4) the number of "high-level" questions asked by parents, and (5) the amount of positive feedback given to the child (Flood, 1977; Snow, 1983).

Another area under scrutiny within the topic of shared storybook reading is the relative power of this experience on children's literacy development. Historically, the practice of shared storybook reading has been thought to have an extremely strong influence. For example, in 1985, the report of the National Institute of Education stated that, "the single most important activity for building the knowledge required for eventual success in reading is reading aloud to children" (Anderson, Hiebert, Scott, & Wilkinson, 1985, p. 23). Moreover, reading to children has been associated with gains in children's vocabulary, syntactic complexity, knowledge of print and book concepts, and story comprehension (Morrow, 2000). Despite these research findings and the popular view that reading to children is a strong facilitator of literacy development, two recent meta-analyses have found that storybook reading between parents and children accounts for 8% of the variance in children's literacy performance (Bus, van IJzendoorn, & Pellegrini, 1995; Scarborough, Dobrich, & Hager, 1994). Interestingly, Bus, van IJzendoorn, and Pellegrini interpreted this effect as a strong predictor of children's literacy performance whereas Scarborough and Dobrich interpreted the same statistic as illustrating that the impact of parent–child storybook reading is less potent than had previously been assumed (Yaden et al., 2000). Nonetheless, the degree to which children's early-literacy foundation is affected by this practice ultimately contributes to the degree to which children are prepared for the reading comprehension task.

Additional home-based factors related to children's literacy development are the uses of print in the home and the parents' educational level. Print knowledge has been found to be related to the frequency with which print is used in the home and especially related to the frequency with which parents explicitly draw their children's attention to it (Baker, Fernandez-Fein, Scher, & Williams, 1998; Purcell-Gates, 1996). Parents' educational level, particularly that of the mother, has been consistently found to be correlated with children's literacy achievement (Purcell-Gates, 2000). Parents' educational level, however, is a factor that is confounded by socioeconomic status (as described earlier) and, in fact, is frequently used as its measure (Leseman & DeJong, 1998).

Thus the home environment is a powerful context for shaping children's early-literacy foundations. The experiences in this realm that each child has or does not have greatly affects the creation of the knowledge sources of oral language, book and print concepts, and attitudes about learning and literacy that will ultimately be available for use during reading comprehension. Children with richer home literacy backgrounds will proceed to school more highly prepared for the work of reading comprehension than those with more impoverished home-literacy experiences.

The "Whole" Child

In addition to being affected by sociocultural, home, and school-based influences, a young child's literacy foundations are influenced by the multiple facets of his or her own being. Many writers, especially early childhood education specialists, have addressed the importance of understanding the functioning of the "whole" child, his or her physical, emotional/social, cognitive, and spiritual aspects, in order to better understand any single dimension of that child (Seefeldt & Barbour, 1994). From this perspective, it is clear that a young learner's literacy development is affected by his or her overall development. The physical dimension affects a child's literacy functioning in that significant differences in the auditory, linguistic, perceptual, or visual systems will dramatically affect literacy learning, and of course, within that realm, the base for reading comprehension. Emotional and social functioning also have implications for literacy learning and comprehension, with children's attitudes toward and experiences with learning and reading greatly affecting their academic progress (Guthrie & Wigfield, 2000). Furthermore, the degree of overall knowledge, both content and procedural, and the experiences that a child possesses significantly impact literacy learning. Maslow goes so far as to suggest a hierarchical schema such that children's literacy learning, centered in the cognitive realm, will not be optimal unless the child also possesses strong physical, emotional, and social bases (Lowry, 1998). In summary, like the sociocultural, school-based, and home-based factors, the personal characteristics of each learner contribute to his or her early-literacy foundation, further differentially preparing him or her for reading comprehension.

The Emergent Literacy Foundation and Comprehension Instruction

To facilitate young learners' preparedness for reading comprehension, a teacher must (1) understand the relationship between children's emergent literacy foundations and their preparedness for the task of reading comprehension, (2) understand the many factors that influence children's literacy foundations, (3) identify and attend to children's individual differences and experiences in these realms, and (4) create learning opportunities that are responsive to children's individual learning and literacy profiles. In addition, teacher attention should be directed at development of the higher order thinking more traditionally associated with comprehension development.

Morrow (2000) identifies learning objectives and activities that will help teachers achieve these goals. She suggests that children are developing reading comprehension when they attempt to read well-known storybooks during "pretend reading," participate in story readings by saying words with adults, retell stories in their own words, respond to texts after reading or listening with activities, questions, or comments, and use reference and study-skill materials. The comprehension experiences we need to provide for young children include predicting what will happen next in stories, relating story episodes to children's life experiences and background knowledge, comparing and contrasting assorted texts, responding to texts in feeling ways, drawing conclusions, problem solving and evaluating reading materials.

OBSERVING EXEMPLARY EDUCATORS FACILITATE THE DEVELOPMENT OF READING COMPREHENSION

The following discussion of the ways in which exemplary educators facilitate the development of comprehension abilities in young children draws on classroom observations from two research studies. In the first project (Morrow et al., 1999), we investigated the instructional practices of first-grade teachers nominated by their building principals as outstanding, based on reputation and students' documented performances. In the second project (Morrow, Smith, & Tracey, 2000), we are documenting the practices of educators nominated as exemplary by their supervisors for their abilities to facilitate standards-based literacy achievements among their students. During our observations for these projects, many dimensions of literacy instruction and learning were captured, and publications on various dimensions of the work are beginning to be generated (for a full discussion of this work, see Pressley et al., 2001). Following we extrapolate a few episodes from our early childhood classroom visitations that we feel are particularly illustrative of the ways in which outstanding educators develop a foundation for reading comprehension in young readers.

Contexts for Comprehension Instruction: A Caveat

Just as a child's preparedness to handle the task of reading comprehension is shaped by his or her sociocultural, home, school, and personal life experiences, a teacher's ability to provide high-quality reading comprehension instruction is affected by the overall context of the classroom. The comprehension instruction we describe here was observed in highly successful classrooms. In brief, these classrooms exuded positive climates characterized by unusually high levels of student engagement, motivation, time on task, and self-regulation and by unusually low levels of classroom management problems. Additionally, the classrooms had exceptionally rich literacy environments. These classroom environments were created deliberately and thoughtfully by master teachers with many years of teaching experience, a high degree of graduate-level training, and clear values and beliefs about literacy learning. The following scenarios depict the ways in which exemplary teachers foster reading comprehension.

One Half-Hour in Ms. Linda Keefe's First-Grade Classroom

After the children have arrived at school, put away their belongings, and independently completed their morning tasks of attendance cards, lunch count, and classroom library responsibilities, Ms. Keefe calls the class to the rug area in her literacy center. She begins by leading the class in reading the morning message that is posted on large chart paper.

"Good morning! Today we will continue with our Southwest centers. We will read a different version of *First Woman and the Strawberry*. We will have music at 10:45 and Spanish at 12:15. Have fun!"

Ms. Keefe then draws the students' attention to particular print concepts embedded within the message. For example, she says, "I see some words that have the 'th' chunk. Can anyone find one?" She also has the students identify key sight words (7 minutes).

Ms. Keefe then turns the class's attention to two pieces of literature, one of which has been read the previous day, *First Woman and the Strawberry*, and one which they would read that day, *The First Strawberry: A Cherokee Story*. Ms. Keefe addresses the students, "Yesterday we read the story, *First Woman and the Strawberry*. Who can tell me what it was about?" After the children have responded Ms. Keefe asks one of them to place a marker on the classroom map showing the southwest region of the country. This is where both stories took place (2 minutes).

Ms. Keefe prints the word "STRAWBERRY" vertically on a fresh piece of chart paper and says to the students, "Let's think a little bit about strawberries before we start our new story. We know this spells 'strawberry,' right? I'd like you to tell me some describing words for the word 'strawberry' using its letters." The children begin with the word "sweet"; they then add "tasty," "red," "amazing," and so on. Ms. Keefe prints the words that the students generate (4 minutes).

Ms. Keefe then reads a section of the new piece of literature to the students. She stops periodically to discuss key ideas and important vocabulary words with the students. She asks questions to link the content of the story with the children's own backgrounds (5 minutes).

At the conclusion of the brief oral reading, Ms. Keefe draws a Venn diagram on a third sheet of chart paper, printing the title of one book on each of the outer circles of the diagram and the word "both" on the portion of the diagram where the circles overlap. The students, obviously familiar with the task, discuss the two pieces of literature, noting that both titles have the words "first" and "strawberry" in them and that both books have women in them and contain arguments. The students generate ideas regarding how the stories are different as well. Ms. Keefe prompts the students with questions, such as asking them to consider how the stories began, their length, their plots, and their settings (7 minutes).

At the conclusion of "rug time" Ms. Keefe explains that the children will now be moving into center time and describes the activities available at each. At the art center children will make a picture using paint made the previous day by crushing strawberries. At the writing center students will be creating their own legends. At the word center students will be making a list of words from the word "Cherokee." The last group of students will be meeting with the teacher at the reading table for small-group reading instruction. The students are then dismissed to their centers (3 minutes).

One Half-Hour in Ms. Veronica Gebesi's Secnd-Grade Classroom

Ms. Gebesi begins her lesson by orienting the students to the specific language arts literacy standards that their work will address that day.

"Good afternoon, boys and girls. Today we're going to take a look at our objective: Students will be able to analyze characters' traits, compare characters, and understand characters' points of view in a fantasy tale. We're working with standards 3.1, 3.3, and 3.4. Now, you know we've already read the story, *Mufaro's Beautiful Daughters*, and there were two main characters in the story, Manyara and Nyasha. What I want to do today is to take a look at their character traits, their personalities, the way they behave, and the way they act. We're going to find out about the characters' feelings—how the characters felt at different points in the story. We're going to find out about the characters' motives—why the characters behaved as they did" (1 minute).

Ms. Gebesi takes out a piece of chart paper with each of the characters' names underlined, points to Manyara's name, and continues. "I want you to raise your hand and tell me a little bit about Manyara. What type of person was she?" A student answers, "selfish." "Yes, good, selfish," Ms. Gebesi responds, and then asks, "At what point of the story was she selfish?" After the student's reply she continues, "What was another of Manyara's characteristics?" A student replies, "impatient," and again, Ms. Gebesi praises the student and asks when Manyara was impatient. The activity continues until several characteristics have been generated for both Manyara and Nyasha (5 minutes).

After separate lists of personality traits have been created for both Manyara and Nyasha, Ms. Gebesi turns to a new page of chart paper containing a Venn diagram. "Okay, we have some character traits of each character. Let's take a look at both of them together. Let's take a look at our Venn diagram. Were they the same in any way?" The students respond that both of the daughters were beautiful and both excited. As the students continue, Ms. Gebesi completes the Venn diagram, filling in the personality traits that the characters shared in the overlapping section of the diagram and filling in the unique traits of each character in the nonintersecting sections. As each defining characteristic is added to the diagram, she discusses with the class the ways in which the personality trait was shared or not shared by the characters (5 minutes).

Ms. Gebesi then turns to a third piece of chart paper and tells the class that they will now be working on their story starters. She reviews a previous assignment that part of the class had already completed in which the students had assumed the character role of either Manyara or Nyasha. Ms. Gebesi continues:

> "Some of you wrote very good story beginnings with this story starter: *My name is [Manyara or Nyasha]. Some people feel that I am* _____, _____, *and* _____. *I am this way because* _____. . . . Some of you are going to continue to work with this story starter and some of you are going to work on our second story starter, the part when the story is over, the part that we didn't see, the part that we're going to imagine."

Ms. Gebesi points to the second starter on the chart paper and reads, "After the wedding I felt. . . ." The teacher questions the class, "Who's going to write from Manyara's point of view?" Students raise their hands. "What did Manyara think and feel at the end of the story? Remember, she didn't get the prize. She wasn't the queen. Who's going to write from Nyasha's point of view?" The remainder of the students raise their hands. "How did she feel after the wedding?" Ms. Gebesi then assigns students to one of three groups for writing workshop. One group still needs to finish the beginning of their stories using the first story starter. The second group has finished the beginning of their stories but needs to elaborate their Venn diagrams. The third group has finished both their story beginnings and their Venn diagrams and are ready to write the next portion of their story (4 minutes).

Ms. Gebesi circulates through the class as the children work on their writing tasks. She stops to respond to students' individual needs and to praise their efforts. The students write for approximately 15 minutes. At the conclusion of the writing workshop the class moves to the rug to hear three students read their stories. Clapping is heard after each child reads (15 minutes).

REFLECTIONS ON BUILDING FOUNDATIONS FOR READING COMPREHENSION IN CLASSROOMS OF EXEMPLARY TEACHERS

Our visits and observations in classrooms of exemplary teachers were exhilarating and informative. We feel fortunate to have had the opportunity to work with such fine educators. We feel continued awe and admiration for the complexity of the work in which they engage, for the myriad of skills they need to do it, and for the outstanding quality with which they complete it. In the next section we reflect on aspects of these observations that we feel were most critical to the teachers' effective support of their students' preparedness for reading comprehension development.

An Integrated, Literature-Based Approach to Literacy Learning

The most striking feature of these teachers' instruction was the degree to which they integrated their language arts literacy program. We saw no worksheets or workbooks to strengthen reading comprehension. We heard no teacher's directions informing the students that it was time to work on reading comprehension. Rather, these teachers were skillful weavers of the many aspects of early literacy that need to be developed to lay the foundation for reading comprehension to occur.

At the center of these educational experiences were invariably one or more pieces of high-quality children's literature. These teachers made careful selections of the pieces of literature they would use, and their selections were then springboards for a variety of literacy-promoting purposes. Often their literature selections were tied to a broader theme that was being studied in the classroom that month, as was the case for Ms. Keefe's literature relating to the Southwest theme of the month. Although not every lesson during the month was thematically linked, the presence of a monthly theme allowed the teachers to integrate the literature selections with at least some activities in other content areas. The presence of the integrated themes and literature then provided the inspiration for ideas for center activities. During interviews, the teachers said that such integrated, thematic teaching resulted from careful planning, including record and note keeping, that was enriched and improved year after year and with experience and practice.

An area in which this integration was very apparent was in linking reading and writing. In the scenarios presented here, and in virtually every exemplary classroom in which we observed, teachers and students consistently connected these two language arts. Teachers' writing assignments were based on what the students had read and were designed to create thoughtful, high-level processing of the texts. Thus much reading comprehension was fostered through the relating of reading and writing assignments.

Meaningful Use of Language to Promote Comprehension

In addition to the integrated approach to literacy learning and comprehension instruction that took place within these classrooms, or perhaps as a result of it, there was a heavy emphasis on the meaningful application of the language arts for literacy learning. The teachers and children constantly used listening, speaking, reading, writing, and viewing within the classroom, but these language arts were consistently used in the context of "making sense" of what they were reading, discussing, listening to, writing, or viewing. Activities were designed to be meaningful to the children and allow them to apply their literacy skills in meaningful ways. Students in these classrooms were surrounded by teaching and activities that reinforced literacy learning as the construction of meaning. In this respect, it seemed as though most instruction during the day was designed to improve students' comprehension.

Use of Established Comprehension Techniques

Within an integrated, literature-based, and meaning-oriented approach to literacy learning, the exemplary teachers we observed also made use of well-established comprehension development techniques. Most notably, we saw an extensive use of questioning. Questions were used before, during, and after reading to promote comprehension. The questions were posed at varying levels of difficulty and promoted a variety of thought processes.

Other commonly known comprehension techniques we observed were use of morning messages, and Venn diagrams. Morning messages were used as a vehicle for making print meaningful and relevant to the children's lives. Venn diagrams were used to compare stories and characters and as graphic organizers for writing workshop.

Teachable Moments

In a more subtle yet no less powerful way, reading comprehension was also fostered through casual conversation focused on concepts related to books, print, and stories. The teachers and students discussed book covers, pages, words, sounds, titles, authors, illustrations, themes, plots, characters, character traits, and points of view. Many of these conversations had an informal, spontaneous feel to them, yet meaningful literacy growth that leads to comprehension development was taking place.

Explicit Instruction

Instruction leading to comprehension growth took place through focused, explicit, teacher-directed lessons as well. Although this teaching was embedded within meaningful, integrated contexts, it was still clearly explicit in nature. Examples of explicit instruction included the lesson on vocabulary development using the word "strawberry," the lesson contrasting the two pieces of literature, and the lesson on characters' traits.

Social Collaboration, Motivation, and Positive Attitudes

Reading comprehension in these classrooms was further facilitated through classroom contexts designed to promote social collaboration, motivation, and positive attitudes toward literacy learning. An emphasis on social collaboration was seen in the arrangement of the physical classroom, including the grouping of desks and use of learning centers. Assignments such as center-based activities and the reading of stories to classmates also promoted an environment of social collaboration. Motivation and positive attitudes were developed through the use of high-quality theme-related children's literature, the use of creative, engaging, hands-on activities, and the general positive climate within the classrooms.

What We Did Not See

As important as what we did see in the classrooms of exemplary teachers is what we did not see. In addition to the absence of the isolated use of reading comprehension workbooks, workbook pages, and activities, we also did not see any evidence of strategy instruction. Strategy instruction, designed to help readers become more metacognitive in their approach to reading as a route toward increasing reading comprehension, is possible to achieve at the early elementary level, though it is infrequently seen (Pressley, 2000). It has been suggested that the reason that strategy instruction is so rare at this level is that teachers and students are focused on first developing more foundational knowledge bases (Alexander & Jetton, 2000; Pressley, 2000).

What We Still Need to Know about Preparing Young Learners for Successful Reading Comprehension

Although much is known about what needs to be done to prepare young learners to be successful comprehenders, there is always a need for further research that provides more depth and detail to our current knowledge bases. Here we suggest several areas in which we feel additional investigation would be fruitful.

- With regard to sociocultural influences on children's preparedness for reading comprehension, educators must learn how to both honor children's cultural differences, including linguistic differences, and simultaneously help children excel in their comprehension of standard oral and written English. Learning to access and build on sociocultural differences may prove to be the most effective route to mastery. Purcell-Gates (2000) states that comparative studies need to be done that evaluate the effectiveness of mainstream literacy programs versus those that are more culturally sensitive.
- With regard to influences of the school, classroom, teacher, and text, a salient research topic is the role of metacognitive (transactional) strategy instruction among emergent literacy learners. Pressley (2000) reports that such instruction has been found to be effective with students in grade 2 but that it is rarely seen in actual practice in classrooms. The effectiveness of this approach, which has been found to be extremely powerful with older students, should be further explored with beginning readers.
- With regard to influences of the home environment, additional research is needed to find ways to help parents learn how to better help their children with preparedness for reading comprehension at home. Although educators have been successful in identifying which home practices are effective in fostering a strong emergent lit-

eracy foundation, additional work needs to be done to find the most efficient methods to help parents implement these recommendations.

- With regard to the needs of the "whole child," research should be conducted to further explore the integrative nature of children's functioning. Differences in rates of literacy acquisition between children in comprehensive programs and those in programs that focus solely on children's cognitive needs should be evaluated. Such information may be critical in helping those children most at risk for failure in reading comprehension.
- With regard to the construct of a child's emergent literacy foundation, much work remains to be done in how to best move this body of information into the public domain. Researchers have compiled an important body of knowledge in this area. Its dissemination is critical to the future reading comprehension success of many children.

CONCLUSIONS

This chapter explores the role of preparedness for reading comprehension success that ideally occurs during a child's emergent literacy period of development. The key points are highlighted in Table 14.1.

It is hoped that the presented information contributes to many children's ultimate success with reading comprehension.

TABLE 14.1. Preparing Young Learners for Successful Reading Comprehension: Key Points

- The roots of reading comprehension are laid during a child's emergent literacy phase of development.
- When working with young learners, the most promising approach to facilitating eventual reading comprehension success is to develop a strong, broad, and rich emergent literacy foundation. Such a foundation enables readers to possess the diverse knowledge sources needed for later reading comprehension competency.
- The stronger and deeper a child's emergent literacy foundation is, the better equipped he or she will be for the eventual job of reading comprehension.
- A child's comprehension development is affected by concentric spheres of influence, including socioeconomic, school-based, home-based, and individual factors. Exemplary educators understand the effects of these influences and, accordingly, differentially respond to children's needs.
- Exemplary early childhood educators foster young children's comprehension development by creating classrooms in which comprehension development is skillfully woven into the fabric of engaging emergent literacy learning experiences.
- Key characteristics of these teachers' practices are an integrated, theme-based, literature-based approach to instruction, meaningful use of language, use of established comprehension development techniques, teachable moments, explicit skill instruction, an emphasis on social collaboration, high motivation, and an overall positive classroom climate.
- Educators, parents, and other interested parties need to understand the close relationship between the development of a child's emergent literacy foundation and his or her eventual success with the task of reading comprehension.

REFERENCES

Adams, M. J. (1996). *Beginning to read: Thinking and learning about print.* Cambridge, MA: MIT Press.

Alexander, P., & Jetton, T. (2000). Learning from text: A multidimensional and developmental perspective. In M. Kamil, P. Mosenthal, P. D. Pearson, & R. Barr (Eds.), *Handbook of reading research* (Vol. 3, pp. 285–310). Mahwah, NJ: Erlbaum.

Anderson, R. C., Hiebert, E., Scott, J., & Wilkinson, I. (1985). *Becoming a nation of readers: The report of the commission on reading.* Washington, DC: National Institute of Education.

Au, K. H. (2000). A multicultural perspective on policies for improving literacy achievement: Equity and excellence. In M. Kamil, P. Mosenthal, P. D. Pearson, & R. Barr (Eds.), *Handbook of reading research* (Vol. 3, pp. 835–852). Mahwah, NJ: Erlbaum.

Baker, L., Fernandez-Fein, S., Scher, S., & Williams, H. (1998). Home experiences related to the development of word recognition. In J. Metsala & L. Ehri (Eds.), *Word recognition in beginning literacy* (pp. 263–287). Mahwah, NJ: Erlbaum.

Bronfenbrenner, U. (1979). *The ecology of human development: Experiments by nature and design.* Cambridge, MA: Harvard University Press.

Bus, A. G., van IJzendoorn, M. H., & Pellegrini, A. D. (1995). Joint book reading makes for success in learning to read: A meta-analysis on intergenerational transmission of literacy. *Review of Educational Research, 65,* 1–21.

Durkin, D. (1966). *Children who read early.* New York: Teachers College Press.

Flood, J. (1977). Parental styles in reading episodes with young children. *Reading Teacher, 30,* 846–867.

Gadsden, V. L. (2000). Intergenerational literacy within families. In M. Kamil, P. Mosenthal, P. D. Pearson, & R. Barr (Eds.), *Handbook of reading research* (Vol. 3, pp. 871–888). Mahwah, NJ: Erlbaum.

Garner, R., & Alexander, P. A. (1991, April). *Skill, will, and thrill: The role of interest in text comprehension.* Paper presented at the Annual Meeting of the American Educational Research Association, Chicago.

Goldman, S. R., & Varma, S. (1995). Caping the construction–integration model of discourse comprehension. In C. Weaver, S. Mannes, & C. Fletcher (Eds.), *Discourse comprehension: Essays in honor of Walter Kintsch* (pp. 337–358). Hillsdale, NJ: Erlbaum.

Guthrie, J. T., & Wigfield, A. (2000). Engagement and motivation in reading. In M. Kamil, P. Mosenthal, P. D. Pearson, & R. Barr (Eds.), *Handbook of reading research* (Vol. 3, pp. 403–424). Mahwah, NJ: Erlbaum.

Knapp, M. S. (1995). *Teaching for meaning in high-poverty classrooms.* New York: Teachers College Press.

Langenberg, D. N., Correro, G., Ehri, L., Ferguson, G., Garza, N., Kamil, M., Marret, C., Samuels, S., Shanahan, T., Shaywitz, S., Trabasso, T., Williams, J., Willows, D., & Yatvin, J. (2000). *Report of the national reading panel: Teaching children to read.* Washington, DC: National Institutes of Health, National Institute of Child Health and Human Development.

Leseman, P., & DeJong, P. F. (1998). Home literacy: Opportunity, instruction, cooperation, and social–emotional quality predicting early reading achievement. *Reading Research Quarterly, 33*(3), 294–319.

Lowry, R. (Ed.). (1998). *Toward a psychology of being* (3rd ed.). New York: John Wiley & Sons.

Morrow, L. M. (1992). The impact of a literature-based program on literacy achievement, use of literature, and attitudes of children from minority backgrounds. *Reading Research Quarterly, 27*(3), 251–275

Morrow, L. M. (2000). *Literacy development in the early years: Helping children read and write* (4th ed.). Needham Heights, MA: Allyn & Bacon.

Morrow, L. M., & Gambrell, L. B. (2000). Literature-based reading instruction. In M. Kamil, P.

Mosenthal, P. D. Pearson, & R. Barr (Eds.), *Handbook of reading research* (Vol. 3, pp. 563–586). Mahwah, NJ: Erlbaum.

Morrow, L. M., Pressley, G. M., Smith, J. K., & Smith, M. (1997). The effect of a literature-based program integrated into literacy and science instruction with children from diverse backgrounds. *Reading Research Quarterly, 32*(1), 54–76.

Morrow, L. M., Smith, M. W., & Tracey, D. H. (2000, December). The GAINS Project: Gaining achievement in the new standards. *Reading On-Line.* http.//www.readingonline.org/newliteracies/morrow/index/.

Morrow, L. M., Tracey, D. H., Woo, D. G., & Pressley, G. M. (1999). Characteristics of exemplary first-grade literacy instruction. *Reading Teacher, 52*(5), 462–476.

Pressley, M. (2000). What should comprehension instruction be the instruction of? In M. Kamil, P. Mosenthal, P. D. Pearson, & R. Barr (Eds.), *Handbook of reading research* (Vol. 3, pp. 545–562). Mahwah, NJ: Erlbaum.

Pressley, G. M., Allington, R. L., Wharton-McDonald, R., Block, C., & Morrow, L. M. (2001). *The good first grade.* New York: Guilford Press.

Purcell-Gates, V. (1996). Stories, coupons, and the *TV Guide*: Relationships between home literacy experiences and emergent literacy knowledge. *Reading Research Quarterly, 31,* 406–428.

Purcell-Gates, V. (2000). Family literacy. In M. Kamil, P. Mosenthal, P. D. Pearson, & R. Barr (Eds.), *Handbook of reading research* (Vol. 3, pp. 853–870). Mahwah, NJ: Erlbaum.

Ruddell, R. B. (1997). Researching the influential literacy teacher: Characteristics, beliefs, strategies, and new directions. In C. K. Kinzer, K. A. Hinchman, & D. J. Leu, (Eds.), *Inquiries in literacy theory and practice: 46th Yearbook of the National Reading Conference* (pp. 37–53). Chicago: National Reading Conference.

Scarborough, H. S., Dobrich, W., & Hager, M. (1994). On the efficacy of reading to preschoolers. *Developmental Review, 14,* 245–302.

Seefeldt, C., & Barbour, N. (1994). *Early childhood education: An introduction* (3rd ed.). New York: Macmillan.

Snow, C. E. (1983). Literacy and language: Relationships during the preschool years. *Harvard Educational Review, 53,* 165–189.

U.S. Department of Education (1992, June). *The condition of bilingual education in the nation: A report to the Congress and the President.* Washington, DC: United States Department of Education, Office of the Secretary.

Yaden, D. B., Jr., Rowe, D. W., & MacGillivray, L. (2000). Emergent literacy: A matter (polyphony) of perspectives. In M. Kamil, P. Mosenthal, P. D. Pearson, & R. Barr (Eds.), *Handbook of reading research* (Vol. 3, pp. 425–454). Mahwah, NJ: Erlbaum.

15

Building Comprehension When They're Still Learning to Read the Words

Gay Ivey

"If I'd known then what I know now." In a presentation at the annual convention of the International Reading Association, Ann Duffy (1997) relayed heartfelt lessons about teaching struggling readers that she learned only after leaving the classroom to pursue a doctorate in reading education on her way to becoming a teacher educator and researcher. Since then, I have thought about my own former students and about realizations that came late. As a teacher I developed a good sense of how to facilitate motivating, productive reading experiences for older struggling readers (Ivey, 1999a), but I had certain nagging questions that I was too distracted, too inexperienced, or not knowledgeable enough to answer. This chapter is devoted to one of those questions and to the answers that make sense to me now.

My priority for the sixth, seventh, and eighth graders I taught in Title I language arts was to lead them to books they could read on their own, especially because most of their past and present reading experiences involved either staring hopelessly into the pages of difficult grade-level texts that were not even in the ballpark of their instructional levels or avoiding reading altogether. Easy-to-read picture books designed for much younger readers seemed to be the answer, and, contrary to popular opinion, the middle school students approached these materials with interest and without embarrassment. For the first time in school, they were actually reading.

But I was always bothered that I knew of no way, except by reading to them, to give them access to the more sophisticated materials that better matched their thinking and experiences. I knew that helping my students read words more efficiently would help them comprehend better in the long run, but because of their limited access to meaning-rich texts, I rarely focused explicitly on comprehension. As my students grew in fluency and engagement in the books they *could* read, I hoped that their abilities to use strategies flexibly to construct meaning would fall into place as they began to read more complex, diverse materials down the line. Nevertheless, I knew that learning to read and reading purposefully required more than just reading the words and that students also need both explicit and implicit instruction in comprehension for reading certain texts, not to mention a real reason for reading.

Since that time I have realized that I was not completely neglecting comprehension in my teaching. Rather, I did not recognize all of the benefits of the kinds of reading my students experienced. But I have also learned new ways of making comprehension instruction count for students who still find reading difficult. In this chapter I first provide some background on the barriers to teaching comprehension when decoding is also a problem. Next, I suggest some meaning-rich reading activities for older readers who are still learning to read the words.

WHAT WE KNOW ABOUT COMPREHENSION INSTRUCTION FOR STUDENTS STILL BREAKING THE CODE

For students in the upper elementary and middle grades who are still learning to decode, high-quality comprehension instruction and meaningful reading experiences probably fall by the wayside. When Johnston and Allington (1991) reviewed the research on remedial reading instruction a decade ago, they found that students with reading difficulties were likely to get instruction that focused mainly on print accuracy rather than on meaning and comprehension. Undoubtedly, this scenario has become even more typical since the mid-1990s as some states began to mandate phonics instruction and as high-stakes testing has driven many districts to adopt commercially available reading programs that typically emphasize decoding over reading for meaning.

Even when teachers include activities intended to bolster comprehension, they may wrongly assume that struggling readers who have limited ability to read the words are incapable of thinking about text in complex ways. Consider my study of Allison (Ivey, 1999b), a sixth grader whose reading was hindered by weak word knowledge and decoding skills. During round-robin readings of texts, Allison sat with her head resting on her desk, jacket hood over her head. She did not follow along in the text but occasionally turned the page when she noticed her classmates turning their pages. In contrast, when the teacher read aloud to the class, Allison was alert and engaged; but unfortunately the level of discussion during and after read-alouds often did not match Allison's high level of thinking about text. For instance, during a teacher read-aloud of *Fly Away Home* (Bunting, 1991), a story about a homeless man and his son who lived in an airport, Allison raised her hand and repeatedly interjected with, "I've got a question," but the teacher kept reading. At the end of the book, the teacher asked for volunteers to recount the gist of the story, and Allison's hand came down. After several other students constructed a summary of the book, Allison's hand went up again: "I've got a question. It seems like [the homeless man] got a little bit of money." Rather than acknowledging Allison's question, the teacher proceeded to her own next question. Throughout the remainder of the discussion, the teacher continued to ask recall questions, and Allison continued to lobby, albeit without much success, for her own higher level questions and comments that in most cases went beyond the text (e.g., "It seems like the homeless man was pretty smart. He had money to buy them hamburgers and stuff"). This kind of thinking and questioning, as well as metacognitive behaviors, were typical for Allison across a range of readings.

Wolf (1998) observed similar incidents in a third- and fourth-grade class in which the teacher focused on comprehension of factual details, and, just as Allison did, struggling readers in this class demonstrated that they were capable of much more sophisticated thinking. For example, in a discussion after reading *Daniel's Duck* (Bulla, 1979), the teacher asked, "Who can tell me, on page 92, where did this story take place?" One student yelled out, "My mom was born in Tennessee!" Although "Tennessee" was the correct response, this student did not answer the question directly, so the student was "hushed" and the question was asked again. When another student responded simply with "Tennessee," the teacher followed up with, "Find the sentence where the word 'Tennessee' is and read me the sentence" (Wolf, 1998, p. 395). Whereas the teacher, in this case guided by the teacher's manual for the basal reader, was concerned about getting verbatim answers, this student and others in similar examples were thinking about stories in more complex ways, such as connecting to personal knowledge.

It may be difficult for teachers to observe this kind of strategic thinking in struggling readers or to teach them strategic comprehension behaviors in the grade-level texts students are expected to read (e.g. class novels, literature anthologies, textbooks) simply because students get sidetracked trying to figure out the words. Laberge and Samuels (1974) stressed the importance of being able to process text automatically because of the connection between fluency and comprehension. In short, they suggest that a reader has a certain amount of mental energy to exert on a reading task and that, if most of their cognitive resources are used to decode words, then little is left for comprehension. If students are dealing with difficult-to-read texts most of the time, high-level comprehension, as well as comprehension instruction, may be lost on them as they get tangled up in reading the words.

Barr, Blachowicz, and Wogman-Sadow (1995), based on Betts's (1954) earlier recommendations, describe criteria for deciding whether or not a passage is too difficult for a child to read. In short, if a student reads a text with less than 90% accuracy in word identification, that text is too difficult, and even 94% accuracy is considered borderline frustrating. In order for students to read fluently and independently, they should be able to read the words nearly effortlessly, with at least 98% accuracy; and this is rarely the case for struggling readers trying to read typical grade-level texts. Nevertheless, this level of fluency is critical for students to be able to focus on meaning and develop strategic behaviors.

Some teachers may perceive, as I did, an either–or dilemma for dealing with fluency and comprehension for older, struggling readers. That is, the teacher must decide whether to concentrate on fluency by making sure students always have texts they can easily read and forgoing comprehension instruction in difficult-to-read texts or to sacrifice instructional-level reading for a higher level comprehension focus in more complex, meaning-rich materials that students might find frustrating to read. But all students, especially those who struggle, need reading experiences and instruction in rich, multidimensional programs that encompass growth in skill, motivation, and the construction of knowledge. In the remainder of this chapter I suggest some ways of combining the development of fluent reading with the development of strategic comprehension behaviors within purposeful reading experiences.

PRACTICES THAT PROMOTE COMPREHENSION
FOR OLDER STRUGGLING READERS

What can teachers do to ensure that students have ample opportunities to cultivate so-phisticated, versatile strategies while they are still learning to read the words? I suggest three principles that might help guide teachers through this dilemma. First, teachers must consider a balanced approach to literacy instruction (e.g., Baumann & Ivey, 1997; McIntyre & Pressley, 1996; Pressley, 1998) that honors the need for a range of instruc-tion within the context of meaningful reading and writing experiences. In other words, inexperienced readers who are poor decoders should not be relegated to a program based predominantly on phonics or decoding. Rather, sound, well-designed phonics and decod-ing instruction (e.g., Bear, Invernizzi, Templeton, & Johnston, 2000) tailored to individ-ual students should be part of a larger framework that connects all of the processes asso-ciated with reading and that fuels students' ability and desire to read independently in a variety of interesting texts.

Second, teachers must not assume that limited decoding ability equals limited ability to think deeply about texts. Although many of these students have had few successful reading experiences with complex materials in school, their knowledge about the world and about reading gained through listening and through exploring alternative forms of print media (e.g., comic books, magazines) and nonprint media (e.g., music, the Internet) should not be underestimated. Third, teachers can include many reading experiences in which the burden of decoding is removed, thus clearing the way for students to read more purposefully, strategically, and reflectively. In the remainder of this section, I offer some practical suggestions that reflect a combination of these three principles.

Reading High-Interest, Easy Texts

In this section, *easy-to-read* books refers to materials that are easy to read at the word level. What is considered *easy* will depend on the individual student's ability and inter-ests. When thinking about comprehension, however, it is critical to consider not only the level of difficulty of the text but also the richness of meaning, and this consideration is es-pecially relevant when identifying books for older readers who are significantly behind their grade-level peers in reading. For instance, although certain predictable pattern books, such as *Earl's Too Cool For Me* (Komaiko, 1988) and *The Book That Jack Wrote* (Scieszka, 1994), are excellent for building fluency, fun for older students to read, and may elicit personal responses from students, they offer neither rich content nor interesting stories. Alternatively, although they are not in great supply, there are some easy-to-read picture books and easy chapter books that contain sophisticated concepts, interesting themes, and rich vocabulary.

Easy-to-Read Fiction

Teachers in the upper elementary and middle grades may be unaware of certain easy-to-read chapter books that are also complex and engaging enough to provide students chances to develop and practice their comprehension strategies. For instance, some of Roald Dahl's books, such as *The Magic Finger* (1966) and *Fantastic Mr. Fox* (1970), are written simply but also cleverly enough to appeal even to adult readers. Scary stories enjoyed by older students (e.g., *In a Creepy, Creepy Place*, Gorog, 1996; *Scary Stories to Tell in the Dark*, Schwartz, 1992) often contain plot twists and mysteries that lend themselves to strategic reading. The *Bullseye Chiller* series includes classic thrillers such as *Frankenstein* (Weinberg, 1982) and *Phantom of the Opera* (McMullan, 1989) that are rewritten at a lower reading level but that still maintain interesting story lines.

Also, teachers should be aware that many easy picture books are better suited for students in the upper elementary and middle grades than for students in the early grades. For instance, *Voices in the Park* (Browne, 1998) offers contrasting narrative perspectives from four different characters who interacted with each other during a visit to the park. *The Happy Hocky Family* (Smith, 1993) is actually a spoof of old basal readers, and the author's subtle humor would probably be lost on a younger student. Scieszka's *The Stinky Cheese Man and Other Fairly Stupid Tales* (1996) and *Squids Will Be Squids* (1998) are similarly appropriate for more mature students and lend themselves to strategic reading and particularly to reading between the lines.

Easy-to-Read Information Books

It is essential to make easy-to-read nonfiction, in addition to narratives, available to struggling readers in the upper elementary and middle grades, in which content reading may start to define the curriculum. In addition to being too difficult for some students, traditional grade-level textbooks also provide students with just one genre of nonfiction. In order to comprehend a variety of informational texts, students need to read and study many different models. Picture books not only come in a range of formats but many are also easy to read. For instance, the *Eyewitness Readers* collection includes high-interest, content-rich nonfiction on a range of science-related topics (*Slinky Scaly Snakes!*, Dussling, 1998; *Micromonsters*, Maynard, 1999; *Plants Bite Back!*, Platt, 1999), and some picture book narratives include scientific information embedded in the text (e.g., *I Took a Walk*, Cole, 1998; *Is This a House for A Hermit Crab?*, McDonald, 1990). There is also a growing number of sophisticated picture books that frame mathematical concepts (e.g., *One Hundred Hungry Ants*, Pinczes, 1993; *Counting on Frank*, Clement, 1991; *Math Curse*, Scieszka, 1995) and historical events such as the Underground Railroad (e.g., *Follow the Drinking Gourd*, Winter, 1988), and the Japanese American internment (e.g., *The Bracelet*, Uchida, 1993). Certain collections of easy-to-read poetry also include important subject area information (e.g., *Bone Poems*, Moss, 1997). Finally, although we typically think of repetitive and cumulative books as fictional in nature, there are some informational pattern books. For example, *Here Is the Wetland* (Dunphy, 1996) details the ecology of a wetland marsh, and *The House That Crack Built* (Taylor, 1992) describes the production, distribution, and detrimental effects of crack cocaine.

A good example of how easy books for diverse learners can be incorporated into whole-class content area study is through concept-oriented reading instruction (CORI; e.g., Guthrie et al., 1996). Instruction is organized around a conceptual, interdisciplinary theme within a framework that includes four phases: (1) immersing students in the thematic topic and having them generate their own questions for further study, (2) having students read a wide range of texts to gather information about the questions they posed, (3) teaching students strategies to comprehend the texts they use, and (4) providing instruction to enable students to create a product based on what they learned. Guthrie and

Cox (1998) point out that a specific benefit of CORI for less experienced readers is that a conceptual theme is accessible to all students and that a range of materials on a variety of difficulty levels can be included to learn about that theme. Also, as students become more knowledgeable about a topic and related vocabulary, they might be able to read materials on that topic that would normally be considered above their reading level.

Repeated Readings

Samuels (1979) recommended repeated readings as an effective way to build reading fluency. For struggling readers, one of the by-products of reading the same text repeatedly is that eventually they can read it fluently and accurately, allowing them to consider the meaning of the passage without the burden of decoding. Even more important, repeated readings give them access to more sophisticated texts than they might be able to manage or comprehend in a single reading. However, repeated readings by themselves may not be enough to sustain older students' motivation. Here I discuss two ways of embedding repeated readings by rehearsing to read for an audience. When students work through decoding issues and unfamiliar vocabulary first, they can get to the more important matter of making their reading comprehensible and interesting to their listeners.

Performance Reading

The goal of Readers Theatre is for students to read a text dramatically and effectively to an audience. In preparation for the performance, students get to practice their parts as many times as needed to work through difficult words and to perfect their fluency, expression, and timing. Several researchers have used analogies of flying to describe how Readers Theatre frees students from the task of decoding. Martinez, Roser, and Strecker (1998/1999) explained, "No longer glued to print, they 'take-off' in reading" (p. 328). Wolf (1998) argued that "flight is possible if children are given the opportunities to construct their own wings and experience the sensation of being able to read text fluently, with sound comprehension and rich interpretation that arises from myriad conversations about potential meanings" (pp. 385–386).

Furthermore, Wolf (1998) described some ways in which one teacher embedded comprehension strategy instruction in reading rehearsals. For instance, she encouraged students to consider the perspectives of their characters and to say a particular line the way a character might say it or to use their own experiences or background knowledge to imagine how a character might express himself or herself. Martinez, Roser, and Strecker (1998/99) argued that Readers Theatre provides a good forum for direct explanation, feedback, and modeling of strategies. For instance, a teacher might discuss the need to be on the lookout for the most critical lines or important information in a text and how to highlight that section in a performance, such as having a large group of students read those lines at once for emphasis. As a follow-up, students can look for critical portions of text in subsequent Readers Theatre scripts they write or arrange on their own. For instance, look at how the arrangement of parts in this script from *Snakes* (Simon, 1992) emphasizes the most important points in this passage. The main idea of the paragraph is read by the entire repertory group at once, and supporting details are read by individual students:

ALL READERS: Almost any animal that is not too big can make a meal for a snake.

READER 1: Small snakes, such as the yellow rat snake, can eat insects, lizards, birds and their eggs, fish, and rodents.

READER 2: Larger snakes can also feed on rabbits, deer, monkeys, pigs, chickens, sheep, and goats.

READER 3: It may take a large snake hours to swallow a really big animal such as a pig or a goat, and weeks or even months before the snake needs another meal.

ALL READERS : The time depends upon the size and the shape of the prey. (p. 10)

There are a number of high-interest texts that are both easily adapted for Readers Theatre and just challenging enough for older struggling readers to manage with some practice. Books that are already written in script form include *Novio Boy: A Play* (Soto, 1997), which is about young adolescents in a Mexican American community, and *Monster* (Myers, 1999) which is a combination of journal entries and a movie script by a teenage boy in prison and on trial for murder. Books written in alternative formats that break up the text into discrete, manageable sections also transform easily into scripts. For instance, *Making Up Megaboy* (Walter, 1998) and *Regarding the Fountain: A Tale, in Letters, of Liars and Leaks* (Klise, 1998) are told through a series of memos, letters, news reports and articles, and firsthand accounts. However, any text can be converted to a script for the upper elementary and middle grades, and nonfiction scripts can be used to focus on comprehension in the content areas. For example, Aliki's (1979) description of the mummification process in *Mummies Made in Egypt* and *Accidents May Happen: Fifty Inventions Discovered By Mistake* (Jones, 1996), a collection of short tales about how certain popular items came to be (e.g., the ice cream soda, dynamite, raisins), are perfect for dramatization.

Cross-Age Tutoring

Older struggling readers who serve as tutors for younger students show overall gains in their reading achievement (e.g., Labbo & Teale, 1990; Taylor, Hanson, Justice-Swanson, & Watts, 1997), but cross-age tutoring has specific potential for the tutees' comprehension abilities. As with Readers Theatre, the older students must practice what they will read before "performing" for the younger students, and as fluency increases, they can focus on how to effectively present it. An added benefit of tutoring, however, is that it forces the students to consider comprehension strategies as they prepare to teach some of those strategies to younger students. In a program described by Taylor and her colleagues (1997), tutors were involved in a series of 3–day preparation cycles taught by the school reading coordinator that included, in addition to fluency practice and strategies for decoding, writing and discussion activities connected to comprehension. In turn, during the tutoring sessions, the older students engaged their younger counterparts in activities focused on comprehension. For instance, after reading a book aloud to the younger students, they worked with them to make a story map that included the main idea and supporting details. They also coached the younger students on self-monitoring strategies when the younger students read to them. Teaching comprehension strategies to others makes students more cognizant of their strategies and more deliberate in their own reading.

Strategy Instruction That Includes Reading Aloud to Students

Although high-interest, easy-to-read books, repeated readings, and reading books on familiar topics provide struggling readers with some access to sophisticated texts with which to hone their comprehension skills, most materials that match their interests and levels of thinking are beyond their reach. Thus an essential component of reading instruction for older struggling readers is the teacher read-aloud, which not only gives students access to what they cannot read alone but also allows them to participate in a common text experience with readers who are more proficient. Here I describe two instructional activities that combine reading aloud and learning to comprehend: (1) teacher modeling and explanations and (2) directed listening–thinking activity (DL-TA).

Teacher Modeling and Explanations

Teacher read-alouds can be a good starting point for introducing critical strategies for comprehension. That is, by just listening first, students can focus on the strategy being introduced without actually having to read. For instance, teachers and researchers report that thinking aloud while reading is effective for enhancing comprehension abilities (Baumann, Jones, & Seifert-Kessell, 1993; Davey, 1983) because the reader must verbally express the mental processes associated with reading that are not readily observable. For students who get caught up in reading the words, a more effective plan is for the teacher to model his or her own mental process as he or she reads aloud to students (e.g., Duffy, Roehler, & Herrmann, 1988). The general idea is that the teacher reads a portion of text and then pauses to describe his or her thinking before continuing to the next portion of text.

Duffy and colleagues (1988) emphasized the importance of teachers' relating their actual thoughts rather than a set of procedures because differences in texts and differences in readers' schemas about a particular topic require that students be flexible in their strategy use. For instance, consider this teacher's comments as she begins to read aloud from *Max the Mighty* (Philbrick, 1998):

"The title is Max the Mighty. On the cover there is a picture of a big guy, almost a giant, carrying a much smaller girl, who is holding a book. She doesn't look younger than him, just smaller. He must be Max the Mighty because he's huge. He's running away from something, but she looks like she's holding on, not trying to get away from him. Now I'm going to read. [Teacher reads aloud] 'My name is Maxwell Kane and the thing you should know about me is this: even though I'm a big dude with a face like the moon and ears that stick out like radar scoops and humongous feet like the abdominal snowman, inside I'm a real weenie. A yellow-bellied sapsucker. A gigantic wuss. A coward.' [Teacher thinks aloud] Maxwell is Max the Mighty, from the cover, because Max is a nickname, and the way he describes himself, you know he's big. I don't think he's a ferocious giant, because he described himself as a coward. He makes me think of that character in *Willy the Wimp* [Browne, 1989] who becomes a bodybuilder but in the end turns out to be a wimp on the inside. I've read stories like this before, so I think he's going to tell about a time when he acted like a coward. But sometimes in books and movies cowards turn out to be heroes. When I look back at the cover, he looks more like a hero than a coward. I predict that he'll do something heroic."

Notice how the teacher includes the reasoning she uses to make sense of this book (e.g., "I've read stories like this before"). Otherwise, students who are listening might be confused about where this teacher was getting her ideas about this book. After teachers model thinking aloud, they can also stop intermittently to allow students to share their own thoughts and reasoning.

Pressley, El-Dinary, Wharton-McDonald, and Brown (1998) caution that, although teacher modeling and explanations are helpful to students, they are not enough for students to fully understand how and when to use strategies. Rather, students will learn most when they are actually making cognitive decisions on their own as they read. Still, when students practice strategies on their own, they need to use materials they can actually manage independently, as discussed in the previous section on easy materials.

Directed Listening–Thinking Activity

The directed listening–thinking activity (DL-TA), an adaptation of the directed reading–thinking activity (DR-TA; Stauffer, 1976), teaches students to use what they already know to help understand the new information they encounter in text. Students learn to set purposes for reading by predicting what the text will be about, then listening to confirm or revise their predictions. If the teacher reads the text, the students are completely freed from the burden of figuring out difficult words, and they can concentrate on building meaning-based strategies they can apply in their own independent reading.

The general framework of the DL-TA is as follows: First, the teacher shows students the cover and title of the selection and asks, "What do you think this might be about?" All responses are accepted as possibilities, but students should provide rationales for their predictions. Next, students are prompted to listen as the teacher reads the first portion of the text to see if their predictions were correct. At a predetermined stopping point, the teacher asks, "Were you correct?" or "What do you think now?" Students should be given an opportunity to revise their predictions if necessary. Students are encouraged to cite proof from the text to support their new or revised predictions. Finally, the next section of the text is read as far as the next logical stopping point. Again, students are asked to evaluate their last predictions. The teacher continues this cycle of reading and predicting to the end of the text. The reading may culminate with an extended discussion of the text, guided by students' own questions.

Materials suitable for DL-TAs with older students are those that build suspense and curiosity in the listener. Short stories and sophisticated picture books with plot twists and surprise endings (e.g., *The Wreck of the Zephyr*, Van Allsburg, 1983; *Hey Al*, Yorinks, 1986) are ideal. However, students may benefit most from hearing the complex young adult novels they might not otherwise know (e.g., *Tangerine*, Bloor, 1997; *Holes*, Sachar, 1998; *When Zachary Beaver Came to Town*, Holt, 1999).

WHAT'S NEXT? : NEW LESSONS TO LEARN ABOUT COMPREHENSION FOR STRUGGLING READERS

The practical suggestions I offer here are just a starting point. The kinds of instruction I recommend for struggling readers obviously require that whole-class, one-size-fits-all instruction, even for comprehension, must be abandoned in response to differences in children. I conclude this chapter with two recommendations for future research.

1. *Documented models of classrooms that include a wide range of reading experiences for a diversity of students.* Although there are a small but growing number of research studies that describe balanced reading instruction for the early elementary grades (e.g., Baumann & Ivey, 1997; Fitzgerald & Noblit, 2000; Hall & Cunningham, 1996), we have little to draw from for older students. In the early elementary classrooms from the previously cited studies, all students, regardless of their levels of word knowledge, were provided with many opportunities daily to engage in rich, meaning-oriented experiences with print. We need similar detailed descriptions of upper elementary and middle grade classrooms in which all students, particularly older struggling readers, benefit from a multidimensional reading program that builds fluency, comprehension, engagement, and learning and that provides students with a well-balanced perspective on what it means to read. For instance, my colleagues and I described how diverse students in one sixth-grade classroom received both teacher-initiated and student-responsive strategy instruction within an overall literacy program that included self-selected independent reading, teacher-guided, whole-class readings, small-group studies of novels, teacher read-alouds, and rehearsed dramatic reading performances (Ivey, Baumann, & Jarrard, 2000).

2. *Research in content-area literacy instruction that takes into account students who are still learning to decode.* We still have much to learn about how to deal with decoding, comprehension, and engagement issues simultaneously in situations in which specific content must also be learned, and this is particularly critical as students move into the upper elementary and middle grades. Although there is a plethora of good strategies for reading to learn (e.g, K-W-L; Ogle, 1986), for studying specific texts (e.g., prereading guides), and for extending content learning through discussion (e.g., discussion web; Alvermann, 1992), students who still struggle with reading the words may find them only marginally useful. Future studies could investigate how teachers might combine principles from developmental reading research with principles from content literacy research in ways that help older struggling readers build knowledge about reading while also building content knowledge. Undoubtedly, notions of content reading would have to be expanded in order to give students along a range of expertise in word knowledge rich, meaning-driven experiences with text. For instance, Guthrie and Cox (1998) explain how concept-oriented reading instruction targets developmental needs within content-area instruction by allowing students to choose from a range of books on a particular theme as opposed to reading from a common text, which might be too difficult or uninteresting to some students. More studies are needed that also examine how other practices to promote effective reading that one might typically find in a language arts classroom (e.g., teacher read-alouds, repeated readings for fluency) might also be used effectively in the content areas to give students access to a variety of texts and especially to promote reading comprehension for students who are still developing the ability to read the words.

REFERENCES

Alvermann, D. E. (1992). The discussion web: A graphic aid for learning across the curriculum. *Reading Teacher, 45*, 92–99.

Barr, R., Blachowicz, C. L. Z., & Wogman-Sadow, M. (1995). *Reading diagnosis for teachers* (3rd ed.). New York: Longman.

Baumann, J. F., & Ivey, G. (1997). Delicate balances: Striving for curricular and instructional equilibrium in a second-grade, literature/strategy-based classroom. *Reading Research Quarterly, 32*, 244–275.

Baumann, J. F., Jones, L. A., & Seifert-Kessell, N. (1993). Using think alouds to enhance children's comprehension monitoring abilities. *Reading Teacher, 47,* 184–193.

Bear, D., Invernizzi, M., Templeton, S., & Johnston, F. (2000). *Words their way: Word study for phonics, vocabulary, and spelling instruction* (2nd ed.). Upper Saddle River, NJ: Merrill/ Prentice Hall.

Betts, E. A. (1954). *Foundations of reading instruction* (Rev. ed.). New York: American Book Company.

Davey, B. (1983). Think-aloud: Modeling the cognitive processes of reading comprehension. *Journal of Reading, 27,* 44–47.

Duffy, A. (1997). *Working with struggling readers and their families in a K–5 Title I program.* Paper presented at the annual convention of the International Reading Association, Atlanta, GA.

Duffy, G., Roehler, L., & Herrmann, B. A. (1988). Modeling mental processes helps poor readers become strategic readers. *Reading Teacher, 41,* 762–767.

Fitzgerald, J., & Noblit, G. (2000). Balance in the making: Learning to read in an ethnically diverse first-grade classroom. *Journal of Educational Psychology, 92,* 3–22.

Guthrie, J. T., & Cox, K. E. (1998). Portrait of an engaging classroom: Principles of concept-oriented reading instruction for diverse students. In K. R. Harris, S. Graham, & D. Deshler (Eds.), *Teaching every child every day: Learning in diverse schools and classrooms* (pp. 77–130). Cambridge, MA: Brookline Books.

Guthrie, J. T., VanMeter, P., McCann, A. D., Wigfield, A., Bender, L., Poundstone, C. C., Rice, M. E., Faibisch, F. M., Hunt, B., & Mitchell, A. M. (1996). Growth of literacy engagement: Changes in motivations and strategies during concept-oriented reading instruction. *Reading Research Quarterly, 31,* 306–325.

Hall, D. P., & Cunningham, P. M. (1996). Becoming literate in first and second grades: Six years of multimethod, multilevel instruction. In D. J. Leu, C. K. Kinzer, & K. A. Hinchman (Eds.), *Literacies for the 21st century: Research and practice* (pp. 195–204). Chicago: National Reading Conference.

Ivey, G. (1999a). Reflections on teaching struggling middle school readers. *Journal of Adolescent and Adult Literacy, 42,* 372–381.

Ivey, G. (1999b). A multicase study in the middle school: Complexities among young adolescent readers. *Reading Research Quarterly, 34,* 172–192.

Ivey, G., Baumann, J. F., & Jarrard, D. (2000). Exploring literacy balance: Iterations in a second-grade and a sixth-grade classroom. *Reading Research and Instruction, 39,* 291–310.

Johnston, P., & Allington, R. L. (1991). Remediation. In R. Barr, M. L. Kamil, P. Mosenthal, & P. D. Pearson (Eds.), *Handbook of reading research* (Vol. 2, pp. 984–1012). Mahway, NJ: Erlbaum.

Labbo, L. D., & Teale, W. H. (1990). Cross-age reading: A strategy for helping poor readers. *Reading Teacher, 43,* 362–369.

Laberge, D., & Samuels, S. J. (1974). Toward a theory of automatic information processing in reading. *Cognitive Psychology, 6,* 293–323.

Martinez, M., Roser, N. L., & Strecker, S. (1998/1999). "I never thought I could be a star": A readers theatre ticket to fluency. *Reading Teacher, 52,* 326–334.

McIntyre, E., & Pressley, M. (Eds.). (1996). *Balanced instruction: Strategies and skills in whole language.* Norwood, MA: Christopher-Gordon.

Ogle, D. (1986). K-W-L: A teaching model that develops active reading of expository text. *Reading Teacher, 39,* 563–570.

Pressley, M. (1998). *Reading instruction that works: The case for balanced teaching.* New York: Guilford Press.

Pressley, M., El-Dinary, P. B., Wharton-McDonald, R., & Brown, R. (1998). Transactional instruction of comprehension strategies in the elementary grades. In D. H. Schunk & B. J. Zimmerman (Eds.), *Self-regulated learning: From teaching to self-reflective practice* (pp. 42–56). New York: Guilford Press.

Samuels, S. J. (1979). The method of repeated readings. *Reading Teacher, 32,* 403–408.

Stauffer, R. (1976). *Teaching reading as a thinking process.* New York: Harper & Row.

Taylor, B. M., Hanson, B. E., Justice-Swanson, K., & Watts, S. M. (1997). Helping struggling readers: Linking small-group intervention with cross-age tutoring. *Reading Teacher, 51,* 196–209.

Wolf, S. (1998). The flight of reading: Shifts in instruction, orchestration, and attitudes through classroom theatre. *Reading Research Quarterly, 33,* 382–414.

CHILDREN'S BOOK REFERENCES

Aliki. (1979). *Mummies made in Egypt.* New York: Harper Trophy.

Bloor, E. (1997). *Tangerine.* New York: Harcourt Brace.

Browne, A. (1989). *Willy the wimp.* New York: Knopf.

Browne, A. (1998). *Voices in the park.* New York: DK.

Bulla, C. R. (1979). *Daniel's duck.* New York: HarperCollins.

Bunting, E. (1991). *Fly away home.* New York: Clarion.

Clement, R. (1991). *Counting on Frank.* New York: Gareth Stevens.

Cole, H. (1998). *I took a walk.* New York: Greenwillow.

Dahl, R. (1966). *The magic finger.* New York: HarperCollins.

Dahl, R. (1970). *Fantastic Mr. Fox.* New York: Knopf.

Dunphy, M. (1996). *Here is the wetland.* New York: Hyperion.

Dussling, J. (1998). *Slinky, scaly snakes!* New York: DK.

Gorog, J. (1996). *In a creepy, creepy place and other scary stories.* New York: HarperCollins.

Holt, K. W. (1999). *When Zachary Beaver came to town.* New York: Holt.

Jones, C. F. (1996). *Accidents may happen: Fifty inventions discovered by mistake.* New York: Delacorte Press.

Klise, K. (1998). *Regarding the fountain: A tale, in letters, of liars and leaks.* New York: Scholastic.

Komaiko, L. (1988). *Earl's too cool for me.* New York: HarperCollins.

Maynard, C. (1999). *Micromonsters: Life under the microscope.* New York: DK.

McDonald, M. (1990). *Is this a house for a hermit crab?* New York: Orchard Books.

McMullan, K. (1989). *Phantom of the opera* [Adaptation]. New York: Random.

Moss, J. (1997). *Bone poems.* New York: Workman.

Myers, W. D. (1999). *Monster.* New York: HarperCollins.

Philbrick, R. (1998). *Max the mighty.* New York: Scholastic.

Pinczes, E. J. (1993). *One hundred hungry ants.* New York: Scholastic.

Platt, R. (1999). *Plants bite back!* New York: DK.

Sachar, L. (1998). *Holes.* New York: Farrar, Straus, & Giroux.

Schwartz, A. (1992). *Scary stories to tell in the dark.* New York: HarperCollins.

Scieszka, J. (1994). *The book that Jack wrote.* New York: Viking.

Scieszka, J. (1995). *Math curse.* New York: Viking.

Scieszka, J. (1996). *The stinky cheese man and other fairly stupid tales.* New York: Viking.

Scieszka, J. (1998). *Squids will be squids.* New York: Viking.

Simon, S. (1992). *Snakes.* New York: HarperCollins.

Smith, L. (1993). *The happy Hocky family.* New York: Viking.

Soto, G. (1997). *Novio boy: A play.* San Diego, CA: Harcourt Brace.

Taylor, C. (1992). *The house that crack built.* San Francisco: Chronicle Books.

Uchida, Y. (1993). *The bracelet*. New York: Putnam.

Van Allsburg, C. (1983). *The wreck of the Zephyr*. Boston: Houghton-Mifflin.

Walter, V. (1998). *Making up megaboy*. New York: Delacorte Press.

Weinberg, L. (1982). *Frankenstein* [Adaptation]. New York: Random.

Winter, J. (1988). *Follow the drinking gourd*. New York: Knopf.

Yorinks, A. (1986). *Hey Al*. New York: Farrar, Straus, & Giroux.

16

Comprehension Instruction in the Primary Grades

P. David Pearson
Nell K. Duke

The terms "comprehension instruction" and "primary grades" do not often appear in the same sentence (Duke & Pearson, in press). In research, the vast majority of studies on comprehension instruction have dealt with learners in third grade and later. In practice, many educators do not consider comprehension instruction to be an important part of primary grade education. There is a widespread belief that it is not possible, or at least not wise, to teach comprehension to young children who are still learning to decode text. This belief may well stem from the assumption, so prevalent in many primary grade programs, that phonics and word identification should be the sole priority in the primary grades.

In this chapter we take the position that the terms "comprehension instruction" and "primary grades" should appear together often—that comprehension instruction in the primary grades is not only possible but wise and beneficial rather than detrimental to overall reading development. Specifically, we intend to document three claims about comprehension instruction in the primary grades:

- Comprehension improves when teachers provide explicit instruction in the use of comprehension strategies.
- Comprehension improves when teachers design and implement activities that support the understanding of the texts that students will read in their classes.
- Comprehension and decoding can exist side by side as instructional goals and valued student outcomes in an exemplary and comprehensive literacy program for primary grade children.

CRITICAL RESEARCH ON COMPREHENSION INSTRUCTION

In this section, we attempt to validate each of these three claims by focusing our attention on a few key studies. The focal grade of the studies varies, but all deal at least in part with students in the primary grades.

Claim 1: Comprehension improves when teachers provide explicit instruction in the use of comprehension strategies.

Three studies anchor our evidentiary base for this claim. In the first, Bauman and Bergeron (1993) posed the question, "Can very young children be taught to use story structure to enhance their ability to identify and recall central story elements?" They compared four classes of grade 1 students. Two classes were provided with explicit instruction in identifying key elements of stories: characters, setting (places and times), problem, events, and solutions. The other two classes listened to and read the same stories but were not taught any specific reading strategies. Groups taught to attend to key aspects of stories outperformed students who engaged only in reading and discussing the stories on all measures employed, including identifying the most important parts of a story and selecting a good summary of a story. A delayed assessment (2.5 weeks later) revealed a continuing effect for the story-structure instruction. Interviews revealed that students in the story groups also provided longer, more coherent, and more sequentially organized retellings with more central story ideas. Moreover, these students were more likely to talk about the importance of looking for key elements of stories read after the end of the study.

Our second focal study demonstrates that even kindergarten-age children's comprehension can be improved through comprehension instruction. In this study (Morrow, 1985), student teachers in 17 kindergarten classrooms read eight storybooks aloud to small groups of children over the course of 8 weeks. Following each read-aloud session, half of the students were asked to draw a picture about the story. The other half were asked to retell the story, on a one-to-one basis, to the student teacher. The student teachers guided the students' retellings, in particular explicitly leading them to attend to major story-structure elements. Following the 8-week period of intervention, children's comprehension of two new stories read aloud to them was assessed through a series of comprehension questions. Students were also asked to retell the stories that had just been read.

Results of the study indicate that practice in guided retelling does improve children's (listening) comprehension of written text. After only 8 weeks of experience, children in the guided-retelling group performed substantially better on both the comprehension test and the retelling than did the children in the drawing group. Even kindergarten children, then, can benefit from well-designed comprehension instruction.

In our third focal study, Brown, Pressley, Van Meter, and Schuder (1996) examined the effectiveness of a comprehensive approach to comprehension instruction known by the acronym SAIL (students achieving independent learning). In SAIL, teachers use explicit instruction, modeling, and discussion to teach comprehension strategies, particularly predicting, visualizing, questioning, clarifying, making associations (e.g., between the text and the students' experiences, between one text and another), and summarizing. Their focus is on not only on what the strategy is but also on when and how to apply it in actual reading. Teachers in SAIL talk very explicitly about particular comprehension strategies and their usefulness. They model the use of these strategies by "thinking aloud" about their own use of comprehension strategies in the presence of students. They encourage students to discuss their comprehension of texts, as well as the strategies they are using to achieve that comprehension. Coming up with "right answers" is less valued in SAIL than is making and justifying interpretations of text. Students are taught to attend to their own reading processes, to the context in which they are reading, and to the text.

Brown et al. (1996) conducted a quasi-experimental study of the effectiveness of SAIL in second-grade classrooms. Small groups of low-achieving students in five SAIL classrooms were compared with similar groups of children in classrooms in which the teacher did not use the SAIL approach but was well regarded as a teacher of language arts. When assessed in the spring of the school year, children in the SAIL classrooms performed considerably better on standardized measures of reading comprehension and word attack. More qualitatively, students in SAIL classrooms were found to be more strategic readers and to make richer interpretations of text. Indeed, SAIL is really one member of a family of approaches to comprehension instruction collectively known as transactional strategy instruction approaches, or TSI (Pressley et al., 1992), because of their concern with transactions between the reader, the text, and the context.

This study demonstrates that explicit comprehension instruction—in this case in the form of the SAIL approach—does indeed improve primary-grade children's comprehension skills. SAIL is a complex approach to the teaching of comprehension strategies. Children are taught several different strategies for use in comprehending text, they are taught to employ these strategies differentially in different reading situations, and they apply these strategies to challenging texts and to deep levels of text interpretation. Yet there is no indication from this research that primary-grade children are unable to handle this instruction. On the contrary, they seem to thrive in it. And this is not limited to second-grade students. Elsewhere, Pressley and his colleagues describe the use of the SAIL program with first-grade children as well (e.g., Pressley et al., 1994). Moreover, the study suggests that comprehension instruction can also improve children's decoding skills. Although SAIL focuses primarily on comprehension, it did not detract from children's decoding development—comprehension and decoding appear to have a reciprocal, even synergistic relationship.[1]

Claim 2: Comprehension improves when teachers design and implement activities that support the understanding of the texts that students will read in their classes.

Several studies demonstrate that comprehension development can be fostered not only by explicit instruction but also by consistently embedding particular kinds of literacy activities in the reading of classroom texts. Some of these activities focus directly on comprehension, such as discussion questions (Tharp, 1982) and prediction activities (Hansen, 1981), whereas others focus more on how the texts are read (e.g., Dowhower, 1987; Eldridge & Reutzel, 1996).

Our first focal study is a classic—an evaluation of the KEEP (Kamehameha Early Education Program) program that was conducted by Tharp in 1982. The KEEP curriculum, which is still used in many native Hawaiian schools despite the demise of the laboratory

---

[1] It should be noted that this process works the other way as well—decoding instruction also improves comprehension (see, e.g., Adams, 1990, and Tan & Nicholson, 1997).

school in which the program was developed, includes attention to comprehension in many of its text activities. The most prominent tool for structuring comprehension and text discussion is the E-T-R (experience–text–relationship) sequence. This sequence involves discussing student *experiences* related to the text ("E"), reading and querying the *text* ("T"), and then discussing *relationships* between experience and text ("R"). E-T-R is used in small group settings, during which the teacher focuses on discussion of text, but also in other classroom activities such as during independent work or at centers. Indeed, 50% of center work in KEEP focuses on comprehension. However, the KEEP curriculum also includes substantial work on phonics, sight vocabulary, and decoding, both at centers and in small groups with the teacher. Continuous monitoring of student progress via curriculum-embedded assessments is also a hallmark of the program.

In the Tharp (1982) evaluation of the program, KEEP consistently outperformed a control curriculum in grades 1, 2, and 3 on standardized measures of vocabulary and comprehension. Although this improvement cannot be traced solely to the attention to comprehension afforded by the program or to the E-T-R structure alone, these were among the most salient differences between KEEP and the control classrooms. Results from a study by Hansen (1981), from the same time period further bolster the interpretation that linking students' prior knowledge to text content and engaging in high-level discussion of text is comprehension-facilitating for young children. Although it was quite different in implementation and duration, like the KEEP evaluation, Hansen's study favored either one of two approaches compared with a control group. Interestingly, both of these approaches were a part of the KEEP curriculum: (1) an approach that encourages children to relate the prior knowledge to text information via predictions from prior knowledge and (2) an approach that dramatically increases the proportion of inferential, higher order questions that children encounter during story discussions.

Our second focal study (Stahl, Heubach, & Cramond, 1997) involved a full-scale reorganization of the second-grade curriculum in order to provide more emphasis on fluency and comprehension than is normally offered to second-grade students. The program was offered to 230 children in 14 classrooms, about half of whom were reading below grade level at the start of the year. The routine for each basal story was modified so that students engaged in the following activities:

1. Listening to the teacher read the story aloud
2. Participating in a whole-class discussion of the story, including teacher-generated questions, student-generated questions, and attention to vocabulary
3. Completing, independently, organizational tools such as story maps, plot charts, and Venn diagrams
4. Echo reading with the teacher if in need of extra help
5. Reading the story to parents or caretakers at home
6. On the next day, rereading the story with a partner
7. Writing a journal entry in pairs or as a whole class
8. Free reading for 15–20 minutes per day in class and at home.

This was not a controlled experiment; instead, Stahl and his colleagues examined growth patterns over the year on the Qualitative Reading Inventory (Leslie & Caldwell, 1995). The most telling result was that of the 190 students who began grade 2 reading at pre-primer level or above, only 5 failed to read the grade 2 passage at criterion level (95% accuracy, with 80% comprehension) in the spring of grade 2. Of the 20 who scored below pre-primer level in the fall, 9 reached or surpassed the grade 2 passage criterion, and only one child could not yet pass the primer-level test. When these results are compared with expected gains, they are truly impressive. In fact, the average gain for students in this program was 1.8 grade levels on a test on which expected growth would be 1.0 grade level.

A study by Dowhower (1987) illustrates the comprehension-facilitating effect of one element of Stahl's intervention—repeated reading. Dowhower engaged 17 second-grade students at a transitional stage of reading development (Chall, 1983) in repeated readings of a set of stories modified from a basal reading series. Students practiced each passage until they reached a reading rate of 100 words per minute on the passage. This entailed between four and six 15-minute sessions per week for 6 weeks. Some students engaged in the practice primarily independently (with word identification assistance on request), whereas others practiced along with a tape of a fluent reader reading the passage.

Results of pre- and posttesting on similar but unfamiliar (that is, not repeatedly read) passages showed gains in reading rate, reading accuracy, and reading comprehension. The percentage of comprehension questions answered correctly rose from 66% to 81% from the pre- to the posttest. Granted, it is difficult to sort out cause and effect in this study (whether improvements in fluency and/or accuracy led to the improvement in reading comprehension or whether the experience of developing better understanding of a series of stories through repeated reading itself led to improvement in reading comprehension or some combination of these). Even so, this study demonstrates a particular reading practice—repeated reading—that may support comprehension development.

Eldredge, Reutzel, and Hollingsworth (1996) provide another illustration of ways in which different types of reading activities may influence young children's comprehension development. They demonstrated that engaging children in shared book experiences, which necessarily entails some (albeit unspecified) attention to comprehension, is of greater value to children's comprehension development, oral reading, fluency, and vocabulary development than round-robin reading practices. Using random assignment, two second-grade teachers were asked to engage students in a shared book experience consisting of a big book reading and discussion and a demonstration of particular print conventions. These were followed by independent, partner, or book-on-tape reading sessions. Another two second-grade teachers provided their students with exposure to the same books, but through traditional round-robin reading. Following 3 months of instruction, children in the shared-book-experience group outperformed the round-robin-reading group on a standardized test of reading comprehension, an oral retelling of a transfer story, and a question-answering task. Assessments of word analysis, vocabulary, and fluency also revealed significant differences favoring the shared book experience.

Claim 3: Comprehension and decoding can exist side by side as instructional goals and valued student outcomes in an exemplary and comprehensive literacy program for primary grade children.

Two recent reviews of literature on primary-grade reading (Snow, Burns, & Griffin, 1998; National Reading Panel, 2000) support attention to both comprehension and decoding in primary-grade curricula. (Notably, both also support a combination of explicit instruction and a great deal of actual reading, precisely consistent with the combination of Claims 1 and 2 herein.) The wisdom of combining comprehension and decoding also emerges in recent research carried out in the tradition of effective schools and teachers. Several studies (e.g., Morrow, Tracey, Woo, & Pressley, 1999; Taylor, Pearson, Clark, & Walpole, 2000; Wharton-McDonald, Pressley, & Hampston, 1998) have documented that exemplary teachers and schools do indeed attend vigorously to comprehension and response to literature, as well as to decoding and word identification in the primary grades. In other words, they implement a comprehensive reading curriculum in which code and meaning are taught in synergistic ways. A recent contribution to this literature is a study reported in Morrow et al. (1999) of six first-grade teachers who are exemplary in their teaching of literacy. The teachers observed in the study were nominated by supervisors and administrators based on an extensive list of criteria, including their students' performance on various measures of literacy achievement, their students' enthusiasm for and engagement with literacy, and their ability to articulate their instructional philosophy and corresponding practices. All teachers were observed for approximately 25 hours during their literacy instruction blocks and were also interviewed about their philosophies and practices. Observation and interview notes were analyzed and synthesized into a model of exemplary literacy instruction that captured the practice of these teachers.

The study yielded a number of important findings (see also Wharton-McDonald et al.'s 1998 report of another set of exemplary first-grade teachers), but most relevant to the topic at hand were findings regarding comprehension instruction in these classrooms. The researchers found that

> the teachers had systematic methods for teaching comprehension skills. Comprehension development was embedded in both the reading of storybooks and in guided reading lessons. Many strategies were introduced to students, from engaging them in story retelling to repeated readings of stories, revisiting the text, making predictions, drawing conclusions, and demonstrating knowledge of structural elements of stories. Students studied styles of authors and illustrators and responded to literature in discussions and writing. (p. 468)

The exemplary teachers in this study clearly saw comprehension strategy instruction as an important part of first-grade literacy instruction. At the same time, these teachers also had strong word-analysis programs and provided a multitude of opportunities for actual reading and writing of high-quality text. A description of practice in these classrooms suggests integrated and mutually supportive attention to multiple aspects of literacy.

Another recent study of exemplary practice, in this case of teachers and schools that are particularly effective in educating high-poverty populations to high levels of literacy, also validates attention to both comprehension and decoding development in the primary grades (Taylor et al., 2000). Researchers found that teachers in the most effective schools and the most accomplished teachers in all the schools were much more likely than less accomplished teachers to ask higher order questions about text and to emphasize writing in response to reading. At the same time, like the teachers in the Morrow et al. (1999) and Wharton-McDonald et al. (1998) studies, these first- and second-grade teachers also had strong word identification and decoding programs. Interestingly, the teachers in the most effective schools were more likely to engage students not only in explicit phonics instruction (as did the moderately and least effective teachers) but also in practice of high-frequency words and to coach students on word recognition strategies during reading. This combination of explicit teaching and coaching during actual reading and writing, apparently so effective in the realm of decoding and word recognition, parallels our recommendations for comprehension work (Claims 1 and 2 herein).

APPLYING WHAT IS KNOWN

The most obvious implication of the preceding studies and others conducted on comprehension instruction in the early grades is that comprehension instruction should have a prominent place in primary-grade curricula. Comprehension can be taught directly by assisting students in acquiring strategies (Claim 1), facilitated by activities surrounding the reading of text (Claim 2), and complemented by important code-based skill instruction (Claim 3). Research shows that it is possible to affect children's comprehension development at least as early as kindergarten.

The studies reviewed for this chapter suggest a wide array of specific techniques for comprehension instruction. We summarize and illustrate these techniques in the examples that follow.

Story Elements

Research by Bauman and Bergeron (1993) suggests that children can be explicitly taught to attend to important elements of stories. In Table 16.1, we recapitulate these elements, along with questions similar to those used by Bauman and Bergeron to promote their awareness. Their work suggests that no special texts, such as those that might be created especially for this sort of instruction, are needed; the authentic stories found in the trade book literature and in good anthologies are preferred (indeed, these were used by Bauman and Bergeron). Also, the approach can be used for stories both read aloud by teachers and read independently by students.

Using Story Retellings to Promote Story Understanding and Retrieval

Morrow's (1985) research supports the practice of explicitly guiding students in retelling stories. To guide students' retellings, teachers in her study used prompts such as, "What comes next?" or "Then what happened?" or asked a question related to the specific stopping point in the student's retelling (e.g., "What was Jenny's problem?"). For children having more difficulty with story retelling, teachers in the study were asked to use the following prompts:

TABLE 16.1. Questions That Promote Story Comprehension

Story element	Questions
Character	• Who was the main character? • What kind of character was XXX? What makes you think so?
Setting	• Where did the story take place? • Why is it important that the story took place there? then?
Problem	• What did XXX want to do? Why was XXX having trouble?
Events	• What happened after XXX did YYY? • Why did XXX do YYY?
Solution	• How did XXX solve the problem? • How did the story turn out? Why?

Note. After Bauman and Bergeron (1992).

- "Once upon a time . . . " or "Once there was . . ."
- "Who was the story about?"
- "When did the story happen?"
- "Where did the story happen?"
- "What was [name the main character]'s problem in the story?"
- "How did she/he try to solve her/his problem? What did she/he do first, next?"
- "How was the problem solved?"
- "How did the story end?" (Morrow, 1985, pp. 659–660)

All of this was done with texts that had been read aloud to children rather than read by the children themselves, suggesting one mechanism for comprehension instruction for prereaders.

Teaching Strategies Directly

Specific practices suggested in the Brown, Pressley, Van Meter, and Schuder (1996) study are described in greater detail elsewhere in this book. But to reiterate briefly, SAIL and other transactional strategies instruction approaches use a combination of explicit instruction, modeling, and discussion to teach comprehension strategies. They have a strong focus on the application of strategies and provide many opportunities for students to become independent in their strategy use. SAIL assumes that comprehension strategy instruction and use is complex; thus instruction is ongoing, deliberate, and intense.

SAIL is best thought of as offering a menu of strategies that teachers, and then students, can flexibly employ as appropriate to the various texts encountered in the ongoing reading program. The clear expectation is that teachers and students will select, from the larger menu, precisely that subset of strategies optimally suited to promoting understanding of and response to each selection. Specific cognitive and interpretive strategies emphasized in SAIL are listed in Table 16.2.

Perhaps the most notable implications of the SAIL research are the complexity of the comprehension instruction provided in this approach and the success experienced by the primary grade—and largely at-risk—population with which the approach has been used.

TABLE 16.2. Basic Components of TSI

Cognitive strategies	Interpretive strategies
- Thinking aloud	- Character development: Imagining how a character might feel; identifying with a character
- Constructing images	- Creating themes
- Summarizing	- Reading for multiple meanings
- Predicting (prior knowledge activation)	- Creating literal–figurative distinctions
- Questioning	- Looking for a consistent point of view
- Clarifying	- Relating text to personal experience
- Story grammar analysis	- Relating one text to another
- Text structure analysis	- Responding to certain text features, such as point of view, tone, or mood

Using Experience–Text–Relationship to Structure Text Discussions in a Comprehension-Rich Classroom

The KEEP evaluation (Tharp, 1992) suggests that the Experience–Text–Relationship (E-T-R) can provide a helpful structure for text discussions. The steps in E-T-R include:

1. *Discussing student experiences related to the text:* How many of you have a little brother like Danno? Does he ever do anything to bother you?
2. *Reading and querying the text:* So how did Danno handle his little brother?
3. *Discussing relationships between experience and text:* So what did you learn about dealing with little brothers (or sisters) that you might use the next time he (or she) does something to bother you?

In the context of an overall literacy program that includes significant attention to comprehension of text, as well as to phonics, sight vocabulary, and decoding, the E-T-R sequence can provide a powerful structure for text discussion.

Using Intensive Study of Text in a Comprehension-Rich Classroom

Research by Stahl et al. (1997) implies that intensive study of text can improve the comprehension abilities of primary-grade learners. Throughout the year, teachers in their study used each of these steps to frame their story-related instruction:

1. Read the focus story aloud.
2. Lead a whole-class discussion of the story, with emphasis on their questions, student-generated questions, and meaning vocabulary.
3. Provide independent story-related activities for students involving organizational tools such as story maps, plot charts, and Venn diagrams.
4. Echo read the story with students most in need of help.
5. Assign students to read the focus story to parents or caretakers at home.
6. Have students reread the story with a partner the next day.
7. Engage students in journal writing in pairs or as a whole class.
8. Assign 15–20 minutes of free reading per day in class and at home.

This package of activities led their second-grade students to make substantial gains in overall reading.

Employing Shared Book Experience

The work of Eldredge, Reutzel, and Hollingsworth (1996) suggests another reading activity that facilitates comprehension development—the shared book experience. As employed by these authors, the shared book experience involved read-aloud and discussion of a big book, with attention to particular print conventions found in the book, followed by independent, partner, or book-on-tape reading of that same text. Their work suggests, in a vein similar to the work of Stahl et al. (1997), that employing a range of reading and rereading techniques promotes greater story understanding. This work is also reminiscent of the work of Dowhower (1987) on repeated reading discussed earlier. It appears as though repeated exposure to the selection content helps students get a better handle on the ideas in the text and that this sense of content mastery promotes transfer to reading other texts.

Attending Comprehensively to Comprehension

Specific techniques for comprehension instruction are somewhat less apparent in the Morrow et al. (1999) study. Still, their description of the comprehension instruction practices of these exemplary teachers suggests some possible qualities of effective comprehension instruction:

- The instruction is systematic.
- It is included in both read-aloud and guided reading.
- It involves a range of comprehension strategies distributed strategically across selections.
- It includes literature-based activities along with cognitive strategies.
- It is part of a comprehensive language arts program, including significant attention to word recognition and decoding.

The Taylor et al. (1999) study suggests some additions to that list:

- There is an emphasis on higher order comprehension questions and discussion.
- There are multiple opportunities for writing in response to reading.

And again, significant attention to word recognition and decoding are also an important part of the curricular package.

WHAT STILL NEEDS TO BE KNOWN
ABOUT COMPREHENSION INSTRUCTION

Although we have written with some confidence in this chapter about what is known about comprehension instruction in the primary grades, we do not wish to give the impression that enough, or even nearly enough, is known. As we noted at the beginning of this chapter, the terms "comprehension" and "primary grades" are not often used conjointly, and the vast majority of published studies of comprehension instruction have been conducted with students in grades 3 and later. Although these studies can certainly suggest promising directions for research and practice in primary-grade settings, they cannot do so on their own merit. We cannot blithely assume that because a particular instructional strategy is effective with fifth graders, it is necessarily going to be effective with first graders. We must conduct comprehension research and practice grounded in the specific characteristics and contexts of primary-grade education. We have three suggestions for research that could move the field forward in a way that focuses specifically on the comprehension development of our youngest readers.

1. *How can comprehension strategy instruction transfer from listening to reading?* Much literacy instruction for young children comes through read-aloud and shared

reading, both activities in which the primary responsibility for processing the *printed* text is in the hands of the teacher rather than the student. How can we help the comprehension strategies children learn when listening to text read aloud transfer to their own reading of text? To take an example from one of the studies discussed earlier in this paper (Morrow, 1985), how can the knowledge kindergarten children develop through guided retellings of stories read aloud to them transfer to their own reading of stories later in schooling?

2. *Are some comprehension strategies more foundational than others?* It may be that some strategies—perhaps relating text to prior experiences or making predictions about text content—are so foundational that they should be emphasized a great deal very early in schooling. It may be that other strategies, such as summarizing, are so difficult for young learners that they should be either backgrounded or given more intensive instruction, in primary-grade education. Unfortunately, presently available research does little to suggest priorities for different comprehension strategies or for the particular challenges young learners may face in learning them.

3. *How can we position young learners to develop comprehension skills for the information age?* Children are typically provided a fairly limited diet of texts to read in early schooling (Duke, 2000), and the body of research on young children's comprehension development is also based on a limited diet of text (almost always fictional narrative). Yet there is growing evidence that children should be provided with a greater diversity of texts in early schooling (e.g., Caswell & Duke, 1998), and certainly the literacy demands posed by this information age are like nothing we have seen before (Kamil & Lane, 1998). There is a particular need for research that examines how to support children's comprehension of nonlinear and nonstory texts, including informational text, procedural text, hypertext, and a multitude of other types of text central to society in the 21st century. [M2]

These significant shortcomings notwithstanding, we know enough about what to teach and how to teach comprehension to our very youngest readers to make a good start at doing so. To delay this sort of powerful instruction until children have reached the intermediate grades is to deny them the very experiences that help them develop the most important of reading dispositions—the expectation that they should and can understand each and every text they read.

REFERENCES

Adams, M. (1990). *Beginning to read: Thinking and learning about print.* Cambridge, MA: Harvard University Press.

Bauman, J. F., & Bergeron, B. S. (1993). Story map instruction using children's literature: Effects on first graders' comprehension of central narrative elements. *Journal of Reading Behavior, 25,* 407–437.

Brown, R., Pressley, M., Van Meter, P., & Schuder, T. (1996). A quasi-experimental validation of transactional strategies instruction with low-achieving second grade readers. *Journal of Educational Psychology, 88,* 18–37.

Caswell, L. J., & Duke, N. K. (1998). Non-narrative as a catalyst for literacy development. *Language Arts, 75,* 108–117.

Chall, J. S. (1983). *Stages of reading development.* New York: McGraw-Hill.

Dowhower, S. L. (1987). Effects of repeated reading on second-grade transitional readers' fluency and comprehension. *Reading Research Quarterly, 22,* 389–406.

Duke, N. K. (2000). 3.6 minutes per day: The scarcity of informational texts in first grade. *Reading Research Quarterly, 35,* 202–224.

Duke, N. K., & Pearson, P. D. (in press). Effective practices for developing reading comprehension. In A. E. Farstrup & S. J. Samuels (Eds.), *What research has to say about reading instruction* (3rd ed.). Newark, DE: International Reading Association.

Eldredge, J. L., Reutzel, D. R., & Hollingsworth, P. M. (1996). Comparing the effectiveness of two oral reading practices: Round-robin reading and the shared book experience. *Journal of Literacy Research, 28*(2), 201–225.

Hansen, J. (1981). The effects of inference training and practice on young children's reading comprehension. *Reading Research Quarterly, 16*(3), 391–417.

Kamil, M. L., & Lane, D. M. (1998). Researching the relation between technology and literacy: An agenda for the 21st century. In D. Reinking, M. McKenna, L. Labbo, & R. Kieffer (Eds.), *Handbook of literacy and technology: Transformations in a post-typographic world* (pp. 323–341). Mahwah, NJ: Erlbaum.

Leslie, L., & Caldwell, J. (1995). *Qualitative Reading Inventory—II.* New York: HarperCollins.

Morrow, L. M. (1985). Retelling stories: A strategy for improving young children's comprehension, concept of story structure, and oral language complexity. *Elementary School Journal, 85,* 647–661.

Morrow, L. M., Tracey, D. H., Woo, D. G., & Pressley, M. (1999). Characteristics of exemplary first-grade literacy instruction. *Reading Teacher, 52,* 462–476.

National Reading Panel. (2000). *Report of the national reading panel.* Washington, DC: Government Printing Office.

Pressley, M., Almasi, J., Schuder, T., Bergman, J., Hite, S., El-Dinary, P. B., & Brown, R. (1994). Transactional instruction of comprehension strategies: The Montgomery County, Maryland, SAIL Program. *Reading and Writing Quarterly: Overcoming Learning Difficulties, 10,* 5–19.

Pressley, M., El-Dinary, P. B., Gaskins, I., Schuder, T., Bergman, J. L., Almasi, J., & Brown, R. (1992). Beyond direct explanation: Transactional instruction of reading comprehension strategies. *Elementary School Journal, 92,* 513–555.

Snow, C. E., Burns, M. S., & Griffin, P. (Eds.). (1998). *Preventing reading difficulties.* Washington, DC: National Academy Press.

Stahl, S. A., Heubach, K., & Cramond, P. (1997). *Fluency-oriented reading instruction* (Reading Research Report No. 79). Athens, GA: National Reading Research Center.

Tan, A., & Nicholson, T. (1997). Flashcards revisited: Training poor readers to read words faster improves their comprehension of text. *Journal of Educational Psychology, 89,* 276–288.

Taylor, B. M., Pearson, P. D., Clark, K. F., & Walpole, S. (2000). Effective schools and accomplished teachers: Lessons about primary reading instruction in low-income schools. *Elementary School Journal, 101,* 121–166.

Tharp, R. (1982). The effective instruction of comprehension: Results and description of the Kamehameha Early Education Program. *Reading Research Quarterly, 17*(4), 503–527.

Wharton-McDonald, R., Pressley, M., & Hampston, J. M. (1998). Literacy instruction in nine first-grade classrooms: Teacher characteristics and student achievement. *Elementary School Journal, 99,* 101–128.

17

Beyond Literature Circles

*Helping Students Comprehend
Informational Texts*

DONNA OGLE
CAMILLE L. Z. BLACHOWICZ

In our work in classrooms, we have seen a growth in classroom approaches to the thoughtful teaching of literature. Approaches such as book clubs (McMahon & Raphael, 1995), literature circles (Morrow & Gambrell, 2000), and other modes of encouraging response to literature have extended and enriched how we look at deepening the ways students interact with text. Yet these emphases, no matter how rich, seem to overlook a major fact about mature reading. Much of what we do every day, by choice or for work, is the reading of informational text.

The influence of literature-based models of reading instruction, drawing on literary studies (Rosenblatt, 1978) and emphasizing fiction, has been enormous. Elementary teachers and district programs seem almost myopic in equating reading with the reading of fiction, stories, and novels. Informational reading, if it is included, is one small strand engulfed by a sea of fictional units—thematic, genre, or author studies—in literature circles, book clubs, or self-selected reading. Very infrequently are students led into the wonderful world of informational books and magazines. At primary levels, little informational text is used for instruction (Duke, 2000). At the middle and secondary levels, at which students are confronted with difficult content-area textbooks and requirements to do much independent research and writing, there is very little support provided students in learning how to ask questions, use resources, and organize and present ideas to others (Alvermann & Moore, 1991).

The discrepancies between current practice and what teachers could do to help students become competent users of informational text concern us. We know much more than we are implementing, and students are the ones being shortchanged. The research that leads us to make such a statement and to propose that we *do* know what to do to provide guidance in informational comprehension comes from a variety of important sources. Given our limited space in this chapter, we are going to focus on a few key questions:

- Why is there a need for greater emphasis on informational reading?
- What are research-based principles and practices for informational reading?
- What does research-based instruction look like?
- What research would move us forward?

WHY THE NEED FOR GREATER EMPHASIS ON INFORMATIONAL READING?

Current research supports our position that informational reading is most representative of mature reading. A recent study by M. Cecil Smith (2000) followed adults through their daily routines by having them keep journals of their reading. Smith found that most reading was informational—both on the job and for pleasure and instrumental purposes, with newspapers and magazines topping the list of materials read. In a study of school-aged children beyond the primary grades, Snowball (1995) found that for them, too, the majority of daily reading was for information. These American reading habits are confirmed by a variety of sources, including the best-seller lists published in newspapers and library journals. As another indicator, standardized tests of reading comprehension and state standards-based assessments now include both fiction (reading for enjoyment or literary purposes) and informational material (to be informed or literary purposes). The Maryland State Performance Assessment Program (MSPAP) also assesses students as they use informational reading and writing during week-long group-problem-solving tasks (Valencia & Wixson, 2000).

Student performance on national assessments provides added support for the notion that we need to do a better job with informational reading. On the National Assessment of Educational Progress (1999) students do less well with informational texts than with narratives; the transition from reading fiction in the primary grades to reading more varied informational materials from fourth grade on may account for the slump in reading scores that shows up between third and fourth grades. As a state example, on the Illinois Goals Assessment Program (IGAP) and now the Illinois Standards Assessment Test (ISAT), student performance on the informational passages regularly falls below scores for the narrative passages (Illinois State Board of Education, 1999).

If informational reading constitutes the majority of reading done by many students and adults, and if nonfiction literacy tasks are being used more widely in tests to measure students' literacy achievement, how are teachers preparing students for these realities? Here we go back to the seminal study of Durkin (1978–1979) that looked at the teaching of reading in social studies classes. As we know well, the data were unsettling; there was almost no instruction in how to read and learn from informational texts. Do students develop needed strategies on their own? Many (1996), working in a Scottish school in which the teacher assigned research with little instructional support, found that students lacked adequate researching skills. Tierney, LaZansky, and Schallert's (1982) work with American students reading content materials yielded similar results.

Watching intermediate-grade teachers "teach" social studies through a fact-transmission process, Ogle was so distressed that she developed the K-W-L (Know, What to Known, Learn) strategy (Ogle, 1986, 1991; Carr & Ogle, 1987). Rather than having teachers teach content by "pouring in" dry, distilled data, students should begin with what they already know and have experienced and then ask their own questions to guide learning. Later, Jennings (1991) working with a volunteer group of teachers established the power of the active stance taken by readers when they used both K-W-L and K-W-L+ (K-W-L+ adds students creating a graphic overview of knowledge and writing a summary of key ideas) with journal writing in social studies. She found the differences in teachers' implementation of the strategies a significant factor in the students' learning. Some teachers did not honor students' input and couldn't seem to create a climate in the classroom that fostered student inquiry.

Two extended projects in urban secondary schools, the National Urban Alliance and Chicago RATE—Goals 2000, were begun because content-area teachers failed to provide instruction in comprehension strategies even when students were failing and lacked reading skills and strategies (George, Moley, & Ogle, 1992; Ogle & Hunter, 2000). In our recent work as part of the Goals 2000 project (Ogle & Hunter, 2000; Boran, 1999) in an urban high school in which nearly all the students speak English as a second language, the faculty is now providing instruction in reading-to-learn strategies as part of a schoolwide commitment. During the course of our project, we developed a core leadership team from the major curricular areas. Through summer institutes, monthly staff development sessions, and weekly support visits by a doctoral student intern, the teachers developed a school reading committee and identified a core set of strategies for all content areas. They also refocused instruction away from a transmission mode toward a social construction mode of learning. Other studies with secondary teachers document similar concerns and possibilities (O'Brien, Stewart, & Moje, 1995; Alvermann et al., 1996; Hinchman & Zalewski, 1996).

Much of the trouble students have comprehending informational material relates to the specific vocabulary that communicates major concepts. Research has documented that students' active involvement in identifying and learning vocabulary is critical to vocabulary learning and related content learning. Yet this same research also documents the paucity of good vocabulary instruction in many classrooms (Blachowicz, 1987; Watts, 1995; Blachowicz & Fisher, 2000). Much of informational vocabulary learning consisted of displaying lists of words for students to look up in the dictionary. Most of this was prereading instruction, done without discussion and teacher dependent in that the list for study was teacher generated (Beyersdorfer, 1991).

Lest this seem too negative a picture, research also has provided information that suggests ways in which we can improve the comprehension of informational text. For vocabulary learning, more active engagement and development of student control of vocabulary learning produces positive results (Fisher, Blachowicz, & Smith, 1991; Finesilver, 1994; Haggard, 1985; Ruddell, 1994). Pressley and his colleagues (1992) provided data on two successful elementary projects that taught students to comprehend materials read for a variety of purposes—both informational and narrative materials. In both Montgomery, Maryland, and at the Benchmark School, in Media, Pennsylvania, the approaches involved sustained, flexible strategy instruction in meaningful learning tasks. Guthrie (see Guthrie & Ozgungor, Chapter 18, this volume), using science as a basis for reading instruction, demonstrated that in-school reading experiences can include a wide variety of activities that sustain students' engagement with informational texts, with increases in student reading achievement and motivation.

Given the clearly established importance of informational reading in today's society, we now turn our attention to research-based principles of informational reading, followed by examples of innovative instructional practices.

WHAT ARE RESEARCH-BASED PRINCIPLES AND PRACTICES OF INFORMATIONAL READING?

Proficient readers of informational text:

- are purposeful and actively engaged in what they read (Stahl & Vancil, 1986; Steffensen, Goetz, & Cheng, 1999).
- attend to both the external physical organization of text and the internal structure of ideas (Meyer & Rice, 1984; Anderson & Armbruster, 1984)
- are strategic and employ a small set of powerful strategies (Pressley et al., 1992; Bereiter & Bird, 1985; Lytle, 1982; Anderson & Roit, 1993)

Purposeful and Active Engagement

From our perspective, the active engagement of students is the most basic requirement of good instruction. Students are more likely to learn when they see the purpose or relevance of what is taught (Goldman, 1997). For this reason, we favor the teaching of reading embedded in the ongoing activities of the content-area classroom (Block & Mangieri, 1997).

Instruction that involves the reader and requires his or her activity can shift the task of comprehending from a memorization exercise to an engagement with the author's ideas and construction of meaning. Both K-W-L (What I Know–What I Want to Know–What I Have Learned) and K-W-L+ (adding graphic organization and summarizing; Carr & Ogle, 1987) have been widely used because they provide an easy and productive way for teachers to involve students in the learning process during content reading. Both approaches are group processes that begin with the teacher engaging the students in a discussion centering on what they know. The group discussion is the catalyst for raising questions that the students might not have formulated on their own. It is these questions and the diversity of ideas and knowledge that capture the students' interest and propel their desire to read and learn. Once students have framed their inquiry around their knowledge and questions, they are stimulated to read the text materials in an active way and to keep notes of their learning and new questions.

"Questioning the author" provides a similar approach (Beck, McKeown, Kucan, & Worthy, 1996). As students read sections of text, they query the invisible author of the text. The discussions can take many directions, from considering why the author included particular information to thinking of better ways of developing the content. Rather than accept the text at "face value," students think more deeply about the text and evaluate both the message and the author's point of view and purpose. Given the increasing use of unreviewed texts and biased sources on the Internet, students need to learn to take an evaluative stance when reading, especially by posing questions of authors, an essential aspect of critical reading.

Other strategies that engage students actively are insert note making (Vaughan & Estes, 1986) and two-column note making (Palmatier, 1973). Students mark the parts of the text that they feel most familiar with, parts that raise questions, and parts that link them to other content and experiences. In both of these strategies, students do not focus only on the text ideas but also on their own relationship to the author.

Scaffolded, participatory approaches, such as project-based learning, problem-based learning, and team learning, also engage and support learners in their reading. They all call for the use of multiple texts and models of real-world interactions with text. Students need to work in groups, an arrangement that allows them to contribute information from which evidence will be collected, weighed, and organized (Moje & Fassio, 1997; Moll, Tapia, & Whitmore, 1993). But these participatory approaches require the scaffolding of teachers to make sure that students have the strategies they need to get the most out of the experience (Evans, 1996; Anderson & Roit, 1993) so that students do not become mired in recycling what they already know as opposed to adding to their knowledge. When the classroom context is guided by principles that ensure everyone reads, that support is provided for a diversity of students, and that students engage in participatory learning and read across texts for learning, teachers can focus on developing a repertoire of strategies to ensure that students become independent.

Attention to Text Organization and Structure

Students create a mental representation of the texts they read. As van den Broek and Kremer (2000) explain, "When reading is successful, the result is a coherent and usable mental representation of the text. This representation resembles a network, with nodes that depict the individual text elements (e.g. events, facts, setting) and connections that depict the meaningful relations between the elements" (p. 2). Many students come to primary schooling already having an internal representation of "story" (Stein & Glenn, 1979) and are thus able to comprehend and retell basic story elements quite easily. The same is not true for expository texts (Goldman, 1997; Stein & Policastro, 1984; Olhausen & Roller, 1988; Chambliss, 1995). Many students have never encountered such texts and their underlying organization prior to schooling.

To provide the knowledge needed to read informational texts with a "road map" in their heads, students need to have many experiences with informational text to develop an understanding of the structures most commonly used to organize these texts. In fact, students who learn to use the internal organization and structure of informational text are more able to comprehend and retain key ideas. The work of several researchers, including Meyer (1975), Armbruster and Anderson (1984), Slater, Graves and Piche (1985), Block (1993), and Taylor and Beach (1984), confirms that students are aided in understanding when they are guided to use the author's underlying text organization. In most of these studies, students were introduced to basic expository structures, such as compare and contrast, description, sequence of events, and problem and solution, and then guided to use those structures to read text and in some cases create graphic or other outlines of key ideas. Although there was support in these studies for teaching students to identify and summarize using top-level structure, the gains produced were not overwhelming.

One key to reading and learning from materials written to inform is to become familiar with the way the ideas are organized by the writer and also with the conventions of organization in presenting a text. Students need to know about informational text features and how such text is organized and structured. As readers of narrative stories, we have learned—often first by listening to stories our parents read to us—that there is a predictable pattern to these tales. We read to find who the characters are, what problem they encounter, and how they go about resolving it, and then we savor their victory at the end. No similar single pattern characterizes informational texts. They can be organized in several ways. Thus predicting and organizing ideas is more difficult for novice readers. Therefore, it is all the more important that we provide guidance so that students can learn to identify and use these writing patterns for their own reading. This guidance provides a powerful background knowledge for anticipating, predicting, and monitoring the text. Young readers need to know how informational texts are organized externally (table of contents, headings, chapters, etc.) and internally (text structure: problem–solution, cause–effect, and so forth; Meyers, 1975; Blachowicz & Ogle, 2001).

Reading Strategically

Given that students are purposeful and actively engaged in what they read and that they attend to both the external physical organization of text and the internal structure of it, they also need to read strategically and employ a small set of powerful strategies. Just as knowing *how* to drive a car (declarative knowledge) does not mean you *can* drive, strategic readers need to develop procedures for actually doing the driving (procedural knowledge) and to make decisions about the right time to use different strategies (conditional knowledge). This necessity suggests that strategy instruction should be taught in a rich milieu in which students can draw and build on existing knowledge and within which they can deploy procedural knowledge and see its effect (Pressley et al., 1992). That means that the learning should be embedded in a rich context, ideally one that is integrated and thematic, a point to which we will return.

When F. B. Davis carried out his groundbreaking research (Davis, 1944), he was interested in narrowing the list of all those things called "comprehension skills" into a list of the most powerful ones. His work stimulated work on comprehension that has helped us, over the past three decades, to get a clearer picture of what strategies, and their supporting subskills, contribute most to effective reading. A small set of strategies used recursively in many different situations can increase comprehension of informational text. These strategies include:

- Using knowledge and text clues to make predictions and to monitor and clarify or extend predictions
- Using internal and external features of informational text to predict and monitor
- Generating questions about informational texts
- Generating elaborations about text
- Organizing and reorganizing texts
- Summarizing texts
- Combining information across texts
- Reflecting critically and personally on informational reading
- Using oral and written language to formulate, express, and reflect on ideas

In effective classrooms, strategy instruction takes both explicit and implicit forms and requires modeling, practice, and reflection. Research showing that one-shot, haphazard instruction is not effective is convincing (Goldman, 1997). Good instruction provides models, practice and reflection and is explicit to the degree necessary for students to see the principles in action, the skull beneath the skin. Strategy instruction also requires time and effort, both on the part of students and teacher. In the next section, we focus on how these research principles might look in action.

WHAT DOES RESEARCH-BASED INSTRUCTION LOOK LIKE?

Setting the Stage for Engaged, Active, Purposeful Reading

How can we convince students that reading informational text can be interesting? One of our best starting places is to share some of our own reading interests with them. We can talk about what we read, share some of our materials with them, and then *read aloud* to them, both from our materials and from good informational texts at their listening comprehension level. A good guideline is to read daily from a variety of kinds of information materials—begin with something you are enjoying or learning about. For example, read interesting pieces from the newspaper, often the human relations stories, sports, or "This Week in History." Later in the day, read aloud something related to your topic of study from a more difficult text than the students would be able to handle themselves—perhaps a biography or magazine article. Bring in materials that encourage students to ask questions or create some new item. Also read aloud from good informational books just to introduce students to the range that is available, just as you do with fiction. In these ways your students begin to appreciate the full range of materials that they can read. They may find some particular topics and genres they will begin to select for themselves, and they will detect more of the structure and format of exposition.

Building Knowledge of External Text Features

One of the first things we notice when we pick up nonfiction or informational materials is that they generally have a format different from that of fiction. (Think of an informational book you have recently read or a children's book such as *Big Bugs*; Gribbin, 1996). One important feature is that such books usually have more pictures and visuals to enhance our interest and to help us understand the concepts. Much of the information is, in fact, presented in the pictures, tables, figures, graphs, diagrams, maps, cartoons, and their captions. In surveying the features of books, we note that, in addition to a table of contents, informational books generally include a glossary and an index. Chapter titles are worth attention because they are important indicators of how the author has organized the information. Within each chapter, there is likely to be a further breakdown of information with headings and subheadings designed to guide our reading to important content or "main ideas".

Many books and articles also highlight key vocabulary with italics, boldface, or marginal notes that provide explanations of the terms. A well-organized informational piece helps us locate the part of the text we want to read when we have particular questions we want answered. In addition, because timely, accurate information is important, readers need to be aware of both the copyright date and the qualifications of the author. Books for very young readers are just now becoming more complete, so looking to be sure there are chapter divisions is important before selecting them for primary students. Check to see if the pages are numbered, because it is hard to locate and return to information without some pagination. As we help children use informational books, we need to be sure that we have quality books available for them. Sometimes the color photographs are stunning, but the rest of the important book features are missing. Particularly troublesome is a lack of tables of contents and indexes in books.

One group of primary teachers in Evanston, Illinois, has been working to build their students' confidence and ability to read informational trade books (Fogelberg, Hiller, Skalinder, Shusterman, & Ogle, 2000). They have noticed that children can have difficulty relating the pictures and other graphic information to the text content. Some books now have graphics inserted in a wide variety of places over the pages, and often on a two-page spread. Some lack captions; in other texts the captions are placed in various locations. Sometimes a caption is beneath a picture, and at other times the captions may be beside or even above the illustrated material. Only by carefully studying the individual pages and mapping the relationship between text and graphics and captions can their relationship be determined. Without support from teachers, much of the richness of these new informational texts would be overlooked by young readers.

As these primary teachers try to use science materials in integrated instruction, they have found they need to be very specific in helping students use the materials. For example, one of the books they use, *Clouds, Rain, and Fog* (Biddulph & Biddulph, 1993), combines photographs with illustrations of clouds. Young readers who have not had experience reading illustrations do not know the differences between the actual photographs and the illustrated drawings. Teachers introduced the big book by explaining to the students,

> "In this book there are both actual photographs of clouds and some pages with pictures that have been drawn to show what is inside the clouds and to explain some things about clouds that the pictures could not show. Look at this page. Is it a photograph like what we could see outside? Look at this next page. Is it a photograph? No, It is really a drawing of what we can't see but helps us understand what is in a cloud."

And so goes the teacher's walk-through of the new book.

In other books, such as *Rice* (Birchall, 1997), there is a combination of full-page photographs and small inserted photographs. One page features a rice harvesting machine and an inserted photo of ducks feeding on the remains of a harvested field. Some children thought that the ducks were going to be killed by the harvester. The teacher, again, had to explain the use of inserted small pictures. She also had to explain how the pictures related to the written text. The way some of the small photos bled from one page to the other was also new to many children, and the teacher explained how the artwork was laid out. She also told some children to look at the pictures before reading a page, then to read the page and look at the pictures when the content was mentioned in the text. Holding the content of the pictures in one's head while reading a page of text and knowing when to refer to the pictures takes real skill. Young readers deserve help in this kind of reading.

At the middle-grade level, some teachers have students identify and use the external structure of chapters they read in textbooks and magazines to make notes (Ogle & Waller, 2000). The children skim through the chapter and create a graphic organizer or map of the chapter, with the title in the center and each of the main headings on one spoke of their "spider map." This graphic organizer is used while students read to help them keep focused on the way the information is related. This mapping of the text can also be used as an interactive guide for reading. The students can brainstorm what they know about each section before reading, write those ideas on the map, and then make notes on their map of new information as they read. This active engagement helps students focus and retain information as they read.

Another strategy teachers use is to have a chapter read in cooperative fashion, in a variation of the jigsaw cooperative learning strategy. The class previews the text by identifying the major sections. The teacher writes these on the board. Then the class is divided into teams. Each team of students reads and creates a visual report of the key ideas of just one section of the text (one heading and elaboration). Many of the informational chapters and articles have such a heavy load of information that asking students to learn just one section from reading makes it manageable. Each group then reports on their section; serving as teachers for the rest of the class both enhances their engagement in reading and creates a shared environment for learning both the content and structure of expository pieces.

Building Knowledge of Internal Text Structure

We can introduce students to the patterns of informational text we noted earlier by collecting several books on the same topic and guiding students to compare the internal structure of the books. For example, in doing a unit on butterflies and migration, one teacher shared several interesting books with his students, focusing on how the authors had chosen to organize their information. The first book he brought was *The Butterfly Alphabet* (Sandved, 1996)—a beautiful book with each page devoted to a letter of the alphabet found in the wings of a butterfly. Information about each butterfly was available in the back of the book, with a poem about butterflies carried through all the pages, A–Z. With this introduction the teacher read *From Caterpillar to Butterfly* (Heligman, 1996), then one on the life cycle and metamorphosis. Next came *Amazing Butterflies and Moths* (Still, 1991), comparing and contrasting the two insect cousins. One book dealt with the problem of loss of habitat for the Carners Blue and how a community in Connecticut is working to create a habitat anew for this endangered species. The authors of these books had chosen different ways of organizing their information, and students began to see these patterns. When they wrote their own reports, they were reminded of the various ways the information could be organized, and their newly focused interest in writing and reading was solidified.

Often vocabulary is useful for these purposes. Using a Vocab-O-Gram (Blachowicz, 1987) organized by structure, one teacher had students arrange both a selected list and a brainstormed list by categories: words describing the habitat (twig, shady, leaf, temperate), words having to do with the life cycle (pupa, chrysalis, cocoon), words having to do with migration (weather, autumn, food source) were discussed and classified and kept on the class word wall. As the unit of study progressed, more words and more categories were added, helping students to create a visual record of the categories of information contained in these informational books, as well as of the concepts and terms common to this domain of study. Such processes also help students see the relationships among words and concepts and provide support for using these words in further reading and writing.

Building Strategies

As teachers help students become familiar with the structure of informational text, we also need to help students develop ways to actively and strategically interact with the authors of those texts and think about the content. Two instructional strategies that have been developed independently but that work well together are the K-W-L+ (Carr & Ogle, 1987) and the I-Chart (Hoffman, 1992).

K-W-L+

Students become much more involved in reading when they and their interests are the starting point for new inquiry and learning. The K-W-L is a process by which the teacher models and guides active engagement and a strategic approach to informational texts. It is a group process using the knowledge and information students bring to help each other build a better starting place for learning and for sharing the results of their reading. The adept teacher weaves together what some class members know and stimulates questions for all to pursue as they develop purposes for reading and learning. The process also helps students who lack confidence in both reading and writing, as the teacher is the first one to write on the board or chart. This permits children to see the written forms of key vocabulary that they will encounter in text later. It also models what the students will write on their own worksheets or in their learning logs.

Once the students have discussed the topic, they are ready to begin their own purposeful reading. As students gain confidence, they can write down on their own worksheets or learning logs those pieces of information they think they *Know* and the questions they *Want* to know more about. In this way both the group and the individual are respected. Some teachers have students work in pairs to do both the writing and reading, as this is more stimulating and supportive for the children who lack confidence in writing and taking risks.

From the class discussion, teachers can determine what texts will be most useful to particular students. It may be that what was anticipated to be an adequate text turns out to be inappropriate or insufficient. For example, a teacher designed a lesson introducing the topic of air pollution to prepare students for reading their fourth-grade science text. By the time the class had brainstormed what they knew, it was clear that most of them could have written a more sophisticated text than the one they had before them. Rather than just reading that one text, the teacher decided to collect other materials for the students to read and learn. As they read the various sources of information, students made notes of what they *Learned*, both answers to their own questions and unexpected information they found interesting and/or important.

Working with students in content areas, teachers know that even motivated and engaged readers will not remember much new information based on a first reading. Therefore, the "plus" in K-W-L+ extends this learning process by asking students to do more reorganizing of what they have learned by making a semantic map or graphic organizer of the key information. The students who were less knowledgeable read the text and made notes of what they learned as their contribution. Bringing the class back together, the teacher then guided the students in the development of a map of the major categories of information on air pollution. After their study and using their map, all students collaborated on writing a chapter for future students in fourth grade.

I-Chart

Using multiple sources of information is wonderful as a way of helping students find texts that meet their own levels of knowledge and interest, find answers to their own questions, and compare and contrast authors' points of view. Yet many students have a difficult time using more than one source effectively, particularly when using the World Wide Web for research. Students need tools to help them organize and evaluate information. Hoffman (1992) has developed a very useful tool in the I-Chart (Inquiry Chart), which provides a framework for students to ask important questions, to select three or four sources of information they want to use to explore those questions, and then to come to their own conclusions about the questions they framed initially.

Once students have used the K-W-L process to activate their knowledge and to interest the class, small groups or individuals select some key questions for more in-depth research and write these on the chart. Then the best sources of information for the questions are selected, usually with teacher help and guidance, and are also listed across the top of the chart. This simple framework establishes the idea that, in seeking answers to questions, multiple sources are needed. Students use the I-Chart to make a systematic search for information and record their findings. The chart also includes a column for "Interesting Information," pieces that don't fit the basic questions but still are relevant to or expand the students' inquiry. This latter process often becomes an important way to take notes on ideas that can be shared with the class later—ideas that are full of potential for more reading and learning.

K-W-L+ and the I-Chart are frameworks through which teachers can engage students personally and corporately in thinking about their relationship to a content to be studied and in setting a course for learning. They also model the important strategies we noted earlier:

- Using knowledge and text clues to make predictions and to monitor and clarify or extend predictions
- Using internal and external features of informational texts to predict and monitor understanding
- Generating questions about informational texts
- Generating elaborations about text
- Organizing and reorganizing texts
- Summarizing texts
- Combining information across texts
- Reflecting critically and personally on informational reading
- Using oral and written language to formulate, express, and reflect on ideas

WHAT RESEARCH WOULD MOVE US FORWARD?

Several important issues need to be addressed in order to develop our knowledge base on instruction in informational reading:

1. Taking a broad view of what constitutes "text" both deals with the reality of real-world informational reading and allows teachers the variety needed to make sure all stu-

dents can read appropriate materials. The definition of text in effective classrooms has been widely expanded over the past years. Internet-based text (Garner & Gillingham, 1996; Bruce, 1997), multimedia texts (Hermanson & Kerfoot, 1994), hypertext (Perfetti, Britt, & Georgi, 1995) student-constructed texts (Moll & Gonzalez, 1994), periodicals, and newspapers all constitute the types of texts that fluent readers handle on a daily basis (Smith, 2000). This same richness of text must be reflected in classroom instruction, and we believe this variety can be motivating to learners. The strategies and processes for dealing with texts that have a richer mix of print and other forms of visual information need to be explored. The use of texts on multiple levels and of different genres, even when a core text is the center of work, can allow all students to do the engaged reading our principles call for. Research that looks at "text" in the broadest senses of the word and that determines the different comprehension demands of these varieties of text should be a line of reading research for this millennium.

2. Similarly, if multiple texts are used, students need to be supported in learning how to read across multiple texts, no easy proposition with school-age readers (Goldman, 1997). Students need to answer their questions not only by drawing from evidence in one source but also by comparing answers to the same question from multiple sources. Then they must weigh that evidence, taking into account and evaluating multiple viewpoints across texts (Hartman & Allison, 1996; Stahl, Hynd, Britton, McNish, & Bosquet, 1996). Along with identifying authors and sources and determining their recency and credibility, readers need to be able to understand the point of view of the text author and the reasons for varied perspectives. They also need to understand how these variables affect our own understanding and point of view. Rather than being seen only as daunting, this task can be seen as a key to interest and motivation, as students can select different texts to contribute to a larger fund of knowledge and engage in the debate and argument that most students enjoy. We would like to see more research on how students learn from multiple informational texts and how teachers can most effectively design instruction to maximize student learning. Also, we would like to see research on the use of varied genres of text and on the ways in which teachers support students in reading, learning, and developing critical approaches to information gathering, synthesis, and evaluation.

3. Further, it may seem gratuitous to say that students actually need to *read* informational texts. However, content-area teachers often have students *listen* to the textbooks being read because they are concerned with making the text accessible to all (Nist & Simpson, 2000). Though we have acknowledged the importance of reading aloud, we feel it is counterproductive to individual reading development not to allow students to grapple with texts through their own reading. Studying ways of dealing with the dilemmas presented in real classrooms by students with varying degrees of reading proficiency is a critical research need, particularly in informational reading.

4. Last, we have been struck by the paucity of research studies on vocabulary in informational reading. We hope to see studies that observe the ways in which teachers incorporate vocabulary instruction into their content classrooms using strategies that develop students' abilities to be independent word learners. This research need seems especially critical because of the explosion of technical vocabulary and the increase in the number of students for whom English is not a first language.

The challenges and the opportunities of expanding the instructional repertoire with informational text is an exciting one. This is a time that is awash in information without the necessary strategies for helping students use it most effectively. Scaffolding students' engagement with and control of informational text is an important challenge for this century.

REFERENCES

Alvermann, D. E., & Moore, D. W. (1991). Secondary school reading. In R. Barr, M. L. Kamil, P. B. Mosenthal, & P. D. Pearson (Eds.), *Handbook of reading research* (Vol. 2, pp. 951–983). New York: Longman.

Alvermann, D. E., Young, J. P., Weaver, D., Hinchman, K. A., Moore, D. W., Phelps, S. F., Thrash, E. C., & Zalewski, P. (1996). Middle and high school students' perceptions of how they experience text-based discussion: A multicase look. *Reading Research Quarterly, 31*, 244–267.

Armbruster, B., & Anderson, T. H. (1984). Studying. In P. D. Pearson, R. Barr, L. Kamil, & P. B. Mosenthal (Eds.), *Handbook of Reading Research* (Vol. 1, pp. 657–679). New York: Longman.

Anderson, T. H., & Armbruster, B. B. (1984). Content area textbooks. In R. C. Anderson, J. Osborn, & R. J. Tierney (Eds.), *Learning to read in American schools: Basal readers and content texts* (pp. 193–226). Hillsdale, NJ: Erlbaum.

Anderson, V., & Roit, M. (1993). Planning and implementing collaborative strategy instruction for delayed readers in grades 6–10. *Elementary School Journal, 94*, 121–137.

Beck, L. L., McKeown, M. G., Sandora, C., Kucan, L., & Worthy, J. (1996). Questioning the author: A yearlong classroom implementation to engage students with text. *Elementary School Journal, 96*(4), 385–414.

Bereiter, C., & Bird, M. (1985). Use of thinking aloud in identification and teaching of reading comprehension strategies. *Cognition and Instruction, 2*, 131–156.

Beyersdorfer, J. M. (1991). *Middle school students' strategies for selection of vocabulary in science texts.* Unpublished doctoral dissertation, National-Louis University, Evanston, IL.

Biddulph, F. J. (1993). *Clouds, rain and fog.* Bothell, WA: The Wright Group.

Birchell, B. (1997). *Rice.* Crystal Lake, IL: Rigby.

Blachowicz, C. L. Z. (1987). Vocabulary instruction: What goes on in the classroom? *Reading Teacher, 41*, 132–137.

Blachowicz, C. L. Z., & Fisher, P. (2000). Vocabulary instruction. In M. L. Kamil, P. B. Mosenthal, P. D., Pearson, & R. Barr (Eds.), *Handbook of reading research* (Vol. 3, pp. 503–524). White Plains, NY: Longman.

Blachowicz, C., & Ogle, D. (2001). *Reading comprehension: Strategies for independent learners.* New York: Guilford Press.

Block, C. (1993). Strategy instruction in a student-centered classroom. *Elementary School Journal, 94*(2), 137–153.

Block, C. C., & Mangieri, J. (1997). *Reason to read: Thinking strategies for life through literature* (Vol. 1). Reading, MA: Addison-Wesley.

Boran, K. (1999). *Rising from the ashes: A dramaturgical analysis of teacher change in a Chicago public high school.* Unpublished dissertation, National-Louis University, Evanston, IL.

Bruce, B. C. (1997). Literacy technologies: What stance should we take? *Journal of Literacy Research, 29*, 289–309.

Carr, E., & Ogle, D. (1987, April). K-W-L Plus: A strategy for comprehension and summarization. *Journal of Reading, 30*, 626–631.

Chambliss, M. (1995). Text cues and strategies successful readers use to construct the gist of lengthy written arguments. *Reading Research Quarterly, 30*, 778–807.

Davis, F. B. (1944). Fundamental factors in reading comprehension. *Psychometrika, 9*, 185–197.

272   PRESCHOOL, PRIMARY, AND INTERMEDIATE GRADES

Duke, N. K. (2000). 3–6 minutes per day: The scarcity of informational texts in first grade. *Reading Research Quarterly, 35*(2), 202–224.

Durkin, D. (1978–1979). What classroom observations reveal about reading comprehension instruction. *Reading Research Quarterly, 15*, 481–533.

Evans, K. (1996). A closer look at literature discussion groups: The influence of gender on student response and discourse. *New Advocate, 9*, 183–196.

Finesilver, M. (1994). *An investigation of three methods to improve vocabulary learning at the middle school level.* Unpublished doctoral dissertation, National-Louis University, Evanston, IL.

Fisher, P., Blachowicz, C. L. Z., & Smith, J. C. (1991). Vocabulary learning in literature discussion groups. In J. Zutell & S. McCormick (Eds.), *Learner factors/teacher factors: Issues in literacy research and instruction: 40th yearbook of the National Reading Conference* (pp. 201–209). Chicago: National Reading Conference.

Fogelberg, E., Hiller, C., & Ogle, D. (2000, May). *Reading informational text: Teacher collaboration in reading.* Paper presented at the annual convention of the International Reading Association, Indianapolis, IN.

Garner, R., & Gillingham, M. G. (1996). *Internet communication in six classrooms: Conversation across time, space and culture.* Mahwah, NJ: Erlbaum.

George, J., Moley, P., & Ogle, D. S. (1992). CCD: A model comprehension program for changing thinking and instruction. *Journal of Reading, 35*(7), 564–570.

Goldman, S. R. (1997). Learning from text: Reflections on the past and suggestions for the future. *Discourse Processes, 23*, 357–398.

Gribbin, M. (1996). *Big bugs.* New York: Ladybird Books.

Haggard, M. R. (1985). An interactive strategies approach to content reading. *Journal of Reading, 29*, 204–210.

Hartman, D. K., & Allison, J. (1996). Promoting inquiry-oriented discussions using multiple texts. In L. B. Gambrell & J. F. Almasi (Eds.), *Lively discussions! Fostering engaged reading* (pp. 106–133). Newark, DE: International Reading Association.

Heligman, D. (1996). *From caterpillar to butterfly.* New York: HarperCollins.

Hermanson, C., & Kerfoot, J. (1994). Technology assisted teaching: Is it getting results? *American Music Teacher, 43*, 20–23.

Hinchman, K. A., & Zalewski, P. (1996). Reading for success in a tenth-grade global studies class. *Journal of Literacy Research, 28*, 91–106.

Hoffman, J. V. (1992). Critical reading/thinking across the curriculum: Using I-Charts to support learning. *Language Arts, 69*, 121–127.

Illinois State Board of Education Reading. (1999). *Reading Report Card.* Springfield, IL: Author.

Jennings, J. H. (1991). A comparison of summary and journal writing as components of an interactive comprehension model. In J. Zutell & S. McCormick (Eds.), *Learner factors/teacher factors: Issues in literacy research and instruction.* Chicago: The National Reading Conference.

Lytle, S. L. (1982). *Exploring comprehension style: A study of twelfth grade readers' transactions with text.* Unpublished doctoral dissertation, University of Pennsylvania.

Many, J. (1996, January–March). Traversing the topical landscape: Exploring students' self-directed reading–writing–research processes. *Reading Research Quarterly, 31*(1), 12–35.

McMahon, S. L., & Raphael, T. E. (Eds.). (1995). *The book club connection: Literacy learning and classroom talk.* New York: Teachers College Press.

Meyer, B. J. F. (1975). *The organization of prose and its effects on memory.* Amsterdam: North-Holland.

Moje, E. B., & Fassio, K. (1997, December). *Revisioning the writer's workshop.* Paper presented at the annual meeting of the National Reading Conference, Scottsdale, AZ.

Moll, L. C., Tapia, J., & Whitmore, K. (1993). Living knowledge: The social distribution of cultural resources for thinking. In G. Solomon (Ed.), *Distributed cognitions: Psychological and educational considerations* (pp. 139–163). Cambridge, England: Cambridge University Press.

Moll, L. C., & Gonzalez, N. (1994). Lessons from research with language minority children. *Journal of Reading Behavior, 26,* 439–456.

Morrow, L. M., & Gambrell, L. B. (2000). Literature-based reading instruction. In M. L. Kamil, P. B. Mosenthal, P. D. Pearson, & R. Barr (Eds.), *Handbook of reading research* (Vol. 3, pp. 563–586). White Plains, NY: Longman.

National Assessment of Educational Progress (1999). *Our nation's report card.* Washington, DC: U.S. Department of Education.

Nist, S. L., & Simpson, M. L. (2000). College studying. In M. L. Kamil, P. B. Mosenthal, P. D. Pearson, & R. Barr (Eds.), *Handbook of reading research* (Vol. 3, pp. 645–666). Mahwah, NJ: Erlbaum.

O'Brien, D., Stewart, R., & Moje, E. (1995). Why content literacy is difficult to infuse into the secondary school: Complexities of curriculum, pedagogy, and school culture. *Reading Research Quarterly, 30,* 442–463.

Ogle, D. (1986). K-W-L: A teaching model that develops action reading of expository text. *Reading Teacher, 40,* 564–70.

Ogle, D. (1991). The Know, Want to Know, Learn strategy. In N. Muth (Ed.), *Children's comprehension of text: Research and practice* (pp. 22–33). Newark, DE: International Reading Association.

Ogle, D., & Hunter, K. (2000). Developing leadership in literacy at Amundson High School. In M. Bizar & R. Barr (Eds.), *Leadership in times of urban reform* (pp. 47–68). Mahwah, NJ: Erlbaum.

Ogle, D., & Waller, S. (2000, April). *Developing engaged readers of social studies and science.* Paper presented at the conference Teaching for Intelligence, Orlando, FL.

Olhausen, M. M., & Roller, C. M. (1988). The operation of text structure and content schemata in isolation and in interaction. *Reading Research Quarterly, 23,* 70–88.

Palmatier, R. (1973). A notemaking system for learning. *Journal of Reading, 17,* 36–39.

Perfetti, C. A., Britt, M. A., & Georgi, M. C. (1995). *Text-based learning and reasoning studies in history.* Hillsdale, NJ: Erlbaum.

Pressley, M., El-Dinary, R. B., Gaskins, I., Schinder, T., Bergman, J. L., Almasi, J., & Brown, R. (1992). Beyond direct exploration: Transactional instruction of reading comprehension strategies. *Elementary School Journal, 92,* 513–535.

Rosenblatt, L. M. (1978). *The reader, the text, the poem: The transactional theory of the literary work.* Carbondale, IL: Southern Illinois University Press.

Ruddell, M. R. (1994). Vocabulary knowledge and comprehension: A comprehensive-process view of complex literacy relationships. In R. B. Ruddell, M. R. Ruddell, & H. Singer (Eds.), *Theoretical models and processes of reading* (4th ed., pp. 414–447). Newark, DE: International Reading Association.

Sandved, K. (1996). *The butterfly alphabet.* New York: Scholastic.

Slater, W. H., Graves, M. F., & Piche, G. L. (1985). Effects of structural organizers on ninth-grade students' comprehension and recall of four patterns of expository text. *Reading Research Quarterly, 20,* 189–202.

Smith, M. C. (2000). The real-world reading practices of adults. *Journal of Literacy Research, 32*(1), 25–32.

Snowball, D. (1995, May). Building literacy skills through nonfiction. *Teaching K–8,* 62–63.

Stahl, S. A., Hynd, C. R., Britton, B. K., McNish, M. M., & Bosquet, D. (1966). What happens when students read multiple source documents in history? *Reading Research Quarterly, 31,* 430–456.

Stahl, S., & Vancil, S. (1986). Discussion is what makes semantic maps work in vocabulary instruction. *Reading Teacher, 40,* 62–69.

Steffensen, M. S., Goetz, E. T., & Cheng, X. (1999). A cross-linguistic perspective on imagery and affect in reading: Dual coding in Chinese and English. *Journal of Literacy Research, 31*(3), 293–319.

Stein, N. L., & Glenn, C. F. (1979). An analysis of story comprehension in elementary school children. In R. O. Freedle (Ed.), *New directions in discourse processing: Vol. 2. Advances in discourse processes* (pp. 53–120). Norwood, NJ: Ablex.

Stein, N. L., & Policastro, M. (1984). The concept of a story: A comparison between children's and teachers' viewpoints. In H. Mandl, N. L. Stein, & T. Trabasso (Eds.), *Learning and comprehension of text* (pp. 113–155). Hillsdale, NJ: Erlbaum.

Still, J. (1991). *Amazing butterflies and moths.* New York: Knopf.

Taylor, B. M., & Beach, R. W. (1984). The effects of text structure instruction on middle-grade students' comprehension and production of expository text. *Reading Research Quarterly, 19,* 134–146.

Tierney, R., LaZansky, J., & Schallert, D. (1982). *Secondary students' use of social studies and biology texts.* Garden City, NY: National Institute of Education.

Valencia, S. W., & Wixson, K. K. (2000). Policy oriented research on literacy standards. In M. L. Kamil, P. B. Mosenthal, P. D. Pearson, & R. Barr (Eds.), *Handbook of reading research* (Vol. 3, pp. 909–936). White Plains, NY: Longman.

van den Broek, P., & Kremer, K. E. (2000). The mind in action: What it means to comprehend during reading. In B. M. Taylor, M. F. Graves, & P. van den Broek (Eds.), *Reading for meaning: Fostering comprehension in the middle grades* (pp. 1–31). Newark, DE: International Reading Association.

Vaughan, J. L.. & Estes, T. H. (1986). *Reading and reasoning beyond the primary grades.* Boston: Allyn & Bacon.

Watts, S. M. (1995). Vocabulary instruction during reading lessons in six classrooms. *Journal of Reading Behavior, 27,* 399–424.

18

Instructional Contexts for Reading Engagement

JOHN T. GUTHRIE
SEVGI OZGUNGOR

In our view, reading comprehension is learned from long-term engagement in reading. When do we mean by reading engagement? When students are using what they already know to build new understandings of the texts they read, they are engaged. When readers use cognitive strategies such as summarizing and self-checking, they are engaged. When students have the desire to comprehend and to share literacy socially in a classroom community, they are engaged. In other words, engaged readers are motivated and strategic in their processes of constructing new knowledge from text.

Collaboratively with teachers, we have developed a reading framework to initiate and sustain reading engagement. The framework is named "concept-oriented reading instruction" (CORI), and it has been found to be successful with low-achieving, multicultural students in the later elementary grades. We first present an example of an 8-week unit of CORI in one third-grade classroom. Second, we present the principles that account for the effectiveness of CORI. We have used this framework with different grades and different schools, and we present the common themes among these applications. Third, we present evidence from longitudinal and cross-sectional studies of CORI, showing its benefits for reading comprehension, reading motivation, and knowledge acquisition. Fourth, we present the implications of this knowledge base for teachers.

AN EXAMPLE OF ONE UNIT OF CORI

Background

This 8-week unit was taught in grade 3 of a Chapter I school with a multicultural population including African American, Hispanic, Asian, and white students. The principal and the media specialists were supportive of Carla Pyne, the third-grade teacher, when she volunteered to teach CORI at the grade 3 level. The principal expected Carla to teach to the goals required in the district but permitted her to use trade books as a primary source of instructional materials rather than the basal reading program. Carla planned her unit collaboratively with the media specialists and with the help of discussions with another third-grade teacher in a different school.

CORI units are built around a large knowledge goal, such as adaptation within life sciences, the solar system within earth sciences, or simple machines in the physical sciences. The knowledge goal for this unit was drawn from the district's science objectives for grade 3. It consisted of adaptation and the interdependence of life, which is a benchmark in the American Association for the Advancement of Science (AAAS) goals. In the context of this knowledge goal, the following reading strategies were taught (1) questioning, (2) activating background knowledge, (3) searching for information, (4) summarizing, (5) comprehension monitoring, and (6) organizing with concept mapping. Instruction followed the four phases of CORI, which consists of (1) observe and personalize, (2) search and retrieve, (3) comprehend and integrate, and (4) communicate to others. These phases are described next.

Observe and Personalize

Carla Pyne decided to organize her reading instruction around the knowledge theme of adaptation. To make this concrete for third graders, she had a bird study unit through which students would learn about birds, their characteristics, and how they survive. In September, as school began, children made bird feeders out of plastic milk bottles and placed them in a tree visible from the classroom. Ms. Pyne formed a 120–minute integrated reading and science period. During the integrated period, students identified and charted birds and their feeding habits and recorded their preferences for different foods. Toward the end of the first week, Carla held a brainstorming session in which students raised their questions about birds. The students wrote their questions in their journals and each chose one question to place on the classroom bulletin board. The teacher taught students how to write a complete interrogative sentence and punctuate it properly. With excitement and pride, students signed their questions and posted them. Questions such as "Where do birds go in winter?" and "How do birds make nests?" became the goals for learning.

Parallel to these science activities, students read stories during this first week of the unit. They read *Owl Moon* by Jane Yolen, which describes owl watching by a child and her grandfather at night. They recorded their thoughts and reactions in a journal. They read *Urban Roost* portraying nesting and bird life in the city. In their journals, students recorded the events and plots of these books, accompanied by reflections on their own experiences. By the end of this initial "observe and personalize" phase toward the close of the first week, students were highly motivated. They had posted their questions, and they wanted to answer them. Having observed birds with the naked eye and through binocular, they were curious about birds' beaks, colors, and migration. Their background knowledge was activated as they shared what they knew to explain the bird behaviors they could see. Having also read relatively simple enjoyable narratives, the stage was set for reading to learn more complex conceptual knowledge.

Search and Retrieve

As the second week began, the teacher entered the phase of searching and retrieving. With the students she took a step back. They had observed birds and written their questions in their journals. Each student had proudly posted one of the questions on the bulletin board. Now they would read to answer their questions and go beyond them to learn more about how birds survive.

With these prevailing knowledge goals in mind, Carla provided instruction on the reading strategy of searching for information. She gave each student a copy of *Birds: The Young Scientist Investigates*, a 25-page trade book on all aspects of birds. Together she and her class identified the table of contents, index, glossary, illustrations, captions, diagrams, graphs, and text in the book. They identified what each element of the expository text communicates to the reader. They compared and contrasted them. Next, students looked at a second expository text, *Birds of a Feather*. They identified the same structural elements of this information book.

The teacher provided direct instruction on how to search for information in an expository book. First, she selected one question from the student list on the bulletin board: "Why do birds sing?" She demonstrated how she might use the table of contents and index to locate relevant text. She showed how she would combine information from two sections in the book to answer this question. Carla led all the students to answer the same question using various texts and structural elements of information texts. They shared their findings in a whole-class discussion. Then she assigned a different question to each team, and the team members collaborated to use the two information books to form answers. After 30 minutes, teams shared their relevant information with the whole class. The teacher charted the elements of the information books that were used (e.g., index), and a class discussion ensued about the benefits of the different features, such as index and captions.

As students learned the basis of searching for information, the teacher added three additional information books to each team's collection, including *Birds* by Gill, *The Bird Atlas*, and *The Rookie Read-About Books*. The difficulty levels ranged from grades 1–4, permitting all students to locate text within their decodable levels. Next, Carla guided the students to answer their own questions from the bulletin board or their journals using the multiple texts available. At this stage, it became necessary to teach note taking. Carla taught students to identify important information in text, to paraphrase in their words, and to combine information from different texts on the same question. Students worked daily for 30 to 40 minutes reading information, taking notes, and learning the information to answer all of their questions.

Toward the end of the third week of the unit, after students had gained familiarity and confidence with information books, the teacher introduced a novel, *White Bird* by Clyde Robert Bulla. In this chapter book, a boy finds a bird with a broken wing and nurses it to health but also faces antagonists who want to steal his bird. For 30 to 40 minutes daily, students read chapters as the teacher helped them chart the plot in their journals. Character study was emphasized, and were encouraged to write personal reactions to text in their journals every other day.

Comprehend and Integrate

By the third week, students had conducted initial observations, formed questions that were motivating for them, learned about the structures of information books, and begun taking notes. However, students' comprehension of the information books was limited. Carla provided direct instruction in gaining the main idea from paragraphs and summarizing. She contextualized this lesson within a student's question and a text. Taking the student question, "Why do some birds have big beaks and others have little beaks?" Carla identified one paragraph on beaks in one information book. She modeled how to summarize this paragraph by: (1) identifying important phrases, (2) eliminating less important information, and (3) integrating information into a synthesis statement. She assigned each student the same new paragraph, and all attempted to complete the processes as she had done. Students shared their results and then tackled a new paragraph. On the following day, Carla asked each student to locate a paragraph relevant to one of their questions. All students wrote summaries of the paragraph, and several students presented their summaries to the class. This process represents peer modeling, which enables other students to see a realistic standard of summarizing performance for themselves. Next, the teacher asked students to write a paragraph summarizing two pages in their journals based on notes taken from information books. Throughout this week, they read, summarized, and took notes from information books for 30 to 40 minutes daily.

In the meantime, students had been reading *White Bird* and recording the actions of the characters in their journals. The teacher extended her summarizing lesson to this novel by asking students to first summarize one paragraph that they all selected together. Next, she raised the summarizing activity to the level of a chapter within the novel. This task posed challenges for locating important points, and synthesizing identified materials. They continued reading to summarize sections of this novel for 30 to 40 minutes daily. Although half of the class improved, the other half needed continuing support on this cognitive reading comprehension strategy.

To reinvigorate the students' reading motivation, Carla provided another "hands-on" science activity. The class went out to the school yard, and each student collected the materials to build a bird's nest, including grasses, twigs, fur, leaves, and dirt or clay. Students brought these materials in plastic containers to the classroom and endeavored to build a bird's nest. Although some students succeeded, other students' nests never "held together." Students concluded that "birds have to be pretty smart to a build a home."

By the sixth week, the students had gained a wealth of specific concepts, propositions, and information about birds. But the teacher was not satisfied that the students had been thinking carefully. She saw gaps in their information. What they had read was not always connected with their questions and their learning goals. Consequently, she attempted to teach comprehension monitoring. She wanted students to keep their minds on their main knowledge goal and to self-check themselves as they read. At the same time, she wanted them to learn how to fix up their misunderstandings or fill in gaps in their knowledge.

In the whole-class lesson on comprehension monitoring, Carla first established a complex knowledge goal—adaptation. Adaptation consists of feeding, defense, reproduction, shelter, and specific characteristics of birds that enable them to survive in their habitat. Carla requested that each team identify a bird they had not already learned about. Different teams located the eagle, falcon, flamingo, blue jay, hummingbird, and Baltimore oriole. Each team was instructed to make a chart on the adaptation of their bird and to read information books to complete the chart thoroughly. They were encouraged to discuss information they had, information they needed, and texts that were useful in their chart building. This procedure enabled students to become aware of the knowledge required, the gaps in information, and the mapping of texts toward their knowledge goal. The teacher believed this process fostered self-checking and repair of misunderstanding or lack of knowledge in a constructive way. She guided students to read and draw concept maps for 40 to 50 minutes daily during the week.

To complement learning from texts, students started a new science activity. The teacher directed students in the process of dissecting owl pellets. They classified the contents and meticulously placed them on display boards. Students were amazed to see skulls of voles and the teeth of rodents in these pellets. This activity sustained motivation for reading and learning about the full range of survival techniques in birds.

To help students monitor their comprehension more fully, the teacher formed teams on the following aspects of adaptation: (1) feeding , (2) breeding, (3) defense, (4) shelter, and (5) habitat. Team members studied all birds and learned about how all adaptations supported these different functions. Then she initiated a new "invent a bird" activity. Students were regrouped, with one expert from each of the preceding groups. The new teams identified a habitat of their own choice (i.e., the snowy peak of Mount Everest or the glen behind the school). They proceeded to "build a bird" that was fully adapted to this habitat. This activity required the reading strategies of comprehension monitoring, summarizing, questioning, and reactivating background knowledge.

The knowledge goal for the last phase of "comprehend and integrate" was "threats to birds' survival." In expository trade books, students located a range of threats such as water pollution (oil spills that poison fish and endanger birds), habitat destruction (cutting the trees that nests are in), and wetlands loss (putting in roads where ducks used to swim). To help students organize this plethora of information, Carla taught organization through concept mapping. In her whole-class activity, she built a concept map on the chalkboard with content volunteered by students. In addition, students named the types of connections among the nodes in the concept map. For instance, water pollution is an abstract concept (poisoned streams are a "type of" water pollution). This map took the form of a pyramid, with the abstract concept of "threats to birds' survival" at the top and more specific concepts, in increasing detail, toward the middle and bottom of the pyramid.

Next, the teacher gave students practice in drawing a concept map. Students chose a section of a science trade book (1–2 pages) relevant to one of their original questions. They drew a pyramid map of the section, and some students shared their maps with the whole class. Carla showed students that there are many types of graphic organizers. She reminded them that they had made a timeline of the events in the chapter book *White Bird*. This is a graphic organizer for the chronology in that narrative. Students made posters of the ingredients in owl pellets, which was a graphic organizer for contents of the pellet. The graphic pyramids showed the organization of knowledge from books. Students seemed to understand that the same information could be displayed in a linear text or in a spatially organized graphic structure.

Communicate to Others

As a culminating activity for the unit, the teacher gave students an opportunity to teach what they had learned to other students. The class identified one grade 2 classroom as the audience for their work. Each team prepared a 20-minute multimedia presentation for the audience. One team elected to present a poster display of three charts. A second team decided to make a videotape of team members explaining their invented bird. A third team used a multimedia computer program titled "On the Brink." (This program permits students to use pictures and audio from existing menus and to enter their own text.) Two other teams elected to make a booklet with separate "chapters" by each team member containing illustrations and explanations about birds, their survival, and their threats. Teams were free to include literary materials such as poems or stories if they chose. Across one week, these reports were given daily to the chosen second-grade classroom. Students returning from their grade 2 presentations were heard to exlaim, "I'm a teacher now!" and "They liked my story," and "They think I'm an expert on birds."

As the unit closed at the end of Week 8, Ms. Pyne looked back in amazement and gratification. She was surprised that students had been able to learn to think and read at a high level. She was proud that these third graders had become such self-directed learners. She was optimistic about the next CORI unit she would teach, and her planning for it had already begun.

CONTEXTUAL FEATURES OF CORI

The framework teachers use for teaching CORI is the following: (1) observe and personalize, (2) search and retrieve, (3) comprehend and integrate, and (4) communicate to others. Throughout these phases, teachers provide explicit teaching of strategies mentioned previously, including activating background knowledge, self-questioning, summarizing, comprehension monitoring, and integrating thorough concept mapping. This direct instruction usually follows the traditional emphasis on modeling, scaffolding, guided practice, and independent use of the strategies. What is most salient about CORI is that the direct instruction of reading strategies is placed in a context. This context consists of supports for both the cognitive and motivational aspects of reading engagement. We believe that direct instruction may be limited in effectiveness if students are not sufficiently motivated to gain mastery of the strategies and apply them frequently (Guthrie & Cox, in press). Therefore, we provide five vitally important contextual features to support strategy instruction, including the following: (1) learning and knowledge goals, (2) real-world interactions, (3) autonomy support, (4) collaboration support, and (5) interesting texts.

Learning and Knowledge Goals

The first feature of the CORI context refers to the goals of the instructional unit. In CORI the most prominent goals are the combination of content knowledge and reading comprehension. First, a knowledge goal in science or social studies is established. This goal should agree with state, district, and school priorities. For example, a life science goal of adaptation or an earth science goal of solar systems may be taught. This becomes a conceptual theme that is learned in depth over an extended period of time. The in-depth knowledge domain enables students to become experts. Learning cognitive strategies is hastened when students possess a rich bank of background information to which they can apply the strategies. Comprehension strategy instruction, such as summarizing, is embedded within a single topic domain such as adaptation. This enables students to build on prior knowledge easily and to apply newly learned strategies to a familiar subject matter (Anderson & Pearson, 1984).

The knowledge goals that form the conceptual theme in CORI are different from the performance goals often used in competitive learning environments. Performance goals refer to objectives in the classroom that are defined by a point system, competition system, or reward structure. If teachers emphasize that 10 points can be obtained by answering 10 questions correctly on a story, a performance goal is prevalent in the classroom. Under the condition of performance goals, students are likely to adapt themselves quickly. With performance goals, students seek recognition and competitive advantage whenever possible. They use strategies for winning the game that the teacher has announced. Although some of these strategies, such as focused effort, will be beneficial, many strategies in a performance orientation are disadvantageous. When they hold performance goals most prominently, students are likely to take short cuts, to stop working when the performance goal has been accomplished (the points have been won), to copy the work of other students, or to procrastinate so they will avoid appearing to be inept to their peers. In sum, knowledge goals foster strategy use, whereas performance goals are not likely to increase frequent use of reading comprehension strategies. In addition, strategies as teaching goals (e.g., comprehension monitoring as a goal for the week) are abstract and not inherently motivating. Therefore, CORI begins with knowledge goals and situates the critically important reading comprehension strategies within a rich subject-matter domain.

Real-World Interaction

The second critical ingredient of the CORI context is real-world interaction in which students observe or manipulate some object or event. In science, this may be a hands-on activity, such as observing birds feeding or dissecting owl pellets. In history, this may be a reenactment of an event or speech from a historical period. There are two cognitive benefits to initiating instruction in reading with real-world interaction. First, real-world interaction is exciting and attention-grabbing for students. During real-world interaction, students automatically perform the extremely vital process of activating background knowledge. They think about what they already know without being asked or prompted. For example, students who are observing a reptile, such as a turtle, in a life science unit on vertebrates will frequently describe experiences they have had or information they possess about turtles. As they keenly observe this turtle or one of its physical features, such as its bony shell, students spontaneously organize what they already hold in memory. In the real-world interaction activities of CORI, students are asked not only to observe but also to draw and to write their current observations. At a later point in the unit, when students are asked to read texts (e.g., about birds), their background knowledge will have been elicited, organized, and written in a form that is immediately applicable to the new text they will be learning from. Therefore, the real-world interaction is a powerful probe into students' memories. It primes them into a state of readiness for new learning from text.

Real-world interaction has another impressive cognitive benefit. Many teachers report that students ask a lot of questions during the hands-on activity. Whether it takes the form of hands-on science activities, historial reenactments, or discussions with a culturally diverse visitor to the classroom, real-world interaction is an opportunity for questioning. In studies of science or other subjects, students in real-world interaction ask more fully formed, sophisticated, generative questions than other students (Ross, 1988). During CORI, when students engage in a hands-on science activity such as dissecting an owl pellet, they ask a deluge of questions, such as, "How does an owl see at night?" "Can it hear its prey?" and "Where does it sleep?" These questions are vital beginning points in the learning process. In CORI, teachers have students write their questions on classroom walls and in student journals. Student questions become guidelines for reading, writing, and literacy activities. Real-world interactions serve to set the stage for text and create a powerful set of purposes for the difficult challenge of reading to learn from expository text. It is evident that the contextual feature of real-world interaction helps students get started in using two of the key strategies for reading, activating background knowledge and self-questioning. With help from the teacher during the reading process, these cognitive strategies can continue and be applied directly to texts.

Real-world interaction influences motivation for reading, as well as cognitive strategies. Student participation in observing an authentic object, such as a bird's nest, or an event, such as a reenacted speech by a historical figure, is often an intrinsically motivated behavior. Students will do it keenly of their own accord. They enjoy it. As students perform the observing activity in a science inquiry unit, they gain a sense of ownership. If they have noticed, for example, that the bird's feet are webbed, they will adopt this information as their own personal knowledge. When they have observed a phenomenon, students take ownership of the information. This sense of perceived control over their knowledge and their learning is integral to intrinsic motivation (Skinner, Wellborn, & Connell, 1990).

The significance of the motivational experience in real-world interaction is that these motivations can be transferred to kindred texts. If students are provided books or multimedia that are readable and related to their real-world experience, they will be motivated to read. Such texts afford an extension of the intrinsically motivated experience of observing a science object or reenacting a historical event. Reading the text becomes intrinsically motivating, just as the real-world interaction was.

One benefit of real-world interaction is that it provides energy for the difficult work of learning cognitive strategies. Strategies such as getting the main idea from paragraphs, monitoring comprehension, and integrating information across texts require effort, energy, and persistence. If students are intrinsically motivated to gain the knowledge and understanding, they will put forth the effort to learn and to use the effective strategies. Intrinsic motivation stemming originally from real-world interaction and from answering the questions related to those interactions can provide a continuing purpose for using strategies that will accelerate cognitive parts of learning to comprehend.

Autonomy Support

The third critical ingredient of the CORI context is autonomy support, which refers to enabling students to make meaningful choices and to take control of their learning and reading. The process of autonomy support directly contributes to the use of cognitive strategies in several ways. First, each student's experience is distinctive. All students may recall their own information and apply it in their own ways to observations or to the text. As students use their own recalled knowledge, they take ownership of the new information connected to their knowledge. The sense of ownership of new knowledge being gained is a motivator for the use of strategies, such as summarizing, which are central to reading comprehension.

Autonomy support is essential to self-questioning. Students should be encouraged to form questions they are interested in and believe are important. In the example, Carla Pyne had students write and post their questions about birds. Of course, the teacher may shape the form of the questions and the direct content to important themes. However, if students believe their questions are personally significant, the question will take on a sense of urgency. If students are reading to answer their own personally formed questions, they will activate their knowledge, summarize, monitor comprehension, and infer more frequently than if they have little autonomy. When the questions are posed by the teacher, the text is supplied by the teacher, and the task is teacher controlled, students' motivation for using strategies will be dramatically reduced. The cognitive strategies of gaining the main idea, comprehension monitoring, and inferring depend on the student's desire to understand the text content.

Suppose students have been afforded a small portion of autonomy in a reading activity. The teacher has given students the opportunity to phrase their own three or four questions and to locate two or three sections of text relevant to those questions. This is motivating. In this condition, students will have high needs for comprehension monitoring. Students will want to determine whether they are selecting appropriate texts. They will need to decide whether they are gaining information from those texts that will answer their questions. The use of strategies is motivated because the students have a personal investment in learning and answering their personally significant questions. Consequently, the condition of autonomy support has created the motivation for using strategies that are essential for reading comprehension. In their essence, cognitive strategies are purposeful and intentional; students must want to use them and know when to use them. To be effective, strategies must be used on certain occasions and avoided on other occasions when they are not valuable. Teachers should provide a clear but limited set of choices and options that enable students to make decisions such as "Do I summarize now?" "Should I spend time connecting information from these two paragraphs now?" "Have I learned everything that is available for me from this text?" Autonomy support prepares the stage for the use of comprehension strategies.

Collaboration Support

The fourth ingredient of CORI context is collaboration support. In the CORI program, students spend approximately equal amounts of time working individually, in pairs, and in teams of three to six. In the CORI phase of comprehend and integrate, when students have located texts relevant to the conceptual theme being studied and to the questions they have posed, collaboration support can be provided (Guthrie & McCann, 1996). For example, teachers may ask students to select partners and to share their background knowledge about the specific texts they are reading with their partners. This request to communicate is automatically a request to recall what they already know. Teachers may ask students to share their questions about the topic with another student. This provides an audience for the questions. Peers are a source of feedback about the content and relevance of the goals students have set for themselves in the form of questions. In the CORI example, Carla Pyne formed teams to take responsibility for learning different subtopics. This procedue can provide a sense of belonging and importance that is integral to intrinsic motivation (Ryan & Deci, 2000). If students believe that they will receive assistance from peers or from the teacher, they will take the risk of trying to use a difficult strategy, such as checking their own understanding or drawing difficult inferences from a text. Thus collaboration support provides a protection against failure that enables students to take the necessary risk to try a new strategy or to use two strategies at the same time.

The process of comprehension monitoring can be aided by collaboration. If two students are requested to share their understanding and to monitor each other's comprehension of a text, strategy use is easier. If one student monitors the text comprehension of another student, the comprehension monitoring process is externalized, allowing both students to see it and discuss it. After discussing the self-monitoring activities during reading, students can more easily perform this strategy independently under their own guidance. Finally, collaboration increases the student commitment to the goals of understanding texts. If students have personal responsibility for part of a group goal, the personal goal for understanding the text and learning the content will be more salient, more enduring, and more sustainable than if they possess solely individual goals for their learning activities. Under collaborative conditions, students' effort and energy devoted to the strategy learning process will be higher than under conditions of exclusively isolated individual reading activities. In the example, students collaborated in reading, note taking, and discussing to "invent a bird" in five 60-minute periods.

Interesting Text

The fifth feature of context in CORI is interesting texts. By this phrase, we refer to trade books, Internet Web sites, and a diversity of materials that are literary or informative. To be regarded as interesting, these materials must be viewed as comprehensible by students. Texts that are so difficult that they are impossible to understand cannot be attractive or interesting. In addition, to be judged as interesting, the materials should be relevant to the intrinsically motivating activities that occur in the real-world-interaction section of CORI. Materials should have relevance to the topic students have selected to read and learn in detail. If students find that texts are too difficult, irrelevant, or remote from their self-selected topics for reading, they will not be judged as interesting.

An abundance of interesting texts in the classroom fosters the use of all of the cognitive strategies. For example, the strategy of activating background knowledge is more likely to occur with interesting than uninteresting texts. Students' use of self-questioning strategies will occur if the texts are appealing and contain content pertinent to their self-stated learning goals. Summarizing and seeking main ideas in texts will be done naturally if students are immersed in the process of choosing among trade books, text selections, or Internet resources for learning. Finally, comprehension monitoring is self-evidently important when students are using multiple resources for reading. They must decide when they have learned all that is relevant from one text and must make a new selection according to their goals and knowledge needs. This is a relatively advanced form of comprehension monitoring. However, this process of text selection and monitoring can be initiated for students at all comprehension achievement levels. The contribution of an abundance of "interesting texts" to increasing reading comprehension has been documented. In a study of 32 schools in Maryland, Guthrie, Schafer, Von Secker, and Alban (2000) found that an abundance of trade books and community resources and the use of multimedia in the classroom predicted gains in statewide tests of reading, writing, and science.

Summary of Contextual Features of CORI

We have proposed that there are five contextual features of CORI. These factors enable students to learn reading comprehension. These five features are: (1) knowledge goals, (2) real-world interaction, (3) autonomy support, (4) collaboration support, and (5) interesting texts. These qualities of the classroom environment can be translated in terms of specific activities for all students. As students perform these activities, they learn reading comprehension. Comprehension of texts is accelerated in this context because comprehension depends on both cognitive strategies and motivation, which are fostered by these contextual features. We have illustrated that the contextual feature of real-world interaction increases the cognitive strategy of activating background knowledge and self-questioning. At the same time, real-world interaction is intrinsically motivating and will enhance motivation for reading text that is related to those intrinsically motivated behaviors. Therefore, real-world interaction contributes simultaneously to the cognitive and motivational parts of reading comprehension. A similar story can be told for all of the contextual features. Although these aspects of the instructional context are challenging for some teachers, they are exceptionally important for students in the acquisition of comprehension.

EVIDENCE FOR BENEFITS OF CORI

To evaluate the impact of CORI on reading comprehension, we performed several experiments. Students who received CORI were compared with other students within the same schools who had received traditional reading and science instruction. To examine whether CORI increased reading comprehension, we used measures of expository text comprehension, narrative text comprehension, and strategies for learning from multiple texts. In order to determine whether students increased in motivation and in reading engagement, we used measures from a questionnaire and a performance assessment of engaged reading activity. Reporting the effects of this instruction on reading comprehension, we used effect sizes that showed the differences between experimental and comparison groups relative to differences within groups. An effect size of .50 signifies that the experimental group was one half (.5) of a standard deviation higher than the comparison group. All of the effect sizes reported here were significant at $p < .05$.

Benefits of CORI for Text Comprehension

We compared CORI students with traditional students on their ability to answer specific questions about main ideas in information text and the plot or character in narrative text. CORI students were significantly higher than traditional students in these text comprehension tasks, with an effect size of .51 for grade 5 students (Guthrie et al., 1998). In a second study, CORI students were compared with traditional students in reading comprehension on material within the topic (life science) that they had studied and also on a new knowledge domain (earth science). CORI students were higher than traditional students on comprehending information texts in the familiar domain, with an effect size of .40. CORI students were higher than traditional students on comprehending information texts in the new domain, with an effect size of .18. CORI students were higher than traditional students on narrative comprehension in the familiar domain, with an effect size of .50, and CORI students surpassed traditional students in narrative comprehension in a new domain, with an effect size of .38 (Guthrie, Anderson, Alao, & Rinehart, 1999).

Benefits of CORI for Comprehending and Integrating Multiple Texts

In today's classrooms, many students read a variety of books and are expected to combine information from them. We examined whether CORI students were successful in reading to locate information, in comprehending specific important texts, and in integrating across multiple sources. In a performance assessment requiring these comprehension strategies, CORI students surpassed the traditionally instructed students, with an effect size of .76 for grade 3 and 1.08 for grade 5. Students in the CORI group were higher in judging which texts were relevant to the topic of study (effect size = .90). They were higher in their reasoning for choosing particular texts for extended reading (effect size = .38) and in the quality of the notes they took while reading multiple texts (effect size = .85; Guthrie et al., 1998). Therefore, in experimental comparisons, CORI students were higher than traditionally instructed students in information text comprehension, narrative text comprehension, and use of strategies for learning from multiple texts over an extended period of time.

Benefits of CORI for Reading Motivation

In investigating whether CORI students increased in motivation for reading, we made several comparisons. In one study, we administered a reading motivation questionnaire to all students following instruction at the end of the academic year. CORI students were higher than traditional students on curiosity (effect size = .86) and involvement in reading (effect size = .33), which are central to intrinsic motivation. It is evident that CORI students became more intrinsically motivated in reading as a result of their year-long experience with this integrated instruction.

Another indicator of motivation is students' self-reported use of strategies during a range of reading activities. In general, students who report using strategies widely are very likely to be intrinsically motivated, and students who report that they use strategies rarely are very likely to be unmotivated. CORI students were much more likely to report using strategies frequently than were traditional students at the end of the academic year. The effect size showing the amount of CORI impact was .64 for grade 3 and .43 for grade 5. When covariates were added to these effect sizes, they increased significantly. For example, the effect of CORI on curiosity had an effect size of 1.94 with covariates added. In addition, the effect of CORI on strategy use had an effect size of 1.71 with covariates added. This indicates that when students were statistically equated for their level at the beginning of the year, CORI had an exceptionally large effect on these motivation indicators (Guthrie, Wigfield, & Von Secker, 2000). We concluded from these findings that CORI increased reading comprehension in comparison with traditional instruction. The benefits of this instructional approach were evident for both aspects of engaged reading. CORI improved the strategies necessary for comprehension and increased motivations that serve to energize and direct the use of those reading strategies.

IMPLICATIONS OF THIS RESEARCH
FOR CLASSROOM TEACHERS

Our research has two implications for teachers. The first is for teachers' thinking. The second is for teachers' practice in the classroom. First, we need to think a bit differently about reading comprehension instruction. Reading comprehension is deeply dependent on motivation. Students have to be highly motivated over a long time to learn the complex cognitive strategies of good comprehension. Motivation cannot be a mere preliminary to the planning of teaching because motivation is not marginal. It is central. Students have to be reading independently and using strategies effectively to become good comprehenders. This requires motivation over time. Because of the need for extended engaged reading, teachers should ask, "How can I sustain long-term engaged reading in my classroom?" Teachers should think of sustained engaged reading as a teaching goal.

Teachers often ask, "How do I teach CORI?" This is our second implication. We have provided a guide that any teacher can use to teach a CORI unit in the classroom (Guthrie, Cox, Knowles, Buehl, Mazzoni, & Fasculo, 2000). Many teachers have used a planning guide to organize their CORI teaching. The guide covers the four phases described previously: observe and personalize, search and retrieve, comprehend and integrate, and communicate to others. These are given as rows in a chart. For each phase, teachers identify the following elements: *Goals, Student Activities Teacher Approaches*, and *Resources*. These are columns in the planning guide (see Guthrie et al., 2000a). In planning, teachers designed an 8-week unit like the one described previously. Over one year, some teachers have taught three 8-week units. The rest of the year was allocated to testing or to specific topics in the curriculum that were not covered in the units but were required in the school.

When teachers write the *goals* of the unit, they form both knowledge goals and reading goals. The knowledge goals may be science goals, such as "adaptation" or "solar system," or the goals may be social science goals, such as "Westward expansion" or "American colonies." In the *student activities* section of the planning guide, teachers make sure they provide for real-world interactions. These might be hands-on science activities, or enactments of a narrative book. Teachers are creative in designing these experiences. This is crucial support for motivation.

In thinking about student activities and *teacher approaches*, teachers think about providing autonomy support. They ask, "Where can I give students academically meaningful choices?" Helping students choose which subtopic to study closely or which text to use is important. Guided choice undergirds students' motivation and sense of self-efficacy as readers.

Teachers plan explicitly to use a lot of interesting texts. These are trade books and other *resources* at the students' level of difficulty. The reading level must be low enough so students can use them independently or with peer support. Some texts must be provided to challenge the higher readers, too. Irrespective of the students' reading levels, the texts must be conceptually informative.

Finally, teachers plan for collaboration support. By forming pairs of students for observing or for reading, teachers increase students' motivation and extend their engaged reading. By forming teams based on a similar interest, teachers can help students read extensively. For example, students who want to observe the moon closely or find out about the sun will work productively together to read texts on those topics. With encouragement, students will spur each other to get more engaged in reading to learn.

Teachers also plan to teach reading strategies. We know from other research that strategies such as summarizing are crucial and are not learned easily. Therefore, direct lessons at prescribed times are needed. However, these lessons can be related to the conceptual goal and to the texts being used in the CORI unit. In fact, embedding these strategy lessons in the context of conceptual goals and motivation support is essential. Engaged reading has roots in both cognitive development (learning strategies to gain knowledge) and motivational development (gaining personal interests and desire to learn about topics).

CONCLUSION

Keeping up with the research literature is a challenge for researchers and teachers alike. In this chapter, we first provided an example of a research-based intervention, concept-oriented reading instruction (CORI). This example shows our belief that reading comprehension depends on a mixture of motivational support and cognitive strategies instruction. The first step in motivating students is to provide a knowledge goal for reading. The following steps are assuring real-world interactions, autonomy support, interesting texts, and collaboration support. We showed how these elements can work together in reading comprehension instruction. When teaching has these qualities, students become deeply engaged in reading. We reported several studies that document the benefit of CORI for reading comprehension, reading motivation, and science knowledge. These gains occurred for traditionally low-achieving students in Chapter I schools. Therefore, we suggest that teachers can confidently try the CORI framework in their own classrooms.

REFERENCES

Anderson, R. C., & Pearson, P. D. (1984). A schema-theoretic view of basic processes in reading. In R. Barr, M. L. Kamil, & P. Mosenthal (Eds.), *Handbook of reading research* (pp. 255–291). New York: Longman.

Bash, B. (1990). *Urban roost*. San Francisco: Sierra Club Books.

Guthrie, J. T., Anderson, E., Alao, S., & Rinehart, J. (1999). Influences of concept-oriented reading instruction on strategy use and conceptual learning from text. *Elementary School Journal, 99*(4), 343–366.

Guthrie, J. T., & Cox, K. E. (in press). Classroom conditions for motivation and engagement in reading. *Educational Psychology Review*.

Guthrie, J. T., Cox, K. E., Knowles, K. T., Buehl, M., Mazzoni, S., & Fasculo, L. (2000). Building toward coherent instruction. In L. Baker, M. J. Dreher, & J. T. Guthrie (Eds.), *Engaging young readers: Promoting achievement and motivation* (pp. 209–237). New York: Guilford Press.

Guthrie, J. T., & McCann, A. D. (1996). Idea circles: Peer collaborations for conceptual learning. In L. Gambrell & J. Almasi (Eds.), *Lively discussions!* (pp. 87–105). Newark, DE: International Reading Association.

Guthrie, J. T., Schafer, W. D., Von Secker, C., & Alban, T. (2000). Contributions of integrated reading instruction and text resources to achievement and engagement in a statewide school improvement program. *Journal of Educational Research, 93*, 211–226.

Guthrie, J. T., Van Meter, P., Hancock, G. R., McCann, A., Anderson, E., & Alao, S. (1998). Does Concept-Oriented Reading Instruction increase strategy use and conceptual learning from text? *Journal of Educational Psychology, 90*(2), 261–278.

Guthrie, J. T., Wigfield, A., & Von Secker, C. (2000). Effects of integrated instruction on motivation and strategy use in reading. *Journal of Educational Psychology, 92*(2), 331–341.

Ross, J. A. (1988). Controlling variables: A meta-analysis of training studies. *Review of Educational Research, 58*, 405–437.

Ryan, R. M., & Deci, E. L. (2000). Intrinsic and extrinsic motivations: Classic definitions and new directions. *Contemporary Educational Psychology, 25*, 54–67.

Skinner, E. A., Wellborn, J. G., & Connell, J. P. (1990). What it takes to do well in school and whether I've got it: A process model of perceived control and children's engagement and achievement in school. *Journal of Educational Psychology, 82*(1), 22–32.

Yolen, J. (1987). *Own moon*. New York: Putnam and Grosser Group.

19

Children Searching and Using Information Text

A Critical Part of Comprehension

Mariam Jean Dreher

> ... while the literacy needs of the adult center primarily on
> obtaining information from non-fictional texts, literacy instruction
> in the schools concentrates almost exclusively on fictional texts
> and literary appreciation.
>
> —Venezky (2000, p. 22)

Venezky's views, recently reprinted, were first published in 1982. In this chapter, I argue that the instructional situation has changed little in the almost 20 years since his essay appeared. And although I love good stories and certainly advocate providing children with access to, instruction about, and extensive opportunities to engage with good stories, I believe that nonfiction must be given similar attention. Indeed, in my view, the notion of balanced reading instruction, currently a hot topic, needs to be extended to include children reading, searching, and using nonfiction. In particular, I argue for systematic, balanced attention to information text throughout elementary school, even with the youngest children.

I use the term *information text* to refer to nonfiction—including books, passages, and documents—that is not primarily narrative in form. I argue that a full consideration of comprehension must include information text—reading it, searching it, using it for varied purposes. In this chapter, I focus on a particular type of comprehension demand—searching for and using information. When children need to locate specific detail to answer a question, find information to satisfy their curiosity or solve a problem, read to write an essay, or carry out research for a report, they are engaged in locating and using information. Search tasks such as these need not involve understanding or recalling the contents of an entire passage, book, or document. In fact, efficient search entails using features (e.g., index, table of contents, headings) and strategies (e.g., selecting sources, skimming, evaluating located information) to eliminate unnecessary information while focusing on the relevant portions.

Although search tasks differ from those of traditional text comprehension, they are an equally vital dimension of reading comprehension if for no other reason than the fact that they are so common a reading demand. A clerk consults product warranty regulations to determine if a repair is covered. A secretary uses a manual to locate the solution to a word processing glitch. A travel agent searches for flight departure time, cost, and restrictions. A vice principal forms a plan of action to increase her school's visibility by locating resources on public relations, selecting information, integrating ideas across multiple resources, and synthesizing what she has found. These types of tasks are widespread in the real-world reading that adults must complete (e.g., Dreher, 1993; Mikulecky, 1982; Secretary's Commission on Achieving Necessary Skills [SCANS], 1992; Venezky, 2000). Search tasks are also common in school, with students expected to engage in tasks such as locating answers to questions, locating evidence supporting their conclusions, and locating specific information for reports (Armbruster & Armstrong, 1993).

Escalating demands for reading achievement mean that even the youngest school children must deal facilely with information text and search tasks. In *Preventing Reading Difficulties in Young Children*, for example, a National Academy of Sciences committee concluded that, by the time children leave third grade, they must be able to read to learn independently and that even in the first three grades, children need instruction that will prepare them to read and comprehend both fiction and nonfiction (Snow, Burns, & Griffin, 1998). Further, the committee concluded that by the third grade children should be able to combine "information from multiple sources in writing reports" (p. 83), a feat that is difficult for many students who are much older (Dreher, 1995; Stahl, Hynd, Britton, McNish, & Bosquet, 1996).

In this chapter I first provide background about what is known about readers searching and using information text. Second, I delineate classroom practices that will improve children's performance, and finally, I discuss what still needs to be known about children locating and using information.

RESEARCH ON SEARCHING AND USING INFORMATION TEXT

Although space does not allow a comprehensive review, in this section I attempt to give a sense of the research relevant to searching and using information text. I present evidence that reading to locate information differs from traditional text comprehension, that tasks requiring readers to locate and use information are difficult and complex, and that instruction relevant to locating information is typically ineffective.

Reading to Locate Information Involves Different Demands Than Does Traditional Text Comprehension

Guthrie and Mosenthal (1987) have argued that reading is multidimensional and that reading to locate information is one of a number of dimensions of literacy, each with different characteristics. A distinction between reading to locate and traditional reading comprehension tasks has been supported in several studies with participants ranging from adults to children. For example, a factor analysis of adults' reading performance showed a clear distinction between traditional text comprehension and locating information (Guthrie & Kirsch, 1987). Similarly, college students' performance on passage recall did not predict success on a document search task (Guthrie & Dreher, 1990), nor did college students' success at searching in textbooks correlate with either passage comprehension or recall performance (Yussen & Stright, 1991).

Working with 9- and 10-year-olds, Neville and Pugh (1975) found low non-statistically significant correlations between reading scores on standardized tests and the children's performance when they were asked to use a book to find answers to straightforward questions. In fact, their teachers were "surprised at the aimless and ineffectual behavior of some of their best pupils, particularly when contrasted with that of other children who were normally not outstanding in class" (p. 30). In other words, being a good reader of passages does not mean that a reader will automatically be good at locating and using information.

Searching for and Using Information Is Not Easy for Many Readers

Whether they are adults or students, many readers find searching for information difficult, especially once the task moves beyond a very basic one. The National Assessment of Educational Progress survey of literacy in young adults indicated that most 21- to 25-year-olds were able to locate a single piece of information in a passage or document but that when the task became more complex performance fell rapidly (Kirsch & Jungeblut, 1986). Only 37%, for example, could answer a question that required locating three pieces of information in a brief newspaper article. Similarly, high school students in a study by Dreher and Guthrie (1990) could locate the definition of a single term in a textbook. But only about half these students were successful when they were given a more complex task involving the location and integration of three pieces of information.

College students have been shown to experience difficulties across diverse search tasks, ranging from the search of documents such as plane schedules and pay stubs (Guthrie, 1988; Guthrie & Dreher, 1990) to tables (Guthrie, Britten, & Barker, 1991) and textbooks (Dreher & Brown, 1993; McGoldrick, Martin, Bergering, & Symons, 1992; Yussen, Stright, & Payne, 1993). For example, college students were able to locate only about half the answers to factual questions when they searched a familiar-topic textbook and were even less successful with a textbook on an unfamiliar topic (Symons & Pressley, 1993).

Elementary school students also find it challenging when they are asked read to locate information. In New Zealand, Brown (1999) assessed the information skills of more than 5,000 students. About half the primary students (aged 10 to 12) were able to select the correct category to search when they were attempting a locating task with one key search term, but only about one third could do so when they had to take into account two or more dimensions. Although the intermediate students (12- to 14-year-olds) did better than the primary students, Brown noted that at all levels students had consistent difficulties with selecting the appropriate category of available information to accomplish a given task.

Children often fail to think of and apply relevant knowledge about locating information (Cole & Gardner, 1979; Kobasigawa, 1983; Neville & Pugh, 1975; Wray & Lewis,

1992). Dreher and Sammons (1994) asked fifth-graders to use a familiar-topic textbook to locate the answers to questions, all of which contained terms that could be looked up in the index. Although the study was limited to those students whose teachers considered them to be at least grade-level readers, only about 30% were able to locate the answers to at least two of the three questions. Students who were not successful usually did not think to use the index. Even those who did often looked up inappropriate terms or had trouble with alphabetical order. Unsuccessful children typically tried to locate the answers to the very specific questions by using the table of contents or paging through the text. Yet these students could find the index and other features and explain their use when asked to do so.

The complex demands of search and using information are also evident when students are asked to use multiple sources to write an essay or report. Because such tasks involve both reading and writing, they have been termed "hybrid literacy acts" (Bracewell, Frederiksen, & Frederiksen, 1982) and have been referred to as "reading to write" (Flower, 1987), "composing from sources," or "discourse synthesis" (Spivey & King, 1989). To compose from multiple sources, students must not only select, process, and evaluate ideas from a given text but also integrate or synthesize ideas across texts.

Armbruster (1994) asked sixth graders to engage in this type of task by having them compose answers to two questions about rain forests. She observed and interviewed the students in individual sessions, during which they had three science trade books to use as they pleased. A few students were quite strategic. But most students, although they appeared to be motivated and on task, were inefficient and ineffective. "Some students had difficulty interpreting the given task and, therefore, establishing a goal. Most students lacked strategies for identifying relevant information in text, processing it effectively, and composing responses that were well-written and contained important information" (p. 41). Although older students and better readers are better at composing from sources than younger and poorer readers (Spivey & King, 1989), high school students still find the process challenging, particularly when the ideas are contradictory across multiple texts (Stahl et al., 1996).

In the studies of locating and using information discussed so far, participants have been given the sources they are to use to accomplish a task. An even more challenging situation occurs when readers have to formulate a specific task and select the sources for themselves. Researchers have investigated this situation by observing students who are completing a research report. Whether they have studied 11- and 12-year-olds (Many, Fyfe, Lewis, & Mitchell, 1996), eighth graders (Lenski, 1998), high school seniors (Kuhlthau, 1988), or college students (Nelson & Hayes, 1988), investigators have compellingly illustrated the obstacles students face as they move recursively from question formulation to finished product.

Moore's (1995) study of sixth graders, for instance, serves to raise awareness of just how demanding a research report is. Moore interviewed and observed students during the initial stages of their work on a research project in the school library; she then interviewed them when their projects were completed. Among other findings, Moore noted that going from a general topic (e.g., birds) to specific questions was fraught with difficulty. Similarly, the students' ability to find the books they needed was limited by many problems, ranging from difficulty determining what to look up in the card catalog to misunderstanding the way books are placed on library bookshelves (from top to bottom within each bookcase rather than in horizontal rows across cases). Throughout their research project, students showed that they had a good deal of metacognitive knowledge but lacked general and specific knowledge about how to take alternate routes when their preferred techniques did not work. The complexity of research tasks and the many decisions children must make at each point in the process highlight the need for effective instruction.

Instruction Relevant to Locating Information Is Typically Not Very Effective

Although we expect students to be able to read to locate and use information, we either do not teach them how to do it at all or we do not teach them very well. Discussing the prevalence of the research project method in Great Britain, Marland put it this way:

> We award the highest academic accolade to a student who can see a question, focus it into an enquiry, trace sources, find relevant information in those sources, collate the information, reorganise that information in a way that meets the question posed, and write up the reorganised material as a report. To those who achieve that pinnacle of scholarship we award a Ph.D. This same process is the one we have adopted as the main teaching method for the less academic and less well-motivated school pupil. . . . Yet we often give no specific help. (1977, p. 208)

Even when we offer research-related instruction, it often does not seem to "stick." In the Dreher and Sammons (1994) study previously discussed, almost all the fifth-graders could locate and explain the book's index, glossary, and table of contents *when asked to do so.* Indeed, in that study, performance went up to a 50% success rate for students who were randomly assigned to receive prompting questions. (For example, before searching they were asked, "Do you think the table of contents might be helpful"? "Do you think the index might be helpful"? "Do you think the glossary might be helpful"? Students were not given answers, only these guiding questions.) Their improved performance suggests that they had received at least some relevant instruction but that the instruction had not become knowledge that they could use independently. (See Dreher & Brown, 1993, for similar results with college students.)

Neville and Pugh's (1975) work, mentioned earlier, illustrates the problem of providing effective instruction. In that study, 9- and 10-year-olds searched for the answers to factual questions in a nonfiction book. Neville and Pugh noted that more than half the children "seemed to be quite bemused by the task, even though they could read both book and questions, seemed able to skim or scan a page, and convinced the experimenter that they knew books contained an index and table of contents" (1975, p. 30). When the headmaster and staff at the school where the study was conducted evaluated the results, they decided "to pay special attention to this aspect of reading in the coming year," and they asked the researchers to return and see how students performed (Neville & Pugh, 1982, p. 34) Thus Neville and Pugh (1977) replicated their initial study with a new group of students whose reading scores were comparable to those in the earlier study (all were average or above average readers). Even with teachers' specific attention to locating information in a book, these students performed no better than those in the first study had.

In short, even students who have received relevant instruction often have difficulty making independent use of what they have been taught. When Wray and Lewis (1992) interviewed British fourth- and sixth-year primary children about finding and using information in books and then later observed the same students doing a research project, they noted a considerable gap between what the children actually did on their own and what they said about how they would use information books. Wray and Lewis concluded that there was a "significant teaching problem" (p. 20)—children may be taught information-seeking lessons but do not get guided practice to help them transfer what they are learning to independent use.

HELPING CHILDREN SEARCH AND USE INFORMATION TEXT

In a recent article, fourth-grade teacher Cathy Tower described her eagerness to involve her students in inquiry tasks (Tower, 2000). She enthusiastically assigned research projects, but she judged her efforts a failure. As Tower reflected on her own and her students' frustration and as she talked about the situation with her class, she concluded that they had little knowledge of the genre of tasks she expected them to complete. In fact, they appeared to have had little exposure to nonfiction text: They were unfamiliar with the features of information books, and none could even remember having heard a nonfiction book read aloud at school. Tower decided to remedy the situation by providing her students with the opportunity to interact with information books and by offering instruction on how to use them.

Tower's experiences mirror the findings of researchers who have investigated instructional contexts and set the context for this section of this chapter. Here I describe practices that make sense based on what we know about reading to locate and use information. I first discuss the need for considerably more opportunity to interact with information text. Then I discuss the need for specific instruction relevant to reading and using information text.

Balanced Attention to Narrative and Information Text Is Needed from the Start

Children's ability to engage in search tasks is likely to be enhanced by balanced exposure to information text and instruction relating to such text throughout the elementary grades. Yet elementary school reading instruction is overwhelmingly narrative. The books teachers read to children are typically stories (Hoffman, Roser, & Battle, 1993). The materials available in basal readers are largely narrative (Moss & Newton, 1998). Teachers report using little information text during instruction (Pressley, Rankin, & Yokoi, 1996). In both literature-based and skills-based classrooms, almost all instruction and materials read or written by students involves narrative text (Fisher & Hiebert, 1990; Hiebert & Fisher, 1990).

To raise children's level of exposure to and familiarity with information text, I recommend that teachers in the elementary grades take the following steps.

1. *Include information books in daily read-alouds.* Young children find information text appealing (Horowitz & Freeman, 1995; Pappas, 1993), making this suggestion easy to implement even in the earliest grades (Kamil & Lane, 1997), and guidance on how to select and present information books is available (Doiron, 1994).

2. Add information books to classroom libraries. Easy access to books makes a difference in literacy achievement (Neuman, 1999). If children have access to information books, they will read them, particularly if their teachers include information books in their read-alouds. Children are more likely to choose books for independent reading that their teacher has read aloud than those that have not been read aloud (Martinez, Roser, Worthy, Strecker, & Gough, 1997).

3. Systematically include information text in the material used for reading instruction. Although stories are typically used for reading instruction, information text can be used successfully as part of reading instruction even in first grade (Kamil & Lane, 1997; Weise, Scharnhorst, & Bransford, 1999).

4. Provide comprehension instruction that includes attention to information text. Although reading to locate information is a distinct dimension of reading, traditional prose comprehension comes into play once readers select a category of a text to examine. Comprehension processes such as integrating and summarizing are particularly important in reading to write from multiple sources.

Dreher (2000) provides a fuller discussion of why and how to balance narrative and information texts. In addition, several recent articles in practitioner journals offer specific tips on broadening students' access to information books (e.g., Camp, 2000; Dreher, 1998–1999; Guillaume, 1998; Yopp & Yopp, 2000).

As fourth-grade teacher Tower (2000) learned, students with little exposure to information text have little opportunity to become familiar with its unique demands. However, if we want to help students become more effective at locating information and in reading to write, they will need more than just opportunity to interact with information text. They also need targeted instruction, as I describe next.

A Cognitive Model of Locating Information Can Be a Valuable Instructional Guide

Although access to information text is important, the research I have reviewed herein makes clear that students also require instruction. In this section, I offer instructional suggestions drawn from a model of reading to locate information.

Many of the studies of reading to locate information have empirically tested a cognitive model of locating information. This model, a modification of one originally proposed by Guthrie and Mosenthal (1987), characterizes efficient search as involving (1) formulating a goal or plan of action, (2) selecting appropriate categories of a document or text for inspection, (3) extracting relevant information from the inspected categories, (4) integrating extracted information with prior knowledge, and (5) monitoring the completeness of the answer and recycling through the component processes until the task is completed. (See explications and variants of the model in Dreher, 1992; Dreher & Guthrie, 1990; Guthrie & Mosenthal, 1987; Guthrie, Weber, & Kimmerly, 1993.) Table 19.1 describes this model as applied to a search task in which a reader is attempting to locate information in a textbook.

If we study the responses of unsuccessful and/or inefficient readers as they try to locate and use information, we find patterns that map onto this model of locating information. For example, the center column in Table 19.2 shows how high school students' difficulties in searching for information in a textbook correspond to the model's components

TABLE 19.1. A Cognitive Model of Text Search

Search processes	Description
Goal formation	Reader forms an objective for which to search. May involve developing own goal or figuring out what to do with a task that has been assigned
Category selection	Categories are structural features of material; reader determines which categories will lead to the information being sought. May entail use of access features such as index, table of contents
Information extraction	Reader must distinguish useful from irrelevant information and either extract relevant data or determine that the category is not helpful
Integration	Reader integrates extracted information in ongoing synthesis of goal-relevant information and prior knowledge
Recycling	Reader assesses whether more information is needed and, if necessary, recycles through all the components until the goal has been met

(Dreher, 1992). The right column in Table 19.2 lists questions derived from the model that can be used to guide students' search processes. Students can be taught to use questions like these to monitor text search tasks.

Using model-based questions such as these as part of instruction is likely to improve students' search performance. Two types of evidence support this notion. First, prompts based on the model have been shown to be effective in improving performance. For college students, the use of prompting questions that zeroed in on goal formation and category selection improved performance on a textbook search task (Dreher & Brown, 1993). And in the Dreher and Sammons (1994) study discussed earlier, fifth graders who received model-based guiding questions as they searched for information in a textbook performed better than those who did not. For example, before they started searching, they were asked a question relevant to goal formation: "Before you start, are there words in this question that you might be able to use to help you find the answer?" Similarly, when students thought they were through, they were asked a question relevant to monitoring success and recycling: "Before we go on, read the question again. Do you think you have all the information you need to answer the question, or do you need to search a bit longer?" The guiding questions improved performance by prompting the children to engage in search processes they might not have thought to do spontaneously.

Second, strategy training based on model components appears to work as well. Third, fourth, and fifth graders improved on text search when they received strategy instruction in category selection, information extraction, and monitoring whether the information they extracted satisfied the goal (Symons, MacLatchy-Gaudet, Stone, & Reynolds, 2001).

In addition to using model-based questions, teachers can use the text search model as a guide or checklist to help them target the skills and strategies involved in each component of the search process. By teaching strategies relevant to each part of model—goal formation, category selection, information extraction, integration, and monitoring/recycling—teachers can help provide the alternate routes that Moore (1995) found her students were lacking when their first efforts were not successful.

TABLE 19.2. How Unsuccessful Searchers' Characteristics Relate to a Model of the Search Process

Search processes	Searchers' problems	Questions for student self-monitoring
Goal formation	Failure to formulate a specific goal before searching (e.g., not using specific search terms when they are present)	Exactly what information do I need?
Category selection	Inability to locate an appropriate text section	How should I approach this material? How is this material organized? What are the available features?
Information extraction	Misuse of potentially helpful text features (e.g., about half of the incorrect responses by high school students were boldface terms that appeared near the correct answers)	Is the information I need located here? Does the information I have located make sense?
Integration	Failure to monitor the appropriateness of the response	Do I need to combine this information with other material that I have located or already know?
Recycling	Failure to evaluate the response and look further	Do I have all the information that I need? If not, I should continue searching.

Note. From Dreher (1992, p. 370). Copyright by the International Reading Association. All rights reserved.

Teachers may modify this model to fit the type of search task their students are engaged in. Doing so may help teachers and their students gain a better understanding of just what demands they will be facing as they complete a locating task. Armbruster (1994), for example, sought a model to describe reading-to-write tasks in which students are expected to search for information to answer a question and then to write a response. She noted the similarities between the text search model in Table 19.1 and Flower and Hayes's (1981) writing process model. Flower and Hayes characterized the writing process as a complex, recursive process of planning (setting goals, generating ideas, and organizing information), translating (transforming ideas into written text), and reviewing (evaluating, editing, and revising what is written). Armbruster (1994, p. 46) combined the text search and writing process models into a hybrid version:

READING-TO-WRITE MODEL

Establishing the goal—establishing or clarifying the goal of reading or writing

Identifying relevant information—locating relevant information in text or from head

Processing selected information—cognitive processing of selected information

Transforming information—transforming information from text, notes, or head to new written product

Evaluating progress toward goal—evaluating goal attainment and repeating preceding steps until goal is achieved

In using such a model or creating a tailored version of it, teachers should help students keep in mind that the process the model describes is recursive rather than linear. Further, although a cognitive model is useful, it must be part of meaningful systematic instruction, as I outline next.

Systematic Instruction and Guided Practice in Meaningful Contexts Can Foster Independence

In the preceding section, I discussed the need for instruction. In this section I elaborate on the conditions of instruction.

Effective instruction is difficult. Teachers complain that they have to teach search-related skills over and over (Dreher & Sammons, 1994). Despite their specific targeting of locating skills, teachers find that many of their students do not apply what they have been taught (Neville & Pugh, 1977, 1982). What can be done to address the "significant teaching problem" (Wray & Lewis, 1992) that leaves even good readers "bemused" (Neville & Pugh, 1975) by seemingly simple tasks? Specifically, I argue for instruction and systematic guided practice in a meaningful context. I believe that such instruction is needed in order to help children become strategic readers, including becoming strategic readers when they need to locate and use information.

Strategic readers possess declarative, procedural, and conditional knowledge (Paris, Lipson, & Wixson, 1994). In the case of reading to locate and use information, it appears that many readers have at least some declarative or factual knowledge about task structures and goals. They also appear to have at least some procedural knowledge of how to accomplish the task at hand. But the fact that they often demonstrate their declarative and procedural knowledge only when specifically prompted to do so suggests that conditional knowledge is lacking. Conditional knowledge involves knowledge of why, when, and where to use these strategies. Without conditional knowledge, readers do not employ strategies appropriately and efficiently.

Strategy instruction seems most likely to be effective if it is systematic and if it is situated in rich, meaningful contexts. The focus here is on research-based suggestions specific to reading to locate and use information. Dreher, Davis, Waynant, and Clewell (1998) worked with fourth graders in a year-long study at two very different schools (one with a largely white middle-income population and the other with a largely minority population and substantial Title I funding). They sought to improve children's ability to carry out research tasks in social studies by integrating research strategy instruction into inquiry-based content-area projects. They worked with the premise that to become strategic readers and researchers, students need both instruction and many opportunities to engage in research. They also assumed that varied task demands would help students develop the conditional knowledge so important to independent strategy use. Thus, during the school year, research projects in meaningful contexts were ongoing—some short, some long, with the topics and products varied. Strategy instruction occurred daily and was based on the difficulties students encountered as they worked. Teachers selected the instructional topics from their observations and from the problems students identified in daily reflection logs. These reflection logs asked students to engage in metacognitive thinking, that is, to evaluate their successes and difficulties as they worked. With this systematic, year-long instruction tied to very meaningful contexts, students at both schools improved in searching for information, in writing answers to research questions, and in applying what they had learned to a new situation.

The instruction Guthrie and his colleagues (Guthrie et al., 1996; Guthrie et al., 1998; Guthrie, Anderson, Alao, & Rinehart, 1999) designed for students has also resulted in growth in students' ability to search for and use information. Concept-oriented reading instruction (CORI) transforms the nature of reading and science instruction (see Chapter 18, this volume, for a lengthier discussion.) CORI involves literacy instruction integrated into science texts and meaningful, socially interactive classroom experiences. By using science content as a major vehicle for teaching reading, CORI makes children's inquiry an integral part of instruction. Children's observations lead them to form questions and to seek answers in multiple sources. CORI has been shown to increase third and fifth graders' literacy engagement and intrinsic motivation for literacy, as well as their concept learning and reading performance. Further, assessments of reading performance have demonstrated children's growth in locating, using, and applying new information.

When teachers use instructional approaches such as CORI, they address head on the problem described earlier of students being unable to apply what they have been taught. When instruction consists of more of the usual approach, student performance does not benefit (Neville & Pugh, 1975, 1977). Teachers who used approaches such as CORI, however, have shown that effective instruction can help students develop conditional knowledge needed for strategic reading. Such knowledge results when instruction is systematic, situated in rich meaningful contexts, and accompanied by many opportunities to practice under varied circumstances.

WHAT STILL NEEDS TO BE KNOWN

Much still needs to be known about children reading, searching, and using information text. To help focus future inquiry, I have identified five areas of concern.

1. *We need to know more about how children select sources when they need information.* As noted earlier, in most of the relevant research, readers are given a source or sources in which they are asked to find something. Such tasks have proven challenging. But reading to locate is even more difficult when readers have to select the source in the first place. Tasks like these are common in adult life; workers, for instance, must very often select the document(s) they need in order to solve a problem. A better understanding of source selection processes might help us more effectively prepare children to be strategic searchers.

2. *We need to investigate the effect on children's comprehension of the changing demands of books.* Today's information books for children look quite different from traditional books. Rather than sequential passages, new trade books are often formatted with bits of information positioned around gorgeous illustrations and activity boxes. Many textbooks have been reconfigured so that they look much like trade books (Walpole, 1998–1999). We need to know more about how changes in books affect not only traditional comprehension but also the way books are used for locating information.

3. *We need research on children's use of the Internet and hypermedia for finding and using information.* Almost all U.S. public schools are now connected to the Internet,

and within those schools, students increasingly have Internet access in their individual classrooms (National Center for Education Statistics [NCES], 2000). Leu (2000) has posited that soon more reading may be done via digital technology networks than in books. If so, major changes in reading demands may occur. For example, Kamil and Lane (1998) concluded that (1) information text predominates on the Internet, even on sites intended for younger students, and (2) the writing found on children's Web sites is substantially more difficult than that in conventional books at the intended grade levels. What are the repercussions for instruction of not only new technologies but also an increase in information text and reading levels? How do new technologies alter comprehension demands in general and research demands in particular?

4. *We need to study how we can help children develop speed and accuracy in searching and using information text.* Leu (in press) pointed out that even in research on new technologies, the outcome measures examined in reading comprehension have been traditional ones, such as recall. But with the Internet and other digital technologies, Leu has argued that we need to look at the speed with which people can locate information relevant to a task and how quickly they can evaluate the worth of various resources for a specific problem. These outcomes are exactly the type of important dimensions of reading comprehension that have been the central focus of this chapter. The new technologies raise the bar.

5. *We need to examine the considerable potential of information text and search tasks for contributing to children's motivation to read and learn* (Dreher, 2000). Motivation to read is an important concern in developing engaged readers who not only can read but also choose to read (Baker, Dreher, & Guthrie, 2000). Guthrie and his colleagues have shown that an emphasis on information books and inquiry influences both students' intrinsic motivation to read and their reading and search performance (e.g., Guthrie et al., 1999). When such results are viewed in the context of new technologies, exciting possibilities emerge. Technologies such as the Internet and hypermedia appear to be more interesting and motivating than traditional text (Leu, in press). As we extend well-done instructional contexts to include locating and using information with new technologies, perhaps these contexts will afford even more possibilities for engaging readers.

Whether dealing with the Internet or with more traditional resources, we need research on how children form questions, how they locate, evaluate, integrate, and use information, and how we can help them become more efficient and independent in doing so. Current and future literacy demands in school and the workplace make such research critically important. Such tasks are often not seen as "real" reading but rather as something taught separately from reading, if at all. Yet with today's growth in information resources, it seems increasingly important that reading to locate information is viewed as an important dimension of literacy. Reading to locate and use information is reading, it is comprehension, and it is important.

REFERENCES

Armbruster, B. B. (1994). *Reading-to-write: Sixth graders and science trade books.* Unpublished manuscript, University of Illinois, Urbana–Champaign.

Armbruster, B. B., & Armstrong, J. O. (1993). Locating information in text: A focus on children. *Contemporary Educational Psychology, 18,* 139–161.

Baker, L., Dreher, M. J., & Guthrie, J. T. (Eds.). (2000). *Engaging young readers: Promoting achievement and motivation*. New York: Guilford Press.

Bracewell, R. J., Frederiksen, C. H., & Frederiksen, J. F. (1982). Cognitive processes in composing and comprehending discourse. *Educational Psychologist, 17*, 146–174.

Brown, G. (1999, December). *Information skills: How information literate are New Zealand children?* Paper presented at the meeting of the New Zealand Association for Research in Education/ Australian Association for Research in Education Conference, Melbourne, Australia.

Camp, D. (2000). It takes two: Teaching with twin texts of fact and fiction. *Reading Teacher, 53*, 400–408.

Cole, J., & Gardner, K. (1979). Topic work with first-year secondary pupils. In E. Lunzer & K. Gardner (Eds.), *The effective use of reading* (pp. 167–192). London, England: Heinemann.

Doiron, R. (1994). Using nonfiction in a read-aloud program: Letting the facts speak for themselves. *Reading Teacher, 47*, 616–624.

Dreher, M. J. (1992). Locating information in textbooks. *Journal of Reading, 35*, 364–371.

Dreher, M. J. (1993). Reading to locate information: Societal and educational perspectives. *Contemporary Educational Psychology, 18*, 129–138.

Dreher, M. J. (1995). *Sixth-grade researchers: Posing questions, finding information, and writing a report* (Reading Research Report No. 40). University of Georgia, Athens, GA, and University of Maryland, National Reading Research Center, College Park, MD.

Dreher, M. J. (1998–1999). Motivating children to read more nonfiction. *Reading Teacher, 52*, 414–417.

Dreher, M. J. (2000). Fostering reading for learning. In L. Baker, M. J. Dreher, & J. T. Guthrie (Eds.), *Engaging young readers: Promoting achievement and independence* (pp. 68–93). New York: Guilford Press.

Dreher, M. J., & Brown, R. F. (1993). Planning prompts and indexed terms in textbook search tasks. *Journal of Educational Psychology, 85*, 662–669.

Dreher, M. J., Davis, K. A., Waynant, P., & Clewell, S. F. (1998). Fourth-grade researchers: Helping children develop strategies for finding and using information. In T. Shanahan & F. V. Y. Rodriquez-Brown (Eds.), *47th yearbook of the National Reading Conference Yearbook* (pp. 311–322). Chicago: National Reading Conference.

Dreher, M. J., & Guthrie, J. T. (1990). Cognitive processes in textbook chapter search tasks. *Reading Research Quarterly, 25*, 323–339.

Dreher, M. J., & Sammons, R. B. (1994). Fifth-graders' search for information in a textbook. *Journal of Reading Behavior, 26*, 301–314.

Fisher, C. W., & Hiebert, E. H. (1990). Characteristics of tasks in two approaches to literature instruction. *Elementary School Journal, 91*, 3–18.

Flower, L. (1987). *The role of task representation in reading to write* (Technical Report No. 6). Berkeley: University of California, Center for the Study of Writing. (ERIC Document Reproduction Service No. ED 285 206)

Flower, L., & Hayes, J. R. (1981). A cognitive process theory of writing. *College Composition and Communication, 32*, 365–387.

Guillaume, A. M. (1998). Learning with text in the primary grades. *Reading Teacher, 51*, 476–486.

Guthrie, J. T. (1988). Locating information in documents: Examination of a cognitive model. *Reading Research Quarterly, 23*, 178–199.

Guthrie, J. T., Anderson, E., Alao, S., & Rinehart, J. (1999). Influences of concept-oriented reading instruction on strategy use and conceptual learning from text. *Elementary School Journal, 99*, 343–366.

Guthrie, J. T., Britten, T., & Barker, K. G. (1991). Roles of document structure, cognitive strategy, and awareness in searching for information. *Reading Research Quarterly, 26*, 300–324.

Guthrie, J. T., & Dreher, M. J. (1990). Literacy as search: Explorations via computer. In D. Nix &

R. Spiro (Eds.), *Cognition, education, and multimedia: Exploring ideas in high technology* (pp. 65–114). Hillsdale, NJ: Erlbaum.

Guthrie, J. T., & Kirsch, I. S. (1987). Literacy as multidimensional: Locating information in text and reading comprehension. *Journal of Educational Psychology, 79,* 220–228.

Guthrie, J. T., & Mosenthal, P. (1987). Literacy as multidimensional: Locating information and reading comprehension. *Educational Psychologist, 22,* 279–297.

Guthrie, J. T., Van Meter, P., Hancock, G. R., Alao, S., Anderson, E., & McCann, A. (1998). Does concept-oriented reading instruction increase strategy use and conceptual learning from text? *Journal of Educational Psychology, 90,* 261–278.

Guthrie, J. T., Van Meter, P., McCann, A., Wigfield, A., Bennett, L., Poundstone, C., Rice, M. E., Faibisch, F., Hunt, B., & Mitchell, A. (1996). Growth of literacy engagement: Changes in motivations and strategies during concept-oriented reading instruction. *Reading Research Quarterly, 31,* 306–333.

Guthrie, J. T., Weber, S., & Kimmerly, N. (1993). Searching documents: Cognitive processes and deficits in understanding graphs, tables, and illustrations. *Contemporary Educational Psychology, 18,* 186–221.

Hiebert, E. H., & Fisher, C. W. (1990). Whole language: Three themes for the future. *Educational Leadership, 47,* 62–64.

Hoffman, J. V., Roser, N. L., & Battle, J. (1993). Reading aloud in classrooms: From modal to a "model." *Reading Teacher, 46,* 496–505.

Horowitz, R., & Freeman, S. H. (1995). Robots versus spaceships: The role of discussion in kindergartners' and second graders' preferences for science texts. *Reading Teacher, 49,* 30–40.

Kamil, M. L., & Lane, D. (1997, December). *Using information text for first-grade reading instruction.* Paper presented at the meeting of the National Reading Conference, Scottsdale, AZ.

Kamil, M. L., & Lane, D. (1998, December). *Informational text, reading instruction and demands of technology in elementary school.* Paper presented at the meeting of the National Reading Conference, Austin, TX.

Kirsch, I., & Jungeblut, A. (1986). *Literacy: Profiles of America's young adults.* Princeton, NJ: Educational Testing Service.

Kobasigawa, A. (1983). Children's retrieval skills for school learning. *Alberta Journal of Educational Research, 29,* 259–271.

Kuhlthau, C. C. (1988). Developing a model of the library search process: Cognitive and affective aspects. *Reference Quarterly, 28,* 232–242.

Lenski, S. D. (1998). Strategic knowledge when reading in order to write. *Reading Psychology, 19,* 287–315.

Leu, D. J., Jr. (2000). Our children's future: Changing the focus of literacy and literacy instruction. *Reading Teacher, 53,* 424–429.

Leu, D. J., Jr. (in press). The new literacies: Research on reading instruction with the Internet and other digital technologies. In S. J. Samuels & A. E. Farstrup (Eds.), *What research has to say about reading instruction.* Newark, DE: International Reading Association.

Many, J., Fyfe, R., Lewis, G., & Mitchell, E. (1996). Traversing the topical landscape: Exploring students' self-directed reading–writing–research processes. *Reading Research Quarterly, 31,* 12–35.

Marland, M. (1977). *Language across the curriculum.* London: Heinemann.

Martinez, M. G., Roser, N. L., Worthy, J., Strecker, S., & Gough, P. (1997). Classroom libraries and children's book selections: Redefining "access" in self-selected reading. In C. K. Kinzer, K. A. Hinchman, & D. J. Leu (Eds.), *Inquiries in literacy theory and practice: 46th yearbook of the National Reading Conference* (pp. 265–272). Chicago, IL: National Reading Conference.

McGoldrick, J. A., Martin, J., Bergering, A. J., & Symons, S. (1992). Locating discrete information in text: Effects of computer presentation and menu formatting. *Journal of Reading Behavior, 24,* 1–20.

Mikulecky, L. (1982). Job literacy: The relationship between school preparation and workplace actuality. *Reading Research Quarterly, 17*(3), 400–419.

Moore, P. (1995). Information problem solving: A wider view of library skills. *Contemporary Educational Psychology, 20,* 1–31.

Moss, B., & Newton, E. (1998, December). *An examination of the informational text genre in recent basal readers.* Paper presented at the meeting of the National Reading Conference, Austin, TX.

National Center for Education Statistics. (2000). *Internet access in U.S. public schools and classrooms: 1994–99* (NCES Report No. 2000–086).Washington, DC: U.S. Department of Education.

Nelson, J., & Hayes, J. R. (1988). *How the writing context shapes college students' strategies for writing from sources* (Technical Report No. 16). Berkeley: University of California, Center for the Study of Writing. (ERIC Document Reproduction Service No. ED 297 374)

Neuman, S. B. (1999). Books make a difference: A study of access to literacy. *Reading Research Quarterly, 34,* 286–311.

Neville, M. H., & Pugh, A. K. (1975). Reading ability and ability to use a book: A study of middle school children. *Reading, 9,* 23–31.

Neville, M. H., & Pugh, A. K. (1977). Ability to use a book: Further studies of middle school children. *Reading, 11,* 13–22.

Neville, M. H., & Pugh, A. K. (1982). *Towards independent reading.* London: Heinemann.

Pappas, C. C. (1993). Is narrative "primary"? Some insights from kindergartners' pretend readings of stories and information books. *Journal of Reading Behavior, 25,* 97–129.

Paris, S., Lipson, M. Y., & Wixson, K. K. (1994). Becoming a strategic reader. In R. B. Ruddell, M. R. Ruddell, & H. Singer (Eds.), *Theoretical models and processes of reading* (4th ed., pp. 788–810). Newark, DE: International Reading Association.

Pressley, M., Rankin, J., & Yokoi, L. (1996). A survey of instructional practices of primary teachers nominated as effective in promoting literacy. *Elementary School Journal, 96,* 363–384.

Secretary's Commission on Achieving Necessary Skills. (1992). *What work requires of schools: A SCANS report for America 2000.* Washington, DC: U.S. Department of Labor.

Snow, C. E., Burns, M. S., & Griffin, P. (Eds.). (1998). *Preventing reading difficulties in young children.* Washington, DC: National Academy Press.

Spivey, N. N., & King, J. R. (1989). Readers as writers composing from sources. *Reading Research Quarterly, 24,* 7–26.

Stahl, S. A., Hynd, C. R., Britton, B. K., McNish, M. M., & Bosquet, D. (1996). What happens when students read multiple source documents in history? *Reading Research Quarterly, 31,* 430–458.

Symons, S., MacLatchy-Gaudet, H., Stone, T. D., & Reynolds, P. L. (in press). Strategy instruction for elementary students searching informational text. *Scientific Studies of Reading, 5,* 1–33.

Symons, S., & Pressley, M. (1993). Prior knowledge affects text search success and extraction of information. *Reading Research Quarterly, 28,* 250–261.

Tower, C. (2000). Questions that matter: Preparing elementary school students for the inquiry process. *Reading Teacher, 53,* 550–556.

Venezky, R. L. (2000). The origins of the present-day chasm between adult literacy needs and school literacy instruction. *Scientific Studies of Reading, 4,* 19–39.

Walpole, S. (1998–1999). Changing texts, changing thinking: Comprehension demands of new science textbooks. *Reading Teacher, 52,* 358–369.

Weise, R., Scharnhorst, U., & Bransford, J. D. (1999). *Developing expository literacy in first grade: A quasi-experimental study of the effects of instruction.* Paper presented at the meeting of the American Educational Research Association, Montreal, Canada.

Wray, D., & Lewis, M. (1992). Primary children's use of information books. *Reading, 19,* 19–24.

Yopp, R. H., & Yopp, H. K. (2000). Sharing informational text with young children. *Reading Teacher, 53,* 410–423.

Yussen, S., & Stright, A. (1991, April). *Simple searching to find information in a textbook.* Paper presented at the meeting of the American Educational Research Association, Chicago, IL.

Yussen, S. R., Stright, A., & Payne, B. (1993). Where is it? Searching for information in a college textbook. *Contemporary Educational Psychology, 18,* 240–247.

20

Imagery

A Strategy for Enhancing Comprehension

Linda B. Gambrell
Patricia S. Koskinen

Comprehension is the process of constructing meaning from written text. Perhaps the most perplexing problem educators face is how to help children develop strategies that will facilitate the comprehension of written text. The research to date suggests that mental imagery is a strategy that can play an important and positive role in enhancing both listening and reading comprehension. The old saying, "A picture is worth a thousand words," may explain why comprehension is increased when visual imagery is employed. When listeners and readers make mental images about information and stories, the mental "pictures" may provide the framework for organizing and remembering the text. This notion is reflected in the conceptual-peg hypothesis (Paivio, 1983; Sadoski, 1983, 1985), which posits that key images serve as mental "pegs" on which associated information is hooked for storage and retrieval.

As research has added to our knowledge base about mental imagery, the "picture-gallery" theory of imagery as static, immobile, and concrete has given way to the current conception of imagery as an active information-handling process (Sadoski, 1985; Sadoski & Paivio, 1994; Paivio, 1986). This view of imagery is based on Kaufmann's (1979, 1980) theory that mental imagery is useful in general problem solving, particularly with respect to unfamiliar or novel situations. Sadoski (1983) has also concluded that imagery is particularly useful in both spatial and verbal problem solving in reading situations.

The research on imagery and reading comprehension is based on the theory that mental imagery is a knowledge representation system that readers can use in organizing, integrating, and retrieving information from written text (Gambrell & Bales, 1986; Lindsay, 1988; Sadoski & Paivio, 1994). One hypothesis is that imagery promotes active processing of text because the reader must construct meaningful images that link prior knowledge with text information (Chan, Cole, & Morris, 1990).

RESEARCH ON IMAGERY AND HOW IT ENHANCES COMPREHENSION

The most comprehensive theory of cognition that explores the relationship between mental imagery and student's comprehension development is Paivio's (1971, 1986) dual coding theory. The dual coding theory posits that cognition occurs through two separate but interconnected coding systems: a verbal system for language and a nonverbal system that deals primarily with imagery. Support for the dual coding theory includes research that demonstrates that imaginable (concrete) information is recalled better than abstract information. Also, memory for imaged verbal information improves relative to information that is only verbalized. Both concrete information and imaged verbalizations result in both verbal and nonverbal representations in memory. Sadoski and Paivio (1994) reviewed research studies that support the dual coding theory as it applies to imagery and comprehension, imagery and learning from text, and imagery as a form of aesthetic appreciation. They concluded that mental imagery improves comprehension, memory, and interpretive understanding of text.

Mental Imagery: Effects on Listening, Reading, and Writing

Instructions to produce mental imagery in listening situations produce a significant increase in comprehension and memory for both children and adults (Guttman & Levin, 1977; Piaget & Inhelder, 1971; Shimron, 1975). The early work of Piaget and Inhelder (1971) revealed that the comprehension and memory of even very young children is enhanced when they are given specific instructions to construct mental imagery while listening.

There is ample evidence that suggests that mental imagery facilitates the reading comprehension of both children and adults (Gambrell, 1982; Pressley, 1976). Several hypotheses have evolved as to why mental imagery enhances reading comprehension. When readers construct mental imagery, the dual processing of both print and images may result in the reader expending additional effort, which results in more in-depth processing of the text (Linden & Wittrock, 1981; Sadoski, 1985: Sadoski & Paivio, 1994). There also appears to be support for the hypothesis that imagery increases the active integration of information across text (Gambrell & Bales, 1987; Linden & Wittrock, 1981).

Visual imagery also helps readers in the crucial task of comprehension monitoring, that is, increasing awareness of whether text is being understood. Older and more proficient readers who encounter a comprehension problem when listening to or reading written text are able to monitor their comprehension and are aware of the processing problems (August, Flavell, & Clift, 1984; Garner, 1980; Paris & Myers, 1981). Younger and less proficient readers do not appear to monitor their comprehension and are unaware of their failure to comprehend (Markman, 1977, 1979). Children get better at comprehension monitoring as they get older (Markman, 1979; Markman & Gorin, 1981). Given the importance of comprehension monitoring in the comprehension process, it is essential that we identify ways to promote monitoring of comprehension. Imagery is one approach to this problem.

Can We Teach Students to Image?

A study by Bales and Gambrell (1985) investigated the effects of mental imagery on the comprehension monitoring of fourth- and fifth-grade poor readers. Students were asked to read passages that contained obvious inconsistencies. Prior to reading the passages, one group received instructions to "make pictures in your mind to help you understand and remember," and the other group received instructions to "do whatever you can to help you understand and remember." All students were specifically told that they were to read to see if there was anything that was not easy to understand in the passage. The most significant finding was that students who were instructed to induce mental imagery were more successful at identifying the inconsistencies in the text than the control group. Also, 70% of the participants in the imagery group reported that they made mental images about what they were reading, whereas less than 1% in the control group reported using mental imagery. Thus, poor readers can successfully use mental imagery to enhance comprehension monitoring. Many students do not spontaneously use mental imagery as a comprehension strategy but will do so if teacher guidance and scaffolding is provided. One reason that children may not spontaneously use mental imagery as a strategy to aid comprehension is that mental imagery is most frequently associated with aesthetic appreciation of prose and is not directly taught as a specific comprehension strategy that is useful with both narrative and expository text (Belcher, 1982).

A number of studies have documented the positive effects of mental imagery on the writing skills of young children. Developing and refining the composing skills of young children is an aspect of instruction that continues to receive a great deal of attention. Composing is the process of selecting, combining, arranging, and developing ideas, and it is therefore a reflection of comprehension. Researchers investigating the writing process have suggested that reflection and contemplation play a significant role in the composing process (Graves, 1978; King, 1978; Stallard, 1974). For example, Gambrell (1983) investigated the effects of mental imagery on the written language expression of young children. Third-grade children were instructed to read a story starter (the brief beginning of an imaginary story) and were then asked to write an ending for the story. Children in the mental imagery group were instructed to use mental imagery while reading the story starter and then, on completing the reading of the story starter, they were instructed to use mental imagery to think through the story ending they were writing. The mental imagery group wrote significantly more than the control group, and the stories were more coherent and well organized. It appears that mental imagery facilitates the written language expression of young children, encouraging reflection and contemplation during the composing process and resulting in improved written expression.

Jampole, Konopak, Readence, and Moser (1991) found similar benefits of instruction when they explored the effects of mental imagery instruction on gifted elementary students' creative writing. Fourth- and fifth-grade students were assigned to either to a mental imagery or control group and then participated in four group lessons over a 2-week period. Students in the imagery group received instruction and practice in imagery using passages with highly imaginable sensory descriptions. Following each lesson, students in both groups completed creative writing assignments. Students in the imagery group significantly outperformed the control group on originality and use of sensory descriptions. Instruction and practice in using imagery can enhance aspects of gifted students' creative writing.

How Early Does Imagery Influence Conceptual Development?

It has long been believed that imagery plays a central role in children's thought processes (Kosslyn, 1980; Bruner, Olver, & Greenfield, 1966) and that imagery influences children's conceptual development and reasoning abilities (Piaget & Inhelder, 1971). Early research by Bruner et al. (1966) and Piaget and Inhelder (1971) supported the contention that the properties of children's imagery would place major constraints on their cognitive abilities. In their research they drew inferences about the ability of children to effectively use imagery based on tasks that the children could not perform. However, they did not provide validation that the properties of children's imagery were responsible for the children's difficulties in task performance. These studies required children to describe or reproduce a visual pattern, and the response mode may have been at the root of the children's difficulties. It may have been that the children were simply unable to describe or draw what they knew. Other studies have found that young children are able to use imagery in ways previously thought impossible. For example, children in Marmor's (1975) study were able to rotate imaged objects, although at a slower rate than older individuals were.

Kosslyn, Van Kleeck, and Kirby (1990) conducted a study to delineate the nature of young children's imagery and compare it with the imagery of older children and adults. The study was based on the work of Kosslyn, Brunn, Cave, and Wallach (1984) that found that imagery ability is based on a relatively small number of components and that not all of these component processes must be used to perform any given imagery task. Kosslyn and his colleagues compared the performance of 5-year-olds, 8-year-olds, 14-year-olds, and adults on four imagery tasks. The four tasks were: generation, the task of forming an image; maintenance, the task of retaining images; scanning, the task of searching for a part, property, or object in the image; and rotation, the task of transforming or rotating images. This study revealed that older participants scanned and rotated objects in images more efficiently than younger children and that older participants were better at generating images. Interesting, there was no age difference in the image maintenance task. The observed age differences in this study provide evidence that imagery is not a single ability and support the imagery component theory. The results also suggest that there may be age differences in some processing components, such as image scanning and rotation, but not in others, such as image maintenance.

The Role of Imagery in Comprehension Monitoring: What Can Be Taught?

Comprehension monitoring is defined as the executive function that directs cognitive processing as the reader strives to make sense of incoming textual information (Flavell & Wellman, 1977; Wagoner, 1983). Reading, by definition, involves active monitoring of one's own understanding of text. One of the most pervasive questions in literacy research is why some younger and poorer readers have difficulty monitoring their comprehension (August, Flavell, & Cliff, 1984; Gambrell & Bales, 1986).

Studies exploring the comprehension monitoring of text typically use the error detection paradigm (Winograd & Johnston, 1980) with the expectation that proficient comprehenders will detect the inconsistencies in text, whereas less proficient comprehenders will not. These studies place greater emphasis on readers' awareness of comprehension failure rather than on the implementation of specific strategies to enhance comprehension monitoring.

In a series of studies in the 1970s, Markman (1977, 1979) investigated the comprehension monitoring of third- through sixth-grade children and found that younger children were not aware of their failure to comprehend inconsistent text in a listening situation. When the children were challenged to "find the problem," their error detection performance improved, suggesting that children have a greater capacity for comprehension monitoring than their spontaneous performance reveals (Markman, 1979).

A number of studies have documented reader ability differences with respect to comprehension monitoring. It appears that children get better at comprehension monitoring as they get older (Garner & Taylor, 1982) and that skilled readers are better at comprehension monitoring than less skilled readers (Garner, 1980; Paris & Myers, 1981; Winograd & Johnston, 1980). Markman (1981) speculated that information about one's comprehension monitoring is a by-product of the active comprehension process and that all that may be necessary to detect one's failure to comprehend is the active attempt to understand. According to Baker and Brown (1984), younger and poorer readers seem to be unaware that they must expend additional effort to make sense of the words they have decoded.

Given the documented importance of comprehension monitoring in the reading process, strategies that facilitate the comprehension monitoring process deserve attention. Gambrell and Bales (1986) explored mental imagery as a reader-induced strategy. They tested the hypothesis that imagery would encourage constructive processing, continued effort, and sustained concentration during the reading of text and would therefore facilitate the comprehension monitoring process. In this study poor comprehenders in grades 3 and 5 were assigned to either an imagery treatment condition or a general-instructions treatment condition. The children read passages that contained explicit and implicit inconsistencies and then responded to questions designed to elicit information concerning their awareness of the inconsistencies embedded in the text. The children who received instructions to induce mental imagery identified both explicit and implicit inconsistencies in text significantly more often than did the children in the general-instructions (control) group. The results of this study were interpreted as demonstrating that poor readers do not spontaneously employ mental imagery as a comprehension strategy, even when they encounter comprehension difficulties. In addition, the results suggest that the capacity of children to successfully monitor their comprehension is much greater than their spontaneous performance indicates. When specifically directed to induce mental imagery, the majority of the poor readers (70%) reported that they did so, and they performed significantly better at the comprehension monitoring task than did the control group. The results of this study support the notion that imagery enhances the reader's ability to comprehend text. More important, imagery may be a particularly effective strategy for poor readers to employ when comprehension difficulties are encountered and more in-depth processing is necessary for complete and adequate comprehension. It appears that imagery as a comprehension strategy supports readers in expending more effort toward effectively integrating information across text, resulting in increased comprehension.

Imagery Increases Time and Effort Expended in Comprehending Text

Imagery is a form of active processing that helps students acquire a more meaningful representation of text. Several researchers have explored the costs and benefits of the extended time required for imagery strategy use. In a series of four experiments, Denis (1982) investigated the effects of imagery on the reading time and memory for informational content of college students. These studies tested the hypothesis that individuals who were identified as high imagers (HIs) would tend to elaborate images expressing the semantic content of the text while reading, thus requiring more time to read imageable text than low imagers (LIs). The results of the experiments revealed that when HIs read a narrative text they read more slowly and remembered the text better than LIs. In contrast, there was no difference between the HIs and LIs on reading time or memory when they read nonimageable text. One interesting finding was that LIs were able to use imagery when instructed to do so (as indicated by the lengthening of reading times) and achieve recognition scores as high as the recognition scores of the HIs. The results suggest that in contexts similar to spontaneous reading conditions, HIs spent more time elaborating images while they read narrative text. Denis (1982) hypothesized that imagery is a prime strategy for encoding information and "thus must be considered as one of the cognitive strategies whose purpose is to maximize the probability of information encoding and storage" (p. 545).

Hodes's (1994) research explored the speed–accuracy tradeoff of using imagery as a comprehension strategy. College-age students were assigned to either an imagery group or a control group. Prior to reading the text, the imagery group received instructions to form images, and the control group received general instructions. Students who received the imagery instructions used significantly more time to learn the material than did the students in the control group. On the other hand, the use of imagery resulted in quicker retrieval speed for information on a recognition posttest. The results of this study suggest that there is an inverse relationship between learning time and retrieval time for imaged information.

The Relationships of Imagery Self-Reports and Measures of Comprehension

Sadoski (1985) replicated and extended his earlier work (1983) regarding the relationships of imagery self-reports to a variety of story comprehension and recall measures. Both the earlier study and the replication and extension study supported the contention that imagery can serve as a comprehension strategy, as a mental peg for memory, and as a repository of deeper meanings that integrate text information. These studies reveal clear and consistent findings that imagery facilitated the understanding of text with students from a range of elementary grades in different locales reading different stories, both illustrated and unillustrated, with climaxes that differ in the amount of imagery evoked.

Taken together, these studies provide strong support for the use of mental imagery as a strategy for enhancing comprehension. Students can be taught to use mental imagery to help them understand and remember information they listen to and read and to help them write in a more organized and descriptive manner. Students need to be made aware of this particular strategy so they will be able to use it with a range of written texts.

APPLYING WHAT IS KNOWN ABOUT IMAGERY
AND COMPREHENSION INSTRUCTION

Studies by Belcher (1984), Gambrell (1982), and Pressley (1976) have documented that elementary-age students know how to induce mental imagery and that only brief training and teacher scaffolding is necessary for most children to effectively use mental imagery as a reading comprehension strategy.

Research clearly points to the benefits of self-regulated reader use of imagery as a comprehension strategy. When teachers assist students in developing the metacognitive skill of imagery, improved levels of comprehension can result. A planned sequence of activities can assist students in using imagery as a strategy for increasing the comprehension and recall of text.

Creating an Awareness of the Value of Imagery as a Comprehension Strategy

1. Using high-image-evoking text, provide students with opportunities to create images during teacher read-alouds of both narrative and informational text. Afterward, have students compare and contrast their images as they discuss the text information.

2. Have students use imagery to recall information from narrative and information text that has been read aloud or read independently. Stop periodically during read-alouds and guided reading and ask students to share their images of the story action and events.

3. Inform students that using mental imagery, or "making pictures in your mind," can help them understand what the text is about. When something is difficult to understand, it sometimes helps to make a picture in your mind. Using mental imagery can help clarify meaning and encourage comprehension monitoring (Gambrell & Bales, 1987). Specific directions, depending on whether the text is narrative or expository, are often helpful. For example, "make pictures in your mind of the interesting characters in this story," "make pictures in your mind about the things that happen in the story," "make a picture in your mind of the solar system." Providing specific suggestions encourages students to integrate information across text as they engage in the constructive processing of information. As a follow-up to story time (listening context) or silent reading, have students share and discuss the mental images they made while listening or reading. Inform students that mental imagery can help you remember what the text is about (Kosslyn, 1976; Pressley, 1976). In listening and reading contexts, encourage students to make mental images about parts of text that they think are important and that they want to remember.

4. Inform students that mental imagery can facilitate their writing. Have them "picture" what they are writing about. Using imagery during the composition process facilitates the constructive processing of information and language elaboration. The use of imagery during the composing process also encourages reflection and increases both the quality and quantity of children's writing (Gambrell, 1983).

Sequential Activities to Build Imagery Competence and Confidence

Fredericks (1986) and Barclay (1990) have suggested the following sequence of activities for assisting students in developing competence and confidence in using imagery as a comprehension strategy.

1. Provide students with opportunities to create images of concrete objects. Have students look carefully at an object, close their eyes, and form a mental picture of the object. Encourage students to compare their mental images with the actual object, noting how they are alike and how they differ.

2. Provide opportunities for guided imagery of concrete objects. For example, have the students make a mental picture of a cat. The teacher then provides guided imagery by refining the picture. ("The cat is all white and has very fluffy fur. The cat's tail is long and fluffy. The cat is looking you right in the eye. It has large gray eyes and long black whiskers.")

3. Encourage students to image and recall familiar objects or scenes. The teacher might ask students to image the outside of their homes and then draw picture of them. The students can then take the pictures home and compare then to the actual place in which they live.

4. Provide guided instruction to support students in making images of events and actions. For example, have the students make a mental picture of a cat, as in activity 2. Extend this activity to include movement and action. Provide guided instructions to support students in imaging movement and action, such as, "The cat is on the back of a large, stuffed chair. The cat suddenly jumps off the chair and lands on the floor. The cat cautiously looks around and then runs into the closet."

5. Develop the use of imagery in listening situations. Have students listen to high-imagery stories or informational text that describes common or familiar experiences. Read aloud to the students and stop periodically to ask students to share their images. At the end of the read-aloud students can work together to create illustrations based on their images.

6. Provide instructions to students to create their own mental images as they read stories. When students read text with illustrations, encourage them to focus on the illustrations and to use them to help make their own images of the events and actions in the story. Specific directions can be helpful (for example, "Look at the picture of the characters on page X. Use this illustration to help you make pictures in your head about what happens when they go camping").

Using the Think-Aloud Procedure to Teach Imagery as a Comprehension Strategy

The think-aloud procedure (Davey, 1983) can be used to help children learn how to use imagery as a comprehension strategy. In this procedure the teacher verbalizes thoughts about using imagery while reading a passage aloud to students. A short passage that is high in image-evoking language should be selected for this activity. As the teacher reads the passage aloud, the students follow along silently, listening to the text as the teacher thinks aloud and comments on his or her use of imagery. Following is an example of a think-aloud activity developed to demonstrate the use of imagery and an appropriate passage for imagery training (Gambrell & Bales, 1987).

> TEACHER: I have a short story, *The Desert Man*, that I am going to read aloud to you. You can use your copy of the story to silently read along with me. I will describe the pictures I make in my head about what I read.

The Desert Man

The old man was hot and tired. His long white robe billowed in the dry desert wind. He wiped his brow as he started to trudge up yet another of the endless dunes of the desert. He saw only a sea of sand surrounding him. The sun beat down on him mercilessly. He would not give up. He knew the camp was near.

At this point in the demonstration the teacher proceeds to read the text aloud and to think aloud about using visual imagery. In the activity below, the text (**bold print**) is interspersed with the teacher's think-aloud comments *(in italics)*.

TEACHER: *The title of the story is* **The Desert Man** . . . *I have a pretty good picture in my mind of what the desert looks like. Miles and miles of sand, blazing hot, very little vegetation.*

The old man was hot and tired. His long white robe billowed in the dry desert wind.

My picture in my head is of a very old man. . . . He is dressed in a long white robe, and the material must be light enough to be blown in the wind. I can see his robe blowing in the wind.

He wiped his brow as he started to trudge up yet another of the endless dunes of the desert. He saw only a sea of sand surrounding him.

I can see in my own mind what the old man sees . . . miles and miles of hot desert . . . perhaps he is wiping his brow because he is so tired and weary.

The sun beat down on him mercilessly. He would not give up. He knew the camp was near.

The look on the old man's face is very clear to me now. He has a look of determination on his face. He is very determined to make it to the camp.

The pictures I made in my head about this passage helped me understand the story, and they will help me remember what I have read. This is a comprehension strategy that good listeners and good readers use to help them learn and remember. It is a strategy that you can use to improve your comprehension.

Using the think-aloud procedure, the teacher models strategy use and the thinking process so that students can realize how the strategy is operationalized (Davey, 1983). Following the teacher modeling, students can use the think-aloud procedure as they read passages with a partner, taking turns reading aloud and sharing the descriptions of the images they make as they read. The teacher can then provide opportunities for students to use imagery with materials of various types (narrative and expository) and lengths. Finally, students should be encouraged to practice using visual imagery as they read silently. The is the final step toward independent application of the imagery strategy.

Guidelines for Using Imagery

The following are research-based guidelines for instruction in the use of imagery.

1. It is important that children understand that everyone's images are unique and are affected by their own experiences. To make this point, teachers can ask students to picture a clock. Students can then share descriptions of the clock they imaged. Some students will describe alarm clocks, and others might describe grandfather clocks or digital clocks.

This activity will help students understand the relationship between experience and imagery.

2. Although children need to understand that there are no "right" or "wrong" images, in reading text it is important that the reader use the clues provided in the text, along with background experience, to form appropriate images that will foster text comprehension.

3. Use listening–reading transfer lessons so that students become independent at using imagery in reading situations. Conduct guided lessons using read-alouds so that students induce imagery while listening to stories and information. Then tell them that they are going to read a text and that you want them to make pictures in their heads about what happens in the story. Research suggests that many students need teacher support to develop independence in using imagery as a comprehension strategy. This means that throughout the school day, in both listening and reading situations, the teacher will need to remind students to use imagery. Practice in using imagery in both listening and reading situations will support students in developing the habit of using imagery as a reading comprehension strategy.

Imagery as a self-regulated comprehension strategy has been shown to be effective with a range of learners, and specifically with less proficient comprehenders. The less proficient comprehenders will benefit most from the imagery strategy because they tend not to spontaneously induce imagery and they tend not to internalize strategic reading behaviors unless they have had direct and explicit instruction and guided practice. Instruction for these students must emphasize the active engagement of the reader in purposefully and selectively applying the imagery strategy in appropriate situations. In addition, imagery appears to be an effective strategy with high-imagery narrative and expository text.

Teachers can take advantage of young children's natural ability to image and teach them to use the imagery strategy for enhancing comprehension. With practice, students can learn to use image to their advantage as an independent strategy in listening, reading, and writing.

WHAT STILL NEEDS TO BE KNOWN ABOUT MENTAL IMAGERY

As previously discussed, there is a strong research base related to mental imagery that informs both theory and practice. As a result, educators have become increasingly interested in the potential of using mental imagery as a self-regulated strategy to enhance reading comprehension. The following section presents a range of new directions for research in the area of mental imagery that have implications for comprehension instruction.

1. *How do we support less skilled comprehenders in constructing images?* It is clear from the research that spontaneous or induced imagery during reading enhances comprehension for both children and adults. One of the major issues that remains unclear, however, is how to support less skilled comprehenders who infrequently employ spontaneous imagery. A number of studies have shed light on the issue and point to future research directions. Pressley's early study (1976) with struggling readers revealed that imagery training enhanced prose comprehension. Studies by Gambrell and Bales (1986) and Oakhill

and Patel (1991) used training procedures similar to those used by Pressley. The features of the imagery training in these studies that deserve attention in future research include scaffolded, direct instruction and extended practice with image-evoking text.

The relationship between mental imagery and text illustrations has provided some insights about the conditions under which readers employ imagery. Gambrell and Jawitz (1993) found that very brief instructions to induce imagery or attend to text illustrations enhanced text comprehension. Not only did students benefit from the brief instructions to induce imagery and attend to text, but also students who were instructed to use the text illustrations to help make mental images outperformed the other groups. This study, with its positive results, warrants replication with younger and less proficient readers.

2. *Does imagery enhance reading motivation?* Although most studies in the area of imagery have focused on having readers create images for the purpose of "remembering" or "understanding" written text, the research by Long, Winograd, and Bridge (1989) and Cariglia-Bull and Pressley (1990) explore other dimensions of imaginal skill that have implications for enhancing comprehension. One finding by Long et al. (1989) was that the strength of images (vividness) was related to reading interest. In light of these results and the findings by Nell (1988) that suggest that imagery influences reading pleasure, there appears to be a need to answer questions of whether imagery training would enhance reading interest or motivation.

3. *Exploring the image-evoking nature of text.* A related area of research that continues to be of interest is the image-evoking nature of text. Although many studies over the past decades have noted the value of using concrete text, few studies have systematically explored the effects of different language features. Long et al.'s (1989) findings of differences in image-evoking qualities among various language features provides a model for the exploration of text features. Information from a replication of this work with less proficient comprehenders would be especially valuable to educators creating textbooks and materials for imagery strategy instruction.

4. *Assessing the ability to image.* Researchers have also noted the need for broadening the types of assessment measures that should be used in future imagery research. Long et al. (1989) and Sadoski (1983, 1985) have raised questions about the assessment of imagery. According to Sadoski (1983), traditional assessment using multiple-choice questions measure verbal representations of knowledge to the exclusion of other representations, such as imagery. Long et al. (1989) also caution that multiple-choice measures are not sensitive to the imaginal mode. As imagery becomes a more integral part of comprehension instruction, it will be important to determine which assessment measures are sensitive to the nonverbal aspects of comprehension.

In summary, the current body of knowledge on imagery provides strong evidence of its facilitating effects on memory and comprehension. Because imagery has been demonstrated to be a viable self-regulated comprehension strategy, it is worthy of inclusion in school curricula, materials developed for students, and instructional methodology texts.

ACKNOWLEDGMENT

We would like to express our appreciation to Yutasha Ballenger of Clemson University for her assistance with the research and editing of this chapter.

REFERENCES

August, D. L., Flavell, J. H., & Clift, R. (1984). Comparison of comprehension monitoring of skilled and less skilled readers. *Reading Research Quarterly, 20,* 39–53.

Baker, L., & Brown, A. L. (1984). Metacognitive skills and reading. In P. D. Pearson (Ed.), *Handbook of reading research* (Vol. 1, pp. 353–394). New York: Longman.

Barclay, K. D. (1990). Constructing meaning: An integrated approach to teaching reading. *Intervention in School and Clinic, 26*(2), 84–91.

Belcher, V. (1982). *Visual imagery in basal manuals.* Unpublished manuscript, University of Maryland, College Park.

Belcher, V. (1984). *The effects of induced visual imagery upon the reading comprehension of above and below average third and fourth grade students.* Unpublished doctoral dissertation, University of Maryland.

Bruner, J. S., Olver, R. O., & Greenfield, P. M. (1966). *Studies in cognitive growth.* New York: Wiley.

Cariglia-Bull, T., & Pressley, M. (1990). Short-term memory differences between children predict imagery effects when sentences are read. *Journal of Experimental Child Psychology, 49,* 384–398.

Chan, L., Cole, P. G., & Morris, J. N. (1990). Effects of instruction in the use of a visual-imagery strategy on the reading-comprehension competence of disabled and average readers. *Learning Disability Quarterly, 13,* 2–11.

Davey, B. (1983). Think-aloud-modeling cognitive process of reading comprehension. *Journal of Reading, 27,* 44–47.

Denis, M. (1982). Imaging while reading text: A study of individual differences. *Memory and Cognition, 10*(6), 540–545.

Flavell, J. H., & Wellman, H. M. (1977). Metamemory. In R. V. Kail & J. H. Hagen (Eds.), *Perspectives on the development of memory and cognition* (pp. 3–33). Hillsdale, NJ: Erlbaum.

Fredericks, A. D. (1986). Mental imagery activities to improve comprehension. *Reading Teacher, 40,* 78–81.

Gambrell, L. B. (1982). Induced mental imagery and the text prediction performance of first and third graders. In J. A. Niles & L. A. Harris (Eds.), *New inquiries in reading research and instruction* (pp. 131–135). Rochester, NY: National Reading Conference.

Gambrell, L. B. (1983). Induced visual imagery and the written language expression of young children. In J. Niles & L. Harris (Eds.), *Searches for meaning in reading/language processing in instruction* (pp. 151–154). New York: National Reading Conference.

Gambrell, L. B., & Bales, R. J. (1986). Mental imagery and the comprehension-monitoring performance of fourth and fifth grade poor readers. *Reading Research Quarterly, 21,* 454–464.

Gambrell, L. B., & Bales, R. J. (1987). Visual imagery: A strategy for enhancing listening, reading and writing. *Australian Journal of Reading, 10* (3), 147–153.

Gambrell, L. B., & Jawitz, P. B. (1993). Mental imagery, text illustrations, and children's story comprehension and recall. *Reading Research Quarterly, 28,* 264–273.

Garner, R. (1980). Monitoring understanding: An investigation of good and poor readers' awareness of induced miscomprehension of text. *Journal of Reading Behavior, 12,* 55–63.

Garner, R., & Taylor, N. (1982). Monitoring of understanding: An investigation of attentional assistance needs at different grade and reading proficiency levels. *Reading Psychology, 3,* 1–6.

Graves, D. H (1978). Balance the basics: Let them write. *Learning, 6,* 30–33.

Guttman, J., & Levin, J. R. (1977). Partial pictures and young children's oral prose learning. *Journal of Educational Psychology, 69,* 473–480.

Hodes, C. L. (1994). The role of visual mental imagery in the speed–accuracy tradeoff: A preliminary investigation. *Journal of Educational Technology Systems, 23*(1), 53–61.

Jampole, E. S., Konopak, B. C., Readence, J. E., & Moser, E. B. (1991). Using mental imagery to enhance gifted elementary students' creative writing. *Reading Psychology: An International Quarterly, 12,* 183–197.

Kaufmann, G. (1979). *Visual imagery and its relation to problem solving.* New York: Columbia University Press.

Kaufmann, G. (1980). *Imagery, language and cognition.* New York: Columbia University Press.

King, M. (1978). Research in composition: A need for theory. *Research in the Teaching of English, 12,* 193–202.

Kosslyn, S. M. (1976). Using imagery to retrieve semantic information: A developmental study. *Child Development, 48,* 684–688.

Kosslyn, S. M. (1980). *Image and mind.* Cambridge, MA: Harvard University Press.

Kosslyn, S. M., Brunn, J. L., Cave, K. R., & Wallach, R. W. (1984). Individual differences in visual imagery: A computational analysis. *Cognition, 18,* 195–243.

Kosslyn, S. M., Van Kleeck, M. C., & Kirby, K. N. (1990). A neurologically plausible theory of individual differences in visual mental imagery. In P. J. Hampson, D. F. Marks, & J. T. E. Richardson (Eds.), *Imagery: Current developments* (pp. 130–139). London: Routledge.

Linden, M., & Wittrock, M. C. (1981). The teaching of reading comprehension according to the model of generative learning. *Reading Research Quarterly, 16,* 44–57.

Lindsay, R. K. (1988). Images and inference. *Cognition, 29,* 229–250.

Long, S. A., Winograd, P. N., & Bridge, C. A. (1989). The effects of reader and text characteristics on imagery reported during and after reading. *Reading Research Quarterly, 24,* 353–372.

Markman, E. M. (1977). Realizing you don't understand: A preliminary investigation. *Child Development, 48,* 986–972.

Markman, E. M. (1979). Realizing that you don't understand: Elementary school children's awareness of inconsistencies. *Child Development, 50,* 643–655.

Markman, E. M. (1981). Comprehension monitoring. In W. P. Dickson (Ed.), *Children's oral communication skills* (pp. 61–84). New York: Academic Press.

Markman, E. J., & Gorin, L. (1981). Children's ability to adjust their standards for evaluating comprehension. *Journal of Educational Psychology, 73,* 320–325.

Marmor, G. S. (1975). Development of kinetic images: When does the child first represent movement in mental images. *Cognitive Psychology, 7,* 548–559.

Nell, V. (1988). The psychology of reading pleasure: Needs and gratifications. *Reading Research Quarterly, 23,* 6–50.

Oakhill, J., & Patel, S. (1991). Can imagery training help children who have comprehension problems? *Journal of Research in Reading, 14,* 106–115.

Paivio, A. (1971). *Imagery and verbal processes.* New York: Holt, Rinehart and Winston.

Paivio, A. (1983). The mind's eye in arts and science. *Poetics, 12,* 1–18.

Paivio, A. (1986). *Mental representations: A dual coding approach.* New York: Oxford University Press.

Paris, S. G., & Myers, M. (1981). Comprehension monitoring, memory, and study strategies of good and poor readers. *Journal of Reading Behavior, 13,* 5–22.

Piaget, J., & Inhelder, B. (1971). *Mental imagery in the child.* New York: Basic Books.

Pressley, M. (1976). Mental imagery helps eight-year olds remember what they read. *Journal of Educational Psychology, 68,* 355–359.

Sadoski, M. (1983). An exploratory study of the relationships between reported imagery and the comprehension and recall of a story. *Reading Research Quarterly, 19,* 110–123.

Sadoski, M. (1985). The natural use of imagery in story comprehension and recall: Replication and extension. *Reading Research Quarterly, 20,* 658–667.

Sadoski, M., & Paivio, A. (1994). A dual coding view of imagery and verbal processes in reading comprehension. In R. B. Ruddell, M. R. Ruddell, & H. Singer (Eds.), *Theoretical models and processes of reading* (4thed., pp. 582–601). Newark, DE: International Reading Association.

Shimron, J. (1975). Imagery and the comprehension of prose by elementary school children. *Dissertation Abstracts International, 36*, 795–A. (University Microfilms No. 75-18, 254)

Stallard, C. K. (1974). An analysis of the writing behaviour of good student writers. *Research in the Teaching of English, 8*, 207–218.

Wagoner, S. (1983). Comprehension monitoring: What it is and what we know about it. *Reading Research Quarterly, 18*, 328–346.

Winograd, P., & Johnston, P. (1980). *Comprehension monitoring and the error detection paradigm* (Technical Report No. 153). Urbana: University of Illinois, Center for the Study of Reading.

21

The Argument Schema
and Learning to Reason

ALINA REZNITSKAYA
RICHARD C. ANDERSON

Reasoned argument is used to resolve a variety of important issues ranging from scientific controversies to guilt or innocence in murder trials. According to Kuhn, "it is in argument that we are likely to find the most significant way in which higher order thinking and reasoning figure in the lives of most people" (Kuhn, 1992, p. 156). Unfortunately, nationwide assessments and research studies consistently show that the majority of young and adult Americans do not have a firm grasp of argumentative discourse (e.g., Kirsch, Jungeblut, Jenkins, & Kolstad, 1993; Langer et al., 1995; Applebee, Langer, Mullis, Latham, & Gentile, 1994; Kuhn, 1991; Means & Voss, 1996).

The academic study of argument is an ancient discipline. Yet it has not received much attention either in contemporary instructional psychology or in the typical classroom. We suggest that schema theory, combined with a sociocognitive perspective on learning, can provide a useful framework for developing a theoretically sound educational environment conducive to the acquisition of argumentative discourse. In this chapter, we review theory and research concerned with schematic structures and present relevant findings from the studies of argumentation. Next, we discuss "collaborative reasoning," an instructional environment that can foster the development of argumentation and reasoning. In the final section, we suggest directions for future research.

ARGUMENT SCHEMAS IN TEXT COMPREHENSION

The idea of schemas as a way to represent and process information has been discussed by cognitive psychologists for decades (e.g., Bartlett, 1932; Ausubel, 1963; Rumelhart & Ortony, 1977; Anderson & Pearson, 1984; Thorndyke, 1984; Reed, 1993). Although definitions of *schema* vary, schemas are generally described as skeleton knowledge structures that can be instantiated with particular details. According to Rumelhart, a "schema is a data structure for representing generic concepts in memory. There are schemata representing our knowledge about all concepts: those underlying objects, situations, events, sequences of events, actions, and sequences of actions" (Rumelhart, 1980, p. 34). Anderson and Pearson explain that "a schema is abstract in the sense that it summarizes what is known about a variety of cases that differ in many particulars. . . . A schema is structured in the sense that it represents the relationships among its component parts" (Anderson & Pearson, 1984, p. 259).

Schemas are theorized to serve a variety of functions, affecting perception, comprehension, learning, inferencing, and remembering. First, schemas direct the allocation of cognitive resources. "Typically, many events occur more or less simultaneously; one perceives some portion of these events, or even some part of one complex event. This selectivity is schema-driven" (West, Farmer, & Wolff, 1991, p. 8).

Second, schemas influence the construction of meaning by integrating new information into existing knowledge structures. "The meaning is not in the message. A message is a cryptic recipe that can guide a person in constructing a representation. The representation that accounts for a message will usually contain elements that are not explicitly contained in the message. These imported elements will be the ones required to maintain consistency with the schemata from which the representation is built" (Anderson, 1977, p. 422).

Third, schemas aid learning by supplying "ideational scaffolding" for assimilating of information. "A schema provides a niche, or slot, for certain information. Information that fits the slots . . . is readily learned, perhaps with little mental effort" (Anderson, 1984, p. 248).

Fourth, schemas enable inferencing. "If the incoming information is incomplete, the schema may allow *predictions* about expected information and guide the interpretation of incoming information to match these expectations" (Reed, 1993, p. 42).

Finally, schemas guide the process of remembering. Rumelhart describes two ways in which schemas influence recollection: "First, they are the mechanisms whereby initial representations are formed and, as such, they determine the form of the memorial fragments. Second, schemata are used to *reinterpret* the stored data in order to reconstruct the original interpretation" (1980, p. 49).

Schema theory gained its credibility through many empirical investigations, which supported the aforementioned tenets of the theory (e.g., Bransford & Johnson, 1972, 1973; Pichert & Anderson, 1977; Anderson & Pichert, 1978; Steffensen, Joag-Dev, & Anderson, 1979). Although not without its critics (e.g., Sadoski, Paivio, & Goetz, 1991; Bigenho, 1992), schema theory continues to provide contemporary psychologists with a useful conception of cognition.

In this chapter, we attempt to connect schema theory and argumentation. To make the connection, we had to assume that argumentation is a knowledge domain in-and-of itself, and that it contains concepts and principles that go across topical domains. This assumption is disputed by those who view arguments as highly discipline specific, claiming that the only requirement for mastery is substantive knowledge, not the general skill of argumentation. "Arguments are usually resolved by bringing into the argument some additional relevant information not given in the original argument. We should notice this is not a matter of skill, but again, a matter of knowledge" (McPeck, 1994, p. 110).

Although we agree that substantive knowledge is necessary for comprehension, evaluation, and production of an argument, it is not the only ingredient. "The story of an expert who reasons poorly is as easy to tell as that of the logician without information, and it is at least as common in actual experience" (Govier, 1987, p. 233). An argument, as a rhetorical and logical form, has a purpose, a structure, and other desirable properties that are independent of specific contexts. With some variations, texts on informal reasoning and written composition agree on general characteristics of a good argument (e.g., Toulmin, 1964; Govier, 1985; Andrews, 1995; Fulkerson, 1996).

The concept of schemas has been previously applied to argumentation and reasoning (e.g., Hidi & Hildyard, 1983; Scardamalia & Bereiter, 1986; Crowhurst, 1988; Cheng & Holyoak, 1985, 1989; Politzer & Nguyen-Xuan, 1992). Researchers in reading and writing have used the term to describe a discourse structure characteristic of persuasion (e.g., Hidi & Hildyard, 1983; Bereiter & Scardamalia, 1982; Scardamalia & Bereiter, 1986; Crowhurst, 1987, 1988; Chambliss, 1995). "Following a general schema-theoretic line (Rumelhart, 1980), we may assume that every sort of discourse production is directed by some schema that specifies types of things to be said and their relationships. An actual discourse 'instantiates' the schema in force at the time—that is, provides particular instances of the kinds of things represented in the schema" (Bereiter & Scardamalia, 1982, p. 8). According to Bereiter and Scardamalia, a discourse schema for persuasion consists of several elements, including a statement of belief, a reason for, an elaboration, an example, a statement on the other side, a reason against, and a conclusion (Bereiter & Scardamalia, 1982).

In the area of formal reasoning, the notion of schemas has been employed to account for people's ability to make several kinds of inferences (Cheng & Holyoak, 1985, 1989; Politzer & Nguyen-Xuan, 1992):

> People reason using abstract knowledge structures induced from ordinary life experiences, such as "permissions," "obligations," and "causations" . . . A pragmatic reasoning schema consists of a set of generalized, context-sensitive rules that, unlike purely syntactic rules, are defined in terms of classes of goals (such as taking desirable actions or making predictions about possible future events) and relationship to these goals (such as cause and effect or precondition and allowable action). (Cheng & Holyoak, 1985, p.395)

The concept of an argument schema proposed in this chapter is broader than the previously outlined notions. It incorporates the rhetorical structure and the inferential rules of reasoning, as well as other cognitive and social practices appropriate for argumentation. According to Angell (1964), a basic argument consists of a conclusion supported by at least one reason. Advanced arguments will contain multiple reasons, qualifiers, counterarguments, and rebuttals. An *argument schema* is a network that connects individual arguments, representing extended stretches of argumentative discourse (Chinn & Anderson, 1998). We hypothesize that the functions of a developed argument schema include (1) directing of attention to argument-relevant information; (2) facilitating argument comprehension, construction, and repair; (3) organizing argument-relevant information; (4) providing the basis for anticipating objections and for finding flaws in one's own arguments and the arguments of others; (5) facilitating retrieval of argument-relevant information from memory.

Our key structural assumption is that an argument schema can be broken down into recurrent patterns, or *argument stratagems*. Argument stratagems are tactics utilized in reasoning and persuasion. They are the building blocks of an argument schema. "A complete argument stratagem is comprised of information about (a) the purpose or function of the stratagem, (b) the conditions in which the stratagem is used, (c) the form the argument takes, (d) the consequences of using the stratagem, (e) the possible objections to this form of argument" (Anderson et al., 2001). Pragmatic reasoning schemas, discussed by Cheng and Holyoak (1985), represent argument stratagems. However, stratagems need not be restricted to deductive or inductive inferences. They can also include informal heuristics that are successful at communicating one's ideas, persuading an opponent, or facilitating a debate.

Readers with developed argument schemas should have quite different experiences when interacting with text. Once the text is recognized as an argument, readers proceed to make use of the "slots" in the activated schema. For example, they can be expected to look for claims, supporting reasons, counterarguments, and rebuttals. Also, knowing the purpose of an argument (i.e., to express and justify a position) and its desirable attributes will encourage readers to take a more critical stance toward a written text. When an argument schema is activated, the reader may start making evaluative judgments regarding the quality of an argument. What is the author's claim? Is the taken position supported by reasons? Are those reasons acceptable? Are they properly connected to the conclusion? What is left unstated? Are alternative points of view taken into account? Are there any objections to the argument stratagems used in the text? According to Govier (1987), recognizing the presence of an argument is "something quite elementary and yet illusive to many not encouraged to think about reasoning, argumentation, and the justification of claims. It is the sense that reasoning is going on, that there is an inference made from some propositions to others, and that this inference can be critically scrutinized" (Govier, 1987, p. 233).

We believe that reading must go beyond mere encoding of information from the page. The reader should interact with the text critically by habitually making judgments regarding the quality of the author's message. Having a well-developed argument schema may help students appreciate what Beck and her colleagues termed the *fallibility of the author* (Beck, McKeown, Hamilton, & Kucan, 1997). Readers need to see argumentative and, eventually, other types of texts as *attempts to persuade,* which are not beyond criticism. Armed with an argument schema, students are able to reason about written material by analyzing its logical consistency, by formulating reasons that oppose or qualify the author's claim, by uncovering implicit assumptions, and by identifying common fallacies.

Unfortunately, the theoretical propositions delineated in the foregoing have not been extensively examined, as empirical studies of argumentative discourse are infrequent compared with investigations of other rhetorical genres (Chambliss, 1995; Goldman & Rakestraw, 2000; Whalley, 1982). However, it stands to reason that at least some principles identified in connection with other types of schemas and discourse structures could be extended to argumentation.

In general, familiarity with structural elements of the text affects comprehension and recall processes and outcomes (for a recent review, see Goldman & Rakestraw, 2000). Knowledge of rhetorical genres is important for the accurate and efficient processing of the text (Meyer, 1985; van Dijk & Kintsch, 1983). Readers can be aware of text structures on multiple levels, including sentences, paragraphs, and discourse types (e.g., Trabasso & van den Broek, 1985; Stein & Policastro, 1984); and their knowledge of schematic patterns influences recall and comprehension (e.g., Kintsch & Greene, 1978;

van Dijk & Kintsch, 1983; Carrell, 1992; Richgels, Mcgee, Lomax, & Sheard, 1987; Meyer, Brandt, & Bluth, 1980; Meyer, 1984).

In order to assist in reading, structural aspects of the text must be learned. "Super-structures must be not only in the text, but also in the reader's or listener's mind" (van Dijk & Kintsch, 1983, p. 251). Readers can develop their knowledge of discourse structures and their attributes through exposure, as well as through direct instruction (e.g, Stein & Trabasso, 1982; Applebee, 1980; Goldman & Rakestraw, 2000). Improved comprehension and memory follows from interventions designed to familiarize students with certain rhetorical forms of the text (e.g., Ouelette, Dagostino, & Carifio, 1999; Samuels et al., 1988; Armbruster, Anderson, & Ostertag, 1987).

We were able to locate only three relevant empirical investigations that focused specifically on analyzing argumentation in relation to reading. The first study examined comprehension of lengthy argumentative texts by senior advanced-placement English students (Chambliss, 1995). Successful readers recognized the claim–evidence–warrant structure for a simple argument proposed by Toulmin (1964) and constructed a gist representation that matched Toulmin's model (Chambliss, 1995). Also, at least some readers appear to have relied on argument schemas taught to them in their composition courses.

The second study was an assessment of the effects of direct instruction in argument concepts and organizational strategies on fifth graders' evaluations of written arguments (Klein, Olson, & Stanovich, 1997). According to this study, students' reading performance improved as a result of instruction that emphasized argument concepts, such as "claim," "evidence," "relevance," and so forth. Also, fifth graders' writing was positively affected as a result of explicit instruction in monitoring procedures for reading an argument, such as figuring out "what the author wants me to believe," or evaluating whether "the author's argument is good" (Klein et al., 1997).

In the third study, Crowhurst examined the effects of teaching persuasion to upper elementary students through practice with persuasive reading, writing, and/or explicit instruction in "persuasion schema" (Crowhurst, 1987). Only students who were exposed to reading practice plus direct instruction improved in text recall. Crowhurst concluded that exposure to texts exemplifying the "persuasion schema" was necessary for internalization of the schema (Crowhurst, 1987).

Based on the theory and research reviewed here, we suggest that readers can benefit from having a well-developed argument schema and that the acquisition and development of such a schema can be affected by instruction. Yet argumentative discourse is rarely practiced in the typical classroom (Langer et al., 1995; Applebee et al., 1994; McCann, 1989; Goodlad, 1983; Cazden, 1988). Current textbooks largely avoid argumentation in favor of narrative and explanatory text (Langer et al., 1995; Calfee & Chambliss, 1988, as cited in Chambliss, 1995; Chambliss, Calfee, & Wong, 1990, as cited in Chambliss, 1995). More than 40% of middle and high school students report never having been assigned to write a persuasive essay (Applebee et al., 1994). Argumentative and persuasive writing tasks are typically absent from the elementary school curriculum (McCann, 1989). Finally, classroom discussions, which can potentially provide an ideal ground for practicing oral argumentation, are generally characterized by short, constrained student answers rather than by open dialogical exchanges (Goodlad, 1984; Cazden, 1988).

Lacking practice with argumentation, students can be expected to have poorly developed argumentation schemas. Frequent reports of children's and adult's unsatisfactory performance on argumentative tasks support this expectation (e.g., Kirsch et al., 1993; Applebee et al., 1994; Kuhn, 1992; Kuhn, Amsel, & O'Loughlin, 1988; Means & Voss, 1996; Scardamalia & Bereiter, 1986; McCann, 1989; Hidi & Hildyard, 1983). People have difficulties comprehending a written argument, writing a well-developed persuasive essay, differentiating between theory and evidence, and generating genuine evidence, alternative theories, counterarguments, and rebuttals. Readers acquainted with only a few rhetorical genres tend to impose familiar superstructures on texts that exemplify different discourse forms (van Dijk & Kintsch, 1983). One can readily imagine undesirable effects of such a tendency, when, for instance, persuasive text is read as a story.

Collaborative reasoning is an instructional method that tries to address the shortcomings of current educational practices by providing elementary school children with an opportunity to develop the schemas necessary for argumentation. In the next section, we describe the collaborative reasoning method, discuss its theoretical underpinnings, and present relevant research findings.

COLLABORATIVE REASONING

The fourth-grade students in the following excerpt are engaged in a collaborative reasoning (CR) discussion. These students have read a story about a girl named Amy, who has been taking care of an injured goose. Now that the goose is healthy, Amy needs to decide whether or not she should let it go. This is a difficult choice for Amy, who has become attached to the goose. After reading the story, children are invited to debate Amy's dilemma in small groups.

SUSAN:[1] Well, maybe Amy wasn't a doctor or anything, so she might not be sure.

TOM: But the goose was already healed.

LORA: And it had been resting for a long time.

SUSAN: No it wasn't. It was just a few days.

JOHN: Where does it say that?

SUSAN: Look, here it says, "for several days Amy was . . . taking care of her goose."

JOHN: (after reading along) But that's not when Amy was deciding whether to let the goose go.

SUSAN: But then she put the goose in the cage, and it was just the next day that the other geese started to leave.

During CR discussions, students are expected to seriously consider multiple and often opposing perspectives on the controversial issue from the stories they read. Texts are carefully chosen to contain topics that are relevant to the students and can provoke a genuine and thoughtful dialogue. A distinct feature of CR discussions is that they have an open participation structure. This means that students don't have to raise their hands and can communicate freely, without being nominated by the teacher. The preference for the

---

[1] Children have been given pseudonyms.

open participation structure is based on the finding that "the higher levels of productive student behavior are probable if there is a balance between the interactional rights of the teacher and children" (Au & Mason, 1981).

Students in CR discussions decide when to talk and what to discuss. The teacher's role is to "promote reflective thinking and collaboration among the students" (Anderson, Chinn, Waggoner, & Nguyen, 1998). Characteristic teaching strategies include: (1) prompting students for their positions and reasoning; (2) demonstrating reasoning processes by thinking aloud; (3) challenging students with countering ideas; (4) acknowledging good reasoning; (5) summing up what students have said; and (6) using the vocabulary of critical and reflective thinking. Specific teacher moves hinge on the degree of control students currently have over thinking strategies, the dynamics of the group, and the direction that the discussion has taken.

Importantly, the emphasis in CR discussions is not on reaching a consensus on the issue but rather on having students experience the process of reflective judgment. The ultimate goal of CR includes "inculcating the values and habits of mind to use reasoned discourse as means for choosing among competing ideas" (Anderson et al., 1998). "Collaborative reasoning discussions offer students opportunities to expand their repertoire of responses to literature by learning to think in a reasoned manner and to explore diverse views prompted by what they read" (Waggoner, Chinn, Yi, & Anderson, 1995).

The key assumption of the CR method is that reasoning and argumentation are best fostered through social interaction. "Reasoning is fundamentally dialogical. Thinkers must hear several voices within their own heads representing different perspectives on the issue. The ability and disposition to take more than one perspective arises from participating in discussions with others who hold different perspectives" (Anderson et al., 2001). The idea that group interaction offers a good context for children's development of reasoning can be traced back to Vygotsky, who asserts that "the higher functions of child thought first appear in the collective life of children in the form of argumentation and only then develop into reflection for the individual child" (Vygotsky, 1981, p. 157). Interaction with peers leads to appropriation of cognitive and social competencies that can later be used by an individual in different contexts and with no external support. Children can benefit from participating in debates because "dialogical thinking is essential for rationally approaching the most significant and pervasive everyday human problems, and because without it we will not develop the intellectual tools essential for confronting our own instinctual egocentric thought" (Paul, 1986, p. 137).

Although many today's psychologists and educators continue to endorse Vygotsky's notion (e.g., Kuhn, 1992; Lipman, 1997; Paul, 1986; Wagonner et al., 1995; Onosko, 1990; Commeyras, 1994), there is little empirical research investigating exactly how group processes can lead to internalization of reasoning (Webb & Palincsar, 1996). A recent study by the CR research group tried to fill this gap by examining the process of appropriation during group discussions (Anderson et al., 2001).

In the Anderson et al. (2001) study, students' oral arguments were broken down into argument stratagems, as described previously. For example, during a CR discussion, a student can refer to story information in support of his or her position by using the stratagem: "In the story, it said [evidence]." As this rhetorical move proves to be a successful strategy, his or her group peers adopt it for use in their arguments. The following are the illustrations of this process from the story about Amy's goose.

CASSY:[2] (*lowers hand*) Um, I think she should let him go, because that goose belongs in the wild, and *in the story she said*, "come on, she said to the goose, I'm going to shut you up, you're, not strong enough for flying, yet." But later on *in the story, she says*, it says that she thinks that, um, he goose really is strong enough, that he can go. She just doesn't want to let him go, because she likes him. . . .

MARY ANN: But *in the story it said* that he was well enough to go and fly. . . .

JAMES: (*lowers hand*) 'Cause, it, um, the gander would probably die too, because, um, *in the story it says*, when they were flying away, all, when they were all far away, all of a sudden [alone] the goose [pulled] back and [sees] the gander, and it was like, and um, the gander had come back many times to the, um, barn uh, calling for his mate.

Importantly, we believe that the children in this excerpt are not merely parroting the inventive group member who initially introduced the argument stratagem. Rather, children adapt those rhetorical moves that prove to be functional. "Children appropriate an argument stratagem when they judge that the stratagem is a useful tool for advancing understanding or adding persuasive force of an argument" (Anderson et al., 2001).

CR researchers termed the process of social propagation in children's development of language and thought the *snowball phenomenon* (Anderson et al., 2001). According to the snowball hypothesis, once a functional argument stratagem has been introduced, it will be picked up by other children in the discussion. The analysis of 48 discussion transcripts led to identification of 13 argument stratagems. The frequency of using a stratagem increased once it was introduced in a discussion by a group member. The observed frequencies conformed to a contagious Poisson distribution, indicating that early occurrences of stratagems influenced later occurrences. An analysis of more than 1000 student turns for speaking gave strong support for the snowball hypothesis:

> The hypothesis holds true for stratagems serving various rhetorical functions: managing participation of classmates, positioning in relation to a classmate's argument, acknowledging uncertainty, extending and personalizing the story world, making arguments explicit, and bolstering arguments with evidence. Snowballing is found for both frequent and infrequent stratagems. It is found in different classrooms and in discussion groups of varying ability. (Anderson et al., 2001)

Anderson et al. (2001) concluded that social interaction helped children to acquire argumentative discourse and use it in group discussions. The question remained, however, whether or not CR students would exhibit improved argumentation in a context other than the one in which the skill was originally learned and practiced. Assuming that a fundamental concern of any educational initiative is transfer of learning, it was important to know whether students would be able to apply newly acquired knowledge and skills in a different context. Another recent study by the CR research group addressed this question by analyzing persuasive writings done by fourth- and fifth-grade students (Reznitskaya et al., in press). In this study, three experimental classrooms participated in CR discussions for a period of 5 weeks, meeting twice a week in small groups. At the end of the 5-week period, students from experimental and matched-control classrooms wrote

---

[2] Utterances that do not contain the strategem have been omitted.

persuasive essays. Their essays were compared in terms of the total number of argument components, such as supporting reasons, counterarguments, rebuttals, and certain argument stratagems (i.e., "In the story it said, [evidence]"). CR students had a significantly higher number of the argument components than their control counterparts (Reznitskaya et al., in press). In addition, a qualitative analysis of the selected essays revealed several superior aspects of the essays written by the CR students.

Consider the following essay of a CR student. It is written in response to story about Jack and Thomas. Briefly, Thomas cheats in the car race and reveals his secret to his classmate Jack. The question presented to the students is whether Jack should tell on Thomas.

> "I think Jack should not tell on Thomas. *It said in the story* that he had never won anything. It looked like Thomas was getting some friends and if Jack tattled Thomas would lose them. There would be other chances for Jack to win something. *Some people might say* that Thomas doesn't deserve the prize. But Thomas was poor because *it said* he smelled strange. Thomas was mean because he didn't have any friends. I think Jack should let Thomas win the prize. *But someone might say* that Thomas has been mean and Jack should tell. The reason Thomas is mean is because no one is nice to him. *But some people might say* that it meant a lot to Jack and that Thomas did not put much effort. (Which is true). This might change my mind."

For a fifth grader, this essay shows a substantial grasp of an argument schema. The student is able to clearly state his position, provide supporting arguments, and consider and rebut counterarguments. The student's propositions are unambiguous, complete, and relevant to the main issue. They are supported with the story evidence that is accurate and is differentiated from claims. Interestingly, the student's opinion on the issue is tentative, as indicated by the last sentence. He is willing to reevaluate his position when presented with compelling reasons.

Note the student's frequent use of argument stratagems, such as "In the story it said [evidence]" and "Some people might say [counterargument]." The latter rhetorical form was suggested by CR researchers to be employed by a teacher when introducing a counterargument. The use of a third person was intended to lessen the authoritative power of the teacher, so that the children would be more likely to offer rebuttals. Apparently, the child who wrote this essay was able to internalize this argument stratagem and successfully use it in a different context and communicative mode (i.e., writing). In a way, the essay represents a dialogue between "some people" and the student, in which counterarguments are not simply dismissed but are seriously considered and responded to. It appears that argument stratagems learned during CR discussions can provide students with useful tools that not only help to communicate but also can help to direct one's thinking.

The instructional method of CR affects the discourse and content of classroom discussions in the intended way (Anderson et al., 1998; Anderson et al., 2001; Anderson, Chinn, Chang, & Waggoner, 1997). Most students' utterances during CR discussions consist of arguments, challenges to the arguments of other participants, and rebuttals (Anderson et al., 1998; Anderson et al., 1997). This is quite different from the conventional discussion approach of recitation, in which students respond to the teacher's questions with specific story information and "almost never express arguments about an issue raised in the story" (Anderson et al., 1998, p. 185). Elementary school children seem to be able to learn the necessary skills for argumentation during group discussions, as well as to transfer the acquired knowledge to other contexts and communicative modes (Anderson et al., 2001; Reznitskaya et al., in press).

DIRECTIONS FOR FUTURE RESEARCH

It is both disappointing and exciting to note how many issues concerned with argumentation remain a matter of speculation rather than a well-documented empirical finding. Although there are obvious challenges in producing rigorous empirical evidence about higher order thinking competencies, many *answerable* questions still have not been addressed. In this section, we highlight the directions for future research in two areas concerned with argumentation: text processing and instruction.

With regard to text processing, as we have already mentioned, argumentative texts have been examined much less frequently than other text types (Chambliss, 1995; Goldman & Rakestraw, 2000; Whalley, 1982). As argued by Whalley, "it is not obvious how solving *all* the problems concerned with the comprehension of one text type, and in particular narrative text, would solve many of the problems with the other (and perhaps more important) text types" (Whalley, 1982, p. 498). Thus research methodologies applied mostly to narrative texts, including eye movement, reading times, verbal protocols, and various recall tasks, should be extended to argumentative texts. There are plenty of questions to be answered. What signaling devices and composition characteristics of the text can improve the comprehension and memorability of an argument? Will comprehension be hampered when the text structure deviates from the typical argument model? Would understanding of an argumentative text be enhanced if argument components, such as claims, reasons, and counterarguments, were explicitly labeled?

In addition to the issues concerned with the properties of the text itself, more research is needed to identify the characteristics of a successful reader of a written argument. How does substantive prior knowledge and an awareness of an argument schema affect comprehension, recall, and processing of an argument? In what ways does content knowledge interact with knowledge of an argument schema and its properties? What other factors influence the process of acquisition of information from a persuasive text?

We cannot seriously talk about argument comprehension without addressing the reader's ability to interact with the text *critically*. What kinds of metacognitive strategies are important for a critical reading of an argument? How do readers' prior beliefs about the content, experiences with argumentation, and epistemological commitments affect their ability to actively engage with a persuasive text? Further, argumentation, as a rhetorical genre, can be aimed at achieving different goals, including persuading an opponent, reaching a compromise, or collaboratively searching for truth. How does a perceived goal or an assumed stance influence one's interaction with an argumentative text? These are important issues that need to be addressed using a variety of measurement methods and designs, demographically diverse populations, and thematically different argumentative texts. Only by combining information from many carefully designed studies can we hope to see the emerging picture of how readers acquire and manipulate information from persuasive texts.

Identifying effective instructional methods for teaching argumentation is another topic that needs more attention from researchers. Educational programs intended to promote the development of reasoning and argumentation are typically evaluated with a pretest and posttest design assessing the effectiveness of the program as a whole (e.g., Nickerson, Perkins, & Smith, 1985). Thus, with the exception of a few quasi-experimental studies (e.g., Crowhurst, 1987; Kuhn, Shaw, & Felton, 1997; Klein et al., 1997; Yen, 1998), there is little information about the particular components of instruction in reasoning and argumentation and their relative contributions to the acquisition of intended skills.

Although group interaction has been shown to be effective in promoting the development of students' argumentation (Kuhn et al., 1997; Anderson et al., 2001), the phenomenon of social propagation needs to be examined in greater detail. For example, what are the characteristics of actors and the features of social networks that impede or facilitate appropriation of an argument schema? What is the teacher's role in this process? What are the limits and possible undesirable effects of social propagation?

Another promising instructional technique for fostering the acquisition of argumentative knowledge is practice with reading and writing argumentative discourse. For example, CR researchers are examining the utility of the World Wide Web for enabling children in distant classrooms to carry on written discussions. Web discussions could serve as a natural bridge between oral and written discourse. Children in diverse classrooms do not share an immediate context of situation and cannot see each other's gestures or facial expressions. Thus Web discussions may lead to greater clarity and explicitness, as well as better organization of students' arguments. In general, there needs to be more research investigating how the experience with reading and writing persuasive pieces affects the development of argumentative discourse. Will students be able to transfer knowledge acquired from writing to reading and vice versa? Will practice in reading and writing persuasive texts influence the way other types of texts are approached?

Also, what are the other instructional techniques and strategies that can enhance the effectiveness of teaching argumentation? For example, it has been argued that reasoning and argumentation are fundamentally metacognitive processes (e.g., Kuhn, 1992). They require the habits of mind to make one's own thought the object of reflection, periodically monitoring and controlling one's cognitive processes. Thoughtful monitoring of mental activities can be essential for successful learning and transfer (e.g., Klein et al., 1997; Bender, 1986, Cross & Paris, 1988; Brown & Palincsar, 1989). What self-monitoring strategies are required for a critical reading of an argument? What are the effective ways of teaching metacognition in the domain of reasoning and argumentation? How can metacognitive efforts be incorporated into group discussions?

Finally, there needs to be more research investigating how the acquisition and transfer of an argument schema can be facilitated through direct instruction in relevant abstractions. In a problem-solving domain, "an abstract rule or schema included with the acquisition instances may facilitate transfer to novel examples, especially when the acquisition and transfer are superficially dissimilar or when the rule is difficult to induce from examples alone" (Gick & Holyoak, 1987). Explicit instruction in abstract rules is especially effective when students already have an informal, approximate grasp of the schema (Fong, Kranz, & Nisbett, 1993; Cheng, Holyoak, Nisbett, & Oliver, 1993). In such cases, students "could take immediate advantage of formal improvements to their intuitive understanding" (Cheng et al., 1993). Further, because rules induced by students through practice may contain flaws or "bugs" (Brown & Burton, 1978), explicit instruction can correct misunderstandings that may occur when students are expected to "discover" general principles (Pressley, Snyder, & Cariglia-Bull, 1987).

Can direct instruction be effective in the area of argumentation? Klein et al. (1997) found that direct instruction in argument concepts affected argument evaluation but not persuasive writing, whereas instruction in argument strategies had just the reverse effect (Klein et al., 1997). Yen (1998) detected small, but statistically significant improvements in the persuasive writings of minority students, as a result of the direct instruction in 'argument heuristics' (Yen, 1998). The latter study, however, employed inappropriate statistical analysis, so the results may be unreliable. Much more research is needed, using various types of direct instruction, measurements, and populations.

The research directions just considered are closely interrelated. Thus learning about the characteristics of a successful reader will affect the development of instructional practices, and examining student contributions to classroom discussions will inform reading researchers and instructional psychologists. Today, the development of higher order reading and thinking represents a pressing national goal. Instructional programs intended to promote reasoning and argumentation need to be widely introduced to classrooms with diverse student populations. The successful development and implementation of such programs, however, is impossible without rigorous and ongoing research concerned with various aspects of argumentation.

REFERENCES

Anderson, R. C. (1977). The notion of schemata and the educational enterprise. In R. C. Anderson, R. J. Spiro, & W. E. Montague (Eds.), *Schooling and the acquisition of knowledge* (pp. 415–431). Hillsdale, NJ: Erlbaum.

Anderson, R. C. (1984). Role of the reader's schema during comprehension, learning, and memory. In R. C. Anderson, J. Osborn, & R. J. Tierney (Eds.), *Learning to read in American schools* (pp. 243–258). Hillsdale, NJ: Erlbaum.

Anderson, R. C., Chinn, C., Chang, J., Waggoner, M., & Yi, H. (1997). On the logical integrity of children's arguments. *Cognition and Instruction, 15*(2), 135–167.

Anderson, R. C., Chinn, C., Waggoner, M., & Nguyen, K. (1998). Intellectually stimulating story discussions. In J. Osborn & F. Lehr (Eds.), *Literacy for all* (pp. 170–196). New York: Guilford Press.

Anderson, R. C., Nguyen-Jahiel, K., McNurlen, B., Archodidou, A., Kim, S., Reznitskaya, A., Tillmanns, M., & Gilbert, L. (2001). The snowball phenomenon: Spread of ways of talking and ways of thinking across groups of children. *Cognition and Instruction, 19*(1), 1–46.

Anderson, R. C., & Pearson, P. D. (1984). A schema-theoretic view of basic processes in reading comprehension. In P. D. Pearson, R. Barr., M. L. Kamil, & P. Mosenthal (Eds.), *Handbook of reading research* (pp. 255–291). New York: Longman.

Anderson, R. C., & Pichert, J. W. (1978). Recall of previously unrecallable information following a shift in perspective. *Journal of Verbal Learning and Verbal Behavior, 17,* 1–12.

Andrews, R. (1995). *Teaching and learning argument.* London: Cassell.

Angell, R. B. (1964). *Reasoning and logic.* New York: Appleton-Century-Crofts.

Applebee, A. N. (1980). Children's narratives: New directions. *Reading Teacher, 34,* 137–142.

Applebee, A. N., Langer, J. A., Mullis, I. V., Latham, A. S., & Gentile, C. A. (1994). *The National Assessment of Educational Progress 1992 Report Card.* Princeton, NJ: Educational Testing Service.

Armbruster, B., Anderson, T., & Ostertag, J. (1987). Does text structure/summarization instruction facilitate learning from expository text? *Reading Research quarterly, 22*(3), 331–347.

Au, K. H., & Mason, J. M. (1981). Social organizational factors in learning to read: The balance of rights hypothesis. *Reading Research Quarterly, 17*(1), 115–152.

Ausubel, D. P. (1963). *The psychology of meaningful verbal learning.* New York: Grune & Stratton.

Bartlett, F. C. (1932). *Remembering.* Cambridge, England: The Cambridge University Press.

Beck, I. L., McKeown, M. G., Hamilton, R. L., & Kucan, L. (1997). *Questioning the author: An approach for enhancing student engagement with text.* Newark, DE: International Reading Association.

Bender, T. (1986). Monitoring and the transfer of individual problem solving. *Contemporary Educational Psychology, 11*(2), 161–169.

Bereiter, C., & Scardamalia, M. (1982). From conversation to composition: The role of instruction in a developmental process. In R. Glaser (Ed.), *Advances in instructional psychology* (Vol. 2, pp. 1–64). Hillsdale, NJ: Erlbaum.

Bigenho, F. W. (1992). *Conceptual developments in schema theory.* (ERIC Document Reproduction Service No. ED 351 392). Peabody College of Vanderbilt University, Nashville, TN.

Bransford, J. D., & Johnson, M. K. (1972). Contextual prerequisites for understanding: Some investigations of comprehension and recall. *Journal of Verbal Learning and Verbal Behavior, 11,* 717–726.

Bransford, J. D., & Johnson, M. K. (1973). Consideration of some problems of comprehension. In W. Chase (Ed.), *Visual information processing* (pp. 383–438). New York: Academic Press.

Brown, A. L., & Burton, R. R. (1978). Diagnostic models for procedural bugs in basic mathematical skills. *Cognitive Science, 2,* 155–192.

Brown, A., & Palincsar, A. (1989). Guided cooperative learning and individual knowledge acquisition. In L. B. Reznick (Ed.), *Knowing, learning, and instruction: Essays in honor of Robert Glaser* (pp. 393–451). Hillsdale, NJ: Erlbaum.

Carrell, P. L. (1992). Awareness of text structures: Effects on recall. *Language learning, 42*(1), 1–20.

Cazden, C. (1988). *Classroom discourse: The language of teaching and learning.* Portmouth, NH: Heinemann.

Chambliss, M. J. (1995). Text cues and strategies successful readers use to construct the gist of lengthy written arguments. *Reading Research Quarterly, 30*(4), 779–807.

Cheng, P., & Holyoak, K. (1985). Pragmatic reasoning schemas. *Cognitive Psychology, 17,* 391–416.

Cheng, P., & Holyoak, K. J. (1989). On the natural selection of reasoning theories. *Cognition, 33,* 285–313.

Cheng, P., Holyoak, K. J., Nisbett, R. E, & Oliver, L. (1993). Pragmatic versus syntactic approaches to training deductive reasoning. In R. E. Nisbett (Ed.), *Rules for reasoning* (pp. 91–135). Hillsdale, NJ: Erlbaum.

Chinn, C. A., & Anderson, R. C. (1998). The structure of discussions that promote reasoning, *Teachers College Record, 100*(2), 315–368.

Commeyras, M. (1994). Promoting critical thinking through dialogical reading thinking lessons. *Reading Teacher, 46,* 486–494.

Cross, D., & Paris, S. (1988). Development and instructional analyses of children's metacognition and reading comprehension. *Journal of Educational Psychology, 80,* 131–142.

Crowhurst, M. (1987). *The effects of reading instruction and writing instruction on reading and writing persuasion.* Paper presented at the annual meeting of the American Educational Association, Washington, DC. (ERIC Document Reproduction Service No. ED 281 148).

Crowhurst, M. (1988). *Research review: Patterns of development in writing persuasive/argumentative discourse* (Report No. 506374.) (ERIC Document Reproduction Service No. ED 299 596.) Vancouver: The University of British Columbia.

Fong, G. T., Krantz, D. H., & Nisbett, R. E. (1993). The effects of statistical training on thinking about everyday problems. In R. E. Nisbett (Ed.), *Rules for reasoning* (pp. 91–135). Hillsdale, NJ: Erlbaum.

Fulkerson, R. (1996). *Teaching the argument in writing*. Urbana, IL: National Council of Teachers of English.

Gick, M. L., & Holyoak, K. J. (1987). The cognitive basis of knowledge transfer. In S. M. Cormier (Ed.), *Transfer of learning* (pp. 9–47). San Diego, CA: Academic Press.

Goldman, S. R., & Rakestraw, J. A. (2000). Structural aspects of construction meaning from text. In M. L. Kamil, P. B. Mosenthal, P. D. Pearson, & R. Barr, (Eds), *Handbook of reading research* (Vol. 3). Hillsdale, NJ: Erlbaum.

Goodlad, J. T. (1984). *A place called school*. New York: McGraw-Hill.

Govier, T. (1987). *Problems in argument analysis and evaluation*. Dordrecht, Netherlands: Foris.

Govier, T. (1985). *A practical study of argument*. Belmont, CA: Wadsworth.

Hidi, S., & Hildyard, A. (1983). The comparison of oral and written productions in two discourse types. *Discourse Processes, 6*, 91–105.

Kintsch, W., & Greene, E. (1978). The role of culture-specific schemata in the comprehension and recall of stories. *Discourse Processes, 1*, 1–15.

Kirsch, I. S., Jungeblut, A., Jenkins, L., & Kolstad, A. (1993) *Adult literacy in America*. Princeton, NJ: Educational Testing Service.

Klein, P., Olson, D. R., & Stanovich, K. (1997). Structuring reflection: Teaching argument concepts and strategies enhances critical thinking. *Canadian Journal of School Psychology, 13*(1), 38–47.

Kuhn, D. (1991). *The skills of argument*. Cambridge, England: Cambridge University Press.

Kuhn, D. (1992). Thinking as argument. *Harvard Educational Review, 62*(2), 155–177.

Kuhn, D., Amsel, E., & O'Loughlin, M. (1988). *The development of scientific skills*. London: Academic Press.

Kuhn, D., Shaw, V., & Felton, M. (1997). Effects of dyadic interaction on argumentative reasoning. *Cognition and Instruction, 15*(3), 287–315.

Langer, J. A., Campbell, J. R., Neuman, S. B., Mullis, I. V. S., Persky, H. R., & Donahue, P. L. (1995). *Reading assessment redesigned*. Princeton, NJ: Educational Testing Service.

Lipman, M. (1997). Education for democracy and freedom. *Wesleyan Graduate Review, 1*(1), 32–38.

Means, M. L., & Voss, J. F. (1996). Who reasons well? Two studies of informal reasoning among children of different grade, ability, and knowledge levels. *Cognition and Instruction, 14*(2), 139–178.

Meyer, B. J. (1984) Text dimensions and cognitive processing. In H. Mandl, N. L. Stein, & T. Trabasso (Eds.), *Learning and comprehension of text* (pp. 3–52). Hillsdale: Erlbaum.

Meyer, B. J. (1985). Prose analysis: Purposes, procedures, and problems. In B. Britton & J. Black (Eds.), *Understanding of expository text* (pp. 11–64). Hillsdale: Erlbaum.

Meyer, B., Brandt, D., & Bluth, G. (1980). Use of top-level structure in text: Key for reading comprehension of ninth-grade students. *Reading Research Quarterly, 1*, 72–103.

McCann, T. M. (1989). Student argumentative writing knowledge and ability at three grade levels. *Research in the Teaching of English, 23*(1), 63–77.

McPeck, J. E. (1994). Critical thinking and the "trivial pursuit" theory of knowledge. In K. Walters (Ed.), *Re-thinking reason: New perspectives in critical thinking* (pp. 101–117). Albany, NY: State University of New York Press.

Nickerson, R. S., Perkins, D. N., & Smith E. E. (Eds.). (1985). *The teaching of thinking*. Hillsdale, NJ: Erlbaum.

Onosko, J. J. (1990). Comparing teacher's instruction to promote students' thinking. *Journal of Curriculum Studies, 22*(5), 443–461.

Ouellette, G., Dagostino, L., & Carifio, J. (1999). The effects of exposure to children's literature through read aloud and an inferencing strategy on low ability fifth graders' sense of story structure and reading comprehension. *Reading Improvement, 36*(2), 73–89.

Paul, R. W. (1986). Dialogical thinking: Critical thought essential to the acquisition of rational knowledge and passions. In J. B. Baron & R. J. Sternberg (Eds.), *Teaching thinking skills: Theory and practice* (pp. 129–148). New York: Freeman.

Pichert, J. A., & Anderson, R. C. (1977). Taking perspectives on a story. *Journal of Educational Psychology, 69*, 309–315.

Politzer, G., & Nguyen-Xuan, A. (1992). Reasoning about conditional promises and warnings: Darwinian algorithms, mental models, relevance judgments or pragmatic schemas. *Quarterly Journal of Experimental Psychology, 44A*(3), 401–421.

Pressley, M., Snyder, B. L., & Cariglia-Bull, T. (1987). How can good strategy use be taught to children: Evaluation of six alternative approaches. In S. M. Cormier (Ed.), *Transfer of learning* (pp. 9–47). San Diego, CA: Academic Press.

Reed, S. K. (1993). A schema-based theory of transfer. In D. K. Detterman & R. J. Sternberg (Eds.), *Transfer on trial: Intelligence, cognition, and instruction* (pp. 39–67). Norwood, NJ: Ablex.

Reznitskaya, A., Anderson, R. C, McNurlen, B., Nguyen-Jahiel, K., Archodidou, A., & So-young, K. (in press). Influence of oral discussion on written argument. *Discourse Processes.*

Richgels, D., Mcgee, L. M., Lomax, R. G., & Sheard, C. S. (1987). Awareness of four text structures: Effects on recall of expository text. *Reading Research Quarterly, 22*(2), 177–196.

Rumelhart, D. E. (1980). Schemata: The building blocks of cognition. In R. J. Spiro, B. C. Bruce, & W. F. Brewer (Eds.), *Theoretical issues in reading and comprehension* (pp. 33–58). Hillsdale, NJ: Erlbaum.

Rumelhart, D. E., & Ortony, A. (1977). The representation of knowledge in memory. In R. C. Anderson, R. J. Spiro, & W. E. Montague (Eds.), *Schooling and the acquisition of knowledge* (pp. 99–136). Hillsdale, NJ: Erlbaum.

Sadoski, M., Paivio, A., & Goetz, E. T. (1991). A critique of schema theory in reading and a dual coding alternative. *Reading Research Quarterly, 26*(4), 463–484.

Samuels, S. J., Tennyson, R., Sax, L., Mulcahy, P., Schermer, N., & Hajovy, H. (1988) Adult's use of text structure in a recall of a scientific article. *Journal of Educational Research, 81*(3), 171–175.

Scardamalia, M., & Bereiter, C. (1986). Research on written composition. In M. Wittrock (Ed.), *Handbook of research on teaching* (3rd ed.). London: Macmillan.

Steffensen, M. S., Joag-Dev, C., & Anderson, R. C. (1979). A cross-cultural perspective on reading comprehension. *Reading Research Quarterly, 15*, 10–29.

Stein, N. L., & Policastro, M. (1984). The concept of a story: A comparison of children's and teacher's viewpoints. In H. Mandl, N. L. Stein, & T. Trabasso (Eds.), *Learning and comprehension of text* (pp. 113–158). Hillsdale, NJ: Erlbaum.

Stein, N. L., & Trabasso, T. (1982). What's in a story: An approach to comprehension and instruction. In R. Glaser (Ed.), *Advances in instructional psychology* (Vol. 2, pp. 213–254). Hillsdale, NJ: Erlbaum.

Thorndyke, P. W. (1984). Applications of schema theory in cognitive research. In J. R. Anderson & S. M. Kosslyn (Eds.), *Tutorials in learning and memory* (pp. 167–191). San Francisco: Freeman.

Toulmin, S. E. (1964). *The uses of argument.* Cambridge, England: Cambridge University Press.

Trabasso, T., & van den Broek, P. (1985). Causal thinking and the representation of narrative events. *Journal of Memory and Language, 24*, 612–630.

van Dijk, T., & Kintsch, W. (1983). *Strategies of discourse comprehension.* Orlando, FL: Academic Press.

Vygotsky, L. S. (1981). The genesis of higher order mental functions. In J. W. Wertsch (Ed.), *The concept of activity in Soviet psychology* (pp. 144–188). Armonk, NY: Sharpe.

Waggoner, M., Chinn, C., Yi, H., & Anderson, R. C. (1995). Collaborative reasoning about stories. *Language Arts, 72*, 582–588.

Webb, N., & Palincsar, A. (1996). Group processes in the classroom. In D. C. Berlinerv & R. C. Calfee, (Eds.), *Handbook of educational psychology* (pp. 841–873). New York: Simon & Schuster Macmillan.

West, C. K., Farmer, J. A., & Wolff, P. M. (1991). *Instructional design: Implications from cognitive science*. Englewood Cliffs, NJ: Prentice-Hall.

Whalley, P. (1982). Argument in text and reading process. In A. Flammer & W. Kintsh, (Eds.), *Discourse processing* (pp. 495–508). Amsterdam: North-Holland.

Yen, S. (1998). Empowering education: Teaching argumentative writing to cultural minority middle-school students. *Research in the Teaching of English, 33*, 49–81.

IV

Intensification of Comprehension Instruction throughout Middle School, High School, and College

22

Straddling Two Worlds

Self-Directed Comprehension
Instruction for Middle Schoolers

RACHEL BROWN

As a middle school learning specialist, I often worked with students who struggle with reading comprehension. On one occasion, I wanted to see how well three middle school students understood the concepts covered in their science chapter on elements, compounds, mixtures, and solutions. The following scenario was the result.

"Oh, we don't need to meet with you today," Bobby, Ahmed, and Jim chimed in unison.[1] "We already studied for our science quiz."

"Prove it!" I said. "Since you're preparing for science, let's conduct our own experiment."

I asked each student how he had prepared for the quiz. I heard variations on a theme: "I checked my stuff over"; "I read the chapter again"; "I looked over the book, my notes, and my papers."

"Okay, here's our experiment. Let's see if you understood what you read and if your studying method really worked."

I began to ask some questions to see if they could define key terms and explain core concepts. Their answers were imprecise. Even when question stems were derived directly from the book, the students gave vague or incorrect answers. When I asked them to summarize a small segment of text, they were unable to reply. They had difficulty with both literal and application comprehension questions.

"Aha!" I said. "So what's the deal with this experiment? Did you understand what you read?"

Sheepishly, they all replied, "No."

---

[1]Student names are pseudonyms. Also, because this episode was recorded immediately after I met with students, the quotations are a close, but not verbatim, account of what transpired during our session.

We then brainstormed strategies they could have used to check their comprehension and to study more effectively.

This scene is noteworthy for several reasons. First, these students selected rereading as a study strategy, not a particularly powerful technique for studying challenging material because students do not engage as deeply with text content as they might with other methods (Anderson & Armbruster, 1991; Anderson & Armbruster, 1984; Caverly & Orlando, 1991; Craik & Lockhart, 1972). These students also failed to check whether they understood what they read. Inability to recall information was not the sole reason these students could not respond. I gave them ample prompts to trigger recall of textual information. They could not summarize facts literally stated in the text, nor could they apply the concepts introduced in the text. Obviously, before students can remember new information from texts, they have to understand what they are reading (Nist & Mealey, 1991; Anderson & Pearson, 1984).

During the middle school years, a marked shift occurs in the teaching of reading. The middle school transitions students from learning more about the fundamentals of reading in elementary school to applying that knowledge to increasingly difficult content-area texts in high school. Thus reading becomes less a subject to be learned in its own right and more a vehicle for learning content in other subject areas (Alvermann & Moore, 1991). In addition, sophisticated comprehension ability is a prerequisite to researching report topics, locating information on the Internet, and preparing for group projects and presentations. To meet these evolving academic demands, students need increasingly to display the goal-directed and skilled comprehension processing of successful readers. (See Borkowski & Muthakrishna, 1992, for more information on the nature of such skillful reading, otherwise known as "good information processing.")

CRITICAL RESEARCH ON COMPREHENSION INSTRUCTION

What constitutes skillful comprehension processing? Researchers have spent much time trying to describe the nature of such proficient reading. By studying highly competent readers, they have identified several characteristics that distinguish skillful readers from less successful ones (Lundeberg, 1987; Shearer, Lundeberg, & Coballes-Vega, 1997; Wyatt et al., 1993).

- Good readers use comprehension strategies when processing various types of text (Pressley, El-Dinary, & Brown, 1992). For example, they make predictions about forthcoming information, paraphrase, summarize and visualize text content, and make connections between textual facts and their background knowledge (Wyatt et al., 1993; Pressley, Johnson, Symons, McGoldrick, & Kurita, 1989).
- Good readers are highly metacognitive (Garner, 1987). Baker and Brown (1994, p. 353) define metacognition as "the knowledge and control the child has over his or her own thinking and learning activities, including reading." That is, students possess knowledge of themselves as readers based on their prior experiences with texts. They know their strengths and weaknesses as readers. Accordingly, good comprehenders exploit this knowledge when accomplishing specific reading tasks. They set goals prior to reading and monitor their understanding. If they encounter

difficulties, they reread or rely on other problem-solving strategies. When they finish reading, good readers evaluate how well they met their goals and how effectively they selected appropriate strategies.

• Good readers are motivated to work hard. They attribute their successes to effort and not to capability (Wigfield & Asher, 1984). They are willing to expend extra time and effort to apply strategies because they understand the benefits of their use (Carr & Borkowski, 1989; Palmer & Goetz, 1988). In addition, good readers are willing to risk failure and to challenge themselves because they know that they can depend on a repertoire of worthwhile strategies to support their construction of meaning.

Given this depiction of self-directed reading, this chapter focuses on the teaching of comprehension strategies that foster active, independent reading. Vocabulary, word recognition, and sentence-level instruction are not discussed, even though these traditionally have been linked to improving comprehension, as Pressley described in Chapter 1 (this volume). Instead, I focus on how to prepare middle school students to become better self-regulated comprehenders of the texts they encounter every day.

In this chapter, I make the distinction between strategies that improve comprehension and those that enhance students' recall of texts, focusing on strategies that support students' on-line reading of texts. That is, I discuss strategies that let students construct text meaning rather than strategies that help students prepare for tests requiring recall. Although comprehension strategies enable students to construct an initial understanding of a text, they may need to apply more elaborative strategies to ensure retention of that material at a level that permits later recall. Readers interested in strategies that foster longer term recall are referred to sources on mnemonic (Willoughby & Wood, 1995; Mastropieri & Scruggs, 1991), note-taking (Caverly & Orlando, 1991; Pressley & McCormick, 1995) and study strategies (Anderson & Armbruster, 1984; Tierney, Readence, & Dishner, 1990; Weinstein & Mayer, 1986).

In this chapter, I also emphasize strategies that are student centered. I do not present strategies that authors or teachers provide to make texts more understandable or memorable, such as advance organizers or guides. Information on aids supplied by authors or teachers is available in books by Tierney, Readence, and Dishner (1990) and by Wood (1994).

Strategies That Improve Text Comprehension

Early strategies instruction research consisted of the teaching of a single strategy designed to improve reading comprehension (Dole, Duffy, Roehler, & Pearson, 1991). In general, one group of students received instruction on a specific comprehension strategy, while another group continued with more conventional reading instruction. When reading measures were given at the conclusion of the study, the strategy-instructed group typically outperformed the group not receiving strategy instruction. Studies such as this validated the teaching of several important reading strategies to middle school students (Pressley, Johnson, et al., 1989; Pressley & McCormick, 1995). These strategies include the following:

1. *Making connections to background knowledge.* Comprehension improves when students actively seek to link text content with prior knowledge stored in memory. Stu-

dents activate their prior knowledge when they make predictions or form associations based on their previous experiences with the presented topic or with similar types of texts (Anderson & Pearson, 1984; Pressley, Johnson, et al., 1989).

2. *Capitalizing on text structures.* Familiarizing students with the common patterns by which an author organizes a chapter helps them grasp how main ideas are presented in text. Common organizational patterns include cause and effect, problem and solution, and description. Additionally, students can use text structure to enhance comprehension in another way. They can use the titles, subheadings, boldfaced words, and pictorial information to generate predictions to guide reading. Moreover, understanding the hierarchical organization of a text can help students keep track of information the author feels is most important for them to understand and remember. Block, Schaller, Joy, and Gaine (Chapter 4, this volume) explain such signaling in more depth, referring to this approach as "Telling the Text."

3. *Self-questioning.* Students can be taught to guide their comprehension by questioning themselves before, during, and after reading. For example, before reading, they can activate their prior knowledge by generating predictions. After reading a segment, they can check their literal comprehension by asking themselves *who*, *what*, and *when* questions to quickly check if they identified essential literal information. They also can ask themselves *why* questions to integrate information across sentences and to elaborate beyond information presented in the text.

4. *Summarizing the most important information.* Considerable research has been conducted on summarizing text, with much of this research centering on devising written summaries. However, teaching students to state in their own words what they read is a useful way to quickly check whether students are grasping the main ideas and most important details.

5. *Creating mental images of text content.* This strategy works best when a text segment is highly descriptive and lends itself to visualization. For example, picturing a nucleus containing plus symbols (+) and concentric circles around the nucleus containing minus symbols (-) may help students better understand the structure of an atom.

Teaching Students to Become Metacognitive

Later research focused on the teaching of single strategies in conjunction with providing metacognitive instruction, for simply teaching students to use strategies was not sufficient for them to become active, autonomous readers (Borkowski & Muthakrishna, 1992; Pressley, Borkowski, & O'Sullivan, 1984). They also needed instruction in when and where to apply strategies and in how to regulate their use of these comprehension strategies during real reading. To meet this goal, students require explicit metacognitive instruction in self-regulating their comprehension processing and selection of strategies. The following components are targeted in such instruction:

- *Teaching students to set goals for reading.* Helping students to identify a goal for reading will enable them to select a strategy that best corresponds to their needs. For example, students can adapt their rate of reading based on their task.
- *Encouraging students to monitor their comprehension.* Students should periodically check whether they understand what they are reading. Comprehension failures can be attributed to text-based difficulties such as coping with poorly written material. How-

ever, comprehension failures can also be student centered because an individual may lack essential background knowledge or be unable to access the appropriate information in memory to understand the text. (Anderson & Pearson, 1984, Garner, 1987). For example, a student may not know a particular word, may fail to understand a specific sentence, or may be unable to integrate information across sentences to build meaning across an entire text.

• *Helping students to find solutions for their problems.* Once a student encounters difficulty, he or she can employ a "fix-up" strategy to bypass the problem. Based on the source and nature of the problem, students can skip over a troublesome word or sentence, make an informed guess based on verbal or pictorial context clues, reread the confusing section, or seek assistance from another individual.

• *Stimulating students to reflect on their performance.* After reading, students can assess how well they met their goals. They can evaluate how well they selected comprehension strategies. Moreover, they can review what they did well, what they might have done differently, and what they might change next time they encounter a similar task.

How can a teacher help students develop more self-knowledge and regulate their text comprehension? Teaching students to think aloud, to use self-instructional statements, and to generate self-questions are three methods that promote self-regulated reading. Since these are important tools for fostering metacognition, I describe these approaches in greater detail.

In the past 20 years, researchers studying self-regulated comprehending often asked readers to verbalize their thinking as they engaged in authentic reading activities (Garner, 1988). This process is known as *thinking aloud*. When readers think aloud, they provide a window on covert activity—that is, how they select strategies, construct meaning, and take control of their text processing.

The think-aloud method can be used for instructional purposes as well. A teacher can use thinking aloud to model for students how a more expert reader tackles a challenging text. For example, while demonstrating how to use a strategy, a teacher simultaneously reveals to her students her thinking as she guides herself while using it. Thinking aloud shows students the thinking that underlies constructing an interpretation, as well as the thinking that guides strategic and self-regulated comprehension of text. In addition, thinking aloud can be used as a diagnostic tool. Students can be taught to think aloud so that their teacher can monitor their growing expertise as they practice using strategies to construct text meaning.

In addition to thinking aloud, metacognition can be promoted through the teaching of positive *self-statements*. Young adolescents, particularly lower achieving students, often harbor negative perceptions of themselves as learners. These views may be attributed to prior academic failures or to a growing emphasis in the middle school on higher achievement (Guthrie, Alao, & Rinehart, 1997). When students fail, they tend to attribute disappointing performance to: (1) not putting in enough effort; (2) lacking sufficient intelligence to succeed; (3) feeling unfair demands were placed on them by a teacher or some other external agent; or (4) experiencing bad luck (Weiner, 1979).

Obviously, in terms of self-regulation, the most positive self-attribution is the belief that successes and failures stem from the amount of effort a reader expends, because this factor is controllable. Thus it is beneficial to expose students' views of themselves as learners to reveal their self-beliefs. For example, Ortiz (1996) asked her college students to visualize themselves with an assigned text. She asked students, "What questions do you ask yourself when you don't want to read something?" (p. 494). She recorded a long list of responses that ranged from avoidance behaviors to negative self-perceptions. Obviously, one goal of teaching self-regulated comprehending is to replace negative self-thoughts that undermine confidence with more positive ones that motivate effort. Self-instructional training is one method to accomplish that aim (Meichenbaum & Biemiller, 1998).

Through self-statement training, students learn how to use affirmations or self-generated statements to guide themselves through the cognitive tasks in which they engage. For example, students can use self-generated statements to plan, self-monitor, select a suitable strategy, evaluate performance, and reward success.

Students also can learn self-instructional statements to replace negative self-beliefs (e.g., "Wow, I can read this type of material well") and inappropriate attributions (e.g., "Okay, if I put in the effort, I can do better"). In addition, students can use self-talk to cope with anticipated failures and to sustain motivation for a task (e.g., "Yes, this is tough, but I can keep going").

Self-questioning also is a tool for facilitating self-regulation. As stated earlier, self-questioning is a cognitive strategy when it serves to improve comprehension of text. However, self-questioning can perform a self-regulatory function as well. By self-interrogating, students can be taught to remind themselves to set goals, focus attention, monitor comprehension, select strategies and reflect on their overall performance.

Bringing It All Together: Interventions That Help Students Coordinate and Self-Regulate Their Use of Strategies

Although the early research on comprehension strategies taught us that teaching strategies was worthwhile, such studies provided little guidance on how to supply students with effective strategies instruction in actual classrooms. Thus attention shifted from identifying beneficial strategies and focused more on describing the nature of effective strategies instruction. Such studies examined the teaching of multiple strategies within the context of far more variegated reading instruction.

In this section, I present several research-based interventions that foster self-regulated comprehension of texts. These approaches provide an example of how to teach students to use several of the previously mentioned strategies in a coordinated fashion, applying them to authentic texts in a collaborative setting. They also describe instruction that emphasizes self-regulation of reading. As such, the instruction is heavily meta-cognitive in nature. That is, students are taught when and where to use these strategies effectively, as well as why learning these strategies is beneficial. In addition, students also learn to set goals, to monitor, to problem solve, and to evaluate, although the degree of explicitness of this instruction varies from one intervention to another. These interventions include reciprocal teaching, collaborative strategic reading, and transactional strategies instruction.

Reciprocal Teaching

In reciprocal teaching (RT), a teacher and students take turns applying four reading comprehension strategies in a small group. Students raise questions, summarize information, make predictions, and clarify confusions while reading segments of expository text. Palincsar and Brown (1984) used this approach to teach seventh graders with poor comprehension. In their study, teachers modeled how to apply the four strategies while students observed the experts at work. Then students took turns as dialogue leaders while using the four strategies. At first the students experienced great difficulties; however, with subsequent practice and subtle teacher prompting and coaching, they became more adept at applying the four strategies. Palincsar and Brown found that students who participated in RT showed marked improvements on a number of reading comprehension measures. Since their initial efforts, other researchers have replicated reciprocal teaching with numerous student populations in diverse settings.

Collaborative Strategic Reading

Collaborative strategic reading (CSR; Klingner & Vaughn, 1999) borrows components from reciprocal teaching and then elaborates on them. In CSR, the teacher, through thinking aloud and whole-class instruction, demonstrates how to make predictions, monitor comprehension, remediate difficulties, identify the gist, and generate self-questions. Once students become competent in the use of these strategies, they are assigned to a heterogeneous group. Each student assumes a role such as leader, clunk expert (this student cues problem-solving strategies), announcer, encourager, reporter, and timekeeper. Students use learning logs to activate prior knowledge before reading and to record their self-questions after reading. Cue cards guide the groups through the comprehension process. As students gain proficiency, the use of cue cards is diminished and eventually eliminated. When students read collaboratively, the teacher moves between the groups, offering assistance as needed.

CSR originally was intended for learning-disabled upper elementary students. However, since its inception, CSR has been tried with heterogeneously grouped students. Although research on the intervention has been conducted with younger students, the approach appears suitable for use with middle school students reading various types of texts.

Transactional Strategies Instruction

Transactional strategies instruction (TSI) is an intervention designed to improve comprehension through the use of cognitive comprehension strategies (Pressley, El-Dinary, et al., 1992; Schuder, 1993). In TSI, students participate in long-term instruction that teaches them how to coordinate a set of strategies to construct text meaning.

TSI is characterized by the explicit teaching of strategic reasoning and self-regulatory practices and is based on a model of direct explanation (Duffy & Roehler, 1987). That is, teachers frequently model, provide explicit explanations, and guide students through corrective feedback. The teacher serves as a model of expert strategy use; she models strategic reasoning, making covert thoughts and motivational self-beliefs visible to students. In addition, she scaffolds students as they use strategies to form and support interpretations. As such, she prompts them to select appropriate strategies, provides clarifying reexplanations and seizes "teachable moments" to reinforce information about when and where to use strategies.

One key element in TSI is the promotion of readers' aesthetic and interpretive responses to authentic texts. Teachers seek multiple, reasonable interpretations from students. They do not direct them toward one favored interpretation.

All this instruction takes place in a highly collaborative environment. Teaching often occurs in small groups so that less self-regulating students can observe the strategic and interpretive processing of more capable peers. Furthermore, the construction of texts is a joint effort among all group members.

Research validating TSI originally was conducted with low-achieving primary students reading narrative texts (Brown, Pressley, Van Meter, & Schuder, 1996). However, the intervention has been implemented in classrooms with low-achieving young adolescents reading expository texts as well (Gaskins & Elliot, 1991).

APPLYING WHAT IS KNOWN

Helping students become self-regulated comprehenders is hard work (Pressley, Goodchild, Fleet, Zajchowski, & Evans, 1989). Learning to teach students to become strategic readers is a long-term process, which requires much commitment (Brown & Coy-Ogan, 1993; Duffy, 1993). Given the challenge of this type of instruction, how can middle-school teachers begin to promote their students' self-regulated reading? In this section, I provide several guidelines to assist teachers as they initiate this process.

1. *Teach a few research-validated comprehension strategies well.* It takes time for students to internalize their use of strategies. Therefore, it is better to teach a few comprehension strategies that are needed most by students rather than to teach a large number superficially. Available resources, such as those cited earlier in this chapter, explain more about research-based strategies (Pressley, Johnson, et al., 1989; Tierney, Readence, & Dishner, 1990). There also are reviews that provide information on validated comprehension strategies geared specifically to secondary students (Alvermann & Moore, 1991; Symons & Richards, 1995).

2. *Analyze your students' needs.* It is important to find out what students already know prior to initiating self-regulated comprehension instruction. Some students, particularly higher achieving readers, may already possess a repertoire of comprehension strategies. Why recreate the wheel, if it is unnecessary? To learn if students use strategies and self-regulate their reading, teachers can set up miniexperiments like the one I conducted with Jim, Ahmed, and Bobby (discussed at the beginning of the chapter). Students also can complete surveys (see Harris & Graham, 1996, pp. 159–161 for a writing example) or participate in interviews (for an example with math students, see Meichenbaum & Biemiller, 1998, pp. 26–27) to assess their metacognitive self-knowledge and their motivational self-beliefs. Observing and questioning students during small-group instruction is another way to discover what students do and do not know. Additionally, a teacher can ask students to complete a checklist or write in a reading journal before, during, or after reading to learn more about students' use of strategies and their motivations for reading.

3. *Try to obtain a commitment from others to teach strategies.* Obviously, the more exposure students have to strategy instruction and the more such teaching is embedded in ongoing instruction, the more likely students will internalize what is taught. Therefore, see if other grade-level, content-area teachers are willing to teach or provide practice in

applying strategies to various text types. Also, collaboration is a great support to teachers who are new to providing this type of instruction.

4. *Plan time for explicit instruction in specific strategies and their self-regulation.* Explicitly explaining, modeling, thinking aloud, and giving many opportunities for practice take a significant amount of class time. This may mean teaching less content in order to focus on the teaching of self-regulated use of strategies.

5. *Do not teach comprehension strategies in isolation.* When providing initial instruction, the teacher should combine it with content that will be presented later in the lesson. At first, a strategy can be taught in a minilesson (such as during a readers workshop) or in relation to a reading task in which students subsequently will employ the strategy. The goal is to integrate strategy instruction as completely as possible into regular classroom teaching.

6. *Do not teach individual strategies in isolation from each other.* Even though strategies may be introduced to students one at a time, they should be taught to use them as a coordinated set. Part of teaching self-regulation is to help students choose the best strategy to meet their needs and the task at hand.

7. *Model use of strategies.* As a more expert reader, the teacher should show how he or she employs the strategy. This can be accomplished while thinking aloud and while using self-statements and self-questioning. In this way, students learn that good reading entails good thinking. They become accustomed to the type of internal monologue that accompanies self-regulated comprehending.

8. *Emphasize self-direction as well as teach strategies*: Teaching metacognitive control is as important as teaching strategies. Therefore, students need explicit instruction in how to set goals, monitor comprehension, problem solve, and evaluate performance. Self-regulation can be taught through the use of thinking aloud. Other tactics, such as self-statements and self-questioning, can be incorporated into the process of thinking aloud. Specific guidance on these three methods can be found in *Nurturing Independent Learners: Helping Students Take Charge of Their Learning* (Meichenbaum & Biemiller, 1998).

9. *Give clear and specific explanations of strategy use.* Self-regulated comprehension instruction is characterized by frequent descriptions and reexplanations of strategic reasoning (Duffy et al., 1987). When first introducing the strategy, the teacher should provide information about how, when, where, and why to use the strategy. Subsequently, the teacher needs to provide explicit, corrective feedback as required. In addition, teachers are encouraged to share their personal experiences of effective strategy use with students. It is important to reiterate the idea that successful readers are active, strategic readers.

10. *Motivate students to use strategies.* Teachers should inspire students to use strategies by letting them observe how their use enhances comprehension. Unquestionably, self-regulation is effortful. Part of instruction should entail showing students that the payoff in terms of succeeding on challenging texts is worth the tradeoff in terms of expending extra time and effort.

11. *Seize every opportunity to reinforce strategies use.* When a student uses a strategy effectively, point out this accomplishment to others in the class. Also, during class reading activities, take every relevant opportunity to highlight when appropriately deploying a strategy would enhance student understanding.

12. *Provide guided practice.* All methods—thinking aloud, self-instructional statements, and self-questioning—take time to learn. Teachers need to provide guided practice

as students use strategies to construct meaning, to form and support interpretations, to monitor their comprehension, to solve problems, and to reflect on their performance. Students need to be given ample opportunities to observe others and to practice on diverse texts.

13. *Provide independent practice.* Students need further opportunities to use their strategies independently and to generalize their strategy use to new contexts and to more complex tasks. Students should be urged to use and talk about their application of strategies when working on homework and when encountering texts in other classes.

14. *Heighten the profile of self-regulated strategy use.* Incorporate methods by which students and teachers can evaluate student progress in learning to become better comprehenders. For example, teachers often use rubrics to assess student projects and presentations. One option is to include a section in the rubric that assesses students' self-regulation on a particular task. In addition, students can track their progress through the use of journal entries, charts, checklists, reflection sheets, and other record-keeping devices. Students should be urged regularly to reflect on how well they believe they learned a strategy and what could be changed to help them learn the strategy better (Harris & Graham, 1996). Involving them in the evaluation process provides the teacher with critical information about tailoring instruction; it also facilitates the kind of evaluative thinking that is part of self-regulating comprehension processes. Essentially, when students see that self-regulated strategy use is important enough to be assessed, they receive the message that it must be important to learn.

WHAT STILL NEEDS TO BE KNOWN ABOUT SELF-REGULATED COMPREHENSION INSTRUCTION

Educational research has taught us much about the nature of expert reading, the instruction of single and multiple comprehension strategies, the need to teach metacognition, and the complexity of strategies instruction. However, more research is needed to answer questions about delivering the best possible self-regulated comprehension instruction to middle schoolers.

We cannot automatically assume that what works for elementary or high school students will work for middle school students (Moje, Young, Readence, & Moore, 2000). Although the same strategies may be taught to students across grade levels, we need to understand how best to reach all types of middle school students whose instruction differs from teaching in elementary and high schools. For example, in the elementary school the same teacher can ensure that self-regulated comprehension is promoted throughout the school day. How does this differ when only one content-area teacher may be teaching strategies in the middle school? Also, instruction in the middle school can be more project oriented and less content driven than classes in the high school. What kinds of strategies-based instruction lend themselves to this kind of teaching? Furthermore, the middle school period can be a time fraught with emotional upheavals as students awaken to a growing sense of self in relationship to their peers. As such, should self-regulated comprehension instruction in middle school focus more heavily on fostering positive attributions for coping with disappointments and on promoting positive self-beliefs than it does in elementary or high schools?

One big issue in middle school is determining where self-regulated comprehension instruction should occur. Perhaps English teachers should take responsibility for strategies-based instruction, as their primary focus is on literacy learning. What is the role of teachers in other content areas who do not necessarily want to view themselves as specialists in reading?

Moreover, recent research has placed a great emphasis on how to deliver this kind of complex, integrated instruction to students. However, additional research needs to focus on teacher acceptance. Since this kind of complex and integrated teaching is so challenging, more research is needed on how to gain and maintain teacher commitment to this type of long-term instruction. One significant conflict faced by teachers is how to balance the competing demands of teaching and assessing subject-area content and of fostering self-regulated comprehension for learning.

Another key question is how to meet the diverse needs of individuals in the middle school classroom. To date, much research on comprehension strategies instruction has focused on at-risk readers. How should teachers interested in this type of instruction meet the needs of students who already use viable strategies and who appear to comprehend quite well on their own? One notion has been to have more expert peers assist or tutor less able students in pairs or small groups. Just as the teacher serves as a model of proficient reading, so, too, these highly competent students can demonstrate how to use reading comprehension strategies successfully. However, one danger is that the better self-regulating students will assume the self-regulation for the entire group. In effect, the less successful students will remain passive and will turn their responsibility for self-regulation over to the more successful students. Therefore, what instructional supports need to be instituted to ensure that high-achieving peers scaffold, rather than dominate, group interactions?

Finally, becoming a self-regulated reader is a long-term process. What happens to students for whom strategy instruction ceases after a year? Do they continue to self-regulate their comprehension after direct instruction and cueing has ceased? Is a year sufficient to ensure that students transfer what they have learned to new tasks in subsequent years? Thus we need longitudinal studies to see whether students persist with self-regulated comprehension when they move on to other classes in which no such instruction exists.

It is true that without years of this type of explicit instruction, some students have become strong comprehenders on their own. However, the goal is to meet the individual needs of as many students as possible during the middle school years. The hope is that the type of instruction portrayed here will support middle schoolers as they leave elementary school en route to becoming more self-regulated comprehenders in high school and beyond.

REFERENCES

Alvermann, D. E., & Moore, D. W. (1991). Secondary school reading. In R. Barr, M. L. Kamil, P. B. Mosenthal, & P. D. Pearson (Eds.), *Handbook of reading research* (Vol. 2, pp. 951–983). New York: Longman.

Anderson, T. H., & Armbruster, B. B. (1984). Studying. In P. D. Pearson, R. Barr, M. Kamil, & P. Mosenthal (Eds.), *Handbook of reading research* (pp. 657–679). New York: Longman.

Anderson, T. H., & Armbruster, B. B. (1991). The value of taking notes during lectures. In R. F.

Flippo & D. C. Caverly (Eds.), *Teaching reading and study strategies at the college level* (pp. 166–193). Newark, DE: International Reading Association.

Anderson, R. C., & Pearson, P. D. (1984). A schema-theoretic view of basic processes in reading comprehension. In P. D. Pearson, R. Barr, M. Kamil, & P. Mosenthal (Eds.), *Handbook of reading research* (pp. 255–292). New York: Longman.

Baker, L., & Brown, A. L. (1984). Metacognitive skills and reading. In P. D. Pearson, R. Barr, M. Kamil, & P. Mosenthal (Eds.), *Handbook of reading research* (pp. 353–394). New York: Longman.

Borkowski, J. G., & Muthakrishna, N. (1992). Moving metacognition into the classroom: "Working models" and effective strategy teaching. In M. Pressley, K. R. Harris, & J. Guthrie (Eds.), *Promoting academic competence and literacy in school* (pp. 478–501). San Diego, CA: Academic Press.

Brown, R., & Coy-Ogan, L. (1993). The evolution of transactional strategies instruction in one teacher's classroom. *The Elementary School Journal, 94,* 221–233.

Brown, R., Pressley, M., Van Meter, P., & Schuder, T. (1996). A quasi-experimental validation of transactional strategies instruction with previously low-achieving, second-grade readers. *Journal of Educational Psychology, 88,* 18–37.

Carr, M., & Borkowski, J. G. (1989). Attributional training and the generalization of reading strategies with underachieving children. *Learning and Individual Differences, 1,* 327–341.

Caverly, D. C., & Orlando, V. P. (1991). Textbook study strategies. In R. F. Flippo & D. C. Caverly (Eds.), *Teaching reading and study strategies at the college level* (pp. 86–165). Newark, DE: International Reading Association.

Craik, F. I. M., & Lockhart, R. S. (1972). Levels of processing: A framework for memory research. *Journal of Verbal Learning and Verbal Behavior, 11,* 671–684.

Dole, J. A., Duffy, G. G., Roehler, L. R., & Pearson, P. D. (1991). Moving from the old to the new: Research on reading comprehension instruction. *Review of Educational Research, 61,* 239–264.

Duffy, G. G. (1993). Teacher's progress toward becoming expert strategy teachers. *The Elementary School Journal, 94,* 111–120.

Duffy, G. G., & Roehler, L. R. (1987). Improving reading instruction through the use of responsive elaboration. *Reading Teacher, 40,* 514–520.

Garner, R. (1987). *Metacognition and reading comprehension.* Norwood, NJ: Ablex.

Garner, R. (1988). Verbal-report data on cognitive and metacognitive strategies. In C. E. Weinstein, E. T. Goetz, & P. A. Alexander (Eds.), *Learning and study strategies: Issues in assessment instruction, and evaluation* (pp. 63–76). San Diego, CA: Academic Press.

Gaskins, I., & Elliot, T. (1991). *Implementing cognitive strategy training across the school: The Benchmark manual for teachers.* Cambridge, MA: Brookline Books.

Guthrie, J. T., Alao, S., & Rinehart, J. M. (1997). Engagement in reading for young adolescents. *Journal of Adolescent and Adult Literacy, 40,* 438–446.

Harris, K. R., & Graham, S. (1996). *Making the writing process work: Strategies for composition and self-regulation.* Cambridge, MA: Brookline Books.

Klingner, J. K., & Vaughn, S. (1999). Promoting reading comprehension, content learning, and English acquisition through collaborative strategic reading (CSR). *Reading Teacher, 52,* 738–747.

Lundeberg, M. A. (1987). Metacognitive aspects of reading comprehension: Studying understanding in legal case analysis. *Reading Research Quarterly, 22,* 407–432.

Mastropieri, M. A., & Scruggs, T. E., (1991). *Teaching students ways to remember: Strategies for learning mnemonically.* Cambridge, MA: Brookline Books.

Meichenbaum, D., & Biemiller, A. (1998). *Nurturing independent learners: Helping students take charge of their learning.* Cambridge, MA: Brookline Books.

Moje, E. B., Young, J. P., Readence, J. E., & Moore, D. W., (2000). Reinventing adolescent literacy for new times: Perennial and millennial issues. *Journal of Adolescent and Adult Literacy, 43,* 400–410).

Nist, S. L., & Mealey, D. L. (1991). Teacher-directed comprehension strategies. In R. F. Flippo & D. C. Caverly (Eds.), *Teaching reading and study strategies at the college level* (pp. 42–85). Newark, DE: International Reading Association.

Ortiz, R. K. (1996). Awareness of inner dialogues can alter reading behaviors. *Journal of Adolescent and Adult Literacy, 39,* 494–495.

Palincsar, A. S., & Brown, A. L. (1984). The reciprocal teaching of comprehension-fostering and comprehension-monitoring activities. *Cognition and Instruction, 1,* 117–175.

Palmer, D. J., & Goetz, E. T. (1988). Selection and use of study strategies: The role of the studier's beliefs about self and strategies. In C. E. Weinstein, E. T. Goetz, & P. A. Alexander (Eds.), *Learning and study strategies: Issues in assessment, instruction and evaluation* (pp. 41–62). San Diego, CA: Academic Press.

Pressley, M., Borkowski, J. G., & O'Sullivan, J. T. (1984) Memory strategy instruction is made of this: Metamemory and durable strategy use. *Educational Psychologist, 19,* 94–107.

Pressley, M., El-Dinary, P. B., & Brown, R. (1992). Skilled and not-so-skilled reading: Good information processing and not-so-good information processing. In M. Pressley, K. R. Harris, & J. T. Guthrie (Eds.), *Promoting academic competence and literacy in school* (pp. 92–129). San Diego, CA: Academic Press.

Pressley, M., El-Dinary, P. B., Gaskins, I., Schuder, T., Bergman, J. L., Almasi, J., & Brown, R. (1992). Beyond direct explanation: Transactional instruction of reading comprehension strategies. *Elementary School Journal, 92,* 513–535.

Pressley, M., Goodchild, R., Fleet, J., Zajchowski, R., & Evans, E. D. (1989). The challenges of classroom strategy instruction. *Elementary School Journal, 90,* 3–32.

Pressley, M., Johnson, C., Symons, S., McGoldrick, J., & Kurita, J. (1989). Strategies that improve children's memory and comprehension of text. *Elementary School Journal, 90,* 3–32.

Pressley, M., & McCormick, C. B. (1995). *Advanced educational psychology for educators, researchers, and policymakers.* New York: HarperCollins.

Pressley, M., Schuder, T., Teachers in the Students Achieving Learning Program, Bergman, J. L., & El-Dinary, P. B. (1992). A researcher–educator collaborative interview study of transactional comprehension strategies instruction. *Journal of Educational Psychology, 84,* 231–246.

Schuder, T. (1993). The genesis of transactional strategies instruction in a reading program for at-risk students. *The Elementary School Journal, 94,* 183–200.

Shearer, B. A., Lundeberg, M. A., & Coballes-Vega, C. (1997). Making the connection between research and reality: Strategies teachers use to read and evaluate journal articles. *Journal of Educational Psychology, 89,* 592–598.

Symons, S., & Richards, C. (1995). Cognitive strategies for reading comprehension. In E. Wood, V. E. Woloshyn, & T. Willoughby (Eds.), *Cognitive strategy instruction for middle and high schools* (pp. 66–87). Cambridge, MA: Brookline Books.

Tierney, R. J., Readence, J. E., & Dishner, E. (1990). *Reading strategies and practices: A compendium.* Needham Heights, MA: Allyn & Bacon.

Weiner, B. (1979). A theory of motivation for some classroom experiences. *Journal of Educational Psychology, 71,* 3–25.

Weinstein, C. E., & Mayer, R. E. (1986). The teaching of learning strategies. In M. C. Wittrock (Ed.), *Handbook of research on teaching* (3rd ed., pp. 315–327). New York: Macmillan.

Wigfield, A., & Asher, S. R. (1984). Social and motivating influences on reading. In P. D. Pearson, R. Barr, M. Kamil, & P. Mosenthal (Eds.), *Handbook of reading research* (pp. 423–452). New York: Longman.

Willoughby, T., & Wood, E. (1995). Mnemonic strategies. In E. Wood, V. E. Woloshyn, & T. Willoughby (Eds.), *Cognitive strategy instruction for middle and high schools* (pp. 5–17). Cambridge, MA: Brookline Books.

Wood, K. D. (1994). *Practical strategies for improving instruction*. Columbus, OH: National Middle School Association.

Wyatt, D., Pressley, M., El-Dinary, P. B., Stein, S., Evans, P., & Brown, R. (1993). Comprehension strategies, worth and credibility monitoring, and evaluations: Cold and hot cognition when experts read professional articles that are important to them. *Learning and Individual Differences, 5*, 49–72.

23

Improving the Reading Comprehension of At-Risk Adolescents

JOSEPH B. FISHER
JEAN B. SCHUMAKER
DONALD D. DESHLER

THE CHALLENGE

Students with high-incidence disabilities (e.g., learning disabilities) have fared poorly in secondary schools. Compared with their peers without disabilities, these students experience a broad array of performance and adjustment problems, including: (1) higher rates of absenteeism, (2) lower grade point averages, (3) higher course failure rates (Wagner, Blackorby, & Hebbeler, 1993,; (4) lower levels of self-confidence, and (5) higher rates of inappropriate social behaviors (Schumaker, 1992). Predictably, more than one third (38%) of these students drop out of high school each year, and only one fourth (25%) pursue postsecondary education (Wagner et al., 1993). In short, many students with high-incidence disabilities are not being prepared to succeed in high school, and they are not likely to succeed when they face the demanding expectations of the global economy or the expected dramatic transformation of work and the workplace (Martin, 1999; Oliver, 1999; Rifkin, 1995).

As discouraging as the present state of circumstances is, a number of current educational trends may exacerbate the situation even further. Foremost among these trends are the expectations that: (1) students with high-incidence disabilities be included in general education classrooms for most if not all of the school day (Kauffman, 1994); (2) all students, including those with disabilities, meet the curriculum standards adopted by states and professional organizations (Erickson, Ysseldyke, Thurlow, & Elliot, 1998; National Research Council, 1997); (3) all students not merely acquire skills and knowledge but apply what they have learned to solve authentic problems (Kameenui & Carnine, 1998).

In order for students with disabilities to succeed within the larger context of these trends, they must be able to learn and apply the challenging content taught in today's secondary schools. Central to this challenge is the expectation that students with high-incidence disabilities will comprehend large amounts of complex content presented in written formats in subject-area classes. Much of this written information is found in students' textbooks. These textbooks not only seem to get thicker each year but also can contain complex information written several readability levels above the students' grade level.

Meeting the expectations associated with comprehending and learning this written information requires students to use a broad array of higher order information-processing skills. Students with such skills (1) plan for their own comprehension; (2) know a large number of comprehension strategies; (3) understand when, where, why, and how to apply these strategies; and (4) monitor their own comprehension (Pressley, Borkowski, & Schneider, 1990). For example, when faced with the task of comprehending a passage from a textbook, good information processors (Pressley & Woloshyn, 1995) first survey it to determine what information is important to learn. During reading, they process important information more deeply than less relevant information. They might paraphrase it, make mental pictures of it, and ask and answer questions about it. They also might relate what they are learning to their prior knowledge. After reading, these students revisit sections that contained particularly important information and work to clarify information they may not have fully understood (Pressley & Afflerbach, 1995).

Unfortunately, research has shown that students with high-incidence disabilities often lack the higher order information-processing skills needed to comprehend complex written content. For example, on tests of reading ability, adolescents with learning disabilities typically score below the 10th percentile (Deshler, Schumaker, Alley, Warner, & Clark, 1982). On average, they read at the fourth-grade level throughout junior and senior high. These students also typically lack knowledge of such comprehension strategies as (1) how to survey text (Schumaker, Deshler, Alley, Warner, & Denton, 1982), (2) how to visualize what is read (Clark, Deshler, Schumaker, Alley, & Warner, 1984), (3) how to ask oneself questions to monitor understanding (Clark et al., 1984), and (4) how to summarize what has been learned (Schumaker & Deshler, 1992).

To help such students meet the expectation that they comprehend complex written information, teachers will have to teach them the necessary strategies. In addition, they will have to deliver subject-area instruction in such a way as to compensate for the information-processing deficits of students with disabilities. Teachers who provide such instruction (1) engage students in the learning process; (2) present abstract, complex concepts in concrete forms; (3) make apparent the structure or organization of information; (4) make explicit the relationships among pieces of information; (5) distinguish between important and less important information; and (6) connect new information to previously learned information (Lenz, Bulgren, & Hudson, 1990) and ensure that students understand the meaning of key vocabulary related to the topic that they will encounter in the readings.

Nevertheless, much of the subject-matter instruction in today's schools is not responsive to the information-processing needs of students with disabilities. For example, research has indicated that lecture and independent seatwork activities are the dominant modes of instruction in secondary-level classrooms (McIntosh, Vaughn, Schumm, Haager, & Lee, 1993; Putnam, Deshler, & Schumaker, 1992). During the teacher-centered instructional method of lecturing, students are provided little opportunity to discuss what they know about a topic and to relate their prior knowledge to new content (McIntosh et al., 1993); they are required to seek their own clarification of information they are not fully understanding (Skrtic, Clark, & Knowlton, 1980); and they receive little feedback about their learning (McIntosh et al., 1993; Skrtic et al., 1980). Additionally, teachers often do not provide advance organizers (Lenz, Alley, & Schumaker, 1987), do not explicitly describe concepts being taught (Bulgren, Schumaker, & Deshler, 1988), and do not monitor student understanding of the information they are to learn (McIntosh et al., 1993).

Clearly, in order for students with high-incidence disabilities to meet the expectation that they comprehend the complex written content associated with subject-area classes, educational practices must be altered. Specifically, these students must be taught the strategies they need to comprehend written information, and their teachers must learn to present information in such a way as to enhance their students' comprehension. Fortunately, in recent years, much has been learned about how the comprehension of students with disabilities can be improved. Two approaches that have been developed and field tested are the learning strategies approach and the content enhancement approach.

THE LEARNING STRATEGIES APPROACH

The learning strategies approach has been designed so that students who lack higher order information-processing skills can be taught directly the skills they need to succeed in school. This approach focuses on the instruction of learning strategies or sets of behaviors that learners use to approach academic tasks. Over the past 20 years, specific strategies and associated instructional methods have been developed to help students to comprehend narrative and expository text, understand and remember important vocabulary words, and interpret visual aids. (See Table 23.1 for descriptions of the learning strategies associated with reading comprehension.)

Each of these strategies actually constitutes a *strategy system*—a complex set of cognitive and metacognitive strategies and other behaviors used in sequence to complete a comprehension task. For example, the paraphrasing strategy is composed of three steps: (1) read a paragraph; (2) ask yourself, "What are the main idea and details in this paragraph?"; and (3) put the main idea and details in your own words. The first step prompts students to approach the reading task in small chunks. The second step prompts students to use the cognitive strategy of self-questioning. To answer the question, students must look the main idea and details in the paragraph, discriminate the main idea from details, and discriminate important details from unimportant details. The final step prompts students to use the cognitive strategy of summarizing to translate the main ideas and details into their own words.

Instructional Methods

Learning strategies such as the paraphrasing strategy are taught to students using an eight-stage instructional model (Ellis, Deshler, Lenz, Schumaker, & Clark, 1991). In Stage 1, Pretest and Make Commitments, students are tested to determine their current ability to comprehend complex subject-area content or to learn vocabulary. If the pretest shows a need to learn a strategy to respond to a particular setting demand, students are asked to

TABLE 23.1. Learning Strategies Associated with Text Comprehension

- The paraphrasing strategy (Schumaker, Denton, & Deshler, 1984). Students use this strategy to focus their attention on the main ideas and most important details in each paragraph in a passage to restate that information in their own words.
- The self-questioning strategy (Schumaker, Deshler, Nolan, & Alley, 1994). Students use this strategy to ask questions about key pieces of the information in the passage, to make predictions, to locate answers to the questions as they read further, and to talk to themselves about those answers in relation to their predictions.
- The visual imagery strategy (Schumaker, Deshler, Zemitzsch, & Warner, 1993). Students use this strategy to make mental movies of the scenes being described, incorporating actors, action, and details.
- The multipass strategy (Schumaker, Deshler, Alley, Warner, & Denton, 1982). Students use this strategy to make three passes through a passage of text, such as a textbook chapter. They survey it to get an overview, systematically scan through it to locate important information and note it, and locate answers to specific questions at the end of the passage.
- The interpreting visual aids strategy (Deshler, Ellis, & Lenz, 1996). Students use this strategy to systematically analyze visual devices such as maps, graphs, pictures, and tables and to talk to themselves about the information.
- The vocabulary strategy (Ellis, 1992). Students use this strategy to create memory devices and study cards to help them understand and remember key vocabulary.

make a personal commitment, in the form of a written goal, to learn that strategy. In Stage 2, Describe, a description of the strategy is provided by the teacher, including where, when, how, and why the strategy should be used. In Stage 3, Model, the teacher demonstrates all aspects of the strategy by thinking aloud while using it. As the model stage progresses, the teacher prompts student involvement in the demonstration, checks understanding of the underlying strategic processes, shapes and corrects student responses, and engineers student success.

During Stage 4, Verbal Practice, students learn to name and explain each of the strategy steps. This is required if they are to prompt themselves through the sequence of strategy steps independently. In Stage 5, Controlled Practice and Feedback, students practice applying the new strategy to materials in which the complexity, length, and difficulty have been controlled. For example, even though the social studies textbook might be written at the 10th-grade level, a student reading at the 5th-grade level might learn in Stage 5 to apply the strategy to a passage written at the 5th-grade level. After each practice attempt, students receive positive and corrective feedback from the teacher.

Once students reach a predetermined level of mastery within controlled materials, they proceed to Stage 6, Advanced Practice with Feedback. In this stage, students are given many opportunities to practice using the strategy with materials and in situations that closely approximate the demands placed on them in their subject-area courses. In Stage 7, Posttest and Make Commitments, students are tested to determine if they have mastered the strategy. The teacher and students take time to reflect on progress and to celebrate achievement of the original goal. Also, students are asked to make a commitment to generalize their use of the strategy to other settings and situations.

During the eighth and final stage of the instructional model, Generalization, teachers provide opportunities to generalize the strategy across tasks, situations, and settings. They first orient students to the various contexts in which the strategy can be applied. Next, students are given opportunities to practice the strategy with new materials and in a variety of settings. Then the teacher prompts students to modify or combine the new strategy with other strategies to comprehend complex content. Finally, teachers periodically administer probes to determine whether students are continuing to use the strategy and whether additional instruction in the strategy is needed.

Research Results

This eight-stage instructional model has been empirically validated through a series of research studies showing that students with disabilities who lack higher order information-processing skills can learn these strategies and can apply them to mediate their own comprehension of subject-area content (Schumaker & Deshler, 1992). For example, when six secondary-level students whose reading comprehension scores ranged between the fourth- and seventh-grade levels were taught the visual imagery strategy in a resource classroom, their reading comprehension scores improved. Prior to mastering the strategy, the students had earned a mean score of 42% correct on reading comprehension tests of passages written at their grade levels when prompted to make visual images of what they read. After learning the strategy, they earned a mean score of 81%. Moreover, on follow-up probes given after students had learned the strategy, students continued to earn, on average, comprehension scores of 77% correct.

This study and others associated with the comprehension strategies (e.g., Lenz & Hughes, 1990; Scanlon, Deshler, & Schumaker, 1996; Schumaker et al., 1982) indicate that students with high-incidence disabilities can learn to mediate their own comprehension of complex subject-area text written at their grade levels through intensive, systematic, and explicit instruction in a learning strategy. Indeed, through strategy instruction, many students have made gains of as many as four to seven grade levels, which have enabled them to meet the reading demands of their general education subject-area classes. These positive results were achieved when students received instruction in one-on-one or small-group formats on a daily basis and had plenty of opportunities to practice the strategy to mastery and to receive individualized feedback on performance.

Because these kinds of conditions are not often present in today's schools, in which resource-room programs have often been eliminated, some researchers have investigated whether these students can be taught learning strategies under the conditions that are typically present in general education classes. For example, Beals (1983) examined whether adolescents could learn the self-questioning strategy and the paraphrasing strategy in a high school English class. The eight-stage instructional model described previously was combined with cooperative group structures (Johnson & Johnson, 1996; Slavin, Stevens, & Madden, 1988) to teach the strategies to a heterogeneous class of students, including those with disabilities. All students mastered the strategies, and their reading comprehension scores increased substantially. Unfortunately, the general education teacher indicated that the time and energy required to deliver the intensive strategy instruction was a significant problem. It was so significant that a part-time assistant was recruited to help the teacher score practice activities. The teacher also indicated that she did not like sacrificing the instruction of other required English content in order to teach the strategies. High-achieving students in the class indicated that they were not satisfied with the instruction (probably because they already comprehended what they were reading before the strategy instruction began) and complained that they did not like having to teach other students in their cooperative groups.

In another study, Wedel, Deshler, and Schumaker (1988) examined the impact of teaching the vocabulary strategy to students in a middle school English class. Students in the experimental class received instruction on the strategy for four to five classes per week, 20 to 30 minutes per class, for 8 weeks. Students in the experimental group understood and remembered definitions of significantly more vocabulary words than did students in the comparison group. Students with mild disabilities, on average, earned a pretest score of 53% correct and a posttest score of 77% correct. However, some of the students with mild disabilities required additional practice time in the resource room in order to reach mastery on the strategy.

In a more recent study in a middle school, Seybert (1998) studied the impact of teaching students the vocabulary strategy and the self-questioning strategy in general education science and social studies classes. Again, although statistically significant differences were achieved on some measures, several students with disabilities had to receive individual instruction in the resource room in order for them to learn the strategies.

In response to general education teachers' complaints that strategy instruction is too time-consuming, Scanlon et al. (1996) worked to streamline strategy instruction. A three-stage instructional model was created. During Stage 1, the teacher introduces students to the concept of strategic learning. During Stage 2, the teacher describes and models a strategy using content-area information. During Stage 3, the teacher provides students opportunities to practice applying the strategy to subject-area information. Thus teachers who use this model simultaneously focus student attention on subject-area content and teach a learning strategy that students can use to mediate their comprehension of that content.

In a study examining the efficacy of this instructional model, students were taught a learning strategy called the Order Strategy (Scanlon et al., 1996). This strategy enables students to identify key information in either written text or notes and to depict graphically how the information is related using one of four major expository structures: sequence, descriptive, compare–contrast, or problem–solution. Recognizing expository structures or organizing content using expository structures aids comprehension (e.g., Darch, Carnine, & Kameenui, 1986; Kinder & Bursuck, 1991; Meyer, Brandt, & Bluth, 1980). Over the course of one semester, social studies teachers introduced, modeled, and had students practice using the strategy to process important content they were to learn.

The teachers' performance of virtually all the teaching behaviors (e.g., describing, modeling, providing opportunities to practice, providing feedback) was limited and decreased over the course of the semester. They provided very few opportunities (i.e., three on average) for students to practice using the strategy after it had been introduced. Student outcomes reflected the low implementation levels by their teachers. At the end of the semester, students on average could name only half of the steps in the strategy. This lack of knowledge inhibited their ability to fully apply the strategy to content. Moreover, though students showed statistically significant gains in achievement after using the strategy, the magnitude of the gains was minimal and could not be considered socially significant (Scanlon et al., 1996).

To summarize, if students with high-incidence disabilities are provided intensive instruction, they can learn higher order information-processing skills for mediating their own comprehension of materials written at their grade levels. However, providing such intensive instruction in general education subject-area courses is very difficult. In order to teach strategies in their general education classes, teachers have had to give up teaching some prescribed content (Beals, 1983). They were not able to deliver strategy instruction as often as they would like because of other demands, such as covering a certain amount of content by the end of the semester (Scanlon et al., 1996). Even when teachers were willing to make this tradeoff, strategy instruction provided in subject-area classes was not sufficient for some students with mild disabilities to master the strategies. They needed additional intensive practice in a separate setting. Thus, if students with disabilities are to benefit from strategic instruction, it must be intensively delivered by someone who views that instruction as a major responsibility, one that does not conflict with other duties.

Implications

These results have certain implications for schools interested in improving students' reading comprehension. First, schools must identify those students whose reading comprehension deficits render them unable to meet the reading demands associated with their general education classes. Second, venues must be provided within which the necessary conditions are present for students to learn comprehension strategies. Third, teachers must be assigned the duties of teaching strategies to students, and they must be held accountable for providing that instruction and for ensuring that students reach mastery. A variety of models can be designed (Hock, Deshler, & Schumaker, 1999). Some schools are currently providing such instruction to students during their regularly scheduled language arts/English periods in small-group settings. Other schools are providing the instruction through specially designed learning strategies courses in which students enroll as an elective. Still other schools are providing the instruction in resource rooms, in summer-school programs, or in before- or after-school programs. Regardless of the model, instruction must be provided in several strategies so that students can comprehend a variety of types of text at their grade levels.

THE CONTENT ENHANCEMENT APPROACH

Another method related to improving the reading comprehension of students with disabilities focuses on the way subject-area teachers present subject-area information in their classes. This method, called the content enhancement approach, enables teachers to compensate for students' information-processing deficits and mediate their comprehension of complex content (Lenz & Bulgren, 1995; Schumaker, Deshler, & McKnight, 1991). Within this approach, teachers can effectively cover important subject-area content and mediate students' comprehension of it simultaneously.

To use this approach, subject-area teachers first examine the outcome standards that students must meet and select the critical content related to those standards that all their students must learn. They then carefully analyze this critical content (including the assigned readings) to determine what information may be difficult for their students to understand. They consider, among other factors, whether the quantity, complexity, abstractness, and/or organization of the content might pose barriers to student comprehension and learning. Once they have identified the critical content and have determined why it may be difficult for students to understand, they then select a content enhancement routine to transform that content into more easily understood formats. They also use the routine to present the content in class in such a way as to prepare students for upcoming reading assignments and lesson activities and to enhance their learning during lessons.

Several content enhancement routines that relate to improving the reading comprehension of students have been developed and field tested over the past 17 years. Two categories of content enhancement routines are organizing routines and understanding routines. Organizing routines are used to create frameworks for understanding the structure of critical course content, whereas understanding routines are used to help students understand important, abstract, and/or complex concepts. (See Table 23.2 for descriptions of specific organizing routines and Table 23.3 for descriptions of specific understanding routines.)

Both types of routines can be used to prepare students for upcoming reading assignments. The organizing routines help students to understand the underlying structures to which all of the pieces of information that they are learning are related. If they understand these structures and relationships, they are more likely to focus on the most important information as they read, and they are more likely to remember it. The understanding routines help students to understand the larger concepts or main ideas to which all the pieces of information are related. Some of them help students to understand and remember key terms (e.g., vocabulary, people, places, events) to which much of the content is related. Thus the routines can be used to prepare students to comprehend their reading assignments because, in essence, they provide a mental "file cabinet" and labeled "file folders" within which students can store the bits of information that they will encounter.

The centerpiece of each routine is its associated teaching device. Most of the devices are graphic depictions of how information is related. Each device has been designed to focus student attention on critical content, to prompt student discussion of that content, to make relationships between pieces of content explicit, and to prompt higher order thinking processes. Figure 23.1 displays an example concept diagram, a graphic device created through use of the concept mastery routine. This diagram displays information related to the target concept "civil war." It was created by a history teacher and her students in an interactive partnership as they analyzed the concept together. Specifically, the concept diagram is used to display: (1) the name of a target concept and the category into which the concept fits, (2) words students associate with the target concept, (3) characteristics that set the examples of the target concept apart from examples of other concepts, (4) examples and nonexamples of the concept, (5) the definition of the concept, and (6) items that

TABLE 23.2. Organizing Routines

- The course organizer routine (Lenz, Schumaker, Deshler, & Bulgren, 1998). Used by teachers to introduce a course and provide mile markers throughout a course.
- The unit organizer routine (Lenz, Bulgren, Schumaker, Deshler, & Boudah, 1994). Used to introduce each unit within a course and the relationships among the content within the unit.
- The lesson organizer routine (Lenz, Marrs, Schumaker, & Deshler, 1993). Used to provide an advance organizer for particularly difficult lessons, including the relationships of information within the lesson and between the current lesson and previous and future lessons and the unit of study.
- The survey routine (Deshler, Schumaker, & McKnight, 1997). Used to provide an advanced organizer for a reading assignment and includes providing an organization for the passage, identifying the critical content, and specifying the relationships among key pieces of information in the passage.
- The framing routine (Ellis, 1998). Used to highlight relationships between main ideas and essential details in text and to help students consider the significance of the content.

TABLE 23.3. Understanding Routines

- The concept anchoring routine (Bulgren, Schumaker, & Deshler, 1994). Used to enhance students' understanding of a new concept by relating it to a concept that they already know and understand.
- The concept mastery routine (Bulgren, Deshler, & Schumaker, 1993). Used to enhance student understanding of a concept by clarifying its definitive characteristics and exploring examples of the concept.
- The concept comparison routine (Bulgren, Lenz, Deshler, & Schumaker, 1995). Used to enhance student understanding of two or more concepts by comparing and contrasting their similarities and differences.
- The clarifying routine (Ellis, 1997). Used to enhance student understanding of important terms (e.g., vocabulary, people, places, events) by listing associated clarifying information and relating that information to prior knowledge.

have not yet been identified as examples so that they can be analyzed to determine if they fit the concept's definition.

Instructional Methods

To facilitate the construction of a device such as the concept diagram, teachers employ a three-stage instructional sequence. During Stage 1, called "cue," teachers explain to their students that a content enhancement routine is going to be used. They also share with the students why the particular routine was selected and how it will improve their understanding of the content. During Stage 2, called "do," teachers and students work collaboratively to build a teaching device to improve student understanding of the difficult content. The teacher asks a series of questions to prompt students to contribute ideas for inclusion in the device. Finally, during Stage 3, called "review," student understanding of both the critical content and the process used to learn it is checked and reinforced by the teacher.

Research Results

The impact of each content enhancement routine on the performance of students with high-incidence disabilities has been evaluated. In a series of studies, Lenz and his colleagues measured the impact of the course organizer (Lenz, Schumaker, Deshler, & Bulgren, 1998), unit organizer (Lenz, Bulgren, Schumaker, Deshler, & Boudah, 1994), and lesson organizer routines (Lenz et al., 1987) on student understanding and retention of subject-area content. Results of these studies indicate that students with disabilities answered more questions correctly about the content that had been taught using the routines than about content that had been taught using traditional instruction. In fact, students with disabilities scored, on average, 10 to 20 percentage points higher on tests following teacher use of each routine than they did when no routine was used. For example, a student who was earning an average test score of 50% before the unit organizer routine was used earned an average test score of 70% after the routine was used.

In another series of studies, Bulgren and her colleagues examined the effects of the concept mastery (Bulgren et al., 1988), concept anchoring (Bulgren, Schumaker, & Deshler, 1994), and concept comparison routines (Bulgren, Lenz, Deshler, & Schumaker,

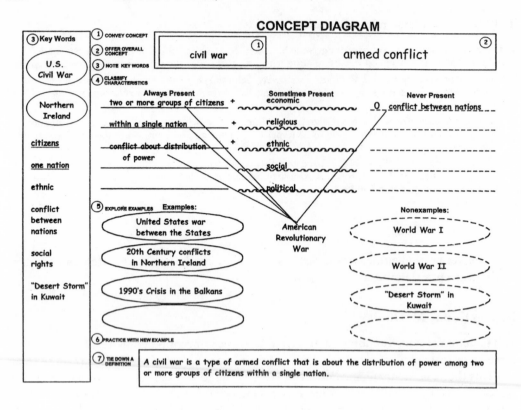

FIGURE 23.1. Concept Diagram.

1995). These routines were designed to enhance student comprehension of complex concepts. Students with mild disabilities answered significantly more questions correctly about the concepts that had been taught using the routines than about concepts that had been taught using traditional instruction. More specifically, on tests measuring student understanding of concepts, the scores of students with mild disabilities improved from a mean of 40% to 62% correct following participation in the concept mastery routine (Bulgren et al., 1988). Students in the experimental group earned a mean score of 63% correct following participation in the concept anchoring routine, in comparison with a mean score of 36% correct earned by the comparison group (Bulgren, Deshler, Schumaker, & Lenz, 2001). Likewise, experimental students earned a mean score of 71% correct following use of the concept comparison routine, whereas comparison students earned a mean score of 57% correct (Bulgren, Lenz, Deshler, & Schumaker, 1995).

To summarize, subject-area teachers can enhance the performance of students with high-incidence disabilities with regard to learning subject-area content by using content enhancement routines. Teachers are able to learn how to implement the routines within a few hours of instruction. They have reported that the routines are easy to use and that they are satisfied with the routines and the devices. Additionally, use of the routines improves the achievement of students with high-incidence disabilities, as well as of other students. Moreover, use of the routines did not require teachers to reduce the integrity of the subject-area content they were required to teach.

Despite these positive findings, there are some limitations associated with the routines. First, although students with high-incidence disabilities score, on average, 10 to 27 percentage points higher on test measures following teacher use of routines, this magnitude of change may not always be large enough for these students to earn satisfactory grades. For example, in the study on the concept anchoring routine (Bulgren et al., 1994), one fourth of the students with disabilities did not earn test scores above 60%. Unfortunately, no data are available on the cumulative impact of a teacher's use of several routines within the same course on the performance of students with disabilities. Perhaps some students need to have information presented through the use of several routines in order to earn passing grades.

Second, whether the amount of time required to prepare a content enhancement routine limits teacher use of the routine is unclear. For example, Bulgren et al. (1988) reported that in the school year following that in which the concept mastery routine study took place, only three of the eight participating teachers reported that they had created new concept diagrams, even though seven of the teachers reported continuing to use the ones they had designed during the study.

Third, no data are available regarding whether students with high-incidence disabilities learn the processes inherent in the routines for organizing and understanding subject-area content and use these processes independently to mediate their own comprehension if they are simply exposed to the routines. Teacher use of the routines may not produce independent learners.

Implications

The positive findings related to the content enhancement approach have important implications for how education is delivered in subject-area classes in which students with high-incidence disabilities and other students with comprehension deficits are enrolled. First, because teachers' use of content enhancement routines can improve student performance, schools need to provide teachers with professional development experiences focusing on the routines. Second, schools need to provide teachers the time they need to plan the devices and the questions that they will ask students so that they can use several of the routines in each course. Schools need to provide time for teachers who teach the same course and who teach courses that relate sequentially to work together on these activities. Finally, schools need to ensure that teachers implement the routines regularly and with high levels of fidelity.

SUMMARY

This chapter has described two of the options that educators have for enhancing the reading comprehension of students with high-incidence disabilities. First, they can teach these students reading comprehension strategies. This requires intensive, explicit instruction. Such instruction can yield gains in reading comprehension that span several grade levels. Alternatively, they can use content enhancement routines to prepare students before they read their assignments. This method does not directly improve students' reading skills; it simply gives students a framework within which they can discriminate important from unimportant information and create relationships among pieces of information, which in turn improves their understanding of content. Ideally, educators will use both options for maximum impact on student performance. That is, they will not only teach students to be strategic readers who can successfully read and understand their textbooks and other assigned passages but will also use content enhancement routines frequently enough that students will become prepared for each assignment and will learn the processes required to understand information. As a result, a large majority of students with high-incidence disabilities will become successful in their subject-area classes. Only then will they begin to feel good about themselves as learners. Only then will they begin to have a vision of themselves as lifelong learners capable of success in today's ever-changing world.

REFERENCES

Beals, V. L. (1983). *The effects of large group instruction on the acquisition of specific learning strategies by learning disabled adolescents.* Unpublished doctoral dissertation, University of Kansas, Lawrence.

Bulgren, J. A., Deshler, D. D., & Schumaker, J. B. (19930. *The concept mastery routine.* Lawrence, KS: Edge Enterprises.

Bulgren, J. A., Deshler, D. D., Schumaker, J. B., & Lenz, B. K. (2001). The use and effectiveness of analogical instruction in diverse secondary content classrooms. *Journal of Educational Psychology, 92*(3), 426–441.

Bulgren, J. A., Lenz, B. K., Deshler, D. D., & Schumaker, J. B. (1995). *The concept comparison routine.* Lawrence, KS: Edge Enterprises.

Bulgren, J. A., Schumaker, J. B., & Deshler, D. D. (1988). Effectiveness of a concept teaching routine in enhancing the performance of LD students in secondary-level mainstream classes. *Learning Disabilities Quarterly, 11*(1), 3–17.

Bulgren, J. A., Schumaker, J. B., & Deshler, D. D. (1994). *The concept anchoring routine.* Lawrence, KS: Edge Enterprises.

Clark, F. L., Deshler, D. D., Schumaker, J. B., Alley, G. R., & Warner, M. M. (1984). Visual imagery and self-questioning: Strategies to improve comprehension of written material. *Journal of Learning Disabilities, 17*(3), 145–149.

Darch, C. B., Carnine, D. W., & Kameenui, E. J. (1986). The role of graphic organizers and social structure in content area instruction. *Journal of Reading Behavior, 18*, 275–295.

Deshler, D. D., Ellis, E. S., & Lenz, B. K. (1996). *Teaching adolescents with learning disabilities: Strategies and methods.* Denver, CO: Love Publishing.

Deshler, D. D., Schumaker, J. B., Alley, G. R., Warner, M. M., & Clark, F. L. (1982). Learning disabilities in adolescent and young adult populations: Research implications. *Focus on Exceptional Children, 15*(1), 1–12.

Deshler, D. D., Schumaker, J. B., & McKnight, P. C. (1997). *The survey routine.* Lawrence, KS: University of Kansas.

Ellis, E. S. (1996). *LINCS: A starter strategy for vocabulary learning.* Lawrence, KS: Edge Enterprises.

Ellis, E. S. (1997). *The clarifying routine.* Lawrence, KS: Edge Enterprises.

Ellis, E. S. (1998). *The framing routine.* Lawrence, KS: Edge Enterprises.

Ellis, E. S., Deshler, D. D., Lenz, B. K., Schumaker, J. B., & Clark, F. L. (1991). An instructional model for teaching learning strategies. *Focus on Exceptional Children, 23*(6), 1–24.

Erickson, R. N., Ysseldyke, J., Thurlow, M. L., & Elliot, J. L. (1998). Inclusive assessment and accountability systems: Tools of the trade in educational reform. *Teaching Exceptional Children, 31*(2), 4–9.

Hock, M. F., Deshler, D. D., & Schumaker, J. B. (1999, Spring). Tutoring programs for academically underprepared college students: A review of the literature. *Journal of College Reading and Learning, 29*(2), pp. 101–122.

Johnson, D. W., & Johnson, R. T. (1996). The role of cooperative learning in assessing and communicating student learning. In T. R. Guskey (Ed.), *ASCD Yearbook 1996* (pp. 25–46). Alexandria, VA: Association for Supervision and Curriculum Development.

Kameenui, E. J., & Carnine, D. W. (Eds.). (1998). *Effective strategies for accommodating students with diverse learning and curricular needs.* Columbus, OH: Merrill.

Kauffman, J. M. (1994). Places of change: Special education's power and identity in an era of educational reform. *Journal of Learning Disabilities, 27,* 610–618.

Kinder, D., & Bursuck, W. (1991). The search for a unified social studies curriculum: Does history really repeat itself? *Journal of Learning Disabilities, 24,* 270–275.

Lenz, B. K., Alley, G. R., & Schumaker, J. B. (1987). Activating the inactive learner: Advance organizers in the secondary content classroom. *Learning Disability Quarterly, 10*(1), 53–67.

Lenz, B. K., & Bulgren, J. A. (1995). Promoting learning in content classes. In P. T. Cegelka & W. H. Berdine (Eds.), *Effective instruction for students with learning disabilities* (pp. 385–417). Boston: Allyn & Bacon.

Lenz, B. K., Bulgren, J. A., & Hudson, P. (1990). Content enhancement: A model for promoting the acquisition of content learning by individuals with learning disabilities. In T. Scruggs & B. Wong (Eds.), *Intervention research in learning disabilities* (pp. 118–146). Boston: Springer-Verlag.

Lenz, B. K., Bulgren, J. A., Schumaker, J. B., Deshler, D. D., & Boudah, D. J. (1994). *The unit organizer routine.* Lawrence, KS: Edge Enterprises.

Lenz, B. K., & Hughes, C. (1990). A word identification strategy for adolescents with learning disabilities. *Journal of Learning Disabilities, 23*(3), 149–158.

Lenz, B. K., Marrs, R. W., Schumaker, J. B., & Deshler, D. D. (1993). *The lesson organizer routine.* Lawrence, KS: Edge Enterprises.

Lenz, B. K., Schumaker, J. B., Deshler, D. D., & Bulgren, J. A. (1998). *The content enhancement series: The course organizer routine.* Lawrence, KS: Edge Enterprises.

Martin, C. (1999). *Net future.* New York: McGraw-Hill.

McIntosh, R., Vaughn, S., Schumm, J. S., Haager, D., & Lee, O. (1993). Observations of students with learning disabilities in general education classrooms. *Exceptional Children, 60*(3), 249–261.

Meyer, B. J. F., Brandt, D. M., & Bluth, G. J. (1980). Use of top-level structure in text: Key for reading comprehension of ninth-grade students. *Reading Research Quarterly, 16,* 72–103.

National Research Council. (1997). *Educating one and all: Students with disabilities and standards-based reform.* Washington, DC: National Academy Press.

Oliver, R. W. (1999). *The shape of things to come.* New York: McGraw-Hill.

Pressley, M., & Afflerbach, P. (1995). *Verbal protocols of reading.* Mahwah NJ: Erlbaum.

Pressley, M., Borkowski, J. G., & Schneider, W. (1990). Good information processing: What it is, how education can promote it. *International Journal of Educational Research, 2,* 857–867.

Pressley, M., & Woloshyn, V. (1995). *Cognitive strategy instruction that really improves children's academic performance.* Cambridge, MA: Brookline Books.

Putnam, M. L., Deshler, D. D., & Schumaker, J. B. (1992). The investigation of setting demands: A missing link in learning strategies instruction. In L. J. Meltzer (Ed.), *Strategy assessment and instruction for students with learning disabilities: From theory to practice* (pp. 325–354). Austin, TX: Pro-Ed.

Rifkin, J. (1995). *The end of work: The decline of the global labor force and the dawn of the post-market era.* New York: Putnam.

Scanlon, D., Deshler, D. D., & Schumaker, J. B. (1996). Can a strategy be taught and learned in secondary inclusive classrooms? *Learning Disabilities Research and Practice, 11*(1), 41–57.

Schumaker, J. B. (1992). Social performance of individuals with learning disabilities. *School Psychology Review, 21*(3), 387–399.

Schumaker, J. B., Denton, P. H., & Deshler, D. D. (1984). *The paraphrasing strategy.* Lawrence, KS: University of Kansas.

Schumaker, J. B., & Deshler, D. D. (1992). Validation of learning strategy interventions for students with learning disabilities: Results of a programmatic research effort. In B. Y. L. Wong (Ed.), *Contemporary intervention research in learning disabilities: An international perspective* (pp. 22–46). New York: Springer-Verlag.

Schumaker, J. B., Deshler, D. D., Alley, G. R., Warner, M. M., & Denton, P. H. (1982). Multipass: A learning strategy for improving reading comprehension. *Learning Disability Quarterly, 5*(3), 295–304.

Schumaker, J. B., Deshler, D. D., & McKnight, P. C. (1991). Teaching routines for content areas at the secondary level. In G. Stoner, M. R. Shinn, & H. M. Walker (Eds.), *Interventions for achievement and behavior problems* (pp. 374–395), Washington, DC: National Association of School Psychologists.

Schumaker, J. B., Deshler, D. D., Nolan, S. M., & Alley, G. R. (1994). *The self-questioning strategy.* Lawrence, KS: University of Kansas.

Schumaker, J. B., Deshler, D. D., Zemitsch, A., & Warner, M. M. (1993). *The visual imagery strategy.* Lawrence, KS: University of Kansas.

Seybert, L. (1998). *The development and evaluation of a model of intensive reading strategies instruction for teachers in inclusive, secondary classrooms.* Unpublished doctoral dissertation, University of Kansas, Lawrence.

Skrtic, T. M., Clark, F. L., & Knowlton, H. E. (1980). Effective inservice education. In J.G. Herlihy & M. T. Herlihy (Eds.), *Mainstreaming in the social studies* (pp. 76–81). Arlington, VA: National Council for the Social Studies.

Slavin, R. E., Stevens, R. J., & Madden, N. A. (1988). Accommodating student diversity in reading and writing instruction: A cooperative learning approach. *Remedial and Special Education, 9*(1), 60–66.

Wagner, M., Blackorby, J., & Hebbeler, K. (1993). *Beyond the report card: The multiple dimensions of secondary school performance of students with disabilities. A report from the National Longitudinal Study of Special Education Students.* Menlo Park, CA: Stanford Research Institute.

Wedel, M., Deshler, D. D., & Schumaker, J. B. (1988). *The effects of teaching at-risk students a vocabulary learning strategy in the general education classroom.* (Research Report No. 73). Lawrence: University of Kansas, Center for Research on Learning.

24

Encouraging Active Reading at the College Level

MICHELE L. SIMPSON
SHERRIE L. NIST

Because we work on a daily basis with college students who are coping with the transition from high school to college, our perspective on reading comprehension may be a bit different from those of most of the authors in this book. That is, our focus is on active reading as a means of learning from text rather than on learning how to read. The students we assist know how to read, but they are passive readers who focus on "doing the reading rather than mastering the content" (Alexander & Jetton, 2000, p. 299). They can comprehend short and considerate pieces of narrative and expository text, especially if instructors provide supports in the form of lectures, overviews, or study sheets. Moreover, most of our students enter college from high school settings in which they averaged only 12 pages of textbook reading a day (Campbell, Voelkl, & Donahue, 1997).

Our research and teaching confirms that the reading tasks in college are far more cognitively demanding (Brozo & Simpson, 1999; Nist & Holschuh, 2000). The major difference between high school and college demands tends to be that college students are expected to understand and remember what they read with few supports and less guidance. For example, we discovered from a survey of 223 professors on our campus that more than 60% expected their students to master textbook concepts through independent silent reading because they were not going to discuss the content during class (Burrell, Tao, Simpson, & Mendez-Berrueta, 1997). Although the amount of assigned material varied significantly across the academic disciplines, students taking humanities and biology had a reading load of 131.7 pages a week for just those two courses. Complicating the reading demands in college is the fact that many professors assign students to read that are less than reader friendly, such as primary sources and edited books, and, on occasion, multiple sources on the same topic. Moreover, research in authentic classroom settings suggests that college students at all levels have difficulties when they are expected to select, organize, and interpret key ideas across a variety of texts (Simpson & Nist, 1997; Simpson & Nist, 1999).

In order to assist students in their quest to learn from text and become successful independent learners, we teach them the importance of becoming active readers who can employ a variety of processes that will match their academic tasks. In planning our curriculum, we have drawn heavily from the research that has characterized mature and skilled readers (e.g., Pressley & Afflerbach, 1995). In the next section, we discuss the critical research concerning three of these characteristics or factors. Then we will describe some practical implications of this research and offer a future research agenda.

CRITICAL RESEARCH ON COMPREHENSION INSTRUCTION

We examine the critical research on comprehension by focusing on three factors we believe to be important to the development of active readers at the college level: (1) personal theories about reading and learning; (2) metacognitive processes; and (3) flexible cognitive processing.

Students' Personal Theories about Reading and Learning

We know from our interactions with college students that they have formed personal theories about reading and learning by the time they graduate from high school, personal theories that are important in situations in which they are asked to comprehend and learn from text (Hofer & Pintrich, 1997; Schommer, 1994; Schutz, Pintrich, & Young, 1993; Wineberg, 1991). For example, if students believe that reading in biology requires focusing on definitions, more than likely they will adopt surface-level reading strategies rather than elaborative reading strategies that involve them in searching for relationships between key concepts.

Even more interesting is the possibility that skilled and expert readers have beliefs about text that cause them to respond to and interpret text in ways different from those of less skilled readers. When Wineburg (1991) examined novices' and experts' beliefs about history texts, he found that the experts in history had an "epistemology of text" that permitted them to understand the writer's point of view and detect the subtexts that most students missed. He suggested that this inability to understand a writer's point of view is based on "an epistemology of text" (p. 510). That is, in order to detect subtexts, students must believe that they actually exist. Wineberg also found what many of us already suspected—that students treat their texts as indisputable sources of information rather than written acts of communication produced by a particular person. In fact, many college students believe that what they read in textbooks is more trustworthy than primary source documents (Stahl & Hynd, 1994).

Our research has focused on the role that students' personal theories play in their interpretation of academic tasks and in the strategies or processes they choose to employ as they read and study (Simpson & Nist, 1997; Simpson & Nist, 1999). In two different case studies of a history class, we found that successful students' (i.e., those who received A's and B's in the course) theories about learning and their theories about what should be learned in history were very much different from those of the less successful students (i.e., those who received *D*'s and *F*'s). The successful students seemed to believe that they were totally or partially responsible for their learning and knowledge acquisition. In contrast, the less successful students viewed the professor as the person who not only controlled what they would learn but also whether they would learn. When asked about what is important to learn in history, successful students said they needed to understand major events, their causes or the "whys" behind those events, and to note trends and patterns across time. The less successful students, however, emphasized the memorization of basic facts, major dates, wars, and presidents. It was clear that students' theories about learning in an academic discipline influenced how they read and studied their textbooks.

Students' Metacognitive Processes

Although some aspects of how we currently define metacognition are anything but new (e.g., Dewey, 1910), the term was not directly related to reading comprehension until the late 1970s (Flavell & Wellman, 1977). Most theorists delineate two (not necessarily independent) aspects of metacognition: knowledge about cognition and self-regulation of cognition. The first key aspect of metacognition, knowledge about cognition, concerns what readers know about their cognitive resources and the regulation of these resources. Regulation includes the ability to detect errors or contradictions in text, knowledge of different strategies to use with different kinds of texts, and the ability to separate important from unimportant information. The second key aspect of metacognition, self-regulation of cognition, involves readers in controlling their actions during reading. Self-regulation includes planning and monitoring, testing, revising, and evaluating the strategies or processes employed when reading and learning from text.

Most of the research on metacognition has targeted younger children. The studies that have been conducted with older students have focused in two areas. The first includes those studies that have compared the metacognitive abilities of skilled and unskilled readers. As expected, researchers have found that unskilled readers generally lack knowledge of comprehension strategies, have misconceptions about the reading process, and do not know what to do when their comprehension breaks down (Gambrell & Heathington, 1981; Malone & Mastropieri, 1992). Our research has differed slightly in that we have collected data about successful and unsuccessful students in authentic classroom settings. When analyzing the data across academic disciplines, we discovered that metacognitive awareness differentiated successful students from their less successful counterparts. Successful students in biology and history identified the concepts they understood and did not understand and used that information to guide their reading and studying. They also made mental or written plans that forced them to keep up with their reading on a daily basis (Nist, Simpson, & Holschuh, 1999). In contrast, unsuccessful students read to locate information or memorize details.

In the second area of metacognitive research, studies have attempted to improve students' metacognitive abilities with strategic interventions (Pressley, Snyder, Levin, Murray, & Ghatala, 1987; Thiede & Dunlosky, 1994; Nist & Simpson, 1990; White & Fredrickson, 1998). In general, the results of these studies indicate that students can improve their planning, monitoring, testing, and evaluating when they are taught a variety of reading strategies and processes. These strategies have included cueing in the form of adjunct questions, cooperative learning pairs, and elaborative verbal rehearsals (Larson et al., 1985; Simpson, Olejnik, Tam, & Supattathum, 1994). We have found from our intervention studies that strategies that have a metacognitive component and promote thinking about the "what" and "how" enable students to enhance their academic performance (Nist, Simpson, Olejnik, & Mealey, 1991; Nist & Simpson, 1988).

Students' Flexible Use of Cognitive Processes

In addition to being metacognitively aware and sophisticated, active readers should flexibly use a variety of cognitive processes that involve them in making sense out of expository text. These essential cognitive processes involve students in selecting, transforming, organizing, synthesizing, elaborating, and interpreting (Mayer, 1996; Pressley & Afflerbach, 1995; Pressley, El-Dinary, Wharton-McDonald, & Brown, 1999). Thus, in order to be both metacognitively aware and be flexible in their strategy use, students must be able not only to modify and apply cognitive processes across the various academic disciplines but also to regulate their cognition by testing, revising, and evaluating. That is, students must understand that the way they read and comprehend their biology assignments is different from the ways they should read and comprehend in courses such as history or economics and they must possess the strategies to carry out these tasks differently.

Although past researchers and instructors have focused their efforts on a particular reading strategy, such as concept mapping, there seems to be a recent effort in researching and teaching the processes embedded in these strategies (e.g., Mayer, 1996). Mayer, for example, has been investigating the impact of teaching students the cognitive processes embodied in a model called SOI, in which students are taught the how to select, organize, and integrate information from text. We believe that such a focus on process rather than product is a positive one, especially for students who often misunderstand the purpose of producing a written artifact such as a map or outline. Trends from the literature would certainly validate our intuitions. For example, Pintrich and Garcia (1991) found in their 5–year correlational study that students who were engaged in deeper levels of processing, such as organization and elaboration, were more likely to do better in terms of grades on assignments or exams, as well as in overall course grades. Our research in history and biology classrooms supports Pintrich and Garcia's research findings (Nist, Simpson, & Holsshuh, 1999). When we examined the academic literacy tasks in these college settings, we determined that there were qualitative differences in how successful and unsuccessful college students thought about and approached their reading tasks (Nist, Simpson, & Holschuh, 1999). Successful students talked about reading for understanding, thinking about the text as they read, and organizing the information into a way that makes sense based on course tasks. Thus their strategies and actions were purposeful, effortful, and facilitative. In contrast, unsuccessful students talked about reading as a task that must be completed. Because they rarely mentioned comprehending and learning new ideas, their actions implied a lack of purpose and effort.

Because the reading tasks that face college students tend to be demanding and complex, a body of current research has focused on factors that can help promote active reading. These factors include students' beliefs about text, the importance of metacognitive development, and students' flexible use of cognitive processes across disciplines. But are these factors evident in classroom settings? We examine this question in the next section.

APPLYING WHAT IS KNOWN

The characteristics of skilled, active readers have been carefully documented and described in the literature. Equally important, however, is to build a bridge from the research studies and theories to classroom practice. In this section we describe several practices that we have used with students who have chosen to take one of the elective courses offered at our university. These students have enrolled in either a 3-hour elective study strategies course (i.e., Learning to Learn) or a 1-hour strategies seminar that has been linked or paired to a specific course and professor (i.e., Adjunct Strategies Seminar).

Provide Activities That Nudge Students into Examining Their Personal Theories

Because we strongly support an interactive model of comprehension, we believe that it is impossible to isolate text from task and students' personal theories about learning in an academic discipline. That is, the strategies that students choose to employ as they read their texts are strongly influenced by what they perceive the task to be, perhaps more so than by the text itself. For example, if students' experiences in biology have always been isolating and memorizing key terms and parroting this information back on a test, they will continue to use these surface-level strategies. Moreover, if students have been successful in the past using this approach, it is going to be difficult for them to change their theory that the text basically contains "just facts" or that biology is a compilation of facts. We believe it is important to nudge students into thinking and reflecting about their personal theories and how these theories relate to active reading and learning in an academic environment. This "nudging" can be orchestrated via a variety of activities. For example, in the Adjunct Strategies Seminar, we teach the students that the first week of class is important because that is the time when professors share their personal theories about an academic discipline and what it means to learn in their course. In a history course linked to one of our seminars, the history professor takes the time on the first day to present the overarching theme for the course and to stress the importance of understanding the significance of historical events. Therefore, we ask students enrolled in the seminar to review their history notes and to brainstorm in small groups what they have learned about this course and their professor. When students leave the seminar on that day, they take with them two important realizations. First, they realize that their personal theories about what is important in history are probably quite different from their professor's theories. Second, they realize that they will have to change the way in which they read historical texts because their assigned material does not explicitly address the "significance" issue. Thus we have nudged our students and set the stage for some "reading between the lines" techniques.

Holschuh (1998) suggests that instructors in Learning to Learn–type courses can encourage more mature theories by incorporating tasks into the curriculum that require maturity and more elaborative processing. They can accomplish this by having students read and discuss ill-structured problems (King & Kitchener, 1994) or by having students explain why they selected a particular answer when solving a problem (Hammer, 1995). Finally, Holschuh recommends that instructors can use belief assessment measures with students and frankly discuss the results, emphasizing where they fall on the beliefs continuum.

Another important factor for practitioners to consider is the link that seems to exist between students' personal theories and the strategies they choose to use as they attempt to understand what they read (Hofer & Pintrich, 1997; Holschuh, 1998; Simpson & Nist, 1997). Although what we know about this link is only in the infancy stage, we believe that enough support exists to build the issue into the curriculum. Because we know that students who possess naïve theories about reading and learning tend to use surface-level strategies regardless of the task, it is important not only to teach students strategies that encourage them to use deeper levels of processing but also to link those strategies with more mature theories. For example, in the Adjunct Strategies Seminar that is linked to a history course, we teach students strategies for interpreting and synthesizing information from multiple sources. We teach those strategies because their professor creates essay exam questions that require students to form historical generalizations. Over time, these lessons have helped to change, in an indirect fashion, our students' theories on what it takes to actively read and learn from history texts. With our students in the Learning to Learn classes, we like to use scenarios or case studies in order to stimulate students into sensing the link between their personal theories and strategy choices (Gibbs, 1990; Nist & Holschuh, 2000). When our students read and discuss these scenarios with their classmates, they not only gain other perspectives on the problem described in the scenario but also begin to understand the link between their actions and personal theories.

Teach Reading Strategies That Involve Both Metacognitive and Cognitive Processes

Because metacognitive and cognitive processes are clearly critical to college students' understanding of texts, it is important to teach strategies that possess both elements. In fact, the more processes encompassed in a strategy, the better. In the Learning to Learn classes, we teach our students two such strategies—textbook annotation and talk-throughs. Both of these strategies have proven to be advantageous to college students as they prepare for exams. More important, surveys of our former students suggest that they have chosen to employ these two strategies several semesters after they took Learning to Learn.

In the reading strategy of textbook annotation, students select what key concepts to annotate in their textbook's margins and organize and elaborate on those concepts. That is the cognitive part. Then, once the students have written their annotations, they read what they have written and ask themselves these questions: (1) Do my annotations make sense?, (2) Do they coincide with what I already know and what I learned in the lecture?, (3) What ideas still confuse me?, and (4) How will I mark these confusing ideas so I can refer back to them? These questions help the students monitor and evaluate their comprehension, metacognitive processes they typically overlook in their reading and studying (Nist & Simpson, 1988; Simpson & Nist, 1990).

The second strategy that embodies both metacognitive and cognitive elements is the talk-through (Simpson, Olejnik, Tam, & Supattathum, 1994). When students prepare talk-throughs, they begin by isolating, organizing, and elaborating on the key ideas of what they have read. We usually recommend that students write these ideas on an index card. Then they externalize and verbally rehearse these ideas as if they were teaching someone. Using a biology chapter excerpt, we place the Learning to Learn students with a study partner to practice their talk-throughs. By talking through an idea or concept out loud, our students can quickly identify what they understand and what remains "fuzzy."

Hence they are monitoring and evaluating their understanding. Once the students have completed their talk-through with their assigned partner, we debrief the experience and help them brainstorm how they might conduct a talk-through without a study partner or how they might modify the strategy for other academic disciplines.

In addition to teaching strategies that involve both metacognitive and cognitive processing, it is also important to make sure that students fully understand the characteristics and responsibilities of active reading. Without such an understanding of what it means to be an active reader and learner, it is difficult for students to select and appropriately apply these reading strategies to their own tasks. We have found it useful to encourage our students in Learning to Learn to reflect on and talk about their reading tasks and what it means to read for understanding and learning. One way to stimulate this reflection is to ask students to write their definitions of reading or studying in a journal or via e-mail. Students can then compare and discuss their definitions among their classmates. Later in the term, after numerous classroom situations requiring their active reading and thinking, the students revisit their definitions and modify their stances. At the beginning of the semester most students write definitions of reading similar to the following: "reading is soaking up information"; "reading involves you in focusing on words and sentences so you will remember everything"; and "reading is memorizing." At the end of the semester the students' definitions have evolved into the following: "reading is thinking about key ideas"; "reading is putting ideas into your own words"; and "reading is thinking like the professor wants you to think."

Teach Students How to Interpret and Synthesize from Multiple Sources

Perhaps the most challenging academic task for college students occurs when they are asked to interpret and synthesize from a variety of primary and secondary sources, especially when those sources offer conflicting information. These tasks are daunting because high school graduates are accustomed to single textbook-based teachers and transmission models of learning, situations in which they are not participants in the construction of knowledge (Jetton, 1994; Moje, 1996). Such tasks are also daunting for instructors because there are many intertwined variables that affect students' abilities to interpret and synthesize from multiple sources. To illustrate, when students are asked to read and interpret three different sources on the impact of the Vietnam conflict in preparation for an analytical essay, they need the following: (1) background or content knowledge about the Vietnam conflict, (2) disciplinary knowledge in order to think like a historian and view text as a historian, (3) organizing strategies that will allow them to identify and understand the links among information presented in the different texts; and (4) an understanding of the requirements of an analytical essay (Stahl, Hynd, Glynn, & Carr, 1995; Wineburg, 1991).

In our Learning to Learn classes, we have attempted to address some of these issues by teaching an issue-based unit on the Vietnam conflict or on the civil rights movement. Both units engage students in reading a variety of primary and secondary sources which "crisscross the conceptual landscape" (Spiro, Coulson, Feltovich, & Anderson, 1994). Once students have a sense of the story of Vietnam, we teach them three processes that have been found to distinguish experts from novices in the way they read and think about history text (Wineburg, 1991). The first process, corroboration, involves students in comparing and contrasting texts with one another. To assist students in their corroboration, we teach organizing strategies such as charts and layered time lines. The second process, sourcing, requires students to analyze the source and to consider how the bias of the source might affect the document. In order to help students judge potential sources and bias, we provide a list of questions they should ask themselves (e.g., What is the background of the individual who wrote this text? What expertise does this individual have on the topic?). The third process, contextualization, asks readers to situate a text in a temporal and spatial context in order to determine how time or place may have had an impact on what the writer wrote. Because we provide students with texts written at the time of the issue, as well as oral and written retrospective texts, students learn how to interpret what they read within a framework of time. The unit culminates with a writing task that requires students to discuss and evaluate. In order to prepare them for this writing, we teach them the steps for writing such an analytical essay and provide them models to critique.

Use Direct Instruction over Time Rather Than Simply Assessing and Evaluating

In her now-classic article on comprehension instruction, Durkin (1978–1979) questioned whether comprehension was being taught in classrooms across the United States. More recently, Carol Santa (2000) reported that things have changed very little since Durkin's article was published. Santa suggested that "assigning activities is not the same thing as teaching them" (p. 30). She also stressed the importance of teacher modeling and guided practice in using new strategies. And although Santa focused on elementary students in her article, we agree with others (e.g., McKeachie, 1988; Pressley, 2000) that the same could be said for college students. We also believe that we should thoroughly teach a limited number of strategies that embody a variety of important cognitive and metacognitive processes rather than try to teach a vast number of strategies in a superficial manner.

In our own research we have reiterated the importance of direct instruction over a period of time. In fact, a key and almost serendipitous finding of our research on PLAE (preplan, list, activate, evaluate; Nist & Simpson, 1990), as well as our research on students' self-selected study processes (Nist et al., 1991), was that the benefits of strategy instruction emerged over an extended period of direct instruction. In both of these studies, data were collected at four points over 10 weeks of direct instruction. Although we found no significant differences between those who received direct strategy instruction and those who did not in the early data collection points, we consistently found significant differences later in the study. For example, at the beginning of the PLAE research study, there were no differences (i.e., 11 correct predictions versus 12 correct predictions) in the knowledge monitoring between the students trained in the PLAE strategy and the students using more traditional methods of time management. However, by the fourth exam, the PLAE students had 23 correct predictions in comparison with 9 given by the time-management students. Had we planned only one or two data collection points, we would have drawn very different conclusions in this study, that being that our intervention failed to aid students in their comprehension, monitoring, and evaluating.

When we teach students a new strategy or process, we use a fairly standard model of direct or explicit instruction. As we teach, we make sure that our lessons emphasize the declarative, procedural, and conditional knowledge (Paris, Lipson, & Wixson, 1983) of each strategy so that students will be able to select and employ the appropriate comprehension strategies for the task at hand. These steps in our model of instruction are inter-related and recursive and include the following:

1. *Model the process.* According to Pressley and Harris (1990), teacher modeling and use of the strategy are what constitute good instruction. The instructor must show the "how" of learning by thinking aloud and showing students how an active reader thinks through an idea.
2. *Provide examples.* When instructors give examples, students can better understand how the strategy works (Pressley et al., 1987). At this stage, it is important to show examples from a variety of contexts so that students can understand the conditional use of the strategy.
3. *Practice strategy use.* At first, strategy use should be guided, by which students repeat the instructor's strategy using new situations or problems. Feedback from the instructor is crucial at this stage so that students can gain a sense of how they are mastering the strategy. Eventually students should practice independently and then, once again, receive feedback on and debriefing of their efforts (Nist & Kirby, 1989).
4. *Evaluate strategy use.* In addition to receiving teacher-provided feedback as a way of evaluating strategy use, students should also learn self-monitoring techniques. Is the comprehension strategy working? If not, do they need to change their choice of strategy or simply to modify it?

We realize that this instructional model is labor intensive, especially in situations in which instructors must provide feedback to more than 100 students. In order to facilitate the process and insure that we could provide specific and timely feedback to our students, we have developed a variety of checklists (see Appendix 24.1). For example, we have a checklist to provide feedback on our students' textbook annotations and another one for their organizational strategies (Nist & Simpson, 1996). Once students begin applying the targeted strategy to their own reading tasks, we then encourage them to use the checklist as a means of self-evaluation and strategy control. The debriefing sessions also help to reduce the necessity of continued feedback from the instructor. During the debriefing sessions, students work in groups to analyze the strategies they employed and the content they used for the practice. We give each group three questions to answer and prepare for whole-class discussion: (1) What problems did you have in understanding the content? (2) What problems did you have in using the strategy? and (3) What do you see as the advantages of this strategy? Both the small-group and large-class discussions provide excellent opportunities for us to emphasize the students' conditional and procedural knowledge of the targeted strategies and to provide students additional feedback on their strategy attempts.

Teach Flexible and Modifiable Comprehension Strategies within the Context of a Discipline

At one time researchers believed that if students knew some general strategies or ways to approach text, they would be able to transfer these skills to a variety of domains. In the college reading arena, this translated into teaching students lockstep heuristics such as SQ3R (survey, question, read, recite, review; Robinson, 1946). In fact, some programs still use this method as the basis for improving their students' reading comprehension. However, as numerous researchers have pointed out, comprehension strategies must be taught in a context rather than in isolation (Alexander, 1996; Garner, 1990; Mayer, 1996; Pressley, 2000; Simpson, Hynd, Nist, & Burrell, 1997), and the strategies taught must be flexible and modifiable. Garner (1990) aptly explained it this way: "One thing that we already know about strategy use is that it is embedded. It does not occur in a vacuum. When context varies, the nature of strategic activity often varies as well" (p. 523). Because approaches to text understanding should be contextualized, we stress with our students that some heuristics or generic strategies are good but that most need to modified in order to match their academic tasks.

One successful way to contextualize strategy instruction is through linking or pairing a strategy course with a demanding core course, such as biology or chemistry, in an Adjunct Strategies Seminar (Simpson et al., 1997). The seminars provide students with the strategies and critical thinking skills they need to be successful in a particular course with tasks outlined by a particular professor. For example, in one seminar linked to a history course, students learn how to think about history in the manner appropriate to the task demands. In addition, they learned strategies that helped them interact with the assigned texts in ways that would promote integration, synthesis, and critical thinking. The questionnaire data we have collected about the seminars have indicated that students view the strategies as relevant and useful. Moreover, when asked if they were applying the strategies or ideas they learned in the seminars to any of their other classes, over 72% of them replied "yes" and described the specific courses and learning strategies (Simpson, 2000).

When we say that strategies should be flexible and modifiable, we mean that they should be generative in nature (Wittrock, 1990). Because reading is an isolated activity, one that generally takes place in privacy without the guidance of others, it is particularly important to teach students comprehension strategies that they can use on their own. Unless students can move beyond teacher dependence (through direct instruction) and apply strategies on their own, they will have a difficult time being academically successful in college. The specific strategies discussed earlier all are strategies that students can use independently; they are transferable and can be modified for effective use in numerous learning situations. For example, when we teach students how to annotate, we begin by discussing the cognitive and metacognitive processes involved in the strategy. Then we brainstorm with the students about how the types of information annotated might vary from course to course. In history, we stress the importance of annotating the significance of an event (not just the event itself), cause–effect relationships, and reasons why a certain event occurred. In biology, on the other hand, we stress functions, processes, and the interrelationships among concepts.

We realize that many instructors are teaching in less than ideal situations, in which incorporating some of our suggestions might seem difficult at best. That is, some instructors may teach large numbers of students each term; in such situations, providing continuous and specific feedback, a key part of direct instruction, is difficult. Or some instructors may be in situations in which they must follow a skills-based prescriptive reading approach that is the antithesis of a strategies-based approach. However, if the goal is to help encourage students to be active readers and involved learners, instruction must focus on ways to meet this challenge. Using a direct instruction model to help students examine their beliefs about reading and to teach them metacognitive and cognitive strategies that are research based is certainly a step in the right direction. Equally important is the contextualizing of instruction so that students view the strategies taught as relevant and useful. In the last section, we outline issues that we view as important next steps to helping college students become active readers and learners.

WHAT STILL NEEDS TO BE KNOWN
ABOUT COMPREHENSION INSTRUCTION

Although we have gained a more in-depth understanding of what skilled, active readers at the college level do when they are reading and learning from text, we have identified four issues in the extant literature that deserves further study.

1. *The need for research on the use of nontraditional texts in college classrooms.* Given the exponential growth of various technologies, we need to examine the cognitive demands of reading and learning on-line and from on-line screen encounters and to address the issues of students' engagement and motivation when assigned to learn from computer technologies such as WebCT instruction. Instructors working with college students also need to know which cognitive and metacognitive processes and reading strategies would be most appropriate for learning from these technologies.

2. *The need for research on strategies for reading multiple sources with multiple perspectives and multiple formats.* More college instructors are choosing to assign primary-source documents and alternative sources (e.g., essays, poems, songs, the Internet) because of their dislike of the textbooks that have been written for their academic discipline. Although we applaud this move from the textbook written by a cadre of authors who typically camouflage their stances and simplify the most complex issues, we also know the problems that students have approaching and interpreting multiple and nontraditional texts. The work of Wineberg (1991) and Stahl et. al. (1995), although useful, is just a beginning point in describing what skilled and less skilled readers do. We think it would be helpful to examine a variety of instructional interventions, much like the strategy research in the 1980s in which college students were taught how to summarize or self-question. For example, it would be interesting to study whether students trained to construct charts or concept maps would be better able to synthesize and evaluate information from primary-source documents than their counterparts who typically read and highlight key ideas as their main approach.

3. *The need for longitudinal research.* We would agree with Alexander and Jetton (2000) that more longitudinal research needs to be conducted on reading and learning from text. We urgently need energetic researchers who would invest the time in describing students' cognitive and metacognitive processing as they move through the grades. Admittedly, longitudinal studies are difficult to fund and pursue, so a compromise might be for researchers to conduct more in-depth, long-term studies in naturalistic settings. It is only through these long-term studies that researchers and instructors can understand strategy transfer and make better sense of the factors that play a role in college students' active reading and learning from text.

4. *The need for additional research on the interactive nature of comprehension.* We need additional research that would describe in more detail the multiple factors that influence students' text comprehension. We mentioned several of these factors earlier (i.e., students' ability to interpret reading tasks, the influence of personal theories), but we

know little about how these factors interact, especially with college students who use reading as a means of learning concepts across a variety of academic disciplines.

REFERENCES

Alexander, P. A. (1996). The past, present, and future of knowledge research: A reexamination of the role of knowledge in learning and instruction. *Educational Psychologist, 31,* 89–92.

Alexander, P. A., & Jetton, T. L. (2000). Learning from text: A multidimensional and developmental perspective. In M. L. Kamil, P. B. Mosenthal, P. D. Pearson, & R. Barr (Eds.), *Handbook of Reading Research* (Vol. 3, pp. 285–310). Mahwah, NJ: Erlbaum.

Brozo, W. G., & Simpson, M. L. (1999). *Readers, teachers, learners: Expanding literacy across the content areas.* Englewood Cliffs, NJ: Prentice-Hall.

Burrell, K. I., Tao, L., Simpson, M. L., & Mendez-Berrueta, H. (1997). How do we know what we are preparing students for? A reality check of one university's academic literacy demands. *Research and Teaching in Developmental Education, 13,* 55–70.

Campbell, J. R., Voelkl, K., & Donahue, P. L. (1997). *Report in brief: NAEP 1996 trends in academic progress.* Washington, DC: National Center for Education Statistics.

Dewey, J. (1910). *How we think.* Lexington, MA: Heath.

Durkin, D. (1978–1979). What classroom observations reveal about reading comprehension instruction. *Reading Research Quarterly, 15,* 481–533.

Flavell, J. H., & Wellman, H. M. (1977). Metamemory. In R. V. Kail, Jr., & J. W. Hagen (Eds.), *Perspectives on the development of memory and cognition* (pp. 3–33). Hillsdale, NJ: Erlbaum.

Gambrell, L. B., & Heathington, B. S. (1981). Adult disabled readers' metacognitive awareness about reading tasks and strategies. *Journal of Reading Behavior, 13,* 215–222.

Garner, R. (1990). When children and students do not use learning strategies: Toward a theory of settings. *Review of Educational Research, 60,* 517–529.

Gibbs, G. (1990). *Improving student learning project briefing paper.* Oxford, England: Oxford Polytechnic University, Oxford Center for Staff Development.

Hammer, D. (1995). Epistemological considerations in teaching introductory physics. *Science Education, 79,* 393–413.

Hofer, B. K., & Pintrich, P. R. (1997). The development of epistemological theories: Beliefs about knowledge and their relation to learning. *Review of Educational Research, 67,* 88–140.

Holschuh, J. P. (1998). *Epistemological beliefs in introductory biology: Addressing measurement concerns and exploring the relationship with strategy use.* Unpublished doctoral dissertation, University of Georgia, Athens.

Jetton, T. L. (1994). *Teachers' and students' understanding of scientific exposition: How importance and interest influence what is assessed and what is discussed.* Unpublished doctoral dissertation, Texas A & M University, College Station.

King, P. M., & Kitchener, K. S. (1994). *Developing reflective judgement.* San Francisco: Jossey-Bass.

Larson, C. O., Dansereau, D. F., O'Donnell, A. M., Hythecker, V. I., Lambiotte, J. G., & Rocklin, T. R. (1985). Effects of metacognition and elaborative activity on cooperative learning and transfer. *Contemporary Educational Psychology, 10,* 342–348.

Malone, L. D., & Mastropieri, M. A. (1992). Reading comprehension instruction: Summarization and self-monitoring for students with learning disabilities. *Exceptional Children, 58,* 270–279.

Mayer, R. E. (1996). Learning strategies for making sense out of expository text: The SOI model for guiding three cognitive processes in knowledge construction. *Educational Psychology Review, 8,* 357–371.

McKeachie, W. G. (1988). The need for strategy training. In C. E. Weinstein, E. T. Goetz, & P. A. Alexander (Eds.), *Learning and study strategies: Issues in assessment, instruction, and evaluation* (pp. 3–9). Orlando, FL: Academic Press.

Moje, E. B. (1996). "I teach students, not subjects": Teacher–student relationships as contexts for secondary literacy. *Reading Research Quarterly, 31,* 172–195.

Nist, S. L., & Holschuh, J. P. (2000). *Active learning: Strategies for college success.* Boston: Allyn & Bacon.

Nist, S. L., & Kirby, K. (1989). The textmarking patterns of college students. *Reading Psychology, 10,* 321–338.

Nist, S. L., & Simpson, M. L. (1988). The effectiveness and efficiency of training college students to annotate and underline texts. In J. E. Readence & R. S. Baldwin (Eds.), *Dialogues in literacy research: 37th Yearbook of the National Reading Conference* (pp. 251–257). Chicago: National Reading Conference.

Nist, S. L., & Simpson, M. L. (1990). The effect of PLAE upon students' test performance and metacognitive awareness. In J. Zutell & S. McCormick (Eds.), *Literacy theory and research: Analyses from multiple paradigms: 39th Yearbook of the National Reading Conference* (pp. 321–328). Chicago: National Reading Conference.

Nist, S. L., & Simpson, M. L. (1996). *Developing textbook fluency.* Lexington, MA: Heath.

Nist, S. L., Simpson, M. L., & Holschuh, J. P. (1999, April). *Looking across domains: Active learning in biology and history.* Paper presented at the annual meeting of the American Educational Research Association, Montreal, Canada.

Nist, S. L., Simpson, M. L., Olejnik, S., & Mealey, D. (1991). The relation between self-selected study processes and performance. *American Educational Research Journal, 28,* 849–874.

Paris, S. G., Lipson, M. Y., & Wixson, K. (1983). Becoming a strategic reader. *Contemporary Educational Psychology, 8,* 293–316.

Pintrich, P. R., & Garcia, T. (1991). Student goal orientation and self-regulation in the college classroom. In M. L. Maehr & P. R. Pintrich (Eds.), *Advances in motivation and achievement: Goals and self-regulatory processes* (Vol. 7, pp. 371–402). Greenwich, CT: JAI Press.

Pressley, M. (2000). What should comprehension instruction be the instruction of? In M. L. Kamil, P. B. Mosenthal, P. D. Pearson, & R. Barr (Eds.), *Handbook of reading research* (Vol. 3, pp. 545–561). Mahwah, NJ: Erlbaum.

Pressley, M., & Afflerbach, P. (1995). *Verbal protocols of reading: The nature of constructively responsive reading.* Hillsdale, NJ: Erlbaum.

Pressley, M., El-Dinary, P. B., Wharton-McDonald, R., & Brown, R. (1999). Transactional instruction of comprehension strategies in the elementary grades. In D. H. Shunk & B. J. Zimmerman (Eds.), *Self-regulated learning: From teaching to self-reflective practice* (pp. 42–56). New York: Guilford Press.

Pressley, M., & Harris, K. R. (1990). What we really know about strategy instruction. *Educational Leadership, 48,* 31–34.

Pressley, M., Snyder, B. L., Levin, J. R., Murray, H. G., & Ghatala, E. S. (1987). Perceived readiness for examination performance (PREP) produced by initial reading of text and text containing adjunct questions. *Reading Research Quarterly, 22,* 219–236.

Robinson, F. (1946). *Effective study* (2nd ed.). New York: Harper & Row.

Santa, C. M. (2000). The complexity of comprehension. *Reading Today, 17,* 30.

Schommer, M. (1994). Synthesizing epistemological belief research: Tentative understandings and provocative confusions. *Educational Psychology Review, 6,* 293–319.

Schutz, P. A., Pintrich, P. R., & Young, A. J. (1993, April). *Epistemological beliefs, motivation, and student learning.* Paper presented at the annual meeting of the American Educational Research Association, Atlanta, GA.

Simpson, M. L. (2000, April). *Challenging the boundaries of academic assistance programs.* Paper presented at the annual meeting of the Georgia Learning Support Conference, Jekyll Island, GA.

Simpson, M. L., Hynd, C. R., Nist, S. L., & Burrell, K. I. (1997). College academic assistance programs and practices. *Educational Psychology Review, 9*, 39–87.

Simpson, M. L., & Nist, S. L. (1990). Textbook annotation: An effective and efficient study strategy for college students. *Journal of Reading, 34*, 122–129.

Simpson, M. L., & Nist, S. L. (1997). Perspectives on learning history: A case study. *Journal of Literacy Research, 29*, 363–395.

Simpson, M. L., & Nist, S. L. (1999, April). *An examination of the factors impacting college students' academic performance in one context and domain.* Paper presented at the annual meeting of the American Educational Research Association, Montreal, Canada.

Simpson, M. L., Olejnik, S., Tam, A., & Supattathum, S. (1994). Elaborative verbal rehearsals and college students' cognitive performance. *Journal of Educational Psychology, 86*, 267–278.

Spiro, R. J., Coulson, R. L., Feltovich, P. J., & Anderson, D. K. (1994). Cognitive flexibility theory: Advanced knowledge acquisition in ill-structured domains. In R. B. Ruddell, M. R. Ruddell, & H. Singer (Eds.), *Theoretical models and processes of reading* (pp. 602–615). Newark, DE: International Reading Association.

Stahl, S. A., & Hynd, C. R. (1994, April). *Selecting historical documents: A study of student reasoning.* Paper presented at the annual meeting of American Educational Research Association, New Orleans, LA.

Stahl, S. A., Hynd, C. R., Glynn, S., & Carr, M. (1995). Beyond reading to learn: Developing content and disciplinary knowledge through texts. In P. Afflerbach, L. Baker, & D. Reinking (Eds.), *Developing engaged readers in home and school communities* (pp. 139–163). Hillsdale, NJ: Erlbaum.

Thiede, K. W., & Dunlosky, J. (1994). Delaying students' metacognitive monitoring improves their accuracy in predicting their recognition performance. *Journal of Educational Psychology, 86*, 290–302.

White, B. Y., & Fredrickson, J. R. (1998). Inquiry, modeling, and metacognition: Making science accessible to all students. *Cognition and Science, 16*, 90–91.

Wineberg, S. S. (1991). On the reading of historical texts: Notes on the breach between school and academy. *American Educational Research Journal, 28*, 495–519.

Wittrock, M. C. (1990). Generative processes of comprehension. *Educational Psychologist, 24*, 345–376.

APPENDIX 24.1. ANNOTATION CHECKLIST

_____ Your annotations are perfect! Keep up the good work.

_____ You have missed many key ideas. I have starred them for you. Go back and annotate them.

_____ You need to put your annotations in your own words. Do not copy from the book!

_____ You need to be briefer in your annotations. Be telegraphic.

_____ You have ignored the graphic aids. Annotate them.

_____ You need to note specific examples. They could reappear on the exam.

_____ You need to enumerate specific facts, characteristics, causes, events, etc., in the margins of the text.

_____ Your annotations need to focus more on key ideas and less on details.

_____ Your annotations need to be better organized.

_____ Your annotations need to show the relationship between ideas.

_____ You are underlining too much. Work more on writing summaries in the margin.

_____ You need to develop some symbols of your own and use them.

_____ Please annotate these sections or pages again.

Page(s) _____   Page(s) _____

Page(s) _____   Page(s) _____

_____ Please see me during my office hours for special assistance on this chapter and your annotations.

V

Conclusion

25

Summing Up

What Comprehension Instruction Could Be

MICHAEL PRESSLEY
CATHY COLLINS BLOCK

As Pressley stated in Chapter 2 of this book, as recently as 1974, many people thought that if was not a good idea to teach comprehension strategies to children. As this book demonstrates, we have come a long way, and we have many goals ahead of us. As we read each chapter, we were uplifted to realize how many actions have been taken to advance comprehension instruction in only 25 years. At the same time, every chapter identifies immediate actions that we can initiate to move us further still.

Today, we are often asked about what is required to improve elementary students' comprehension of texts they read. Thus we have developed a stock answer to the question, an answer that is completely defensible based on available evidence (e.g., Pressley, 2000):

1. *Do all possible to ensure that the young reader learns how to decode well.* It is impossible to understand the meaning of words, sentences, and paragraphs until such text is decoded. Beyond being able to sound out words per se, the young reader needs to be able to do so fluently. The more fluent the recognition of words, the less mental capacity consumed by word recognition. This is critical because mental capacity is limited, and the capacity available for comprehension is the capacity left over from decoding efforts.

2. *Teach vocabulary.* It is impossible to understand the meaning of running text if the meanings of individual words are not known.

3. *Teach students to relate relevant prior knowledge to what they read.* Because such associating to prior knowledge depends on having prior knowledge, a related point is that schooling should be knowledge intense, with kids reading and writing about ideas and events that are familiar to literate people.

4. *Teach students to use well-validated comprehension strategies*, such as predicting what will be in text, self-questioning while reading, constructing mental images representing the meaning of text, and summarizing.

5. *Teach students to monitor whether what is being read makes sense*. Does the word just read make sense given the paragraph context? Does the overall message make sense? If it does not, then the reader should reread and clarify the meaning of the text.

6. *Encourage students to read extensively*, for such reading provides practice in decoding as it builds vocabulary and prior knowledge. If readers are taught comprehension strategies and use them when reading on their own, there is the potential for creating fluent comprehenders (i.e., readers who effortlessly and automatically use the comprehension processes used by skilled readers).

All of the processes in our stock answer about encouraging comprehension are covered extensively in this volume. That is, at least some agreement exists among members of the comprehension research community about how to develop readers who comprehend well. Even so, a number of novel themes also appear in this volume.

NEW AND EXPANDED THEMES

In discussing these new and expanded themes, we do not attempt to cite chapters exhaustively, for the result would be a chapter cluttered with references to other chapters in the volume. That said, occasionally we cite some chapters that seem particularly apt to some of the points being made, and we cite sources outside this volume that convinces us of points made by contributors to this volume.

Decoding

Although authors in this volume recognize that skilled decoding is necessary for skilled comprehension, they also recognize that decoding is not sufficient to assure comprehension. This is an important point to emphasize at the present historical moment, for there has been much emphasis on the primacy of word recognition processes in recent years. Decoding skill—and eventually, fluent decoding—is a prerequisite to skilled comprehension; skilled decoding does not guarantee high comprehension.

Early Teaching of Comprehension Skills

Historically, comprehension instruction often was conceived of as developing after word recognition competencies. That is, decoding was a primary-grade skill, with development of comprehension something that should be targeted in the later elementary grades.

Challenges to this position are offered in this volume. Duffy (Chapter 3) provides extensive evidence that direct teacher explanation of strategies results in significant achievement gains, especially for struggling readers. Duffy presents three reasons why teachers have not yet emphasized explicit and less explicit techniques as much as desired, even though these findings were reported more than 13 years ago.

Tracey and Morrow (Chapter 14) convincingly remind us that much goes on during the preschool years that affects later reading competence. This sets the stage for the beginning reading instruction encountered in school, with children who are rich in emergent literacy experiences better prepared for beginning reading instruction than those who did not have such rich language experiences during the preschool years.

Several researchers in this volume relates their experiences with beginning comprehension instruction in the primary grades. For example, Smolkin and Donovan (Chapter 10) discuss how a grade 1 teacher can model and explain comprehension processes in the context of storybook read-alouds. They believe that by starting early, readers naturally internalize higher order comprehension processing as the way a reader should approach a text. Ogle and Blachowicz (Chapter 17) offer concrete suggestions about how to increase primary-level children's understanding of informational texts. Williams (Chapter 9) writes about how development of the theme scheme could be taught at the primary levels. Pearson and Duke (Chapter 16) review a set of studies confirming that comprehension can be taught in the early grades, a set of investigations that seems to us to be a must-read for anyone interested in development of higher order thinking as part of reading for young children.

Individual Strategies and Packages of Strategies

A number of individual comprehension strategies can be taught to students with benefit (e.g., imagery, summarization). Gambrell and Koskinen (Chapter 20) provide a thorough review of research concerning imagery, for instance. They propose more than 10 instructional practices that can be used in our classrooms today. Not surprisingly, many other contributors to this volume endorse the teaching of individual comprehension strategies. Also, research continues on some individual strategies (e.g., imagery, organizing, K-W-L), including new individual strategies identified in recent years (e.g., content enhancement as described by Fisher, Schumaker, & Deshler in Chapter 23). Since the publication of Keene and Zimmerman's (1997) *Mosaics of Thought*, teaching of individual strategies has enjoyed a renaissance, seen as a good way to introduce strategies to young readers.

In addition, however, this book contains a good deal of discussion about the teaching of repertoires of strategies, with students learning how to coordinate processes such as prediction of upcoming text, self-questioning, clarifying when confused, and summarizing. One appeal of the package approach is that highly skilled readers never use only one strategy but rather fluidly coordinate a number of strategies to make sense of text (Pressley & Afflerbach, 1995). Yes, even in these package approaches, there is some teaching of individual strategies, but such teaching is typically very brief compared with the time devoted to teaching of individual strategies in the Keene and Zimmerman (1997) approach. We suspect that there is room for both approaches in elementary classrooms, with some teachers and students more comfortable mastering individual strategies and later learning to coordinate them and others preferring to work with multiple processes from the very beginning of strategies instruction.

Challenges in Teaching Comprehension Strategies

Despite the plethora of research establishing the efficacy of comprehension strategies instruction, very little comprehension strategies instruction occurs in elementary schools. One reason is that comprehension strategies instruction is long-term rather than a type of teaching that promises rapid results or that can be memorized in one lesson and practice session, as Block, Schaller, Joy, and Gaine (Chapter 4) describe. Also, it is a complicated form of instruction, a point made frequently in this volume. Ivey (Chapter 15) voices many of these concerns by referring to her own distractions and inexperience as a first-year middle school teacher. She also cites numerous studies and practices that can be referenced to decrease the complexity of comprehension instruction for future teachers and students.

Teacher modeling and explanations of strategies yield to student practice, which must be scaffolded by the teacher. The scaffolding teacher monitors the reading of students and offers prompts and hints as to points at which strategies might be applied. Such scaffolding often takes place in the context of small groups of children applying comprehension strategies to an assigned reading. The idea is that long-term participation in such groups will lead individual members of the group eventually to internalize the comprehension strategies and to use them on their own when reading.

As complicated as comprehension strategies instruction is, we were struck by the indications in this volume that it perhaps should be even more complicated. Perhaps strategies packages would be more effective if there were much more emphasis on coordinating comprehension strategies with one another and if there were more information included in instruction and practice about where and when to use particular strategies.

It definitely takes a while for teachers to feel comfortable with this type of instruction, and many who try it decide not to stick with it. One reason that comprehension strategies instruction is unpopular with some teachers is because it is so different from traditional classroom discourse, in which the teacher is definitely in control and instruction consists of endless cycles of teacher's questions, student's responses, and teacher's feedback. Students using strategies are much more autonomous and much more active than those experiencing the traditional model.

In addition, using comprehension strategies is foreign to many teachers. That is, they do not use strategies such as prediction, relating to prior knowledge, seeking clarification, and summarization as they read. Thus, for these teachers, a first productive step can be to persuade them to try comprehension strategies themselves (Keene & Zimmerman, 1997). Comprehension strategies instruction can become more acceptable to teachers when they see it work, either for themselves as readers or, even more compelling, for their students. Thus we think a great deal can be accomplished in motivating teachers to become comprehension teachers by developing experiences that make clear to them that their students need and benefit from comprehension instruction.

Criticality of Monitoring

Good readers monitor whether they are reading well, whether what they are reading makes sense, as detailed, for example, by Baker (Chapter 6). When they perceive that reading and comprehension are not going well, they change reading tactics, perhaps rereading or reading more slowly and carefully. As important as monitoring is in the regulation of reading, relatively little is known about how to encourage readers to monitor better. Guthrie and Ozgungor (Chapter 18) found that students monitor when they (1) are using what they already know to build new understandings of the texts they read, (2) use cognitive strategies such as summarizing and self-checking, and (3) have the desire to comprehend and to share literacy socially in a classroom community.

Afflerbach (Chapter 7) is particularly informative about additional ways that students can be encouraged to monitor their reading more, as are Baker (Chapter 6) and Simpson and Nist (Chapter 24). Smolkin and Donovan (Chapter 10) and Pearson and Duke (Chapter 16) provide evidence that teaching of monitoring can begin in the lower primary grades. Much work needs to be done to determine just how monitoring can be best encouraged in students; for the present, researchers and practitioners should be thinking hard about how monitoring instruction can become a regular part of reading instruction.

Monitoring is a critical step in self-regulation of comprehension processes. That is, it is not enough for students to be taught comprehension processing; students must also come to understand where and when to use the processes and be motivated to do so. There is much motivation potential in being aware of when reading is going well and when it is not and in being aware of when comprehension processes that one knows can be deployed to improve understanding of text. Although there was a start in the 1980s on research to heighten student awareness of learning and comprehension and awareness of how and when particular strategies positively affect learning and understanding (Pressley, Borkowski, & O'Sullivan, 1984, 1985), there is a real need to revisit such research and expand on it. There just is not enough yet known about how to develop readers who monitor well and who, in turn, self-regulate their comprehension processes well. The need to add to this database is urgent, as Brown (Chapter 22) describes. By the middle school years, students must apply these monitoring processes to increasingly difficult content-area texts, often written at high school readability levels.

Cognitive Overload

Comprehension strategies and monitoring both consume cognitive capacity, as does decoding. Cognitive capacity is limited, with conscious thought often considered to be limited to 7 ± 2 pieces of information at a time. The many processes required to carry out any given cognitive act compete with one another for the available capacity. Thus, when reading a word, word recognition, comprehension, and memory processes compete. If the word recognition is effortless and if the word is easily comprehended as a vocabulary item familiar to the reader, there is plenty of capacity left over to remember the word and to integrate its meaning with the text that came before.

If readers are to have sufficient capacity to do all that skilled reading entails, then comprehension and word recognition processes need to be fairly automatic. The more automatic these processes, the less capacity they consume. When comprehension and decoding processes are not automatic, it is possible for readers to carry them out with little benefit. That is, so much capacity is used carrying out the comprehension and word recognition processes that there is no capacity left over to remember what was read.

Thus it is striking that so little is said in this volume about fluency issues, for the more fluent a comprehension process, the less capacity consumed in executing it. The reason so little is said is that there has been relatively little study of fluency of comprehension processes. For the present, it is safe to hypothesize that comprehension instruction needs to be sufficiently long term so that readers will become fluent in their execution of comprehension strategies, monitoring, access of vocabulary meanings and so forth.

Importance of Prior Knowledge

During the late 1970s and early 1980s, the group at the Illinois Center for the Study of Reading spearheaded research on the criticality of background knowledge to reading comprehension (e.g., Anderson & Pearson, 1984). Specifically, they found that what readers knew about the topic of a text before reading it very much influenced the messages they took away from reading a text. Although the heyday of research on prior knowledge effects seems to have passed, this volume acknowledges the effects of prior knowledge on comprehension. A striking example was offered by Narvaez (Chapter 11), who discusses how moral discourses are filtered through readers' general understanding of morality. Narvaez also contends that many cultural interpretations reflect prior knowledge processes, with the members of a culture applying their views of the world as they attempt to understand ideas in text.

Despite the relative lack of research attention to prior knowledge processes in the recent past, it is essential to remember that developing rich knowledge plays a prime role in schooling and is an important goal of instruction. Getting students to apply their prior knowledge appropriately can be more challenging. Students with reading difficulties are apt to associate knowledge irrelevancies with a text being read, hence undermining comprehension (as Williams reports in Chapter 9).

Prior knowledge is a double-edged sword. When relevant prior knowledge is used appropriately, readers go well beyond the text as given, making inferences and elaborations that permit sophisticated understanding of text. When inappropriate prior knowledge is tapped and related to text, the reader's thinking can go off on tangents, with the content of the text ignored in favor of the reader's dwelling on the irrelevant associations she or he made in reaction to a word or isolated phrase in a text (e.g., when reading "The Little Egine That Could," thinking about how packed the subway is with people). Approaches such as Williams's theme scheme (Chapter 9) are powerful because they orient struggling readers to the big ideas in text rather than stimulating them to think about details that are irrelevant to higher order understandings of the messages in text.

Processing Diverse Texts

Several chapter authors lament the paucity of research on comprehension of expository texts compared with narrative texts. That said, some research has been done with expository texts, with comprehension strategies proving effective in promoting comprehension of and memory for such materials. Even so, the need for research on a greater variety of text types is real. For example, Spires and Estes (Chapter 8) contention that much needs to be known about comprehension of Web-based and hypertext documents is definitely valid, given that such documents are becoming extremely commonplace even in the world of elementary readers. Ogle and Blachowicz (Chapter 17) comment that children should be taught to coordinate across several types of texts to find information, including both traditional and Internet-based texts. Simpson and Nist (Chapter 24) made similar points with respect to college-aged readers, for contemporary college classes already require students to be facile with Web materials and to compose based on integration of ideas across texts.

Diverse Text Tasks

A point made by several authors in this volume is that reader purpose matters in text processing. That said, relatively little work has been done on reader purpose and the effects of purpose on comprehension. One purpose—besides simple comprehension and memory of text—has been explored in more detail than others. As Dreher (Chapter 19) points out, text search is a very complicated activity but one that deserves much researcher attention, because searching text is such a common reader purpose in school and in the workplace.

Diverse Populations

Comprehension strategies, in particular, have often been studied with respect to their impact on weaker comprehenders, such as in the work described by Fisher, Schumaker, and Deshler (Chapter 23) and Simpson and Nist (Chapter 24). We really do not know the effects of attempts to improve comprehension on good and average readers. Given that many college-level readers do far less than they could do to comprehend text (Pressley & Afflerbach, 1995), it is reasonable to hypothesize that even good and average readers might benefit from instruction to be more active during text processing.

In addition, there has been far more study of children's than of adolescents' responses to comprehension instruction. In part, the reason is that reading instruction is viewed as an elementary school concern, rather than a proper curriculum direction for middle and high school educators. The fact that so many college students are not active comprehenders makes it obvious that there is plenty of room for improvement of comprehension processing after the elementary years.

An overarching theme in this volume is that comprehension instruction should vary with the needs and characteristics of the learner. This flies in the face of efforts to identify comprehension instruction that "works" across the board, with that instruction then provided uniformly to all students.

Comprehension Research Has Been Good Science, But It Could Be Better Science

Trabasso and Bouchard (Chapter 12) highlight the fact that much of the work on comprehension instruction has been done in true experiments, permitting cause-and-effect conclusions. Trabasso and Bouchard see this methodological feature as indicative of the research excellence of work on comprehension instruction. We note, however, that there have also been distinguished qualitative efforts, and it seems to us that more such work will be helpful. For example, with respect to getting an initial idea of the processes used in hypertext environments, it is easy to imagine informative studies involving think-alouds and assessments of qualitative decision making. Such work would permit the development of a theory of text processing in a Web-based environment, which, in turn, could result in well-controlled experiments to evaluate the theory.

A real strength of qualitative approaches is that they force dealing with reading as it naturally occurs. Qualitative studies of literacy are studies of the real texts children read and the real ways they read them (e.g., curled up in the classroom reading corner versus reading line-by-line from a computer screen in a true experiment). An excellent science of comprehension instruction will be a science that often involves real children reading real texts in real settings. In short, although the many true experiments on comprehension instruction do signal methodological rigor, future progress depends on a healthy interaction between qualitative and quantitative approaches, with qualitative studies offering advantages of naturalism often not afforded by true experiments.

SUMMING UP: WHAT SHOULD COMPREHENSION
INSTRUCTION BE THE INSTRUCTION OF?

We began this chapter with comprehension instruction recommendations that seem indisputable based on available evidence. That was a conservative, data-driven list of recommendations. In this section, we offer a set of recommendations that collapses across the thinking presented in this book about comprehension instruction, recognizing that the points made here vary with respect to the amount of empirical support they enjoy. So what should comprehension instruction be the instruction of, according to the authors in this book?

1. *Begin teaching comprehension skills during the primary grades*, even if that is only through teacher modeling during kindergarten and grade 1. *Continue to teach comprehension processing for as long as students need it.* Certainly, that means at least middle school and high school. In many cases, college students can benefit from instruction in effective comprehension processing.

2. *Develop decoding skills in readers*, providing sufficient instruction and practice reading that word recognition becomes fluent and hence demands low capacity.

3. *Teach vocabulary.* Knowing the meanings of the words decoded improves overall comprehension, and hence there is plenty of motivation to make certain that young readers know the meanings of at least the most frequently encountered words in English.

4. *Have students read diverse and worthwhile texts as they perform diverse and worthwhile text processing tasks.* Strategies need to be practiced with narratives and expository texts, as well as with Web-based documents. Students need to learn strategies for remembering important details in text, comprehending the main ideas, finding important facts, and integrating information across texts. Moreover, the texts that students read and search should be carefully selected for their worthwhile content, for incidental learning from text is an important source of world (prior) knowledge, and rich prior knowledge is essential for readers to be capable comprehenders of text. Although prior knowledge effects have not been studied as much in the past decade as they were in the 1970s and 1980s, that is not because they are not important in skilled comprehension. New work such as that described by Reznitskaya and Anderson (Chapter 21) is likely to launch renewed interest in the development of prior knowledge as part of teaching of comprehension, including knowledge of argument structures, which is the specific form of knowledge those authors highlight in their contribution to this volume.

5. *Teach students to relate their prior knowledge to new texts when prior knowledge can increase understanding of new texts.* One of the most critical findings in my research group in the past decade is that readers often do not relate even closely associated prior knowledge to new text they encounter, with the result that the text is not remembered later (Pressley et al., 1992). Having prior knowledge is only half the battle; using it appropriately to understand newly encountered ideas does not automatically follow from having prior knowledge.

6. *Teach students the well-validated comprehension strategies*, including relating text to prior knowledge, self-questioning during reading, imagery, setting purposes, determining cause and effects, and summarization. If initial teaching is of individual strategies, then teach students to coordinate their repertoire of strategies as they actively process text. Comprehension strategies instruction starts as teacher modeling and explanations,

with responsibility for strategy use gradually transferred to students. Teachers must learn how to group students according to the types of strategies and comprehension processes they do *not* know. Strategies instruction should continue until use of strategies is fluent and students can and do elect to use them appropriately.

Until fluent, self-regulated use of comprehension strategies is achieved, benefits of strategies will be limited. Learning a repertoire of comprehension strategies so that the strategies can be gainfully employed is a long-term enterprise, because the strategies must be acquired to the point at which they can be executed effortlessly, and learners must come to recognize automatically when it makes sense to use the strategies in the repertoire.

7. *Teach students to monitor whether they are understanding text* and to check whether what they are reading is making sense and whether they are understanding and remembering what is read. Teach them as well to make adjustments when they detect that reading is not going well.

In summary, comprehension instruction is complex and long term. As Block, Schaller, Joy, and Gaine (Chapter 4) point out, it certainly cannot be reduced to one particular process that should be encouraged (e.g., merely reminding students before they read to "think about a comprehension strategy that was just taught"). These researchers describe how students must be taught how to relate multiple strategies together at specific points in a text at which they are needed, such as setting a purpose before they begin, sequencing single facts, recognizing a main idea, relating main ideas vertically throughout a reading, verifying connections within a text, and then applying relevant data to their lives. Such work subsumes both lower order processes, such as learning to decode and acquiring vocabulary, and higher order processes, such as use of student-initiated comprehension strategies and monitoring. Because so much is known about how to empower students to accomplish all of this and to reach an enriched understanding, it is especially disheartening that it is so easy to find so many elementary classrooms in which very little comprehension instruction occurs (Wharton-McDonald, Pressley, & Hampston, 1998).

One likely reason for this lack of comprehension instruction is that teachers are not aware of how much can be done to increase readers' understanding of text. We think one of the most profound insights about comprehension instruction in recent years was provided by Keene and Zimmerman (1997), who argued that if teachers are not sold on comprehension strategies and monitoring instruction, they should be persuaded to try using comprehension strategies and to monitor their own understanding and memory of text as they read and to assess the difference comprehension strategies and monitoring make in their own reading.

This point makes sense especially in light of the analysis El-Dinary (Chapter 13) contributed to this volume. A parallel argument could be made with respect to all of the processes covered earlier in this concluding section: Teachers are more likely to teach comprehension processing if they are convinced that such processing improves their own reading. This point is consistent with a more general perspective that commitment to effortful intellectual processing depends on the thinker believing the effort will pay off in terms of improved performance (Pressley et al., 1984, 1985).

In short, we close this volume with a few main hypotheses. A key to improving student readers' comprehension is improving the comprehension processing of their teachers with a variety of mechanisms detailed in this volume that should go far in improving the reading of many adults (i.e., teachers) and children. We can increase the amount of comprehension instruction that is provided to children. This instruction can begin in the preschool years and should continue throughout their high school and college years. There are many methods in this book that can be used reliably. We will work to encourage educators to do so. We also believe that the directions for future research cited by every author in this volume are important. When we examine in a scientific manner the issues that they raise, we can touch the lives of even more students. When we do this, the joy of reading can become a more permanent state for countless generations to come. Comprehension will forever fall more directly and completely under their control.

REFERENCES

Anderson, R. C., & Pearson, P. D. (1984). A schema-theoretic view of basic processes in reading. In P. D. Pearson (Ed.), *Handbook of reading research* (pp. 255–291). New York: Longman.

Keene, E. O., & Zimmerman, S. (1997). *Mosaic of thought: Teaching comprehension in a reader's workshop*. Portsmouth, NH: Heinemann.

Pressley, M. (2000). What should comprehension instruction be the instruction of? In M. L. Kamil, P. B. Mosenthal, P. D. Pearson, & R. Barr (Eds.), *Handbook of reading research* (Vol. 3, pp. 545–561). Mahwah, NJ: Erlbaum.

Pressley, M., & Afflerbach, P. (1995). *Verbal protocols of reading: The nature of constructively responsive reading*. Hillsdale, NJ: Erlbaum.

Pressley, M., Borkowski, J. G., & O'Sullivan, J. T. (1984). Memory strategy instruction is made of this: Metamemory and durable strategy use. *Educational Psychologist, 19*, 94–107.

Pressley, M., Borkowski, J. G., & O'Sullivan, J. T. (1985). Children's metamemory and the teaching of strategies. In D. L. Forrest-Pressley, G. E. MacKinnon, & T. G. Waller (Eds.), *Metacognition, cognition, and human performance* (pp. 111–153). Orlando, FL: Academic Press.

Pressley, M., Wood, E., Woloshyn, V. E., Martin, V., King, A., & Menke, D. (1992). Encouraging mindful use of prior knowledge: Attempting to construct explanatory answers facilitates learning. *Educational Psychologist, 27*, 91–110.

Wharton-McDonald, R., Pressley, M., & Hampston, J. M. (1998). Outstanding literacy instruction in first grade: Teacher practices and student achievement. *Elementary School Journal, 99*, 101–128.

Author Index

Abelson, R., 159
Adams, M. J., 22, 69, 183, 220, 222
Adesman, P., 160
Afflerbach, P., 14, 15, 16, 17, 37, 42, 44, 51,
    78, 79, 85, 88, 97, 98, 100, 109, 123,
    158, 176, 210, 352, 366, 385, 386,
    389
Alao, S., 285, 299, 341
Alban, T., 284
Albertson, L. R., 89
Alexander, P. A., 62, 63, 68, 78, 83, 89, 100,
    160, 222, 230, 365, 374, 375
Alley, G. R., 352, 353
Allington, R. L., 31, 42, 129, 221, 235
Allison, J., 270
Almasi, J. F., 78, 177, 210
Alvermann, D. E., 30, 78, 243, 259, 261, 338,
    344
Amsel, E., 324
Anderson, D. K., 371
Anderson, E., 285, 299
Anderson, J. R., 67
Anderson, R. C., 19, 22, 23, 29, 30, 62, 159,
    161, 165, 167, 176, 180, 203, 223, 319,
    320, 321, 322, 323, 325, 326, 327, 328,
    329, 338, 340, 341, 388, 390
Anderson, T. H., 262, 263, 323, 338, 339
Anderson, V., 21, 43, 185, 186, 262, 263
Andrews, R., 321
Angell, R. B., 321
Applebee, A. N., 319, 323, 324
Armbruster, B. B., 262, 263, 290, 292, 297, 323,
    338, 339
Armstrong, J. O., 290
Asher, S. R., 339
Au, K. H., 28, 30, 219, 221, 223, 319, 325
August, D. L., 141, 306, 308
Ausubel, D. P., 319

Babbitt, N., 71
Bacigalupa, C., 168
Baker, K., 129
Baker, L., 29, 77, 78, 79, 80, 82, 83, 85, 87, 89,
    97, 98, 223, 300, 309, 338
Baldwin, L. E., 89, 149
Bales, R. J., 305, 306, 307, 308, 309, 311, 312,
    314
Barbour, N., 224
Barclay, K. D., 311
Bargh, J. A., 67
Barker, K. G., 291
Barksdale-Ladd, M. A., 84, 89
Barr, R., 236
Barrentine, S. J., 145, 146
Barron, B. J., 78
Barry, A., 146, 147
Bartlett, F. C., 159, 161, 163, 168, 319
Battle, J., 147, 294
Baumann, J. F., 80, 83, 84, 88, 237, 241, 243,
    248, 253
Baumann, J., 30, 33
Bazerman, C., 98
Beach, R. W., 263
Beach, R., 123, 127
Beal, C. R., 80
Beals, V. L., 355, 356
Bear, D., 237
Bebeau, M., 161
Beck, I. L., 22, 23, 43, 62, 66, 70, 83, 85, 86,
    99, 101, 140, 183, 322
Beck, L. L., 262
Belcher, V., 307, 311
Bell, J. A., 17
Bell, R. Q., 202
Bender, T., 329
Bennett, W., 158
Bentley, J., 162

Subject Index